Revisiting Prussia's Wars against Napoleon

In 2013, Germany celebrated the bicentennial of the so-called Wars of Liberation of 1813–15. These wars were the culmination of the Prussian and German struggle against Napoleon between 1806 and 1815, which occupied a key position in both German national historiography and memory. Although these conflicts have been analyzed in thousands of books and articles, much of the focus has been on the military campaigns and alliances, emerging sovereign states and reform movements and early articulations of modern nationalism. Karen Hagemann argues that we cannot achieve a comprehensive understanding of these wars and their importance in collective memory without recognizing how the interaction of politics, culture and gender influenced these historical events and continues to shape later recollections of them. She thus explores the highly contested discourses and symbolic practices by which individuals and groups interpreted these wars and made political claims, starting in the period itself and ending with the centenary in 1913.

Karen Hagemann is the James G. Kenan Distinguished Professor of History at the University of North Carolina at Chapel Hill. She has published widely in Modern German and European history and gender history. Her recent co-edited books include *Gendering Modern German History: Rewriting Historiography* (2007); *Representing Masculinity: Male Citizenship in Modern Western Culture* (2007); *Gender, War, and Politics: Transatlantic Perspectives, 1775–1830* (2010); and *War Memories: The Revolutionary and Napoleonic Wars in Modern European Culture* (2012).

Revisiting Prussia's Wars against Napoleon

History, Culture and Memory

KAREN HAGEMANN

University of North Carolina at Chapel Hill

(Translations by Pamela Selwyn)

CAMBRIDGE
UNIVERSITY PRESS

CAMBRIDGE
UNIVERSITY PRESS

One Liberty Plaza, 20th Floor, New York, NY 10006, USA

Cambridge University Press is part of the University of Cambridge.

It furthers the University's mission by disseminating knowledge in the pursuit of
education, learning and research at the highest international levels of excellence.

www.cambridge.org
Information on this title: www.cambridge.org/9780521152303

© Karen Hagemann 2015

First published 2015
Reprinted 2020

Printed in the United Kingdom by TJ Books Limited, Padstow Cornwall

A catalog record for this publication is available from the British Library.

Library of Congress Cataloging in Publication data
Hagemann, Karen.
Revisiting Prussia's wars against Napoleon : history, culture and memory / Karen Hagemann,
University of North Carolina, Chapel Hill; translations by Pamela Selwyn.
pages cm
Includes bibliographical references and index.
ISBN 978-0-521-19013-8 (hardback) – ISBN 978-0-521-15230-3 (pbk.)
1. Germany – History – 1806–1815. 2. Collective memory – Germany. 3. Napoleonic
Wars, 1800–1815 – Influence. 4. Wars of Liberation, 1813–1814 – Influence. 5. National
characteristics, German. 6. Prussia (Germany) – History, Military – 19th century. I. Title.
DD419.H27   2015
940.2'70943–dc23   2014043086

ISBN 978-0-521-19013-8 Hardback
ISBN 978-0-521-15230-3 Paperback

"It is a dreadful barbarism to which we have forced our enemies, through which they in turn forced us to commit atrocities that would never have happened otherwise. Oh, my beloved friend, my heart stops when I think of this pernicious circle, which coils itself around millennia of history! Will there never come a time when Man will fully enjoy the privilege of being ennobled above all creatures through the gift of reason; will freely and cheerfully live up to the duties that flow from this highest form of nobility; will be allowed to be human, without inhumanity being demanded of him in the name of familial love, welfare, the fatherland, national honor?"

The French officer Marquis Hypolit Drouot d'Hericourt
in a letter to his German fiancé Minna Warburg in the winter of 1812,
cited in Friedrich Spielhagen's novel *Noblesse oblige* (Leipzig, 1888)

Contents

Figures and Maps

Abbreviations

AB	*Amts-Blatt der königlichen kurmärkischen Regierung*
ADB	*Allgemeine Deutsche Biographie*
AFZ	*Allgemeine deutsche Frauen-Zeitung*
AHR	*American Historical Review*
ALZ	*Allgemeine Literatur Zeitung*
AMZ	*Allgemeine Militär-Zeitung*
BHMW	*Beihefte zum Militär-Wochenblatt*
BLU	*Blätter für Literarische Unterhaltung*
BN	*Berlinische Nachrichten von Staats- und gelehrten Sachen*
CEH	*Central European History*
DB	*Deutsche Blätter*
DBO	*Deutscher Beobachter*
EHQ	*European History Quarterly*
FB	*Freimüthige Blatter für Deutsche, in Beziehung auf Krieg, Politik und Staatswesen*
FBPG	*Forschungen zur brandenburgischen und preußischen Geschichte*
G&H	*Gender & History*
GB	*Die Grenzboten*
GG	*Geschichte und Gesellschaft*
GMP	*Gemeinnütziges Magazin für Prediger auf dem Lande und in kleinen Städten*
GWU	*Geschichte in Wissenschaft und Unterricht*
HWJ	*History Workshop: A Journal of Feminist and Socialist Historians*
HZ	*Historische Zeitschrift*
IASL	*Internationales Archiv für Sozialgeschichte der Literatur*
JfP	*Journal für Prediger*
JMH	*The Journal of Modern History*

JWH	*Journal of Women's History*
LB	*Literaturblatt*
MfP	*Magazin für Prediger*
MGM	*Militärgeschichtliche Mitteilungen*
MW	*Militair-Wochenblatt*
ND	*Das neue Deutschland*
NDB	*Neue Deutsche Biographie*
NF	*Neue Fakkeln*
NM	*Neuestes Magazin von Fest-, Gelegenheits- und andern Predigten*
ÖZG	*Österreichische Zeitschrift für Geschichtswissenschaft*
PC	*Der Preussische Correspondent*
PF	*Preußische Feldzeitung*
PFB	*Politische Flugblätter*
PrJb	*Preußische Jahrbücher*
RDVB	*Russisch-Deutsches Volks-Blatt*
RM	*Rheinischer Merkur*
RT	*Rußlands Triumpf 1812 oder das erwachte Europa*
SP	*Schlesische Provinzialblätter*
SPZ	*Schlesische Privilegierte Zeitung*
TB	*Teutsche Blätter*
TG	*Tageblatt der Geschichte*
UP	*University Press*
VM	*Vaterländisches Museum*
VZ	*Vossische Zeitung*
WiH	*War in History*
ZaF	*Zeitung aus dem Feldlager*
ZfeW	*Zeitung für die elegante Welt*
ZfG	*Zeitschrift für Geschichtswissenschaft*
ZnG	*Zeitschrift für die neueste Geschichte, die Staaten- und Völkerkunde*

Acknowledgments

Every book has a history and is tied to memories. This project has accompanied me for ten years. A membership at the Institute for Advanced Studies in Princeton for 2001–02 gave me time to prepare for publication my habilitation thesis on the nation, the military and gender at the time of Prussia's Anti-Napoleonic Wars – which I had submitted to the Technical University in Berlin – and allowed me to start working on the recollections of these wars. From the beginning, I was very interested in the comparative and transnational dimensions of these memories, and I therefore initiated a larger European project: the Anglo-German research group "Nations, Borders and Identities: Experiences and Memories of the Revolutionary and Napoleonic Wars in Europe, 1792–1945," which began work in 2004. The project explored the images and narratives that shaped war experiences and memories and helped form collective identities across much of nineteenth- and twentieth-century Europe. Alan Forrest (University of York) and Étienne François (Free University of Berlin and University of Paris-I, Panthéon-Sorbonne) directed the project with me. Arnd Bauerkämper (Free University of Berlin), Richard Bessel and Jane Rendall (both University of York) joined us on the project board. Funded by the project, eight postdoctoral and doctoral researchers worked on France, England and Ireland, Austria and Germany, and Russia and Poland. The whole team collaborated closely through a joint working group, which met regularly and organized a series of five workshops and three international conferences held in association with institutions such as the German Historical Institutes in London and Washington, DC, the Military History Research Institute in Potsdam, the Free University of Berlin, the University of Mannheim, the University of North Carolina at Chapel Hill and the University of York. Between 2005 and 2008–09, the German Research Foundation (*Deutsche Forschungsgemeinschaft*, or DFG) and the British Arts and Humanities Research Council generously funded the project. I would like to express my appreciation to all of these institutions, as well as to the two foundations and those scholars who have contributed to the project, which culminated in several joint publications. Not only did the project influence my approach to this book, but the DFG grant also provided me with the help of research assistants, and I am especially grateful to Friederike Brühöfener.

Last but not least, I would like to thank the Department of History at the University of North Carolina (UNC) at Chapel Hill, which I joined in the summer of 2005, the UNC Institute for the Arts and Humanities (IAH) and the National Humanities Center (NHC) for their support. An IAH fellowship in the fall of 2008 allowed me to develop the first outline for this book. During the academic year 2011–12, I was invited to become the John G. Medlin, Jr. Fellow at the NHC. There, I finally had the time to write. At the NHC, Karen Carroll was a very helpful editor. I am also indebted to other colleagues and friends who kindly agreed to read the entire manuscript, especially Stefan Dudink, Alan Forrest and Sonya Rose, or chapters, like Tim Carter, Annegret Fauser and Paula Michels. The book combines old and new work on the subject that I have done over the last ten years. Different versions of some of the chapters, but mostly only of parts, have already been published in other books and journals. I note at the beginning of the chapters which material I have used, and I would like to thank the original publishers for permission to do so.

My final thanks must go to Michael Grutchfield who helped me with the production of the index, and most importantly Pamela Selwyn, my longtime editor and translator. She translated major parts of the book and edited its English, because I still think and write in German. Without her work and our intensive cooperation, my transatlantic German-American academic existence would not have been possible. She has helped me translate texts, cultures and memories.

Revisiting Prussia's Wars against Napoleon

PRELUDE

WAR, CULTURE AND MEMORY

In November 1816, an article on the latest exhibition at the Berlin Academy of Arts appeared in the *Zeitung für die Elegante Welt*. Held one year after the end of the 1813–15 wars against Napoleon, this exhibition was entirely devoted to "patriotic art."[1] One of the works introduced in the report was the diptych *On Outpost Duty – The Wreath-Maker* (see Figures 1 and 2), painted in 1815 by the Saxon artist Georg Friedrich Kersting, who had joined the artistic group of "Dresden Romanticism" some years before.[2] During and after the wars of 1813–15, Kersting expressed his German-national and early-liberal convictions in his paintings more explicitly than most of his artist friends.[3] When he painted the diptych, the wars against Napoleonic France were coming to an end, and hopes for a German-national rebirth and greater political liberty were running high in the circles of "patriots"[4] to which he belonged: reform-oriented, educated middle- and upper-class civil

[1] "Analekten: Die Berliner Akademieausstellung," *ZfeW*, no. 228, 19 Nov. 1816.
[2] On Kersting's biography and oeuvre, see also Hannelore Gärtner, *Georg Friedrich Kersting* (Leipzig, 1988); Werner Schnell, *Georg Friedrich Kersting (1785–1847): Das zeichnerische und malerische Werk mit Oeuvrekatalog* (Berlin, 1994); and Helmut Börsch-Supan, "Kersting, Georg," *NDB* 11 (1977): 539–541.
[3] On patriotic German art in this period, see Renate Hartleb, ed., *1813: Die Zeit der Befreiungskriege und die Leipziger Völkerschlacht in Malerei, Graphik, Plastik*, exhibition catalogue (Leipzig, 1989); Gerd Biegel and Christof Römer, eds., *Patriotische Flugblätter, 1800–1815 und ihr Umfeld*, exhibition catalogue (Braunschweig, 1990); Veit Veltzke, ed., *Napoleon: Trikolore und Kaiseradler über Rhein und Weser*, exhibition catalogue (Cologne, 2007); Michael Eissenhauer, ed., *König Lustik!? Jérôme Bonaparte und der Modellstaat Königreich Westphalen*, exhibition catalogue (Kassel, 2008); Veit Veltzke, ed., *Für die Freiheit – Gegen Napoleon: Ferdinand von Schill, Preußen und die deutsche Nation*, exhibition catalogue (Cologne, 2009); and Bénédicte Savoy, ed., *Napoleon und Europa: Traum und Trauma*, exhibition catalogue (Munich, 2011).
[4] On the significance of this self-description, which was extremely widespread in the literature of the late eighteenth and early nineteenth centuries, see Bernhard Giesen, *Die Intellektuellen und die deutsche Nation: Eine deutsche Achsenzeit* (Frankfurt/M., 1993), 122–125.

servants, officers, clergymen, educators, writers and artists whose objectives
were the "liberation of the fatherland" and frequently more political liberty
as well. His diptych depicts the complementary figures that embodied those
hopes: young military volunteers and a "German maiden."[5]

On Outpost Duty, which Kersting himself had entitled "Theodor Körner,
Karl Friedrich Friesen and Christian Ferdinand Hartmann on Outpost
Duty," portrays three men who, like Kersting, served as volunteers in the
Lützower *Freikorps* (Lützow Free Corps), which had been authorized
by the Prussian King Friedrich Wilhelm III one month before his declaration of war against France on 15 March 1813. The corps was to enlist
into its ranks mainly "young men from abroad" – that is, from German
regions outside Prussia – who could arm and outfit themselves. Because of
its all-German composition and the activities and publications of its best-
known members, for the contemporary public and in collective memory
it symbolized the German-national and early-liberal goals of the struggle
for liberation.[6] Among the most enthusiastic propagandists of the volunteer corps were Friedrich Ludwig Jahn, Friedrich Friesen and Theodor
Körner.[7] Jahn, a Prussian teacher and journalist who is today known as the
Turnvater – "the truly German father of gymnastics" – was one of the most
influential activists of the early national movement. In 1810, together with
his friend Friedrich Friesen, a teacher from Magdeburg, he began to build
up a group of national-minded male gymnasts – the *Turner*.[8] In the spring
of 1813, Jahn's and Friesen's attempts to mobilize young men throughout
Germany for the Lützowers were supported in no small part by an appeal
from the popular young Saxon poet Theodor Körner, which had been distributed as a leaflet in Dresden, among other places, in early April 1813.
Körner also supported the war effort with poems and songs, which became
extremely popular in the volunteer movement. Körner's appeal challenged

[5] For the following, see Karen Hagemann, "Gendered Images of the German Nation: The
  Romantic Painter Friedrich Kersting and the Patriotic-National Discourse during the Wars of
  Liberation," *Nation and Nationalism* 12 (2006): 653–679.
[6] Peter Brandt, "Einstellungen, Motive und Ziele von Kriegsfreiwilligen 1813–14: Das
  Freikorps Lützow," in *Kriegsbereitschaft und Friedensordnung in Deutschland, 1800–1814*,
  ed. Jost Dülffer (Münster, 1995), 211–233. One of the many popular publications on the
  Lützowers in the nineteenth century was Karl von Lützow, *Adolf Lützows Freikorps in den
  Jahren 1813–1814* (Berlin, 1884).
[7] On their biography, see Horst Ueberhorst, ed., *Friedrich Ludwig Jahn: 1778/1978* (Munich,
  1978); idem, "Jahn, Friedrich Ludwig," *NDB* 10 (1974): 301–303; Christa Janic, "Ausgegraben:
  Friedrich Friesen oder Wie wird man ein deutscher Held?," *WerkstattGeschichte* 6 (1993):
  22–34; Marianne Leber, "Friesen, Karl Friedrich," *NDB* 5 (1961): 613–614; René Schilling,
  "Kriegshelden": Deutungsmuster heroischer Männlichkeit in Deutschland, 1813–1945
  (Paderborn, 2002), esp. 126–151; and Hans-Wolf Jäger, "Körner, Theodor," *NDB* 12 (1980):
  378–379.
[8] On the early gymnastic movement, see Dieter Düding, *Organisierter gesellschaftlicher
  Nationalismus in Deutschland, 1808–1847: Bedeutung und Funktion der Turner- und
  Sänger-Vereine für die deutsche Nationalbewegung* (Munich, 1984).

the "arms-bearing young men of subjugated Saxony" to join the struggle for liberation and enter the ranks of the Lützow Free Corps, which he described as follows: "In our company there is no distinction of birth, station or country. We are all free men, defying hell and its confederates, whom we will drown, if need be with our own blood."[9] Using similar rhetoric, he sought with his lyric poetry to mobilize young men for the wars as a struggle for both liberation and political liberty.[10] By August 1813, the corps had grown to 3,666 men, with three-fifths of them from German-speaking "foreign countries," primarily from the Protestant areas of northern, central and western Germany.[11] Five hundred young men from Saxony alone joined the corps, among them the penniless Kersting, whose uniform and weapons were financed by his older and more-established painter friends Carl Gustav Carus, Caspar David Friedrich and Gerhard von Kügelgen.[12] In the corps he befriended Heinrich Hartmann, a law student and member of the patriotic student associations (*Burschenschaften*) from Thuringia.

Educated contemporaries in Berlin and elsewhere were well aware of the Lützow Free Corps; had surely heard of Jahn, Friesen and Körner; and very likely had read, listened to or personally sung some of Körner's lyrics, which were not only popularized in the poetry collection *Lyre and Sword*, published only one year after his death in August 1813, but also quickly set to music by such well-known composers as Carl Maria von Weber in 1814 and Franz Schubert in 1815.[13] Contemporaries who saw Kersting's painting *On Outpost Duty* in the exhibition at the Berlin Academy of Arts in 1816 or read about it in a journal or newspaper understood its iconography.

The painting represented for them the German-national and early-liberal agenda of the wars of 1813–15 epitomized by the three bearded volunteers dressed in the black, red and gold uniform of the Lützowers and an "old German beret," all symbolizing their German-national aims.[14] Kersting's

---

[9] [Theodor Körner], "An das Volk der Sachsen, anonyme Flugschrift, 5. April 1813," in *Die Erhebung gegen Napoleon 1806–1814/15*, ed. Hans-Bernd Spies (Darmstadt, 1981), 269–270.

[10] Karen Hagemann, "Of 'Manly Valor' and 'German Honor': Nation, War and Masculinity in the Age of the Prussian Uprising against Napoleon," *CEH* 30 (1997): 187–220.

[11] Brandt, "Einstellungen."

[12] On these painters, see Wolfgang Genschorek, *Carl Gustav Carus: Arzt, Künstler, Naturforscher* (Leipzig, 1980); Bernhard Knauß, "Carus, Carl Gustav," *NDB* 3 (1957): 161–163; Wolfgang Hofmann, *Caspar David Friedrich* (New York, 2000); Herbert Einem, "Friedrich, Caspar David," *NDB* 5 (1961): 602–603; Gerhard Schöner, *Gerhard v. Kügelgen: Leben und Werk* (Kiel, 1982); and Bernt von Kügelgen, "Kügelgen, Gerhard," *NDB* 13 (1982): 184–185.

[13] Theodor Körner, *Leyer und Schwert* (Berlin, 1814, 2nd edn.); see also Susan Youens, *Schubert's Poets and the Making of Music* (Cambridge, 1999), 51–150. On Weber, see Wilhelm Joseph von Wasielewski, "Weber, Karl Maria," *ADB* 41 (1896): 321–333; on Schubert, see Ernst Hilmar, "Schubert, Franz Seraph Peter," *NDB* 23 (2007): 609–612.

[14] Hans Hattenhauer, *Deutsche Nationalsymbole: Zeichen und Bedeutung* (Munich, 1984), 9–39.

diptych, however, was not merely an emphatic declaration of his belief in this agenda. At the same time, he created in it a memorial to three fallen friends, all of whom had died during the fighting of 1813–14: from left to right Hartmann, Friesen and Körner. The three Lützowers – marked as heroic by the Iron Cross medal on their chests – are keeping watch at an advance post on the frontier of the German fatherland, symbolized by the oak forest. They represent the German nation to the outside world as a valorous, manly community of brothers who are restoring their national and thereby their virile honor by liberating the fatherland from the French. Theodor Körner in particular was quickly stylized in contemporary discourse and collective memory as the very embodiment of the young German-national hero (*deutscher Heldenjüngling*) who voluntarily sacrifices his life to protect the "fatherland" from its enemies.[15]

The companion piece, *The Wreath-Maker*, represents the complementary interior image. The German oak forest, symbolizing the unified German nation, connects the two paintings. This nation is shared by both sexes, but assigns men and women different, gender-specific spheres of activity. Whereas the three men in *On Outpost Duty* are represented as individuals whose names are carved in the oak trees close to the young woman, her portrayal lacks individuality. In her plain, white, national dress and pinned-up blonde hair, she is the allegorical incarnation of the moral and domestic German maiden who emboldens men's fighting resolve, upholds virtue and modesty at home, greets and honors the returning victors with wreaths and commemorates the fallen heroes. For that very reason she is the ideal visual embodiment of the German-national war aims for which the three young heroes are fighting. The allegory of Germany as a young woman was quite widespread in the art, literature and poetry of the time.[16]

Kersting's complex diptych thus represents a gendered vision of the German nation that was popular in the patriotic circles of the small elite of educated middle- and upper-class men and women in Prussia and beyond at the time of the wars against Napoleon. They not only aspired to the liberation of their fatherland, but also to national unity within a confederation and greater political rights, especially a constitution. This German-national and early-liberal idea of the nation competed during and after the wars with a far more widespread notion of a Christian-conservative regional patriotism focused on the territorial state and its monarchical ruler, which was propagated by the Prussian and other territorial governments, the churches

[15] Karen Hagemann, "German Heroes: The Cult of the Death for the Fatherland in Nineteenth-Century Germany," in *Masculinities in Politics and War: Gendering Modern History*, ed. Stefan Dudink et al. (Manchester, 2004), 116–134.

[16] Monika Wagner, "Germania und Ihre Freier: Zur Herausbildung einer deutschen nationalen Ikonographie um 1800," in *Volk – Nation – Vaterland*, ed. Ulrich Hermann (Hamburg, 1996), 244–267; and Bettina Brandt, *Germania und ihre Söhne: Repräsentationen von Nation, Geschlecht und Politik in der Moderne* (Göttingen, 2010), 166–206.

and army leaders. The two approaches thus represented competing visions of the future of the German nation and its political order that were debated with increasing vehemence during the wars of 1813–15 and the first postwar decades. Despite all political differences, the supporters shared an understanding of patriotism[17] as the self-sacrificing "love of the fatherland," an adoration of German culture and language and similar ideas about the gender order. In the context of the war, these common ideas, which are also present in Kersting's diptych, created the unity beyond all political conflicts that was necessary for a successful war against Napoleon.[18]

After 1815, Kersting continued to paint explicitly patriotic subjects. In 1821 he exhibited *The Soldier's Farewell to His Family*, now lost, in the Dresden Academy exhibition, and in 1829 he showed his oil painting *The Outpost* there (see Figure 3). In this picture Kersting again portrays a volunteer. This time, however, he shows a solitary and isolated soldier on sentry duty, lying alone on a hill, far from his comrades and the civilization that is still suggested by the houses vaguely visible in the background. The middle-aged man, whose beret and full beard reveal his German-national allegiance, appears to be more melancholy than valorous. The color blue dominates the picture, intensifying the lonely, cold aspect of the volunteer, who is wrapped in his cape and clearly shivering. He no longer radiates the middle-class, manly self-confidence of the subjects in Kersting's earlier drawings and paintings. The nameless volunteer appears to be more doubtful, broken and ambivalent, mirroring Kersting's own situation at the time and that of the nation in general.

Kersting's paintings were not as well received by art critics in the 1820s as they had been during and immediately after the wars of 1813–15. A period of restoration had set in after the final victory over Napoleon in June 1815, and the national opposition movement increasingly became the target of conservative criticism and censorship. The *Turner* and the *Burschenschaften* as the vanguard of this movement were outlawed and their leading proponents persecuted following the Carlsbad Decrees of September 1819. In Prussia alone, 345 trials were held in the wake of these decrees.[19] Kersting's paintings no longer fit the zeitgeist. Through his art, he had tried to support the

---

[17] "Patriotismus," in *Conversations-Lexicon oder Encyclopädisches Handwörterbuch für gebildete Stände*, ed. Friedrich A. Brockhaus, 10 vols. (Altenburg and Leipzig, 1814–1819), 9:306–307 (1817).

[18] On the patriotic-national discourse of the time, see Jörg Echternkamp, *Der Aufstieg des deutschen Nationalismus, 1770–1840* (Frankfurt/M., 1998); Matthew Levinger, *Enlightened Nationalism: The Transformation of Prussian Political Culture, 1806–1848* (Oxford, 2000); and Karen Hagemann, *"Mannlicher Muth und Teutsche Ehre": Nation, Militär und Geschlecht zur Zeit der Antinapoleonischen Kriege Preußens* (Paderborn, 2002). Important early studies of the national movement are Düding, *Nationalismus*; and Karin Luys, *Die Anfänge der deutschen Nationalbewegung von 1815 bis 1819* (Münster, 1992).

[19] Düding, *Nationalismus*, 130–135.

FIGURE 3 Georg Friedrich Kersting, The Outpost (*Auf Vorposten*), oil painting, 1829, Nationalgalerie, Staatliche Museen zu Berlin.

early-liberal demand that the territorial states of the German Confederation created by the Congress of Vienna in 1815 award more political rights to the men who had valorously protected their fatherland and approve the promised constitutions. After the final victory, the conservative governments of the restoration period increasingly attempted to suppress such dangerous ideas. In 1818 Kersting had to abandon his attempts to make a living as a freelance artist and accept a position as supervisor of the designers at the Royal Porcelain Manufactory in Meissen, near Dresden, which allowed him to marry and support a family. Kersting continued to paint in his leisure time, but he never again achieved the same reception as in the period during and immediately after the wars of 1813–15. He responded to the conservative political climate by changing his *sujet*, increasingly painting middle-class men and women performing gender-specific tasks in appropriate interiors. His German-national and early-liberal paintings were forgotten as the nineteenth century wore on. Kersting's name surfaced only sporadically in writings about art. *On Outpost Duty – The Wreath-Maker* was not shown again until the Third Reich, when it resurfaced as part of a 1936 exhibition on German Romanticism in Rostock. The reception in the Nazi press emphasized the nationalist aspects of the iconography in the two paintings and suppressed their liberal agenda.[20] After 1945 the two paintings were included in the permanent exhibition first of Charlottenburg Palace and later of the Old National Gallery in Berlin. Only recently have art historians rediscovered Kersting's oeuvre, although they usually continue to overlook its gender dimensions.

Kersting, his paintings and their changing reception (to the point of total oblivion) are a fitting starting point for a book on war, culture and memory focusing on the history of Prussia's wars against Napoleon between 1806 and 1815 and how they were remembered up to the First World War. Kersting's story encapsulates several themes that this book explores. Its aim is to rewrite the history of the wars by emphasizing the importance of the era's political culture for war mobilization; connecting the analysis of this culture and the contested contemporary perceptions of the wars with the study of the creation of collective memories; and focusing on the significance of gender and other constructed differences in these intertwined processes of the creation of meaning and memory. I use the concept of "political culture" here, broadly defined as the concepts, "values, expectations, and implicit rules that expressed and shaped collective intentions and actions."[21] The focus of the study is on the highly contested discourses and symbolic practices by which individuals and groups made political claims in the broadest sense.[22] The construction of competing memories played an important role in this hard-fought process. Although art and other visual representations were obviously very important in the intermedial creation of the collective memories, I decided to concentrate my analysis on textual representations and cultural practices to give the book a clearer focus. In the following Introduction I discuss in more detail the framework of the study, reflecting on the place of the wars in history, historiography and memory, and outlining my own approach.

[20] Kunstverein Rostock, ed., *Ausstellung Deutsche Romantik: Malerei und Zeichnung. 18. Oktober – 15. November 1936 im Städt. Kunst- und Altertumsmuseum* (Rostock, 1936); and "Kersting im Kreis der Romantiker," *Mecklenburgische Tageszeitung*, no. 281, 1 Dec. 1936.

[21] Lynn Hunt, *Politics, Culture, and Class in the French Revolution* (Berkeley, CA, 1984), 10.

[22] Here I follow Keith Michael Baker, *Inventing the French Revolution: Essays on French Political Culture in the Eighteenth Century* (Cambridge, 1990), 4; for a more developed discussion of his approach, see 4–7.

INTRODUCTION

REVISITING THE WARS AGAINST NAPOLEON

In 2013, the media and museums throughout Germany began to mark the bicentenary of the last, ultimately victorious wars against Napoleon in 1813–15, which are usually referred to as the "Wars of Liberation."[1] Several academic conferences have debated the history of the period and a plethora of public events – including a vast reenactment of the central battle at Leipzig in October 1813, lectures, readings and "history festivals" – have recalled the wars.[2] Documentaries and other programs on television,[3] newspapers and magazines,[4] popular history books and bestselling historical

---

[1] See *1813. Auf dem Schlachtfeld bei Leipzig: Ein Rundgang durch das Gemälde "Siegesmeldung" von Johann Peter Krafft*, exhibition catalogue, ed. German Historical Museum Berlin (Berlin, 2013); Volker Rodekamp, ed., *Helden nach Maß: 200 Jahre Völkerschlacht bei Leipzig*, exhibition catalogue (Leipzig, 2013); Gerhard Bauer, Gorch Pieken and Matthias Rogg, eds., *Blutige Romantik: 200 Jahre Befreiungskriege – Essays*, exhibition catalogue (Dresden, 2013); and Andrej Tchernodarov, ed., *"Und Frieden aller Welt gebracht." Russisch-Preußischer Feldzug 1813–1814*, exhibition catalogue (Berlin, 1813). The following introduction is to some extent based on Karen Hagemann, "Occupation, Mobilization and Politics: The Anti-Napoleonic Wars in Prussian Experience, Memory and Historiography," *CEH* 39 (2006): 580–610, "'Desperation to the Utmost': The Defeat of 1806 and the French Occupation in Prussian Experience and Perception," in *The Bee and the Eagle: Napoleonic France and the End of the Holy Roman Empire*, ed. Alan Forrest and Peter Wilson (Basingstoke, 2008), 191–214, and "The Military and Masculinity: Gendering the History of the French Wars, 1792–1815," in *War in an Age of Revolution, 1775–1815*, ed. Roger Chickering and Stig Förster (Cambridge, 2010), 331–352.

[2] See for example, http://www.mgfa-potsdam.de/html/aktuelles/54.itmg?teaser=0&PHPSESSID=55b1336eeabbc69be4c65f1a34bd0da0; http://www.voelkerschlacht-jubilaeum.de/home.html; and http://www.leipzig1813.eu/de/home.html (Accessed 17 December 2013).

[3] See for example, http://www.mdr.de/voelkerschlacht/index.html (Accessed 17 December 2013).

[4] For example, Jan Fleischhauer, "Der Parvenue als Kaiser," *Der Spiegel* 32 (5 May 2013); Gerd Fesser, "Die Stunde der Befreiung," *DIE ZEIT* 39 (16 October 2013); and "1813: Für Freiheit und Einheit! Die Deutschen gegen Napoleon," special issue of *Geschichte* 5 (2013).

novels have re-narrated them.[5] The hype around the anniversaries of the Napoleonic Wars began in 2005 in Britain, occasioned by the anniversary of the Battle of Trafalgar with a major exhibition on *Nelson & Napoleon*. Exhibitions in Austria, Germany, Italy, Russia and Sweden followed.[6] The most recent include *Napoleon and Europe: Dream and Trauma*, a Franco-German project that was shown in Bonn in 2011 and in Paris in 2013. It explores "the close connection between the level of expectation that Napoleon created and the deep distress he caused."[7] This book also emphasizes the ambivalence, frictions, ruptures and contradictions that marked the period of the wars of the Napoleonic Empire and the preceding French Revolution – which raged across and beyond the Continent between 1792 and 1815 – and its legacy. The sometimes sudden and dramatic transformations in the economy, politics, the military and society that characterized this time occurred unevenly across Europe and were accompanied by stagnation and the persistence of tradition in other areas of work and life, particularly in the culture of everyday life and mentalities. Contemporaries had to cope with the coexistence of accelerated change and cultural continuities, and the contradiction between universalist rhetoric and exclusionary practices.[8] These ambivalences also formed the memories of the Napoleonic Wars from 1803 to 1815, which were at once national and European. The nation – defined, following Benedict Anderson, as an "imagined community" – was the main framework in which most memories of these wars were initially constructed and in which they then evolved and circulated.[9] Many European

[5] For example, Steffen Poser, *Die Völkerschlacht bei Leipzig: "In Schutt und Graus begraben"* (Leipzig, 2013); Gerd Fesser, *1813: Die Völkerschlacht bei Leipzig* (Jena, 2013); Hans-Ulrich Thamer, *Die Völkerschlacht bei Leipzig: Europas Kampf gegen Napoleon* (Munich, 2013); and Andreas Platthaus, *1813: Die Völkerschlacht und das Ende der Alten Welt* (Berlin, 2013). The bestselling novel is Sabine Ebert, *Kriegsfeuer: 1813* (Munich, 2013).

[6] For Germany, see Veltzke, *Napoleon*; Eissenhauer, *König Lustik!?*; Veltzke, *Für die Freiheit*; Savoy, *Napoleon*. Other important exhibitions include Margarette Lincoln, ed., *Nelson & Napoléon*, exhibition catalogue (London, 2005); and Jan Berggren, *Bernadotterna och Helsingborg: 200 år sedan Karl XIV Johan landsteg i Helsingborg*, exhibition catalogue (Helsingborg, 2010). Two of the major books that remember the Russian campaign are Adam Zamoyski, *Moscow 1812: Napoleon's Fatal March* (New York, 2004); and Dominic Lieven, *Russia against Napoleon: The Battle for Europe, 1807 to 1814* (London, 2009).

[7] Savoy, *Napoleon*, 16–17.

[8] Reinhart Koselleck, *Futures Past: On the Semantic of Historical Time* (New York, 2004), 246.

[9] Benedict R. Anderson, *Imagined Communities: Reflections on the Origin and Spread of Nationalism* (London, 2006). For the state of research, see Lloyd Kramer, *Nationalism in Europe and America: Politics, Cultures, and Identities since 1775* (Chapel Hill, NC, 2011); and Stefan Berger and Chris Lorenz, eds., *The Contested Nation: Ethnicity, Class, Religion and Gender in National Histories* (Basingstoke, 2011). On nation and war in the nineteenth century, see Jörn Leonhard, *Bellizismus und Nation: Kriegsdeutung und Nationsbestimmung in Europa und den Vereinigten Staaten, 1750–1914* (Munich, 2008). A still useful introduction to the development of the conceptual debate is Geoff Eley and Ronald Grigor Suny, "Introduction: From the Moment of Social History to the Work of

countries recall the era even today as a "formative period" in the history of their nation.[10] This "nationalization" of memory, which is also reflected in the research, is, however, accompanied by the emergence and formation of a "shared and entangled," specifically European memory of the same wars.[11]

This dual national and European dimension of the memories of the wars between 1792 and 1815 stems from their specific character: They were the first modern world wars, or as David A. Bell has put it, the first "total wars," to be conducted by mass armies that used patriotic and national propaganda to mobilize men for fighting.[12] For Bell, this "fusion of politics and war" characterizes the period and led to a "cataclysmic intensification of the fighting" that justifies the description of "total war" mainly for three reasons: the much larger size of armies and the dramatic increase of the frequency of battles; the changing relations between the military and civilians; and a new "culture of war," which used a nationalized rhetoric to legitimate the proclaimed aim to annihilate the enemy.[13] It relentlessly pushed states toward "an inexorable spiral of escalation that ultimately" ended "with the collapse of one side or the other from sheer exhaustion and exsanguinations."[14]

In many ways Bell's approach, which emphasizes the importance of the culture of war, can help us to understand the specific dynamic of the period. In using the contentious concept of "total war," we risk, however, projecting an ideal definition drawn from present-day scholarship onto a historical period that was marked by a rapid and contradictory transformation.[15]

Cultural Representation," in *Becoming National: A Reader*, ed. eidem (Oxford, 1996), 3–39. See also Jörg Echternkamp and Sven Oliver Müller, "Perspektiven einer politik- und kulturgeschichtlichen Nationalismusforschung," in *Die Politik der Nation: Deutscher Nationalismus in Krieg and Krisen, 1760–1960*, ed. eidem (Munich, 2002), 1–24.

[10] Monika Flacke, ed., *Mythen der Nationen: Ein europäisches Panorama*, exhibition catalogue (Munich, 1998); and Nikolaus Buschmann and Dieter Langewiesche, eds., *Der Krieg in den Gründungsmythen europäischer Nationen und der USA* (Frankfurt/M., 2003).

[11] For an overview of the research on European memory, see Alan Forrest et al., eds., *War Memories: The Revolutionary and Napoleonic Wars in Modern European Culture* (Basingstoke, 2011), esp. Alan Forrest et al., "Introduction: Memories of the Revolutionary and Napoleonic Wars in Modern European Culture," 1–37.

[12] See Chickering and Förster, *War*; and Paul Fregosi, *Dreams of Empire: Napoleon and the First World War, 1792–1815* (London, 1989); see also Charles Esdaile, "Recent Writing on Napoleon and His Wars," *The Journal of Military History* 73 (2009): 209–220; and his *Napoleon's Wars: An International History, 1803–1815* (London, 2009).

[13] David A. Bell, *The First Total War: Napoleon's Europe and the Birth of Warfare as We Know It* (Boston, 2007), 9.

[14] David Bell, "The Limits of Conflict in Napoleonic Europe – And Their Transgression," in *Civilians and War in Europe, 1618–1815*, ed. Erica Charters, Eve Rosenhaft and Hannah Smith (Liverpool, 2012), 201–208, 203.

[15] For a critical discussion of the concept for this period, see Roger Chickering, "Introduction: A Tale of Two Tales. Grand Narratives of War in the Age of Revolution," in Chickering and Förster, *War*, 1–17; Karen Hagemann et al., eds., *Gender, War and Politics: Transatlantic*

If we wish to understand the interplay between the complex processes at work, we need to historicize them. Only then can we recognize that the related political and military goals of these wars and the different forms of mass mobilization had far-reaching structural consequences with significance far beyond the military and the conduct of war. Most important, compared to earlier periods, was the trend to deploy mass armies of a size previously unknown.

The number of soldiers deployed surpassed anything ever before seen in Europe. In 1813 the Grande Armée was around 440,000 men strong, and the coalition field army around 510,000.[16] In order to defeat Napoleon, his enemies had to build up mass armies and appropriate French military strategy with its general aim of annihilating the troops of the adversary. This development had far-reaching consequences not only for the military but also for civilian society. For the wars between 1792 and 1815, scholars estimate up to five million war dead in Europe; in relation to the size of the population this matches the death rate of the First World War.[17] The magnitude of the armies meant that war casualties rose to previously unheard-of levels. Only a minority of the victims were soldiers who died in battle; most perished from injuries, diseases and epidemics that also affected the civilian population. Thousands of veterans returned home disabled and faced the prospect of survival without adequate state support.[18]

Civilians experienced more troop movements combined with military engagements, occupation and annexation than in all of the eighteenth-century wars put together. They had to pay the costs of mass warfare. Old forms of supply through state repositories were replaced by new requisitions systems. The lands crossed and occupied by mass armies also had to feed and house them; in this respect, these armies did not distinguish between friend and foe. The civilian population had to finance the wars not only by means of higher taxes and tariffs, but also by providing all kinds of goods: weapons and uniforms, along with food, animals and carts. Occupied territories were exploited and compelled to make financial contributions, intensifying economic hardship. Economic warfare became an

Perspectives, 1775–1830 (Basingstoke, 2010), 7–9; and Charters et al., *Civilians and War*, 3–13.

[16] Karen Hagemann, "'Unimaginable Horror and Misery': The Battle of Leipzig in October 1813 in Civilian Experience and Perception," in *Soldiers, Citizens and Civilians: Experiences and Perceptions of the French Wars, 1790–1820*, ed. Alan Forrest et al. (Basingstoke, 2009), 157–178.

[17] David Gates, *The Napoleonic Wars, 1803–1815* (London, 1997), 272.

[18] See also Stuart J. Woolf, *Napoleon's Integration of Europe* (London, 1991); Michael Broers, *Europe Under Napoleon, 1799–1815* (London, 1996); Philip G. Dwyer, ed., *Napoleon and Europe* (London, 2001); and Dwyer and Alan Forrest, eds., *Napoleon and his Empire: Europe, 1804–1814* (Basingstoke, 2007); Forrest et al., *Soldiers, Citizens*.

important strategy to defeat the enemy; the Continental Blockade is the best-known example of this strategy.[19]

Warfare on this scale necessitated the support of large segments of the population. Larger and smaller states, monarchies and republics alike appealed to patriotic sentiment to mobilize men to volunteer for military service. They also needed the support of male and female civilians to provide equipment for the armies, medical services for sick and wounded soldiers and charitable contributions for invalids, widows and orphans. The war as a situation of declared "national emergency" thus opened up opportunities especially for noble and middle-class women to become active in arenas of public life that had previously been closed to them. The *levée en masse* that Revolutionary France introduced in August 1793 set the model for other states. It demanded that young men of military age become soldiers, and that older men support the war effort with material and ideas. Women, by contrast, were to ensure that the warriors were equipped with tents and uniforms, care for sick and wounded soldiers and bolster the men's fighting resolve. Political differences notwithstanding, the same ideas about the gender order of war informed the propaganda that accompanied military mass mobilization in the various belligerent countries.[20]

Influenced by the experiences of these new forms of mass warfare as well as the political culture of the time, self-perceptions and perceptions of the Other by the inhabitants of many European regions and nations changed fundamentally. Because these wars led to the circulation of millions of people – soldiers, prisoners of war and civilians – throughout Europe and beyond, many men and women experienced the otherness, but also similarities, of different European cultures for the first time. The increased use of a highly gendered "patriotic-national"[21] rhetoric in war propaganda provided a discursive framework for the articulation of these differences and similarities that seems to have led to a nationalization of

---

[19] Katherine Aaslestad, "The Continental System and Imperial Exploitation," in Dwyer and Forrest, *Napoleon*, 114–32; and Aaslestad and Johannes Joor, eds., *Revisiting Napoleon's Continental System: Local, Regional, and European Experiences* (Basingstoke, 2014).

[20] On the gender dimension of the levée en masse, see Harriet B. Applewhite and Darline G. Levy, "Women and Militant Citizenship in Revolutionary Paris," in *Rebel Daughters: Women and the French Revolution*, ed. Sara E. Melzer and Leslie W. Kabine (New York, 1992), 79–101. More generally, see Katherine Aaslestad et al., eds., *Gender, War and the Nation in the Period of the Revolutionary and Napoleonic Wars – European Perspectives*, special issue of *EHQ* 37.4 (2007); Waltraud Maierhofer et al., eds., *Women Against Napoleon: Historical and Fictional Responses to His Rise and Legacy* (Frankfurt/M., 2007); Hagemann et al., *Gender, War and Politics*.

[21] Following Miroslav Hroch, I use the term "patriotic-national" to express the ambivalence, simultaneity and diversity of nationalized notions in the contemporary discourse. See Hroch, "From National Movement to the Fully-Formed Nation: The Nation-Building Process in Europe," in Eley and Suny, *Becoming National*, 60–77, 62.

collective identities. Traditional stereotypes about the differing character of peoples (*Völkerstereotype*) now became modern ideas about disparate national characters (*Nationalcharaktere*).[22] As a result, to an extent unprecedented in previous wars, the discourse of the time created ideas of ethnic and national identity that would continue to define European culture well into the twentieth century. At the same time, in this discourse the idea of a European identity that united the included "civilized" nations against their external "Others" in the "barbaric East" and the "uncivilized South" as well as the "savages" in the colonized world were further developed. These wars, therefore, had an enduring influence on the creation of the collective identity and memory of most European regions and nations, and the ways in which they were remembered had both regional and national as well as transnational dimensions.[23] They shaped the thinking about Europe and the world beyond, but the collective recollections of the wars themselves were constructed mostly as regional and national memories.[24]

THE ANTI-NAPOLEONIC WARS IN HISTORIOGRAPHY AND MEMORY

For these reasons, the exploration of the history of the Anti-Napoleonic Wars, specifically how they were experienced and remembered, needs to start on the level of the region and the nation, even though most European countries were involved in the wars of the Napoleonic Empire between 1803 and 1815. Only on the regional and national levels can the many factors that influenced the perception and recollection of the wars against Napoleon be carved out in greater detail. The focus of this study is German-speaking Central Europe, especially Prussia. For the Prussian monarchy and other parts of Germany, the period of the Anti-Napoleonic Wars that began in 1806 with a devastating defeat and ended in 1815 with a decisive victory occupied a key position in both historiography and memory up to 1945. Several contesting interpretations emerged and competed for hegemony in

[22] See Winfried Schulze, "Die Entstehung des nationalen Vorurteils: Zur Kultur der Wahrnehmung fremder Nationen in der europäischen Frühen Neuzeit," *GWU* 46 (1995): 642–665. On the "nationalization" of the political discourse that started in the eighteenth century and intensified after the French Revolution, see Michael Jeismann, *Das Vaterland der Feinde: Studien zum nationalen Feindbegriff und Selbstverständnis in Deutschland und Frankreich, 1792–1918* (Stuttgart, 1992); Linda Colley, *Britons: Forging the Nation, 1707–1837* (London, 2003); Hans-Martin Blitz, *Aus Liebe zum Vaterland: Die deutsche Nation im 18. Jahrhundert* (Hamburg, 2000); and David A. Bell, *The Cult of the Nation in France: Inventing Nationalism, 1680–1800* (Cambridge, MA, 2001).
[23] Forrest et al., *War Memories*, esp. Étienne François, "Conclusion: The Revolutionary and Napoleonic Wars as a Shared and Entangled European *lieu de mémoire*," 386–402.
[24] See Forrest et al., *War Memories*; and Wolfgang Koller, *Historienkino im Zeitalter der Weltkriege: Die Revolutions- und Napoleonischen Kriege in der europäischen Erinnerungs* (Paderborn, 2013).

the German-speaking regions during the nineteenth century, the period in which the historiographical "master narratives"[25] and collective memory of the period were formulated.

In the German historiography, two master narratives became most influential. Both focused on the wars of 1813–15. The monarchic-conservative Prussian narrative spoke of "Wars of Liberation" (Befreiungskriege) fought by "subjects" who were "monarchical to their very marrow," followed the king's call to resist, and were led by his generals.[26] The liberal German-national interpretation, in contrast, spoke of "Wars of Liberty" (Freiheitskriege) conducted by "the German people" (primarily understood as the educated classes) as a "free, autonomous movement" and a "struggle for liberty" against external and internal forces.[27] A third interpretation challenged both approaches following the Democratic Revolution of 1848–49, as Marxists viewed the wars of 1813–15 as "people's wars." Unlike the liberal reading, however, the Marxist interpretation featured the active, autonomous conduct of the "popular masses," including the urban and rural poor.[28] The debate on the name and meaning of the wars of 1813–15, which had already begun during the wars themselves, centered on whether they were simply a struggle for liberation from French rule led by the Prussian king or had been instigated by the German people, who forced the Prussian monarch and other German princes into a movement for national liberation and political liberty. Until the foundation of the German Empire in 1871, this distinction was politically vital because it legitimated liberal and democratic demands for more political rights, particularly the granting of a constitution; justified the borders envisioned for a united Germany (that is, whether to include or exclude Austria in a gross- or kleindeutsch model

---

[25] On the term "master narratives," see Konrad H. Jarausch and Michael Geyer, Shattered Past: Reconstructing German Histories (Princeton, NJ, 2003), 38–39.

[26] Heinrich von Treitschke, Deutsche Geschichte im Neunzehnten Jahrhundert, 5 vols., (Leipzig, 1886, 4th edn.), 1:269, 417, 429–430 and 434–445. See also Johann Gustav Droysen, Das Leben des Feldmarschalls Grafen York von Wartenburg, 2 vols. (Leipzig, 1975, 7th edn.); and Leopold v. Ranke, Denkwürdigkeiten des Staatskanzlers Fürsten v. Hardenberg, 4 vols. (Leipzig, 1877).

[27] Karl von Rotteck, Allgemeine Geschichte: Vom Anfang der historischen Kenntnis bis auf unsere Zeiten, 10 vols. (Braunschweig, 1851), 9:425–426. See also the young Johann Gustav Droysen, Vorlesungen über die Freiheitskriege, 2 vols. (Kiel, 1846); Heinrich Beitzke, Geschichte der Deutschen Freiheitskriege in den Jahren 1813 und 1814, 3 vols. (Berlin, 1854 and 1855); Friedrich Förster, Geschichte der Befreiungs-Kriege, 1813, 1814, 1815, 3 vols. (Berlin, 1856, 1858 and 1861); Max Lehmann, Freiherr vom Stein, 3 vols. (Leipzig, 1902 and 1905); and Friedrich Meinecke, Die Deutschen Gesellschaften und der Hoffmannsche Bund: Ein Beitrag zur Geschichte der politischen Bewegungen in Deutschland im Zeitalter der Befreiungskriege (Stuttgart, 1891).

[28] Friedrich Engels, "Ernst Moritz Arndt," in Karl Marx and Friedrich Engels, Werke, Ergänzungsband, pt. 2 (Berlin, 1967), 118–131, 120–121; and Franz Mehring, "Zur deutschen Geschichte von der Zeit der Französischen Revolution bis zum Vormärz (1789–1847)," in Gesammelte Schriften, ed. Thomas Höhle et al., vol. 6 (Berlin, 1965).

of the empire); and raised questions about Prussia's influence in any future German confederation. After the unification, the distinction, and with it different political traditions, were mainly used to legitimate competing vision of the German nation.[29]

These political conflict lines were complicated by the quite different regional experiences and thus recollections of the period between 1792 and 1815. Some regions, especially in the southwest of German Central Europe, had already encountered war in the 1790s and since then had either belonged to the Napoleonic Empire, been affiliated with Napoleon and become members of the Confederation of the Rhine in 1806 or, like Austria, continued to resist. Other regions, particularly in the northeast of Germany, did not face war and occupation before 1806 and were afterward either incorporated into the French Empire, integrated into the Confederation of the Rhine or tried to stay independent like Prussia.[30] As a consequence Germans fought against Germans: First the male inhabitants of military age in the German *départements* of France were conscripted for the Grande Armée. This began in 1797 with the recognition in the Treaty of Campo Formio of the extension of France's borders up to the Rhine, and after 1806 the same happened to the men liable for military service in the member states of the confederation. The German soldiers and officers who fought for Napoleon until he was defeated on German territory in the Battle of Leipzig in October 1813 mainly remembered the struggle as the "wars of Napoleon." Their recollections were quite different than the memories of their German opponents in the Austrian and Prussian armies, who recalled the occupation by the Napoleonic Empire as "the time of the French" and their struggle against France as the "wars against Napoleon." In the analysis of German experiences and memories of the time it is therefore important to keep this difference in mind and clearly differentiate between the period of the Napoleonic Wars and the Anti-Napoleonic Wars as one part of it.

Political controversies and regional differences dominated academic historiography throughout the nineteenth century.[31] Its master narratives were not only complemented by conflicting recollections of the wars in different

---

[29] For more on this debate, see Helmut Berding, "Das geschichtliche Problem der Freiheitskriege, 1813–1814," in *Historismus und moderne Geschichtswissenschaft: Europa zwischen Revolution und Restauration, 1797–1815*, ed. Karl Otmar Freiherr von Aretin and Gerhard A. Ritter (Wiesbaden, 1987), 201–215. Because of this debate, historians today need to be careful about the terms they use. The common designation "Wars of Liberation" reflects one specific historical interpretation. I will therefore use the contemporary terms only in quotations and will speak instead simply of the wars of 1813–15. When I discuss the entire war period between 1806 and 1815 in Prussian history, I use the term "Anti-Napoleonic Wars."

[30] See Katherine Aaslestad, and Karen Hagemann, eds., "Collaboration, Resistance, and Reform: Experiences and Historiographies of the Napoleonic Wars in Central Europe," special issue of *CEH* 39.4 (2006).

[31] See Ferdi Akaltin, *Die Befreiungskriege im Geschichtsbild der Deutschen im 19. Jahrhundert* (Frankfurt/M., 1997).

regions and social groups as expressed in autobiographies and war memoirs; several other media of memory, too, were part of the process of memory construction. The most important literary media were novels, biographies, textbooks, songs and poems. Together with pictorial media (paintings, prints, book illustrations, postcards and collectors' cards), commemorative festivities and rituals as well as monuments and symbols, they had a decisive influence on the collective memory of the period of the Napoleonic Wars.[32]

Together these media of memory created nuanced and conflicting interpretations of the Anti-Napoleonic Wars in nineteenth-century collective memory. These conflicts were especially developed before the foundation of the German Empire in 1871. Thereafter, the democratic and liberal interpretations of the wars of 1813–15 increasingly lost influence. A unifying metanarrative became pervasive: that of the wars of 1813–15 as the "birth of the German nation." It revolved around the notion that the period of the Anti-Napoleonic Wars was a "glorious era" and a "truly heroic time"[33] that "Germans cannot recall often enough,"[34] because the German people had rediscovered their own manly valor and warlike power along with the strength of unity. This interpretation, which glorified the "heroes of the Wars of Liberation" as models for succeeding generations, gained increasing influence, especially in popular culture, and stood at the center of the celebration of the centennial in 1913–15. Its major function was to create national unity across political, regional and social differences as well as to

[32] Akaltin, *Befreiungskriege*; Christopher Clark, "The Wars of Liberation in Prussian Memory: Reflections on the Memorialization of War in Early Nineteenth-Century Germany," *JMH* 68 (1996): 550–576; Katherine B. Aaslestad, *Place and Politics: Local Identity, Civic Culture, and German Nationalism in North Germany during the Revolutionary Era* (Leiden, 2005), 321–349; Ute Planert, *Der Mythos vom Befreiungskrieg: Frankreichs Kriege und der deutsche Süden: Alltag – Wahrnehmung – Deutung, 1792–1841* (Paderborn, 2007), 620–664; and Angelika Bethan, *Napoleons Königreich Westphalen. Lokale, deutsche und europäische Erinnerungen* (Paderborn, 2012). With a focus on individuals, see Reinhard K. Sprenger, *Die Jahnrezeption in Deutschland, 1871–1933: Nationale Identität und Modernisierung* (Schorndorf, 1985); Schilling, "*Kriegshelden*," 126–151; Philipp Demandt, *Luisenkult: Die Unsterblichkeit der Königin von Preussen* (Cologne, 2003); Sam A. Mustafa, *The Long Ride of Major von Schill: A Journey through German History and Memory* (Lanham, MD, 2008); Heinz Duchhardt, *Mythos Stein: Vom Nachleben, von der Stilisierung und von der Instrumentalisierung des preußischen Reformers* (Göttingen, 2008); and Birte Förster, *Der Königin Luise-Mythos: Mediengeschichte des "Idealbilds deutscher Weiblichkeit," 1860–1960* (Göttingen, 2011). On monuments, see Meinhold Lürz, *Kriegerdenkmäler in Deutschland*, vol. 1: *Die Befreiungskriege* (Heidelberg, 1985); and Katrin Keller and Hans-Dieter Schmid, eds., *Vom Kult zur Kulisse: Das Volkerschlachtdenkmal als Gegenstand der Geschichtskultur* (Leipzig, 1995). On the battle of Jena and Auerstedt as one key event in collective memory, see Konrad Breitenborn und Justus H. Ulbricht, eds., *Jena und Auerstedt: Ereignis und Erinnerung in europäischer, nationaler und regionaler Perspektive* (Dössel, 2006).
[33] Julius v. Pflug-Hartung, *1813–1815, Illustrierte Geschichte der Befreiungskriege: Ein Jubiläumswerk zur Erinnerung an die große Zeit vor 100 Jahren* (Stuttgart, 1912), ii.
[34] Engels, "Ernst Moritz Arndt," 120.

foster the population's willingness to make sacrifices for the nation, which was especially needed during World War I.[35]

During the Weimar Republic, the story of Prussia's defeat by the Napoleonic army in 1806 and of Germany's national "regeneration" in the "Wars of Liberation" continued to be very popular among nationalists and conservatives, since it was well suited to the situation of the defeated nation. In the mass media of the time, particularly historical novels and films, conquered Germany after 1918 was compared to routed and occupied Prussia after 1806. The myth of a successful "national uprising" against the French between 1806 and 1815 was used to foster nationalism and anti-French sentiments more than a hundred years later. Now the national-conservative reading of "Wars of Liberation" clearly dominated scholarship and public culture. The period between 1806 and 1815 remained a popular subject in the mass media as well as academic historiography after 1933 and was used to create a historical tradition for the Third Reich. Any liberal interpretation was completely suppressed in historiography and cultural memory. The Nationalist Socialist reading stressed the idea of a "national community" (*Volksgemeinschaft*) and its heroic willingness to fight and sacrifice in the struggle against internal and external enemies.[36] Before 1945, whenever national conservatives believed that nationalism needed a boost, recollections of the "German heroic age of the Wars of Liberation" and the cultivation of the songs, symbols and rituals of that period reemerged in public life.

After the Second World War, the period of the Anti-Napoleonic Wars soon became a focus of historical research in the German Democratic Republic (GDR). Taking up the tradition of Marxist interpretation, interest centered on the role of the "popular masses."[37] The GDR styled itself the

[35] Wolfram Siemann, "Krieg und Frieden in historischen Gedenkfeiern des Jahres 1913," in *Öffentliche Festkultur: Politische Feste in Deutschland von der Aufklärung bis zum Ersten Weltkrieg*, ed. Dieter Düding, Peter Friedemann and Paul Münch (Reinbek, 1988), 298–320; Stefan-Ludwig Hoffmann, "Mythos und Geschichte: Leipziger Gedenkfeiern der Völkerschlacht im 19. und frühen 20. Jahrhundert," in *Nation und Emotion: Deutschland und Frankreich im Vergleich 19. und 20. Jahrhundert*, ed. Etiénne François et al. (Göttingen, 1995), 111–132; Ute Schneider, "War in Mind: Celebrations and War Enthusiasm in the Rhineland, 1913," in *Festive Culture in Germany and Europe from the Sixteenth to the Twentieth Century*, ed. Karin Friedrich (Lewiston, NJ, 2000), 265–280; and Kay Wenzel, "Befreiung oder Freiheit? Zur politischen Ausdeutung der deutschen Kriege gegen Napoleon von 1913 bis 1923," in *Griff nach der Deutungsmacht: Zur Geschichte der Geschichtspolitik in Deutschland*, ed. Heinrich August Winkler (Göttingen, 2004), 67–89.

[36] Berding, "Problem"; Sprenger, *Jahnrezeption*, 109–216; Wenzel, "Befreiung"; Koller, *Historienkino*; and idem, "Heroic Memories: Gendered Images of the Napoleonic Wars in German Feature Films of the Interwar Period," in Forrest et al., *War Memories*, 366–385.

[37] Andreas Dorpalen, "The German Struggle against Napoleon: The East German View," *JMH* 41 (1969): 485–516; and Karl Heinz Schäfer, "1813 – Die Freiheitskriege in der Sicht der marxistischen Geschichtsschreibung der DDR," *Geschichte in Wissenschaft und Unterricht* 21 (1970): 2–21.

"living custodian" of the "legacy of the movement for liberty of 1813" and sought to legitimize itself in this way as a "people's state" based on liberty.[38] GDR historiography shifted the focus from the military, political and intellectual history that was dominant until 1945 to social history. In particular, regional studies yielded new information on the form and scope of popular uprisings before and during the wars of 1813–15.[39] Ideological and political strictures, however, limited the possible insights of this scholarship from the outset, because interpretations not in keeping with Marxist dogma were deemed to be unacceptable.

In the Federal Republic (FRG), in contrast, historians lost interest in the era as a kind of counterreaction to its earlier preeminence and to the dominance of a pro-Prussian and nationalist interpretation. In the late 1960s, however, scholars began to rediscover the period between 1806 and 1820. Initially, their research focused once again on Prussia, but increasingly encompassed the Confederation of the Rhine and Austria as well.[40] The tenor of many publications was rather critical of the role of Prussia, which was now perceived as the center of militarism and conservatism in Germany. This interpretation reflected the politics of the Allies, who had enforced the abolition of Prussia after 1945. Firmly distancing themselves from the older conservative and liberal Prusso-centric historiography, some historians, in their attempts to create a counternarrative, even denied that any broader patriotic-national mobilization had occurred in Prussia during the wars of 1813–15.[41] Today, most scholars interpret Prussian history in a more balanced way and emphasize the regional differences within Germany.[42] All agree that the "Wars of Liberation" were not, as earlier generations of national-liberal historians like

[38] Albert Norden, "Das Volk stand auf und siegte," in *Der Befreiungskrieg 1813*, ed. Peter Hoffmann (Berlin, 1967), 1–10, 6; and Fritz Straube, *Das Jahr 1813: Studien zur Geschichte und Wirkung der Befreiungskriege* (Berlin, 1963).

[39] Heinz Heitzer, *Insurrection zwischen Weser und Elbe: Volksbewegungen gegen die französische Fremdherrschaft im Königreich Westfalen (1806–1813)* (Berlin, 1959); and Percy Stulz, *Fremdherrschaft und Befreiungskampf: Die preußische Kabinettspolitik und die Rolle der Volksmassen in den Jahren 1811 bis 1813* (Berlin, 1960).

[40] On the development of research on German Central Europe since 1945, see Peter Brandt, "Die Befreiungskriege von 1813 bis 1815 in der deutschen Geschichte," in *Geschichte und Emanzipation*, ed. Michael Grüttner et al. (Frankfurt/M., 1999), 17–57; and Katherine Aaslestad and Karen Hagemann, "1806 and Its Aftermath: Revisiting the Period of the Napoleonic Wars in German Central Europe," *CEH* 39 (2006): 547–579. On the historiography on Prussia, see Stefan Berger, "Prussia in History and Historiography from the Nineteenth to the Twentieth Centuries," in *Modern Prussian History, 1830–1945*, ed. Philip G. Dwyer (Harlow, 2001), 21–40.

[41] Hans-Ulrich Wehler, *Deutsche Gesellschaftsgeschichte*, 5 vols. (Munich, 1987–2008), 1:525–526; Echternkamp, *Aufstieg*, 216; recently also Planert, *Mythos*, 23–24.

[42] Three excellent studies on Prussia are Bernd von Münchow-Pohl, *Zwischen Reform und Krieg: Untersuchungen zu Bewußtseinslage in Preußen* (Göttingen, 1987); Christopher Clark, *Iron Kingdom: The Rise and Downfall of Prussia, 1600–1947* (Cambridge, MA, 2006); and Peter Paret, *The Cognitive Challenge of War: Prussia 1806* (Princeton, NJ,

Friedrich Meinecke had claimed, the "natal hour" of "German nationalism."[43] The history of the discourse on the "German nation" begins four hundred years earlier, in the period of the Reformation and Renaissance, but, as this book argues, it gained a new quality during the war years.[44]

As scholarship on Napoleonic Germany revived in the FRG, it moved in three directions, focusing on military campaigns and alliances, emerging sovereign states and reform movements, and early articulations of "modern nationalism."[45] These three thematic areas, however, were often treated in isolation from one another. Studies either featured specific campaigns, military organizations and diplomatic relations or focused on the political and social consequences of Napoleonic conquest by highlighting structural transformations, state-building and reform policies or explored the emergence of nationalism. Moreover, this scholarship often ignored the economic, social and cultural dimensions of the wars. Only recently have historians begun to explore the wide variety of war experiences in Central Europe. Their studies emphasize the differences between soldiers and civilians as well as friends and foes of Napoleon, but also the importance of geography, social status and profession, education and linguistic skills, ethnicity and gender for war experiences.[46] What most scholars tend to overlook, however, is

2009). For the regional difference, see Monika Lahrkamp, *Münster in Napoleonischer Zeit, 1800–1815: Administration, Wirtschaft und Gesellschaft im Zeichen von Säkularisation und Französischer Herrschaft* (Münster, 1976); Reinhard Köpping, *Sachsen gegen Napoleon: Zur Geschichte der Befreiungskriege, 1813–1815* (Berlin, 2001); Michael Rowe, *From Reich to State: The Rhineland in the Revolutionary Age, 1780–1830* (Cambridge, 2003); Aaslestad, *Place*; Robert Beachy, *The Soul of Commerce: Credit, Property and Politics in Leipzig, 1750–1840* (Leiden, 2005); James M. Brophy, *Popular Culture and the Public Sphere in the Rhineland, 1800–1850* (Cambridge, 2007); and Planert, *Mythos*.

[43] Friedrich Meinecke, *Das Zeitalter der deutschen Erhebung, 1795–1815* (Leipzig, [1906]; repr. Göttingen, 1957, 6th edn.). On Meinecke, see Ernst Schulin, "Friedrich Meinecke," in *Deutsche Historiker*, ed. Hans-Ulrich Wehler, 7 vols. (Göttingen, 1971–80), 1:39–57.

[44] As research overviews, see Reinhard Stauber, "Nationalismus vor dem Nationalismus? Eine Bestandsaufnahme der Forschung zu 'Nation' und 'Nationalismus' in der Frühen Neuzeit," *GWU* 47 (1996): 139–165; Dieter Langewiesche and Georg Schmidt, eds., *Föderative Nation: Deutschlandkonzepte von der Reformation bis zum Ersten Weltkrieg* (Munich, 2000); and Ute Planert, "Wann beginnt der 'moderne' deutsche Nationalismus? Plädoyer für eine nationale Sattelzeit," in Echternkamp and Müller, *Politik*, 25–59.

[45] To distinguish older forms of national thinking from more modern forms, I follow Dieter Langewiesche's terminology. "Modern nationalism" will be defined here functionally as "all behaviors" that have as their aim "the creation or preservation of a nation-state." Langewiesche, "Reich, Nation und Staat in der jüngeren Deutschen Geschichte," *HZ* 254 (1992): 341–381, 341–342.

[46] See, Planert, *Mythos*; Julia Murken, *Bayerische Soldaten im Russlandfeldzug 1812: Ihre Kriegserfahrungen und deren Umdeutungen im 19. und 20. Jahrhundert* (Munich, 2006); Aaslestad and Hagemann, "Collaboration"; "Karl J. Mayer, *Napoleons Soldaten: Alltag in der Grande Armeé* (Darmstadt, 2008); Hagemann, "Unimaginable Horror"; Leighton S. James, "Invasion and Occupation: Civilian-Military Relations in Central Europe during the Revolutionary and Napoleonic Wars," in *Civilians and War in Europe, 1618–1815*, ed.

that Prussia itself was marked by extreme differences in the experience of the wars. The monarchy was (next to Austria) the largest German state, with a population of more than ten million in 1816 that included Poles and Germans, Protestants, Catholics and Jews. After the Congress of Vienna, Prussia had extensive territories in the east as well as the west because it not only recovered major parts of its pre-1806 territory, but also acquired the rest of Swedish Pomerania, the northern parts of the Kingdom of Saxony, the province of Westphalia and large areas of the Rhineland.[47]

If we want to understand the specific character of the Napoleonic period with all of its ambiguities and the construction of its memories, a more comprehensive approach is needed, one that links the analysis of the military and warfare with political and cultural history. This approach has to recognize that the contemporaries seem to have perceived the era as both a traumatic time of ongoing warfare, military occupation and economic hardship *and* an epoch of opportunity that offered new ways to engage in society and state and allowed for novel political claims.[48] The political culture of the time reflects this ambivalence; shaped by the needs and possibilities of the day, it was a mix of old and new ideas and practices, borrowed from all available sources – even the enemy.[49]

The present study contributes to this agenda by revisiting the history and memory of Prussia's wars against Napoleon between 1806 and 1815 with a focus on the political culture that formed the perception of contemporaries and their memories. Its aim is a multilayered analysis of the contested

Erica Charters et al. (Liverpool, 2012), 225–240, and *Witnessing the Revolutionary and Napoleonic Wars: The Experience of German Central Europe* (Basingstoke, 2012); and Daniel Furrer, *Soldatenleben: Napoleons Russlandfeldzug 1812* (Paderborn, 2012).

[47] On Prussia in this period, see Reinhart Koselleck, *Preußen zwischen Reform und Revolution: Allgemeines Landrecht, Verwaltung und soziale Bewegung von 1791 bis 1848* (Stuttgart, 1967); Rudolf Ibbeken, *Preußen, 1807–1813: Staat und Volk als Idee und in Wirklichkeit* (Cologne, 1970); Münchow-Pohl, *Reform*; Levinger, *Nationalism*; Michael V. Leggiere, *Napoleon and Berlin: The Franco-Prussian War in North Germany, 1813* (Norman, OK, 2002); Clark, *Kingdom*, 284–418; and Paret, *Challenge*. On Jews in Prussia, see Albert Bruer, *Geschichte der Juden in Preußen, 1750–1820* (Frankfurt/M., 1991).

[48] Werner K. Blessing, "Umbruchkrise und Verstörung: Die Napoleonische Erschütterung und ihre sozialpsychologische Bedeutung (Bayern als Beispiel)," *Zeitschrift für Bayerische Landesgeschichte* 42 (1979): 75–106; Ernst Wolfgang Becker, "Zeiterfahrungen zwischen Revolution und Krieg: Zum Wandel des Zeitbewusstseins in der Napoleonischen Ära," in *Die Erfahrung des Krieges: Erfahrungsgeschichtliche Perspektiven von der Französischen Revolution bis zum Zweiten Weltkrieg*, ed. Nikolaus Buschmann and Horst Carl (Paderborn, 2001), 67–95; and Ute Planert, ed., *Krieg und Umbruch in Mitteleuropa um 1800: Erfahrungsgeschichte(n) auf dem Weg in eine neue Zeit* (Paderborn, 2009). On the experience of this period and the invention of a "nostalgia about the past" – that is, the longing for what was lost in the transition to more modern times – see, more generally, Peter Fritzsche, *Stranded in the Present: Modern Time and the Melancholy of History* (Cambridge, MA, 2004).

[49] See Ernst Weber, *Lyrik der Befreiungskriege 1812–1815: Gesellschaftspolitische Meinungs- und Willensbildung durch Literatur* (Stuttgart, 1991); and Jeismann, *Vaterland*, 27–102.

long-term process of constructing meaning and memory that began during the wars themselves. By concentrating on the period until World War I, it explores how competing discourses and cultural practices influenced both historical events and the perception and collective memory of them, how these memories changed over time and which factors influenced the changes. I argue that only by incorporating the dimensions of political culture and memory into the interpretation of the period of the Napoleonic Wars and Prussia's and Germany's anti-Napoleonic struggle, and by taking account of the interplay among the constructed differences that defined belonging and exclusion, can we understand the extent of the patriotic-national mobilization for these wars and their conflicting perceptions and memories. Only then can we comprehend how the many contesting voices in the political discourse and the recollections of contemporary witnesses in communicative memory within Prussia and beyond were increasingly overshadowed by a hegemonic master narrative that lastingly shaped cultural memory of these wars in Germany since the late nineteenth century.

GENDERED EXPERIENCES, PERCEPTIONS AND MEMORIES OF WAR

The question of how to define the terms "experience," "perception" and "memory" has been widely debated in recent decades by scholars who pushed for a linguistic and cultural turn of history.[50] One of the most influential historians in the debate on "experience" was Joan W. Scott, who, in the early 1990s, challenged "the appeal to experience as incontestable evidence and as an originary point of explanation" for subjective perceptions, identities and practices. Her criticism was that historians who seek to make experiences visible take meaning as transparent and reproduce rather than contest given ideological systems in the belief that the "facts of history speak for themselves."[51] She suggested that we instead look beyond subjects' experiences, defined as the process by which subjectivity is constructed, and focus on the way in which individuals and groups perceive a historical situation and try to make sense of it for themselves. Thus, we need to analyze the discursive systems underpinning experience, the forms of representation those systems use and the ways they operate, because

---

[50] For a critical debate of the development of the scholarship, see "AHR Forum: Historiograhic 'Turns' in Critical Perspective," *AHR* 117 (2012): 688–813.

[51] Joan W. Scott, "Experience," in *Feminists Theorize the Political*, ed. Judith Butler and Joan W. Scott (New York, 1992), 22–40, 25 and 37; and idem, "The Evidence of Experience," *Critical Inquiry* 17 (1991): 773–797; see also the critique by Kathleen Canning, "Feminist History after the Linguistic Turn: Historicizing Discourse and Experience," in her *Gender History in Practice: Historical Perspectives on Bodies, Class, and Citizenship* (Ithaca, NY, 2006), 62–100, 72–73.

"discourses position subjects," thereby producing experiences and forming perceptions.[52] Accordingly, experience is a linguistically shaped process of weighing and assigning meaning to events as they happen, which is embedded in the "cultural understandings and linguistic capacities" of historical subjects and thus is time-specific, relative and changeable.[53] "Experience" in this sense is more like an individual or collective narrative of the perception of a historical event or development. This definition leads to two methodological consequences: on the one hand, the need to focus on the specific forms of the articulation of perceptions and their narratives, and the conditions of their production. The forms used and their literary traditions had an important effect on what was said in a particular style of writing. The imagined audience mattered as well, as did the distance in time between the experienced event and the writing of the record. On the other hand, it leads to the necessity to historicize and differentiate the accounts of perceptions as time-specific and born of particular circumstances.[54]

This approach not only allows us to conceptualize "perception" as an evolving construct – a narrative that can take a number of different forms and be changed and enriched by the passage of time and the process of reflection – but also enables us to examine the entanglement of contemporary perceptions and constructed memories.[55] For the exploration of this relationship, the distinction between "communicative" and "cultural memory," introduced by Jan Assmann, is fruitful. For him, the former is generational and based on collective communication, and spans no more than two or three generations. It is socially framed – that is, it depends on the respective group that produced it – and is much less structured and hierarchical than cultural memory, which is sustained by social and cultural institutions in the form of buildings, monuments, symbols, rituals, art and texts, and

---

[52] Scott, "Experience," 37–39.

[53] William H. Sewell, *Gender, History, and Deconstruction: Joan W. Scott's Gender and the Politics of History*, CSST Working Paper 34 (Ann Arbor, MI, 1989), 19. On the term "war experiences" (*Kriegserfahrungen*), see Nikolaus Buschmann and Horst Carl, "Zugänge zur Erfahrungsgeschichte des Krieges: Forschung, Theorie, Fragestellung," in *Die Erfahrung des Krieges: Erfahrungsgeschichtliche Perspektiven von der Französischen Revolution bis zum Zweiten Weltkrieg*, ed. eidem (Paderborn, 2001), 11–26; and Alan Forrest et al., "Introduction: Nations in Arms, People at War: Analyzing War Experiences and Perceptions," in Forrest et al., *Soldiers, Citizens*, 1–22.

[54] On the study of experience, see also Martin Jay, *Songs of Experience: Modern American and European Variations on a Universal Theme* (Berkeley, CA, 2005), esp. 261–400.

[55] For an overview of the extensive theoretical and methodological literature in the field of memory studies, see Astrid Erll and Ansgar Nünning, eds., *A Companion to Cultural Memory Studies* (Berlin, 2010); Christian Gudehus et al., eds., *Gedächtnis und Erinnerung: Ein interdisziplinäres Handbuch* (Stuttgart, 2010); and Christoph Cornelißen, "Was heißt Erinnerungskultur? Begriff – Methoden – Perspektiven," *Geschichte in Wissenschaft und Unterricht* 54 (2003): 548–563. An interesting early critical comment on the research is Alon Confino, "Collective Memory and Cultural History: Problems of Method," *AHR* 102 (1997): 1386–1403; as well as Forrest et al., "Introduction: Memories."

constitutes remembrance and belonging in a more lasting and normative mode. The main function of cultural memory is to create the identities of collectives (communities, nations, states etc). Both forms of memory together make up "collective memory."[56] Along with the distinction between communicative and cultural memory, Aleida Assmann suggested differentiating between "storage memory" and "functional memory." The former is the reservoir of texts and rituals that were in the past, or will become in the future important for the historical legitimation of a community. The latter refers to the public use of history and memory for the construction of the collective identity of a political/social group, state or nation.[57] This study focuses on functional memory and is based on the assumption that emotions play an important role in its use for identity construction.[58] People's connection to a group, state or nation and their specific culture is emotional, not rational. Their "emotional attachments are shaped, tapped into and evoked through the mobilization of symbols and images." They are therefore a crucial part of the political memory culture.[59]

Although recollections tell us more about the time when they were produced than about the remembered past, at least in communicative memory, the narratives must still reflect important pieces of this past if they are to become and remain influential. Thus, we need to connect the analyses of history and memory. The historical context in which producers of narratives work, the competing narratives of the past that they face and the specific media they use, as well as the market for which they produce all shape the narratives in contemporary discourse and memory. In the process of memory construction, which is a continuous reinterpretation of historical remembrance in the context of changing presents, "intermediality" – the interplay of different media as "carriers of memory" and their narratives – is a key element because it ensures a particularly successful construction of emotionally loaded collective memories and the creation of a sense of belonging.[60] The

[56] Jan Assmann and John Czaplicka, "Collective Memory and Cultural Identity," New German Critique 65 (1995): 125–133; see also Aleida Assmann, Erinnerungsräume: Formen und Wandlungen des kulturellen Gedächtnisses (Munich, 1999), Engl.: Cultural Memory and Western Civilization: Functions, Media, Archives (New York, 2011). On the "social framing" of collective memories, see Maurice Halbwachs, Les cadres sociaux de la mémoire (Paris, 1925).

[57] Assmann, Cultural Memory, 1–17.

[58] On the emerging field of the history of emotions, see William M. Reddy, The Navigation of Feeling: A Framework for the History of Emotions (Cambridge, 2001), and "Historical Research on the Self and Emotions," Emotion Review 1 (2009): 302–315; and Ute Frevert, "Was haben Gefühle in der Geschichte zu suchen," GG 35 (2009): 183–208.

[59] Ruth Roach Pierson, "Nations: Gendered, Racialized, Crossed with Empire," in Gendered Nations: Nationalisms and Gender Order in the Long Nineteenth Century, ed. Ida Blom et al. (Oxford, 2000), 41–61, 42; see also François et al., Nation.

[60] On the importance of media for memory construction, see Astrid Erll and Ansgar Nünning, eds., Medien des kollektiven Gedächtnisses: Konstruktivität, Historizität, Kulturspezifität

German-national imagery in Kersting's patriotic paintings is an excellent illustration of how intermediality works in memory culture. Kersting and his patriotic paintings are also an example of the continuous and contested process of memory construction and the importance of the suppression and forgetting of memories. This process leads to the coexistence of multiple and differing hegemonic and marginal memories and their related cultures, which legitimize and organize contemporary hierarchies of power. Politics, ethnicity, class and gender play an especially important role in the hierarchical construction of collective identities.[61] Historically specific cultures of memory are closely related to the development of nation-states, their distinct political cultures and constructions of national identities.[62] Based on these reflections, I ask who produced discourses and memories and with what aims; what media were chosen to disseminate them and what were the conditions of their production on the literature market; and finally why certain interpretations of the present and recollections of the past became "hegemonic" while others were suppressed, rewritten or forgotten.

One dimension of the history and memory of the Anti-Napoleonic Wars that was forgotten until recently was the highly gendered nature of discourses and cultural practices.[63] Just as most of the extensive historiography on these wars has ignored the gendered character of their history and recollection, the theoretical debate on memory has overlooked the importance of gender for the construction of remembrance. Only recently has feminist scholarship begun to discuss the close interrelationships between gender and memory.[64] In this study, "gender" is understood as both an important subject

(Berlin, 2004); on intermediality, see Kirsten Dickhaut, "Intermedialität und Gedächtnis," in *Gedächtniskonzepte der Literaturwissenschaft: Theoretische Grundlagen und Anwendungsperspektiven*, ed. Astrid Erll and Ansgar Nünning (Berlin, 2005), 203–226.

[61] Jay Winter, *Remembering War: The Great War and Historical Memory in the Twentieth Century* (New Haven, CT, 2006), 1–13.

[62] Sylvia Paletschek, "Opening up Narrow Boundaries: Memory, Culture, Historiography and Excluded Histories from a Gendered Perspective," in *Gendering Historiography: Beyond National Canons*, ed. Angelika Epple and Angelika Schaser (Frankfurt/M., 2009), 163–177.

[63] On the theoretical and methodological debate on gender, culture and nation, see Mrinalini Sinha, "Gender and Nation," in *Women's History in Global Perspective*, ed. Bonnie G. Smith, 3 vols. (Urbana, IL, 2004), 1:229–312; Blom et al., *Gendered Nations*, 3–80. On the state of research in German history, see Angelika Schaser, "The Challenge of Gender: National Historiography, Nationalism, and National Identities," in *Gendering Modern German History: Rewriting Historiography*, ed. Karen Hagemann and Jean H. Quataert (New York, 2007), 39–62.

[64] On the state of research on gender and memory, see Marianne Hirsch and Valerie Smith, eds., "Gender and Cultural Memory," special issue of *Signs* 82 (2002), esp. 1–19; and Sylvia Paletschek and Sylvia Schraut, "Introduction: Gender and Memory Culture in Europe – Female Representations in Historical Perspective," in *The Gender of Memory: Cultures of Remembrance in Nineteenth- and Twentieth-Century Europe*, ed. eidem (Frankfurt/M., 2008), 7–30.

of investigation and a method of doing research. As the latter, gender "is above all an invitation to think critically about how the meanings of sexed bodies are produced, deployed, and changed."[65] Scholarship suggests that, while a pattern of hierarchy and complementarity shapes gender relations to some degree, concepts of masculinity and femininity depend on their historical context, are never constant and are continually being negotiated.[66]

In this process of cultural negotiation, the invention of tradition and the construction of memories each play an important role. Not only is memory always gendered, as Aleida Assmann has emphasized, but gender is also one of the most important interpretive patterns (*Deutungsmuster*) that structure the process of memory production. She observed that women are often the "subjects of memory" because they transmit more differentiated, complex and often ambiguous communicative memories; but at the same time they are the "objects of oblivion" by men who dominate the production of cultural memory.[67] In this gendered process of memory construction, women's memories tend to disappear in perceptions, not because they did not exist, but because they were regarded as insignificant. This is especially true of nineteenth-century national cultures of memory, which – based on the constructed division between "the public" and "the private sphere" – associated men with "public" and women with "private memory." This distinction subsequently framed female memories as less important and excluded them from the national memory culture.[68] For that reason, war memories, which in most European countries were at the center of national memory culture, are usually narrated in a highly gendered way. One important function of the gendering of national war memories is the restoration of the social and gender order in postwar societies. War as a "gendering activity" – one that ritually marks the gender of every member of a society in war propaganda

---

[65] Joan W. Scott, "Unanswered Questions," *AHR* 113 (2008): 1422–1430, 1423, and *The Fantasy of Feminist History* (Durham, NC, 2012). Her classic essay is "Gender: A Useful Category of Historical Analysis," in her *Gender and the Politics of History* (New York, 1989), 28–50. For the development of the debate, see, for example, Leonore Davidoff et al., eds., *Gender and History: Retrospect and Prospect* (Oxford, 2000); "*AHR* Forum: Revisiting 'Gender: A Useful Category of Historical Analysis,'" *AHR* 113 (2008): 1344–1430; and Alexandra Shepard and Garthine Walker, eds., *Gender and Change: Agency, Chronology and Periodization* (Oxford, 2009).

[66] For the period between 1750 and 1850, see most recently Sarah Knott and Barbara Taylor, eds., *Women, Gender and Enlightenment* (Basingstoke, 2005); Ulrike Gleixner and Marion W. Gray, eds., *Gender in Transition: Discourse and Practice in German-Speaking Europe, 1750–1830* (Ann Arbor, MI, 2006); Hagemann et al., *Gender, War and Politics*.

[67] Aleida Assmann, "Geschlecht und kulturelles Gedächtnis," *Freiburger FrauenStudien* 19 (2006): 29–46.

[68] Sylvia Schraut and Sylvia Paletschek, "Remembrance and Gender: Making Gender Visible and Inscribing Women into Memory Culture," in eidem, *Gender of Memory*, 267–287; and Marianne Hirsch and Valerie Smith, "Feminism and Cultural Memory: An Introduction," *Signs* 28.1 (2002): 1–19.

and at the same time questions these discursively constructed gender lines in everyday practice – destabilizes dominant prewar ideas about the gender order. Thus, in the postwar period, it becomes all the more necessary to stabilize the gender order and with it the social order.[69]

A striking example of this complex process is the history and memory of women's patriotic activities during the wars of 1813–15. Women participated as authors in the patriotic-national discourse, even if their numbers were still very small, and founded their own patriotic associations – some 600 in Germany alone – that collected money and material and organized wartime nursing and relief work.[70] Although most of these women's associations ceased their activities after the wars, thereby reestablishing "proper" gender relations, and their memory was suppressed in the immediate postwar decades not just in the public arena but also in historiography, women recalled them in their oral narratives and some even described them in their memoirs or novels. Only because some women kept alive the memory of female patriotic activism during the wars of 1813–15 could it become a model for the middle-class women's movement that emerged in the 1840s. Its members used this memory to give their challenging political agenda a tradition that created continuity. In the second half of the nineteenth century, with the rise of the women's movement, female and male novelists who wrote about the period of the Napoleonic Wars finally included female forms of patriotism more regularly in their historical novels. This example also helps us to understand the relationship between history, historiography and memory. Paul Ricoeur has described them as at once distinct and complementary, interactive and overlapping modes of interpreting the past and relating it to the present and the future.[71]

Based on these reflections, the five parts of this book connect history and memory and follow the process of memory construction. In the first part, "A History of Defeat, Crisis and Victory," I provide a brief overview of the main developments in Prussia and other parts of Germany between 1806 and 1820, emphasizing the dimensions of political culture and contemporary perception. The second part, "Discourses on the Nation, War and Gender," assesses the often controversial and highly gendered public debates in the years during the wars of 1813–15 and the first postwar years, their media and the war-specific literary market, which allows me to touch on continuities

---

[69] Margaret R. Higonnet et al., eds., *Behind the Lines: Gender and the Two World Wars* (New Haven, CT, 1987), 31–50; also Karen Hagemann, "Reconstructing 'Front' and 'Home': Gendered Experiences and Memories of the German Wars against Napoleon – A Case Study," *WiH* 16 (2009): 25–50.

[70] Dirk Reder, *Frauenbewegung und Nation: Patriotische Frauenvereine in Deutschland im frühen 19. Jahrhundert, 1813–1830* (Cologne, 1998); and Jean H. Quataert, *Staging Philanthropy: Patriotic Women and the National Imagination in Dynastic Germany, 1813–1916* (Ann Arbor, MI, 2001).

[71] Paul Ricoeur, *La mémoire, l'histoire, l'oubli* (Paris, 2000).

and disruptions of the discourse in nineteenth-century collective memory. The focus here is on Prussia and the central, northern and western regions of Germany. In the third part, "Collective Practices of De/Mobilization and Commemoration," I examine the degree of political and social mobilization for war and the cultural practices (festivities, celebrations, rituals and symbols) that the Prussian monarchy and its military, churches and communities in particular used to mobilize during the wars and to demobilize and commemorate during the early postwar years. Such practices of the political culture became a lasting blueprint for the subsequent mobilization for and commemoration of war in Germany, as demonstrated in the last chapter of this part, on the invention of the tradition of the cult of death for the fatherland and with it the honoring and commemorating of war heroes. The first three parts of the book are mainly based on an extensive study of the political literature (newspapers, journals, brochures, pamphlets, sermons, songs and poems) and printed documents on and by the military (memoranda, decrees, regulations and instructions, field newspapers) published between 1806 and 1820 and afterward, but also include several autobiographical accounts. Parts four and five focus on the process of literary memory production. In part four, "Literary Market, History and War Memories," I explore first the conditions that formed this process during the nineteenth century, especially the changing political culture and the transformation of the literature market. Then I examine the nostalgic invention of history and the development of academic, military and "popular historiography"[72] on the period of the Napoleonic Wars, which provided the master narratives that informed all other media of memory. Afterwards I analyze how these wars were narrated in autobiographies and war memoirs written by military and civilian eyewitnesses from different parts of Germany and published in great numbers during the nineteenth century.[73] Finally, in part five, "Novels, Memory and Politics," I study how the most popular media of literary memory production – novels – narrated the Prussian and German history of the years between 1806 and 1815. I examine novels of the recent past (*Zeitromane*)[74]

---

[72] For the term, see Sylvia Paletschek, ed., *Popular Historiographies in the 19th and 20th Centuries: Cultural Meanings, Social Practices* (Oxford, 2011), esp. 1–18.

[73] Following Mary Jo Maynes, I prefer an open and flexible definition of the two genres: a memoir "can be limited to describing or explaining a particular phase of a life or a limited range of (often public) activities"; an autobiography "ranges more widely thematically and temporally to fulfill its promise to explain the development of a personality." Idem et al., *Telling Stories: The Use of Personal Narratives in the Social Sciences and History* (Ithaca, NY, 2008), 77; see also Yuval Noah Harari, "Military Memoires: A Historical Overview of the Genre from the Middle Ages to the Late Modern Era," *WiH* 14 (2007): 289–309.

[74] A "novel of the recent past" or *Zeitroman* reflects contemporary history and/or the social reality of the present; see Dirk Göttsche, *Zeit im Roman: Literarische Zeitreflexion und die Geschichte des Zeitromans im späten 18. und im 19. Jahrhundert* (Munich, 2001), 20–21.

and historical novels[75] published between 1815 and 1914 and their varied narratives and ask how these narratives changed over time and which factors influenced this change. The study ends before the First World War because the national myth of the "Wars of Liberation" as the birth of the German nation had been formed by that point and was the master narrative of German history.

---

[75] Following Günther Mühlberger and Kurt Habitzel, I define the "historical novel" broadly as a "work of prose fiction of at least 150 pages, set for the most part in a time before the author's birth." Eidem, "The German Historical Novel (1780–1945): The German Historical Novel from 1780 to 1945 – Utilising the Innsbruck Database," in *Travellers in Time and Space: The German Historical Novel*, ed. Osman Durrani and Julian Preece (Amsterdam, 2001), 5–23, 5–6. As an introduction, see Hartmut Eggert, *Studien zur Wirkungsgeschichte des deutschen historischen Romans, 1850–1875* (Frankfurt/M., 1971); Hugo Aust, *Der historische Roman* (Stuttgart, 1994); and Brent O. Peterson, *History, Fiction, and Germany: Writing the Nineteenth-Century Nation* (Detroit, 2005). On historical novels and the construction of memory, see Erll and Nünning, *Gedächtniskonzepte*.

PART ONE

A HISTORY OF DEFEAT, CRISIS AND VICTORY

The events of 1806 and their aftermath were one of the most important subjects in German historiography until 1945 because they stood at the heart of the national myth of Germany's "renewal" after the "debacle" of the crushing Prussian-Saxon defeat. If we want to understand the importance of this defeat and its aftermath for the history and memory of the period of the Anti-Napoleonic Wars, we need to understand more fully the experiences of war and occupation and to take into account the distinct regional differences within German Central Europe. These variances can explain why in Prussia and other parts of northern Germany the hatred of Napoleon and all things French was more intense in 1813 and the patriotic-national movement more developed than elsewhere in German Central Europe – in particular the south and west. These northern regions had suffered more during the war of 1806–07 and the subsequent occupation by the French army under Napoleonic rule than the southern and western territories belonging to the Confederation of the Rhine.[1] The experiences of warfare and occupation fed anti-French sentiment far beyond "educated circles."[2] The distinction between an "inner" and "outer fringe" of the Napoleonic Empire introduced by Michael Broers is helpful here. The southern and western territories of Germany, alongside the Low Countries and Northern

---

[1] On the regional differences, see Hagemann, "Occupation"; Aaslestad, *Place*, 225–271; idem, "Paying for War: Experiences of Napoleonic Rule in the Hanseatic Cities," *CEH* 39 (2006): 641–675; Planert, *Mythos*, esp. 544–595; and idem, "From Collaboration to Resistance: Politics, Experience, and Memory of the Revolutionary and Napoleonic Wars in Southern Germany," *CEH* 39 (2006): 676–705.

[2] The "educated circles" (*Stand der Gebildeten*), included in contemporary understanding both the educated middle and upper classes and the aristocracy. See Hans Erich Bödeker, "Die gebildeten Stände im späten 18. und frühen 19. Jahrhundert: Zugehörigkeit und Abgrenzungen – Mentalitäten und Handlungspotentiale," in *Bildungsbürgertum im 19. Jahrhundert*, pt. 4: *Politischer Einfluß und gesellschaftliche Formation*, ed. Jürgen Kocka (Stuttgart 1989), 21–52; and Wehler, *Gesellschaftsgeschichte*, 1:202–217.

Italy, belonged to the "inner empire." These territories profited from French rule; here, the Napoleonic system left a powerful institutional heritage. In the "outer empire," to which the old Prussian and other northern and eastern territories belonged, Napoleonic rule "was traumatic and destabilizing." It was "ephemeral, in that it left few institutional traces."[3] This difference was felt not only by contemporary politicians but also by the people, a fact that has been ignored in some of the recent scholarship.[4]

In this first part I cannot analyze in detail the concrete military and civilian experiences and perceptions of the wars of 1806–07, the French occupation and the subsequent developments in Prussia and other parts of northern Germany that led to the wars of 1813–15, but I will include them more systematically in the following overview of the main developments between 1806 and 1820 than is often the case, because we cannot understand 1813 without 1806. In the beginning was not "Napoleon" but a defeat.[5]

---

[3] Broers, *Europe*, 266–267.

[4] Especially in Planert, *Mythos*.

[5] Thomas Nipperdey, *Germany from Napoleon to Bismarck, 1800–1866* (Princeton, NJ, 1996), 1. This first part is to some extent based on Hagemann, "Occupation," "Desperation," and *Muth*, 17–44 and 71–104. For the following, see also Paret, *Challenge*; Clark, *Kingdom*, 296–387; James J. Sheehan, *German History, 1770–1866* (Oxford, 1989), 209–451; and Nipperdey, *Germany*, 1–85. For the war experiences, see also, James, *Witnessing*.

The Defeat of 1806 and Its Aftermath

On 9 October 1806, Prussia declared war on France. This was the first time since 1795 that the monarchy had joined in a coalition war against France. In the separate Peace of Basel of 5 April 1795, Prussia had made a pact of neutrality and left the fight against the French army above all to Britain, Austria and Russia. As a consequence of this decade of neutrality, large parts of central, eastern and northern Germany, unlike the south and southwest, had escaped war. But when the Prussian government learned in August 1806 that Napoleon was engaged in alliance negotiations with Britain and had unilaterally offered the return of Hanover as an inducement, an unambiguous response seemed unavoidable. Hanover, a German electorate in personal union with the British monarchy, had been occupied by France in 1803. When French troops in 1805 violated the neutrality of Ansbach in Prussian territory on their march to face the Austrians and Russians, Prussia had remained at peace with France because of a formal treaty promising to give Hanover to Prussia in exchange for Ansbach being awarded to France's ally Bavaria. Thus, when Napoleon offered Hanover to Britain, the path to war seemed inevitable for the Prussian monarch Friedrich Wilhelm III, who saw no "honorable" alternative.[1]

His decision met with the support not just of the "war party" in his own entourage, which had been promoting war against France since 1805, but also of a broader public. When Napoleon had assumed power, educated people throughout Germany had welcomed him because they hoped that he would promote peace and reform. In 1805–06, however, the mood began to change. Because of his imperialist policy, the French emperor was increasingly detested, especially in Prussia. The French Lieutenant Colonel Marcellin de Marbot, who spent late August 1806 in Berlin, recalled in his memoirs: "Before my departure from Berlin I had evidence of the frenzy to which their hatred of Napoleon carried the Prussian nation, usually so calm. [...] The officers whom I knew ventured no longer to speak to me or salute me; many Frenchmen were insulted by the populace."[2] The Prussian

---

[1] On Prussia between 1789 and 1806, see Clark, *Kingdom*, 284–311; and on the German Southwest, Planert, *Mythos*, 125–473.

[2] Jean-Baptiste Antoine Marcellin Marbot, *Memoirs of Baron de Marbot Late Lieutenant General in the French Army* (London, 1894), 173.

public seems to have perceived the upcoming war as a struggle in which the "honor and continued existence of the fatherland were at stake."[3] According to eyewitnesses, public opinion was dominated by a "great thirst for war" and "the certain hope of victory."[4] Among the army, the political administration and the population at large, the Seven Years' War was still remembered as a time of glory. The Prussian army felt invincible, and marched to battle with "high hearts, drums beating and trumpets sounding."[5]

Nevertheless, the timing could hardly have been worse for Prussia: the coalition with Russia remained largely theoretical; the army corps promised by Tsar Alexander failed to materialize; and apart from Saxony, Saxony-Weimar, Brunswick and Hanover, no other German powers were willing to join the coalition. Thus, its army of 142,800 soldiers was no match for the French foe with 208,563 soldiers: 177,376 of them French and 31,187 Germans who belonged to the troops of the Confederation of the Rhine, which Napoleon had established on 12 July 1806 as a military alliance and federation of Germans under his protectorate.[6] The confederation originally included only 16 German territorial states. After the last emperor of the Holy Roman Empire, Franz II, had abdicated and dissolved the empire on 6 August 1806, and Napoleon had triumphed in his struggle against the fourth coalition, 23 more states joined. Only Prussia, Danish Holstein and Swedish Pomerania remained outside it, alongside the Austrian Empire (see Map 1).[7]

The devastating defeat of 14 October that the anti-French coalition suffered at the battles of Jena and Auerstedt – just five days after war was declared – came as a terrible shock to the Prussian monarchy. Over the following fortnight, the French broke up a smaller Prussian force near Halle and occupied the city of Halberstadt. Soon thereafter the commanders of the Prussian fortresses of Küstrin (1 November) and Magdeburg (8 November) surrendered without a fight. The conquest and occupation of central and northern Germany as well as large portions of Prussia by the Grande Armée took just a few weeks. On 27 October 1806, Napoleon's troops entered Berlin, where France then declared the Continental Blockade against Britain. The royal family and their court fled along with the central administration to Königsberg, where Friedrich Wilhelm III arrived on 10 December, only to continue his flight to Memel in East Prussia with his

[3] Ludwig Rellstab, *Aus meinem Leben*, 2 vols. (Berlin, 1861), 1:45.
[4] Agnes von Gerlach, "Brief vom 30. August 1806 and ihre Schwester," in *Aus den Jahren preußischer Not und Erneuerung: Tagebücher und Briefe der Gebrüder Gerlach und ihres Kreises, 1805–1820*, ed. Hans Joachim Schoeps (Berlin, 1963), 347–348.
[5] Großer Generalstab, Kriegsgeschichtliche Abteilung II, ed., *1806: Das Preußische Offizierkorps und die Untersuchung der Kriegsereignisse* (Berlin, 1906), 70.
[6] Esdaile, *Napoleon's Wars*, 268–272; see also Gerd Fesser, *1806: Die Doppelschlacht bei Jena und Auerstedt* (Jena, 2006); and Paret, *Challenge*, 1–32.
[7] Wehler, *Gesellschaftsgeschichte*, 1:362–369.

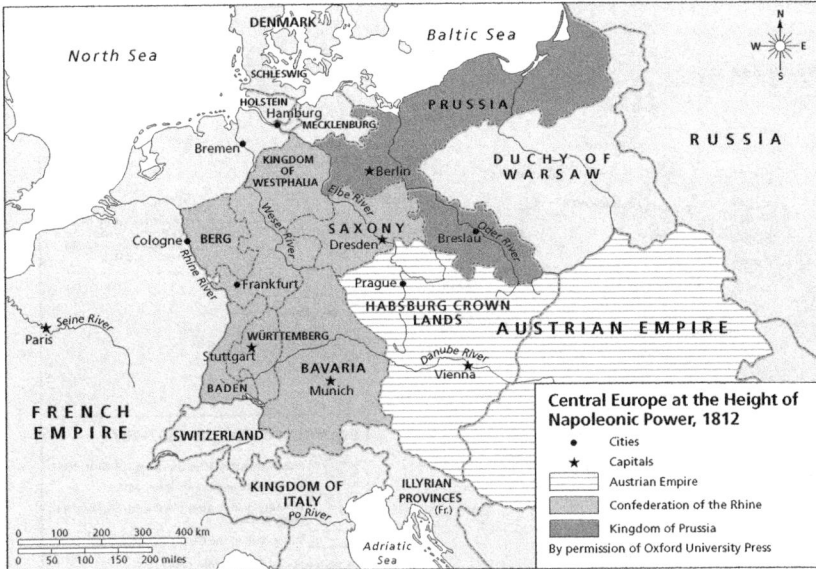

MAP 1. Central Europe at the Height of Napoleonic Power, 1812.

retinue. On 11 December 1806, Napoleon made peace with Saxony.[8] The magnificent success of the Grande Armée continued in the course of the subsequent campaign. The traditional Prussian and Russian armies had no chance against the foe's modern mass army. After the Prusso-Russian defeat at Friedland on 14 June 1807, Russia and Prussia were forced on 9 July to sign the Peace of Tilsit, which exposed the debacle of the Prussian monarchy to the whole world. Its territory diminished from 314,448 to 158,008 square kilometers, and the population dropped from approximately 10 million in 1804 to 4.6 million in 1808 (see Map 2).[9]

The Paris Treaty of 8 September 1808 ended the occupation of Prussia, but also set tribute payments at 140 million francs. This sum, on whose payment in installments the withdrawal of the last French troops depended,

---

[8] On Prussia between 1806 and 1813, see Clark, *Kingdom*, 312–344. On developments in Saxony during this period, see Roman Töppel, *Die Sachsen und Napoleon: Ein Stimmungsbild 1806–1813* (Cologne, 2008). On the importance of Jena and Auerstedt at the time and in European memory, see Breitenborn and Ulbricht, *Jena und Auerstedt* and Jürgen Kloosterhuis, and Sönke Neitzel, eds., *Krise, Reformen – und Militär: Preussen vor und nach der Katastrophe von 1806* (Berlin, 2009).

[9] Ilja Mieck, "Preußen von 1807 bis 1850: Reformen, Restauration und Revolution," in *Handbuch der Preußischen Geschichte*, ed. Otto Büsch, 3 vols. (Berlin, 1992), 2:3–292, 17–21; and Wilhelm Treue, "Preußens Wirtschaft vom Dreißigjährigen Krieg bis zum Nationalsozialismus," in ibid., 2:449–604, 497–498.

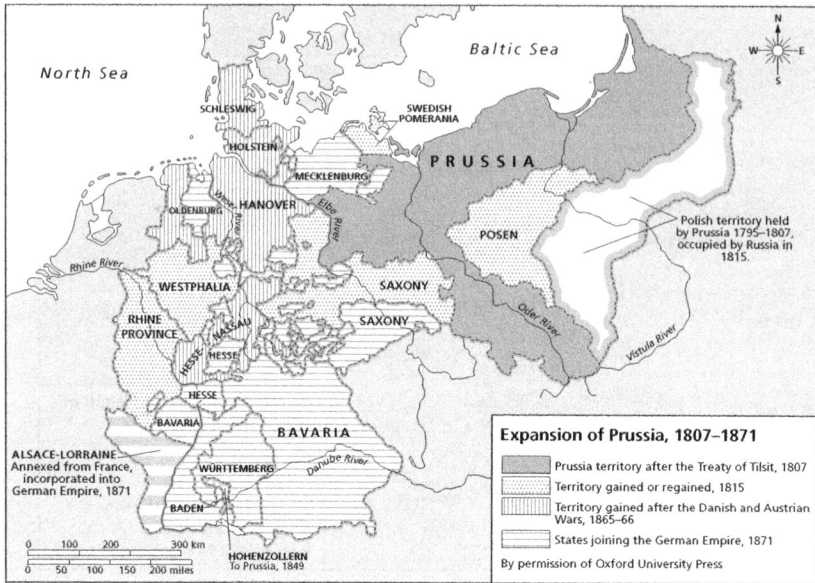

MAP 2. The Expansion of Prussia, 1807–71.

was soon reduced to 120 million, but with interest, interest on arrears and bank transfer costs at an extremely unfavorable exchange rate, amounting to more than 34 million taler, payable over 30 months. These payments were difficult to realize because of the state's substantial financial problems. Between 1807 and 1815, the monarchy was constantly on the verge of bankruptcy. State spending during the war years 1806–07 and 1812–15 was at least twice the usual peacetime level. Income fell between 1807 and 1812 to less than half the 1805 level. For example, according to official calculations, the Prussian state took in about 15 million taler in 1807–08. The budget, however, was more than 28.1 million taler, of which the military claimed 16.6 million (or 59 percent). Such a discrepancy between income and outlay remained the norm for more than a decade.[10] The financial shortfall of the Prussian state was so great that many bureaucrats had to be dismissed, and salaries and pensions went unpaid for months at a time. The situation for lower civil servants and pensioners, in particular, worsened dramatically. Their hardship, which contemporaries described vividly, was so great that they gradually had to sell all of their possessions.[11]

---

[10] Hanna Schissler, "Preußische Finanzpolitik 1806–1820," in *Preußische Finanzpolitik 1806–1810: Quellen zur Verwaltung der Ministerien Stein und Altenstein*, ed. Hanna Schissler and Hans-Ulrich Wehler (Göttingen, 1984), 13–64.

[11] "Zeitungs-Bericht der Immediat-Friedens-Vollzugs-Kommission, Berlin, 1 November 1807," in *Berichte aus der Berliner Franzosenzeit 1807–1809, nach den Akten des Berliner Geheimen Staatsarchivs und des Pariser Kriegsarchivs*, ed. Herman Granier (Leipzig, 1913), 37–44, 41.

Even middle- and higher-level civil servants suffered visibly from the non-payment of their salaries.[12]

The monarchy also lost important material bases for its military power as the French took the Prussian fortresses of Stettin, Küstrin and Glogau with their stocks of weapons and munitions as a security.[13] Six secret articles of the Paris Convention stipulated that for ten years, the strength of the Prussian army could not exceed 42,000 men. Any additional recruitment of militias or civil guards was prohibited. The army was thus reduced to one-sixth its peacetime size in 1806, which had been 247,000. A large number of soldiers and officers had to be discharged. These men lost their livelihoods and represented a substantial source of political unrest.[14] They perceived the defeat not only as a "national debacle" but also as a dramatic loss of military and personal honor as men.

PERCEPTIONS OF THE DEFEAT AMONG THE MILITARY AND THE PUBLIC

The campaign of 1806 revealed to the bewildered public a Prussian army in a very sorry state. It had not merely been defeated; it had been ruined. In the words of an officer who had been at Jena, "The carefully assembled and apparently unshakeable military structure was suddenly shattered to its foundations."[15] The many public and private accounts by contemporary witnesses painted an unflattering portrait of an army convinced of its invincibility, which had severely underestimated the enemy. Nearly half of the 108,000 mobilized soldiers came from other German-speaking lands, many recruited by dubious methods, pressed into service as mercenaries and disinclined to fight. They were ill prepared after years of peacetime service, during which emphasis had increasingly been placed on elaborate forms of parade drill and appearance. A mechanically drilled and slow-moving army with a vast train dependent on magazine provisioning was no match for the larger, more flexible and fast-moving French forces, which requisitioned necessities from the lands they invaded.[16] The result was a disastrous defeat and a chaotic retreat. Commanded by elderly and incompetent generals, and with officers in the middle and lower ranks drilled in obedience and incapable of independent leadership and action, the confused soldiers had fled headlong and in droves after the first blows by the French army. The military train blocked the roads with hundreds of carts and coaches, preventing

---

[12] Heinrich and Amalie von Beguelin, *Denkwürdigkeiten aus den Jahren 1807–13, nebst Briefen von Gneisenau und Hardenberg*, ed. Adolf Ernst (Berlin, 1892), 171.

[13] Mieck, "Preußen," 33; Treue, "Preußens Wirtschaft," 501.

[14] See Heinz Stübig, *Armee und Nation: Die pädagogisch-politischen Motive der preußischen Heeresreform, 1807–1814* (Frankfurt/M., 1971), 13.

[15] Clark, *Kingdom*, 298.

[16] Ibid., 296–311.

an orderly retreat. Thus the troops withdrew in chaos, and all military order dissolved.[17]

The Prussian press soon harshly criticized the army's "failure." This began on 4 November 1806 with the publication of an anonymous open letter from "a citizen to the duke of Brunswick" (the commander of the Prussian forces) in the *Berlinische Nachrichten*, one of the capital's two most important newspapers. It was followed by a long series of public complaints, critiques, slander and sarcasm but also rebuttals and justifications in newspapers and magazines. A rapidly growing number of pamphlets and articles were devoted solely to the events of the recent war. Civilians and military men alike participated in this passionate public exchange.[18]

Among the harshest critics of the old Prussian army and the "downfall of its own making" were those officers who had already intensely debated the causes of the "French fortunes in war" before the defeat of 1806–07 and had repeatedly but unsuccessfully called for army reform.[19] Only in the context of discussions of the military causes of the defeat, which permanently shook the foundations of the state and the army, did they gain a hearing. This group of officers included the later Prussian General Field Marshal Neidhardt von Gneisenau, who was a second lieutenant in 1806.[20] He reached devastating conclusions in his November 1806 exposé *On the War of 1806*:

The inability of the duke of Brunswick to design a solid campaign plan, [...] the army's distrust of him, the disunity among the luminaries of the general staff, the neutralization of some of its most able members, our army, unaccustomed to war, the lack of preparation for war visible in nearly all its branches, the fixation on worthless details of elementary tactics that had become habitual in the years of peace, our recruiting system, with all its exemptions, which demands military service of only a portion of the nation and extends their period of service inordinately, so that they serve reluctantly and can be held together only by discipline; [...] the sorry state of our regimental artillery; [...] the poor quality of our weapons; [...] and to sum it all up, the arrogance that prevented us from moving with the times, [all this] causes the patriot to heave a silent sigh.[21]

---

[17] See Generalstab, *1806*; Carl von Clausewitz, *Nachrichten über Preußen in seiner großen Katastrophe (1823–25)*, ed. Großer Generalstab, Abtheilung für Kriegsgeschichte (Berlin, 1888); Neidhardt von Gneisenau, "Über den Krieg von 1806," in *Ausgewählte militärische Schriften*, ed. Gerhard Förster and Christa Gudzent (Berlin, 1984), 50–62; and Johann Rühle von Lilienstern, *Bericht eines Augenzeugen von dem Feldzug der während den Monaten September und Oktober 1806 unter dem Kommando des Fürsten zu Hohenlohe-Ingelfingen gestandenen königlich-preußischen und kurfürstlich sächsischen Truppen* (Tübingen, 1807).

[18] Generalstab, *1806*, 17–18; Stübig, *Armee*, 39–41.

[19] Hagemann, *Muth*, 75–77.

[20] On Gneisenau, see Hermann Teske, "Gneisenau, August Wilhelm Anton Graf Neidhardt von," *NDB* 6 (1964): 484–487.

[21] Gneisenau, "Über den Krieg," 50–51.

In his memorandum, which he submitted to the Prussian king, Gneisenau analyzed all of these weaknesses of the Prussian army in detail. In closing, he referred to a further central point that aroused general criticism: "Our blindness toward what measures the bold foe could undertake against us played an important role, however. We assumed it would be easy to overcome *this* enemy" (emphasis in the original).[22]

The public debate on the causes of the "debacle" indicates that the overestimation of their own military abilities, coupled with the national chauvinism fostered by many officers, was brought down by the defeat of 1806, but that the officer corps still clung to the underlying military arrogance, which made it hard for them to stomach the discussion over the causes of defeat.[23] For generations, Prussian military men had been raised to see their "pride" and "honor" in the army, and they therefore believed that the defeat had robbed them of everything they held dear. The insult to their individual and collective sense of honor, which they drew from the regiment, the army and the "Prussian nation," seems to have been the most painful one.[24] In their haste to save their personal honor, officers began with wild mutual recriminations and denunciations soon after the defeat. They fought veritable verbal duels, which often enough ended in actual duels.[25]

In order to restore the lost honor of the army and with it that of the "Prussian nation," in November 1807 the king set up a Royal Commission to Study the Capitulations and Other Events of the Recent War, which he charged with "investigating the causes that led to the unfortunate events of the recent war" and "discovering, on the one hand, those officers who contributed by violating their duties, and on the other those who, despite the accidents that befell the army, distinguished themselves personally."[26] The monarch intended this commission and the "regimental tribunals" established shortly thereafter – which as corporative courts were elected by the officers of each regiment for the purpose of assessing the conduct of

---

[22] Ibid., 61; see also Johann von Borcke, "Kriegerleben des Johann von Borcke, weiland Kgl. Preuß. Oberstlieutenants, 1806–1815 (1888)," in *Deutschland unter Napoleon in Augenzeugenberichten*, ed. Eckart Kleßmann (Düsseldorf, 1965), 129.

[23] See "Brief Scharnhorsts, an Clausewitz, Memel, 27. Nov. 1807" (333–336), "Brief Scharnhorsts an Müffling, Königsberg, 27 März 1808" (340–341) and "Brief Scharnhorsts an Götzen, Königsberg, 25. Sept. 1808" (347–350), in Gerhardt von Scharnhorst, *Briefe*, vol. 1: *Privatbriefe*, ed. Karl von Linnebach (Munich, 1914); also Johann von Hüser, *Denkwürdigkeiten aus dem Leben des Generals der Infanterie von Hüser größtenteils nach dessen hinterlassenen Papieren* (Berlin, 1877), 64–65.

[24] "Brief Scharnhorsts an seinen Sohn Wilhelm, 29. Dez. 1806," in Scharnhorst, *Briefe*, 1:309–311.

[25] Generalstab, *1806*, 86–87; and, in the same volume, " 'Pflichtmäßiger Bericht über die Ereignisse vom 15.–28. Oktober 1806,' Major von der Marwitz, Friedersdorf, 24. Sept. 1808," 202–240, 209–210.

[26] "Instruktion für die zur Untersuchung der Capitulationen und sonstigen Ereignisse des letzteren Krieges niedergesetzte Commission," in Generalstab, *1806*, 13–15.

each of them in the recent war – to effect a "self-cleansing" of the Prussian military.[27] All officers "whom the regimental tribunals found to be above reproach" were to receive a certificate stating "that they had been determined to be blameless." This certificate was a prerequisite for their reinstatement or pension.[28] Younger officers in particular participated vigorously in the "self-cleansing" process. Unlike many older, higher-ranking officers, they had little to lose. They wanted to justify themselves – "cost what may" – "so they might continue to serve."[29]

The work of the "self-cleansing commission" led to the dismissal of a large number of incompetent officers and a significant restructuring of the officer corps, including a considerable lowering of their average age. At the start of the war of 1806–07, the Prussian army numbered 7,096 officers (among them 142 generals and 885 staff officers). Of these, 4,933 had left by 1813 (including 103 generals and 635 staff officers); 208 were forced to leave in the course of criminal proceedings. Only 3,898 officers of the 1806 army also fought in the subsequent wars of 1813–15.[30] By restructuring the officer corps, the "self-cleansing" process significantly contributed to reducing inner-military resistance to army reform. It was also intended to improve the army's greatly diminished reputation in civilian society and to promote the necessary public support for military reforms.[31] The latter two objectives, however, were not attained to the hoped-for degree.

Public criticism of the army's "disgraceful failure" did not end in 1807–08. For that reason, the king tried in September 1808 to stop it by a cabinet decree prohibiting any form of oral or written "argument" by military or civilian individuals that "might compromise" the state and the army. This measure proved rather counterproductive, especially because it could only be enforced in the Prussian rump monarchy, but not in the territories controlled by France.[32] Critiques of the army, and with it implicitly of the government, were one outlet for the desperate mood of crisis caused by the experiences of war and occupation that had swept up broad strata of Prussia's civilian population after the 1806–07 defeat.

---

[27] Generalstab, *1806*, 50–86

[28] "Schreiben Friedrich Wilhelms III an die Immediatskommission zur Untersuchung der Kapitulationen und sonstiger Ereignisse des letzten Krieges, 9. Juni 1808," in ibid., 29–30.

[29] "Bericht des L. von Trillitz," in ibid., 82; also Herman von Boyen, *Erinnerungen aus dem Leben des Generalfeldmarschalls Hermann von Boyen*, ed. Dorothea Schmidt, 2 vols. (Berlin, 1990), 1:366.

[30] Generalstab, *1806*, 104–106.

[31] See "Kabinettsorder, 26 Dez. 1807," in Generalstab, *1806*, 57; for more on the agenda and organization of the "self-cleansing" process, see ibid., 17–18; and Hagemann, *Muth*, 92–96.

[32] "Kabinettsorder an den Generalleutnant von Blücher, Königsberg, 27 Sept. 1808," in Rudolph Vaupel, *Das Preussische Heer vom Tilsiter Frieden bis zur Befreiung, 1807–1814*, 2 vols. (Berlin, 1938), 1:592.

CIVILIAN EXPERIENCES OF THE WAR OF 1806–07
AND FRENCH OCCUPATION

The experience of war, defeat and occupation came as a shock to broad segments of the population in Prussia and in central and northern Germany who, after many years of peace, experienced for the first time at close range what the violence of war meant for everyday life. The residents of those regions through which the Grande Armée passed, and which they besieged and occupied, were particularly affected. French troops did not hesitate to bombard contested villages and towns continuously and to set fire to homes and farms. The writer Willibald Alexis, who experienced the shelling of Breslau during the French siege of 6 November 1806 to 5 January 1807 as a young boy, recalled, "The foe showered bullets upon the city and not upon its fortifications, and while few soldiers remained there, all the more citizens came to harm. Serious fires both day and night; the fire alarm vied with the rattle of the guns. Single bombs shattered entire houses."[33] Since Breslau, unlike most other fortified cities, did not surrender without a fight, the city felt the full force of the enemy's destructive fury. After the capitulation, a veritable orgy of pillaging erupted, in which, according to Alexis, the "German compatriots" serving under Napoleon proved "more despotic and crueler still than the French."[34] Eyewitnesses in other Prussian regions reported similar occurrences. The old conflicts between Catholic southern Germany and Protestant northern and eastern Germany apparently resurfaced here.

The rampant pillaging of conquered villages and towns was an everyday wartime experience in 1806–07. In a letter to her son Arthur from the embattled city of Weimar in late October 1806, the widowed author Johanna Schopenhauer reported:

> The hardship in the city is terrible. [...] The town has been literally abandoned to pillaging; the officers and cavalry remained innocent of atrocities and did what they could to protect and to help. But what could they achieve in the face of 50,000 furious men who were left to do as they pleased that night, since the first leaders permitted it, at least passively! Many houses have been completely plundered; the shops, naturally, were first; linens, silverware, and money were carried off; the furniture, and anything that could not be transported left to rot. [...] All those who abandoned their houses have lost nearly everything. Some were so fortunate as to be given officers to billet right away, who offered them some protection, often at peril to their own lives. Those who came off best were those who, like us, had courage, showed no fear and were acquainted with the French language and customs.[35]

---

[33] Willibald Alexis, *Eine Jugend in Preußen: Erinnerungen* (Berlin, 1991), 23. On Alexis, see Walter Heynen, "Alexis, Willibald," *NDB* 1 (1953): 197–198.

[34] Alexis, *Eine Jugend*, 30.

[35] "Johanna Schopenhauer, Brief von Okt. 1806," in Kleßmann, *Deutschland*, 149; on Schopenhauer, see Ulrike Bergmann, "Schopenhauer, Johanna Henriette, geborene Trosiener," *NDB* 23 (2007): 470–471.

Similar scenes were repeated everywhere. Frequently, the accounts noted that officers had tried to maintain military discipline, but the troops had been impossible to control, particularly while the fighting was still going on. Since the Napoleonic army lived off the land and was billeted in town houses, estates, farms and cottages, people of all classes whose regions were touched by the war were affected.[36] Fear of the conquering troops of the Grande Armée spread quickly throughout Prussia and northern Germany, although the censored newspapers tried every means of preventing panic.[37]

The Grande Armée occupied Prussian territory for more than two years. Only after the amount of the contributions that remained to be paid had been agreed upon did the last French units leave the country in December 1808, with the exception of the fortresses on the Oder at Glogau, Küstrin and Stettin. It is impossible to reconstruct precisely the material costs to the population of the presence of the approximately 150,000-man occupying force, which was distributed across the monarchy in four *commandements* (only East Prussia, which had been evacuated in August 1807, was exempted). In any case, it represented a significant economic and social burden for the inhabitants, who had already financed Prussian arms and the war. The Continental Blockade weakened the economy, contribution payments burdened the entire country, and with the peace treaty even the most remote corners of Prussia, which had previously known the French troops only from hearsay, had to billet and provision soldiers, and provide forage as well as horses and servants for transport. Few people profited from the war, chief among them army suppliers, carters, moneylenders and smugglers.[38]

The effect of war and occupation was an economic and social crisis that encompassed broad segments of the Prussian population, 80 percent of whom still lived in the countryside, as they did elsewhere in Central Europe. The majority of the urban population resided in small towns with fewer than 1,000 residents. Only 5 percent of the cities had more than 2,000 inhabitants.[39] In 1810, Berlin, with a population of 145,000 civilian and 13,500 military inhabitants, was the sixth largest city in Europe after London, Paris, Vienna, Amsterdam and St Petersburg.[40] Around 1800, more than two-thirds of the population in Prussia worked in agriculture. The vast majority of them owned no land. Fewer than one-fifth of Prussians earned their living from the trades. The nobility, upper and middle classes were a small elite in the cities and countryside. Only 1 percent of the population belonged to the aristocracy, and, on average, 1–10 percent to the urban upper class and

---

[36] Granier, *Berichte*.
[37] François Gabriel de Bray, "Aus dem Leben eines Diplomaten alter Schule (1901)," in Kleßmann, *Deutschland*, 159–161.
[38] See Münchow-Pohl, *Reform*, 227–282.
[39] Wehler, *Gesellschaftsgeschichte*, 1:142.
[40] Theodore Ziolkowski, *Berlin: Aufstieg einer Kulturmetropole um 1810* (Stuttgart, 2002), 33.

10–35 percent to the urban middle classes. Most people in towns and villages (40–65 percent) were poor.[41]

As suggested earlier, the economic conditions of the vast majority of the Prussian populace deteriorated dramatically after 1806. The economy all over Europe suffered as a result of the many wars and the trade and tariff policies that accompanied them. But the situation of the monarchy was particularly precarious in comparison to the states of the other German-speaking regions that belonged to the Confederation of the Rhine or were directly annexed to France. The economy of rump Prussia, especially the export sectors, suffered severely from the Continental Blockade. Areas particularly affected were grain production in the eastern provinces and textile manufacturing in the Mark Brandenburg and Silesia. As elsewhere on the Continent, the demand for iron products, in contrast, remained relatively stable as a result of the wars. Unlike in the western and southern regions of Germany, cutting off the Prussian market from English goods gave only a limited boost to domestic production. France sought to create a new market for its own industry in the monarchy by fostering the import of French manufactured goods at a very modest tariff. This measure led to a severe depression in the Berlin and Potsdam silk-weaving industry, among others. [42]

In addition, the enormous tribute payments in cash and in kind that Prussia had to make to France, the significant burdens of the French occupation and the continuing march-through of French troops exercised a chilling effect on economic and social life. Cities and counties amassed enormous debts in a very short time with no prospect of relief. Where no money could be borrowed, all payments had to be tendered in cash or in kind, or directly distributed among the population. The two-year sojourn of Napoleonic troops in Berlin from 1806 to 1808 alone cost 15.1 million taler in contributions and billeting expenses.[43] During this period, the capital's 145,900 inhabitants had to support 15,000 French soldiers and officers.[44] As a result, many firms and estates went bankrupt. Heinrich von Béguelin, a high official in the Prussian financial administration, summarized the precarious economic situation in his political memoirs, which were published posthumously in 1819:

The plight of private citizens was just as terrible [as that of the state]. The estate owners were drained by the contributions, delivery of supplies, and billeting of troops. House owners suffered a similar fate, their properties also lost half their value, and it was only

---

[41] Wehler, *Gesellschaftsgeschichte*, 1:140–217, esp. 171–172, 180, 183, 188–189.

[42] Ibid., 1:486–505; Treue, "Preußens Wirtschaft," 496–509; and Friedrich-Wilhelm Henning, *Handbuch der Wirtschafts- und Sozialgeschichte Deutschlands*, 3 vols. (Paderborn, 1991, 1996 and 2003), 2:190–195. On the effects of the Continental Blockade from a comparative perspective, see Aaslestad and Joor, *Revisiting*.

[43] Treue, "Preußens Wirtschaft," 507.

[44] Granier, *Berichte*, 44, 148–149 and 453.

with great effort that they could let some of them for half the previous rent. Holders of government stocks received no interest and feared losing their capital, for which they were offered 50 percent. The manufacturer was compelled, for lack of sales, to give notice to his workers. The merchant sold nothing, or did so only on credit. The civil servant daily feared dismissal, and many had received no salary for years.[45]

In fact, not only were many manufacturers, craftsmen and merchants – and their employees with them – affected by Prussia's economic crisis, but so were the owners of houses, agricultural land, and stocks and bonds.[46]

The situation in the countryside was even more dramatic.[47] A "Memorandum of the Committee of the Kurmark Estates" of May 1808 poignantly summarized the desolate state of the province under occupation:

Thus is the situation in the countryside, where the helpless peasant, bereft of animals, grain and bread in vain entreats his no less devastated landlord to help him, and at last, hard-pressed by billeting, desperately leaves the paternal farm – just as in all villages many farms already stand utterly empty. Thus is the situation in the towns where the lack of bread daily arouses insurrection; where within a few days the growing want and dearness of provisions must drive desperation to the utmost.[48]

In some regions agriculture came to a complete standstill. Peasants left their homes and farms. Rural poverty increased substantially, and with it petty crime, violence and prostitution rose. Reports to the government complained not only about "immorality, the abandonment of obedience [and] tampering with other people's property as natural consequences of war," but they also described the increasing "wantonness" of the female sex and the rise in venereal disease as signs of destitution.[49] Here the sources use the suffering of the civilian population not only to emphasize the brutality and ruthlessness of the French enemy, but also to describe its "demoralizing" effects on the population, especially the female part, which had become out of control and "immoral."

Misery, starvation and epidemic disease (especially typhus, dysentery and cholera) spread. In their wake, the death rates in town and country alike skyrocketed. In Königsberg, where soldiers, unemployed civil servants and other refugees from all parts of Prussia lived crowded together, the weekly number of deaths in August 1807 rose to 230–240 from a pre-war figure of 30–40.[50] Even in the relatively prosperous regions around

---

[45] Beguelin and Beguelin, *Denkwürdigkeiten*, 171.
[46] Hanna Schissler, *Preußische Agrargesellschaft im Wandel: Wirtschaftliche, gesellschaftliche und politische Transformationsprozesse von 1763 bis 1847* (Göttingen, 1978), 83–90.
[47] Granier, *Berichte*, 279, 350–354 and 360–361.
[48] Ibid., 246–251.
[49] Münchow-Pohl, *Reform*, 53.
[50] Ibid., 51.

Berlin and in the capital itself, the situation became so dire that the first
food riots began to break out in April 1808 in response to grain and bread
shortages.[51]

Such unrest over food remained rare, however. There were virtually
no protest actions against the French occupiers between 1806 and 1808
in Prussia. The population stayed extremely calm and lived through the
"time of the French" passively. The economic and social effects of the
war and the occupation nevertheless led to radical changes in the civilian
population's attitude toward Napoleon and the French. Indifference and
antipathy were transformed into rejection and hostility well beyond military and patriotic circles.[52] This development is well documented in the
status reports compiled regularly for the Prussian king during the French
occupation, beginning in July 1807, by the financial official Johann August
Sack, who served as chairman of the Commission on the Implementation
of the Peace.[53]

The reports of this commission as well as the letters and diaries of educated contemporaries indicate that a strong sense of crisis had gripped not
only the government and the administrative and military elites but also
the Prussian population more generally after 1806, which increased until
1812. This sense of a "fundamental crisis" was fueled by the experiences
of social, economic and political downfall in the wake of the defeat and
occupation and intensified by the already widespread collective feeling of
living in a "time of upheaval," which was a reaction to the economic,
social and political changes accelerated by the French Revolution and the
wars that accompanied it.[54] It led to the questioning of accepted patterns
of interpretation, norms and values, thereby revealing their contingency
and fragility.[55]

---

[51] "Büsching an Stein, Berlin, 26. April 1808," in Heinrich Friedrich Karl Freiherr vom
Stein, *Briefe und Amtliche Schriften*, ed. Erich Botzenhart and Walther Hubatsch, 10 vols.
(Stuttgart, 1957–1974), 2:714–716.

[52] Granier, *Berichte*, 377, 387, 390, 393–394, 466–468, 505, and 510–511; see also Münchow-
Pohl, *Reform*, 49–62. On the different response in the kingdom of Saxony, see Töppel,
Sachsen, esp. 79–115.

[53] See Granier, *Berichte*; on the history of status reports, see ibid., v–xiii; and Andrea
Hofmeister-Hunger, *Pressepolitik und Staatsreform: Die Institutionalisierung staatlicher
Öffentlichkeitsarbeit bei Karl August von Hardenberg, 1792–1822* (Göttingen, 1994),
184–185.

[54] See Fritzsche, *Stranded*, 11–54; and also chapter 16 in the fourth part.

[55] Wehler, *Gesellschaftsgeschichte*, 1:398; also Blessing "Umbruchkrise"; and Münchow-Pohl,
Reform, 385–409. With the concept of "crisis" I want to emphasize that, at the time, it was
a matter not of the insecurity of single individuals or larger groups of individuals, but of a
collective sense of crisis, which was also explicitly formulated as such. This understanding
follows Kurt Imhof, "Vermessene Öffentlichkeit – vermessene Forschung? Vorstellung eines
Projektes," in *Zwischen Konflikt und Konkordanz: Analyse von Medienereignissen in der
Schweiz der Vor- und Zwischenkriegszeit*, ed. Imhof et al. (Zurich, 1996), 11–60.

The educated male elites in Prussia's administration and army overwhelmingly reacted to the crisis of the monarchy's state, army and society with calls for "revenge"; that is, they hoped for the opportunity of another war against France under more auspicious circumstances and thus not just for the restitution of the Prussian monarchy in its pre-1806 borders, but also of the nation's honor, their military's honor and their own "manly honor."[56]

---

[56] See Echternkamp, *Aufstieg*, 167–169; Hagemann, *Muth*, 85–87.

2

Reform and Revenge: Political Responses

Looking back at the aims of Prussian reformers and patriots between 1807 and 1813, to whom he had belonged, the Prussian statesmen Baron vom Stein wrote:

Our chief idea was to rouse a moral, religious, patriotic spirit in the nation, to inspire it anew with courage, self-confidence, a readiness to make any sacrifice for independence from foreigners and national honor, and to seize the first opportunity to begin the bloody and hazardous struggle for both.[1]

As he had before, Stein emphasized in his reminiscences written in 1823 that, after the devastating defeat in the 1806–07 war, all aims of Prussian policy were subordinated to one "universal objective" – military liberation from Napoleonic domination. All Prussian reform initiatives were dedicated to the "chief idea" of a "national rising" (*Erhebung*).[2] In his view, this applied not just to policies for which he was responsible as Prussian Minister of State between October 1807 and November 1808; the governments under Baron vom Stein zum Altenstein and Burggrave zu Dohna-Schlobitten (1808–10) as well as Baron von Hardenberg (1810–22), who followed him in this leading position, set similar priorities.[3]

Some historians share this assessment, stressing that Prussia "had to rebuild a state which had been defeated and sliced in two, and which was still bleeding from its wounds," and that, until 1813, the three governments differed only in their specific responses to this challenge.[4] Other scholars place more emphasis on the political differences between these governments

---

[1] Stein, "Erinnerungen ans Vergangene (Autobiographische Aufzeichnungen aus den Jahren 1823–24), 1757–1824," in idem, *Briefe*, 9:864–910, 878; on Stein, see Alfred Stern, "Stein, Heinrich Friedrich Karl," *ADB* (1893): 614–641.

[2] Stein, *Briefe*, 9:878–880.

[3] On Stein vom Altenstein, see Heinz Gollwitzer, "Altenstein, Karl Sigmund Franz Freiherr von Stein zum Altenstein," *NDB* 1 (1953): 216–217; on Dohna-Schlobitten, see Karl Otmar Freiherr von Aretin, "Dohna-Schlobitten, Friedrich Ferdinand Alexander, Burggraf und Graf zu," *NDB* 4 (1959): 53; and on Hardenberg, see Hans Haussherr and Walter Bußmann, "Hardenberg, Carl August Fürst von," *NDB* 7 (1966): 658–663.

[4] See, for example, Nipperdey, *Germany*, 21 and 23; and Paul Nolte, *Staatsbildung als Gesellschaftsreform: Politische Reformen in Preußen und den süddeutschen Staaten, 1800–1820* (Frankfurt/M., 1990), 97.

and the various reform groupings in the administration and army. They stress that Stein's supporters tended to pursue a "conservative modernization" of the state administration and military structure. In so doing, they were strongly oriented toward the old society of estates and the traditional institutions and corporative liberties under the Holy Roman Empire. The reformers around Hardenberg, in contrast, according to these historians pursued a reform policy oriented toward modern political concepts, which grappled with the French model and for that reason tended to be more open to ideas of political and economic liberalism.[5] What most scholars overlook, though, is that, despite differences of opinion, the small circle of reformers in the administration[6] and the military[7] agreed on the paramount immediate goal: the self-assertion of the Prussian state. This goal was based on their assessment of the causes of the defeat of the monarchy and more generally of Napoleon's domination of Germany.

THE DEBATE OVER THE CAUSES OF THE DEFEAT

The objective of regenerating the Prussian state was at the heart of most discussions of the "Prussian debacle" in educated patriotic circles, which began with a critique of the causes of the Prussian military defeat but quickly proceeded to place the army's failure in a broader political, social and cultural context. Everywhere in Prussia, as in other regions of Germany, these circles perceived the defeat as one of many indicators of the "decline" of the German nation, manifested in the dissolution of the Holy Roman Empire.[8] Severe censorship by the French and Prussian authorities meant that the main sites of this discussion were letters and internal memoranda exchanged outside the censorship system, as well as private social gatherings and patriotic associations, on the one hand, and books, brochures and journals published

---

[5] See Barbara Vogel, *Allgemeine Gewerbefreiheit: Die Reformpolitk des preußischen Staatskanzlers Hardenberg, 1810–1820* (Göttingen, 1983). For the development of research on Prussian reform policies, see Bernd Sösemann, ed., *Gemeingeist und Bürgersinn: Die preußischen Reformen* (Berlin, 1993), esp. his "Die preußischen Reformen: Forderung und Herausforderung," 11–24.

[6] Around 25 higher Prussian civil servants belonged to the inner circle of reform officials. See Walther Hubatsch, *Die Stein-Hardenbergschen Reformen* (Darmstadt, 1977), 97–130; as well as the names listed in "Denkschrift des Generalmajors von Scharnhorst [Aug. 1808]," in Vaupel, *Heer*, 1:555–557. The importance of this small group is evident from the fact that, in the summer of 1808, the circle of civil servants on the king's Königsberg administrative staff consisted of only 52 persons, including the lower officials. See Vogel, *Gewerbefreiheit*, 74.

[7] Aside from Scharnhorst, the inner circle of army reformers included seven officers; see Heinz G. Nitschke, *Die Preußischen Militärreformen, 1807–1813: Die Tätigkeit der Militärreorganisationskommission und ihre Auswirkungen auf die preußische Armee* (Berlin, 1983), 49–52; and "Denkschrift des Generalmajors von Scharnhorst."

[8] For a much more detailed analysis of the social profile of this group of patriotic publishers and writers, see Hagemann, *Muth*, 158–202.

abroad – in other German-speaking states or even foreign countries – and smuggled in illegally, on the other. [9]

Two basic lines of argumentation emerged in this debate. The first attributed the collapse of the traditional state and military order primarily to political failings. The disintegration of German unity was seen as the chief cause of the defeat, and particular reproach was directed at the "treachery" of the German princes. Fearing the ideas unleashed by the French Revolution, they had increasingly suppressed the liberties and rights of their subjects and made "dishonorable" alliances with France for the sole purpose of maintaining their individual power. The Prussian government, in particular, had clung to a rigid corporative organization of estates, an obsolete military system and outmoded methods of warfare, refusing to institute necessary reforms. Like the other German states, Prussia had resisted the zeitgeist for all too long.

In keeping with this idea, the Pomeranian historian Ernst Moritz Arndt, a leading German-national publicist of the time, noted in his pamphlet *The Prussian People and Army in 1813* that the most recent history had shown once more that those who cling to the old ways and fail to move with the times would be swept away by their tempests. [10] The politicians of Revolutionary France, and later Napoleon, had been mere instruments of God for the realization of a "higher plan of world history." The devastating defeat of 1806–07 had brought down Prussia's decaying edifice of state and promoted the internal forces of political and military renewal. [11] Other reform-minded patriots wrote similar things about Prussia, but also about other German states. These reflections on the times were frequently accompanied by harsh criticisms of the princes and their governments, which were accused of unwillingness to enact reforms. [12] Instead of "buttressing the tottering edifice with strong new supports," they had "merely [clung] more tightly to the crumbling ruins," wrote the Bavarian jurist Anselm von Feuerbach in his 1813 pamphlet *On the Repression and Re-Liberation of Europe*. Exaggerated fears of revolution and rebellion had prevented them from recognizing the signs of the times. Instead of "jumping onto the back" of the "winged horse" of history and guiding its flight with the "master's sure hand," they had reined it in, and even tried "to yoke it like an ox." Out of the same fear they had also failed to fight the "enemy with his own weapons" and to make the cause of their crowns the cause of their nations. [13]

---

[9] On the form and influence of censorship, see ibid., 112–127; on the debate itself, 206–221. On the press policy of the Prussian government in this period, see Hofmeister-Hunger, *Pressepolitik*, 181–250. For more, see chapter 4 in the second part.

[10] On Arndt, see Hellmuth Rößler, "Arndt, Ernst Moritz," *NDB* 1 (1953): 358–360.

[11] Ernst Moritz Arndt, *Das preußische Volk und Heer im Jahr 1813* ([Leipzig], 1813), 10–13.

[12] See Orion [Joseph Görres], "Reflexionen," *VM* 1 (Aug. 1810): 154–172.

[13] Anselm Feuerbach, *Ueber die Unterdrückung und Wiederbefreiung Europens* (Deutschland, n.p., [1813]), 16–21. On Feuerbach, see Friedrich Merzbacher, "Feuerbach, Paul Johann Anselm Ritter von," *NDB* 5 (1961): 110–111.

It was mainly authors of early-liberal and German-national leanings who sought to explain the "Prussian debacle" and the fall of the Holy Roman Empire in this political and reform-oriented manner.

The other line of argumentation explained the debacle mainly in terms of the "decay" of "German customs and morals," and the absence of a "national spirit" of self-sacrifice, combined with the lack of a "valorous" attitude and religiosity. There was much lamentation about "citizens'" absent sense of "patriotic" responsibility toward society and the state, and deficient sentiments of "honor and valor." They had thus not lived up to their roles as "protectors of home and fatherland" and had therefore also "failed as men."[14] This second, cultural explanation, quite compatible with the first, not only dominated in Prussia's patriotic circles but was also shared by many German-national authors from other regions. It was so widespread because it offered a meaningful interpretation of a defeat that had seemed incomprehensible to many, and that had had such catastrophic results. It took up dominant, religiously colored patterns of thought and feeling and did not fundamentally challenge existing political authority in Prussia or elsewhere.[15] Only in combination with the first line of argumentation did it become dangerous for the authorities.

At first it was mainly patriotic Protestant clerics who tried to explain the defeat in these terms. One of them was the Hessian pastor Friedrich Wilhelm Kleinschmidt, who published his sermon "The Evil Spirit of Our Age Is an Enemy of the Word of God" in the theological journal *Magazin für Prediger* in late 1807. In the sermon, which he had given a few months previously, he accused his fellow mankind of frivolousness, false enlightenment, unbelief, prodigality, hedonism, covetousness, unfairness, selfishness and pride and admonished them to repent. In particular those who "might influence others through their reputation" should do everything in their power to counteract this "harmful spirit." Without repentance, the corruption would only increase, and the enemy would gain more and more influence.[16] As in many sermons after 1806, the argument here is still limited to the traditional religious interpretation of the defeat as a result of godless and sinful deviation from the path of Christian virtue.

This interpretation was quickly taken up in historical and political magazines, broadsides and pamphlets and charged with patriotic-national rhetoric, which in turn influenced later sermons. Before 1813 the writings of pioneering German-national thinkers such as Ernst Moritz Arndt, Johann Gottlieb Fichte or Friedrich Ludwig Jahn already had a substantial impact

---

[14] See Anonymous, *Frauensteuer an der Wiege des wiedergeborenen Vaterlandes: Von Elisabeth von F.* (n.p., [1814]), 10–12.

[15] See Ibbeken, *Preußen*, 50–61; Münchow-Pohl, *Reform*, 37–48.

[16] Friedrich Wilhelm Kleinschmidt, "Am Sonntage Seragesima, ueber Luc. 8, v. 12: Der böse Geist unseres Zeitalters als ein Feind des Wortes Gottes," *MfP* 3.2 (1807): 116–123.

on patriotic-minded educated people.[17] Journals such as the *Vaterländisches Museum* brought out in 1810–11 by the Hamburg publisher Friedrich Perthes,[18] or *Minerva*, edited by the former Prussian officer and historian Johann Wilhelm Archenholz also helped set the tone. The monthly *Minerva*, in particular, which appeared beginning in 1792 first in Hamburg and from 1808 in Jena, was a journalistic institution because of its long tradition and large print-run of 5,000. The journal was extremely popular with the educated public in central, eastern and northern Germany. Many Prussian officers and state officials were subscribers; even Friedrich Wilhelm III is said to have been a regular reader. Between 1806 and 1813 it developed into a leading periodical for the discussion of economic, social, political and military reforms, with particular attention to Prussia. Many authors published their contributions anonymously, as was common at the time, in order to shield themselves from state repression.[19]

An intense debate over the causes of the "national debacle" began in *Minerva* immediately after the Prussian defeat, and continued for many years. Apart from contributions criticizing the outmoded political and military system, the magazine also regularly published articles discussing immorality and unbelief as important reasons for the defeat. Unlike in sermons, however, in the magazine this accusation was combined with a criticism of German men for abandoning patriotism. Thus, for example, an author wrote in the September 1811 issue, "Nowhere does one see the decisiveness that befits a man in storms and among the ruins of a world; everywhere there is an absence of self-sacrifice for the common good, which maintains states, and all love of country has been extinguished."[20] Apart from patriotism, understood as self-sacrificing "love of country,"[21] German men also lacked "manly courage" and a "sense of honor," the critic continued. Men's "dishonorability" had turned into "defenselessness." In this contribution, a sense of honor was no longer expected only of princes and the aristocratic elites, but of all men. A central cause of the lack of patriotism and manly

---

[17] See, in particular, Ernst Moritz Arndt, "Geist der Zeit, Theil I und II (1806 und 1809)," in *Arndts Werke: Auswahl in zwölf Teilen*, ed. August Lesson and Wilhelm Steffens (Berlin, n.d.), pt. 6; Johann Gottlieb Fichte, *Reden an die deutsche Nation* (Berlin, 1808); and Friedrich Ludwig Jahn, *Deutsches Volksthum* (Lübeck, 1810). On Fichte, see Hermann Zeltner, "Fichte, Johann Gottlieb," *NDB* 5 (1961): 122–125.

[18] On Perthes, see Franz Menges, "Perthes, Friedrich Christoph," *NDB* 20 (2001): 203–204.

[19] *Minerva* appeared from 1792 to 1858. See Hubert Max, *Wesen und Gestalt der politischen Zeitschrift: Ein Beitrag zur Geschichte des politischen Erziehungsprozesses des deutschen Volkes bis zu den Karlsbader Beschlüssen* (Essen, [1942]), 113–114; and Boris Bovekamp, *Die Zeitschrift "Minerva" und ihre Herausgeber Johann Wilhelm von Archenholz (1743–1812) und Friedrich Alexander Bran (1767–1831): Ein Beitrag zur Kompatibilität von Militär, Aufklärung und Liberalismus* (Kiel, 2009).

[20] "Betrachtungen," *Minerva* 3 (Sept. 1811): 486–505, 494–495.

[21] "Patriotismus," in *Conversations-Lexicon*, 9:306–307.

courage and honor, the author believed, was the lack of faith and trust in God.[22]

Arndt had argued similarly in 1809 in the second part of his work *Spirit of the Times*, when he wrote that nothing gives a man more strength than trust in God, and nothing fills him with as much enthusiasm for great and difficult undertakings as a sense of religion.[23] Other authors in *Minerva* – but also well-known political writers such as the Saxon-Gotha court counselor Friedrich Jacobs, the Hessian professor Philipp Friedrich Boost or Friedrich Ludwig Jahn in his popular 1810 work *German Folkdom* – attributed the lack of patriotism to "perverse cosmopolitanism" and a "slavish desire to emulate" all things foreign, whose most extreme expression they criticized as "Gallomania," which led people to "ape" all things French, even to the extent of giving up their own language.[24] This cultural-political explanation became increasingly popular before and during the wars of 1813–15, far beyond German-national circles.[25] The small number of female authors who participated in this debate argued similarly. They, too, like the German-Swedish translator, poet and salonnière Amalie von Helvig, criticized the "failure of men" and their "loss of honor."[26]

Both the political and cultural explanation of Prussia's defeat and the "downfall" of Germany influenced the politics of the Prussian reformers in the government, administration and army after 1806–07.

AN AGENDA OF REVENGE AND REFORM

Faced with catastrophic conditions in the Prussian rump monarchy, there was, between 1807 and 1813, very little room for political maneuvering. Therefore, leading reform-oriented government and military officials agreed, despite all other differences, that in the medium term only military victory over France could restore the state's autonomy, as Stein stressed in retrospect. The central political objective was, consequently, to turn Prussia into

---

[22] "Betrachtungen," 495–496.

[23] Arndt, "Geist der Zeit," pt. 2, 12–16.

[24] Friedrich Jacobs, *Deutschlands Gefahren und Hoffnungen: An Germaniens Jugend* (Gotha, 1813, 2nd edn.), 23–24; see also "Und noch einige Bemerkungen über den deutschen Volkscharakter," *Minerva* 2 (May 1810): 193–204; Karl Gottlieb Prätzel, "An die Deutschen," *Minerva* 3 (Aug. 1810): 332–338; Jahn, *Volksthum*, 187; and [Philipp Friedrich] Boost, *Ueber die National-Ehre der Deutschen: Eine historisch-philosophische Untersuchung* (Wiesbaden, 1812).

[25] See, for example, Heinrich Burdach, *Ueber die endliche Erhebung Germaniens oder wie kann die Hoffnung auf eine bessere Zukunft in Erfüllung gehen* (Berlin, 1814), 27–30; and Friedrich Ehrenberg, *Das Volk und seine Fürsten: Volkswesen und Volkssinn* (Leipzig, 1815), 149–152.

[26] [Amalie von Helvig,] *An Deutschlands Frauen von einer ihrer Schwestern* (Leipzig, 1814), 9–10; on Helvig see, Adalbert Elschenbroich, "Helvig, Anna Amalie von, geborene Freiin von Imhoff," *NDB* 8 (1969): 508–509.

a "valorous nation" (*wehrhafte Nation*) able to lead the liberation struggle against Napoleon in Central Europe. The ideas about the nation that developed in these debates on the causes of the Prussian defeat and the necessary steps toward liberation remained quite open and ambiguous. The small circle of patriotic-minded educated men who dominated the discussion used the word "nation" synonymously with the terms "people" (*Volk*) and "fatherland" (*Vaterland*) and applied them to both the Prussian territorial state and the German nation as a whole. In these circles, the vision of a German "cultural nation" (*Kulturnation*) whose unity rested on primordial factors such as shared history, language and culture was tied either to a Christian-conservative regional state patriotism or a more liberal version of it. Prussia was generally regarded as a "monarchical nation" that stood above the various ethnic groups in the population of the territorial state and formed the heart of the German cultural nation. Many of these ideas had already been developed in the eighteenth century, and some went back still further. What was new in Prussia under the specific conditions of French rule after the defeat of 1806–07, however, was the discourse's focus on a single major objective: the struggle for liberation from Napoleon. This was accompanied not just by further politicization, but also by a militarization and virilization of the concepts of "the nation," "the people" and "the fatherland" as well as an intensification of the exclusionary aspect of patriotic-national ideas. Political argumentation using patriotic-national rhetoric became increasingly commonplace in the educated classes after 1806–07.[27]

Reform-oriented circles in the Prussian government, administration and military tried to realize their aim of remaking Prussia as a "valorous nation" that would be able to triumph over Napoleon and his empire primarily by tackling five tasks. First and foremost, financial policy had to ensure that the Prussian state could afford to settle the demanded reparations to France, which would end the occupation, and support the occupying French army. Furthermore, a cautious financial policy was necessary to fund the planned military reforms and the costs of the hoped-for next war.[28]

Second, a new approach to military policy was needed. After 1806–07, reformers in the state and army largely agreed that the monarchy would be able to withstand the French foe only if it recast its own military system along the French model and introduced universal conscription, at least during wartime. To realize this aim, they worked on a rapid reorganization of the Prussian army.[29] They believed that two preconditions would be

---

[27] On the national discourse in the eighteenth century, see Blitz, *Liebe*; Echternkamp, *Aufstieg*, 41–159 on the early nineteenth century, see 163–381; more in chapter 5 in the second part.

[28] Henning, *Handbuch*, 2:276–282.

[29] On the Prussian military reforms, see Dierk Walter, *Preußische Heeresreformen, 1807–1870: Militärische Innovation und der Mythos der "Roonschen Reform"* (Paderborn, 2003), 235–324; and Ute Frevert, *A Nation in Barracks: Modern Germany, Military Conscription and Civil Society* (Oxford, 2004), 10–30.

necessary for its success: On the one hand, its "self-cleansing," which would bring a younger generation of officers who supported military reform into positions of responsibility; and, on the other hand, greater acceptance for the army by the population, especially the middle class. The military system needed to correspond better to middle-class notions of freedom and honor. An army with draconian punishments and compulsion was no longer considered up-to-date.[30] Against stiff resistance in the army and the administration, the Military Reorganization Commission set up by the king on 15 July 1807 under the leadership of General Gerhardt von Scharnhorst managed by 1813 to reform not just the military administration and justice system, but also the system of training, recruitment and provisioning.[31] Old privileges of the nobility, above all preferred access to officers' commissions and the principle of seniority, were abandoned in favor of a more meritocratic commissioning and promotion of officers. Military law was adapted to middle-class legal concepts and special rights largely dismantled. In the interest of a necessary improvement in troop motivation to fight and readiness for duty, the legal position of soldiers and noncommissioned officers was also strengthened. The "Articles of War for Non-Commissioned Officers and Common Soldiers" of 8 August 1808, as the basic legal order of the Prussian army, were especially important here. They replaced the old military regulations of 1797, whose emphasis on "the strictest obedience" and Christian "fear of God" made them as out-of-date as the threats of draconian corporal punishment such as running the gauntlet for the most minor offenses.[32] The new "Articles of War" programmatically announced, "that in future, any subject of the state, without regard to birth [...] shall be obliged to perform military service." For the first time, noncommissioned officers and soldiers were explicitly addressed as "men of honor."[33] The "Regulation on Military Punishments," issued together with the "Articles of War," accordingly removed all corporal punishments for noncommissioned officers and soldiers.[34] These reforms created a decisive precondition for the

---

[30] On everyday life in eighteenth-century German armies, see Peter H. Wilson, *German Armies: War and German Politics, 1648–1806* (London, 1998). On Prussia, see the classic study by Otto Büsch, *Military System and Social Life in Old-regime Prussia, 1713–1807: The Beginnings of the Social Militarization of Prusso-German Society* (Atlantic Highlands, NJ, 1997).

[31] On Scharnhorst, see Johannes Kunisch, "Scharnhorst, Gerhard Johann David von," *NDB* 22 (2005): 574–575.

[32] See [Scherbening], ed., *Die Reorganisation der Preußischen Armee nach dem Tilsiter Frieden*, 2 vols. (Berlin, 1862 and 1866) (also in *BHMW*, 1854–1866), 1:554–557.

[33] *Kriegs-Artikel für die Unter-Offiziere und gemeinen Soldaten, den 3ten August 1808* (Königsberg, 1808), Art. 1, 3–4; more in [Scherbening], *Reorganisation*, 1:553–580; "Entwicklung der Preußischen Kriegsartikel," in *BHMW* 7 (1890): 351–394.

[34] *Verordnung wegen der Militair-Strafen, den 3ten August 1808* (Königsberg, 1808), 3–4 and 10–14; more in [Scherbening], *Reorganisation*, 1:553–580; on the legal position of soldiers in the nineteenth-century Prussian army, see Manfred Messerschmidt, "Die preußische

introduction of universal conscription, which only became possible when war was declared on France, because it violated the Treaty of Paris.

In conjunction with this military reorganization, the reformers in the Prussian state and military believed, third, that it was necessary to create "military readiness" in broad segments of the male population, who were to be mobilized for military service by means of universal conscription for the first time. Up to that point the canton system of recruitment, introduced in 1733, called only a relatively small proportion of Prussian men of military age to do service, and these had mainly been from the rural lower classes. Not just aristocrats, civil servants and members of the educated and propertied middle classes, but also the male inhabitants of entire regions and industrial districts – such as the western territories of the monarchy, as well as large cities, including Berlin and Potsdam, Brandenburg, Breslau and Magdeburg – had been exempted from conscription. The canton system was abolished in Prussia on 9 February 1813.[35] For a military based on universal conscription, a new type of soldier was necessary: "subjects of the king" (*Untertanen*) had to become autonomous "citizens of the state" (*Bürger des Staates*)[36] who were prepared to take up arms and defend their home and country. The universal obligation to do military service was linked early on with the promise of increased political rights, albeit mostly for men of property.[37]

Fourth, the reformers were convinced that a "warlike national spirit" of "patriotic self-sacrifice" also had to be fostered in large segments of the population, not just in men of military age. They regarded this as essential, since the virtually bankrupt Prussian state needed broad financial and practical support to make war on France. The population was not only expected to pay high taxes and dues and to buy war bonds, but also to equip and supply the militia and volunteer units, care for the sick, wounded and crippled

---

Armee," in *Handbuch zur deutschen Militärgeschichte 1648–1939*, ed. Militärgeschichtliches Forschungsamt, 9 vols. (Munich, 1964–1981), vol. 4, pt. 2:10–225, 122–201.

[35] Rainer Wohlfeil, "*Vom stehenden Heer des Absolutismus zur Allgemeinen Wehrpflicht, 1789–1814*," in *Handbuch zur deutschen Militärgeschichte*, 2:86–87.

[36] In the German-language discourse of the time, the term *Bürger* encompassed the private individual, the town citizen (*Stadtbürger*) possessing municipal citizenship (*Bürgerrecht*), but also the public, political state citizen (*Staatsbürger*) on the French model of the *citoyen*. Between the latter two meanings was the term "citizen of the state" (*Bürger des Staates*), which was far more common in the early nineteenth-century German-speaking region than the relatively rarely used term *Staatsbürger*. See Manfred Riedel, "Bürger, Staatsbürger, Bürgertum," in *Geschichtliche Grundbegriffe: Historisches Lexikon zur politisch-sozialen Sprache in Deutschland*, ed. Otto Brunner et al., 8 vols. (Stuttgart, 1972–1997), 1:672–725, 700–705; and Michael Stolleis, "Untertan – Bürger – Staatsbürger: Bemerkungen zur juristischen Terminologie im späten 18. Jahrhundert," in *Bürger und Bürgerlichkeit im Zeitalter der Aufklärung*, ed. Rudolf Vierhaus (Heidelberg, 1981), 65–100.

[37] See more in chapter 7 in the second part.

soldiers, and support the civilian victims of war, particularly widows and orphans. Both the organization of the militia and volunteer units and war charity were left to the provincial estates, municipalities and churches and thus to the local population. To mobilize the inhabitants, an intensive propaganda campaign had to be waged before and during the war that promoted a "bellicose spirit" and patriotism. The debate on the options for such a campaign was part of a wider discourse in patriot circles on German "national education."[38] The patriots saw five routes to this objective: the promotion of "publicity" (*Publicität*) – today we would say an uncensored public sphere – by means of which patriotic-minded writers were first and foremost to influence the educated men who shaped public opinion; the furtherance of patriotism among the "common people" by popular enlightenment; the education of male youth, whose "civic and bellicose spirit" was to be awakened as early as possible by schoolteachers and professors; the development of a public culture of patriotic-national symbols, rituals and festivities that created community and collective identity; and the strengthening of the general population's "religious faith." The Prussian reformers, like many patriots, believed that the willingness to sacrifice life and property for the fatherland was mostly based on a strong Christian faith.[39] Therefore, they allotted to the state-controlled established church and its Protestant clergy the task of an intensive religious-patriotic education from the pulpit. Although it has often been overlooked in scholarship, the Protestant Church and religion thus played an important role in the reformers' plans for "national education." Given the precarious diplomatic and domestic circumstances, they considered religion to be the central and safest means for the state to promote a "bellicose spirit" and "self-sacrifice" well beyond the small, educated elite.[40]

Last but not least, reforms in the state, economy and society had to be initiated in order to reduce Prussia's modernization deficit, keep pace with the performance and efficiency of the French state, and put the monarchy in a political and economic position to conduct a successful war. As in the field of military reforms, here, too, it was only the defeat of 1806–07 and the subsequent profound crisis that forced an "anti-revolution": catching up with the economic, social and political changes that had already been made by the French foe through energetic reforms.[41] The Prussian reformers

---

[38] See Helmut König, *Zur Geschichte der bürgerlichen Nationalerziehung in Deutschland zwischen 1807 und 1815*, 2 vols. (Berlin, 1972 and 1973), 1:298–356; and Stübig, *Armee*, 239–256.

[39] See "Denkschrift Steins, Brünn, März 1810," in Stein, *Briefe*, 3:292–298; and König, *Geschichte*, 2:81–177 and 286–302.

[40] For more, see Karen Hagemann, "A 'Valorous Nation' in a 'Holy War': War Mobilisation, Religion and Political Culture in Prussia, 1807 to 1815," in *The Napoleonic Empire and the New European Political Culture*, ed. Michael Broers et al. (Basingstoke, 2011), 186–200.

[41] Clark, *Kingdom*, 313; and Levinger, *Nationalism*, 3–17.

agreed in principle on the need to tackle these five tasks, but their opinions differed about the best means of handling them. In the implementation of their reform project, however, they faced not just massive misgivings on the part of the king and the highest court circles, but also opposition in parts of the administration and the noble elite.[42]

A similar reform agenda was pursued by the states in the Confederation of the Rhine. Different and especially challenging, for the Prussian reformers, was the fact that the monarchy was faced with the trifold necessity of coping with the consequences of war, preparing for another war and reforming the state, economy and society.[43] Military reforms and the attendant question of financing the substantial costs of the army and war had therefore a far more central status within overall modernization measures in Prussia than in the Confederation of the Rhine.[44] Even here, though, the constantly growing French demands for war financing and the resulting dramatic rise in war debts left the reformers under pressure to embark on radical new paths: in the states of the Confederation of the Rhine and Prussia alike the war and its financing were the *nervus rerum* of reforms in state and society.[45]

THE RESPONSE OF THE PRUSSIAN PUBLIC

The reforms that the Prussian government began to introduce in 1807 did little to change the massive loss of authority and popular confidence, which increased steadily until 1812.[46] Apart from the military reorganization, the immediate practical effects of most reform projects before 1812–13 – administrative, financial, educational and agrarian reform, trade regulations, the emancipation edict and the laws regulating municipal government – remained too limited or brought instead of relief new burdens (in particular special taxes and compulsory loans) to the broader population. The reform policy thus appears to have increased people's sense of crisis and widened the chasm between subjects and the Prussian state instead of fostering support.[47]

In light of the desperate mood of the population, all plans for a popular uprising against Napoleon – which leading army reformers around Gerhard

---

[42] On political differences within the group of reformers, see Vogel, *Gewerbefreiheit*, 30–72.

[43] See Wehler, *Gesellschaftsgeschichte*, 1:397–485.

[44] See Barbara Vogel, "Staatsfinanzen und Gesellschaftsreform in Preußen," in *Privatkapital, Staatsfinanzen und Reformpolitik im Deutschland der napoleonischen Zeit*, ed. Helmut Berding (Ostfildern, 1981), 37–57.

[45] Horst Carl, "Der Mythos des Befreiungskrieges: Die 'martialische Nation' im Zeitalter der Revolutions- und Befreiungskriege 1792–1815," in *Föderative Nation: Deutschlandkonzepte von der Reformation bis zum Ersten Weltkrieg*, ed. Dieter Langewiesche and Georg Schmidt (Munich, 2000), 63–82, 69.

[46] See Münchow-Pohl, *Reform*, 89–384.

[47] Ibid., 171–312; Ibbeken, *Preußen*, 254–304.

von Scharnhorst and Neidhardt von Gneisenau in particular had considered after 1807, pointing to the Spanish uprising of 1808–09 – appeared unlikely to succeed and were therefore rejected by the Prussian king.[48] The lack of support for an armed uprising in Prussia and northern Germany is evident in the short-lived military adventure of the extremely popular Hussar Major Ferdinand von Schill, who had commanded the successful defense of the fortress of Kolberg in 1807. He led his own regiment against the Kingdom of Westphalia in a campaign begun on 28 April 1809, which ended in bloody defeat only one month later.[49] Friedrich Wilhelm III was also unwilling to support Austria when it declared war against France on 9 April 1809. The king's realistic skepticism was confirmed by the devastating defeat of Austria. Only seven months after Franz II had started the war, with British support, he was forced to agree to the Treaty of Schönbrunn with France on 14 October 1809.[50]

Between 1806 and 1812, regional patriotism and loyalty to the Prussian king were expressed only on a few extraordinary occasions. These included the reentry of the army in Berlin, led by the garrison troops under the command of Ferdinand von Schill, in December 1808; the return of the royal family to the capital in December 1809; and especially the death of Queen Luise on 19 July 1810, which was popularly perceived as a very disconcerting stroke of fate.[51] The elaborate obsequies, which were carefully staged by the state and churches and went on for two weeks, became the most important events in the kingdom between 1807 and 1813 in which the entire country publicly displayed its patriotism and loyalty to the royal family.[52] The ceremonies throughout the kingdom reunited the royal family with the people for the first time since the defeat of 1806–07. A plethora of poems, sermons and commemorative broadsheets expressed the subjects' sorrow.[53] Autobiographical texts indicate that the queen's death in fact moved contemporaries profoundly. When they mourned the loss of the much-loved queen, it was not just as the "mother" of the Prussian nation, but also as a symbol of hope for national renewal.[54]

---

[48] On the Prussian king and his role at this time, see Thomas Stamm-Kuhlmann, *König in Preußens großer Zeit: Friedrich Wilhelm III. – Der Melancholiker auf dem Thron* (Berlin, 1992), esp. 267–364.

[49] See Ibbeken, *Preußen*, 146–173; Münchow-Pohl, *Reform*, 132–170; on Schill and his role in history and collective memory, see Mustafa, *Long Ride*; Veltzke, *Freiheit*.

[50] Esdaile, *Napoleon's Wars*, 391–396.

[51] Granier, *Berichte*, 320, 512–513 and 544. On Queen Luise, see Daniel Schönpflug, *Luise von Preussen: Königin der Herzen – Eine Biographie* (Munich, 2010); Demandt, *Luisenkult*; and Förster, *Königin*.

[52] See Paul Czygan, "Totenfeier für die Königin Luise 1810," *Altpreußische Monatsschrift* 54 (1917): 347–359; and Friedrich Emanuel Sack, "Verkündigung des Todes der Königin Luise von Preußen," in *Zum Angedenken der Königin Luise von Preußen* (Berlin, 1810).

[53] *Zum Angedenken*, 29–35 and 47–49.

[54] See Boyen, *Erinnerungen*, 1:337–338; Henrich Steffens, *Was ich erlebte*, ed. Willi A. Koch (Leipzig, 1938), 205.

The brief burst of regional patriotism on the occasion of the queen's death did little to change the persistent sense of crisis in Prussia, which peaked in 1812 during mobilization for the Grande Armée's invasion of Russia. On 4 March the Prussian king ratified a military alliance with France, which turned the entire region into a deployment and march-through area for the invasion troops, and burdened it with substantial armaments contributions for the war against Russia that Napoleon began on 24 June 1812. Prussia was expected to muster an auxiliary corps of 30,000 men for the Grande Armée, which was 457,000 and later 600,000 men strong and moving eastward through Prussian territory. One of the most affected regions was East Prussia. In order to provision the assembled armies, which had been promised free passage, the exhausted country had to deliver 600,000 hundredweight of flour, two million bottles each of beer and brandy, one million hundredweight of hay and straw, six million bushels of oats, 15,000 horses, 44,000 oxen, 3,600 horse-drawn wagons with carters as well as field-hospital supplies and munitions. The costs were to be settled later against the remaining contribution payments (at that time only 12 million taler were left), but the total sum of all payments made during the renewed occupation came to 85 million taler. The alliance with France was tantamount to a total surrender by Prussia, imposed renewed heavy burdens on the population and, because of requisitions and pillaging, it painfully reminded people of the French occupation of 1806–08. When the Grande Armée marched off to Russia, the Prussian monarchy was once again economically and financially on the verge of state bankruptcy and had relinquished the last vestiges of its political reputation.[55]

Public opinion in Prussia began to change only in the autumn of 1812. With Moscow in flames in September, but above all with the withdrawal and retreat of Napoleon's army, which in the winter of 1812 was moving toward an ever more obvious defeat, hope awakened everywhere. A universal and final reversal of the mood came with the march-through of the ragged remains of the Grande Armée in eastern Prussia, and Napoleon's official admission of defeat in December 1812. At this point, reports from East Prussia as well as Berlin and the surrounding marches indicated "that only a spark is needed to ignite a flame."[56] Within just a few years, the negative experiences with French domination had created an anti-French mood, which, now that the defeat of France finally seemed possible, was transformed into a willingness to fight for liberation from French domination. Thus, more and more voices were raised in addresses, letters and petitions to the Prussian king demanding an alliance with Russia.[57] The first signal for the Prussians to rise up came with the Convention of Tauroggen,

[55] Mieck, "Preußen," 38–40; Münchow-Pohl, *Reform*, 352–384.
[56] Droysen, *Leben*, 1:4–5.
[57] See Ernst Müsebeck, *Freiwillige Gaben und Opfer des preußischen Volkes in den Jahren 1813–1815: Nach der amtlichen Statistik zusammengestellt* (Leipzig, 1913), 113–145.

which General Hans David Ludwig von Yorck signed on his own authority as commander of the Prussian auxiliary corps on 30 December 1812. The chief content of this agreement with Russian headquarters, of which the king publicly disapproved, was the temporary neutralization of the auxiliary corps.[58]

In February 1813 public outrage in Prussia reached the boiling point. "The king is no longer in a position to suppress the enthusiasm that has taken possession of nearly all hearts," the English privy agent in Berlin, the future Hanover minister of state and cabinet minister Baron Ludwig von Ompteda wrote to London on 20 February.[59] The mood was fired not just by the advance of the Russian army, which had reached Königsberg in January 1813, but also by the king's appeal of 3 February to form volunteer units and the resolution of the diet (*Landtag*) of the East Prussian estates of 7 February to establish a provincial militia and arm the population of its territory, which was not authorized by the monarch. Prussia did not openly declare war on Napoleon until 16 March 1813, however.[60]

[58] Peter Paret, *Yorck and the Era of Prussian Reform, 1807–15* (Princeton, NJ, 1966), 191–196.

[59] Mieck, "Preußen," 49.

[60] Ibid., 38–57.

3

Liberation and Restoration: The Wars of 1813–1815 and Their Legacy

The wars of 1813–14 were the first in Prussian history to be conducted based on universal conscription. A first step was the enactment on 9 February 1813 of the "Edict Lifting Previous Exemptions from Cantonal Duties for the Duration of the War," drafted by General Scharnhorst, which introduced compulsory military service for all men between the ages of 17 and 24 who had previously been exempt. Those who volunteered for a rifle detachment on foot or horseback or an artillery detachment within eight days could choose their own units. Those who came later had to serve in the unit assigned to them by the military authorities. Young men in frail health; those whose fathers had died and who had inherited the running of a town house, farm or larger property; the sons of widows without older brothers who were not serving in the military; those who were known as the sole breadwinners of their families; and "active and salaried officials" of the Prussian state as well as clerics remained exempt. The edict thus retained broad exemptions from service in the standing army. As the military reformers intended, service in the standing army became exclusively a matter for young, unmarried men with no domestic establishment of their own. In order to make service attractive, they were assured that "every man in the military, without regard to estate and wealth, shall be given the chance, according to his abilities and conduct, to be promoted to officer or non-commissioned officer as soon as he has served one month and the opportunity arises, and shall have a preferred claim to a position in the civil service."[1] In addition, more political rights were promised to all men who willingly fulfilled their military duties.[2]

In his appeal "To My People," issued one day after Prussia declared war on France, on 17 March 1813, Friedrich Wilhelm III called upon all men capable of bearing arms to defend their country and announced the immediate introduction of a militia (*Landwehr*) for the duration of the war

---

[1] "Verordnung über die Aufhebung der bisherigen Exemtion von der Kantonpflichtigkeit für die Dauer des Krieges," in *Das Preußische Heer der Befreiungskriege*, ed. Großer Generalstab, Kriegsgeschichtliche Abteilung II, 3 vols. (Berlin, 1912 and 1914), 2:386–387.

[2] See chapter 5 and 6 in the second part.

and the later establishment of a general levy (*Landsturm*). That same day, he issued the "Edict on the Organization of the Militia," also drafted by Scharnhorst, which regulated the implementation of the *Landwehr*. It stipulated that the provincial estates had to set up the militia as an autonomous military organization alongside the standing army. All men between the ages of 17 and 40 who were capable of bearing arms and did not belong to the standing army or the special units of the rifle detachments were obliged to serve in the militia. The "Conscription Act" of 3 September 1814 retained general conscription without proxies for peacetime as well.[3] By 15 March, Prussia had already been divided into four military governorates (*Militär Gouvernements*) (between the rivers Elbe and Oder, between the Oder and the Vistula, between the Vistula and the Russian border, and Silesia), each headed by one civilian and one military governor, with the latter having the final say in case of "imminent danger." These military governorates, which were joined by the governorates between the Elbe and the Weser and later on between the Weser and the Rhine were responsible for organizing the war on the ground.[4]

The Prussian field army managed to mobilize 245,000 men by early August 1813. Of those, 119,000 belonged to the troops of the line (among them more than 9,000 volunteers in rifle detachments), 113,000 to the militia, 11,000 to the various volunteer formations and 2,000 to the train and craft units. Therefore 46 percent of all soldiers in the field army were militiamen and 8 percent volunteers. Prussia had 281,000 men under arms, including 6,900 officers. Thus, in 1813 not only did Prussia have twice as many soldiers fighting as it had in 1806, but the army consisted almost exclusively of "locals." More than 10 percent of the male population was deployed in 1813, compared to only about 2 percent in 1806.[5] This enormous mobilization was only possible because the kingdom had already begun rearming secretly before 1813, in contravention of the Paris Convention. Two cabinet orders of 6 August and 24 December 1808 had introduced the so-called *Krümper* system.[6] It stipulated that each month, five of the oldest trained "inlanders" – that is, local recruits – in every infantry company would be granted a furlough, and the same number would be newly inducted. Those on furlough assembled on Sundays and holidays for further training. This system of recruitment, which was later extended to the artillery and cavalry,

[3] Wohlfeil, "Heer," 102–153.
[4] Max Lehmann, *Scharnhorst*, 2 vols. (Leipzig, 1886 and 1887), 2:556; and Mieck, "Preußen," 56.
[5] The difference in size between the field army (first line) and the army as a whole reflects the 36,000 men of the garrison and reserve troops (second line); see Generalstab, *Heer*, 2:458–551, esp. 548–551; and Wohlfeil, "Heer," 86–87 and 159–161.
[6] The word *Krümper* comes from the vocabulary of the standing armies, and refers to the regiments' hidden reserves of supernumerary recruits on leave.

established a trained military reserve without officially expanding the army. It thereby created the preconditions for rapid general mobilization. By August 1811, some 80,000 men were under arms, and another 35,000 to 40,000 could be mobilized on short notice. Fortified storehouses had been set up to outfit them in Pillau, Kolberg, Spandau and Silesia. The price of this secret rearmament was a further rise in the state debt. The Prussian state could only raise the requisite funds through daring financial transactions and extensive private loans.[7]

This military mobilization received political support from an intense patriotic-national propaganda campaign beginning in early 1813. With the advance of the Russian army, which reached Königsberg in January and Berlin in March 1813, rigid French and Prussian censorship was essentially abolished.[8] Russian headquarters insisted, as Berlin's Chief Commissioner of Police Paul Ludwig Le Coq complained in a report to the central government on 8 March 1813, "that any and all printed matter directed against France should appear and be distributed by all means, even if it contains slanders."[9] The resentment and hatred that had built up against Napoleon were expressed in the subsequent period in a large number of anti-French cartoons, satirical poems, farces, and calls to arms. Soon, more and more pamphlets appeared containing war songs and poems intended to mobilize the population. Beginning in the spring of 1813, a whole wave of patriotic-national newspapers and journals were also founded.[10] After the official declaration of war, this flood of publications was also promoted by the Prussian army leadership, the military and civilian governors of liberated regions, and the central administrative council of the allied powers under Baron vom Stein, which were all equally interested in mobilizing for war. As a result, they not only supported the printing and distribution of leaflets but also disregarded government censorship. In the war years 1813–14, censorship was largely abolished in practice, especially for individual books and pamphlets. The "war of swords" – to cite the much-used phrase of the time – was accompanied by an intensive "war of quills."[11]

The rapid and relatively successful mobilization of Prussian men for the volunteer units and the militia, as well as of the rest of society for the various forms of support necessary for the war effort, would have been impossible without the broad and intensive attempts to mobilize public

---

[7] See Generalstab, *Heer*, 1:1–374; Treue, "Preußens Wirtschaft," 509; and Wohlfeil, "Heer," 100–104 and 122–123.

[8] See Karl-Heinz Schäfer, *Ernst Moritz Arndt als politischer Publizist: Studien zu Publizistik, Pressepolitik und kollektivem Bewußtsein im frühen 19. Jahrhundert* (Bonn, 1974), 59–65.

[9] Paul Czygan, *Zur Geschichte der Tagesliteratur während der Freiheitskriege*, 3 vols. (Berlin, 1909–1911), 2:49–60.

[10] See Hagemann, *Muth*, 128–157.

[11] For more, see chapter 4 in the second part.

opinion. Coercion by the state and the army was not enough. They urgently needed to win public support in 1813. Thus, in the propaganda of the time, the term "people's war" (*Volkskrieg*) was one of the most frequently invoked *Pathosformeln* (pathos formulas), or highly emotional national slogans.[12] It represented the idea of a war based on universal conscription and supported by the entire population, whose success derived from the unity between princes, their governments, the army and the subjects of the Prussian and German nation.[13]

PRUSSIA AND GERMANY DURING THE WARS OF 1813–15

Austria provided the greatest number of troops to the allied forces during the wars of 1813–15. The allied coalition fought under the main command of Austrian Field Marshal Karl Philipp, Prince of Schwarzenberg, but Prussia was the driving force among the German powers. The kingdom began the war in alliance with Russia. On 14 March, the Duchy of Mecklenburg-Schwerin joined the coalition of Kalisch of 28 February 1813, followed by Sweden on 22 April, Great Britain during the ceasefire of 4 June to 10 August and Austria a short while later. Thus, 500,000 allied soldiers in three armies confronted the Grande Armée, whose strength had returned to 440,000. Through skillful delay tactics that were also flexible, the coalition succeeded in capturing the initiative, winning a whole series of battles from late August and uniting the three armies by the beginning of October 1813.[14] Recognizing the coalition's likely military success, Bavaria also joined on 8 October. After the Battle of the Nations near Leipzig, which began on 16 October and ended on 19 October with an overwhelming defeat for Napoleon, who lost one-third of his men, his army had to retreat across the Rhine. Within a few weeks, the Confederation of the Rhine had been dissolved. In accord with the Leipzig Convention of 21 October 1813,

---

[12] Aby Warburg introduced the term *Pathosformel* in 1911 to refer to an artistic mode of expression that speaks to the emotions and passions. See Philippe-Alain Michaud, *Aby Warburg and the Image in Motion* (New York, 2004), esp. 7–19. In 1921, Max Weber defined the "national" as "a specific kind of pathos that links a human group with a common language, religion, customs or shared destiny to the idea of a political power organization of their own, whether already existing or desired." Weber, *Wirtschaft und Gesellschaft: Grundriß der verstehenden Soziologie* (Tübingen, 1972, 5th edn.), 244 and 530, as well as 240–245 and 527–531. It is in this dual sense that I use the term *nationale Pathosformeln*.

[13] See the second part.

[14] The most important victories were won on 23 Aug. at Großbeeren, 26 Aug. at Katzbach, 26–27 Aug. at Dresden, 29–30 Aug. at Kulm, 6 Sept. at Dennewitz and 3 Oct. 1813 at Wartenburg. For the history of the 1813–14 military campaigns in Central Europe and France, see Leggiere, *Napoleon*; and idem, *The Fall of Napoleon*, vol. 1: *The Allied Invasion of France, 1813–1814* (Cambridge, 2007). On the situation in Prussia during the war, see Clark, *Kingdom*, 358–378.

pending territorial reorganization the coalition set up four general governorates (*General Gouvernements*) in the liberated northern and western
regions: one in the region between the Weser and the Rhine, which was
already controlled by Prussia, one in the Grand Duchy of Berg, one in the
Grand Duchy of Frankfurt am Main, and one in the Kingdom of Saxony.
Each was headed by one civilian and one military governor and placed under
a central administrative department located in Frankfurt am Main, directed
by Baron vom Stein. This body replaced the central administrative council
of the coalition powers, which had been established on 4 April following
an agreement between Prussia and Russia, also with Stein at the helm. On
19 November, universal conscription was introduced in the new general
administrative districts and the roundup of recruits began immediately. On
24 November, Colonel Otto August Rühle von Lilienstern, who had been
among the Prussian army reformers, was appointed Commissioner General
for German Armaments. He was responsible for overseeing recruitment and
ensuring the uniform organization of the system of defense on behalf of the
central administrative department.[15]

Napoleon's forced retreat to French territory raised the question of
whether the war was over, or should be continued until the emperor was
toppled. While Austrian Chancellor Prince Klemens von Metternich and
his government favored peace negotiations with France, the Prussian and
Russian army leadership wanted to destroy the enemy utterly and for that
reason pushed for a quick march on Paris. In fact, Napoleon decided this
conflict by ignoring the allies' peace overtures. On 31 December 1813, the
coalition troops crossed the Rhine. Three months later, they marched into the
French capital. Prussia had begun the war of 1813–14 under the rhetorical
auspices of a "people's war" with the declared aim of national "liberation."
In the first year, the war indeed could not have been successfully conducted
without the broad mobilization of men for military service and the support
of much of the general population in Prussia. After the victorious Battle of
the Nations in October 1813, however, Austria became increasingly influential in the coalition against Napoleon. From the beginning, Metternich tried
not merely to cool patriotic-national tempers in Germany, among other
things by pushing for the return to a strict enforcement of censorship laws,
but at the same time also to pursue a policy of moderation toward France.
In the period that followed, the war increasingly became a traditional cabinet war over the German and European balance of powers.[16]

[15] See in particular, Johann Jakob Otto August Rühle von Lilienstern, ed., *Die Deutsche
Volksbewaffnung in einer Sammlung der darüber in sämmtlichen Deutschen Staaten ergan-
genen Verordnungen*, ed. General-Kommissair der Deutschen Bewaffnungsangelegenheiten
(Berlin, 1815); on his biography, see Bernhard von Poten, "Rühle von Lilienstern, Johann
Jakob Otto August," *ADB* 29 (1889): 611–615.
[16] See Leggiere, *Fall*, vol. 1.

In order to restore this power balance, the 30 May 1814 Treaty of Paris avoided dividing Europe into victors and vanquished. France's 1792 borders were confirmed, with the addition of a few captured territories. The rulers of the states of the Confederation of the Rhine (with the exception of Saxony, which had fought on France's side to the end) were guaranteed their possessions as well as their sovereignty. This recognized the territorial changes that had occurred since 1803 and prevented a return to the conditions of the Holy Roman Empire that had been dissolved in 1806. At the Congress of Vienna, held from 18 September 1814 to 9 June 1815, which decided on the future political organization of Europe, too, Metternich succeeded in pushing his politics of restoration. The aim of the Congress was to settle the many issues arising from the Revolutionary and Napoleonic Wars. The Holy Roman Empire was replaced by the German Confederation with 39 member states, which in 1815 encompassed some 630,100 square kilometers with a population of approximately 29.2 million.[17]

The war of 1815, which was unleashed by Napoleon's return to France and began officially on 25 March with the declaration of war by the old coalition partners, was even more clearly an old-style cabinet war. This no longer applied only to the war aims, which the rulers had already sought to enforce with diplomatic negotiations that ran parallel to the war, but also to the manner in which the war was conducted. On 7 April 1815 Friedrich Wilhelm III once again called the "Prussian people" to arms. The other German states also mobilized their populations, but the war was fought mainly with the regular troops of the standing armies, who were the first to be deployed, because the conflict already ended on 3 July 1815 with the capitulation of the provisional French government.[18]

The second Treaty of Paris of 20 November 1815 did not challenge the great land consolidation of the Napoleonic era, but it was less favorable to France, which now lost the border regions that its revolutionary armies had gained in 1790–92; the state was reduced to its 1790 boundaries. The old powers were restored throughout Europe. The politics of restoration did not, however, go so far as to reestablish Germany in the borders of the Holy Roman Empire, reintroduce the emperorship or reinstitute the mediatized and secularized imperial principalities. There were also substantial shifts of territory between the German states. Austria relinquished its possessions and claims in southern and western Germany in favor of its possessions in the Alps, Hungary and Galicia as well as Italy. The petty states went empty-handed. Saxony survived only in greatly reduced form. Bavaria was able to expand its position in southern Germany and Hanover greatly enlarged its territory. Prussia had to cede

[17] Wolfram Siemann, *Vom Staatenbund zum Nationalstaat: Deutschland 1806–1871* (Munich, 1995), 313–315.
[18] Siegfried Fiedler, *Kriegswesen und Kriegsführung im Zeitalter der Revolutionskriege* (Koblenz, 1988), 252–279.

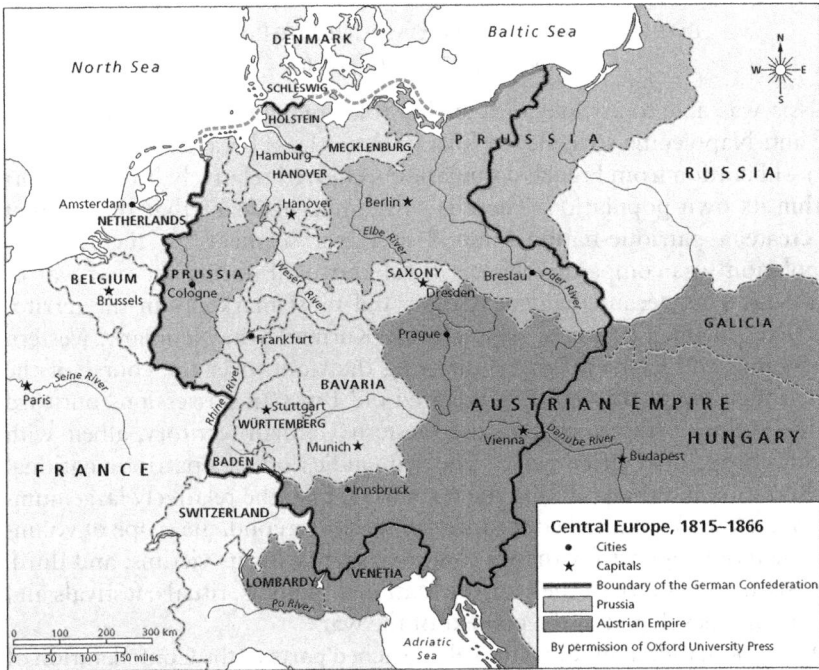

MAP 3. Central Europe, 1815–66.

the majority of its acquisitions from the Polish partitions to the newly created Kingdom of Poland, which was dependent on Russia, and failed to enforce its demand for a total annexation of Saxony, but did acquire two-thirds of the Saxon kingdom and a substantial part of Rhineland-Westphalia as well as the Saar. At 278,000 square kilometers, the Prussian state returned to nearly 90 percent of its former size in 1806, while its population of 10.3 million surpassed the old levels. Following the "Edict on the Improved Organization of the Provincial Authorities" of 30 April 1815, Prussia's state territory was divided into ten provinces: East Prussia, West Prussia, Posen, Pomerania, Silesia and Brandenburg in the old state territory and Saxony, Westphalia, the Lower Rhine and Jülich-Cleves-Berg in the newly acquired territory. This growth, which was mostly in the west, integrated Prussia, which had previously expanded mainly in the east, more than ever before into the center of Central European politics. Alongside Austria, it became the leading power in the German Confederation. In the immediate postwar period and the decades that followed, the power competition between the two monarchies substantially influenced German policy. (See Map 3)[19]

[19] See Elisabeth Fehrenbach, *Vom Ancien Régime zum Wiener Kongreß* (Munich, 1986, 2nd edn.), 125–130; and Siemann, *Staatenbund*, 314–320.

POLITICS AND POLITICAL CULTURE DURING
AND AFTER THE WARS

Prussia was able to assume a leadership role among the German powers in
the anti-Napoleonic struggle for liberation not least because its central war
aim – liberation from French domination – enjoyed relatively broad support
within its own population. There is substantial evidence that the attempt
to create a patriotic-national mood in larger segments of the Prussian
population was comparatively successful above all during the first war of
1813–14. This became evident earliest and most markedly in the territories that remained Prussian, especially the Kurmark, the Neumark, Western
Pomerania and East Prussia.[20] Following the front, over the course of the
war it then swept through the liberated old Prussian possessions outward
to the entire northern, central and western German territory, albeit with
significant regional differences.[21] The main indicators of a patriotic-national
mobilization in Prussia during the wars were, first, the relatively large number of men who volunteered for military service; second, the scope of voluntary material support for the war and relief work for its victims; and third,
the broad acceptance of the patriotic-national symbols, rituals, festivals and
ceremonies developed in the context of the war.[22]

Patriotic-national mobilization also reached parts of the Confederation of
the Rhine in 1813–14. At first, the existing reservations against Napoleonic
domination were balanced out here by the new circumstances in economic
and political life created by the French. Many educated people had even
welcomed the Napoleonic regime because they hoped for rapid reforms
under French influence.[23] As it became increasingly obvious that Napoleon
was pursuing quite traditional dynastic power politics, educated people in
particular became more and more critical. The growing costs of the army
and the war also fostered anti-French attitudes in broader parts of the population, which is indicated by the protests that began in some regions of the
Confederation of the Rhine in early 1813 and the growing number of young
men of military age who refused to fight under the French flag.[24] Anti-French
unrest was reported in 1813–14 from Bremen, Hamburg, Lübeck, Lüneburg,

[20] See Münchow-Pohl, *Reform*, 49–63 and 227–241.
[21] See Heitzer, *Insurrection*, 236–293; Stulz, *Fremdherrschaft*, 102–299; Aaslestad, *Place*,
273–320; Rowe, *Reich*, 216–223.
[22] See the third part.
[23] See Gerhard Schuck, *Rheinbundpatriotismus und Politische Öffentlichkeit zwischen
Aufklärung und Frühliberalismus, Kontinuitätsdenken und Diskontinuitätserfahrung in den
Staatsrechts- und Verfassungsdebatten der Rheinbundpublizistik* (Stuttgart, 1994).
[24] See Josef Smets, "Von der 'Dorfidylle' zur preußischen Nation: Sozialdisziplinierung der
linksrheinischen Bevölkerung durch die Franzosen am Beispiel der allgemeinen Wehrpflicht
(1802–1814)," *HZ* 262 (1996): 695–738, 735–738; also Planert, *Mythos*, 419–473; and
Rowe, *Reich*, 159–192.

Oldenburg, Dresden, Erfurt, Hanau, the region of Lippe, Hesse-Darmstadt, the Kingdom of Westphalia and the Grand Duchies of Berg and Frankfurt am Main, among other places.[25] This economically and socially motivated protest, however, should not be equated with patriotism or nationalism. It more closely resembled early-modern social riots. From the summer of 1814 on – after the first victory over Napoleon – patriotic-national mobilization generally started to wane. The main reason for this was the altered political climate. Even in Prussia, the "patriotic collective experience" of 1813 was not repeated at the start of the second war in spring 1815.[26]

In light of the new form and breadth of patriotic-national engagement, historians consider the war years 1813–15 to be the phase in German history in which a broader national movement emerged for the first time.[27] The regional dissemination and scope of this movement and its influence remain subject to debate, however. Historians emphasize, on the one hand, that a national discourse already existed among the elites in the German-speaking lands long before the period of the wars against Napoleon, and that, during the war years 1813–15, too, this discourse mainly involved educated circles.[28] Moreover, scholars warn against equating Prussia with Germany.[29] These two caveats are vital, but they cannot really diminish the importance of the patriotic-national movement itself, which went beyond Prussia, at least briefly touching North, Central and West Germany, and for the first time extended beyond the educated elite. That this quite diverse movement was locally based and had no unifying political program contributed to its success. The very vagueness of political concepts held political controversies at bay, and the combination of regional patriotism with a vision of a German cultural nation had an integrative effect because it represented the complexity of German identity formation in the conflicted field between *Heimat* (local home region), territorial state, nation-state and nation.[30]

---

[25] See Heitzer, *Insurrection*, 240–245; Aaslestad, *Place*, 262–271; and Rowe, *Reich*, 216–223; more generally, see Charles J. Esdaile, *Popular Resistance in the French Wars: Patriots, Partisans and Land Pirates* (Basingstoke, 2005).

[26] Eckhard Trox, *Militärischer Konservativismus: Kriegervereine und "Militärpartei" in Preußen zwischen 1815 und 1848/49* (Stuttgart, 1990), 56–57.

[27] See Otto Dann, *Nation und Nationalismus in Deutschland, 1770–1990* (Munich, 1996, 3rd edn.), 68–84; for a more critical view, see Hagen Schulze, *States, Nations, and Nationalism: From the Middle Ages to the Present* (Oxford, 1996), 137–196.

[28] See Planert, *Mythos*, 20–21; and Echternkamp, *Aufstieg*, 216. On earlier forms of nationalism, Stauber, "Nationalismus"; and Blitz, *Liebe*.

[29] See James J. Sheehan, "State and Nationality in the Napoleonic Period," in *The State of Germany: The National Idea in the Making, Unmaking and Remaking of a Modern Nation-State*, ed. John Breuilly (London, 1992), 47–59; and John Breuilly, "The National Idea in Modern German History," in ibid., 1–28.

[30] See Celia Applegate, *A Nation of Provincials: The German Idea of Heimat* (Berkeley, CA, 1990); Alon Confino, *The Nation as a Local Metaphor: Württemberg, Imperial Germany, and National Memory, 1871–1918* (Chapel Hill, NC, 1997); and Abigail Green, *Fatherlands: State-Building and Nationhood in Nineteenth-Century Germany* (Cambridge, 2001).

Against the backdrop of a liberalization of censorship practice, the national *Pathosformeln* repeatedly invoked in war propaganda – such as the "unity" and "fraternity" of the German national community (*Volksgemeinschaft*) in a "people's war" – appear at first to have nourished hopes that liberation from the Napoleonic yoke would be followed by a more liberal reorganization of Germany in consensus with the princes.[31]

Only when victory over Napoleon seemed increasingly likely and the question of the postwar political order moved onto the agenda did a greater discursive specification of political concepts begin, accompanied by the eruption of political differences. This process, which intensified parallel to negotiations at the Congress of Vienna, was decisively promoted by the growing disappointment with political developments. Not only did the governments of the German states increasingly attempt to roll back the de facto press freedom of wartime by tightening censorship in 1814–15, but the Congress of Vienna also produced – against all hopes for more political liberties and territorial unification in a single German federal state – only a weak compromise.[32] The German Confederation (*Deutscher Bund*) was merely a loose federation of German territorial states, an association of "Germany's sovereign princes and free cities," whose objective, according to the Federal Act of 8 June 1815, was to preserve the external and internal security of Germany and the independence and inviolability of the individual German states. There was to be neither a common head of state nor a federal government. The only constitutional organ provided for in the Federal Act was a Federal Convention (*Bundesversammlung*) in Frankfurt am Main, a permanent congress of envoys of all 39 member states under the Austrian presidency. But a federal army was created, under the authority of a federal military commission, which conducted business on behalf of the federal diet. Of the ten army corps in the federal armed forces, Austria and Prussia provided three each. In addition, in 1819 a state police agency was set up in Mainz for the purpose of political surveillance.[33] Instead of national unity and political liberty the German Confederation brought more united military forces and stronger police control.

In order to respond to demands for political reform, Article 13 of the Federal Act vaguely announced that "All states of the Confederation will have a constitution based on the provincial estates (*Landständische Verfassung*)."[34] While this established the duty of the individual states to create constitutions in their territories, it neither set a date nor specified any

---

[31] See chapter 6 in the second part.
[32] See Hagemann, *Muth*, 112–128.
[33] Siemann, *Staatenbund*, 320–329.
[34] Ernst Rudolf Huber, *Deutsche Verfassungsgeschichte seit 1789*, 8 vols. (Stuttgart, 1957–1991), 1:640–658, 640–641.

content. The central question, and with it *the* potential for conflict inherent in Article 13, was and remained whether "provincial estates" referred to chambers of the old corporative type or to a modern form of popular representation. By 1824, 15 states of the German Confederation had made good on the Federal Act's promise of constitutions. They included Bavaria (on 26 May 1818), Baden (on 22 August 1818), Württemberg (on 25 September 1819) and Hanover (on 7 December 1819).[35] The Prussian king, too, had promised more political rights in exchange for the nation's willingness to perform military service in his constitutional declaration of 22 May 1815. He had even announced the formation of a "popular representation," which would more firmly anchor the state of civil rights and liberties and just administration based on order, and further strengthen harmony between the sovereign and the "Prussian nation."[36] These promises, however, were not realized until the Revolution of 1848–49. All that existed were estate assemblies (*Ständeversammlungen*) in the various Prussian provinces.[37]

From 1815 on, a growing national opposition movement tried to resist the politics of restoration, and above all the German system of petty states and neo-absolutism. Its members demanded the civil rights and liberties that monarchs had promised them as compensation for their wartime service, and were particularly committed to the provincial estates announced in the Federal Act. A significant portion of the universally male and mainly young activists of this movement had fought in the recent wars as volunteers and now joined forces in various patriotic-national men's clubs, the most important of them being the gymnastic associations (*Turnvereine*), the student associations (*Burschenschaften*) and the nascent choral societies (*Gesangsvereine*), along with the German Societies (*Deutsche Gesellschaften*) and the Committees for a National Festival. Their organized political activities were quickly and radically ended by the Carlsbad Decrees of 20 September 1819, which had the status of provisional federal laws. They banned the national-liberal opposition of the *Turner* and *Burschenschaften*, removed liberal- and national-minded university professors from their academic positions, expanded the censorship of the press and set up the *Central-Untersuchungs-Commission*, a central commission for the "joint investigation, as thorough and extensive as possible, of the facts relating to the origin and manifold ramifications of the revolutionary plots and demagogical associations directed against the existing constitution and the domestic peace of both the Confederation and the federal states."[38]

---

[35] Ibid., 656–666.
[36] Ernst Rudolf Huber, ed., *Dokumente zur deutschen Verfassungsgeschichte*, 3 vols. (Stuttgart, 1961–1966), 1:61–62.
[37] Huber, *Verfassungsgeschichte*, 1:302–313; and Siemann, *Staatenbund*, 343–426.
[38] Huber, *Verfassungsgeschichte*, 1:732–734; see also Siemann, *Staatenbund*, 332–333.

The first wave of an intensive persecution of the demagogues followed in the wake of the Carlsbad Decrees, although it proved impossible to suppress the oppositional national movement altogether. The nationalization of political culture continued apace, accompanied by a greater ideological differentiation of national political concepts.[39]

---

[39] On the development of early German nationalism up to the 1840s, see Echternkamp, *Aufstieg*, 297–479; Düding, *Nationalismus*; Luys, *Anfänge*; Levinger, *Nationalism*, 97–159; Dann, *Nation*, 85–160. On early liberalism, see Dieter Langewiesche, *Liberalism in Germany* (Princeton, NJ, 2000), 1–55. For an overview up to 1871, see John Breuilly, *The Formation of the First German Nation-State, 1800–1871* (Basingstoke, 1996), 1–55.

Conclusion

The first two decades of the nineteenth century in Central Europe were decisively shaped by the political hegemony and military expansionism of the Napoleonic Empire. The new form of warfare already introduced during the French Revolutionary Wars – national war conducted with mass armies – which Napoleon retained after he assumed power in November 1799, left its mark on the age. It not only forced the princes of the ancien régime and their governments to make at times far-reaching reforms of army and state, and indeed even the economy and society, in the interest of defending or regaining full state sovereignty, but also shaped the process of political and cultural nation-building.[1] In the German-speaking region, the form and content of this process were influenced in a highly ambivalent manner by experiences with the French Revolution and Napoleonic rule: many protagonists of the early national movement were well aware of the modernizing character of the Napoleonic reforms in the armed forces, society and state, and some of them even propagated elements of these reform ideas in modified form and adopted modes of political culture and national mobilization that had been successfully tested in Revolutionary and Napoleonic France, while still distancing themselves from the enemy with increasing vehemence in response to France's policy of expansion. As the second part demonstrates, the early-liberal protagonists of the German national movement combined liberal political demands for themselves and their kind with national chauvinism, anti-Semitism and conventional views of the gender order, which they shared with conservatives of every stripe. Their nationalism, like the political thinking of most conservatives, also bore a thoroughly Christian stamp. Such ambivalences had a lasting influence on the political culture not just of the era itself, but also of the entire nineteenth century.

[1] See Bell, *Total War*, 263–301.

PART TWO

DISCOURSES ON THE NATION, WAR AND GENDER

In his "List of Historical-Political Writings Censored in the Month of February 1815," the Prussian censor Heinrich Renfner complained once more about the monotony of the literary products he was compelled to read.[1] The occasion for his lament was an article by the Berlin history professor Friedrich Rühs, "On the Unity of the German People," in the *Zeitschrift für die neueste Geschichte, die Staaten- und Völkerkunde*. This journal of contemporary history and politics was published by Georg Andreas Reimer, one of the leading publishers in the Prussian capital, from 1814 to 1816.[2] In his article Rühs supported the reconstitution of a German empire. As long as political circumstances rendered this impossible, unity could only be created and maintained by the agreement of the German people. To this end, all Germans must be regarded as compatriots and attain the same rights in each German state, for which universal legislation was necessary. Rühs suggested establishing a federal council of German states with Austria and Prussia at the helm. The states would have a common foreign policy toward non-German states, and henceforth no individual member would be permitted to maintain envoys at foreign courts. The defense of the German fatherland would be secured by a reorganization of military affairs, with a general militia as its main element. To make German men better able to defend their country, they should undergo regular military training during peacetime. Fostering a sense of common purpose among all Germans, Rühs believed, demanded instruction in German history, the promotion of German language and customs and the introduction of a German national costume and festivals.[3] As

[1] Heinrich Renfner, "Verzeichnis der im Monat Februar 1815 censierten historisch-politischen Schriften," in *Zur Geschichte der Tagesliteratur während der Freiheitskriege*, ed. Paul Czygan, 3 vols. (Leipzig, 1909–1911), 2:162–166, 165.
[2] Doris Reimer, *Passion & Kalkül: Der Verleger Georg Andreas Reimer, 1776–1842* (Berlin, 1999); on Rühs, see Hans Schleier, "Rühs, Christian Friedrich," *NDB* 22 (2005): 221–222.
[3] Friedrich Rühs, "Ueber die Einheit des teutschen Volkes," *ZnG* 3.1 (1815): 21–40.

Renfner commented tersely on the essay, "All in all, the same suggestions we have already read in a hundred pamphlets and presumably will read again *ad nauseam usque*."[4] In fact, we can find similar recommendations in many other pamphlets, broadsheets, magazines and newspapers of the time. If we look at the range of political literature, it soon becomes apparent that much of what Arndt, Fichte or Jahn – the best known German-national authors of their time – wrote in their texts was also shared by many less famous contemporary authors.

In the political discourse of the years 1806 to 1819, opinion makers used different media – from newspapers and journals, leaflets, brochures and books, to proclamations, sermons, songs and poems – to determine what constituted "Germanness" and how best to represent it. While the characteristics of the national identity defined in this process were constructed as primordial, they were de facto highly dependent on situation and context. The discourse took up the eighteenth-century debate on patriotism, people and nation, combining old ideas with more current ones, and because of this mix could fulfill the intended purpose: bringing order into a "disordered world."[5] This combination was a prerequisite for the acceptance and relatively quick dissemination of the new national ideas as organizing principles for the perception and interpretation of a world shaken by war and crisis. After all, concepts generally only gain broad currency when they substantiate and intensify existing value judgments and attitudes and enrich them with new ideas. A second prerequisite was their open and vivid quality. In order to render the order of the national community comprehensible to broader circles, arguments were couched in metaphors and *Pathosformeln*, which condense complicated argumentation into complex and vivid images that are generally open to interpretation, and are far easier to communicate and remember. For that reason they were used especially in calls to action, proclamations, songs and poems, as well as sermons – intended to reach broad segments of the population and appeal to the emotions. The political-historical journals, for their part, were devoted mainly to intellectual exchange among educated men, while the main task of the newspapers was to provide information on current events. This interplay among the various media formed published opinion.[6]

The following analysis is therefore based on a wide variety of the media that participated in the contemporary patriotic-national discourse aimed at a broad mobilization for war. I begin this second part by introducing the most important of these media and the conditions of their production and

---

[4] Renfner, "Verzeichnis der im Monat Februar 1815," 165.

[5] Siegried Weichlein, "Nationalismus als Theorie sozialer Ordnung," in *Geschichte zwischen Kultur und Gesellschaft: Beiträge zur Theoriedebatte*, ed. Thomas Mergel and Thomas Welskopp (Munich, 1997), 171–202, 181–183.

[6] Jeismann, *Vaterland*, 280–282; and Echternkamp, *Aufstieg*, 442–443.

distribution, which allows for an understanding of the extent, forms and limitations of the contemporary discourse.[7] Then I analyze the discourse itself, which centered on models of the nation, war and gender. I ask what images and notions these models transported, how they were shaped and nuanced in religious, political, social, ethnic, racial and gender-specific terms, and how they were interrelated. First, I focus on the constructions of the nation and the people and with them the drawing of external and internal boundaries; here nationality, gender and race became crucial. Afterward, I examine the debate concerning the nation, military and war, and explore how this debate was intertwined with concepts of masculinity. Finally, I study the discussion of competing concepts of the nation and citizenship; here the political visions of patriotism, citizenship and gender for war- and peacetime will be the center of attention, because politics at this time was constructed as a highly gendered matter, mainly a "men's affair."

A study of the media, the conditions of their production and distribution, and the concepts of nation, war and gender they provided is crucial if we want to understand the intellectual framework for the contemporary political culture and its uses for the mobilization for war in the time between 1806 and 1815 and the cultural demobilization in the postwar period. It also helps us to comprehend the reasons for the long-term legacy of many of the ideas from that time that continued to influence not only memories of the period but with them also the patriotic-national discourse and military culture until the First World War.

[7] The most important groups of printed sources for the following analysis are the press, sermons, brochures and leaflets, as well as patriotic songs and poems. I have analyzed 61 newspapers and historical-political, military and theological journals and magazines, mostly published between 1800 and 1830; 91 editions of sermons and 310 editions and collections of patriotic poetry, with 2,885 poems and songs published between 1806 and 1820 and their reprints in anthologies of the nineteenth century. In addition, I assembled a large collection of brochures and leaflets of the time. See more on this media in Hagemann, *Muth*, 539–559.

4

Mobilizing Public Opinion: Propaganda, Media and War

"A nation that does not dare to speak boldly will dare still less to act boldly," wrote the Prussian officer and military reformer Carl von Clausewitz in a letter of December 1808 in which he reflected on the future of Prussia and Germany.[1] Like most patriots, he believed in the power of "public opinion" (*öffentliche Meinung*). Without its mobilization, he supposed, it would be impossible to turn Prussia into a "valorous nation."[2] This belief reflected the enlightened quest to probe and grasp the world rationally, which since the end of the eighteenth century had increasingly included political and social phenomena, and was decisively fed by the experience of the French Revolution and Napoleonic rule. Both had impressively demonstrated the power of public opinion.[3] Views of what constituted this power and how it should be handled differed, to be sure. There was, however, a broad consensus in patriotic circles that the formation of "public opinion" was the "most important and indispensable pillar of any well-ordered state organization," as the Prussian official Baron Friedrich Ludwig von Vincke wrote in his August 1808 memorandum for the king, titled "Aims and Instruments of Prussian State Administration." For that reason, Vincke supported the systematic promotion of "publicity" or free access to the public sphere. His model was England with its extensive press freedom, where only abuses were prosecuted. He firmly opposed preventive censorship such as existed in Prussia.[4]

[1] This chapter is based in part on Hagemann, *Muth*, 105–157. On Clausewitz, see Werner Hahlweg, "Clausewitz, Carl Philipp Gottlieb von," *NDB* 3 (1957): 271–276.

[2] "Clausewitz an Marie von Brühl, Königsberg, 27. Dez. 1808," in *Carl und Marie von Clausewitz: Ein Lebensbild in Briefen und Tagebuchblättern*, ed. Karl Linnebach (Berlin, 1917, 2nd edn.), 194–196. See also Hofmeister-Hunger, *Pressepolitik*, 195–250.

[3] Holger Böning, ed., *Französische Revolution und deutsche Öffentlichkeit: Wandlungen in Presse und Alltagskultur am Ende des 18. Jahrhunderts* (Munich, 1992).

[4] Friedrich Ludwig Freiherr von Vincke, "Zwecke und Mittel der preußischen Staatsverwaltung, welche dieselbe verfolgen, deren dieselbe sich bedienen dürfte," in *Das Reformministerium Stein: Akten zur Verfassungs- und Verwaltungsgeschichte aus den Jahren 1807/1808*, ed. Heinrich Scheel, 3 vols. (Berlin, 1968), 3:704–717, 714. For the contemporary debate, see Lucian Hölscher, *Öffentlichkeit und Geheimnis: Eine begriffsgeschichtliche Untersuchung zur Entstehung der Öffentlichkeit in der frühen Neuzeit* (Stuttgart, 1979); and James Van Horn Melton, *The Rise of the Public in Enlightenment Europe* (Cambridge, 2001).

In the imagination of patriots and reformers, public opinion was a supervisory and mediating authority between the monarchical state and the society of citizens. It was at the same time a precondition for the implementation of "publicity," and its expression. The nation thus found its most important manifestation and its medium in public opinion.[5] Its "bearers" could only be the educated male elite from the middle classes and aristocracy, for only they possessed the requisite knowledge and virtues. The "common people" or men of the "working classes," like women, were considered too uneducated and easily controllable to be allowed to influence the formation of public opinion.[6] Jürgen Habermas's construction of the "bourgeois public sphere" (*bürgerliche Öffentlichkeit*) in his 1962 classic *The Structural Transformation of the Public Sphere* reflects this contemporary understanding. In contrast to the older res publica, he deems it to be the site for the political regulation of civil society, and credits its willingness to challenge the established authority of the monarch. The bourgeois public sphere is for Habermas both private and political from the outset. Analytically he differentiates between the "political" and "literary public sphere" (the "world of letters"), but emphasizes that "in the educated classes the one form of public sphere was considered to be identical with the other; in the self-understanding of public opinion the public sphere appeared as one and indivisible." This differentiation is, however, important if we want to include women in the analysis. Women were often "factually and legally excluded from the political public sphere," whereas female writers and readers could very actively participate in the literary public sphere.[7]

Nevertheless, the male patriots and reformers in the early nineteenth century assumed that the agents in the public sphere were all men. And indeed, at first glance, its activists and authors seem to be all male. Among the most prominent writers who sought to influence German-speaking public opinion in the period of the Anti-Napoleonic Wars were – alongside Arndt, Fichte and Jahn – men such as the well-known Berlin theology professor Friedrich Schleiermacher, who edited the newly founded newspaper *Der Preussische*

---

[5] Arndt, "Geist der Zeit," pt. 2, 19.

[6] Hagemann, *Muth*, 106–112.

[7] Jürgen Habermas, *The Structural Transformation of the Public Sphere: An Inquiry into a Category of Bourgeois Society* (Cambridge, 1989), 56; idem, *Strukturwandel der Öffentlichkeit: Untersuchungen zu einer Kategorie der bürgerlichen Gesellschaft* (Neuwied, 1962). After the publication of the translation, an intensive discussion about the concept of the "bourgeois public sphere" and its shortcomings started. See Craig Calhoun, ed., *Habermas and the Public Sphere* (Cambridge, MA, 1992); Joan Landes, ed., *Feminism, the Public and the Private* (Oxford, 1998); Brophy, *Popular Culture*, 1–17; most recently, Karen Hagemann, "Gendered Boundaries: Civil Society, the Public/Private Divide and the Family," in *The Golden Chain: Family, Civil Society and the State*, ed. Paul Ginsborg, Jürgen Nautz, and Ton Nijhuis (New York, 2012), 43–65.

Correspondent in 1813;[8] the Saxon publisher Friedrich Arnold Brockhaus, who had made a name for himself as editor of the very popular encyclopedia, the *Conversations-Lexikon* and from 1813 to 1815 edited the political-historical journal *Deutsche Blätter*;[9] the Rhenish schoolmaster, writer and journalist Joseph Görres, who published the weekly *Rheinischer Merkur* from 1814 to 1816;[10] and the Thuringian history professor Heinrich Luden, who brought out the political-historical journal *Nemesis* from 1814 to 1818.[11] They were trailblazers and opinion leaders of a patriotic-national discourse carried out by a much larger number of political writers, which included very few female authors.

Women who wrote as a profession still encountered massive social disapproval. They faced even more resistance when they wrote texts that explicitly commented on politics in the widest sense. Thus, many female authors of such "topical literature" (*Tagesliteratur*), the contemporary term for all historical and political texts and media that focused on issues of the present, published anonymously. Among the very few who dared to bring out such texts under their own names were the Rhenish journalist Helmine von Chézy, the Prussian writer Caroline de la Motte Fouqué, the Bremen educator Betty Gleim, the Weimar poet Amalie von Helvig and the Hamburg author Christine Westphalen. All came from upper-class, often aristocratic families and were well educated and financially independent.[12] The fact that at best 5 percent of all known writers in this period were women, and even fewer wrote about politics, does not mean, however, that they were not interested and involved in politics. Rather, middle- and upper-class women participated in the public sphere in gender-specific ways.[13]

It is impossible to know exactly how many authors produced topical literature between 1806 and 1815. In 1806 there were approximately 10,600

[8] Nowak, *Schleiermacher: Leben, Werk und Wirkung* (Göttingen, 2001); Matthias Wolfes, *Öffentlichkeit und Bürgergesellschaft: Friedrich Schleiermachers politische Wirksamkeit*, 2 vols. (Berlin, 2004).

[9] *Friedrich Arnold Brockhaus, Sein Leben und Wirken nach Briefen und anderen Aufzeichnungen*, ed. Heinrich Eduard Brockhaus, 3 vols. (Leipzig, 1872–1881).

[10] Jon Vanden Heuvel, *A German Life in the Age of Revolution: Joseph Görres, 1776–1848* (Washington, DC, 2001).

[11] On Luden, see Irene Crusius, "Luden, Heinrich," *NDB* 15 (1987): 283–285.

[12] Katherine R. Goodman and Edith Waldstein, eds., *In the Shadow of Olympus: German Women Writers around 1800* (Albany, NY, 1992); Caroline Bland and Elisa Müller-Adams, eds., *Frauen in der literarischen Öffentlichkeit, 1780–1918* (Bielefeld, 2007), esp. 9–100; Karin Baumgartner, *Public Voices: Political Discourse in the Writings of Caroline de la Motte Fouqué* (Oxford, 2009), esp. 117–151. On Chézy, see Fritz Martini, "Chézy, Wilhelmine von, geborene von Klencke," *NDB* 3 (1957): 202–203; on Gleim, see Sander, "Gleim, Betty," *ADB* 49 (1904): 390–384; on Fouqué, see Arno Schmidt, "Fouqué, Friedrich Heinrich Karl Baron de la Motte-Fouqué," *NDB* 5 (1961): 306–307; on Westphalen, see Max Mendheim, "Westphalen, Engel Christine," *ADB* 42 (1897): 217–218.

[13] See chapter 5 and 6 in the third part; as well as Reder, *Frauenbewegung* and Gleixner and Gray, *Gender*.

authors in the German-speaking region – this included anyone who had published at least one independent work.[14] The number of authors of topical literature was probably far smaller. During my research, I came across the names of 420 men and 19 women.[15] Of them, 81 percent came from the middle classes and 13 percent from the aristocracy. Fifty-one percent were born after 1775, 29 percent between 1775 and 1784, 17 percent between 1785 and 1794, and only 5 percent after 1795. Thus, when the war began in 1813, the overwhelming majority was younger than 38 years old. Of this age group, about one-half of the men fought actively in the wars as volunteers or militiamen. Nearly all of the male authors in the sample had an academic secondary education, and 75 percent had been to university. A substantial 29 percent were clergymen by profession, 18 percent were booksellers and publishers, 14 percent high- and middle-ranking civil servants, 10 percent teachers at academic secondary schools and 5 percent university professors. The proportion of professional authors among them, 5 percent, corresponded to the average among published writers more generally. In the early nineteenth century very few authors could live from their writing alone.[16]

While these opinion makers recognized only men like themselves as "bearers" of public opinion, the circles they addressed were far broader. Most of them also wanted to reach the men of the "working people," which for them included not just small farmers and artisans and the lower ranks of the military and administrative hierarchy but also domestic servants and day laborers. Their aim, as the Hessian pastor Karl Christian Gehren noted in an article "On the Training of Country Folk in Patriotism," published in the *Journal für Prediger* in 1810, was to awaken "loyal devotion and firm affection for their fellow citizens, the constitution and rulers of the land" and to promote the "patriotic willingness to sacrifice and fight."[17]

In order to reach broader strata of the population, the patriotic opinion makers believed they had to abandon the usual "mere enlightenment of reason" and address "feelings" as well. For them, only those who understood the art of "arousing emotions, guiding inclinations, setting passions in motion, making a cause pleasing, [and] captivating by habit" were assured

---

[14] Reinhard Wittmann, *Geschichte des deutschen Buchhandels: Ein Überblick* (Munich, 1991), 147; Wehler, *Gesellschaftsgeschichte*, 1:313–316.

[15] I was able to collect more precise biographical information for 374 men and 12 women. For a far more extensive analysis of the data and description of the collective social profile of this group, see Hagemann, *Muth*, 158–204.

[16] On the situation of writers around 1800, see Wittmann, *Geschichte*, 143–170; on journalists in nineteenth-century Germany, in particular, see Jörg Requate, *Journalismus als Beruf: Entstehung und Entwicklung des Journalistenberufs im 19. Jahrhundert – Deutschland im internationalen Vergleich* (Göttingen, 1995), 117–236.

[17] Karl Christian Gehren, "Ueber die Bildung des Landvolks zum Patriotismus durch Schulunterricht," *JfP* 37.1 (1810): 36–60, 39.

of success.[18] For that reason, they assigned media such as appeals, songs and sermons a special importance in mobilizing opinion.[19] The practice of the "war of quills" between 1806 and 1819 that will be studied in this chapter corresponded to this view. After focusing on the literary market, readers and censorship, the most important media of the patriotic-national discourse will be introduced.

LITERARY MARKET AND READERSHIP

During the period of the Anti-Napoleonic Wars, the production of and demand for topical literature in the German-speaking region were higher than ever before.[20] The development of the literary market is one indicator of this trend. To be sure, book production, which had been rising continually since the mid-eighteenth century, fell by nearly half between 1805 and 1815, as measured by the number of titles in the book fair catalogues (from 4,181 in 1805 to 2,323 in 1813), but at the same time the type of books changed significantly. While sales of *belles lettres* (poetry, novels, novellas, short stories and plays) as well as theological literature dropped sharply and literature in other areas stagnated at best, sales of topical literature, including periodicals, rose extraordinarily. The growth rates outstripped those of all other genres of literature. This development further intensified during the war years 1813–15 and suggests a growing politicization of the reading public.[21]

Since historical and political books, brochures and periodicals were less strictly censored in practice than newspapers, the reading public seems to have abandoned the latter for the former in the years between 1806 and 1813. That, at least, is what the few existing circulation figures for the press in those years seem to indicate. While the print runs of newspapers fell between 1806 and 1813 and only rose again during the wars of 1813–15, the number and total print run of the historical-political periodicals grew continuously.[22] The following figures underline the development: some ten

[18] Ehrenberg, *Volk*, 102.
[19] For example, see "Eingesandt," *RDVB*, no. 20 (1813), 189–190.
[20] The following is partly based on Karen Hagemann, "Literaturmarkt, Zensur und Meinungsmobilisierung: Die politische Presse Preußens zur Zeit der Napoleonischen Kriege," in *Agenten der Öffentlichkeit: Theater und Medien im 19. Jahrhundert*, ed. Maike Wagner (Bielefeld, 2012), 171–196.
[21] Johann Adolf Goldfriedrich, *Geschichte des deutschen Buchhandels*, 4 vols. (Leipzig, 1886, 1909 and 1913, repr. Leipzig 1970), 4:14–16.
[22] Statistics on the development of newspaper and magazine circulation in the early nineteenth century are very fragmentary. The circulation figures for *BN* and *VZ* give some indication: *BN*: 1776: 1,780; 1804: 4,000; 1813: 3,150; 1814: 4,500; *VZ*: 1776: 2,000; 1804: 7,100; 1813: 4,000; 1814: 4,250. Based on Horst Heenemann, "Die Auflagenhöhe der deutschen Zeitungen: Ihre Entwicklung und ihre Probleme" (Phil. Diss., University of Berlin, 1930),

new journals of this type were founded between 1799 and 1805, 19 between 1806 and 1812 and around 30 between 1813 and 1819, 20 of them in the years 1813–15 alone. The most important places of publication for these political-historical periodicals between 1806 and 1820 were Berlin (19 titles), Leipzig and Weimar (6 each) and Königsberg (4). Far fewer such journals appeared in southern and western Germany. In general, these new journals were significantly shorter-lived, at a scant two years, than in the period before and after the wars.[23]

An important precondition for the distribution of literature of all kinds was the relatively dense network of bookshops, of which 473 are said to have existed in the German-speaking region in 1802. Most of them no longer belonged to publishers, but rather were retail shops that sold books on consignment.[24] Regional centers of the book trade were Saxony, Prussia and the rest of northern Germany. One-tenth of the booksellers who regularly visited the book fairs around 1800 came from Leipzig, the most important center of the book trade in the German-speaking world. Berlin and Frankfurt am Main came second and third.[25] Most bookshops and publishing companies were concentrated in the larger princely capitals, or in university and commercial towns. Smaller towns and large stretches of rural areas, in contrast, were underserved. The main reason for this was the practice of granting concessions, which the governments of many German states treated very restrictively until the introduction of the freedom to practice a trade. The concession system – along with pre- and post-publication censorship, prohibition on distribution through the post, import restrictions and high customs duties on printed materials – was an important instrument for controlling and censoring the literary market. All branches of the book trade were affected by compulsory concessions, not just the establishment of printing houses, publishing companies and retail bookshops, but also the publication of newspapers and magazines and the opening of reading clubs and lending libraries. Even itinerant book traders and peddlers were subject to concessions, which in these cases were generally handled even more strictly. For most literate people in rural areas and small towns, peddlers and itinerant booksellers at country and local trade fairs were often the only options for purchasing reading material, provided

---

13–14, 36 and 64; and Erich Widdecke, *Geschichte der Haude- und Spenerschen Zeitung 1734 bis 1874* (Berlin, 1925), 105.

[23] Hubert Max, *Wesen und Gestalt der politischen Zeitschrift: Ein Beitrag zur Geschichte des politischen Erziehungsprozesses des deutschen Volkes bis zu den Karlsbader Beschlüssen* (Essen, [1942]), 278–285.

[24] Wittmann, *Geschichte*, 130 and 111–142.

[25] The next most important cities were Vienna, Nuremberg, Halle, Hamburg, Augsburg, Basel, Breslau, Jena, Dresden, Prague, Göttingen and Copenhagen, in that order; see ibid., 113.

they could afford it in the first place. This situation changed little until the mid-nineteenth century.[26]

Increases in literacy were an important precondition for the sale of the growing number of printed products. The extremely fragmentary figures suggest that literacy was already comparatively widespread in the German-speaking region in the early nineteenth century.[27] Rudolf Schenda estimates that in 1800, an average of 25 percent of the Central European population were competent readers, and that the level had risen to 40 percent by 1840.[28] His figures are controversial, however. Contemporaries like the popular author Jean Paul Richter, for example, estimated that the German-speaking reading public around 1800 numbered no more than 300,000 persons, or less than 1.5 percent of a population of 20–22 million. In arriving at this figure, he was probably mainly thinking of the readers of books.[29] The estimated number of newspaper readers is a good deal higher. Martin Welke assumes their numbers at around 3 million for the same period, or about 14 percent of the population.[30] All we know for certain is that there were significant variations in literacy rates. Literacy was generally higher in the cities and the better-off strata, as well as among soldiers and civil servants; on average, fewer women could read because less value was placed on educating them. There is also a striking gap between east and west. West of the line running from Stralsund to Dresden, significantly more people were able to read and write, which can be attributed, among other factors, to higher population density and greater urbanization and the higher frequency of schools that went along with them.[31]

[26] Ibid., 111–142.

[27] See Martin Lyons, *A History of Reading and Writing in the Western World* (Basingstoke, 2010), 88–104 and 119–136, esp. 90; also Roger Chartier, *The Order of Books: Readers, Authors, and Libraries in Europe between the Fourteenth and Eighteenth Centuries* (Stanford, CA, 1994); Reinhard Wittman, "Was There a Reading Revolution at the End of the Eighteenth Century?," in *A History of Reading in the West*, ed. Guglielmo Cavallo and Roger Chartier (Amherst, MA, 1999), 284–312.

[28] Rudolf Schenda, *Volk ohne Buch: Studien zur Sozialgeschichte der populären Lesestoffe, 1770–1910* (Frankfurt/M., 1970), 444–445; see also Rolf Engelsing, *Analphabetentum und Lektüre: Zur Sozialgeschichte des Lesens in Deutschland zwischen feudaler und industrieller Gesellschaft* (Stuttgart, 1973), 69–116.

[29] Wittman, *Geschichte*, 197.

[30] Martin Welke, "Gemeinsame Lektüre und frühe Formen von Gruppenbildungen im 17. und 18. Jahrhundert: Zeitungsleser in Deutschland," in *Lesegesellschaft und bürgerliche Emanzipation: Ein europäischer Vergleich*, ed. Otto Dann (Munich, 1981), 29–53, 45.

[31] On the wide variation in reading ability in Germany, see Wittmann, *Geschichte*, 171–199; Brophy, *Popular Culture*, 18–53; Etienne François, "Alphabetisierung und Lesefähigkeit in Frankreich um 1800," in *Deutschland und Frankreich im Zeitalter der Französischen Revolution*, ed. Helmut Berding et al. (Frankfurt/M., 1989), 407–425; Norbert Winnige, "Alphabetisierung in Brandenburg–Preußen, 1600–1850: Zu den Grundlagen von Kommunikation und Rezeption and in Europe," in *Wissen ist Macht: Herrschaft und*

The incipient expansion of the reading public was an important prerequisite for the expansion of the literary market described here. In the larger cities, printed matter, if it was cheap and written in an accessible manner, found readers beyond the narrow stratum of the educated, who on average made up no more than 5 percent of the population. For the majority of people from the middle and lower classes, however, various forms of collective reading were more common than the purchase of books or periodicals, which few could afford. This included not only reading aloud in the workplace, taverns or among friends or family, but also joint subscriptions to newspapers or magazines and their circulation within the group, as well as membership in one of the many reading societies and the growing use of lending libraries and reading rooms. At the end of the eighteenth century some 600 to 1,000 reading societies existed in the German-speaking region, with an average of 50–100 members each.[32] In light of this situation, the talk of "rampant reading mania" popular mainly among conservative contemporaries seems very much exaggerated. An actual "numerical democratization of reading" was only attained about a century later.[33] This notwithstanding, governments regarded the growing interest in reading above all in the cities as potentially dangerous.

CENSORSHIP, WAR AND POLITICS

The governments of the German territorial states responded to the increasing interest in reading with stricter censorship laws.[34] Prussia became the model for censorship practice with Wöllner's Censorship Edict of July 1788, which was further tightened by two decrees of March 1792 and April 1793.

Kommunikation in Brandenburg-Preußen, ed. Ralf Pröve and Norbert Winnige (Berlin, 2001), 49–67; Lyons, *History*, 89–104.

[32] Wittmann, *Geschichte*, 191; Welke, "Gemeinsame Lektüre," 45; Irene Jentsch, "Zur Geschichte des Zeitungslesens in Deutschland am Ende des 18. Jahrhunderts: Mit besonderer Berücksichtigung der gesellschaftlichen Formen des Zeitungslesens" (Phil. Diss., University of Leipzig, 1937); Erich Schön, *Der Verlust der Sinnlichkeit oder Die Verwandlung des Lesers: Mentalitätswandel um 1800* (Stuttgart, 1987), esp. 99–122 and 177–187; on lending libraries, see Alberto Martino, *Die deutsche Leihbibliothek: Geschichte einer literarischen Institution, 1756–1914* (Wiesbaden, 1990), 57–133; and on reading societies, Marlies Prüsener, *Lesegesellschaften im achtzehnten Jahrhundert* (Frankfurt/M., 1972); Dann, *Lesegesellschaft*.

[33] Wittmann, *Geschichte*, 199.

[34] On the history of censorship in Germany, see Franz Schneider, "Presse, Pressefreiheit, Zensur," in Brunner et al., *Grundbegriffe*, 4:899–927; idem, *Pressefreiheit und politische Öffentlichkeit: Studien zur politischen Geschichte Deutschlands bis 1848* (Neuwied, 1966), esp. 171–217; Wolfgang Siemann, "Ideenschmuggel: Probleme der Meinungskontrolle und das Los deutscher Zensoren im 19. Jahrhundert," *HZ* 245 (1987): 71–106. On the practice before 1806, see Ulrich Eisenhardt, *Die kaiserliche Aufsicht über Buchdruck, Buchhandel und Presse im Heiligen Römischen Reich deutscher Nation (1496–1806): Ein Beitrag zur Geschichte der Bücher- und Pressezensur* (Karlsruhe, 1970), esp. 142–146.

The edict stipulated that anything to be printed had to be submitted to the censors first in order to suppress all texts that appeared to be detrimental to the "general principles of religion," the state or the "moral order of society" or that aimed to insult an individual's "personal honor and good name." All political and historical writings, wherever they were being published, had to be submitted to the Department of Foreign Affairs. In Berlin, it also scrutinized political newspapers; in the provinces this was the task of the regional governing bodies, the *Landeskollegien*. There were substantial fines for works printed without permission. If they had prohibited and indictable content, the entire print run was to be confiscated and destroyed. Prussian printers were liable for the works of publishers from outside the monarchy. In cases of repeated offenses, printers faced the loss of their privilege and permission to exercise a trade as well as prison.[35] These regulations formally determined Prussian censorship policy up to the Carlsbad Decrees of September 1819.

In practice, however, it was the Napoleonic Empire that defined censorship policy throughout the German-speaking region between 1806 and 1812. In Prussia, from the defeat of October 1806 until the end of the French occupation in December 1808, censorship was the province of the Napoleonic administration, which controlled the letter post, mail service, publishing and the book trade. Anything written and printed was strictly supervised, and any criticism of Napoleonic rule was harshly punished, while critical reporting on the government policies of other monarchs was permitted. Publications of an educational, scholarly or artistic nature had little to fear from the French censors.[36] To forestall French sanctions, the Prussian government tightened censorship during the occupation even in unoccupied West and East Prussia. Here, too, anything that might arouse Napoleon's anger or suspicion had to be silenced. The monarchy retained this policy even after the withdrawal of the French occupation troops.[37]

The French government demanded a similar censorship policy from the states of the Confederation of the Rhine and the nine *départements* of the annexed German territories from the west bank of the Rhine to Hamburg. With two decrees of February and August 1810, a centralized system of political censorship was finally introduced for the entire Napoleonic Empire.[38]

---

35 "Wöllnerschen Zensuredikt," in Czygan, *Geschichte*, 1:3–5.

36 Paul Czygan, "Ueber die französische Zensur während der Okkupation von Berlin und ihren Leiter, den Prediger Hauchecorne, in den Jahren 1806 bis 1808," *FBPG* 21 (1908): 99–137; idem, *Geschichte*, 1:7–31.

37 Gertrud Braun, "Die Königsberger Zeitschriften von 1800 bis zu den Karlsbader Beschlüssen: Ein Beitrag zur Publizistik" (Phil. Diss, University of Königsberg, 1936).

38 Heribert Gisch, " 'Preßfreiheit' – 'Preßfrechheit': Zum Problem der Presseaufsicht in napoleonischer Zeit in Deutschland (1806–1818)," in *Deutsche Kommunikationskontrolle des 15.–20. Jahrhunderts*, ed. Heinz-Dietrich Fischer (Munich, 1982), 56–74; Daniel Moran, *Towards the Century of Words: Johann Cotta and the Politics of the Public Realm in Germany, 1795–1832* (Berkeley, CA, 1990), 87–115.

The most important new regulation for the annexed German territories was that only one newspaper would be tolerated in each *département*. Only in large cities were more papers permitted, as long as they treated only literature, scholarship and art; or trade, industry and agriculture; or contained only advertisements. A supplementary ordinance of May 1811 also stipulated that, effective immediately, "any paper" would be banned that printed "different political news" than that published in the Napoleonic state newspaper, the *Moniteur*.[39]

The decree of August 1810 had already recommended that Napoleon's allies adopt similar measures. Accordingly, in November 1810 the Prussian king ordered the centralization of responsibility for the entire censorship system, which occurred in February 1811. The section chief of the general police in the Interior Ministry was now charged with supervising the censorship of all political and nonpolitical works, an authority previously held by the Department of Public Worship and Education.[40] At the same time, he ordered the establishment of a "higher censorship" for all "writings and essays appearing [in the monarchy] that dealt with government and administration," which was placed under Prime Minister Hardenberg.[41] The states of the Confederation of the Rhine enacted similar laws. Growing French pressure meant that censorship in the Prussian monarchy and the other German states was stricter than ever in 1811–12. Particularly harsh was the prepublication censorship of newspapers.[42] The censors allowed somewhat more leeway to the editors of historical-political journals that were directed exclusively at an educated audience. The authors of political brochures and books had the best chance of evading censorship, since they could produce and sell the works in concert with printers, booksellers and publishers without the censors' approval. They either had their works printed illegally and anonymously or they chose to print where censorship practice was more liberal and then smuggled the work into the territorial state in question. Sales were assured in any case, since the censors could not control the complete literature market.[43]

The restrictive censorship practice only began to change gradually in the winter of 1812–13. With massive support at first from the Russian and then in March 1813 from the Prussian headquarters, joined later by the central administrative department of the coalition powers, the censorship laws of the German territorial states were de facto undermined everywhere with the advance of the troops.[44] The army leaders were only interested in censoring

[39] Goldfriedrich, *Geschichte*, 4:46.
[40] Czygan, *Geschichte*, 1:14–15.
[41] Ibid., 1:17–18.
[42] Ibid., 1:19–20.
[43] Siemann, "Ideenschmuggel," 82–86 and 93–96; Martino, *Leihbibliothek*, 30–50 and 157–150.
[44] Schäfer, *Arndt*, 59; Schneider, *Pressefreiheit*, 190–191.

texts on the military, especially inofficial reports on military affairs and the progress of the war.[45] In the period that followed, the number of political leaflets, brochures and books grew exponentially.[46] The press, too, increasingly adopted a critical tone toward the French.[47] From early April 1813 on, a wave of new journals appeared, beginning in Prussia. The government tried to continue enforcing press censorship, facilitated by the fact that periodical licenses depended on prepublication censorship.[48] Friedrich Wilhelm III was strictly opposed to any "publicity."[49] But given the necessity of a patriotic-national mobilization for the recently begun war, his government was compelled to make concessions in censorship policy and thus to attempt a balancing act. As Prime Minister Hardenberg wrote in his instructions to the censors in late April 1813, given the current situation, "political writings" were "an object of such interest" to the broad public that "it is impossible to exercise enough vigilance regarding their distribution." However, in order not to arouse the public's ire or interest, the censors should keep a low profile. Any ban only increased demand. The aim must be instead to intensify censorship slowly and "thus gradually wean the spirit of the public away from the outbursts of writers."[50] In practice, it proved quite difficult to implement this policy.[51]

Over the course of 1814, censorship was again applied more strictly not only in Prussia but also in most of the other German territorial states in order to prevent a further politicization of published opinion. Not just the press, but also single publications on current affairs were increasingly subject to censorship. This politics of restoration brought the Prussian government, in particular, into increasing conflict not only with patriotically engaged writers, who repeatedly tried to evade censorship, but also with higher officials in the provinces. The Prussian governors, particularly in the liberated regions of the north and west, had already pursued a relatively liberal press policy during the war of 1813–14 in order to promote patriotism among the inhabitants, whose mobilization for war was their responsibility. They continued this policy after the war as a means of strengthening the population's ties to the Prussian monarchy, under whose authority these regions were again, or newly, placed.[52]

[45] Czygan, *Geschichte*, 2:87–88; Hofmeister-Hunger, *Pressepolitik*, 264–273.

[46] Czygan, *Geschichte*, 2:39–64.

[47] Ibid., 1:36–61, 66–75 and 262–285.

[48] Hofmeister-Hunger, *Pressepolitik*, 256–264.

[49] Czygan, *Geschichte*, 2:130–131.

[50] "Hardenberg an das Minist. f. ausw. Angel., Dresden, 30. April 1813," in Czygan, *Geschichte*, 2:86–87, 82–84 and 81–82.

[51] See, for example, Czygan, *Geschichte*, 1:262–276, 304–316 and 335–351, 3:299–370; and Hagemann, "Literaturmarkt."

[52] Czygan, *Geschichte*, 3:299–370 and 2:249–256. See Hagemann, "Literaturmarkt."

After the second victory over Napoleon in June 1815, the reactionary censorship policy was further intensified. Now that Napoleon had been vanquished and the support of the population was no longer needed for the war effort, governments in Berlin, Vienna and elsewhere were no longer prepared to tolerate oppositional opinions anywhere in their sphere of influence. To be sure, the Federal Act signed at the Congress of Vienna in June 1815 stated that at its first session, the federal assembly would tackle the matter of uniform regulations concerning freedom of the press, but it was only the Carlsbad Decrees, which had the status of provisional federal laws, that laid out a uniform censorship policy for the entire German Confederation. They stipulated obligatory prepublication censorship for all newspapers and magazines as well as all books up to 20 sheets long (320 pages in octavo format) and remained in force until 2 April 1848, when the Federal Assembly of the German Confederation abolished the Carlsbad Decrees under the political pressure of the Revolution of 1848. For the greater part of book and periodical production, this meant that manuscripts or galleys had to be submitted to the relevant censor before final printing.[53] Given the widespread belief among educated people when the war began in 1813 that they had finally attained the long-hoped-for state of "publicity," this politics of restoration led to massive political dissatisfaction. Quite a few producers of literature during the period had hoped that those in power would recognize their media campaign of support for the war of 1813–15, leading to more political rights.

THE MEDIA OF THE PATRIOTIC-NATIONAL DISCOURSE

A first sign of the impending "war of quills" was the appearance in January 1814 of anti-Napoleonic leaflets and cartoons.[54] Patriotic-national songs and poetry soon followed, first mainly as broadsheets and later as pamphlets of several pages. All of these texts evaded censorship and made use of the prevailing de facto press freedom that the invasion of Russian troops ushered in on Prussian soil. After Prussia declared war on France, the newspapers could again report on current events in more detail, printing appeals by governments and military leaders as well as official army reports and poetry. They also informed their readers about patriotic-national festivals and ceremonies held by the government and local communities, churches

---

[53] Wittmann, *Geschichte*, 206; see Huber, *Verfassungsgeschichte*, 749–750; Siemann, "Ideenschmuggel," more generally, 36–56, on Prussia, 57–71; idem, "Von der offenen zur mittelbaren Kontrolle: Der Wandel in der deutschen Preßgesetzgebung und Zensurpraxis des 19. Jahrhunderts," in *"Unmoralisch an sich ...": Zensur im 18. und 19. Jahrhundert*, ed. Herbert G. Göpfert and Erdmann Weyrauch (Wiesbaden, 1988), 293–308.

[54] Czygan, *Geschichte*, 2:37–70; and Biegel and Römer, *Patriotische Flugblätter*.

and the army, which became a part of wartime culture, and the activities of the many patriotic associations that were founded to support the war effort. Last but not least, they printed lists of decorated officers and soldiers from the region and the obituaries of fallen officers. All of this reawakened the interest of the reading public. Beginning in April 1813, a number of historical-political journals were also founded. Thus during the wars of 1813–15, a broad variety of media shaped the patriotic-national discourse, which targeted different groups of the population.

Proclamations, Leaflets and Pamphlets

Early on, the Russian army leadership accompanied the military campaign against Napoleon with war propaganda. It hired, as Prussian, Swedish and Austrian headquarters would do later, German writers to produce propaganda texts. Two of them were popular dramatist and journalist August von Kotzebue, who supported the war as a state secretary in Russian service, and Ernst Moritz Arndt, who worked as secretary to Baron Stein in Petersburg starting in September 1812. Kotzebue was the author of one of the first leaflets that Russian headquarters commissioned in German – the brief farce *The River-God Niémen and Someone Else*, a satire on Napoleon and his devastating defeat in Russia, which appeared in January 1813 and quickly gained great popularity as a puppet show in taverns and at fairs.[55] This text was typical of Kotzebue's ironic style. He ignored all attempts at censorship and "firmly [maintained] his own tone," as the Prussian censor complained.[56] With his leaflets and his two journals, the *Russisch-Deutsches Volks-Blatt* and the *Politische Flugblätter*, he became one of the most critical and independent early-liberal writers during and after the wars of 1813–15.[57]

Arndt, who continued to work for Stein during the wars, was by far the most productive and influential political author of his day with nearly 300 titles and editions published between 1812 and 1815 alone. He was the only political writer with works that attained mass print runs and were distributed throughout the German-speaking region. After his return to Königsberg in early 1813, Arndt published new texts in rapid succession, systematically evading the censors.[58] Among his first pamphlets with mass circulation was

55 "Der Flußgott Niemen und Noch Jemand," in Spies, *Erhebung*, 209–224; see also Czygan, *Geschichte*, 1:87–89.

56 "Der preußische Zensor Himly an Raumer, Berlin, 6. Mai 1814," in Czygan, *Geschichte*, 2:205–207.

57 On Kotzebue, see George S. Williamson, "What Killed August von Kotzebue? The Temptations of Virtue and the Political Theology of German Nationalism, 1789–1819," *JMH* 72 (2000): 890–943.

58 Schäfer, *Arndt*, 231, also 164–179 and 207–234; idem, "Kollektivbewußtsein am Beginn des 19. Jahrhunderts, dargestellt am Beispiel der Verbreitung der Schriften Ernst Moritz Arndts,"

What Are the Reserves and the Militia? in February, in which he propagated arming all "valiant men throughout the German land" for a war against Napoleon.[59] Fifty thousand copies of this text were printed and distributed free of charge after Prussia introduced the militia, financed by donations collected in Berlin. Reprinted more than 20 times with a total of 76,000 to 100,000 copies, this work probably had the largest edition size of any publication during and after the war years. The Russian and Prussian army leaderships saw to its distribution.[60]

Another very widely disseminated text was Arndt's *Soldier's Catechism*, which appeared in three updated versions between 1812 and 1815.[61] The main purpose of the work was not only to explain the war aims to men who were going to war for the first time on the basis of universal conscription, but also to formulate binding soldierly norms for them to follow. This text, too, was printed and distributed free of charge, first by the headquarters of the Russian and then of the Prussian army as well as the central administrative department of the coalition forces. A variety of advertisements and reviews printed in newspapers and magazines – especially after the appearance of the third edition in August 1813 – also helped to spread the word, so that this edition alone went through at least ten printings with a total of 60,000 to 80,000 copies. The places of printing followed the string of victories of the coalition troops.[62]

Most broadsheets and pamphlets, however, had print runs of only a few thousand. This applied even to official appeals and proclamations. High-ranking officers and government circles, and indeed monarchs, now followed the French model and used pamphlets as a means of propaganda.[63] The trailblazer here was the appeal "To My People" of 17 March 1813 by

in *Presse und Geschichte*, 137–148; James Elstone Dow, *A Good German Conscience: The Life and Time of Ernst Moritz Arndt* (Lanham, MD, 1995).

[59] [Ernst Moritz Arndt], "Was bedeutet Landsturm und Landwehr?, Febr. 1813," in Spies, *Erhebung*, 229–236.

[60] Rudolf Müller, "Geschichte von Arndts Schrift: Was bedeutet Landsturm und Landwehr?," *Nord und Süd* 123 (1907): 224–253; Schäfer, *Arndt*, 178 and 257.

[61] Ernst Moritz Arndt, *Kurzer Katechismus für teutsche Soldaten, nebst einem Anhang von Liedern* ([Petersburg], 1812); repr. in Arndt, *Drei Flugschriften: Kurzer Katechismus für teutsche Soldaten – Zwei Worte über die Entstehung und Bestimmung der Teutschen Legion – Was bedeutet Landsturm und Landwehr?*, ed. Rolf Weber (Berlin, 1988); Arndt, *Kurzer Katechismus für teutsche Soldaten, nebst zwei Anhängen von Liedern* ([Königsberg], 1813); and idem, *Katechismus für den teutschen Kriegs- und Wehrmann, worin gelehret wird, wie ein christlicher Wehrmann seyn und mit Gott in den Streit gehen soll* ([Leipzig], 1813); see also Albrecht Dühr, "Die Text- und Druckgeschichte des 'Soldaten-Katechismus' E. M. Arndts," *Zeitschrift für Bibliothekswesen und Bibliographie* 8 (1961): 337–349; and Schäfer, *Arndt*, 176–180.

[62] Schäfer, *Arndt*, 179.

[63] See Jentsch, "Geschichte." On early modern forms of Prussian war propaganda, see Sylvia Mazura, *Die preußische und österreichische Kriegspropaganda im Ersten und Zweiten Schlesischen Krieg* (Berlin, 1996).

King Friedrich Wilhelm III of Prussia, which shows how his government had to respond to the patriotic-national mood at the beginning of the wars of 1813–15. The fact that a monarch turned directly to "his people" in this way, explaining the reasons for and aims of the war and calling upon them to support it, was unprecedented in Germany. This appeal, which every Prussian newspaper was required to reprint, thus became a public sensation and motivated other German rulers to issue similar proclamations in 1813.[64]

Among the first military appeals was "To the Inhabitants of Saxony" by Prussian General Gebhardt Leberecht von Blücher, which was distributed as a broadsheet in late March 1813 when the Prussian troops marched into the Kingdom of Saxony and praised the invasion as liberation from "foreign oppression." The appeal offered the Saxons "the fraternal hand" of alliance and called upon them to cooperate with the Prussian occupation troops, support them in every way and unite with Prussia to raise "the flag of insurrection against the foreign oppressors."[65] Other military leaders followed this example.

Poems and Songs

The only genre even more widely distributed during the war years than proclamations, leaflets and pamphlets was probably patriotic-national song and poetry,[66] which was disseminated in broadsheets, handy songbooks, poetry collections and the periodical press as well as orally. Thousands of songs and poems have survived. The songs were generally printed without music, but frequently with the names of popular hymns or secular tunes to which they could be sung.[67] At first, Prussia was the main region in which patriotic-national poetry was produced, but over the course of the war it quickly spread to all German states.[68] Most of these political songs and poems were written

---

[64] Friedrich Wilhelm III, "An Mein Volk, Breslau, 17. März 1813," in Spies, *Erhebung*, 254–255; see also Julius von Pflugk-Hartung, "Die Aufrufe 'An mein Volk' und 'An Mein Kriegsheer,' 1813," in *FBPG* 26 (1913): 265–274; and Schäfer, *Arndt*, 59.

[65] "An Sachsens Einwohner, Bunzlau, 23. März 1813," in Spies, *Erhebung*, 261–262, see also 268–269.

[66] See Weber, *Lyrik*; Hasko Zimmer, *Auf dem Altar des Vaterlands: Religion und Patriotismus in der deutschen Kriegslyrik des 19. Jahrhunderts* (Frankfurt/M., 1971); and Albert Portmann-Tinguely, *Romantik und Krieg: Eine Untersuchung zum Bild des Krieges bei deutschen Romantikern und "Freiheitssängern"* (Freiburg, 1989).

[67] Of the 310 poetry and song sheets and anthologies I surveyed, 70 suggested melodies to which they should be sung. On contrafacture, see Susanne Engelmann, "Der Einfluß des Volksliedes auf die Lyrik der Befreiungskriege" (Phil. Diss., University of Heidelberg, 1909); Karl Scheibenberger, "Der Einfluß der Bibel und des Kirchenliedes auf die Lyrik der deutschen Befreiungskriege" (Phil. Diss., University of Frankfurt/M., 1936).

[68] Of the lyric poetry I surveyed, 48 percent appeared in Prussia, 20 percent in the Hessian states, and 7 percent in the Kingdom of Saxony, with the rest published in a variety of German regions. See also Weber, *Lyrik*, 145–281.

by anonymous or little-known amateur poets.[69] For that reason, literary scholars have long ignored their specific function as a political mass medium: They played a major role in mobilizing large segments of the population for war, since they expressed in a universally accessible manner the aim of liberation as a national task, and sought to create a common – mainly culturally defined – national identity for all groups in society beyond regional, social and generational differences.[70] This function was powerfully facilitated on the one hand by the works' use of *Pathosformeln* and with them their appeal to emotion and their vagueness, and on the other by their utilitarian nature. Most poems and songs were written for specific target groups and concrete occasions, and were intended to be read aloud or sung collectively. The fact that they could be sung – and their rapid dissemination in the context of typical wartime situations such as marches and encampments as well as various state, church and military festivals and ceremonies – appears to have contributed significantly to their circulation.[71]

Scholars have claimed that "the poetry of the Wars of Liberation" was overwhelmingly German-national, which they equate with oppositional.[72] This thesis is based on the work of a few poets such as Arndt and Körner, who are still known today. Given the extremely wide dissemination of their songs and poems well beyond the period of the wars of 1813–15, their influence was indeed quite significant. Arndt's poetry occupied a special place; particularly influential were the 30 songs in the appendix to his *Soldier's Catechism*, many of which were repeatedly reprinted as broadsheets and in newspapers, magazines and song anthologies.[73] Arndt's German-national songs and poems with their popular Old Testament language became the model for patriotic-national poetry at the time and decisively shaped the current *Pathosformeln* for patriotism, military valor and masculinity. Also influential were the "volunteers' lyrics," written primarily by and for the young men who signed up voluntarily in the spring and summer of 1813 with the aim of mobilizing them for the fighting, which explains the appellative tone of the poems and songs. The volunteers seem to have found Theodor Körner's lyric poetry particularly appealing. His 1814 collection *Lyre and Sword* attained extraordinary popularity, which it retained into the twentieth century.[74]

---

[69] One-third of the 310 song sheets and anthologies appeared anonymously.

[70] See Weber, *Lyrik*; idem, "Zwischen Emanzipation und Disziplinierung: Zur meinungs- und willensbildenden Funktion politischer Lyrik in Zeitungen zur Zeit der Befreiungskriege," in *Volk – Nation – Vaterland*, ed. Ulrich Herrmann (Hamburg, 1996), 325–352. On the political importance of poems and songs during the French Revolution, which became a model for the patriots, see Laura Mason, *Singing the French Revolution: Popular Culture and Politics, 1787–1799* (Ithaca, NY, 1996).

[71] Weber, *Lyrik*, 23–35 and 94–118.

[72] Ibid., 12.

[73] See Schäfer, *Arndt*, 174, also 165–170; and Weber, *Lyrik*, 169–197.

[74] Weber, *Lyrik*, 169–197.

A broad analysis of the patriotic-national poetry of the period itself, however, shows that between 1813 and 1816 it was regional-patriotic poetry that not only made up the largest group, but was also the most widely disseminated. Its compositions quite conventionally invoke loyalty to king and love of country in the form of the territorial state as the main motives for taking up arms.[75] A more precise analysis of the lyrics published at the time also reveals changes in the text corpus that reflect the shifting political culture of the era. The greatest number of song sheets and anthologies appeared in 1813; afterward, the number of poems published fell.[76] At first, German-national songs and poems dominated, among them a striking number by and for volunteers.[77] Only after the great victories of autumn 1813 did a rapidly growing amount of regional-patriotic poetry come on the market, including a striking number of works celebrating victories or praising princes and generals. At the same time, the proportion of anonymous, mainly German-national texts declined. The authors of regional-patriotic poetry had no reason to fear the censors.[78]

After the war ended, the production of patriotic-national songs and poems waned. Like the appeals and broadsheets, they had largely fulfilled their purpose as a mobilizing medium for the time being, but unlike the former they retained their importance as a medium of collective memory, which still had a role to play in creating and maintaining community. Into the twentieth century, the most popular songs from the period of 1813–15 belonged to the song repertoires of the army, schools and nationalist organizations such as the *Burschenschaften* and *Turner*, and choral associations, but they were also frequently sung as part of patriotic-national celebrations.[79]

Newspapers and Journals

While calls to arms and other proclamations like songs and poems overwhelmingly spoke to the emotions, the most important media for

---

[75] For example, *Kriegslieder für die Königlich Preußischen Truppen vorzüglich den Jäger-Detachements gewidmet. Beym Ausmarsch den 23sten März 1813* (Breslau, 1813). My analysis of the 310 surveyed song sheets and collections revealed that some 15 percent belonged to the category of "volunteers' lyric," 32 percent to that with a generally German-national tendency and 42 percent to regional-patriotic poetry in the broadest sense. See also Weber, *Lyrik*, 198–207.

[76] Of the 310 sheets and collections surveyed, 137 appeared in 1813 alone, 87 in 1814 and 48 in 1815. Six collections were published between 1806 and 1812 and 17 between 1816 and 1818.

[77] Of all the song sheets and collections surveyed, some 45 percent appeared in 1813. Of volunteers' lyric, however, the figure was 59 percent. Around 16 percent of all volunteers' lyric appeared in 1814 and 21 percent in 1815.

[78] Weber, *Lyrik*, 33 and 53; Czygan, *Geschichte*, 2:244 and 275–276.

[79] Weber, *Lyrik*, 282–292; Dietmar Klenke, *Der singende "deutsche Mann": Gesangvereine und deutsches Nationalbewußtsein von Napoleon bis Hitler* (Münster, 1998).

political information and debate, in addition to a wealth of pamphlets, were
newspapers and journals. During the wars of 1813–15 most of the newly
established periodicals were weekly or monthly historical-political journals edited by an individual, whose aims and interests – along with those
of the authors, who were usually his friends – determined the contents. It
was economically far more costly and risky to introduce a new newspaper,
which the public expected to appear three to five times a week and provide
comprehensive information. Production of a newspaper was dependent on
a professional editorial staff and a larger print shop.[80] Furthermore, the first
military newspapers (*Feldzeitungen*) produced by the army leadership for
soldiers and officers in the field appeared at this time.[81]

Among the first new periodicals were *Der Preussische Correspondent*
and the *Russisch-Deutsches Volks-Blatt*. *Der Preussische Correspondent*
was founded in Berlin at the beginning of April 1813, edited first by Prussian
official and historian Barthold Georg Niebuhr and later by Schleiermacher,
among others, and published by Reimer's Realschulbuchhandlung in
Berlin.[82] The *Russisch-Deutsches Volks-Blatt* was edited by Kotzebue on
behalf of Russian military headquarters and distributed by the Berlin book-
seller-publisher Julius Eduard Hitzig.[83] Outside Berlin, the two most influential new journals were the *Deutsche Blätter* and the *Rheinischer Merkur*.
The *Deutsche Blätter* started in November 1813, edited and published by
Brockhaus, who wanted to produce a committed, partisan German-national
magazine with an early-liberal character. He ignored censorship as much as
he could, which was possible because his publishing company cooperated
with printers in two different cities and states – Altenburg in Saxe-Gotha
and Leipzig in Saxony – and he could thus exploit the differences in censorship practices.[84] Only Görres pursued a similar agenda with the same

---

[80] On the distinction between the newspaper (*Verlegerzeitung*) and the journal
(*Herausgeberzeitschrift*), see Requate, *Journalismus*, 118–123. On the history of the
press in Germany, see Rudolf Stöber, *Deutsche Pressegeschichte. Einführung, Systematik,
Glossar* (Konstanz, 2000), 113–257; Peter Ufer, *Leipziger Presse 1789 bis 1815: Eine
Studie zu Entwicklungstendenzen und Kommunikationsbedingungen des Zeitungs- und
Zeitschriftenwesens zwischen Französischer Revolution und den Befreiungskriegen* (Münster,
2000).

[81] Hagemann, *Muth*, 155–157; and Karl Heinz Schäfer, "Zur Frühgeschichte der Feldzeitungen,"
Publizistik 18 (1973): 160–164.

[82] Hermann Dreyhaus, "Der Preußische Correspondent von 1813/14 und der Anteil seiner
Gründer Niebuhr und Schleiermacher," *FBPG* 22 (1909): 55–126; and Czygan, *Geschichte*,
1:262–276 and 304–327.

[83] Czygan, *Geschichte*, 1:236–249 and 2:78–81; and Klaus Meyer, "Das 'Russisch-Deutsche
Volks-Blatt' von 1813," in *Russen und Rußland aus deutscher Sicht. 19. Jahrhundert: Von
der Jahrhundertwende bis zur Reichsgründung, 1800–1871*, ed. Mechthild Keller (Munich,
1992), 400–416.

[84] Ufer, *Presse*, 182–186; and Karl Reiber, "Die Deutschen Blätter von Brockhaus 1813–1816"
(Phil. Diss., University of Cologne, 1937).

consistency in his *Rheinischer Merkur*, founded in January 1814 and published in Koblenz.[85]

In 1815 nearly 300 newspapers and some 57 political-historical journals were being published in the German-speaking region (excluding Austria).[86] While the commercially run newspapers sought to reach the widest possible audience in their region and thus largely limited themselves to simple information on all areas of politics, economics, society and culture, the historical-political journals usually addressed a supraregional educated audience.[87] The different functions and target audiences of the two formats are evident in circulation figures. As a rule, the larger newspapers printed no more than 1,000 copies, in smaller towns sometimes only 600 to 700.[88] Only the largest papers had higher circulations. In 1813 the conservative *Berlinische Nachrichten*, with close ties to the Prussian court, attained a print run of 3,150, while the *Vossische Zeitung*, which addressed a more liberal middle-class readership, had an edition size of 4,000. *Der Preussische Correspondent* reached 1,250 copies. In northern and central Germany, only the *Hamburgische Correspondent* with a circulation of 10,000 and the *Leipziger Zeitung* with a print run of 5,000 produced more copies.[89] Historical-political journals had an average print run of 1,000, which was surpassed only by the *Deutsche Blätter* and the *Rheinischer Merkur* in their heyday, with a circulation of 4,000 and 3,000, respectively.[90] During the war years both journals experienced a substantial drop in sales along with most other newly founded periodicals, which contemporaries attributed to the public's waning interest. In fact, there was a close connection between the fall in demand, the increase in press censorship and the short-lived nature of many periodicals.[91]

In retrospect, the era of the wars of 1813–15 appears to have been an exceptional period that vividly showed contemporaries the power of a

[85] Czygan, *Geschichte* 1:335–350; Hofmeister-Hunger, *Pressepolitik*, 300–309; Portmann-Tinguely, *Romantik*, 59–106.

[86] The figure for the newspapers is based on Martin Welke, "Zeitung und Öffentlichkeit im 18. Jahrhundert: Betrachtungen zur Reichweite und Funktion der periodischen deutschen Tagespublizistik," in *Presse und Geschichte*, 71–99, 78; for the journals, see Joachim Kirchner, *Bibliographie der Zeitschriften des deutschen Sprachgebietes bis 1900* (Stuttgart, 1969), 1:105–107.

[87] Requate, *Journalismus*, 118–123.

[88] Welke, "Zeitung," 78.

[89] Hans-Friedrich Meyer, "Berlinische Nachrichten von Staats- und Gelehrten Sachen, Berlin (1740–1974)," in *Deutsche Zeitungen des 17.–20. Jahrhunderts*, ed. Heinz-Dietrich Fischer (Munich, 1971), 103–114; Erich Widdecke, *Geschichte der Haude- und Spenerschen Zeitung 1734 bis 1874* (Berlin, 1925), 104–105; and Hans-Friedrich Meyer, "Zeitungspreise in Deutschland im 19. Jahrhundert und ihre gesellschaftliche Bedeutung" (Phil. Diss., University of Münster, 1967), 529–540; see also Hagemann, "Litersturmarkt."

[90] Schäfer, *Arndt*, 254.

[91] Czygan, *Geschichte*, 1:262–285.

media public and gave them their first taste of what freedom of the press might mean. Such an intensive deployment of topical literature to mobilize for war had no precedent in German history. As had already been demonstrated in Revolutionary France when the levée en masse was introduced, the enforcement of universal conscription and with it a "people's war" legitimated by national interests evidently demanded intensive mobilization of the public by all available forms of media. Only a broad-based analysis of the different media used to mobilize for war – from proclamations, leaflets and pamphlets, poems and songs to newspapers and journals – however, can reveal the extent of the efforts to mobilize different groups in society with the declared common goal of the "liberation" and "unity" of the "nation." Only such an analysis can, furthermore, show the wide variety of quite divergent political aims and ideas that were discussed under the umbrella of these generic terms.

5

Defining the Nation: Belonging and Exclusion

One of the few poems from the wars of 1813–15 still known today is Arndt's "The German's Fatherland," which was written in early 1813 and became a kind of German national anthem.[1] No poem was reprinted and recited more frequently during this era. Wherever people wished to demonstrate national belonging they chose this poem, which was soon also set to music.[2] It begins with the rhetorical question "What is the German's Fatherland?" For Arndt, the answer was obvious. The "German fatherland" should extend to everywhere that "the German tongue rings out." There, the same virtues and customs would prevail:

> There is the German's fatherland!
> Where oaths attest the grasped hand,
> Where truth beams from the sparkling eyes,
> And in the heart love warmly lies.
> That is the land!
> There, brother, is thy fatherland!
>
> That is the German's fatherland,
> Where wrath pursues the foreign band,
> Where every Frank is held a foe,
> And Germans all as brothers glow.
> That is the land!
> All Germany's thy fatherland![3]

In this song, Arndt defines the main objective of the patriots: to reestablish the external and internal unity of the German nation. In addition to

---

[1] This chapter is based in part on Hagemann, *Muth*, 204–270.
[2] See Weber, *Lyrik*, 166. The setting by Gustav Reichardt was especially popular.
[3] Ernst Moritz Arndt, "Des Teutschen Vaterland," in idem, *Lieder für Teutsche im Jahr der Freiheit 1813* (Leipzig, 1813), 99–101. Engl.: "The German Fatherland," in *The Poets and Poetry of Europe*, with introductions and biographical notes by Henry Wadsworth Longfellow (Philadelphia, PA, 1845), 322–333.

military liberation from French domination, this primarily meant a return
to the German language, culture and virtues as well as the Christian faith,
which together formed German identity. The song's popularity suggests that
Arndt's vision of the German fatherland struck a chord with many of his
educated contemporaries.

In this chapter I explore in more detail how the nation and national identity were defined in the discourse of the era. Apart from the topical literature of the time, I survey encyclopedias, since they provide information on
how terms and concepts commonly used at a time were defined and understood especially in middle- and upper-class circles, where most readers of
lexica stemmed from.[4] First, I explore the changing definitions of *Nation*,
Volk (people) and *Vaterland* (fatherland) then I analyze the gendering of the
national discourse and examine the contemporary debates over the national,
ethnic and racial borders of the nation.

NATION, *VOLK* AND FATHERLAND

In the German-speaking region, it was only in the late eighteenth century
that the terms *Nation* and *Volk* began to evolve into central concepts that
were used as synonyms in patriotic-national discourse. While both terms had
been in use for far longer, and were discussed with growing intensity among
the educated elite, this left no mark on the German-language encyclopedias,
where their meaning remained rather vague.[5] Most eighteenth-century
encyclopedias, such as Johann Zedler's popular *Great and Complete
Universal Lexicon,* defined *Nation* simply as a community of citizens who
shared a culture and a legal system. Its 1754 edition states, for example, "In
its proper and primary definition, nation means a united number of citizens
sharing the same habits, customs and laws."[6] Until the end of the eighteenth
century, similarly brief definitions dominated in the encyclopedias. Culture
and language, which became increasingly significant in the Enlightenment
debates on national literature and national culture, and which scholars
increasingly counted among the central determining characteristics of a

[4] On the importance of encyclopedias as a source for intellectual history, see Ute Frevert, "*Mann
und Weib, und Weib und Mann.*" *Geschlechter-Differenzen in der Moderne* (Munich, 1995),
17–18; and Kirsten Belgum, "Documenting the Zeitgeist: How the Brockhaus Recorded
and Fashioned the World for Germans," in *Publishing Culture and the "Reading Nation":
German Book History in the Long Nineteenth Century,* ed. Lynne Tatlock (Rochester, NY,
2010), 89–117.
[5] Reinhart Koselleck et al., "Volk, Nation, Nationalismus, Masse," in Brunner, *Geschichtliche
Grundbegriffe,* 7:141–431, 315–320 and 307–310.
[6] "Nation," in *Grosses vollständiges Universal-Lexicon aller Wissenschaften und Künste,* ed.
Johann Heinrich Zedler, 64 vols. and 4 suppl. vols. (Halle, 1732–1754; repr. Graz, 1961–
1964), 23:901.

nation, are mentioned only occasionally in the encyclopedias.[7] The term *Volk*, too, was long used only in the traditional manner, either politically as *Staatsvolk*, that is, the community of all "subjects" of a state, or sociologically to refer to social groups of various sizes and compositions, including the entire propertyless and uneducated population of a society.[8]

The term *Vaterland* appears to have been the most common one in eighteenth-century political discourse, or at least it is here that we find the most extensive encyclopedia entries.[9] Unlike the terms *Nation* and *Volk*, the encyclopedias directly associated *Vaterland* with the territorial state in which a man was born and closely tied it to duties, particularly the defense of country. Accordingly, a *Patriot* was a man who "stands before land and people with loyalty and honesty and takes the common good to heart."[10] These notions of patriotism to a state, which dominated in encyclopedias up to the end of the eighteenth century, corresponded to contemporary texts on constitutional law.[11]

Only after the French Revolution did the terms *Nation* and *Volk* take on a new quality through their democratization. Henceforth, they not merely could potentially encompass *all* members of a people or a nation in the modern sense, but the collective of the *Volk* or the nation itself was conceived of as a historical subject, which could actively intervene in history. Both notions referred only to men. In this modern definition, formed along the French model and its concept of the *peuple*, for the first time *Volk* constituted a *Staatsvolk* encompassing all male inhabitants of a state, whose citizens (*Staatsbürger*) were entitled at least theoretically to the same political rights and were subject to the same duties to the state. The nation was correspondingly conceived of as a nation of state citizens (*Staatsbürgernation*).[12]

As a sort of countermodel to this French-inspired concept of "the nation" and "the people," which was political in the stricter sense of the word, the two terms came to be used more frequently and emphatically in a cultural sense in later eighteenth-century Germany, in a continuation of humanist discourse and encouraged by debates on national culture and language. Most influential here was the philosopher Johann Gottfried Herder, whose 1770 *Essay on the Origin of Language* already promoted the idea that each people's individuality is rooted in its language, so that its mentality,

[7] "Nation," in *Reales Staats-Zeitungs- und Conversations-Lexicon. Neue verbesserte u. stark vermehrte Ausgabe*, ed. Johann Hübener (Leipzig, 1782), col. 1658.

[8] See "Volck," in Zedler, *Universal-Lexicon* (1746), 50: cols. 378–379. The 1782 edition of Hübener's encyclopedia contains no entry for "*Volck*," the usual spelling of Volk at that time.

[9] "Vaterland," in *Allgemeines Lexicon der Künste und Wissenschaften*, ed. Johann Theodor Jablonskie (Königsberg, 1767), 1627–1628.

[10] "Patriot," in ibid., 1027.

[11] An example is Thomas Abbt's well known text *Vom Tode für das Vaterland* (Berlin, 1761); see also Koselleck, "Volk, Nation," 309–312.

[12] Koselleck, "Volk, Nation," 321–325; Kramer, *Nationalism*, 29–56.

character and way of life are recognizable in its original texts.[13] For Herder, language and poetry served to constitute the "people" and the "nation"; they created them as spiritual, human communities, based primarily on a harmony of inner values. Thus being outwardly united in a state was unnecessary for the communal life of a *Kulturnation*. At the same time, Herder proceeded from the assumption that the multiplicity of languages and thus of peoples was divinely ordained and natural, and he therefore argued for coexistence in equality, without any form of mixing. The main causes of linguistic differences, he believed, were external factors, in particular varying climates and geography and the living and working conditions that went along with them. He thereby took up the long-standing model of climate theory, which had been used since antiquity to explain ethnic differences and enjoyed renewed popularity in the eighteenth century, and integrated it into his historical-philosophical theory of language.[14]

Like Herder, a growing number of poets, writers and scholars in the second half of the eighteenth century considered the national language and literature to be the highest expressions of national culture. More and more, language was accorded central significance in distinguishing between peoples and nations.[15] From the early nineteenth century on, this cultural understanding was backed up with the argument of "nature"; the nation was now not only defined by language and culture but also by biology. It was constructed as a "community of descent" (*Abstammungsgemeinschaft*). This did not yet change the old belief that national unity and identity were possible without political unification in a centralized state – and indeed even without a confederation of states. It was still constructed as a collective act of autonomous individual wills. This conceptualization of "the nation" reflects the political situation in German Central Europe at that time, which was a patchwork of smaller and larger territorial states.[16] An example of this understanding is the 22-page article "Nation" in Krünitz's *Economic Encyclopedia* of 1806. It begins:

"Nation, [...] *the native-born inhabitants of a country*, to the extent that they share common origins, speak a common language and distinguish themselves from other

---

[13] Johann Gottfried Herder, "Abhandlung über den Ursprung der Sprache, welche den von der Königl. Academie der Wissenschaften für das Jahr 1770 Gesetzten Preis erhalten hat (1772)," in *Herder Werke*, vol. 1: *Frühe Schriften, 1764–1772*, ed. Ulrich Gaier (Frankfurt/M., 1985), 695–810.

[14] Johann Gottfried Herder, "Briefe zur Beförderung der Humanität", Brief 115, in *Herder Werke*, vol. 7, ed. Dietrich Irmscher (Frankfurt/M., 1991), 686–689. See, also, Koselleck, "Volk, Nation," 283 and 316–320.

[15] See Echternkamp, *Aufstieg*, 91–126; and Hinrich C. Seeba, "So weit die deutsche Zunge klingt": The Role of Language in German Idenity Formation," in *Searching for Common Ground: Diskurs zur deutschen Identität, 1750–1870*, ed. Nicholas Vazsonyi (Cologne, 2000), 45–57.

[16] Koselleck, "Volk, Nation," 325–330.

peoples in a somewhat stricter sense by a distinct manner of thought and action or national spirit, whether they constitute their own state or are distributed among several."(Emphasis in the original.)[17]

At this point in time, the topic of "the nation" had apparently become so important to broad segments of the educated public that encyclopedias like the *Krünitz* devoted long articles to interpreting the term. The entry in the *Krünitz* already contains all of the central elements that defined the *Nation* in the discourse of the period of the Anti-Napoleonic Wars in Central Germany: common descent (*Abstammung*), history, language and culture and, mediated through them, a shared "national spirit" (*Nationalgeist*) and "national character" (*Nationalcharakter*) as well – both terms are interchangeable in the entry. Three main factors formed this national spirit: first, the "natural constitution of a country," especially its geography and climate, which determined not only the people's dominant means of earning a living, richness of invention and willingness to work, but also its soul and temperament, quite an old idea based on Enlightenment "climate theory"; second, the form of government, which decisively influenced the striving for freedom and manner of thinking; and third, language and culture, which shaped character mainly through religion and education. While the "physical causes," geography and climate, influenced the "ineradicable basic traits" of national character, the "moral causes" of the form of government, language and culture lent the national character an "eradicable tendency."[18]

This concept of the fixed "geographical" and "physical" and mutable "moral" causes of the shape that a national character assumed followed eighteenth-century Enlightenment traditions.[19] In the context of the intense debate about the causes of the Prussian defeat of 1806, however, the emphasis of the argument shifted more and more to language. To the extent that the adoption of French culture and language was deemed the "chief cause" of the "decline" of German culture and manners, language as a marker of national differences gained even more importance in the political discourse than it had had before. Two publications by Jahn and Arndt proved pathbreaking here. The first seminal text was Jahn's 1810 work *German Folkdom*, in which he brings old notions of the "physical" and "moral causes" of the differences between peoples/nations together with new ideas on ethnicity and biological anthropology. For him, the *Volk* was a community of descent, culture and common faith with a long shared history that encompassed all

[17] "Nation," in *Oeconomische Encyclopädie oder allgemeines System der Staats-Stadt-Haus- und Landwirthschaft in alphabetischer Ordnung*, ed. Johann Georg Krünitz, 242 vols. (Berlin, 1806), 101:393–415.
[18] "Nation," in Krünitz, *Oeconomische Encyclopädie* (1806), 101:395–400 and 414–415.
[19] Michael Maurer, "Nationalcharakter und Nationalbewußtsein: England und Deutschland im Vergleich," in Herrmann, *Volk*, 89–100; Hans-Dietrich Schultz, "Land – Volk – Staat: Der geographische Anteil an der 'Erfindung' der Nation," *GWU* 54 (2000): 4–16.

social strata. Unlike most patriots, Jahn counted among the *Volk* not just the educated and propertied, but also the "working strata" in the cities and countryside. He defined "folkdom" (*Volksthum*) as "that which is common" to a people – "its intrinsic essence, its activity and life, its regenerative force, its reproductive capacity."[20] For him language played a crucial role in the formation of a folkdom, therefore he called for abandoning "foreign" terms such as nation, nationality and national character and propagated instead "German" words such as *Volk*, *Volksthum* and *Volkscharakter*.[21] Many other patriots followed his call for "linguistic purity."[22]

The second paradigmatic work was Arndt's *The Rhine, Germany's River, but Not Germany's Border* published at the end of 1813, which raised the question of how Germany's future borders should be drawn. Arndt vehemently opposed the old view of the Rhine as a "natural frontier" between Germany and France. He only accepted "language as the valid natural frontier." Set by God, it defined the internal difference between peoples – their "folk character." Alongside it he recognized only mountains and oceans and to a lesser extent large deserts and swamps as natural borders, because they generally marked linguistic boundaries. Rivers, in contrast, he argued, connect more than they separate.[23] From this he concluded that the territories on the left bank of the Rhine up to the great mountain ridges in the west had to be recaptured. If the Rhine remained Germany's border, the risk of the ultimate "annihilation" of all things German was very great indeed. The Francophile "degeneracy" of recent years, which now needed to be undone, would lead to total "extinction."[24] Since the French, unlike the Germans, were conquerors by virtue of their "folk character," there was always a danger, even under a different rule than Napoleon's, that they would invade Germany from the Rhine. For that reason, "the honor of the *Volk*" demanded that the struggle be conducted not with half measures, but unto victory or death.[25] Arndt's work was widely read and discussed too and met with the assent of many fellow authors.[26] The notion of language as a "natural frontier" was repeatedly invoked even in poetry and song.[27] For many political writers, as for Arndt, the logical consequence was clearly that

[20] Jahn, *Volksthum*, 7.
[21] Friedrich Ludwig Jahn, "Subskriptionsanzeige zum 'Deutschen Volksthum,'" in *Literarischer und artistischer Anzeiger* of *Der Freimüthige*, no. 5 (Sept. 1809).
[22] See Hagemann, *Muth*, 231–233.
[23] Ernst Moritz Arndt, *Der Rhein, Teutschlands Strom, aber nicht Teutschlands Gränze* (Leipzig, 1813), 7 and 11.
[24] Ibid., 67–70; see also Jeismann, *Vaterland*, 51–59; Schultz, "Land."
[25] Arndt, *Rhein*, 46–47, 49, 53 and 55.
[26] See, for example, "Der Rheinstrom," *DB* 2.70 (1814); Johann Christian Gottfried Jörg, *Ahndungen für Deutsche bei Eröffnung des Feldzuges von 1814* (Leipzig, 1814), 5–9.
[27] See Friedrich Klotz, "Der Rhein," *Der Freimüthige*, no. 220, 4 Nov. 1814; "Rheinweinlied," *PF*, supplement to no. 51, 31 Jan. 1814; Max v. Schenkendorf, "Das Lied vom Rhein," *RM*, no. 86, July 1814; Friedrich Leopold Graf zu Stolberg, "Die Gränze," *RM*, no. 28, 1814.

the territories west of the Rhine had to be liberated, for the sake of "German honor" alone, and Germany had to be extended to the mountain ridges on the left bank.[28]

The encyclopedias reveal how rapidly the nationalization of political thought spread in the German-speaking region in the context of the Anti-Napoleonic Wars. In 1817 the following appeared in Brockhaus's *Conversations-Lexicon* under the keywords "Nation, Nationality, National Character":

Nature constitutes a number of differences among humankind, which are only recognized and ever more freely developed at a higher stage of *culture*. These also include *nationality* (the state of being a nation) or human life in the form and quality of a *nation*, from which emerges *national character* or the peculiarity of a nation formed over the nation's life and history. [...] The components of nationality, however, or that which constitutes nationality, is shared *descent* and *language*.[29]

In keeping with contemporary discourse, in this seven-page entry it is on the one hand language that defines the borders of a nation and its national character. In addition, unlike texts of the late eighteenth century, the entry also refers to "descent." The word itself already appears in the definition in Krünitz's *Economic Encyclopedia* of 1806, but now for the first time an encyclopedia also offers a physiological explanation for the asserted "naturalness" of linguistic and cultural differences:

Descent, in concert with the particular climates and parts of the earth to which the growing mass of humanity spread, is what fosters a particular bodily form. The latter generally emerges visibly as the family resemblance of a nation, for example in national physiognomies. This particularity of formation is in turn connected with a particular relationship of human beings to nature, particular inclinations, predominant temperaments and the like. Of primary importance, however, is the influence on the *speech organs*, without whose diversity among human beings different languages would be impossible.[30](Emphasis in the original.)

In this entry, "nature" is ultimately the central argument for the differences. It leads to different cultures and languages. This indicates how strongly an

[28] For an example, see "Deutschlands Gefahren," *DB* 2.55 (1813); "Der Rhein ist nicht die natürliche Gränze zwischen Deutschland und Frankreich," *Blüthen der Zeit* 1 (1814): 43–48; "Das linke Rheinufer muß wieder an Deutschland fallen," pts. 1–5, *TB*, nos. 20, 21, 24–26, 1814; "Ideen zu einer künftigen Befestigung der Grenzen Deutschlands gegen Frankreich," *RT* 2.1 (1815): 18–36; "Deutschlands Naturgränze gegen Frankreich," pts. 1–2, *RM*, no. 318 and 319, Oct. 1815; as well as several brochures, for instance *Welche Aussichten eröffnen sich für Deutschland wenn der Rhein die künftige Gränze zwischen ihm und Frankreich bilden sollte?* (Nürnberg, 1814); Georg Arnold Jacobi, *Natürliche Gränzen* (Düsseldorf, 1814).
[29] "Nation," in *Brockhaus Conversations-Lexicon oder Encyclopädisches Handwörterbuch für gebildete Stände* (1817), 6:728–752.
[30] Ibid., 729.

anthropologization of political thought was already shaping ideas about *Volk* and *Nation* in this period. This was an important step in the construction of the nation. Culture can be a choice and is open to change, but nature is inevitable destiny. With *descent* one is *born* in a nation. This made the constructed borders between nations more solid and the traits of a "national character" universal for all people of a nation.[31]

In a second point, too, the *Brockhaus* article deviates strikingly from the earlier terminology, reflecting the political developments of the preceding war years, especially the debates on the future shape of Germany at the Congress of Vienna: *Volk*, *Nation* and "state" were no longer coterminous. The *Volk* was now defined as an "indeterminate mass of human beings" who "live together in a certain clime." "The term 'Volk' in the stricter sense" refers both to "a state, which (like the Prussian) can encompass several nations and to a single nation (e.g., the German) that can encompass several states." The most favorable circumstance for the development of nation and state is when the two are congruent, for the "existence of a nation" can "only be completely secured by a unified state, national virtue and religion."[32] The entry in the *Brockhaus* thus mirrors the most recent development in the patriotic-national discourse. During the war years 1813–15 a growing number of German-national patriots had argued for a politics aimed at congruence between the borders of the *Kulturnation* and the *Staatsvolk* – that is, an extension of Germany's frontiers to include the German-speaking territories in France, Alsace and Lorraine – because "mixing" always carried the risk of "pollution" and "degeneration."[33]

The aim of identical borders for state and nation became increasingly accepted in the German-national movement after 1815. In the period that followed, a common constitution became an ever more frequent defining characteristic of the "nation," which was now also conceived of as a "nation-state," unlike 20 years earlier. In 1826 the *Rheinische Conversations-Lexicon* accordingly published the following definition: "Nation is a collective term meaning a larger or smaller group of people bound together by descent, language, religion, manners, customs and constitution into a

---

[31] Honegger, Claudia, *Die Ordnung der Geschlechter: Die Wissenschaft vom Menschen und das Weib 1750–1850* (Frankfurt/M., 1991), 107–125; Gerhard Kaiser already discussed contemporary notions of state and nation as "natural organisms" in *Pietismus und Patriotismus im literarischen Deutschland: Ein Beitrag zum Problem der Säkularisation* (Wiesbaden, 1961), 139–159.

[32] "Nation," in *Brockhaus Conversations-Lexicon* (1817), 6:730; there is a similar article on "Volksthum" in *Brockhaus Conversations-Lexicon* (1819), 10:377–378.

[33] Heinrich Luden, "Das Vaterland, oder Staat und Volk," pts. 1–2, *Nemesis* 1.1 (1814): 14–39 and 1.2 (1814): 192–233; see also Rühs, "Ueber," 21–40. Both Luden and Rühs, however, did not use the term *nation*. Instead, following Jahn and his call for linguistic purity, they spoke of *Volk*, *Volkstum* and *Volkscharakter*. In fact, however, their position was precisely that the cultural nation (*Volkstum*) must be congruent with the political nation (*Staatsvolk*).

social whole."[34] This new expectation that the politically defined borders of a state would coincide with the culturally and ethnically defined borders of a nation unleashed the potential for political and military conflict. In Central Europe, it led to the forging of the German Empire 50 years later in the Wars of Unification between 1864 and 1871, which resulted in the establishment of a *kleindeutsch* nation-state under Prussian domination in January 1871. The new German Empire annexed previously French Alsace and Lorraine, which were defined as "German," as the national movement had already demanded in 1813–15.

NATIONAL CHARACTER AND GENDER CHARACTER

One common core of the ideas of a German nation discussed during and after the Anti-Napoleonic Wars was thus the notion of a "natural," specifically German national character articulated in German language, culture and virtues.[35] While taking up traditional *Völkerstereotype*, the constructed collective character assumed a new quality through the process of anthropologization. By grounding national differences in "nature," they became universal. At the same time they became gendered and racialized in new ways, because the constructed differences of gender and race too were now increasingly explained by "nature." The contemporary discourses on nation, gender and race were completely intertwined.

In addition, the discourse on the German nation was during period of the Anti-Napoleonic Wars increasingly politicized and militarized, because the patriots and reformers sought to prepare the Prussian and German nation for a new war against Napoleon. Since, after the debacle of 1806, they were primarily concerned with shaping Prussia and Germany into a national community capable of fighting a successful battle for liberation from the Napoleonic yoke, the initial emphasis was on formulating those dimensions of national identity that would strengthen a sense of common purpose and a willingness to fight. How these processes were related and led to the construction of a German national identity that was projected as a male-connoted counterimage to the "national enemy" (France), while internally it was further differentiated by class, gender and race, will be examined in this chapter.

---

[34] "Nation," in *Rheinisches Conversations-Lexicon* (1826), 8:74–78; see also "Nation," in Hübener, *Reales Staats-Zeitungs- und Conversations-Lexicon* (1827), 3:277.

[35] "Ideen über Entstehung, Ausbildung und verschiedene Verhältnisse der Nationen und Staaten," *Minerva* 2 (June 1808): 522–544. *Minerva* was among the journals that began quite early on to conduct an extensive debate on "national character." See, for example, "Hat der Deutsche wirklich keinen Charakter?," *Minerva* 3 (July 1806): 1–10; "Über Nationalität. Von einem Deutschen," *Minerva* 4 (Oct. 1807): 24–37; "Über den deutschen Volkscharakter," *Minerva* 4 (Nov. 1808): 291–307.

Because the patriots and reformers believed that ideas about the nation needed to address first and foremost those men who had to be won over for the first time for a "people's war," especially middle-class men, the topical literature of the time described with monotonous regularity the German character traits with supposedly male middle-class values that "for several millennia had been the treasures" of the "German folkdom." Aside from the constantly repeated core qualities of patriotism, valor and Christian piety, these traits were "vigor, moral uprightness, rectitude and an aversion to trickery as well as fairness and earnest good intentions."[36] In this way German men were equipped with the virtues deemed to be desirable for adult male citizens.

The external counterimage to the "good German men," who represented the German nation, were "the French," who were described and devalued as sham, adroit and subtle, glib, false and superficial, lascivious and unchaste – that is, in terms of traits generally referred to as "effeminate"[37] and attributed to the court nobility.[38] The internal counterimage was all those men who supported French policy or even cooperated with the French. They were denounced as selfish, greedy, dishonorable, servile and unmanly Francophiles and excluded from the community of adult, honorable and valorous German men using epithets such as *Bube* (a weak, effeminate and not seldom aristocratic boy), *Knecht* (an adult bondsman) or even *Sklave* (a man in a state of total dependence). In the political literature of the war years, both the external counterimage of the effeminate French foe and the internal one of the "unmanly" "Francophile" (*Franzosenfreund*) were widespread.[39] They fell on fertile ground not least because feminizing and thus

---

[36] Jahn, *Volksthum*, 10; see also Arndt, "An die Preußen," in Spies, *Erhebung*, 224–228; "Volksstimmung im Rheingebiet," *RM*, no. 1, Jan. 1814; Karl Hoffmann, *Des Teutschen Volkes feuriger Dank- und Ehrentempel oder Beschreibung wie das aus zwanzigjähriger französischer Sklaverei durch Fürsten-Eintracht und Volkskraft gerettete Teutsche Volk die Tage der entscheidenden Völker- und Rettungsschlacht bei Leipzig am 18. und 19. October zum erstenmale gefeiert hat* (Offenbach, 1815), 10–13; Jacobs, *Deutschlands Gefahren*, 28; Friedrich Kohlrausch, *Deutschlands Zukunft: In sechs Reden* (Elberfeld, 1814), 16–20; Johann Lorenz Friedrich Richter, *Vaterlandskatechismus der Teutschen aus den höheren Ständen* (Erlangen, 1814), 150–153.

[37] The contemporary discourse distinguished between the positively connoted "feminine" (*weiblich*) and the negatively connoted "effeminate" (*weibisch*); see "Wahrheiten und Zweifel," pt. 2, *TG*, no. 51, 13 March 1815.

[38] "Was halten die Franzosen von sich selbst?," *DB*, NS 1.14 (1815): 209–222; "Vorwort," *Leuchtkugeln* 1.1 (1815): 3–5; Ernst Moritz Arndt, *Noch ein Wort über die Franzosen und über uns* (n.p., 1814).

[39] Theodor Körner, "Männer und Buben," in Ernst Moritz Arndt und Theodor Körner, *Lob teutscher Helden* (Frankfurt/M., 1814), 57–60; Ernst von Grabitz, "Waffenlob," in *Lob teutscher Helden*, ed. Ernst Moritz Arndt and Theodor Körner (Frankfurt/M., 1814, 2nd edn.), 29–31; "Warum haben die Franzosen so viel Anhänger?," *ND* 1.2 (1813): 154–167; "Die Franzosenfreunde in Deutschland," *DB*, NS, 1.8 (1815): 113–228.

devaluing one's military and political opponent had a long tradition in the early modern period.[40]

Within the nation, the manly German national character was, furthermore, counterposed to the complementary model of a middle-class female national character.[41] The topical literature stylized the essential characteristics of "German women" as solicitousness and charitableness, domesticity, gracefulness, simplicity, depth of soul and piety, as well as chastity and morality.[42] These stereotypical ascriptions, too, were projected against a double image of the enemy: the external counterimage of the "Gallic cocotte," the luxury and fashion-mad Frenchwoman who allowed men to support her and surpassed the vices already attributed to "the French" with her specifically feminine "frivolity" and "unchastity," and the internal counterimage of the "neo-Frankish coquette," a German woman who adopted French fashions, gave in to "immorality" and "unchastity" or even fraternized with the enemy.[43]

In respect of the main character traits of the ideal German man, male and female authors of the topical literature agreed. When it came to defining the ideal female national character, however, the small number of women writers accentuated different aspects than their male colleagues. Three of the best known of these female authors were Caroline de la Motte Fouqué, Betty Gleim and Amalie von Helvig, who during the wars of 1813–15 all published patriotic pamphlets that explicitly addressed women: Fouqué's *Call to the German Women* appeared in 1813 and Gleim's *What Should Reborn Germany Demand of Its Women* and Helvig's *To German Women by one of their Sisters* in 1814.[44] These texts projected an ideal image of German femininity that expected more of German women and girls than the generally demanded domestic "virtues." Gleim, for example, appealed to them, "German Woman! Gird thyself with simplicity, dignity [and] capability. May public spirit and love and pride of country no longer be alien to thee!"[45] Here, she additionally equipped the female national character with active political traits that many contemporaries doubtless regarded as genuinely masculine.[46] She rooted her demands in a reference to the

---

[40] See Isabel V. Hull, *Sexuality, State, and Civil Society in Germany, 1700–1815* (Ithaca, NY, 1996), 400.

[41] See Ehrenberg, *Volk*, 113–114.

[42] "Wahrheiten und Zweifel," pts. 1–3, *TG*, nos. 47, 51 and 52, 7, 13 and 14 March 1815; Jahn, *Volksthum*, 259.

[43] "Die Deutsch-Franzosen [...]," *NF* 2.2 (1814): 268–269.

[44] Caroline de la Motte Fouqué, *Ruf an die deutschen Frauen* (Berlin, 1813); [Betty Gleim], *Was hat das wiedergeborne Deutschland von seinen Frauen zu fordern? Beantwortet durch eine Deutsche* (Bremen, 1814); and [Helvig,] *Deutschlands*.

[45] [Gleim,] *Deutschland*, 6.

[46] See also Cyane [pseudonym of Phillipine von Calenberg], "Ich bin ein deutsches Weib," *Die Musen*, no. 2, 1814, 227–228.

"Teutonic era," when women had been held in high esteem. Women then had been brave and strong and had shared men's cares, woes and dangers. Both had loved their fatherland and fought for it together. Very few texts, with the exception of the brochures by Fouqué and Helvig, made similar arguments.[47]

For Gleim, as for most fellow authors, both female and male, the central cause of the gender-specific shaping of national character was "natural differences" between the sexes. This viewpoint was based on a discourse that had begun to gain currency in the second half of the eighteenth century, which drew upon new Enlightenment insights in the natural sciences and medicine. While until then gender differences had been understood primarily as social differences – that is, derived mainly from men's and women's respective positions and specific tasks in the society of estates – physicians, scientist and philosophers now rooted them in the newly discovered physiological differences between men and women, particularly their different anatomies and functions in the reproductive process.[48] The biological explanation of the differences between the sexes appears to have become so widespread among educated people in the early nineteenth century that it found its way into the educational advice manuals and encyclopedias of the time.[49] The *Brockhaus* article on "sex/gender" (*Geschlecht*) in the 1815 edition offers a typical example of such argumentation.[50] It states that physical gender differences gave rise to specific "gender characters" (*Geschlechtscharaktere*), which were posited as opposite but associated.[51] These "basic characters of the two sexes" were already revealed in human physiology, the entry argued. Men's bodies were stronger, had more mass, firmer and more powerful musculature, broader chests and larger and more robust hearts. Women, in contrast, had a more delicate bone structure, softer muscles and so on. The series of dichotomous attributions of physical differences continues for half a page.[52] The article then went on to derive gender-specific virtues and tasks in culture and society from these physiologically defined "basic gender characters":

Noisy desire bursts forth from man; woman harbors silent yearning. Woman is restricted to a small circle, which she however surveys; she has more patience and endurance in small tasks. Man must acquire, woman seeks to maintain; man with force, woman with kindness – or cunning. The former belongs to resounding, public

[47] [Gleim,] *Deutschland*, 7–8; and "An Teutschlands Frauen und Jungfrauen," *RM*, no. 250, June 1815.

[48] Honegger, *Ordnung*, 107–125 and 186–199.

[49] See Friedrich Ehrenberg, *Der Charakter und die Bestimmung des Mannes* (Elberfeld, 1808; 2nd edn., 1822), 10–15.

[50] "Geschlecht," in *Brockhaus Conversations-Lexicon* (1815), 4:206–208, 207; "Frau," in ibid. (1815), 3:780–784.

[51] "Geschlecht," in ibid., 4:207–208.

[52] Honegger, *Ordnung*, 107–125 and 186–199.

life, the latter to the quiet domestic circle. Man works by the sweat of his brow, and, exhausted, needs profound rests; woman is always busy, in incessant activity. Man resists fate, and defies violence even when lying on the ground; woman willingly bends her head, and finds comfort and aid in her tears.[53]

Over three pages, Brockhaus's *Conversations-Lexicon* unrolls the entire range of gender stereotypes popular at the time. The only place in which society's assignment of tasks to the two sexes was formulated in more extreme form was in the advice manuals on education and behavior specifically targeting boys and men that appeared in large numbers and editions after the turn of the nineteenth century.[54] This suggests an urgent need among educated men for masculine reassurance and a demand for texts in which the gender order was structured hierarchically and male dominance in politics, the economy and society was fortified, at least rhetorically.[55]

In the early nineteenth century, though, this gendered division of tasks did not mean that the household and family assigned to women were considered unimportant – on the contrary. There was a broad consensus in the literature that they were the foundation, the "nursery," of state and nation, which were both envisioned as *Volk* families.[56] For the majority of contemporary writers, despite all political differences, "domestic life" was the foundation and source of "public life." In their view, public virtues and values could develop only on the basis of domestic ones. Relationships within a people reflected the relationships in the family. Just as the ties of marriage and love united household and family, the people and the nation were strengthened by their concurrence with the state, and connected by love of country. Domestic and public lives alike were created by all members working together, each with specific tasks according to their social position, marital status, age and sex.[57] Women were thus assigned a task that was regarded in the contemporary discourse as politically significant and central to the common good. They were to fulfil it, however, not in the arena defined as public but primarily in the domestic realm. Their task was to perform their duties as spouses, housewives and mothers in a manner consistent with the honor, manners and culture of the German nation. Domesticity was henceforth elevated to the foremost "patriotic female duty" of German women.[58]

53 "Geschlecht," in *Brockhaus Conversations-Lexicon* (1815), 4:208.
54 The most important of these were Ehrenberg, *Charakter*; Johann Ludwig Ewald, *Der gute Jüngling, gute Gatte und Vater, oder Mittel um es zu werden: Ein Gegenstück zu der Kunst ein gutes Mädchen zu werden*, 2 vols. (Frankfurt/M., 1804); Carl Friedrich Pockels, *Der Mann: Ein anthropologisches Charaktergemälde seines Geschlechts*, 4 vols. (Hanover, 1805 and 1806).
55 Ehrenberg, *Charakter*, 11–15.
56 For example Kohlrausch, *Deutschlands*, 160–163; for more, see Colley, *Britons*, 237–321; Hagemann et al., *Gender, Politics and War*.
57 For example, Jahn, *Volkstum*, 354–357.
58 See [Gleim,] *Deutschland*, 18–19.

Similar to the anthropologization of the causes of national differences, this anthropologization of the cause of gender differences rendered them immutable and inevitable. It turned bourgeois notions of a gender order into an inescapable, naturally ordained certainty that claimed universal validity across class lines for the first time.[59] This offered an excellent foundation for the politically desired virilization and militarization of notions of masculinity. The political catalogue of manly virtues – already defined by warlike and active characteristics – now applied to all men because of their universal character, based on nature. The militarization of the image of masculinity, in turn, intensified and cemented the idea of the "nature-based" polarity of the sexes. In this intertwined process, valor became the masculine character trait par excellence, which was juxtaposed with loving, caring and kindly domesticity and morality as its feminine counterpart.[60] Accordingly, women's wartime role of sacrifice, mourning and commemoration became the necessary precondition for both men's individual valor and the nation's collective capacity to conduct war.

At the same time, these new ideas helped to reconsolidate a gender order that had appeared to be unstable since the French Revolution, which had not merely made it conceivable that men's demands for political equality and individual freedom could be extended to women as well, but also demonstrated that women could intervene radically, violently and by force of arms in the formation of public opinion, an arena of action and power connoted as genuinely masculine.[61] Women's demands and activities during the Revolution were followed intently in Germany. Educated men in particular seem to have perceived them here, too, as a danger to the gender order and the male predominance it safeguarded. They used anthropologized gender images to define the political arena as a male sphere – following the example of their enemies, the French revolutionaries, who had already utilized it in 1795 to push women out of the political public sphere and back to home and hearth.[62]

The simultaneously emerging ideas about national and gender character thus shaped and reinforced one another reciprocally. The process of constructing a contemporary gender order that cemented the hierarchy of political power between the sexes and at the same time defined nationally specific gender characters, conceived of as universal and complementary, gave rise to a purportedly natural gender-specific division of labor in family

[59] Frevert, *Mann und Weib*, 13–60; and Hull, *Sexuality*, 229–256 and 294–298.
[60] See "Wahrheit und Zweifel," pt. 1, in *TG*, no. 47, 7 March 1815.
[61] Joan B. Landes, *Women and the Public Sphere in the Age of the French Revolution* (Ithaca, NY, 1988); and Sara E. Melzer and Leslie W. Kabine, eds., *Rebel Daughters: Women and the French Revolution* (New York, 1992).
[62] Peter Kuhlbrodt, "Die Französische Revolution und die Frauenrechte in Deutschland," *ZfG* 38 (1990): 405–421.

and society. It was imbedded in the process of shaping Prussia and Germany into a valorous nation that was accompanied by a virilization of notions of the nation and a militarization of models of masculinity. The constructed national identity was rooted in a doubly dualistic basic structure of definitions of the self and the other through national and gender stereotypes. At least in its most radical political variant, it became increasingly xenophobic and anti-Semitic during and after the wars of 1813–15.

GERMANOMANIA, FRANCOPHOBIA AND ANTI-SEMITISM

One effect of the intertwined processes of anthropologization and militarization of the discourse on the nation in the era of the Anti-Napoleonic Wars was the escalation of national exclusion in its most extreme version into national chauvinism based on Christian faith and paired with Francophobia and "early anti-Semitism," which was already labeled by its contemporary critics as "Germanomania" (*Germanomanie*).[63] Previous scholarship tends to view this Germanomania as peculiar to the trailblazers of German-national thinking around Arndt, Fichte and Rühs.[64] A broader analysis of the political literature, however, shows on the one hand how widespread national-chauvinist and anti-Semitic thinking was in the years from 1813 to 1819; on the other hand, it helps us to identify the critics of this ideology.[65]

One of the most explicit was the Jewish philosopher and political author Saul Ascher, who introduced the term *Germanomania* with his 1815 work

---

[63] See Nicoline Hortzitz, *"Früh-Antisemitismus" in Deutschland, 1789–1870/72: Strukturelle Untersuchungen zu Wortschatz, Text und Argumentation* (Tübingen, 1988), 2; and Rainer Erb and Werner Bergmann, *Die Nachtseite der Judenemanzipation: Der Widerstand gegen die Integration der Juden in Deutschland 1780–1860* (Berlin, 1989), 10–12. The question of what should be referred to as "anti-Semitism" and at what point in history we can start speaking of anti-Semitism is a controversial one among scholars. See Anthony J. La Vopa, "Jews and Germans: Old Quarrels, New Departures," *Journal of the History of Ideas* 54 (1993): 675–695. My use of the term follows Hortzitz and Erb and Bergmann, who use it to refer to religiously, economically and racially-anthropologically based anti-Jewish sentiment that regards Jews as aliens incapable of being integrated and emancipated who exert a pernicious influence on the state, society and culture. On traditional anti-Judaism, see Helmut Berding, *Moderner Antisemitismus in Deutschland* (Frankfurt/M., 1988), 11–19; Jacob Katz, *From Prejudice to Destruction: Anti-Semitism, 1700–1933* (Cambridge, MA, 1980), 13–51.

[64] See Erb and Bergmann, *Nachtseite*; Hortzitz, *Früh-Antisemitismus*; Katz, *Prejudice*, 51–106; and Paul Lawrence Rose, *Revolutionary Antisemitism in Germany from Kant to Wagner* (Princeton, NJ, 1990), 10–15, 61–69 and 116–132.

[65] See Peter Fasel, *Revolte und Judenmord: Hartwig von Hundt-Radowsky (1780–1835): Biografie eines Demagogen* (Berlin, 2010).

Germanomania: Sketch for a Portrait of the Times. In this brochure he addressed its function and dangers:[66]

The highest interests of human nature, religion, fatherland, law, now acquired their own stamp in the minds of German thinkers, expressed in a mental manifestation that may conveniently be dubbed *Germanomania*. The fixed tendency or sole aspiration of the *Germanomanes* was and remains the attainment of a counterweight, in Germandom, to *Gallomania*.[67] (Emphases in the original.)

He describes the main objective of the "Germanomanes" as reestablishing "Christian Germandom." With the idea of an ecumenical Christianity, they sought to unite a country that was split into two confessions – Catholicism and Protestantism – by stressing Christian roots alongside a common history, language and culture and at the same time glorifying Germanness itself as quasi-religious. Thus, "Christianity and Germandom" were "fused and became one."[68] This spawned a new variant of the old anti-Judaism, an antipathy to Jews justified in Christian nationalist terms:

The Jews, it is said, are neither Germans nor Christians, and hence can never become Germans. As Jews they are opposed to Germandom, and hence the Christians cannot accept them as their equals, and can at most tolerate them if they are convinced they will not get in the way of Germandom.[69]

Ascher equates the exclusionary "fanaticism" against Jews with that against the French. Both were based on the intention to "erase anything alien from German soil."[70] He clear-sightedly diagnosed the heart of Germanomania as hatred of all things different and foreign, based on antithetical thinking in friend/foe categories. Proceeding from the notion of "nature"-based specific national characters that lead to differences in language and culture as the core of national identities, this manner of thinking understood "the Jews" and "the French" alike as "enemy nations." Since the "peculiarities of character" attributed to these two nations were increasingly regarded as "natural," they appeared to be rather immutable, which was used to justify the necessity of eternal hatred of the French on the one hand and a rejection of general Jewish emancipation on the other.[71] The related discourse on both, Francophobia and anti-Semitism, will be further explored in the following.

---

[66] On Ascher, see Marco Puschner, *Antisemitismus im Kontext der politischen Romantik: Konstruktionen des "Deutschen" und des "Jüdischen" bei Arnim, Brentano und Saul Ascher* (Tübingen, 2008), 442–457; Jonathan M. Hess, *Germans, Jews and the Claims of Modernity* (New Haven, CT, 2002), 137–168.

[67] Saul Ascher, *Die Germanomanie: Skizze zu einem Zeitgemälde* (Berlin, 1815), 10–11.

[68] Ibid., 13 and 10–15.

[69] Ibid., 14–15.

[70] Ibid., 16.

[71] See Lutz Hoffmann, "Die Konstruktion des Volkes durch seine Feinde," *Jahrbuch für Antisemitismusforschung* 2 (1993): 13–37.

Hatred of the French

The wanton injuries that the French troops inflicted in Germany rallied everyone against them; the mental imprint that weighed upon all products of the mind nourished the most bitter resentment of the French government, and the humiliations the French nation visited upon us in their arrogance fomented the bloodiest hatred in all noble German souls.[72]

These words introduced an article on "Germany's Liberation and Salvation" that appeared in *Minerva* in November 1813, in which the author demonstrates in minute detail why hatred of the French was so universal among the Germans. At first, Francophobia could be expressed openly only in Prussia, but now it was palpable all over Germany, for "news that the French had lost the battle at Leipzig" had struck "all German hearts like an electric shock." Princes and peoples had felt "revived and free" now that their disgraceful fetters had fallen away. Nothing could hold back "fiery youth and cool-headed men" from "cursing all things French-minded":

A cry sounded throughout Germany: 'bloody hatred to the French and ruin to their disgraceful tyranny!' Everyone felt awakened to new strength, boy and man breathed nothing but war against the French, and all are determined to fall in the battle for what is most sacred rather than embrace the yoke that is as pernicious as it is dishonorable.[73]

The article describes hatred of the French as a universal sentiment during the first year of the war. An analysis of the public discourse shows that it was indeed a central component of the war propaganda.

Among the earliest broadsheets preaching "bloody hatred of the French" was Arndt's widely disseminated *Appeal to the Prussians* of late January 1813. He calls upon Prussian men to give free rein to their hatred of the enemy, for only it could "unite German strength and restore German splendor, bringing forth the people's noblest drives and burying all ignoble ones." For Arndt this hatred was a "palladium of German liberty," because it set the "kindhearted German" in motion and ensured that he would be ready in future to defend his borders.[74] As the front advanced, a large number of such appeals appeared beyond Prussia's borders as well, disseminated mainly by the Russian and Prussian armies to promote the fighting spirit.[75] The press also printed pages of descriptions of Napoleon's "reign of terror" and the "atrocities" of the French under his command.[76] A 15-page "Compilation

[72] "Teutschlands Befreiung und Rettung," *Minerva* 4 (October 1813): 222–240, 222.

[73] Ibid., 225–226.

[74] Arndt, "An die Preußen," 228.

[75] A frequently reprinted example is the "Appeal to German Youths and Men to Fight for Germany's Liberty," which Justus Gruner issued on 29 November 1813 as provisional governor of the newly established General Gouvernement of Berg. See *RT* 1.1 (1814): 71–77.

[76] See, for example, "Schändliche Beispiele französischer Grausamkeiten," *NF* 3.2 (1814): 235–253; "Rückerinnerung an die Jahre 1806, 1813 und 1814, enthaltend Anekdoten,

of the Reasons Why the French Are Hated," for example, which appeared at
the end of 1813 in the journal *Das neue Deutschland* and whose tone was
relatively moderate, culminated in the allegation that French soldiers had
not shied away from "violating" the "virginal daughters" of the "most honorable citizens." Here, as in other texts, the "dissolute" seduction or rape of
German women and girls was interpreted as the symbol par excellence of
the "baseness" and "depravity" of the French.[77]

One of the most inflammatory pamphlets was penned by Arndt and
appeared in May 1814 under the title *Another Word about the French and
Us*. It treats the question of what needed to happen after military victory
over the French to safeguard that victory. For Arndt, the two most urgent
tasks were on the one hand to secure the regained unity and "freedom of
the Germans" and on the other to struggle against all "worship of things
foreign" (*Ausländerei*) and return to the values of Germandom. The basic
precondition for both was, for Arndt, a permanent and passionate hatred of
the French, all Francophiles and indeed anything French, which seemed to
him to be the surest safeguard against the many dangers proceeding from
"conquest-mad" France.[78] What sets this text apart from all previous anti-
French pamphlets, aside from the call to indefinite hatred of the French, was
the equation of the French with the Jews. He not only resorts in the text
once again to contrasting "manly Germans" and "effeminate Frenchmen,"
but also describes the French as a "people of Jews," of "criminals and
knaves," marked by a "disgraceful greed for gold," "duplicity," "lechery"
and "immorality."[79] This equation defamed Frenchmen and Jews equally,
devaluing both as "false," "effeminate" and "lustful."[80] This text seem to
have been widely read in educated circles, but after the first victory over
Napoleon, criticism of this extreme form of Francophobia was increasingly
published in the press.[81] Not only did civil servants such as the Prussian
censor Renfner strictly rejected Arndt's text; moderate early-liberal writers

Charakterzüge und Bemerkungen über die französische Soldateska," *Leuchtkugeln* 1.2
(1815): 186–212. Three journals were dedicated mainly to documenting French "atrocities": *Janus: Ruinen und Blüthen, bei Deutschlands Wiederauferstehung 1814*, ed. G. A.
Wundermann alias Hermann Germanus in 1814 in Leipzig; *Neuen Fakkeln*, ed. Karl Nicolai
in 1813–15 in Quedlinburg; and *Der Wächter*, ed. Ernst Moritz Arndt in 1815–16 in
Cologne.
[77] "Zusammenstellung der Ursachen, warum die Franzosen gehaßt werden," *ND* 1.1 (1813):
45–60, 56–57.
[78] Arndt, *Wort*, 10.
[79] Ibid., 4, 12–15 and 22–23.
[80] On the tradition of anti-Jewish stereotypes, see Berding, *Antisemitismus*, 7–20; on their gender dimension in the German discourse, although not in this early period, see Gender-Killer
AG., ed., *Antisemitismus und Geschlecht: von "effeminierten Juden," "maskulinisierten
Jüdinnen" und anderen Geschlechterbildern* (Münster, 2005).
[81] For example, "An Herrn E. M. Arndt," *RT* 2.4 (1815): 75–87.

and patriotic Protestant clerics also called for peace and reconciliation with France now that Napoleon had been vanquished.[82]

Those who took a particularly early and prominent position against Germanomania and Francophobia included August von Kotzebue, in his journal *Politische Flugblätter*, published by Friedrich Nicolovius in Königsberg from 1814 to 1816. Here, he had already sharply criticized Arndt's *The Rhine, Germany's River, but Not Germany's Border* in early 1814, emphasizing that "natural borders" no longer existed for the people of his day. Still less could language be a "natural border," since the history of all frontier regions demonstrates the mutability of boundaries, and presents the phenomenon of linguistic blending.[83] Kotzebue's confrontation with Germanomania did not end there. In the series of articles "The Sharper the Blade, the Easier it Cracks," which appeared in the *Politische Flugblätter* in autumn 1814, he vehemently rejected Arndt's call for permanent hatred of the French, since "burning hatred" was a "very active passion" and risked "permanent war between France and Germany."[84] Kotzebue also criticized the notion of a "natural" national character, believing national differences to be merely products of differences in historical-political development.[85] He consequently wrote in 1815 under the heading "Are We Free Now?" that what was needed after the final victory over Napoleon was not a battle against "the worship of things foreign" but rather the safeguarding of regained liberty. First and foremost he called for the introduction of freedom of profession and trade, complete legal equality between the nobility and middle classes, and total freedom of opinion.[86] With his call in the *Politische Flugblätter* for tolerance and civil and political liberties, Kotzebue, whom Arndt and his fellow travelers denounced as a "traitor" because of his critique of Germanomania, revealed a firmly independent and undogmatic early-liberal mindset, a fact that is generally overlooked by most scholars today.[87]

With this position, Kotzebue certainly made no friends among the Germanomanes of 1815. Instead, they felt vindicated by the return of Napoleon, which led to a second wave of anti-French publications. The Prussian censor Renfner accordingly complained in his "Inventory of the Historical-Political Writings Censored in April 1815" that all the

---

[82] Heinrich Renfner, "Verzeichnis der im Monat November 1814 censierten historisch-politischen Schriften," in Czygan, *Geschichte*, 3:97–98. See also Burdach, *Erhebung*, 114–116; Ehrenberg, *Volk*, 206–209; G. W. Mundt, *Einige Reden und Predigten bei wichtigen Veranlassungen des Krieges gehalten* (Halle, 1816), 81–83.

[83] "Die natürliche Grenze der Völker," *PFB* 1.2 (1814–15): 25–31, 31.

[84] "Allzuscharf macht schartig," pts. 1–2, *PFB* 1.4 (1814–15): 69–71 and 1.5 (1814–15): 88–93, 91–92.

[85] "Noch ein paar Worte über die Franzosen und über uns," *PFB* 2.16 (1816): 17–30, 20.

[86] "Sind wir jetzt frei?," *PFB* 1.12 (1814–15): 244–247.

[87] Williamson, "What Killed."

writers he was given to assess devoted particular wrath to Napoleon and the French nation. As he wrote to Prime Minister Hardenberg, however, under the prevailing circumstances he would allow them complete freedom "To snort vengeance and arouse indignation against Napoleon and his followers."[88] After the rapid second victory over Napoleon, however, censorship intensified again and the critics of Francophobia gained increasing influence in the public, too. Moderate patriotic periodicals such as *Das erwachte Europa, Freimütige Blätter für Deutsche* or *Leuchtkugeln* now regarded Germanomania as one of the many "exaggerations of the era."[89] Even Heinrich Luden criticized the "widespread clamor for hatred" in his journal *Nemesis*.[90] The spokesmen for the restoration, who were anxious to see a return to the old balance of power in Europe and stable relations with the reinstalled French dynasty, also increasingly attacked Francophobia and sought to suppress it through censorship. This was evidently successful, since the number of inflammatory anti-French pamphlets fell sharply after 1815.

While the Francophobe texts published during the war of 1813–15 are unlikely to have turned peaceful folk into rabid Francophobes, they may well have intensified existing prejudices and legitimized feelings of antipathy based on the bad experiences during years of French occupation and rule. Letters, diaries and memoirs indicate that anti-French feeling was widespread among the military and the civilian population in Prussia and other areas of central and northern Germany in the war years. With regard to the army, for example, the civilian governor of the military governorate between the rivers Elbe and Oder, Johann August Sack, complained in a letter to Princess Marianne of Prussia in late August 1813 that Frenchmen and Prussians had to be separated in the military hospitals because they were so "rancorous" toward one another.[91] In his epistolary diary, the Prussian military chaplain Karl August Köhler, who served with a Silesian militia brigade in 1813–14, noted that the hatred of the militiamen was so great that they gave the foe "no quarter" even when their officers and generals demanded that they exercise more "discipline" and threatened to punish their violent excesses and pillaging.[92] As to the civilian population, the writer Karl August Varnhagen von Ense, who had served during the wars of

[88] Heinrich Renfner, "Verzeichnis der im Monat April 1815 censierten historisch-politischen Schriften," in Czygan, *Geschichte*, 3:238–41, 240–241.

[89] See "Uebertreibungen der Zeit," *Leuchtkugeln* 2.2 (1815): 257–277; "An Herrn E. M. Arndt," *RT* 2.4 (1815): 75–87; "Merkwürdige Sinnes-Änderung," *PFB* 2.20 (1816): 105–122; "Rückblick auf die nächste Vergangenheit Preußens," *FB* 3.9–12 (1816): 65–86.

[90] Heinrich Luden, "Einige Worte gegen einen Aufsatz im zweiten Stück des vierten Bandes der Nemesis. Mit einer Nachschrift des Herausgebers," *Nemesis* 4.3 (1815): 453–459 and 460–467.

[91] "Brief von Sack an Prinzessin Marianne, 29 August 1813," quoted in Reder, *Frauenbewegung*, 75.

[92] Karl August Köhler, *1813–14: Tagebuchblätter eines Feldgeistlichen*, ed. Kadettenhauspfarrer Jäkel (Berlin, 1912), 36, 45 and 166.

1813–15 first as a Russian officer and later as a Prussian diplomat, reported quite critically in 1842 in his *Memorabilia* that hatred of the French had been extremely widespread during the war, bringing together people of the "most varied ranks" and viewpoints and shared equally by the two sexes.[93] His fellow author Willibald Alexis also described the universal hatred of the French in 1813 in the memoirs of his youth. In retrospect he took no pride in it. At the same time, there was no doubt in his mind that without "this smoldering hatred, the work of liberation" would have been impossible: "a *juste milieu* enthusiasm would not have sufficed to bind together a torn and devastated Prussia and impress upon it the moral awareness of its existence."[94] Alexis points here to a very central function of the emotionalization and nationalization of friend/foe thinking in the period before and during the wars of 1813–15: It served both to unite the Prussian and German nation internally and to set it off from the military foe, as well as aiding in the necessary mobilization for the war. For that reason, the explosion of Francophobia in the media at the beginning of the war was promoted by the Russian and Prussian armies and even tolerated by governments and their censors. Public critics like Ascher and Kotzebue were at first a small minority. Increasingly, however, the authorities too sought to rein in this dangerous nationalist demon, since it unleashed spirits that would ill serve the peaceful coexistence among the European peoples that the Congress of Vienna sought to establish after more than 20 years of war.

They were only partially successful; in the long run, as Michael Jeismann has shown, German-French enmity marked relations between the two nations well into the twentieth century: "In France and Germany alike" the "enemy became a constitutive element of national consciousness."[95] However, as the study of the collective memory of the Anti-Napoleonic Wars in parts four and five will reveal, this was a quite contested development and critiques of Germanomania and Francophobia competed in collective memory with hatred of the French. It was mainly in situations of war and national crisis that nationalized friend/foe thinking and with it Francophobia became dominant again in German history up to 1945. And only because this thinking was anthropologized, and thus encompassed the entire French people, who were constructed as different not only by language and culture, but also by "nature," – could it extend far beyond the war of 1815 and become the core of a nationalist culture that attained dominance at the latest after the Franco-Prussian War of 1870–71 and was based on the fundamental structure of inclusion and exclusion. The old hatred of the French was revived

---

[93] Karl August Varnhagen von Ense, *Denkwürdigkeiten des eignen Lebens*, ed. Joachim Kühn, 2 vols. (Berlin 1922–1923), 2:106.

[94] Alexis, *Jugend*, 32–34.

[95] Jeismann, *Vaterland*, 374.

especially in the context of the Rhine crisis of 1841, the wars of 1870–71 and 1914–18, the annexation of the Palatinate by the French between 1918–19 and 1930, the French occupation of the Ruhr in 1923–24 and the occupation of the Saar under French and British rule after 1920.[96]

Old and New Anti-Semitism

The anthropologization, and with it the nationalization of political thought also shaped the discourse on "Jewish emancipation"[97] before, during and after the wars of 1813–15. To the degree that articulations of Francophobia in the media waned after the wars, discussions of the so-called "Jewish questions" gained in importance, since the political focus now shifted from external to internal nation building. The matter of whether or not Jews could and should belong to the German nation was especially controversial. In this debate, the opponents of any form of Jewish emancipation combined old Christian anti-Judaism and its religious and economic prejudices against Jews with the anthropologically based German-national thinking of the time into "early anti-Semitism," which became the "dark side of Jewish emancipation."[98]

The debate on Jewish emancipation had already begun during the eighteenth-century Enlightenment. Among its earliest propagandists was the Prussian official Christian Wilhelm Dohm, whose *On the Civil Improvement of the Jews* was published in 1781. In it he argued for legal equality for Jews and their extensive assimilation, as well as for educating non-Jewish society about their incorrect anti-Jewish ideas.[99] Austrian Emperor Joseph II became one of the first monarchs to adopt such enlightened ideas when he issued his 1782 "Edict of Toleration," which lifted the capitation tax for Jews, dissolved their ghettos and granted them freedom to exercise a trade without citizenship rights or master artisan status.[100] Revolutionary France was far more radical in implementing the idea of Jewish emancipation. In

[96] Ibid., 299–388; Margaret Pawley, *The Watch on the Rhine: The Military Occupation of the Rhineland, 1918–1930* (London, 2007); Wilhelm Kreutz and Karl Scherer, eds., *Die Pfalz unter französischer Besetzung, 1918/19–1930* (Kaiserslautern, 1999).

[97] On the term *Judenemanzipation* (Jewish emancipation), see Reinhard Rürup, "Emanzipation. Anmerkungen zur Begriffsgeschichte," in idem, *Emanzipation und Antisemitismus: Studien zur "Judenfrage" der bürgerlichen Gesellschaft* (Frankfurt/M., 1987, 2nd edn.), 159–166. On its history in Germany, see Michael A. Meyer, ed., *German-Jewish History in Modern Times*, vol. 2: *Emancipation and Acculturation, 1780–1871* (New York, 1996); and Albert A. Bruer, *Aufstieg und Untergang: Eine Geschichte der Juden in Deutschland, 1750–1918* (Cologne, 2006).

[98] Erb and Bergmann, *Nachtseite*; Berding *Antisemitismus*, 7–19.

[99] Christian Konrad Wilhelm von Dohm, *Über die bürgerliche Verbesserung der Juden*, 2 vols. (Berlin, 1781–83, repr. Hildesheim, 1973, 2 pts. in one vol.), 1:v and I: 34–38; on Dohm, see Hess, *Germans*, 25–50.

[100] Meyer, *History*, 2:15–19.

September 1791 the National Assembly proclaimed complete legal equality for all French Jews, which was extended in 1798 to the territories west of the Rhine that were conquered by France, and was also introduced, along with the *Code Civil*, in the occupied and dependent German states. Although Napoleon placed broad restrictions on the freedom of movement granted to Jews in 1808, especially regarding their economic activities, French legislation remained relatively liberal.[101] Prussia and the other German states introduced legal equality for Jews only in stages. The first farther-reaching "Emancipation Edict," which proclaimed Jews to be "Inlanders" and "Prussian state citizens," was not issued until March 1812. While it did not bring Jewish men complete legal equality in the Prussian monarchy, it did grant them more civil rights and integration into society via new duties such as military service. A central aim of the Prussian government in granting these rights was to secure the financial support of the Jewish communities that was needed to fund the war.[102]

In response to increasing efforts at Jewish emancipation, the number of anti-Jewish publications had been rising significantly since the late eighteenth century. This so-called "pamphlet war" reached an initial high point in Prussia in 1803, when the writer and court commissioner at the Berlin Superior Court of Justice, Carl Wilhelm Friedrich Grattenauer, unleashed his brochure *Against the Jews: A Word of Warning to All of Our Christian Fellow Citizens*. Grattenauer had already made a name for himself with anti-Jewish pamphlets in the 1790s. The 1803 text reproduced the entire range of traditional anti-Jewish prejudices and met with a remarkable response. The work was reprinted six times in only one year and, with 13,000 copies, was probably one of the most widely distributed publications of the time. Grattenauer had apparently hit a nerve with the educated public, which may be attributed not least to the fact that he presented anti-Jewish views in a novel form as biting satire. He caricatured Jewish attempts at assimilation while at the same time denouncing the emancipation efforts of the proponents of Enlightenment. This satirical style would become typical of many anti-Semitic texts in the years that followed.[103]

---

[101] Ibid., 2:19–24.

[102] Ibid., 2:24–27; Bruer, *Geschichte*, 226–305; Annegret H. Brammer, *Judenpolitik und Judengesetzgebung in Preußen 1812 bis 1847 mit einem Ausblick auf das Gleichberechtigungsgesetz des Norddeutschen Bundes von 1869* (Berlin, 1987).

[103] Carl Wilhelm Friedrich Grattenauer, *Wider die Juden: Ein Wort der Warnungen an alle unsere christlichen Mitbürger* (Berlin, 1803), 52; see also his *Über die physische und moralische Verfassung der heutigen Juden: Stimme eines Kosmopoliten* (Germanien [Leipzig], 1791). On Grattenauer, see Bruer, *Geschichte*, 197–200 and 207–210; Erb and Bergmann, *Nachtseite*, 111–112; and Günter Oesterle, "Juden, Philister und romantische Intellektuelle: Überlegungen zum Antisemitismus in der Romantik," *Athenäum* 2 (1992): 55–89, 73–75.

Other authors seconded Grattenauer's attacks on Jews and Jewish emancipation.[104] Only rarely did they encounter criticism.[105] The Prussian government watched the growing dissemination of anti-Jewish pamphlets with concern and regarded it as demagoguery aimed at counteracting the main objective of the official policy of better integrating the Jews in Enlightenment tradition. In order to stem the pamphlet war, a royal cabinet order of September 1804 forbade the publication in Prussia of polemical writings on the "Jewish question."[106] Only in internal administrative papers did a lively debate about the pros and cons of Jewish emancipation continue, which led in 1812 to the Prussian "Emancipation Edict."[107]

Among the few anti-Jewish publications that appeared before 1813 in Prussia and caused a sensation was *The Philistine before, in and after History: Compiled, Accompanied and Reflected from Divine and Secular Writings and Personal Observation* by Clemens Brentano, who had made his name as a Romantic poet. This was the published version of a speech he had given at the inaugural meeting of the "German Christian Table Society" (*Christlich-Teutsche Tischgesellschaft*) in January 1811. This Berlin club accepted only "Christian and German men" as members.[108] The biting satire on Philistines and Jews appeared in May 1811 at the request of the Table Society members, printed anonymously in an edition of 200 copies, which soon sold out in Berlin's bookshops. Public protest against the tract arose only when excerpts were reprinted in a newspaper, the *Breslauer Zeitung*. The Prussian censor banned the work, but could not stop its dissemination.[109]

Even after censorship for single publications was de facto lifted in 1813, no anti-Jewish works appeared at first. During the war the clear priority

---

[104] See Christian Ludwig Paalzow, *Über den Juden-Staat (de civitate Judaeorum) oder über die bürgerlichen Rechte der Juden: Eine historische Abhandlung* (Berlin, 1803); and Friedrich Buchholz, *Moses und Jesus, oder über das intellektuelle und moralische Verhältnis der Juden und Christen* (Berlin, 1803).

[105] For an example, see Johann W. Andreas Kosmann, *Für die Juden – Ein Wort zur Beherzigung an die Freunde der Menschheit und die wahren Verehrer Jesu* (Berlin, 1803).

[106] See Bruer, *Geschichte*, 206–210. Two examples of brochures from the later perod are Friedrich Buchholz, ed., *Chauffour's, des Jüngeren, Betrachtungen über die Anwendung des kaiserlichen Dekrets vom 17ten März 1808 in Betreff der Schuldforderungen der Juden* (Berlin, 1809); and August Ferdinand Lüder, *Über die Veredelung der Menschen, besonders der Juden durch die Regierungen* (Braunschweig, 1808).

[107] See Bruer, *Geschichte*, 257–305.

[108] On its history, see Stefan Nienhaus, *Geschichte der deutschen Tischgesellschaft* (Tübingen, 2003), esp. on their anti-Semitism, 182–272.

[109] Clemens Brentano, "Der Philister vor, in und nach der Geschichte: Scherzhafte Abhandlung," in *Clemens Brentano's Gesammelte Schriften*, ed. Christian Brentano, vol. 5: *Der kleinen Schriften zweiter Theil* (Frankfurt/M., 1852), 371–446. On anti-Semitism among Romantic authors, see Oesterle, "Juden"; Puschner, *Antisemitismus*, esp. on Brentano, 377–436, and on the *Tischgesellschaft*, 268–298; and Hans Peter Herrmann et al., *Machtphantasie Deutschland: Nationalismus, Männlichkeit und Fremdenhaß im Vaterlandsdiskurs deutscher Schriftsteller des 18. Jahrhunderts* (Frankfurt/M., 1996), 123–159.

for political writers was mobilizing the nation against the external enemy. In this national emergency, even the participation of Jewish volunteers in the war, the material support of the Jewish communities and Jewish war charities were welcome.[110] Only when the external foe had been vanquished did a public debate begin over the question of who belonged to the German nation and should be recognized as citizens of the state. This debate accompanied arguments over the Jewish question at the Congress of Vienna, which had held out the prospect of improved legal status for Jews in Article 16 of the Federal Act and affirmed the status quo of laws enacted in the federal states, but did not apply this to the territories that France had annexed to its empire, which the Hanseatic cities in particular had championed.[111]

Once again, Arndt was among the authors who launched this debate. He devoted himself to the Jewish question in his *View of Our Time from Our Time* of autumn 1814 and developed a twofold line of argument against equal rights. He characterized the Jews as an "alien people" whose peculiar "*Volk* character" was marked by "meanness, pettiness, cowardice and miserliness." To be sure, he conceded that the Jewish "*Volk* character" was not purely a product of ancestry, but also derived from language, culture and religion as well as the political history of Jewry. The "persecution, humiliation and detestation" inflicted on the Jews in the diaspora had smothered everything "noble, great, brave and magnanimous" in them. He did not believe, however, that their "common *Volk* character" could change anytime soon, because it was based on "descent" and thus "nature." Since he fundamentally opposed "the mixing of peoples" as "bastardization" and wished to keep "the Germanic tribe as pure as possible from alien elements," he believed that an acceptance of Jews into the "German nation" on equal terms might lead to "degeneracy."[112] Arndt supplemented this anthropological argument with a religious-political one. For him the Christian faith was a genuine component of Germanness. The "Germans" were a "Christian tribe," and the German states were also built on Christianity and its doctrines. "The Jews with their harsh, hostile manner and exclusiveness" were "completely outside of Christianity." Therefore only conversion

[110] Horst Fischer, *Judentum, Staat und Heer in Preußen im frühen 19. Jahrhundert: Zur Geschichte der staatlichen Judenpolitik* (Tübingen, 1968), 32–62.
[111] Anti-Jewish texts included Martin Judo and Johann Isaak Freihr. von Gerning, *Ansichten und Bemerkungen über die bürgerlichen Rechts-Verhältnisse der Juden in der freyen Stadt Frankfurt a. M.* (Teutschland [Frankfurt/M.], 1816); and *Die Juden in Lübeck* (Frankfurt/M., 1816). Pro-Jewish texts included Carl August Buchholz, *Über die Aufnahme der jüdischen Glaubensgenossen zum Bürgerrecht* (Lübeck, 1814), and *Actenstükke, die Verbesserung des bürgerlichen Zustandes der Israeliten betreffend* (Stuttgart, 1815). See also Erb and Bergmann, *Nachtseite*, 86–90 and 97–111; and Meyer, *Geschichte*, 2:27–35.
[112] Ernst Moritz Arndt, *Blick aus der Zeit auf die Zeit* (Germanien [Frankfurt/M.], 1814), 188 and 194–197.

to Christianity would permit Jews to be "absorbed" into the "tribe of the Christian-German *Volk*."[113]

On this issue, too, Arndt's views were widely read in patriot circles and soon gained influence. His friend Friedrich Rühs had a good deal to do with this. In the February 1815 issue of the *Zeitschrift für die neueste Geschichte, die Staaten- und Völkerkunde*, he published a long article, "On the Claims of Jews to German Citizenship," which took up and further developed Arndt's arguments. Rühs accused the humanistically inclined proponents of Enlightenment of equating human rights with citizenship rights. In the case of the Jews, too, one must distinguish between the two. Jews were entitled to full human rights, for the "duty and dignity of any good government" demands that "they be protected from injustices and abuse, that hatred against them not be nourished, and that the way to improvement and participation in the benefits of Christianity be open to them." It was "the old doctrine and hope of the Christian church that all of the Jews will be converted." The right of citizenship, in contrast, could be accorded to them only *after* conversion. Since for Rühs, as for Arndt, Christianity was an indispensable part of Germanness and the foundation of the German states, he believed it necessary to tie citizenship for Jews to baptism.[114]

In his argument, Rühs, like most political authors of his time, constructed the Jews as a people/nation and at the same time as a state. They were a nation since they were connected with their "compatriots throughout the world" through "descent, attitudes, duty, faith, language and inclinations" and together with them "constituted a unit," to which they "were naturally more warmly devoted than to the people among whom they live." At the same time, he thought of the Jews as a "state" since the basic laws of the Jewish religion were also those of the Jewish state. Since political citizenship demanded exclusive identification with one state, it could not for this reason be granted to the Jews.[115] From these considerations, Rühs derived the necessity of a clear segregation of the Jews. It must be impressed upon them generally, but particularly in the regulation of their legal situation, that their status in Germany was that of "metics," resident foreigners without political rights. The rights accorded to them by the Prussian Emancipation Edict of 1812 must thus be significantly curtailed. In particular, their access to public office, "honors and dignities" and the "duties" of a "citizen" at all levels of the state should be made dependent on their baptism and "solemn naturalization."[116]

---

[113] Ibid., 189, 193 and 198; also idem, *Ansichten und Aussichten der Teutschen Geschichte*, pt. 1 (Leipzig, 1814).

[114] Friedrich Rühs, "Ueber die Ansprüche der Juden auf das deutsche Bürgerrecht," *ZnG* 3.2 (1814): 129–161 and 130–133.

[115] Ibid., 133 and 134–143; see also idem, "Die Rechte des Christenthums und des deutschen Volks, vertheidigt gegen die Ansprüche der Juden und ihre Verfechter," *ZnG* 4.5 and 6 (1816): 393–474 and 417–420.

[116] Rühs, "Ansprüche," 153–154.

Despite recognition by leading generals of the achievements of Jewish soldiers during the war of 1813–14, Rühs wanted to exclude Jews from universal conscription once again. He cited two arguments for this. First, the duty to perform military service was a duty of honor, which gave access to civil rights; second, the German army, as the "flower of the nation," must "unite the noblest forces" and thus be wholly characteristic of the *Volk* (*volksmäßig*). Apart from a legal reorganization of citizenship duties and rights, he also called for a halt to immigration and restrictions on local rights of settlement. In addition, he favored the payment of a special "Jew tax" to defray the costs of the many benefits that German governments had offered to the foreign people.[117]

Friedrich Rühs's text met with a broad and mainly positive response. Even Prussian ministers Friedrich von Schuckmann and Friedrich Leopold von Kircheisen, who were responsible for the Interior and Justice Departments, respectively, approved of his arguments.[118] For that reason, his essay was republished in 1816 by Reimer's Realschulbuchhandlung in Berlin, augmented by an appendix on the history of the Spanish Jews.[119] A review by Heidelberg philosophy professor Jacob Friedrich Fries appeared that same year in the *Heidelberger Jahrbücher der Literatur* and was published not long afterward as a pamphlet entitled *On the Endangerment of the Well Being and Character of the Germans by the Jews*.[120] Fries largely agreed with Rühs, except on one central point: he separated national-political and religious concepts and thus detached the ideas of *Volk*, nation and state from their Christian foundations. He rejected Christian and Jewish dogmas alike, and thus demanded a complete separation of church and state. As a consequence of this secularization, unlike Rühs he did not want the bestowal of citizenship on Jews to depend on baptism alone. He demanded complete acculturation. The Jews should wholly emancipate themselves from their religion and their traditions, commandments and ceremonies, give up their outmoded system of norms and values, adapt their educational and occupational careers, integrate completely into social life – in short, cease being Jews and existing as a "Jewish people."[121] Given the Jewish "*Volk* character,"

[117] Ibid., 156–159.

[118] Bruer, *Geschichte*, 333–335.

[119] Friedrich Rühs, *Ueber die Ansprüche der Juden auf das deutsche Bürgerrecht. Mit einem Anhang über die Geschichte der Juden in Spanien* (Berlin, 1816).

[120] Jacob Friedrich Fries, "Rezension der Schrift, Ueber die Ansprüche der Juden an das deutsche Bürgerrecht, Berlin 1816," pts. 1–2, *Heidelberger Jahrbücher der Litteratur*, nos. 16 and 17, 1816. On Fries, see Gerald Hubmann, *Ethische Überzeugung und politisches Handeln: Jakob Friedrich Fries und die deutsche Tradition der Gesinnungsethik* (Heidelberg, 1997).

[121] Jacob Friedrich Fries, *Über die Gefährdung des Wohlstandes und Charakters der Deutschen durch die Juden: Eine aus den Heidelberger Jahrbüchern der Litteratur besonders abgedruckte Recension der Schrift des Professors Rühs in Berlin: "Ueber die Ansprüche der Juden an das deutsche Bürgerrecht"* (Heidelberg, 1816, 2nd edn.), 15–16.

however, Fries believed that this was possible only as a conscious act of cultural adaptation. If the Jews showed no willingness for "improvement," he wanted to "utterly root them out." Apart from a strict ban on immigration, marriage restrictions and the wearing of a special yellow symbol such as had been usual in the Middle Ages, the method he suggested was a strict prohibition on any activity in commerce and finance. If the Jews refused to submit to these measures, the German governments should banish them from their territories as "blights on the people" (*Volksschädlinge*).[122]

Fries was thus one of the most militant early anti-Semites of his era. Interestingly, the difference between Rühs and Fries, which seems so significant in retrospect, was not much discussed publicly at the time by the two men or others. All Rühs had to say on the subject in his second major writing on the "Jewish question," which appeared in 1816 under the title "The Rights of Christianity and the German People, Defended against the Claims of the Jews and Their Champions" in his *Zeitschrift für die neueste Geschichte, die Staaten- und Völkerkunde*, was that he "by no means agreed with all of Professor Fries's opinions," but was pleased that he and Fries, despite "approaching the subject from quite opposite directions" agreed on the main conclusions.[123] The contemporary public thus perceived them as united opponents of Jewish emancipation. The politically explosive nature of secularized anti-Semitism went unrecognized.[124] The writings of Rühs and Fries appear to have been "disseminated in a variety of ways" beyond the educated strata and were even read aloud "in public taverns," as one contemporary commentator notes.[125] Between 1816 and 1819, the "Jewish question" developed into a hotly debated topic.[126] Scholars have suggested that anti-Jewish pamphleteering played a decisive role in heightening the

---

[122] Ibid., 16–25.

[123] Rühs, "Rechte," *ZnG* 4.5 (1816), 397.

[124] Rürup, "Emanzipation," 93–119, 93, and 120–144.

[125] Sigmund Zimmern, *Versuch einer Würdigung der Angriffe des Herrn Professor Fries auf die Juden* (Heidelberg, 1816), 4; see also Erb and Bergmann, *Nachtseite*, 183–185 and 262–265.

[126] See, for example, Judo and Gerning, *Ansichten*; Konrad Georg Friedrich von Schmidt-Philseldek, *Über das Verhältnis der jüdischen Nation zum christlichen Bürgerverein* (Wiesbaden, 1816); Zimmern, *Versuch*; Christian Ludwig Paalzow, *Helm und Schild: Gespräche über das Bürgerrecht der Juden* (Berlin, 1817); Hartwig von Hundt-Radowsky, *Judenspiegel: Ein Schand- und Sittengemälde alter und neuer Zeit* (Würzburg, 1819); Johann Matthias Schütt, *Was giebts nach achtzehn Jahrhunderten vergeblichem Warten auf einen anderen Messias noch für gerechte Mittel, die im Lande Christi und also unter Christen Befehl stehenden Juden zu ihm zu bekehren, damit sie das jüdische Land in Segen wieder besitzen?* (Hamburg, 1819); Anonymous, *Über Juden-Reformation* ([Augsburg], 1819). The subject was also widely discussed in the political-historical journals. Heinrich Luden dedicated a whole issue of *Nemesis* to the topic, "Ueber das Judenthum und die Juden," *Nemesis* 8.1 (1816); see also *Wetterfahnen* 1.3 (1817): 55–70; and *Kieler Blättern* 1.2 (1819): 122–165. For more on this debate, see Brammer, *Judenpolitik*, 78–88; and Katz, *Prejudice*, 74–104.

"'nasty mood' and complaints against the Jews," thus lending ideological legitimacy to the anti-Jewish Hep-Hep riots of 1819.[127]

Very few non-Jewish authors publicly defended Jewish emancipation. One of them was Justus Gruner, governor-general of the territory of Mittelrhein since February 1814, who had already spoken out in favor of legal equality for Jews in the spring of 1814 in a two-part essay "On Germany's Future Constitution," published in the journal *Nemesis*. There, he called for unconditional citizenship rights and a consistent policy of integration.[128] Another was the Prussian senior official and writer Friedrich von Cölln, who edited the journal *Freimüthige Blätter für Deutsche, in Beziehung auf Krieg, Politik und Staatswesen*. In an article titled "Look Back at the Most Recent Past," published in 1816, he noted concisely, "Among all of the excesses of our time, the persecution of the Jews and the French is the most foolish."[129] August von Kotzebue also criticized the anti-Jewish tirades of the Germanomanes in his *Politische Flugschriften*.[130]

The majority of the writings that fought for Jewish emancipation were by Jewish authors.[131] One of the first and best known among them was Saul Ascher with his 1815 pamphlet *Germanomania*. He devoted particular attention to Rühs, sharply criticizing his objective of making the state and the *Volk*/nation one. The notion that a state was based on the "individuality of a people, soil and climate" was for him outmoded. In future, following the French model, only the "principle of law" would determine membership in a state: "One does not, or should not, ask: What does the newcomer think, but rather, what does he do, how does he live? If he obeys the state's laws, he is a good citizen."[132] For Ascher, the idea of the "insularity of

---

[127] See Erb and Bergmann, *Nachtseite*, 262–265; Jacob Katz, *Die Hep-Hep-Verfolgungen des Jahres 1819* (Berlin, 1994); and Stefan Rohrbacher, *Gewalt im Biedermeier: Antijüdische Ausschreitungen in Vormärz und Revolution, 1815–1848/49* (Frankfurt/M., 1993), 35–156.

[128] Justus Gruner, "Ueber Teutschlands zukünftige Verfassung: Aussichten und Erwartungen (Geschrieben vor dem Abschlusse des Friedens)," pts. 1–2, *Nemesis* 2.2 (1814): 176–206 and 303–328, esp. 312.

[129] "Rueckblicke auf die nächste Vergangenheit," *FB* 3.9–12 (1816): 65–86, 68; on Cölln, see Großmann, "Cölln, Friedrich von," *ADB* 4 (1876): 411–412.

[130] "Noch ein paar Worte über die Franzosen und über uns," *PFB* 2.16 (1816): 17–30, 29. See also, Johann Ludwig Ewald, *Ideen über die nöthige Organisation der Israeliten in Christlichen Staaten* (Karlsruhe, 1816); Alexander Lips, *Über die künftige Stellung der Juden in den deutschen Bundesstaaten, ein Versuch, diesen wichtigen Gegenstand endlich auf die einfachen Prinzipien des Rechts und der Politik zurückzuführen* (Erlangen, 1819); and Brammer, *Judenpolitik*, 88–90.

[131] Michael Hess, *Freimüthige Prüfung der Schrift des Herrn Professor Rühs, über die Ansprüche der Juden an das deutsche Bürgerrecht* (Frankfurt/M., 1816); Jacob Weil, *Bemerkungen zu den Schriften der Herrn Professoren Rühs und Fries über die Juden und deren Ansprüche auf das deutsche Bürgerrecht* ([Franfurt/M.], 1816); Joseph Wolf and Gotthold Salomon, *Der Charakter des Judenthums* (n.p., 1817); more in Brammer, *Judenpolitik*, 90–99.

[132] Ascher, *Germanomanie*, 47–70, esp. 54.

nations" corresponded to a historically obsolete "lower stage of cultivation" that needed to be overcome. He believed that "Germanomania" would one day adorn the "gallery of German aberrations of judgment" alongside "Gallomania" and "Anglomania."[133]

Adherents of the German-national movement responded very aggressively to the critiques of Francophobia and anti-Judaism by enlightened authors such as Ascher and Kotzebue. The two writers, who were friends, became a favorite target of scorn from the ranks of the patriotic student associations and the gymnastics movement.[134] The reaction was probably so extreme not least because the two men's critique of Germanomania was also an attack on such much-admired German-national pioneers as Fichte, Jahn and Arndt and popular professors as Rühs and Fries. This aroused massive resistance and hatred, which led to the notorious book burning at the Wartburg Festival mounted by student fraternities on 18 and 19 October 1817 in Eisenach. Amid the cheers of the crowd, 28 books were cast into the flames, including works by Ascher, Cölln and Kotzebue.[135]

National chauvinism, Francophobia and anti-Jewish sentiment formed a unity in the thinking of the Germanomanes, the core of which was fear and hatred of anything different and foreign. The marginalization of anything purportedly "non-German" followed the dualist patterns of interpretation running through the entire German-national discourse of the early nineteenth century, which served four essential purposes: First, it offered cognitive orientation in a historical situation that was experienced as crisis-ridden and unstable. The possibility of uncomplicated classification structured perception in simple ways, thus reducing the bewildering complexity of reality. Second, it served the purposes of collective and individual self-definition. National identity was, as it were, defined negatively by its boundaries. Third, through respective negative and positive connotations, it promoted emotional stabilization by devaluing the alien/enemy and valorizing the familiar. At the same time, it defined a clear and unchallengeable hierarchy of social groups and of the two sexes, thereby creating unambiguous power structures. Fourth, and finally, it contributed significantly to the creation and control of aggression. This behavior-regulating function was especially important during the prewar and war years, when the Prussian and German nation had to be formed into a fighting community that was prepared to face the Napoleonic foe, and a spirit of self-sacrifice had to be awakened in the volunteers and militiamen stylized as "national warriors." When the will to damage and destroy could be attributed to the alien/enemy, this pugnacity could evolve into hatred. Xenophobia and with it anti-Jewish sentiment were thus constitutive components of German-national thought in parts of

---

[133] Ibid., 40 and 70.
[134] See Williamson, "What Killed," 921–925.
[135] Luys, *Anfänge*, 218–235; Brandt, "Die Befreiungskriege," 285–333.

the early national movement.[136] But at the same time in the period during and immediately after the wars of 1813–1815 we can also identify "voices of reason": national-liberal writers and politicians, who supported early-liberal demands for national unity and a constitution that guaranteed basic political rights and equal citizenship, and at the same time argued against all extreme forms of national chauvinism.

[136] On the political function of concepts of the enemy, see Christoph Weller, "Feindbilder – zwischen politischen Absichten und wissenschaftlichen Einsichten," *Neue Politische Literatur* 54 (2009): 87–104.

6

Debating War: The Military, Warfare and Masculinity

"Who is a Man?" asked Ernst Moritz Arndt, in a poem that first appeared in February 1813 in the appendix to the *Brief Catechism for German Soldiers*.[1] This question occupied not only him but also his contemporaries to a degree hardly imaginable today. Diverse images of masculinity were developed in the patriotic-national discourse of the time. Arndt, for example, defined a "German man" in the poem as follows:

> He is a man prepared to fight,
> For his wife and his dear child;
> For a cold breast lacks will and might,
> And its deeds will be as wind.
>
> He is a man prepared to die,
> For liberty, duty, and right:
> A God-fearing heart knows all is well,
> His step is ever light.
>
> He is a man prepared to die,
> For God and fatherland,
> Until the grave he'll carry on
> With heart and voice and hand.
>
> So, German man, so, free man,
> With God thy lord to the foe!
> For God alone can aid thy cause,
> And luck and victory bestow.[2]

Here, as in other songs in the *Catechism*, Arndt entreated German men to recall their core virtues. Apart from military valor, these included love of liberty and country, piety, strength and courage – manly virtues, he asserted,

---

[1] This chapter is partly based on Hagemann, *Muth*, 271–349.
[2] Arndt, *Katechismus* (2nd edn.), song appendix.

that their Germanic forefathers had demonstrated. At the heart of this model of masculinity was the inseparable equation of masculinity, military valor and patriotism. While these masculine virtues had been propagated, especially in poetry, since the Seven Years' War,[3] it was only in the war years 1813–15 that they became the core of the dominant model of masculinity that served to bolster recently introduced universal conscription ideologically.[4] A closer analysis of the contemporary discourse, however, reveals complementary and competing variants of this model, each with its own specific political notions of war and military service. In this chapter, I first examine the changing ideas of warfare and the debate over the character of the wars of 1813–15 – which had a lasting influence on the contested construction of war memories and the political claims related to them – and then explore the variant models of valorous masculinity.

OLD AND NEW IDEAS OF WARFARE

In the period of the Anti-Napoleonic Wars, images of war and war aims were by no means topics of discussion for the military alone. Civilians, too, intensely debated the questions of under what circumstances war is justified, which aims should be pursued and how war could be conducted successfully under altered political and military conditions. The military and civilian debates alike were marked by the opposition between the "people's war" (*Volkskrieg*) and the "war of princes" (*Fürstenkrieg*). The educated zeitgeist accepted only "defensive war" fought as a war of the people on the basis of temporary universal conscription introduced for the duration of the conflict

---

[3] Emil Horner, ed., *Deutsche Literatur: Sammlung literarischer Kunst- und Kulturdenkmaler in Entwicklungsreihen*, vol. 1: *Vor dem Untergang des alten Reichs, 1756–1795* (Leipzig, 1930); Robert F. Arnold, ed., *Deutsche Literatur: Sammlung literarischer Kunst- und Kulturdenkmäler in Entwicklungsreihen*, vol. 2: *Fremdherrschaft und Befreiung, 1795–1815* (Leipzig, 1932). On the concept of martial masculinity in early modern Germany more generally, see Ann B. Tlusty, *The Martial Ethic in Early Modern Germany: Civic Duty and the Right of Arms* (Basingstoke, 2011).

[4] I avoid the widely discussed term "hegemonic masculinity" that was introduced by R. W. Connell because even a concept of masculinity that is dominant in the discourse and culture of a specific time period is relational and context-specific and defined in distinction to other competing and complementary images of masculinity and the related images of femininity. For more on this concept and the related debate, see R. W. Connell, *Masculinities* (St Leonards, 1995); John Tosh, "What Should Historians Do With Masculinity? Reflections on Nineteenth-Century Britain," in idem, *Manliness and Masculinities in Nineteenth-Century Britain: Essays on Gender, Family, and Empire* (Harlow, 2004), 29–60; idem, "Hegemonic, Masculinity and the History of Gender," in Dudink et al., *Masculinities*, 41–60; and Anna Clark, "The Rhetoric of Masculine Citizenship: Concepts and Representations in Modern Western Culture," in *Representing Masculinity: Male Citizenship in Modern Western Culture*, ed. Stefan Dudink et al. (New York, 2007), 3–24. For the state of research, see Robert A. Nye, "Western Masculinities in War and Peace," *AHR* 112.2 (2007): 417–438.

only, not a "war of princes" fought with a "mercenary army" dedicated to the interests of rulers.[5]

Carl von Clausewitz formulated the most influential definition of "people's war" long before the posthumous publication of his classic work on military theory *On War* in 1832. Clausewitz, who belonged to the leading group of military reformers, taught at the Prussian Military Academy from 1810 and served as its director from 1818 until his death in 1831. He outlined his ideas on war more fully for the first time in his "Political Declaration" of February 1812, in which he analyzed Prussia's political and military situation and proposed alternatives to government policy:

The war of present times is a war of all against all. The king does not wage war against the king, nor the army against another army, but rather one people against another and king and army are part of the people. The war will scarcely change this character. [...] Every war is regarded as a national affair and conducted in this spirit, according to the degrees of effort that the force of the national character and the government determine.[6]

For Clausewitz, a "people's war" legitimized by national interests was *the* future form of warfare between the emerging nation-states. He proceeded from the assumption that this "national war," which he believed was justified only as a "war of defense," had to aim to destroy the enemy and thus could only be conducted as an "absolute war." In order to win such a war, one had to mobilize the entire population, for which "the organization of a military state" with "a universal duty to perform military service" was necessary.[7] It was from these reflections that he derived his commitment to the "people's war":

---

[5] "Der heilige Krieg," *DB* 2.91 (1814): 598–599. On German thinking about war in military theory and literature in the late eighteenth and early nineteenth centuries, see also Johannes Kunisch and Herfried Münkler, eds., *Die Wiedergeburt des Krieges aus dem Geist der Revolution: Studien zum bellizistischen Diskurs des ausgehenden 18. und beginnenden 19. Jahrhunderts* (Berlin, 1999); Leonhard, *Bellizismus*, 181–281; Patricia Anne Simpson, *The Erotics of War in German Romanticism* (Lewisburg, PA, 2006); Paret, *Challenge*; Elisabeth Krimmer and Patricia Anne Simpson, eds., *Enlightened War: German Theories and Cultures of Warfare from Frederick the Great to Clausewitz* (Rochester, NY, 2011). For more general accounts of thinking about war in this period, see, esp. Azar Gat, *A History of Military Thought: From the Enlightenment to the Cold War* (Oxford, 2001), 56–382; and Mary Favret, *War at a Distance: Romanticism and the Making of Modern Wartime* (Princeton, NJ, 2010).

[6] Carl von Clausewitz, "Bekenntnisschrift, Februar 1812," in Carl von Clausewitz, *Schriften – Aufsätze – Studien – Briefe: Dokumente aus dem Clausewitz, Scharnhorst- und Gneisenau-Nachlaß sowie aus öffentlichen und privaten Sammlungen*, ed. Werner Hahlweg, 2 vols. (Göttingen, 1965–1990), 1:682–750, 750. Excerpts have been published in English in Clausewitz, *Historical and Political Writings*, ed. and trans. Peter Paret and David Moran (Princeton, NJ, 1992), 285–303.

[7] Clausewitz, "Bekenntnisschrift," 698.

I believe and confess that a people can value nothing more highly than the dignity and liberty of its existence.

That it must defend these to the last drop of blood.

That there is no higher duty to fulfill, no higher law to obey.

That the shameful blot of cowardly submission can never be erased.

That this drop of poison in the blood of the nation is passed on to posterity, crippling and eroding the strength of future generations.

That the honor of the king and the government are at one with the honor of the people, and the sole safeguard of its well-being.

That a people courageously struggling for its liberty is invincible.

That even the destruction of liberty after a bloody and honorable struggle assures the people's rebirth. It is the seed of life, which one day will bring forth a new, securely rooted tree.[8]

Clausewitz defined liberty and honor as a people's highest possessions, which it must defend to the death, not least because the shame of "dishonorable disgrace" is inherited by subsequent generations. In a genuine people's war, the danger of defeat, he believed, was small, since the desire for freedom would be a powerful motivation to fight. The soldiers' fighting spirit could compensate for inferior firepower, and for that reason the state and the army must take all possible measures to strengthen it.[9] Clausewitz was well aware of the negative sides of such a "war of liberty," which was bloodier than any other kind of war and rarely "without dreadful scenes." In it, "all the misfortune and perdition" of every war were heightened to the highest degree, both by the mass of the soldiers going to war and their emotional involvement and by the manner in which the war was conducted. This could not, however, be blamed on the people's war as such. Instead, it was the "fault" of those who wantonly provoked it.[10]

In his "Political Declaration," Clausewitz thereby formulated for the first time the idea of the primacy of politics, which he elaborated theoretically in his later major work *On War* that he started to write in 1816 but was unable to finish. His widow Marie von Clausewitz was left to publish his magnum opus on the philosophy of war, in which he defined the military and war as results of political will and described people's war as a nationally justified form of the absolute war of defense, which incorporates all of society.[11] In 1812 Clausewitz believed that such a situation prevailed and

---

[8] Ibid., 688–689; English translation in Clausewitz, *Writings*, 290.

[9] Clausewitz, "Bekenntnisschrift," 703–704.

[10] Ibid., 740–741.

[11] Carl von Clausewitz, *Vom Kriege: Hinterlassenes Werk: Ungekürzter Text* (Frankfurt/M., 1991); Engl.: *On War*, trans. Michael Howard and Peter Paret, abridged with an introduction and notes by Beatrice Heuser (Oxford, 2006). For more on Clausewitz, see Peter Paret, *Clausewitz and the State: The Man, His Theories, and His Times* (Princeton, NJ, 2007); Gat, *History*, 139–269; Hew Strachan, *Clausewitz's On War: A Biography* (New York, 2007); and Andreas Herberg-Rothe, *Clausewitz's Puzzle: The Political Theory of War* (Oxford, 2007).

therefore pleaded for a military alliance between Prussia and Russia against France. He strongly opposed Prussia's support of a campaign of the Grande Armée against the tsardom.[12]

In the period before and during the wars of 1813–15, only few other members of the Prussian military publicly advocated such a modern image of war. One of them was Colonel Rühle von Lilienstern, Commissioner General for German Armaments since November 1813, who became head of the newly established Department of War History of the General Staff of the Prussian Army in 1815.[13] He formulated his ideas in *On War: A Fragment from a Series of Lectures on the Theory of the Art of War*, published in autumn 1814.[14] While accepting that war was "evil" from the perspective of the "private individual," he juxtaposed it with the "viewpoint of the state," which he defined as of higher value. From this perspective, war was "a boon, not a political disease, but a political remedy":

> For among "all of the bonding agents that hold together the institution of the state, true war [that is, war for liberty] is the most effective and lasting, because shared hardship and tears bind better and more tightly than good fortune. [...] There is no question that every war demands great sacrifice even from the state. But without this constant willingness to sacrifice the individual member for the whole, the state would be utterly inconceivable.[15]

Only "in the war of national vigor against national vigor," does "the most essential and finest aspect of national existence emerge: namely, the idea of the people itself; the feeling of one's own value as a people." Here, Rühle von Lilienstern postulates the necessity of national wars for building the nation and the nation-state. In his opinion, nations emerge as valorous and sacrificial communities for and in war, and must be prepared "to be trained for war" in peacetime.[16] He accordingly propagated the goal of "the nation at arms," for which reason he not merely advocated the introduction of universal conscription in peacetime, which in fact occurred in Prussia with the September 1814 law on compulsory military service, but also vehemently supported military and at the same time patriotic-religious education for young men.[17] Rühle von Lilienstern believed that only two factors civilized

---

[12] Hagemann, *Muth*, 273–274.

[13] On Rühle von Lilienstern, see Jean-Jacques Langendorf, "Rühle von Lilinenstern und seine Apologie des Krieges," in Kunisch and Münkler, *Wiedergeburt*, 211–225.

[14] [Johann Rühle von Lilienstern], *Vom Kriege: Ein Fragment aus einer Reihe v. Vorlesungen über die Theorie der Kriegskunst* (Frankfurt/M., 1814). The text is based on the article "Apologie des Krieges, besonders gegen Kant. Vom Obersten Rühle," which was published in the spring of 1813 in the journal *Deutsches Museum*. See also his *Kriegs-Katechismus für die Landwehr* (Breslau, 1813).

[15] Rühle von Lilienstern, *Vom Kriege*, 51–52.

[16] Ibid., 49.

[17] Ibid., 74–77.

war: the laws of the Christian religion and chivalry, which is why he idealized people's war as "a duel of nations, a great tribunal and trial by ordeal, a sublime public feud in the chivalric sense."[18] In short, Rühle von Lilienstern promoted a patriotic-national bellicism that focused on the continuous militarization of the nation.

During and after the wars of 1813–15 Clausewitz's and Rühle von Lilienstern's ideas met with approval especially in the circles of the Prussian military reformers and younger officers, as is evident in their writings, among other places.[19] One of its best-known supporters was Major-General Neidhardt von Gneisenau, Blücher's quartermaster-general during the wars, who became commander of the VIII Prussian Corps in 1816, governor of Berlin and a member of the Prussian Council of State in 1818 and General Field Marshal in 1825.[20]

Most civilian patriots, in contrast, rejected such bellicism, since their objective was not to militarize the nation but to civilize the military and thus war itself. This was also true of leading German-national authors such as Arndt, Fichte and Jahn. They agreed that war as such was "a heinous evil," "a menace more terrible than floods, crop failure and the Plague, because it contained all of these menaces within it or brought them in its wake."[21] Of the many texts that expressed this position was the 1814 pamphlet *What Was the German Warrior under Napoleon? And What Is He Today?* Its anonymous author declared:

An unnecessary war is a mortal sin against liberty, justice, equitableness, humankind and God; a sin that 'will not be forgiven, neither in this world nor the next.' Whoever begins a war is an enemy of man and God, a nefarious disrupter of all human tranquility, the happiness of families, humanity, morality and religiosity. Those who participate voluntarily make themselves slaves; those compelled to do so are unfortunates who deserve our sympathy.[22]

This attitude followed the eighteenth-century Enlightenment tradition, the majority of whose authors had branded "war the greatest crime of the rulers of this earth and the eternal scourge of its inhabitants." This did not mean that they condemned war on principle, but rather that they rejected wars

---

[18] Ibid., 55–56.
[19] See Stübig, *Armee*, 94–96. For more on this widespread thinking in military circles, see Johannes Kunisch, "Die Denuzierung des Ewigen Friedens: Der Krieg als moralische Anstalt in der Literatur und Publizistik der Spätaufklärung," in Kunisch and Münkler, *Wiedergeburt*, 57–74.
[20] On Gneisenau, see Gerhard Thiele, *Gneisenau: Leben und Werk des königlich-preussischen Generalfeldmarschalls – eine Chronik* (Potsdam, 1999); and Georg Heinrich Pertz, *Das Leben des Feldmarschalls Grafen Neidhardt v. Gneisenau*, 4 vols. (Berlin 1864–80).
[21] Anonymous, *Was war der deutsche Krieger unter Napoleon? Und was ist er jetzt?* ([Heidelberg], 1814), 3.
[22] Ibid.

of aggression, while accepting as "just," wars of defense.[23] Even after 1806, most civilian patriots agreed that in general, war was justifiable only if the fatherland was in danger and the liberty and independence of the nation had to be defended against attacks from outside. Given France's policy of military conquest, this appeared to be the situation. They, too, juxtaposed the negative image of the traditional "war of princes," which is what they believed Napoleon was conducting, with the positive image of a "people's war" fought by "warriors for the nation."[24]

This position, which can be found in many texts by patriotic-national authors of the period, was formulated in a paradigmatic way by the early-liberal Freiburg professor of history Karl von Rotteck in his 1816 *On Standing Armies and National Militias*, which was soon discussed broadly in the press and recommended as a standard work on the subject.[25] It concisely summarizes the discussion among civilian patriots up to that point, and begins by asking, "Do we want to make the nation itself the army, or do we want to make the soldiers into citizens?" – a question that assumed central significance in the German territorial states after the war ended in 1815 in light of the impending implementation of the military system for the German Confederation that was resolved at the Congress of Vienna. Rotteck argued vehemently for the "abolition of the standing armies" and "introduction of a national defense force" (*Nationalwehr*). Standing armies with paid mercenaries or conscripted soldiers corroded virtue and morals and encouraged princes to conduct wars of conquest.[26] For him, the traditional system of conscription with sweeping exemptions and proxies was merely the despotic version of a standing army, which universalized the latter's corrosive effects.[27] Only when "the whole nation – that is its combative element – [...] [constitutes] the army or the armed force," which every citizen would belong to "as soon and as long as he was capable of

---

[23] [Johann Valentin] Embser, *Die Abgötterei unseres philosophischen Jahrhunderts: Erster Abgott: Ewiger Friede* (Mannheim, 1779), quoted in Wilhelm Janssen, "Krieg," in Brunner et al., *Grundbegriffe*, 3:567–615, 593. Embser himself was one of the first to argue against the pacifist stance of many of his educated contemporaries; see Janssen, "Johann Valentin Embser und der vorrevolutionäre Bellizismus in Deutschland," in Kunisch and Münkler, *Wiedergeburt*, 43–55.

[24] Arndt, *Katechismus* (2nd edn.), 21–24; Jahn, *Volksthum*, 296–298; "Soldaten," in *Brockhaus Conversations-Lexicon* (1917), 9:203–215, 213.

[25] Karl von Rotteck, *Ueber stehende Heere und Nationalmiliz* (Freyburg, 1816). Rotteck himself stressed in this text that, although there was no "complete agreement" on the military question among the authors of topical literature, the differences related only to questions of detail. All patriotic authors generally agreed "on fundamental matters," and still more "in the innermost sentiments of their hearts." Ibid., 129–130; on Rotteck, see Hermann Kopf, *Karl von Rotteck, zwischen Revolution und Restauration* (Freiburg/Br., 1980); and Manfred Friedrich, "Rotteck, Karl Wenceslaus Rodeckher von," *NDB* 22 (2005): 138–140.

[26] Rotteck, *Heere*, 55–84.

[27] Ibid., 85–87.

bearing arms," and when this "national army" was mobilized only for wars conducted on the basis of the common resolution of a "popular representation" could one speak of a "people's war." In order to turn all men into national fighters in such a national army and render them "efficacious" in case of war, they should train with weapons regularly "without interrupting their civilian occupations."[28] A decisive aspect of Rotteck's argumentation for him and other German-national and early-liberal patriots was that only a war decided on by a "popular representation" could truly be called a "people's war." In articulating this position, on the one hand, he criticized the widespread and often vague rhetoric of the "people's war" that even princes had used in 1813–14 to mobilize for the struggle against Napoleon. On the other hand, he explicitly linked the call to introduce universal conscription in wartime with the demand for popular political representation.

One of the most important early theorists and popularizers of such a civil and civic notion of the people's war, to whom Rotteck explicitly referred, was Johann Gottlieb Fichte. In particular, his 1813 lectures "On the Concept of True War," which Reimer published as a brochure after Fichte's death in 1815, had a lasting impact. In them, he reflected not just on the general relationship between politics and war, but also analyzed the historical significance of the anti-Napoleonic struggle for liberty. He picked up where his *Addresses to the German Nation* of 1807–08 had left off. While it had been Fichte's primary aim in the *Addresses*, which he held before large audiences in Berlin, to win over the "German nation" to the project of "national education" and thus contribute to shaping Prussia and Germany into a "valorous nation," his lectures of 1813 promoted active support for the war against France. Fichte had already presented an initial short version of the lectures at the University of Berlin in February 1813; three months later he delivered a more elaborated version to a much larger audience.[29] For Fichte, too, war was only justified if a people were defending its external and internal freedom as its "highest good." This "fight for freedom" must be conducted as a matter of "life or death" by all men of a people equally. In light of Napoleon's imperial politics, he believed this situation existed in 1813 and therefore called upon his audience to join the universal struggle "for the liberty and autonomy of nations" without reservation.[30] Given the magnitude of the task at hand, "citizens" (*Bürger*) must disregard the "inconsistencies" of their government, which while calling for a "people's war" continued to speak of "subjects" and to place the

---

[28] Ibid., 128–130.

[29] Johann Gottlieb Fichte, *Über den Begriff des wahrhaften Krieges in Bezug auf den Krieg im Jahre 1813* (Tübingen, 1815); see also idem, *Reden*. On Fichte's theory of war, see Herfried Münkler, "'Wer sterben kann, wer will den zwingen' – Fichte als Philosoph des Krieges," in Kunisch and Münkler, *Wiedergeburt*, 241–260.

[30] Fichte, *Begriff*, 39.

monarch before the fatherland, as if he had none. These were "old, bad habits." Should it become evident after the war that the rulers had only misused "the people" for their own interests, then the fight for freedom would have to continue within the states.[31]

Thus, in 1813, Fichte was one of the few people who were already expressing public skepticism about the rhetoric of "people's war" as it was articulated in official calls to arms. This realistic foresight ensured that the published lectures would attract great attention in 1815, especially in German-national circles, since the text affirmed their view that the fight for freedom within their own countries must, if necessary, be conducted against the princes and their governments. They had fought the wars of 1813–15 from the beginning as "Wars of Liberty" waged by the people and, now that victory over Napoleon had been achieved, they realized that their demands for liberty at home met with significant resistance and were blocked with the rhetoric of the "Wars of Liberation" for which the princes had called them up. This motivated early liberals like Rotteck to explicitly demand popular representation in 1815 and insist that only a war of defense resolved by such a parliamentary body was truly a people's war. With this position, he intervened directly in the increasingly intense debate about the nature of the wars of 1813–15, which would prove to be of lasting significance. This debate revolved around the question of whether the wars had been waged as "Wars of Liberation" or "Wars of Liberty."

WARS OF LIBERATION OR WARS OF LIBERTY?

The military necessity to mobilize broad segments of men for the war against France forced the Prussian King Friedrich Wilhelm III to address his male subjects directly on 17 March 1813, one day after the declaration of war, in his appeal "To My People," in which he explicitly addressed them as a historical subject – a "people" – to recruit them for war. The rationale of the proclamation, which calls "the people" to fight in "Wars of Liberation," became paradigmatic of regional-patriotic justifications for war. The text begins by recalling the "sad fate" of the Prussian monarchy over the preceding seven years, then describes the failure of all attempts to resolve the conflict peacefully, which made the fight for liberation necessary. It addresses the monarchy's male subjects first as "Brandenburgers, Prussians, Silesians, Pomeranians [and] Lithuanians" and reminds them of Prussia's glorious shared history, creating a relationship to the monarchy first through attachment to their home regions and second through a common past. The war aims, for which their forefathers had already engaged in bloody battle, are then derived from Prussia's past historical greatness: "freedom of conscience, honor, independence, trade, artisanship and scholarship." In order

[31] Ibid., 31.

to heighten the courage and will to fight, the address points not just to the "great example" of the "mighty Russian allies," but also to the liberation struggles of the Portuguese and Spanish against Napoleon. Following this model, the king calls upon Prussian men to also wage a self-sacrificing life-or-death battle.[32] The appeal's rhetoric makes the king part of the Prussian and German people:

Great sacrifices are demanded of all estates, for *our* beginning is great, and the number and means of *our* enemies are not small. [...] But whatever sacrifices may be demanded of the individual, they do not balance out the sacred goods for which *we* surrender them, for which *we* must fight and win if *we* do not wish to cease to be *Prussians* and *German*.[33] (Emphases in the original.)

In this way, the fight for liberation not only becomes a matter for the entire Prussian and German nation, but also a "holy war" that can only be waged with God's help. At the end of the appeal, the idea that the coming war is a life-or-death struggle is further intensified. It is a matter of the very "existence" and "independence" of the state and thus also of saving the national honor: "The only alternatives are honorable peace or glorious downfall. You would also stride confidently to meet the latter for the sake of honor, for the Prussian and the German cannot live without honor."[34] Thus here, too, as in the texts of military officers, the honor of the Prussian and German "nation" is a key argument for the called-for masculine self-sacrifice unto death.

Like most other texts of the period, this appeal seamlessly intertwines regional, territorial-state and German identity, thus opening up three access routes for motivating men to fight, which coexisted on an equal footing: a local one – the war as defense of farm, home and hearth; a regional-patriotic one – fighting for the king and the Prussian fatherland; and a German-national one – the struggle for the liberty, honor and independence of Germany. This open quality of the text and, with it, of the war aims that it propagated explains the wide influence of the appeal, which met with much approval even among German-national patriots. The battle cry "With God for King and Fatherland" proclaimed in the appeal did not yet encounter resistance in 1813, since great hopes were still placed in the willingness of princes to make reforms.[35]

De facto, in March 1813 this slogan and the appeal itself already cemented the interpretation of the impending struggle as "Wars of Liberation," which would only be intensified by the subsequent proclamations of the Prussian

[32] Friedrich Wilhelm III, "An Mein Volk.",
[33] Ibid.
[34] Ibid.
[35] See, for example, the enthusiastic reaction of Barthold Georg Niebuhr in his letter of 21 March 1813 from Berlin to Dore Hensler, in *Barthold Georg Niebuhr: Die Briefe, 1776–1816*, ed. Dietrich Gerhard and William Norvin, 2 vols. (Berlin, 1926 and 1929), 2:374–380.

king.[36] This becomes obvious in comparison with the monarch's call to arms for the second war, which was published in April 1815, and contains significantly less patriotic-national rhetoric. The appeal simply refers to the first campaign and the achievements of "Prussia's people, army and generals" and, in light of Napoleon's return, calls "the people" to arms again.[37] The language of the appeal thus plainly reflects the altered balance of power in domestic politics.

The institution, apart from the army, that was most responsible for mobilizing for the "Wars of Liberation" in Prussia and that participated intensively in propagating the regional-patriotic notion of war was the Protestant Church. Its clerics regularly had to read out government appeals and proclamations in church and interpret them in their sermons based on prescribed biblical passages.[38] In Prussia, the war began with the "general service of worship to celebrate the departure of the patriotic warriors" of 28 March 1813 mandated by the Department of Public Worship and Education, during which the appeal "To My People" was to be read aloud along with the "Decree on the Organization of the Militia." The surviving sermons from these services, which were required to address the appeal and the decree, are illuminating documents of Protestant regional-patriotism in the war years 1813–15.[39]

Characteristic of these early sermons is the "Preparatory Sermon for the Establishment of the Prussian Militia," which Carl Friedrich Ferdinand Nicolai, pastor and schoolmaster at the Züllichau orphanage in Brandenburg, gave on 28 March 1813.[40] In it he spoke of the "most sacred duty to hasten to defend our fatherland" and enjoined his listeners to trust in God during this struggle. This war of defense, for which the king himself, inspired by the "voice of the people," had issued a call to arms, must be conducted in the spirit of trust in God and his just order of all things. For God embraces those peoples that rise up against godless tyrants and stands by them in their fight.[41] In keeping with the idea of the Prussian nation as a *Volk* family, Nicolai called on the entire people – young and old, men and women – to defend the

[36] Particularly important was Friedrich Wilhelm III, "An Mein Heer, Berlin, 18. Juni 1814," *SPZ*, no. 73, 23 June 1814; and *VZ*, no. 73, 18 June 1814.
[37] Friedrich Wilhelm III, "An Mein Volk, Wien, 7. April 1815," *AB*, no. 15, 21 April 1815, 92–93.
[38] Hagemann, *Muth*, 143–148.
[39] Gerhard Graf, *Gottesbild und Politik: Eine Studie zur Frömmigkeit in Preußen während der Befreiungskriege 1813–1815* (Göttingen, 1993).
[40] For examples, see Carl Friedrich Ferdinand Nicolai, *Vaterlands-Predigten im Jahre 1813 gehalten in der Kirche des Waisenhauses bei Züllichau* (Züllichau, 1814); "Entwurf zur Predigt, das Volk zur Teilnahme am Kriege aufzufordern, März 1813," *GMP* 7.2 (1813): 30–34; C. F. W. Herrosee, *Rede bei der Vereidigung einiger Kompagnien der Züllichauschen Landsturmmänner, gehalten in der königlichen Schloßkirche am 3ten Junius 1813* ([Züllichau, 1813]).
[41] Nicolai, *Vaterlands-Predigten*, 8 and 5–8.

fatherland.[42] Those "whom the law of the land calls up as valorous and liable to conscription" must "take up arms without misgivings," but those who "were not called" had a "sacred duty" to promote "the holy cause of the struggle" for the "dear fatherland" as "vigorously as possible":

Go forth and give and gather, and search out anything not absolutely essential for the most urgent needs of domestic life, which might serve in some way to clothe, nourish, heal and care for the brave defenders of our fatherland. Officeholders should now seek more than ever to ensure that the internal business of the country continues in an orderly fashion, and wives and daughters at home should joyfully relinquish their expendable jewelry, and even children should gladly offer their collected pennies – for the fatherland![43]

The whole nation should be prepared for great sacrifices of all kinds, even risking their own lives. As in the Prussian king's appeal, the rhetoric of sacrifice is also pronounced in Nicolai's sermon, albeit with an explicitly religious justification, which addressed not just men of military age but the entire population.

A similar tone runs through many other war sermons of the period, in which theological and political differences play only a very minor role. They universally demand the entire people's unconditional self-sacrifice as a precondition for God's help in the war.[44] The tenor of Protestant war sermons scarcely changed over the course of the war, although the emphasis did shift. Until the positive outcome of the Battle of the Nations in Leipzig, exhortations to religious repentance and active proof of patriotic sentiment and pleas for divine succor dominated. Thereafter, the sermons took on a more optimistic tone. Victories were interpreted as "signs from God," proof of having passed the divine test. The sermons preached profound gratitude for the lord's mercy and kindness and the hopeful belief in his continuing assistance, along with admonitions not to stop reflecting on virtuous piety and the willingness to engage in patriotic self-sacrifice and battle, in order to ward off new calamity.[45] This tendency intensified with the beginning of the second war, which was interpreted as a renewed divine trial.[46]

Official calls to arms and proclamations and the many Sunday war sermons were thus the central media with which the regional-patriotic image

[42] See more in chapter 7 in the second part.
[43] Ibid., 14–15.
[44] Graf, *Gottesbild*, 37–44 and 98–104.
[45] For examples, see Leonhard Bertholdt, *Zwei Predigten am Siegesfeste und dem darauf eingefallenen gewöhnlichen allgemeinen Buß- und Bettage in der Universität zu Erlangen gehalten* (Sulzbach, 1814); Friedrich Wihelm Offelsmeyer, *Predigt in Anwesenheit der großen Hauptquartiere, zu Frankfurt in der St. Katharinenkirche am 28. November 1813* (Frankfurt/M. 1814, 3rd edn.).
[46] Franz Theremin, "Predigt zur Feier der am 3. Juli erfolgten Kapitulation von Paris, am 16. Juli 1815: Die Pflichten eines siegreichen Volks, Berlin 1815," in idem, *Werke*, 4 vols. (Berlin, 1828), 4:269–289, 276.

of war – also popularized in poetry – was propagated to broad effect.[47] This idealized image was used to portray the wars of 1813–15, in contrast to the traditional "wars of princes," as "people's wars" at the behest of and in alliance with the princes, in which volunteers and militiamen fought side by side with soldiers of the standing army; this fight was supported by the entire "nation" as a valorous *Volk* family. The war was described as a "just war of defense," in which the aim was not gold, money or power, but outward liberty and independence, and as a "holy war" according to God's will, dedicated not just to defending home and hearth, the king and the Prussian and German fatherland, but also to the struggle for piety, virtue and morality. For this reason valorousness – that is, the willingness to sacrifice one's life – had to be demanded of all men, as in the glorious past.

In the German-national and early-liberal image of war, too, the wars of 1813–15 were consistently described as "just" and "holy." The religious rhetoric was as strong in the German-national texts, especially poems, as it was in the regional-patriotic ones.[48] From the beginning, the primary war aim was defined as recapturing liberty and independence, and accordingly the term "Wars of Liberty" gained acceptance among German-national patriots in the course of the wars. Naturally, the war was also considered a people's war in these circles, but in the years 1813–15, the German-national interpretation of this term increasingly diverged from the regional-patriotic one. The war was described as a "war of the people," who had forced the princes to fight for liberty, and without whom they could not successfully wage the struggle. The central German-national wartime slogan was, accordingly, "For Liberty, Unity and Justice!"[49]

While the notion of liberty was still diffuse in the beginning, as the war went on it was more precisely defined in three areas: First, it referred to freedom from French domination – that is, liberation from outside oppression; second, to the freedom of the male individual to act in a self-determined manner, which culminated – in the tradition of classical antiquity – in the freedom of patriotic surrender to the state, of sacrificial death for the fatherland; and third, to political liberty, not only in the sense of freedom from

---

[47] For examples, see [Christian Christoph Bodenburg], *Preußische Kriegslieder und einige andere Gedichte von B., Erstes Heft* (n.p., 1813); Friedrich Baron de LaMotte Fouqué, *Kriegslied für die freiwilligen Jäger im Brandenburgischen Kürassier-Regiment* ([Berlin, 1813]); idem, *Kriegslieder für die Königlich Preußischen Truppen, 1813*. For more, see Weber, *Lyrik*, 198–207.

[48] Engelmann, "Der Einfluß," 12–16; and Scheibenberger, "Der Einfluß," 16–33.

[49] This slogan was a quite conscious departure from the French Revolutionary "liberty, equality, fraternity." See Hans Erich Bödeker, "Zur Rezeption der französischen Menschen- und Bürgerrechtserklärung von 1789/1791 in der deutschen Aufklärungsgesellschaft," in *Grund- und Freiheitsrechte im Wandel von Gesellschaft und Geschichte: Beiträge zur Geschichte der Grund- und Freiheitsrechte vom Ausgang des Mittelalters bis zur Revolution von 1848*, ed. Günter Birtsch (Göttingen, 1981), 258–286.

the tyranny of the authorities, but also in more modern terms of liberty as a basic value of the state constitution. The initial focus was on the demand for freedom of opinion and the press, and only later for a constitution. In the course of the war, this was accompanied by increasingly concrete elaborations of and calls for "unity" and "law."[50]

In the first year of the war, the German-national notions of a "War of Liberty" were articulated particularly distinctively and memorably in the political poetry of Arndt and Körner, both of whom used songs and poems – alongside appeals and longer pamphlets – quite deliberately as vehicles for political propaganda. An especially influential example is Körner's poem "Appeal" which was first published in late March 1813. Its second stanza reads:

> 'Tis no war as crowned heads know it,
> It is a crusade, 'tis a holy war!
> Law, morality, virtue, faith and conscience
> Hath the tyrant ripped from thy breast:
> Save them with thy freedom's victory!
> The whining of thy old men calls: 'Awake!'
> The ruined cottages curse the thieving rabble!
> The dishonor of thy daughters cries out for vengeance,
> The treacherous murder of thy sons cries for blood.[51]

While here, too, the battle is waged with God's help, it is for the "German fatherland" alone, not for the princes. It is a "crusade" by the people for liberty, for "law, morality, virtue, faith and conscience," a campaign of vengeance for French misdeeds. In his "Appeal" Körner explicitly calls on men of all social strata to participate in the fight to the death for liberty, and accordingly he writes in the third stanza:

> Smash the plowshare, drop the chisel,
> Let the lyre be silent, the loom stand still!
> Leave thy farms, thy halls!
> He before whose face thy banners wave,
> Will see his people arrayed in armor.
> For thou shalt build a great altar
> In the eternal dawn of his freedom;
> With thy sword shalt thou break the stones!
> May the temple be founded on heroic death![52]

With such *Pathosformeln* targeting the emotions, Körner sought to motivate farmers, laborers and artisans, artists and university graduates alike to go

---

[50] On the German tradition of the debate about the concept of *Freiheit* (freedom, liberty), see Werner Conze, "Freiheit," in Brunner et al., *Grundbegriffe*, 2:425–542; see also Echternkamp, *Aufstieg*, 268–276.

[51] Theodor Körner, "Aufruf," in *Gedichte vor und im heiligen Kriege gesungen von Theodor Körner* (n.p., 1814), 10–11. On the broad reception of this song, see Arnold, *Literatur*, 277.

[52] Körner, "Aufruf."

to war and to propagate the idea of a fighting community of valorous men across class lines. To attain this goal and not produce differences in a situation that demanded unity, German-national poetry during the war of 1813–14 left the definition of the war aims very vague. The liberty they aspired to, for example, was referred to as the "star of hope" or "dawn of the people."[53] This open-ended quality is also evident in many German-national calls to arms from the first year of the war.[54] Arndt's *Appeal to the Prussians* of late January 1813, for example, asks:

And what will be the objective of struggle in this great battle? That which is holiest and most venerable, honor, justice, science and the arts, all the finest virtues and the highest possessions of the human race, which the most despicable tyrant seeks to wipe off the face of the earth; our nearest and dearest, our parents and children, wives and sweethearts, the present generation and those yet to come, who will be miserable slaves unless you choose to be bold men.[55]

The patriotic-national opinion makers appear to have used such open-ended and emotional metaphors quite deliberately, chiefly in the media intended to appeal to a broader audience. At first, they were primarily interested in creating national unity, bridging not just social but also regional and political differences. That is why the notion that "all Germans are brothers" and that only disunity had led to enslavement appears repeatedly in their texts, along with the call to abandon regional and religious prejudices and animosities.[56]

It was only in the media primarily targeting the educated male elite (especially books, pamphlets and historical-political journals) that a clarifying political discussion of German-national war aims (and, as described earlier in this part, of national identity more generally) began in the autumn of 1813 after the Battle of the Nations, when victory over Napoleon became likely – a discussion that intensified parallel to the Congress of Vienna. This debate produced not only a more precise formulation of the early-liberal program, but also growing criticism of the rhetoric of people's war. In the autumn of 1814 in the journal *Nemesis*, Heinrich Luden sharply denounced the hopes that the war had been pursued with the same aims by princes and people, and that rulers would accord their people more political liberties in recognition of their wartime service. He believed these hopes to be illusory: The "previous faith in the future [persists] at most among boys and dreamers [...], who form the world in their minds without attention to the world."[57] It was impossible to overlook the fact that the princes,

---

[53] Körner, "Lied zur feierlichen Einsegnung des preußischen Freicorps," in idem, *Leyer*, 26–27.
[54] See the many examples reprinted in Spies, *Erhebung*, 209–294.
[55] Arndt, "An die Preussen," in ibid., 224–228, 228.
[56] Arndt, *Katechismus* (2nd. edn.), 35–37.
[57] "Die Zeichen der Zeit," *Nemesis* 3.1 (1814): 4–45, 5.

having achieved victory with the help of the people, now sought to return as quickly as possible to traditional political power relations:

At the time when the thrones were tottering and the nobility was in danger, the spirit of the people was called and conjured up; and the spirit appeared in all its grandeur and splendor. [...] The people rose up for prince and fatherland. Never had Europe's princes been greater than they were at this time through the liberty and the love of the peoples. Order and discipline prevailed everywhere, and voluntary obedience was the honor of a man.[58]

Now that victory had been won, however, the governments believed they could "turn back the clock" and return to the old state of affairs "that had been destroyed by the course of world events." The people "who had acted nobly," deserved "to be treated nobly"; they had, after all, "risen up not only against the tyrant Napoleon, but against tyranny as such."[59] Such criticism of princes received further impetus after Napoleon's return in 1815. A second war could have been avoided, one could read in the press, if only princes had listened to the voice of the people and proceeded more firmly against Napoleon and the French.[60]

The debate on the character of the wars of 1813–15 and the question of whether they had been "Wars of Liberty" sustained by the people or "Wars of Liberation" led by princes continued in the pamphlet literature and journals after the renewed victory over Napoleon. It also influenced the writing of the history of this period in the century that followed, since liberals and later democrats derived demands for extensive political reforms from the German-national and early-liberal interpretation of the wars as a "struggle for liberty." The notion of "Wars of Liberation" was in turn used by conservatives to deny the legitimacy of these demands. This controversy was closely connected with the propagation of competing images of masculinity during and after the war years.[61]

IMAGES OF PATRIOTIC AND MILITARY MASCULINITY

In the contemporary discourse, masculinity, patriotism and valor were inextricably linked. These three concepts were at the heart of the model of patriotic-valorous masculinity that reform-oriented members of the

[58] Ibid., 8–9.
[59] Ibid., 10–12.
[60] "Wie ist der Krieg gegen die Franzosen mit Einigkeit zu führen?," *DB*, NS, 1.2 (1815): 25–31.
[61] One early escalation of this conflict in Prussia was the so-called *Tugendbundstreit* of 1815–16. This public quarrel was started by a pamphlet written by the conservative Prussian jurist Theodor Schmalz. See Otto Dann, "Geheime Organisierung und politisches Engagement im deutschen Bürgertum des frühen 19. Jahrhunderts: Der Tugendbund-Streit in Preußen," in *Geheime Gesellschaften*, ed. Peter Christian Ludz (Heidelberg, 1979), 399–428; and Hans-Christof Kraus, *Theodor Anton Heinrich Schmalz (1760–1831)* (Frankfurt/M., 1999), 189–242.

military and civilian patriots formulated and propagated in the context of the Anti-Napoleonic Wars. This model combined the old values of soldierly honor, aristocratic officer virtue and Christian-civic ethics with new notions of political participation, national identity and Romantic heroism. At its core was the myth of "death for the fatherland." We can distinguish between two versions of the model in contemporary discourse: on the one hand, the "man at arms" (*Waffenmann*) as a patriotic-minded soldier who served "king and fatherland" in a standing army defined as a "permanent national defense force" (*ständige Nationalwehr*); and on the other, the "citizen as national warrior" (*Bürger als Nationalkrieger*) who dutifully took up arms in case of war to defend home and fatherland.[62] The analysis that follows will focus on the civilian version, since many of its notions would retain their significance into the twentieth century, primarily for "military culture" – that is, the "habitual practices, default programs, hidden assumptions, and unreflective cognitive frames" that form "military practices and the basic assumptions behind them."[63] The civilian version of this patriotic-valorous ideal of masculinity was formulated in three age- and class-specific variants that complemented and competed with each other: "the citizen in uniform" fighting to defend his nation which mainly aimed at middle-class men; the "young war hero" (*Heldenjüngling*) who volunteered for a "people's war"; and the common "Christian militiaman" (*Landwehrmann*) who sought to protect home and country and was fighting with God for his king.

The Citizen in Uniform

One of the first texts that intensively propagated the new image of patriotic-valorous masculinity was the pamphlet *What Are the Reserves and the Militia?* written by Arndt. It appeared anonymously in Königsberg, the capital of East Prussia, in February 1813.[64] The region was the center of the resistance against Napoleon at that time. On 7 February, the provincial assembly of the East Prussian estates had autonomously decided to establish a militia in the province and to arm all men who were capable of fighting. Two days later, the "Decree on the Abolition of Existing Exemptions from Cantonal Obligations for the Duration of the War" created the legal framework for introducing universal conscription throughout the Prussian monarchy.[65] Arndt's 16-page pamphlet, like many other publications of the time, supported this policy. Accordingly, it suggested to all men of military

---

[62] The section that follows is based on Hagemann, *Muth*, 204–349; and idem, "Of 'Manly Valor.'"

[63] Isabel V. Hull, *Absolute Destruction: Military Culture and the Practice of War in Imperial Germany* (Ithaca, NY, 2005), 2.

[64] Hagemann, *Muth*, 28.

[65] [Ernst Moritz Arndt], "Was bedeutet Landsturm und Landwehr," repr. in Spies, *Erhebung*, 229–236.

age that defending the fatherland was their foremost manly duty, an idea that was new to most men previously exempt from military service. It called on "all valorous men of the German lands" to prepare for a "people's war" against Napoleon. Participation in this "people's war" must be an "honor and duty" for every man. Any man who "did not wish to share good fortune and bad, suffering and death with his people" was "unworthy to live among them" and must "be expelled or eradicated as a scoundrel or weakling." In the very widely distributed booklet, Arndt establishes a direct connection between "love of country," "valor" and "manfulness." He not merely denies any man unwilling to bear arms his masculinity, but also brands him a "traitor to his country" who should be excluded from the "people's community" of adult men.[66]

Arndt further elaborated this new ideal of masculinity in the second and third editions of his anonymously published and equally widespread *Soldier's Catechism*. The first version was published in St. Petersburg by the Russian army in late October 1812. It was intended for the troops of the nascent Russian-German Legion, which assembled German officers and soldiers under Russian banners to fight against Napoleon. Arndt proposed a new national code of honor for them, which justified taking up arms against their former German commanders and territorial princes in the Grande Armée.[67] The second version, which appeared in February 1813 in Königsberg under the title *A Brief Catechism for German Soldiers, with Two Appendices of Songs* was intended for soldiers of the Prussian army, volunteers and militiamen. In this version, Arndt developed an extensive catalogue of conduct and norms for the "citizen in uniform," who, as a "national warrior" bound by middle-class Christian ethics, was fighting for his "fatherland" and with it, ultimately, also for himself, his family and his property. Every man should be a "virtuous citizen," a "patriot willing to make sacrifices" and "a warrior ready to fight," glad to "shed his last drop of blood" for "his fatherland and his people." The *Catechism* glorifies war as a test of manliness: only through the common struggle to liberate the "fatherland" could German men demonstrate that they had retained the "manfulness" so harshly battered by the defeat of 1806–07 and restore both their masculine and their national honor.[68]

In August 1813 the third version appeared under the new title *Catechism for the German Warrior and Militia Man, in Which Is Explained How a Christian Warrior Is to Behave and Enter the Battle with God at His Side*, now addressed to all members of the allied troops.[69] By this time Sweden,

---

[66] Ibid.
[67] The first version is reprinted in Arndt, *Drei Flugschriften*; on the history of the "soldier's catechism," see 7–30.
[68] Arndt, *Katechismus* (2nd edn.).
[69] Arndt, *Katechismus* (3rd edn.).

England and Austria had joined the coalition against Napoleon that sought to win over the rulers of the German states in the Confederation of the Rhine and their subjects to the liberation struggle. This version therefore toned down the criticism of the German princes who were still collaborating with Napoleon and, even more than earlier editions, emphasized unity and fraternity within Germany across regional differences, as well as the Christian values that defined the national identity and united all German men.[70] The originally slim 36-page *Catechism* had grown into a substantial brochure of 126 pages, half of them devoted to the song appendix, which contains Arndt's best-known and most loved patriotic-national lyrics. One of the most famous of these is "Song for the Fatherland" (*Vaterlandslied*), which like many others in the *Catechism* was widely distributed as a broadsheet and reprinted in newspapers, journals and songbooks. The composer Albert Methfessel set it to music the same year.[71] Its first stanza, which became iconic in German-national culture during the nineteenth century, reads:

> The God who once let iron grow
> Did not want us as slaves
> 'Twas for this reason that he gave
> Men saber, sword and spear
> 'Twas for this he gave men hearts so bold
> And passion to speak free,
> That in battle they might hold their own
> Unto their last blood, unto death.[72]

This stanza neatly summarizes the core ideas of this German-national variant of patriotic-valorous masculinity and contains many of the metaphors that were omnipresent in the media of the time, especially in poetry.[73]

Interestingly, neither in this song nor in the many other German-national proclamations, pamphlets and poems addressed to men of broader social strata – but especially the middle class – was the concept of the "citizen in uniform" elaborated more precisely. These texts, even if they called for a "War of Liberty," only very vaguely associated the duty of every German man to defend the fatherland with the promise of more political "liberty." The main reason for this was that most German-national and early-liberal patriots did not aspire to equal political rights for all men. They demanded it mostly for themselves and their educated peers, and articulated their political demands more precisely only in texts addressed to their equals, especially in historical-political journals and longer booklets and books, which had to be purchased. This limited the access to these texts to propertied and educated men.

[70] Ibid, 42.
[71] Ibid., 116–118.
[72] Ibid., 116.
[73] Ibid., 116–118.

The Young War Hero

The image of the "young war hero" was an age-specific variant of the model of the "citizen in uniform." It is most clearly developed in "volunteers' lyrics." The first and most successful collection of this poetry was *German Military Songs for the Royal Prussian Volunteer Corps* (which was known as the Lützow Free Corps).[74] The editor of this collection, which came out in March 1813 in Berlin, was Friedrich Ludwig Jahn, one of the founders and propagandists of the legendary unit. In the introduction to the collection he explains the German title *Deutsche Wehrlieder*, which has a specific meaning, and indicates the agenda of the songbook and the genre of volunteers' poetry more generally:

In Old German, *Wehr* means a man who bears arms for his own honor and that of his people. The terms *wehrbar* and *wehrhaft* have always recalled this old form of manhood, which disappeared only for a time [...] Wehrlieder are the voices of the bards, songs of manliness, and a prelude to the new age, where every man will be a man once again, and the people no herd doing forced labor for foreign masters. No being of the male sex who is not a *Wehr* can be considered a man, but only a male, a manikin. *Wehrlos! Ehrlos!* (Emphases in the original)[75]

While traditional collections of military and soldiers' songs (which continued to appear in the period between 1812 and 1815 and were directed primarily at soldiers of the standing army) still described the army as an "estate" that fights for king and fatherland and aspires to military honor and fame,[76] this and later collections of volunteers' lyric poetry characterized military service for the "imperiled fatherland" as the duty of every man capable of bearing arms (*wehrfähig*), but especially of youth. A defenseless (*wehrlos*) man was perceived as an effeminate, dishonorable (*ehrlos*) one – in other words, as no man at all. The defense of the fatherland thus became a matter not only of national but also of individual manly honor. Both needed to be restored by victory in the wars against Napoleon. According to volunteers' lyrics, this was the particular task of male youth. Hence the appeal "To German Youth Capable of Bearing Arms" by Lützow volunteer Mill in the *Deutsche Wehrlieder* begins:

> Come on, come on, to victory or death!
> Young men heed the fatherland's distress!
> If ye fail to vanquish the foe now
> The day of deliverance shall never return
> Young men make good what your elders neglected
> The portals of honor stand open to you.[77]

---

[74] [Friedrich Ludwig Jahn], ed., *Deutsche Wehrlieder für das Königlich-Preussische Frei-Corps herausgegeben. Erste Sammlung* (Berlin, Easter 1813).

[75] Ibid., 5.

[76] For example, *Lieder für Preußische Soldaten* (Berlin, 1812).

[77] Ibid., 11.

It was the duty of the young generation to vanquish the enemy and liberate the fatherland, because – so the song suggests – the "elders" had failed at this task in 1806–07 and had forfeited their manly honor as well as the national honor.

Like this appeal, other volunteer poems also suggest a generational conflict. Their authors distance themselves in form and content from the generation of their fathers, whom they deemed to be "sluggish in thought" and "poor in deed." They emphasize a more emotionally vivid, enterprising, virile manliness inspired by Romanticism. For the young men like Mill or Körner who propagated it, there was no contradiction between "virility" and "tender sensibility." On the contrary, they regarded the two as reciprocally and mutually reinforcing. "Sensibility" (*Empfindsamkeit*) was an important masculine virtue in the interior space of emotional relationships – for both romantic love affairs and friendships with like-minded men and women of their generation. But it was also the necessary precondition for passionate, active, and "truly manly" behavior in the exterior spaces of the political sphere and warfare, since it made men more sensitive to the problems and needs of community and "fatherland" and was the basis of "brotherly" comradeship not only in the "young men's associations" of the *Burschenschaften* and *Turner*, but also the volunteer corps.[78] Accordingly, these military units were repeatedly described in volunteers' lyrics as harmonious "bands of brothers" – that is, men of similar origins and culture and close emotional bonds, whose "equality" was embodied in their "equal freedom" to die a "sacrificial death for the fatherland." This topos was of great significance throughout patriotic-national poetry, for it promised a chance to rise to the status of "heroes."[79] In their thinking, emotionality and passion – hatred of the enemy and love of the fatherland – were important preconditions for this manly will to fight, persevere and sacrifice in warfare.

This generation-specific model of patriotic-valorous masculinity is apparent not only in the many calls to arms directed at male youth, but also in the genre of *Jägerlieder* (riflemen's/huntsmen's songs), which were particularly popular in volunteer units.[80] No fewer than five of the twelve poems in the *Deutsche Wehrlieder* belong to this genre. The best known was "The Band of Volunteers" (*Die Freischaar*) by Körner. Its first stanza reads:

> Step lively riflemen, free and bold
> Take down your rifles from the walls!

---

[78] On the meaning of the term *Empfindsamkeit* at that time, see Gerhard Sauder, "'Bürgerliche' Empfindsamkeit," in *Bürger und Bürgerlichkeit im Zeitalter der Aufklärung*, ed. Rudolf Vierhaus (Heidelberg, 1981), 149–164; and Anne-Charlott Trepp, "The Emotional Side of Men in Late Eighteenth-Century Germany (Theory and Example)," *CEH* 27 (1994): 127–152.

[79] For example, see *Schlachtgesänge und Vaterlandslieder für deutsche Jünglinge* (Berlin, 1813).

[80] In German, the word *Jäger* means both hunter and rifleman.

The brave man frees the world,
On against the foe! On to the field
The German fatherland calls![81]

Like other volunteer songs, it painted a portrait of war and warriors that corresponded closely to the sentiments and notions of young volunteers. With the multilayered metaphor of the hunt, Körner sketches an image of war as a sporting contest, a playful game. The enemy appears as a vanquished animal, "boldly" and "bravely" bagged by riflemen-hunters. In this way, the horrors and dangers of war, and not least the risk of one's own death, were repressed, simultaneously banishing any ethical scruples about killing in battle. At the same time, this metaphor sketches the image of a freewheeling life in the field as part of a comradely male community. Voluntary military service was thus also portrayed as offering freedom from paternal control and domination and an escape from the rigid daily round.[82]

The images and metaphors employed here and in other *Jägerlieder* point to additional, more personal generation-specific motives that were offered to young volunteers. Military service was presented to them as an initiation period in which they could test and demonstrate their manliness and at the same time gain more personal freedom. In fulfilling their "duty to serve" they proved their competence as "protectors of home and fatherland" and thus their "marriageability," because only a man who was able and willing to bear arms and protect his loved ones would make a good husband. At the same time, military service gave them the right to join the community of adult men, who could hope to be rewarded with more political rights after the war. Thus volunteers' lyrics presented the struggle not only as a crusade for liberation *and* liberty, but also as a path to national *Ermannung* (restoration of national masculinity and honor) and individual *Mannwerdung* (a rite of passage to manhood).[83]

The Christian Militiaman

The third variant of the propagated model of patriotic-valorous masculinity was the "Christian militiaman" who protects his home and country and fights for his king with God's blessing. This model primarily targeted members of the militia and reserves – that is, men of the rural and urban lower classes who were previously exempt from military service, but also addressed regular soldiers of the standing army. More than the other two versions of the model of patriotic-valorous masculinity, this version was based on Christian-conservative values. It propagated the idea of the wars as a struggle for liberation. The chief motives for participating in the

---

[81] Jahn, *Wehrlieder*, 12.
[82] Weber, *Lyrik*, 187–198.
[83] Hagemann, *Muth*, 331–339.

struggle emphasized here were thus "loyalty" to the king and "love" of the "fatherland" (in this case, the territorial state). The "War Song for Marching Out" from the anonymous collection *War Songs for the Royal Prussian Troops* of March 1813 expresses it thus:

> Boldly comrades, let us take to the field!
> Our lives belong to the King!
> Trust and love, not gold and silver
> Inspire our resolve!
> Devoted to king and fatherland
> Man for man, here we stand![84]

At the same time, regional-patriotic songs like this one constantly emphasized that soldiers and militiamen of the Prussian army were fighting out of conviction, not "contemptible greed" – an attempt to distance them from the universally reviled "mercenaries" of the old "princely armies."[85]

This regional-patriotic variant stressed that the men had only taken up arms in response to the king's call to defend the fatherland, not out of their autonomous and manly free will, as in the other two versions. This idea was prototypically formulated in "Song of the Prussians" by Aulic Councilor Carl Heun, who had written it on behalf of his monarch. This song, which became quite a popular ditty soon after its publication in May 1813, propagated the motto that Friedrich Wilhelm III had issued for the war: "With God for King and Fatherland."

> The king called and all men came
> Arms courageous in their hands
> And each Prussian in God's name
> Fought for the beloved fatherland.
> And all gave whate'er they could
> Child, property, health, blood, and life.
> With God for King and Fatherland![86]

Regional-patriotic poems and sermons, which also propagated this variant extensively, frequently offered three further reasons for men to support the struggle. First, songs in particular emphasized recapturing old Prussian military glory and soldiers' honor. At the same time, as in the other two versions, the "stalwart fighters" were promised immortality should they die a "hero's death."[87] Second, sermons and songs underlined the urgent need to

---

[84] *Kriegslieder für die Königlich Preussischen Truppen vorzüglich den Jäger Detachements gewidmet: Beym Ausmarsch den 23. März 1813* (n.p., 1813), 7–8.

[85] Ibid.

[86] Carl Heun, *Lied der Preussen: Der König rief, und alle, alle kamen, mit Begleitung des Forte-Piano und der Guitarre* (Hamburg, 1813); on Heun, who published very popular novels under the pseudonym Heinrich Clauren, see Karl Richter, "Clauren, Heinrich," *NDB* 3 (1957): 267–268.

[87] Ibid.

liberate one's own homeland and protect home, farm and family. The anonymous author of a song reprinted in the 1815 edition of the extraordinarily popular *Mildheim Songbook*, edited by the well-known publisher and proponent of the popular Enlightenment Rudolph Zacharias Becker, for example, wrote:[88]

> We fight for our parents' peace
> And our children's happiness
> For our brothers' safety,
> This arm is dedicated to the sword,
> We shall not turn back!
>
> We fight for our own hearths,
> For a roof and for bread
> Oh brothers, not a hut did stand
> Safely in our fatherland;
> How great was our distress![89]

The topos of the man as "protector" and "rescuer" was at the core of all versions of the model of patriotic-valorous masculinity, but was especially emphasized in this variant. All men, regardless of family status, were expected to protect wives and daughters, mothers and sisters and their homes. Behind this image were male fears that the French foe, who was deemed "immoral," intended to violate the "womanly honor" of their sweethearts, wives and daughters, and thus the "German honor" that female virtue symbolized and that needed to be protected.[90] The lines cited above stress two other important motivations: resistance to the existential threat posed by the enemy and "revenge for long humiliation."[91] For many ordinary men, the experience of exploitation and oppression during the occupation and war as well as the need to protect their homes and farms may well have been the primary arguments that made participation in the war seem a sensible course of action.

This third variant and the related regional-patriotic interpretation of the wars of 1813–15 was the most widespread model of masculinity in war propaganda, especially in patriotic-national poetry and sermons. This more conservative version, which propagated a God-fearing patriotism and demanded that men be loyal to the king and sentimentally devoted to the homeland (*Heimat*), seems to have corresponded more closely to the thoughts and feelings of broad segments of the male population than the two other variants, and would have lasting influence in nineteenth-century Prussia.

[88] Rudolph Zacharias Becker, *Mildheimisches Liederbuch: Faksimiledruck nach der Ausgabe von 1815* (Stuttgart, 1971); on the history of this extremely widely distributed songbook, see the afterword by Georg Häntzschel and Gottfried Weissert, *Das Mildheimische Liederbuch: Studien zur volkspädagogischen Literatur der Aufklärung* (Tübingen, 1966).
[89] Becker, *Liederbuch*, no. 765, 508.
[90] See, for example, Friedrich Wilhelm Stargardt, "Landwehr," in Jahn, *Wehrlieder*, 18–20.
[91] "Ermannung," in *Kriegslieder der Deutschen: Erstes Dutzend* (Breslau, 1813), 21–22.

Not surprisingly, criticism of the model of patriotic-valorous masculinity was publicly voiced only very rarely during the wars of 1813–15. Pacifism of any kind was certainly not part of any version of masculinity propagated at the time. At most, texts described the destructive and violent side of war for men: parting and death, mourning and hardship. One of the rare surviving examples is an anonymous song that seems to have been very popular among the Prussian troops.[92] It begins:

> Delicate night, thy dark veil covereth
> My face, perhaps for the last time
> Tomorrow I shall already be laid low
> Struck from the list of the living.
>
> Tomorrow we go into battle
> For brethren and fatherland;
> But alas! Many a man will not return
> To the place where friends embrace.[93]

This eight-verse song was heard frequently around Prussian campfires and apparently affected the soldiers so deeply that the army command forbade it to be sung because of its "morale-destroying" effect.[94]

Any realistic description of the war was censored as long as the fighting continued. Death was to be described and imagined only as a heroic sacrifice for the "fatherland." This myth, along with the topos of man as "protector" and "rescuer," was at the heart of all versions of the model of patriotic-valorous masculinity. The myth produced reciprocal meanings: The sacrifice of death affirmed the reality of the fatherland, which needed to be liberated, or created in the first place. The fatherland, in turn, imbued death in battle with a higher meaning, sanctifying it and promising those who went to war prepared to fight and lay down their lives that their glorious memory would live on in those they left behind. It is no accident that the veneration and commemoration of heroes gained great significance in the time of the wars of 1813–15, when universal conscription was introduced in many German states for the first time, and became one of its important legacies during the nineteenth century.[95] Now that every man of military age was expected to become a "defender of the fatherland" who might die in battle, death "on the field of honor" had to be made socially acceptable by exalting all soldiers, militiamen and volunteers, no longer focusing solely on high-ranking aristocratic army leaders.[96]

---

[92] Wolfgang Steinitz, *Deutsche Volkslieder demokratischen Charakters aus sechs Jahrhunderten*, 2 vols. (Berlin, 1955), 1:315–499.

[93] Ibid., 442.

[94] Ibid., 440.

[95] See chapter 7 in the second part.

[96] See Jeismann, *Vaterland*, 95–102; and Reinhart Koselleck and Michael Jeismann, eds., *Der politische Totenkult: Kriegerdenkmäler in der Moderne* (Munich, 1994), esp. 9–50.

7

Regulating Participation: Patriotism, Citizenship and Gender

A few days before the Prussian King Friedrich Wilhelm III officially declared war against Napoleonic France in March 1813, the Silesian newspaper *Schlesische Provinzialblätter* wrote:

If the feeling for domestic happiness, paternal care, quiet, unadorned and thus all the truer and more profound religiosity must be awakened in the people from above, moving and urging them to emulation, then the image of our beloved king in the circle of his family rises before us, splendid and edifying; a dignified, deeply loved and loving father to his children, resting from the heavy and burdensome business of an eventful era in the company of his offspring, a model of every civic virtue.[1]

The article called on male readers to follow the king's example and "ennoble and improve" both their public activities and their domestic lives according to his model.[2] In this way they would prove themselves to be "worthy" sons of the "beloved father of the country [...] So that the German spirit and way of thinking may arise ever more amongst us, and we may increasingly reject the tattered, shallow and undomestic life with which foreigners have sought to inoculate us, and turn away in contempt."[3]

Like many other publications at the time of the Anti-Napoleonic Wars, this article propagated the image of the Prussian nation as a *Volk* family. This image organized the participation of men and women of different generations, familial statuses and regional and social backgrounds in the nation in a seemingly "natural" fashion, while simultaneously serving to contain demands for increased political participation in the state. At the head of the Prussian *Volk* family was the monarch as the "father," and at his side the queen as the "mother of the people"; the two were bound to each other,

---

[1] "Chronik. Breslau," *SP*, no. 3, March 1813, 254–261, 256–257.
[2] This chapter is based on Karen Hagemann, "The First Citizen of the State: Paternal Masculinity, Patriotism and Citizenship in Early Nineteenth-Century Prussia," in Dudink et al., *Representing*, 67–88.
[3] "Chronik. Breslau," 257.

as to their children and subjects, in love and solicitude. At the same time, in his role as supreme military commander, the father of the people also led the fraternal community of valorous male "citizens of the state." He was even stylized as the "first citizen of his state." The mother of the people served as a model and teacher for the fatherland's daughters, who, like her, performed their patriotic duties in the domestic and familial sphere.[4] Together with their subjects/children, the royal couple thus promoted the liberation of the Prussian nation with their readiness to act and make sacrifices. The key figure in this image was Friedrich Wilhelm III rather than his very popular wife Queen Louise, a circumstance that scholars have ignored up until now.[5]

In the following chapter, I explore the contemporary discourse on patriotism, citizenship and gender, in which opinion leaders from different political camps tried to define the desirable forms of participation for various social groups in the nation and the state. The focus will be on the image of the nation as a *Volk* family and the contested concept of paternal masculinity represented by the king, which vied with more liberal ideas of male citizenship. The analysis of this discourse is important if we wish to understand the diverse meanings of citizenship in the political culture of the period. At the turn of the nineteenth century, when Europe was constrained by revolution and war, different concepts of and paths to citizenship coexisted and competed. Britain and France are only two important examples; despite all differences in their political systems and cultures, they were both centralized states that were evolving into nation-states. German Central Europe, with its very different form of political organization, is another equally important case.

Although the German Confederation of 1815 with its 39 territorial states had only a relatively small number of members compared to the hundreds of German states and principalities of the Holy Roman Empire, it was still a variegated patchwork. Unlike in France, the idea of a centralized nation-state found very little support in German Central Europe during and after the Anti-Napoleonic Wars, for the political aims of the elites were strong territorial states in a federative nation (*Föderative Nation*), represented politically by a German federation and unified culturally by the idea of the Christian-German *Kulturnation*. Even the German nationalists supported this agenda. Because of this specific political landscape, historical analysis needs to distinguish between nation and state, which helps us to understand not only the political developments in this region, but also

---

[4] Wilhelm Anton von Klewitz, ed., *Denkmal der Preußen für ihre verewigte Königin Luise, durch weibliche Erziehungsanstalten* (Halberstadt, 1814), 6–7.

[5] Thus far, the research has focused solely on Queen Louise; see Demandt, *Luisenkult*, 11–16; important new publications aside from Demandt's book include Regina Schulte, "The Queen – A Middle-Class Tragedy: The Writing of History and the Creation of Myths in Nineteenth-Century France and Germany," *G&H* 14 (2002): 266–293; Schönpflug, *Luise*; Förster, *Königin*.

the gendered rhetoric of political discourse. Furthermore, an awareness of important national differences in the terminology is necessary. The English terms "citizen" and "citizenship" do not represent the German discourse of the nineteenth century, which distinguished between *Bürger* (members of the educated middle class), *Stadtbürger* (approved members of a municipality), *Staatsangehörige* (subjects of a territorial state or nation-state), *Staatseinwohner* (all people living in a territorial state), *Unterthanen* (subjects of a king) and *Staatsbürger* (citizens of a territorial state or nation-state with political, civil and social rights).[6] These peculiarities formed the discourse on patriotism, citizenship and gender, especially masculinity.

SUBJECTS, BÜRGER AND CITIZENS

There is widespread agreement in the literature that the law of descent (*ius sanguinis*) has always been a characteristic of German legislation and practice related to citizenship and nationhood. Rogers Brubaker and others explain this as a consequence of the "peculiarities" of German nationalism.[7] This statement needs further nuancing for the period of the early nineteenth century because of the complicated relationship between the nation and the state(s). In Prussia, as in other territorial states at that time, *Staatsangehörigkeit* was defined mainly by the law of birthplace (*ius soli*) or functions of it – that is, naturalization – which was granted on the basis either of military or civil service or residence in the state for a certain number of years (normally ten). The definition of *Staatsangehörigkeit* in the Prussian legal code, the General State Law for the Prussian States (*Allgemeines Preußisches Landrecht*) of 1794, however, was still an ambivalent mixture of these systematic modern regulations and the older regulations of the estate regime. Men could become *Staatsangehörige* without being *Staatsbürger* possessing equal political citizenship rights.[8]

The term *Staatsangehöriger* was a further elaboration and generalization of the older term *Stadtbürger*.[9] In the early modern municipalities, only a very small number of male inhabitants were approved as *Stadtbürger*. The Prussian Municipal Ordinance (*Städteordnung*) enacted on 19 November 1808 to arouse "a sense of public spirit" represented a first step toward greater

---

[6] For a recent discussion of the terms, see Andreas Fahrmeir, *Citizens and Aliens: Foreigners and the Law in Britain and the German States, 1789–1870* (Oxford, 2000), 16–42; and Dieter Gosewinkel, *Einbürgern und Ausschließen: Die Nationalisierung der Staatsangehörigkeit vom Deutschen Bund zur Bundesrepublik Deutschland* (Göttingen, 2001), 27–66.

[7] Rogers Brubaker, *Citizenship and Nationhood in France and Germany* (Cambridge, MA, 1992), 72; and Huber, *Verfassungsgeschichte*, 1:351.

[8] *Allgemeines Landrecht für die Preußischen Staaten* (ALR) (Berlin, 1 Juni 1794), pt. 2, 1 and 2 (http://opinioiuris.de/quelle/1621) (Accessed 11 November 2013); see also Gosewinkel, *Einbürgern*, 67–69.

[9] Koselleck, *Preußen*, 87–88 and 660–662.

political participation on the local level. In the future, all "respectable" male business or property owners with sufficient income (the amount depended on the size of the town) would be recognized as citizens (*Bürger*); the regulation no longer used the old term "town citizen" (*Stadtbürger*). However, the percentage of citizens in Prussian towns remained small after 1808; in Berlin, for example, the proportion was only 7 percent. This percentage increased, after the wars of 1813–15, when the Prussian government awarded all men who had fulfilled their military duties in these wars the status of *Bürger* in their municipalities.[10]

Military service had already been one of the most important duties of a *Stadtbürger* in older town regulations.[11] When the Prussian government introduced universal conscription in March 1813 for the duration of the wars, it also promised all men who willingly fulfilled their military duties a constitution and increased political rights, at least on the municipal level.[12] Especially important was an ordinance of 9 February 1813, which outlined what would happen to those who sought to evade the "obligation of each citizen capable of bearing arms to defend his fatherland." Men who did not yet have citizenship rights in their municipality were to be "excluded from citizenship (*Bürgerrecht*) for their entire life." Those who were already town citizens were threatened with the loss of those rights and, in some cases, of their license to engage in a trade. In addition, evaders would be "excluded from the honor" of "ever being allowed to hold public or municipal office." Fathers or guardians "who deliberately hindered their sons or wards from entering military service or, if they wished to volunteer," refused "to supply them with the necessary equipment according to their means," faced the same punishment. With this provision, for the first time the Prussian state created a direct legal connection between compulsory military service and citizenship rights. In the future, only men who fulfilled their obligation to defend the fatherland would enjoy the rights of active and passive citizenship in their municipalities, then later in the territorial states and finally in the nation-state.[13]

In the context of this development, the term *Bürger* had a double meaning: on the one hand it applied to men with political rights (in the sense of citizens of a town or the state), and on the other it referred to any man who belonged to the socially and culturally defined *Bürgertum*, the middle class, which shared a style of living that crossed the borders of the territorial states.[14] The first time the word *Staatsbürger* was used in a Prussian law

[10] Bruer, *Geschichte*, 269.
[11] Hagemann, *Muth*, 299–302.
[12] Walter, *Heeresreformen*, 235–325.
[13] "Nähere Bestimmung zur Verordnung vom 9. Februar 1813," in Generalstab, *Heer*, 2:388.
[14] Jürgen Kocka, ed., *Bürger und Bürgerlichkeit im 19. Jahrhundert* (Göttingen, 1987), 21–30.

was in 1812, when the government enacted the Jewish emancipation edict, which declared all Jewish men to be *Staatsbürger* of the Prussian territorial state without granting them equal civil and political rights. The edict used the word more in the sense of *Staatsangehöriger*. Not until 1814–15, in the context of debates about the political constitution of the German Confederation stimulated by the Congress of Vienna, did early-liberal publicists start to use the word *Staatsbürger* in a manner similar to the English word "citizen." Political citizenship in the territorial state and the German Confederation created by the Congress of Vienna in June 1815 now became one of their key aims.[15]

A grasp of this complex German terminology is important for understanding the political discourse of the time, which clearly distinguished between the nation, the nation-state and the territorial state. Because of the broad acceptance in patriotic circles of the ideas of a federative nation and a constitutional monarchy as the best paths to greater national unity and a more democratic government in the territorial states and the future German Federation, the image of the nation as a *Volk* family and the king as the "father of the nation" and the "first citizen of the state" became more important in the political discourse.

THE NATION AS VALOROUS VOLK FAMILY

The notion of the state and nation as a family had already been formulated in ideal-typical terms for Prussia in the 1790s. Contemporary political discourse increasingly glorified Friedrich Wilhelm III and Louise of Prussia, who had married in December 1793, as the model of a loving couple representing enlightened middle-class family virtues.[16] After Friedrich Wilhelm III succeeded to the throne in September 1797, this idea was propagated in particular in the *Jahrbücher der preußischen Monarchie unter der Regierung Friedrich Wilhelms III.*, edited by the Romantic writer Friedrich Schlegel.[17] This periodical, published between 1798 and 1801 in Berlin, painted a picture of Prussia under Friedrich Wilhelm III as an enlightened monarchy, a *Volk* family, with the loving royal couple as "father and mother of the people," in contrast to the former King Friedrich Wilhelm II, whose mode of rule it criticized as absolutist and whose court and lifestyle it deemed to be dissolute, ostentatious and wasteful. The *Jahrbücher* used the programmatic juxtaposition of absolutist and enlightened styles of rule to propagate the

---

[15] See Fahrmeir, *Citizens*, 16–42; and Gosewinkel, *Einbürgern*, 27–66.

[16] Wulf Wülfing, "Die heilige Luise von Preußen: Zur Mythisierung einer Figur der Geschichte in der deutschen Literatur des 19. Jahrhunderts," in *Bewegung und Stillstand in Metaphern und Mythen: Fallstudien zum Verhältnis von elementarem Wissen und Literatur im 19. Jahrhundert*, ed. Jürgen Link and Wulf Wülfing (Stuttgart, 1984), 233–275.

[17] "Die Herausgeber der Jahrbücher u.s.w. an ihre Leser," *Jahrbücher der preußischen Monarchie* 1 (1798): 1–6. On Schlegel, see Jure Zovko, "Schlegel, Carl Wilhelm Friedrich von," *NDB* 23 (2007): 40–42.

community-building image of a "great family of the people," which shared middle-class values within and stood together against all threats and perils from without.[18] This image became increasingly popular in educated circles of the monarchy at the turn of the century.

After the Prussian defeat of 1806–07, a new dimension was added in the context of the patriotic-national mobilization for a war of revenge against France. The romantic image was increasingly nationalized and militarized. Patriotic writers now declared the royal family to be the model par excellence for the desired rejection of *Ausländerei*, the worship of all things foreign, and a re-embracing of "Prussian- and Germanness" in the home and family. Friedrich Wilhelm III and Queen Louise were stylized as a counter-model to Napoleon and his first and second wives, who, it was said, incarnated all the negative attributes of the "Gallic foe" and "dissolute" French family life.[19] In this way, the public presentation of the royal family was adapted to the changing demands of the times.[20] In order to foster a broad patriotic-national mobilization of the whole nation, the government and its patriotic supporters increasingly propagated the image of the Prussian nation as a "valorous" *Volk* family, which became dominant during the wars of 1813–15.[21]

Of course, the notion of the state and nation as an extended family looked back on a long tradition.[22] What was new in the late eighteenth- and early nineteenth-century German discourse, however, was the specific form this idea took: The relationship between the "father of the people" and his subjects/children was now no longer to be based on fear and obedience, but on love and loyalty. The modern middle-class family ideal, and with it the hierarchical and complementary model of the gender order, which for the first time was justified in biological-anthropological terms and claimed universal validity, was thus integrated into the old doctrines of the state. The anthropologization and emotionalization of political concepts that accompanied their nationalization was intended to help in this context to level the opposition between monarch and subjects, and at the same time to legitimize as natural the inequalities between ranks, strata, generations

---

[18] Stamm-Kuhlmann, *König*, 148.

[19] Hagemann, *Muth*, 222–271.

[20] For more on this, see Karen Hagemann, "A Valorous *Volk* Family: The Nation, the Military, and the Gender Order in Prussia in the Time of the Anti-Napoleonic Wars, 1806–15," in Blom et al., *Gendered Nations*, 179–205.

[21] See Hagemann, *Muth*, 271–303; and the first part.

[22] On the early modern discourse, see Gotthardt Frühsorge, "Die Begründung der 'väterlichen Gesellschaft' in der europäischen oeconomia christiana: Zur Rolle des Vaters in der 'Hausväterliteratur' des 16. bis 18. Jahrhunderts in Deutschland," in *Das Vaterbild im Abendland I: Rom, Frühes Christentum, Mittelalter, Neuzeit, Gegenwart*, ed. Hubertus Tellenbach (Stuttgart, 1978), 110–123; and Paul Münch, "Die 'Obrigkeit im Vaterstand' – Zu Definition und Kritik des 'Landesvaters' während der frühen Neuzeit," *Daphnis* 11 (1982): 15–40.

and genders, and to bridge them through emotional ties. This was supposed to do more than merely encourage the patriotic-national readiness to fight and sacrifice that was necessary for a "people's war." At the same time, it was intended to prevent the population from following the American and French examples, calling into question the monarchy as a political form more generally and demanding fundamental changes in the political system. On the one hand, the patriotically and nationally charged patriarchal and hierarchical concept of the *Volk* family took up patriotic-national rhetoric and adapted government language to the zeitgeist, which was necessary to obtain broader support. On the other, the politically explosive nature of this rhetoric was mitigated by the concept's inherent idea of the "natural quality" of the various differences and hierarchies, which corresponded to differing duties and rights. Thus, for example, exclusions of all sorts from the community of *Bürger* in the municipality, the territorial state and the nation-state could easily be justified as "natural," as could exclusion from the nation, as we have seen. The central role in this model of the Prussian monarchy as a family was played by the image of Friedrich Wilhelm III, which underwent a remarkable modernization in the context of patriotic-national mobilization for the "Wars of Liberation" and postwar discourse and played a very important but overlooked role for the development of competing contemporary concepts of male citizenship and their complex political, social and cultural meanings.

FATHER OF HIS COUNTRY AND FIRST CITIZEN OF HIS STATE

The image of Friedrich Wilhelm III as the caring and pious father of his country and of Louise as the loving mother dominated in the Prussian media until 1813. The royal couple's return to Berlin in December 1809 was the first major event after the defeat of 1806 that was used to shape and popularize this image in the whole monarchy. Since the withdrawal of the French troops in December 1808, many committed patriots had pinned their hopes on the royal family's imminent return from Königsberg to Berlin, which they interpreted as a sign of a general turn for the better. The preparations were accordingly intensive. Sermons preached from pulpits up and down the country sought to prepare the public for this event. All of the towns and villages that the royal couple was expected to pass through prepared celebrations.[23] After the court announced that the royal family would remain in Königsberg for the time being, preparations were put on hold, but they resumed one year later when the return became definite. In early December of 1809, Friedrich Wilhelm III himself laid down precise instructions for

---

[23] "Immediat-Bericht des Staats-Ministers von Voss, Berlin, 7. Dez. 1808," in Granier, *Berichte*, 317–319, also 324–325 and 334–336.

the festivities. He was particularly concerned that they be kept "plain and simple" and integrate all elements of the "citizenry" (*Bürgerschaft*) of Berlin, for he wished to present himself to his subjects as a solicitous and pious father of his people.[24] The royal couple's entry was to form the centerpiece of the festivities. The monarch wanted to enter Berlin at the head of his troops – followed by his wife and children. Unlike his father and grandfather, he insisted that his family be part of the procession because he wanted to present himself not primarily as a military leader, but as a good head and father of his family, and his country as well. A civic guard and rifle associations were to maintain order and the city authorities, town councilors and clergy were permitted to form a "portal of honor" to greet the king.[25] Apart from the queen and her daughters, the actors in this ceremonial ritual were exclusively male, foremost among them the generals and the educated official elite of the capital. Their appearance in full dress uniform or gala official robes marked their respective significance in the power structure of public space as well as their specific relationships to the monarch. Through their parade or march-past, the military, civic guard and rifle associations demonstrated the valorousness of the Prussian nation assembled around the steadfast father of the people.

The sermons preached throughout the kingdom on the occasion of the ruler's return also glorified the caring and pious father of his country. Typical of these was a homily already given in December 1808 in honor of the hoped-for event and published nearly a year later in a popular journal for clergymen. The sermon describes the monarch as the father of his country who, like any good paterfamilias, manages his nation and the royal household justly, frugally and with an eye to the common good.[26] It suggests to the congregation that, regardless of all the misery and sorrows of recent years, they should trust cheerfully in the king's return, for he had proved himself throughout his "entire reign" to be a "kind friend of humanity" and "loving father of the people." This offered hope for the future. But one could not expect too much of the king. The "decline of the fatherland" was too great, "its wounds" too deep and "the exhaustion" too universal "for recovery and improvement to occur soon without patient persistence, constant laborious effort and willing sacrifice." Then God, too, would stand by the fatherland, for the emergency could only be mastered if everyone worked together.[27] The poetry of the interwar years praised Friedrich Wilhelm III in a similar way.[28] Deviating from the tradition of panegyric, the monarch

---

[24] Friedrich Wilhelm III, "Instruktion zum Einzuge SM des Königs in Berlin, Königsberg, 5 Dez. 1809," in ibid., 563–564.

[25] Ibid., 561–563, 551–554 and 559–560.

[26] "Predigt am 1. Adventssonntage 1808," *GMP* 3.3 (1809): 41–48; "Predigt am 2. Adventssonntage 1808," in ibid., 48–56.

[27] Ibid., 44–45; on the later period, see Herrosee, *Rede*, 6.

[28] *Lieder für Preußische Soldaten*.

is lauded not as a glorious, mighty ruler and a strong and courageous general to whom soldiers owed allegiance and obedience.[29] Praise was reserved instead for his patriotism and devotion to the welfare of his people, his sense of duty and his virtue, decency, piety, kindness and fairness, and even his "domesticity."[30]

During the wars of 1813–15 the image of the king changed. The official war propaganda now increasingly emphasized his role as a courageous military leader alongside that of a caring father.[31] Typical of the many royal proclamations that were distributed as leaflets by the army, reprinted in newspapers and read aloud in church services is the appeal "To the Inhabitants" of the liberated western Prussian territories of September 1813. It presents Friedrich Wilhelm III as both a heroic military commander and a compassionate father and ends with an appeal to the inhabitants of the former Prussian territories to commit themselves to the liberation of Prussia and Germany under the leadership of the beloved father of their country.[32] This proclamation, like others published during the wars, lent a new facet to the image of the king. He now became a masculine role model for the sons of his people not just as a paterfamilias, but also as a warrior. After the great victories of the coalition troops in the late summer and fall of 1813, the media stylized the Prussian monarch, along with the Russian tsar, more and more as *the* war hero par excellence.[33] An excellent example is the victory celebration for the entry of the coalition armies into Paris on 31 March 1814. The numerous songs and poems published for this occasion no longer praised Friedrich Wilhelm III merely as the liberator of Prussia, but also as the heroic savior of all of Germany, a "hero king" of all Germans and "tutelary god of German liberty."[34]

The glorification of the Prussian king reached a climax with the monarch's solemn entry into Berlin on 7 August 1814 on the occasion of the return of the first victorious troops. To be sure, the king had refused to allow any celebrations that referred exclusively to his person and suggested

[29] "Es lebe das Haus wohl von Berlin," in *Die Historischen Volkslieder des siebenjährigen Krieges nebst geschichtlichen und sonstigen Erläuterungen*, ed. Franz Wilhelm Freiherr von Ditfurth (Berlin, 1871), 76–78.

[30] "Heil dem König," in *Lieder für Preußische Soldaten*, 6–7; and "Unser König," in ibid., 5–6.

[31] Hagemann, *Muth*, 97–105 and 128–157.

[32] "An die Bewohner der Altmark, des Herzogthums Magdeburg, des Fürstenthums Halberstadt und der übrigen preußischen Staaten jenseits der Elbe, September 1813," *PC*, no. 110, 9 Oct. 1813.

[33] Christian Wilhelm Spieker, "Altarrede bei der Vereidigung der Frankfurter Landwehr im Frühjahr 1813," in idem, *Gebete, Predigten und Reden: Zur Zeit der Erhebung des Preußischen Volks gegen die Tyrannei des Auslandes, im Felde und in der Heimath gehalten* (Berlin, 1816), 93–107.

[34] "Geburtstagsfest unseres allerverehrten Königs in Halberstädt 1814," supplement to *BN*, no. 93, 4 August 1814.

instead an honorable welcome for the "guards, as representatives of the whole army returning triumphant from the field."[35] He nevertheless entered the city at the head of the guards as supreme commander of the army, and was greeted with loud cheers by the massed populace lining the road. The extraordinarily lavish celebrations now centered only on the regular army and its heroic commander Friedrich Wilhelm III.[36]

This took up an eighteenth-century tradition going back to the monarch's great-uncle Friedrich II: the celebration of the Prussian king as a heroic leader of his army. The manner in which Friedrich Wilhelm III was presented was different, however. The newspapers reported that the sermons at the center of the worship services to be held in every church to mark this event praised him as a model not only for other monarchs, but also for all "citizens of the state." A typical sermon, preached during the celebrations and reprinted in a theological magazine as a model for other pastors, paid homage to Friedrich Wilhelm III as the father of his people and a "heroic leader" and praised him as "prudent and daring, courageous and valiant, manly and firm." The sermon went on to note that he had performed deeds "worthy of his throne and his forefathers," which "enrapture and render his name great before the peoples and princes of the earth." Yet he had remained humble and, thus, in the eyes of citizens,

great and admirable above all others: through the modesty with which he clothes them [his deeds], the humility with which he adorns them, the leniency and gener-osity toward the conquered foe with which he crowns them; when he returns home to his people from perils and battles as a hero and victor the like of which the world rarely sees, saved and protected, glorified and exalted by an invisible hand, he stands before our eyes as a wonder.[37]

The mythologizing of the Prussian king could hardly have been taken any further: the king as a "wonder" in the eyes of his subjects. This recalls the old belief in the ability of kings to perform miracles[38] and yet differs substan-tially from it, for part of the mythologizing of Friedrich Wilhelm III was his embourgeoisement. He appeared to be a wonder precisely because, despite his noble origins, he had preserved the middle-class virtues and performed his heroic deeds not for the sake of glory, but for his country, which he led valiantly as the father of his people. Even the man, praised as a princely hero, remained a citizens' king (*Bürgerkönig*) and was, as it were, the chief

---

[35] "Feierlicher Einzug Sr. Maj. des Königs und der königlichen Garden zu Berlin am 7ten August," pts. 1–2, *ZfeW*, no. 163, 28 Aug. 1814, and no. 164, 19 Aug. 1814.

[36] Ibid.

[37] "Predigt am 9. Sonntage nach Trinitatis, den 7. Aug. 1814: Als der König seinen feyerlichen Einzug hielt," pt. 2, *NM* (1817): 227–236, 231.

[38] See Marc Bloch, *The Royal Touch: Sacred Monarchy and Scrofula in England and France,* trans. J. E. Anderson (London, 1973; first publ. Paris, 1924).

national warrior. He set off to battle at the head of his people to free the fatherland.

During and even after the wars of 1813–15 it was not just the large number of conservative monarchist journalists, but also the small group of German-national authors who enthusiastically contributed to this image. The latter long exercised remarkable reticence in their criticisms of Friedrich Wilhelm III, despite the fact that he did nothing to put into practice the promises of a constitution that he had made several times during the war, nor was there any hope of realizing even the modest early-liberal demands of freedom of speech and assembly. Instead, from 1814 on, German-national authors increasingly criticized government policy while continuing to publish prose and poetry glorifying Friedrich Wilhelm III as a popular citizens' king. A typical example is *The Celebrations of Allegiance at Aachen on 14 May 1815* by Arndt.[39] In the introduction to this pamphlet about the festivities held in the Rhine province on the occasion of their incorporation into the Prussian kingdom in the spring of 1815, he formulates his expectations of the Prussian king: "The new ruler has made a great vow to his people, which receives him as a prince and a father. He will neither weaken nor break his royal word."[40] Arndt emphasizes that the king had "taken on an honorable but perilous office with his Rhenish territories." He was now the "champion and frontier guardian of the Germans against mighty kingdoms in the east and west." This office could "be worthily maintained only through a noble cultivation of the German spirit and German virtue, a just administration, a great military order and a constitution appropriate to the requirements of the epoch and the character and education of the German people." A "government that had grown great through the early liberation of the human spirit could not refuse" these "loud demands" of the age.[41]

As Arndt's remarks demonstrate, German-national authors adopted the image of the Prussian king as the father of his people and a model for subjects and monarchs alike, but pursued their own interests in the process. In this way they sketched their ideal of a "good prince and ruler" who governed in an enlightened manner and was prepared to make the political reforms they called for and to recognize the achievements of "the people," defined as the community of *Bürger* (conceived of here as educated middle-class men), in the "Wars of Liberty," in which they had fought for both liberation and liberty. At the same time, they formulated a counterimage to the many rulers, great and small, in the other territorial states who believed that once Germany was liberated they could return, unaltered and unhindered, to their old absolutist style of governing. This countermodel also

[39] Ernst Moritz Arndt, *Die Huldigungsfeier in Aachen am 15ten Mai 1815* (Aachen, 1815); and "Übersicht der neuesten Zeitereignisse," *RM*, no. 104, Aug. 1814.
[40] Arndt, *Huldigungsfeier*, I.
[41] Ibid., II.

allowed the German-national writers to raise criticisms of those elements of the Prussian government that tended toward restoration without fundamentally calling into question the king or the system of monarchy. They did so by distinguishing between the citizen-king and the conservative noble camarilla in high court positions, which tried to influence the king's politics in their own interest. German-national and early-liberal political journalists thus promoted their program of political reform using the idealized image of the Prussian monarch.[42]

This becomes clear in a comparison with texts that reflected generally on the desired form of a monarchy and the requirements of a "good prince."[43] These included *What Is to Be Done at the Rebirth of Germany and Europe?* by Arnold Mallinckrodt, a member of the Düsseldorf provincial council. The piece appeared as a pamphlet in Dortmund in December 1813 and was also reprinted in several journals.[44] In this work, Mallinckrodt proceeds from the assertion that the "awakening spirit" of the German tribes (*deutsche Volksstämme*) and their altered relationship to one another rendered "political constitutions" necessary. He demands them for the territorial states as well as for the aspired-to German federation, then goes on to develop the entire early-liberal catalogue of reforms, closing with the "fine image" of a "good ruler" as the first servant and citizen of the state (*Diener und Bürger des Staates*):

Oh, it is a lofty, honorable lot to be a prince! The visible image of God here on earth. The Eternal has entrusted great things to him, the happiness of the people at whose helm he stands. Good himself, he desires only the good: Truth and justice are the principles of his striving and actions; to ennoble his people and make them happy his highest aims. He sees in himself the first civil servant of the state, there for the people, and not the people for his sake. Though filled with manly valor in the defense of the fatherland, never will he be a conqueror, nay, but like the deity a friend of peace. Suffused with true religious sentiment, he honors and promotes religious sentiment everywhere, without bigotry. [...] Strictly moral, he is a model and example of good and decent behavior to his subjects, permitting himself nothing that is not allowed by law and morality to each of them.[45]

Mallinckrodt's expectations corresponded to the idealized image of Friedrich Wilhelm III. Like him, the good prince should be characterized by a will to truth and a sense of justice, concern for the welfare of his people, religiosity and morality, courage and manliness, a desire for peace and a readiness

[42] Ibid., 5–7 and 14–20.
[43] See, for example, "Ueber das Verhaeltnis der Religion zum Kriegszustand," *Leuchtkugeln* 1.2 (1815): 269–287; and "Zum neuen Jahr," *Wächter* 3 (1816): 13–206, 42–46.
[44] Arnold Mallinckrodt, "Was thun bey Teutschlands, bey Europas Wiedergeburt? I–III," *TB*, no. 46, 21 April 1814, no. 48, 25 April 1814, and no. 51, 2 May 1814; on Mallinckrodt, see Silvia Backs, "Mallinckrodt, Arnold," *NDB* 15 (1987): 732–733.
[45] Mallinckrodt, "Was thun bey Teutschlands," no. 46.

to fight when necessary and thus serve as an example for his subjects as a citizen of the state. Mallinckrodt expected of the subject, in turn, that he would be a "good man" and a "good citizen" in the sense of *Bürger* as a middle-class man. The heart of this *Bürger* should beat "warmly" for his country and monarch, and should be enlarged by "public spirit and love for the common good," so that he would follow the laws "faithfully" and pay the taxes and duties imposed on him by the state honestly. Moreover, he should willingly do his duty to defend the fatherland, fight openly for truth and justice, earn his bread honorably in his profession and, not least, be loving and considerate toward his fellow human beings.[46]

This ideal of a "good citizen" (*Bürger*) was that of an all-around perfect man who fulfilled the demands made upon him by society, the economy and his family in his own small circle of work and life, just as the prince did in his larger world. The ideal became especially popular in the postwar period and was the demilitarized complement to the wartime model of patriotic-valorous masculinity. Unlike during wartime, this version no longer focused on valor as the key male virtue, but instead on active patriotism. The following five basic ideas made up the normative foundation of this postwar model: First, adult men were conceived of as married; only after founding a family was a man accepted into their community.[47] Associated with this was, second, the right and duty to be the head, breadwinner and protector of the family.[48] Third, a man could only fulfill the last function if he was "valorous" – that is, prepared and willing to risk his life to defend family, home and fatherland. Tied to this was, fourth, masculine honor, which, at least theoretically, was for the first time accorded to, and also demanded of, all men and not just aristocrats. Finally, only the adult man prepared to bear arms could claim the political rights of a citizen. Military service was made a precondition of citizen status. Men who shirked this duty were considered to be "dishonorable" and "unmanly." In the thinking of educated patriots, the claim to citizen status was also inevitably tied to education and property as well as the Christian faith. In this way, all men were required to perform military service if they wanted to become citizens (*Bürger*) in their municipalities, while the overwhelming majority of them were excluded from political citizenship on the level of the territorial state and the future nation-state. For young men in this construct, military service, as proof of the ability to bear arms, became a rite of passage not just to adult masculinity but also to male citizenship. Later, especially during the Democratic Revolution of 1848–49, the demand of democrats to extend political citizenship rights to

---

[46] Ibid.
[47] Hull, *Sexuality*, 409.
[48] *ARL*, pt. 2, 1 and 2; see Marion Gray, "Men as Citizens and Women as Wives: The Enlightenment Codification of Law and the Establishment of Separated Spheres," in *Reich oder Nation? Mitteleuropa 1780 – 1815*, ed. Heinz Duchhardt and Andreas Kunz (Mainz, 1998), 279–298.

all men would become a source of political conflict. Such radical ideas were not very widespread during and after the wars of 1813–15, however.

One of the rare examples is the anonymous booklet *A German Word Spoken to German Citizens* (*Staatsbürger*), which appeared at the end of 1813 in Leipzig. It addressed all "candid" men of every rank who were ready and able to bear arms, and included in this "league of citizens" (*Bund der Staatsbürger*) the "citizen on the throne" (*Staatsbürger auf dem Thron*). Because the term *Staatsbürger* was still quite unusual in the German-speaking lands and awakened associations with the political discourse in enemy France and its key term *citoyen*, its author felt compelled to emphasize that it was a term not of disapproval, but of the utmost respect. Princes could receive no higher praise from a German man than this:

You are the first citizens of the state (*Staatsbürger*), to whom, presuming higher wisdom, the loftiest and most important duties in leading the whole have been entrusted; and as the first citizens of the state you are, in the faithful and conscientious fulfillment of your duties, men before whom he joyfully bows his head in the deepest veneration.[49]

Such formulations and the use of the term *Staatsbürger* in its political meaning were very new and clearly influenced by the French Revolution. They signaled a departure from the image of the nation as a father-centered *Volk* family. The pamphlet focuses on the state, does not discuss the nation, and no longer addresses the monarch as the father of his people. He has been wholly divested of his divine nature and turned into a primus inter pares in the state, understood in the German context as a territorial state. This state had evolved into a male club. It is therefore hardly surprising that the entire pamphlet speaks exclusively of *men* as citizens (*Staatsbürger*) and brothers, each with specific tasks in the community of brothers (*Gemeinschaft der Brüder*) according to rank and generation. Women, whom contemporary German discourse conceptualized as an important part of the nation, but not of the state, are mentioned not at all. A fraternal concept of masculinity and citizenship has replaced a paternal one here.

During and after the wars against Napoleon, scarcely any of the German-national and early-liberal authors followed the virile radicalism of this text, which constructs the state as a fraternity and demands equal political citizenship rights for all men regardless of rank. In their visions of the future political order, even after the war, most continued to use the topos of state and nation as a family and to perceive the German nation as a cultural one whose political framework should be a monarchical confederation of states, the German Federation.[50] But they began to demand more political

[49] *Wort zu deutschen Bürgern* (n.p., 1813), 5.
[50] Ludwig Wachler, *Ernste Worte der Vaterlandsliebe an alle, welche Deutsche sind und bleiben wollen* (Deutschland [Marburg], 1813), 24; and Friedrich Jacobs, *Deutschlands Ehre:*

rights on the national level, too. Since the political debates remained within the framework of the monarchical system, early-liberal authors – similar to more conservative propagandists – deployed the model of the ideal king as first citizen to promote their own political demands in a manner that conformed to the system and the rules of censorship. Furthermore, after the Anti-Napoleonic Wars, both groups were interested in adapting the universally accepted model of patriotic-valorous masculinity to the requirements of peacetime societies. Therefore, they now emphasized the civilian virtues more. Thus an article on "Monarchism and Despotism" that appeared in June 1815 in the journal *Rußlands Triumpf 1812 oder das erwachte Europa*, edited by the Prussian official and writer Karl Müchler, asserted:

As the father of his people, a noble prince is to his country what the paterfamilias is to the members of his household; the former guards, protects and cares for the whole kingdom as the latter does for his entire domestic establishment. He keeps order everywhere and guides everything to a good and noble end, the ennoblement of the people.[51]

For "the good prince" as for "the good citizen" (*Bürger*), the degree of his patriotic virtuousness in peacetime depended decisively on his qualities as a paterfamilias. Only a prince who cared for his people and his family and defended and managed the state like his own household was considered to be truly good and noble; only a man who headed his household in an orderly fashion, and cared for and protected his family was a "good citizen," for a "bad paterfamilias" could never be a good citizen.[52]

The analysis of the discourse on patriotism, citizenship and gender shows, first of all, that the dominant model of patriotic-valorous masculinity was so strongly "generalized" in the context of the Anti-Napoleonic Wars that it applied even to the Prussian king. He was glorified as the very incarnation and exemplar of this model for all men, and thereby democratized. In the process, he lost the unattainability and inviolability that had been his in the ancien régime and he could now be measured by the same yardstick as other men. It reveals, second, how open and complex the dominant image of masculinity still was in the early nineteenth century. Only in combination with other categories of social and cultural difference (including social stratum, age and marital status) and in association with varying political concepts did it take on specific meanings. This openness not only facilitated its rapid spread and generalization, but also permitted different political groups to make widely disparate use of it. Thus, different versions coexisted, which competed with one another or complemented each other in group- and

---

Dem Andenken der in dem heiligen Kriege gegen Frankreich gefallenen Deutschen gewidmet (Gotha, 1814), 47.

[51] "Monarchismus und Despotismus," *RT* 2.6 (1815): 81–105, 86–87; on Müchler, see Ernst Weber, "Müchler, Karl Friedrich," *NDB* 18 (1997): 261–262.

[52] Jacobs, *Deutschlands Ehre*, 52.

generation-specific terms. Third, an analysis of the image of the king makes clear how large a role "sensibility," "domesticity" and "solicitude" still played in the dominant image of masculinity in early nineteenth-century Germany. These virtues did not stand in contradiction to the qualities of patriotism and valorousness that were now demanded of all men, including the king. They were, rather, the preconditions for these qualities. Without ardent love and concern for the family and provision for an orderly domestic establishment, a man could be neither a patriotic citizen nor a protector of home and defender of country.

Conclusion

In the first two decades of the nineteenth century in Prussia and other parts of Germany, the patriotic-national discourse was to a remarkable extent shaped by war and used for the intellectual mobilization for war. The new form of mass warfare was distinguished not merely by the size of the armies, but also by its infusion with patriotic and national ideologies, which facilitated the mobilization of vast forces, now increasingly composed of conscripts, militias and volunteers, as well as long-service professionals. As conservative regimes like Prussia also deployed mass armies, not only was the conduct of warfare transformed, but the social and gender order and political culture along with it. Soldiers and civilians of all classes – men and women alike – had to be mobilized for war on an unprecedented scale. In 1813–15 the Prussian and other German governments thus promised men political rights in return for military service. They had to use a highly gendered patriotic-national rhetoric in their war propaganda to serve the zeitgeist and gain the support from society, which they needed to be able to win the war against Napoleonic France. Not just conservative-monarchic regents and regencies, but also their early-liberal and German-national opponents used such rhetoric, which led to intensive debates about the meaning of key concepts in the political discourse on nation and state, military and warfare and the social and gender order, both in war and in peacetime.

As this second part has shown, it is crucial not only to understand the contested meanings of these concepts but also the variety of media in which they were discussed and the conditions of their production and distribution. Only if we include this dimension in our analysis can we understand the extent and forms of the patriotic-national mobilization for war in the time between 1806 and 1815, the postwar process of political demobilization and the causes of the long-term legacy of many of the ideas of the time of the Anti-Napoleonic Wars, which influenced the construction of war memories in the future and provided a kind of blueprint for the political and cultural mobilization for subsequent wars based on universal conscription. The influence of the patterns of thinking that were developed in and provided by the patriotic-national discourse in the period of the Anti-Napoleonic Wars in Prussia and Germany are evident in the practical attempts at mobilization and demobilization, the patriotic-national festival culture of the time, and war commemoration, all of which will be explored in the third part.

PART THREE

COLLECTIVE PRACTICES OF DE/MOBILIZATION AND COMMEMORATION

It was one of the finest evenings of my life, when, on the 18th of October, I joined several thousand merry people to stand on the Feldberg, the peak of the Taunus, and saw the sky reddened all around for a great distance by more than five hundred blazes; for the glow of the fires burning on the highest peaks of the Spessart, the Odenwald, the Westerwald and the Donnersberg was visible to us. The news that came later, that on that evening flames glowed in the farthest reaches of the fatherland, was sweet as well.[1]

Ernst Moritz Arndt offers this comment in the preface to the second edition of his *On the Celebrations of the Battle of Leipzig*, which appeared in the late summer of 1815. In this text he describes his emotions on the first evening of the "National Festival of the Germans" (*Deutsches Nationalfest*) which was celebrated in hundreds of towns and villages on 18 and 19 October 1814 to mark the anniversary of the Battle of the Nations at Leipzig. For Arndt, the widely visible fires on the mountaintops linking Germany's various regions must have been a very remarkable experience, since the initiative for these festive bonfires as well as the celebration more generally came largely from him and a small circle of likeminded men, including Jahn. They had met in early May 1814 to discuss the next two projects of the nascent national movement, the initiation of "German Societies" (*Teutsche Gesellschaften*) and the introduction of an annual "Festival of the Battle of Leipzig."[2] Arndt had already suggested both in his pamphlet *Another Word About the French and Us,* and intended them to foster the "preservation and invigoration of German nature and German thought," the "awakening of German strength and discipline" and the "revival of new and old memories"

---

[1] Ernst Moritz Arndt, *Ueber die Feier der Leipziger Schlacht* (Frankfurt/M., 1815, 2nd edn.), 3–4.

[2] Dieter Düding, "Das deutsche Nationalfest von 1814: Matrix der deutschen Nationalfeste im 19. Jahrhundert," in Düding et al., *Öffentliche Festkultur,* 67–88; and Luys, *Anfänge,* 49–50.

of German history.[3] The German Societies were to be founded in all of the larger towns and to accept as members any "German man of blameless reputation." One of their central tasks was to organize the annual National Festival of the Germans, which was supposed to keep alive memories of the period of the "Wars of Liberty" more generally and the outstanding event of the Leipzig Battle of the Nations more specifically, with an emphasis on the role of the people.[4]

The German-national patriots began promoting both projects widely immediately following the meeting in May 1814.[5] Arndt's pamphlets *Sketch for a German Society*, which appeared in August 1814, and *A Word on the Celebration of the Battle of Leipzig*, which came out one month later and soon reached a printing of 7,500, were important vehicles.[6] In their initiative, the patriots took up suggestions that had been discussed for some time. It was apparently not until these two pamphlets by Arndt, however, that the argument proved persuasive enough to find broad support in patriot circles, and the plans were implemented with remarkable speed.[7]

On 18 and 19 October 1814 the suggested National Festival of the Germans, and with it the victory over Napoleon, was celebrated in broad areas of the German-speaking region. The account of the festival, entitled *The German People's Fiery Temple of Gratitude and Honor*, which the Rödelheim counselor of justice Karl Hoffmann[8] compiled on behalf of the initiators, runs to 1,146 pages and documents more than 780 celebrations.[9] A look at the regional newspapers suggests that the total number was far higher, since the report fails to mention events in many small towns and villages. The largest number of ceremonies seems to have taken place in Central and West Germany, where the military governors supported them very actively.[10] But communities throughout North and East Germany also celebrated the national festival. In Prussia the 19th of October was declared an official holiday, on which at least a religious service of thanksgiving was

[3] Arndt, *Noch ein Wort*, 34–38.

[4] Ernst Moritz Arndt, *Ein Wort über die Feier der Leipziger Schlacht* (Frankfurt/M., 1814), 3–4 and 36–37.

[5] On these activities and the *Teutsche Gesellschaften*, see Luys, *Anfänge*, 29–122, esp. 50 and 62–65.

[6] Ernst Moritz Arndt, *Entwurf einer teutschen Gesellschaft* (Frankfurt/M., 1814); and idem, *Wort*; see Schäfer, *Arndt*, 257 and 268.

[7] Kohlrausch, *Deutschlands Zukunft* 24 and 103–132, 110; and Jörg, *Ahndungen*, 87–88; more in Hagemann, *Muth*, 481–497.

[8] On Hoffmann, see Wolfgang Klötzer, "Hoffmann, Karl," *NDB* 9 (1972): 431.

[9] Karl Hoffmann, *Des Teutschen Volkes feuriger Dank- und Ehrentempel oder Beschreibung wie das aus zwanzigjähriger französischer Sklaverei durch Fürsten-Eintracht und Volkskraft gerettete Teutsche Volk die Tage der entscheidenden Völker- und Rettungsschlacht bei Leipzig am 18. und 19. October zum erstenmale gefeiert hat* (Offenbach, 1815), 1133–1146.

[10] Hoffmann, *Volkes*, 209–255, 545–549, 765–829, 1087–1092 and 1123–1131.

to be held.[11] The anniversary of the Leipzig Battle of the Nations continued to be marked in subsequent years as well. With the emerging restoration, however, the support of governments, the military and local authorities waned considerably and the celebrations were halted for the time being in 1818.[12]

The initiative by Arndt, Jahn and other patriots to set up German Societies and create an annual national festival commemorating the Battle of the Nations at Leipzig was an attempt to keep alive the patriotic-national mobilization of the war years – as expressed in such collective practices as the volunteers' movement, extensive local activities to support the newly established militia, war charity, patriotic women's associations and the many patriotic-national celebrations, rituals and symbols – and to continue this young national movement in a new form in postwar society. At the same time, their initiative served to bear in remembrance the wars of 1813–15 as "Wars of Liberty" and "people's wars."

In this third part I explore with a focus on Prussia the varied collective practices of patriotic-national mobilization during the wars of 1813–15 and of cultural demobilization and commemoration in the postwar era. These collective practices were to a great extent shaped by the political discourse of the time in the different print media, which contributed significantly to patriotic-national mobilization before and during the wars. At the same time, festivals, rituals and symbols, in particular, represented central ideas of this patriotic-national discourse in an emotionally accessible manner to broad audiences and thus played a key role in disseminating them beyond the educated strata of society. Early on, the patriots recognized and discussed the significance of festivals, rituals and symbols not only for promoting national spirit, self-sacrifice and the willingness to defend one's country during war, but also for cultural demobilization and commemoration in the postwar era.

A more detailed analysis of these collective practices shows that, at least in Prussia, the intended patriotic-national mobilization appears to have been quite successful during and after the wars of 1813–15, albeit with substantial regional and social variations. Three indicators point to this, which I explore in the first three chapters of this part: First, the extent of mobilization for the militia and the volunteers' movement; second, the scope of wartime charity work, especially the activities of the many patriotic women's associations; and third, the broad acceptance of patriotic-national and military festivals, rituals and symbols developed during and after the wars, whose effects were still felt in the twentieth century. In the fourth chapter of this part I study the legacy of patriotic-national practices developed during the wars of 1813–15 by focusing on the cult of death for the fatherland and the honoring and commemoration of war heroes.

[11] Ibid., 680–764.
[12] Hagemann, *Muth*, 481–497.

8

Military Service: Mobilizing Militiamen and Volunteers

The extent to which men were marshaled for the militia and volunteered in Prussia in 1813 is one indicator of the scale of the population's mobilization for war. Even in retrospect, it is remarkable how quickly the monarchy succeeded in the spring and summer of 1813 – despite all adverse circumstances – in marshaling a large field army that, in coalition with the Russian troops, matched the rapidly reconstructed Grande Armée. As a result of mobilization for the militia and volunteer units, the Prussian army grew from 67,000 men in March 1813 to 245,000 in August 1813; 113,000 of them were in the militia. An additional 49,372 volunteers signed up, of whom 24,841 served in the "national regiments," volunteer rifle (*Jäger*) detachments and volunteer units such as the Lützow Free Corps and 24,531 in the regiments of the standing army and the militia.[1] Resistance to the introduction of universal conscription among the male population was in general astonishingly small. Many young men even volunteered.

Recruitment for the militia and the volunteer units and their equipment, arming and outfitting were all funded and organized by the local communities and thus required the broad support of the civilian population. The militia and volunteer movement, therefore, needs to be conceptualized as a collective practice of patriotic-national war support. The volunteer movement in particular can only be understood in this way, because each volunteer was only accepted as such if he enlisted fully equipped, armed and outfitted. In the equestrian units, the volunteers themselves, their families and friends or sponsors in the community even had to buy their horses, which was quite expensive. The level of this form of war support naturally differed significantly between the various regions, social strata and ethnic groups of the Prussian monarchy. It correlated, as I will demonstrate in this part, with disparities in support for war charity, the spread of the patriotic

---

[1] Generalstab, *Heer*, 2:458–551, esp. 548–551; Müsebeck, *Gaben*, 112.

women's associations and the level of acceptance of patriotic-national culture.[2] A more detailed analysis of the regional and social differences in military mobilization within Prussia thus helps us to understand the complex interplay of factors that influenced more general patriotic-national mobilization for war in the old and new territories of the monarchy and far beyond.

THE PRUSSIAN MILITIA

The introduction and organization of the militia was regulated in Prussia by an edict of 17 March 1813 and its supplementary provisions, which stipulated that any man between the ages of 17 and 40 capable of fighting was liable for military service. The militia was conceived of primarily as a volunteer force, whose members would immediately attain the rank of lance corporal (*Gefreiter*). Only if the number of volunteers was insufficient were additional militiamen to be chosen by lot "without regard to status and service." Overall responsibility for recruiting, provisioning and arming the militia was in the hands of the military and civil governors of the four Prussian military governorates that were created on 15 March 1813.[3] In a conscription plan, the central government distributed the troops and horses, which had to be provided, among the individual districts in these four military governorates. The individual districts had to organize the local recruitment, equipment, arming and outfitting of the militia independently.[4]

The central government set very tight deadlines. On 31 March 1813 a cabinet order was issued calling for the greatest possible speed in executing the militia edict. Provisioning of troops, their division into companies, and the selection of officers was to be completed by 15 April. They were to be fitted out, "horsed" and equipped by 30 April. As the reports from the provinces and descriptions from individual districts show, given the shortness of time but also the desolate financial and economic situation, mobilizing the militia was an extraordinary task imposed upon the responsible local committees and thus ultimately their population. The central government provided only weapons and munitions – and only if they were obtainable.[5] The limited means and time available meant that the training and equipment of militia soldiers remained insufficient. Their training lasted three weeks

[2] This chapter is based on Hagemann, *Muth*, 397–405; on the militia, see also Dorothea Schmidt, *Die preußische Landwehr: Ein Beitrag zur Geschichte der allgemeinen Wehrpflicht in Preußen zwischen 1813 und 1830* (Berlin, 1981).

[3] Mieck, "Preußen," 56; see also the first part.

[4] Generalstab, *Heer*, 2:243–246.

[5] Ibid., 2:234–307; see also Maximilian Schultze, *Die Landwehr der Neumark von 1813 bis 1815*, 2 vols. (Landsberg, 1912 and 1914); and Manfred Laubert, "Die schlesische Landwehr der Befreiungskriege," *Zeitschrift des Vereins für Geschichte Schlesiens* 47 (1913): 1–21.

at best.[6] They lacked even the most necessary clothing and weapons, because rural communities especially were bereft of the financial means to pay for equipment and uniforms. Only in the autumn of 1813, after persistent protest by citizens about the poor treatment of the militiamen, did the Prussian government supply more of them with durable boots and coats and better arms.[7]

Because of the vast regional disparities in economic resources within Prussia, in particular between urban and rural communities, the equipment that the district committees could provide the militiamen differed widely. These differences, however, not only reflected disparities between city and countryside and the level of economic development, but also indicated local support for the war and the level of patriotic-national mobilization more generally, which depended on the interplay of multiple additional factors – notably the average educational level, the history of the region (especially its past territorial affiliation), experiences with French warfare and occupation, the ethnic composition of the population and the dominant religion.

The interaction of these same factors seems to have influenced the degree of military mobilization as well. The available figures for the Prussian militia in the different regions are incomplete, but they help us at least to identify some trends. The information on the size of the Prussian army in the territories remaining to Prussia after the Peace of Tilsit merely tells us the size of the militia contingents that were provided by the individual provinces during the war years. Of all the officers and soldiers of the militia that were mobilized by mid-August 1813, 42 percent belonged to the East Prussian, 20 percent to the Kurmark, 15 percent to the Silesian, 9 percent to the Pomeranian, 7 percent to the West Prussian, 6 percent to the Neumark and 1 percent to the Lithuanian militia. The proportion of the overall Prussian population serving in the militia was about 10 percent of the male population, and 3 percent on average, but the proportion differed markedly from region to region.[8]

There seems to have been little difficulty recruiting militia troops in the easternmost military governorate between the Vistula and the Russian border, which encompassed the old Prussian provinces of Lithuania and East Prussia as well as the sections of West Prussia east of the Vistula. Since the inhabitants had suffered particularly badly from the French presence in 1812–13, the degree of mobilization was exceptionally high.[9] During the first ten months of the war, the military government was able to recruit

---

[6] Generalstab, *Heer*, 2:246–247.
[7] Ibid., 2:180–181.
[8] Ibid., 2:500–539.
[9] See Christian Anton Krollmann, ed., *Landwehrbriefe 1813: Ein Denkmal der Erinnerung an den Burggrafen Ludwig zu Dohna-Schlobitten* (Danzig, 1913), vii–xxxix.

45 percent of men between the ages of 18 and 45, or 16 percent of the total male population. A large number of them volunteered.[10]

The military governorate between the Oder and the Vistula, which included the parts of West Prussia west of the Vistula, the parts of Pomerania east of the Oder, and the Neumark, presented a very different picture. Resistance to military service was intense primarily in the West Prussian areas inhabited mainly by Kashubians and Poles, where there was a good deal of aversion to Protestant Prussia, most of which can probably be explained by ethnic differences, intensified by religious differences. More than 60 percent of the population was Catholic, and there were also large Mennonite and Jewish communities. Unlike their coreligionists in the western regions of Prussia, the latter tried to buy their men's way out of military service, which was permitted by a royal ordinance of 29 May 1813. This so-called Jewish ransom money (*Juden-Loskaufgelder*) was used to finance a large part of the equipment for the militia. This resistance to recruitment meant that West Prussia's troop contingent could only be assembled by forced conscription.[11] Similar problems arose in the poor agrarian region of East Pomerania, with a majority population of Kashubians and Wends, where massive state force was required to bring men into the militia.[12]

The situation was quite different in the Neumark, which also belonged to the military governorate between the Oder and the Vistula.[13] Here, as in the entire district between the Elbe and the Oder, which included Hither Pomerania and the Kurmark, the degree of mobilization in town and country was disproportionately high. As everywhere in Prussia's core provinces, the young men of the urban middle classes and the petty bourgeoisie were the most willing to take up arms, regardless of their religious affiliation. Unlike in the East, however, here men of the rural lower classes, whose aversion to military service was great in other regions, also heeded the call to arms.[14] The old urban middle class in Berlin, Potsdam, Brandenburg and Frankfurt an der Oder, which had previously enjoyed exemption from compulsory military service, was the only group in this military province to protest the introduction of universal conscription.[15]

In the military governorate of Silesia, which encompassed the two largest and most populous Prussian provinces (Upper and Lower Silesia) and had been only indirectly affected by the war since 1806, the willingness to perform military service was comparatively low. Historical, political and religious reasons were probably the main factors. Upper and Lower Silesia

---

[10] Generalstab, *Heer*, 2:252 and 250–257.
[11] Ibid., 2:258–267.
[12] Ibid., 2:268–275.
[13] Ibid., 2:275–279; Schultze, *Landwehr*.
[14] See Fischer, *Judentum*, 39–40.
[15] See Generalstab, *Heer*, 2:278–292.

had belonged to Prussia only since 1742, when the kingdom had defeated Austria in the first Silesian War, which it had started in 1740. Both powers continued the struggle over the region in the second and third Silesian Wars in 1744–45 and 1756–63. The majority Catholic population in Silesia still tended to feel a deep antipathy for Protestant Prussia in 1813. The Catholic nobility sympathized with the Austrian emperor, or harbored hopes of a Greater Polish state. Large sections of the population followed the example of the noble elite. Even in Breslau, which became the temporary residence of the Prussian court on 22 January 1813, initial enthusiasm for the Prussian war effort soon waned so sharply that on 1 July 1813 the king ordered that the city be "punished for its obvious lack of patriotism [...] in order to prevent the bad example of the Breslauers from exerting a deleterious effect on other cities."[16] The aversion to serving in the Prussian army was particularly marked in Upper Silesia; here, recruits fled to Austria in droves to avoid conscription. The rate of desertion was so high that the king reintroduced flogging, which had been abolished in the course of military reform only a few years before, along with incarceration: the penalty for desertion was to be 50–100 cane strokes; repeat offenders even faced death by firing squad. Given these massive problems, the number of recruits that the province of Silesia managed to muster was quite impressive.[17]

The extent of military mobilization was and remained uneven in the two western military governorates between the Elbe and the Weser and between the Weser and the Rhine, which Prussia recaptured and claimed during the war, as well. Three factors seem to have come together in these two military governorates: their specific experiences with Napoleonic France, religious differences and how long the area had previously belonged to Prussia.[18] While mobilization for the militia was implemented relatively smoothly in the largely Protestant military governorate between the Elbe and the Weser, which included many formerly Prussian territories, it proved to be a good deal more difficult in the heavily Catholic governorate between the Weser and the Rhine, which also encompassed substantial non-Prussian possessions. Here, as in the three other general governorates – the Grand Duchy of Berg, the Grand Duchy of Frankfurt am Main and the Kingdom of Saxony – created by the Leipzig Convention in late October 1813, the willingness of men of military age to fight Napoleon appears to have been far less developed, as is also indicated by the complaints about desertion and the comparatively low level of mobilization of volunteers.[19] The main reason

---

[16] Ibid., 2:295.
[17] Ibid., 2:292–299.
[18] See Müsebeck, *Gaben*, 92–107.
[19] See Generalstab, *Heer*, 3:25–74; on the organization of the militia, see also Historische Abtheilung des Generalstabes, ed., "Geschichte der Organisation der Landwehr," pts. 1–2, in *BHMW* (Berlin, 1857).

was probably that the population of the territories previously occupied by France and formerly part of the Confederation of the Rhine was heartily sick of war, since the young men had been permanently conscripted for service under Napoleon and deployed in nearby or distant lands.[20] Moreover, these regions, which had belonged to the "inner empire," had suffered less under Napoleonic domination and rule. They had been spared war since 1806, and greater revenues more than compensated for the financial burdens imposed upon them. Unlike in the territories that remained Prussian, the Continental Blockade had promoted the development of local industry here and the easing of commerce between the states of the Confederation of the Rhine and the French Empire increased the wholesale trade.[21] Nevertheless, the patriotic-national mobilization of 1813–14 reached parts of the population in these regions, too.[22]

In light of these substantial regional differences in the degree of military mobilization, one cannot speak of a universal acceptance of compulsory militia service in Prussia and the regions over which it gained control during the war of 1813–14 as a sign of broad patriotic-national mobilization. The latter was, rather, limited to certain regions and population groups. The regions where support was most developed were the old core territories of the Prussian monarchy, which were mainly Protestant and had suffered greatly under the French occupation. The social groups that were most supportive of the war effort were the educated strata; the urban middle classes in smaller towns and cities, including artisans and merchants; civil servants and military of all ranks. These groups were one major target of patriotic-national propaganda. The other was ordinary men in town and countryside who composed the majority of the militiamen.

Despite all propaganda, the number of militia volunteers remained small, which is not surprising because service in the volunteer units appeared far more attractive to most young men who were able to equip and arm themselves. As a result, throughout the kingdom the majority of militiamen came from the lower social strata and had to be chosen by lot. The greatest proportion of those recruited in this manner were penniless young men of rural origin whose clothing, equipment and provisions had to be provided entirely by the local communities. Thus, in the Pomeranian militia, for example, 40 percent of the men were under 25; married men represented a minority of recruits.[23] Despite all of these difficulties, mobilization for the militia in the spring and summer of 1813 remains an achievement of the Prussian

[20] Smets, "Dorfidylle," 734–735; Michael Sikora, "Desertion und nationale Mobilmachung: Militärische Verweigerung 1792–1813," in *Armeen und ihre Deserteure: Vernachlässigte Kapitel einer Militärgeschichte der Neuzeit*, ed. Ulrich Broeckling and Michael Sikora (Göttingen, 1998), 112–140; and Rowe, *Reich*, 158–192.

[21] See Rowe, *Reich*, 193–210.

[22] See Echternkamp, *Aufstieg*, 191–194; and Rowe, *Reich*, 213–242.

[23] See Generalstab, *Heer*, 2:299–301.

state. It is remarkable how many men who had not previously been subject to military service, particularly in Prussia's core provinces, accepted conscription. These men had to learn how to fight in wartime under the worst possible conditions.

In the first months after the introduction of universal conscription, negative reports on the militia dominated in army circles. The military leadership complained in particular about "unreliability" and the high rate of desertion. We do not have any precise figures on the percentage of militiamen who tried to desert during the wars of 1813–15; in any case, the rate was certainly nowhere near the average of 20–30 percent frequently cited for the eighteenth-century Prussian army and fluctuated significantly from region to region and unit to unit.[24]

The perception of the militia by army leaders changed after the end of the armistice in August 1813. According to their unanimous view, once the militia units had gained more practice, they increasingly developed surprising military strength under fire. At the same time, they noted that the losses in these inexperienced units were still disproportionately high.[25] Even the Prussian king, who harbored substantial prejudices against the militia, had to concede in his October 1813 order for the four Prussian army corps that the militia regiments had "acquitted themselves splendidly" in the victorious battles of August and September. The order stated that the militiamen had "quickly made people forget" that "they were beginners in the exercise of soldierly virtues" and "thereby also earned an equal claim to [the king's] greater confidence" as supreme commander of the army.[26] In other words, the militiamen fought bravely and courageously, as the army leadership expected of its soldiers. Criticism continued to focus primarily on the militiamen's deficient stamina on long marches and their tendency to be "undisciplined" in camp and on the battlefield. Officers especially criticized their lack of military discipline (*Mannszucht*), which led to unrestrained rage in battles, caused higher death rates and could endanger an operational plan.[27]

The few surviving autobiographical texts on everyday life in the militia confirm some of these concerns, but suggest at the same time that the majority of those who stuck it out fought with extraordinary dedication. They also offer hints of the effects of war on the psychology and conduct of civilians who were fighting in a conflict legitimized by highly emotional propaganda. These rare documents include the journal of Silesian pastor Karl August Köhler, who served as chaplain to a militia brigade

[24] Ibbeken, *Preußen*, 409; and Sikora, "Desertion."

[25] "Armee-Befehl für die vier Armeekorps, Teplitz 1.10.1813," *AB*, no. 45, 22 Oct. 1813.

[26] Ibid. This army order was widely published in the press; see, for example, *PF*, no. 1, 6 Oct. 1813; and *PC*, no. 112, 13 Oct. 1813.

[27] See Mieck, "Preußen," 55.

in 1813–14. Köhler had volunteered as a chaplain and harbored strong patriotic sentiments, but his critical distance grew considerably as the war went on. In the epistolary journal he wrote for his parents and siblings, he repeatedly reflects on the effects of the war on civilians who had been recruited for military service for the first time in the context of universal conscription.[28] To his dismay, Köhler found that whatever their social background, war affected the mass of militiamen similarly – increasing their feelings of hatred and their thirst for revenge, destroying their civilian system of values and norms and "hardening them" emotionally.[29] In one of his first entries of 21 August 1813, he writes:

The enemy was superior to us in both numbers and marksmanship; for, since nearly the entire army consisted of militias, which had served only a few months, their shooting was uncertain and slow. Since, however, none of the rifles functioned [because of constant heavy rains], almost everything was decided by cannon and bayonets, and the foe could not resist, because our regiments threw themselves with fury upon their ranks and gave no thought to death. Thousands fell, run through, or beaten to death with rifle butts. The soldiers appeared to be animals, not men; several smashed their rifle butts against the skulls of the enemy and took their rifles as booty to continue the bloody work.[30]

Köhler notes uneasily how strong the hatred of the French was in his militia unit, and that it only increased during the war. It led the militiamen to uncontrolled rage, which could not even be disciplined by the orders of their officers and generals. They were, for example, not willing to give pardon to their French enemies when ordered to do so.[31] Köhler observes at the same time that the war "dulled" the men, leading to "foolhardy behavior" during battle and causing needless bloodshed in their own ranks.[32] On 12 January 1814 he observes:

The troops show unparalleled bravery and daring. Thus they went not through the approaches, but straight across the open fields to the defensive works, until the general forbade it. When they carried away the wounded or dead, they returned immediately with the greatest calm, as if fearing no battle. Daily they beg the general to order them to charge.[33]

The experience of war changed the men in Köhler's brigade. They lost all qualms and soon thought nothing of plundering wounded and dead enemy soldiers. He describes the increasing breakdown of "military discipline" (*Mannszucht*) as the war went on and moved to enemy territory. In France,

---

[28] See Köhler, *1813–14*.
[29] Ibid., 45 and 168.
[30] Ibid., 31.
[31] Ibid., 36, 45 and 166.
[32] Ibid., 46 and 175.
[33] Ibid., 173–174.

plundering, violence and the maltreatment of civilians, even rape, became common.[34] Köhler himself became increasingly war-weary, not least because of the feeling that he as a chaplain could do little to stop the "savagery" around him.

The stirring up of the emotions of newly recruited militiamen that was the aim of so much war propaganda in 1813 appears to have been more effective than many leading Prussian politicians and generals may have wished. The ordinary men who fought in the militia were mainly addressed by sermons and songs in church services, patriotic-national festivals and military rituals. The patriotic-national propaganda gave them words for their often devastating experiences with the French since 1806. It legitimated hatred of the enemy and his "destruction," which was useful for rousing the fighting spirit and war support by the population in 1813, but could lead to uncontrollable and hazardous behavior during battle and was politically dangerous once the enemy had been defeated and Europe needed to be demobilized and pacified again.

THE VOLUNTEERS' MOVEMENT

The public greeted the high degree of mobilization among volunteers in the war years 1813–15 with great enthusiasm. Contemporary journalism elevated the volunteers' movement to *the* symbol par excellence of the "uprising" of the Prussian and German nation.[35] The catalyst for this movement was the royal "Decree on the Establishment of Rifle Detachments" issued on 3 February 1813, more than a month before the official declaration of war on France, which called on young men who could provide their own clothing and horses to volunteer for military service, with the following explanation:

The perilous situation in which the state finds itself demands a rapid increase in the existing troops, while the financial means permit no great expenditure. Given the patriotism and loyal devotion to the king that has always inspired the inhabitants of the Prussian monarchy, and which has consistently expressed itself most vigorously in times of danger, all that is needed is a suitable occasion to channel these sentiments and the thirst for action peculiar to so many doughty young men, so that they might strengthen the ranks of older defenders of the fatherland and vie with them in the fine fulfillment of the first of those duties that resides with us.[36]

The decree ordered the establishment of rifle detachments in the infantry battalions and cavalry regiments, which were primarily to serve the light

---

[34] Ibid.,151.

[35] The following is based on Hagemann, *Muth*, 496–516; Brandt, "Einstellungen"; Ibbeken, *Preußen*, 393–452; and Generalstab, *Heer*, 2:381–389.

[36] "Verordnung wegen der zu errichtenden Jäger-Detachements, 3.2.1813," repr. in Generalstab, *Heer*, 2:381–383.

troops and be trained in the use of weapons for this purpose. They were freed of garrison duties as well as work details, service details and transport and baggage details. They were to receive preferred opportunities for honors and the chance of an officer's career was to be opened to them where appropriate. The call to volunteer for military service was combined with the announcement that

No young man who has attained the age of seventeen and not yet completed his twenty-fourth year and is not in active royal service [...] shall, if the war continues, attain a post, a dignity, an honor (a medal or the like) unless he has served one year with the active troops or in one of the rifle detachments.[37]

Exceptions were made only for frail young men or the sole adult sons of widows, if their domestic circumstances demanded the presence of their sons. Those who "distinguished themselves through bravery, zeal and patriotism" in their detachments were also to receive "preferred consideration one day in the civil service," qualifications permitting. Any "foreigner" who joined one of the detachments was promised the privileges of an "inlander" if he served well.[38] Given the miserable employment market, this offered educated young men in particular a strong incentive to serve as volunteers, since it held out the promise of a position in the public service and better career opportunities.

For the government, this decree was an initial test of responsiveness to the mobilization of those segments of the male population that had previously been exempt from conscription. The unclear political situation, however, at first kept many young men from volunteering for military service. Until 17 March 1813, when Friedrich Wilhelm III publicly declared war against France with his "Call to My People," nobody was really sure on which side the volunteers would have to fight. Therefore, up to 15 March, only 9,000 volunteers were mobilized in all of Prussia, of which 26 rifle detachments of 100 to 300 men were formed in the infantry and 17 in the cavalry. But the situation changed immediately after the declaration of war; now the number of volunteers rose rapidly. Considering that volunteers had to equip and arm themselves very quickly, the response was quite impressive. Since the Prussian army could muster only 66,963 soldiers and 1,766 officers when the war began, the proportion of volunteers was initially relatively high, at some 13 percent, but later made up 8 percent of troops on average.[39]

In all, during the war years 1813–14 alone nearly 50,000 volunteers from all over Germany were deployed in Prussia.[40] Including the war of

---

[37] Ibid.
[38] Ibid.
[39] See ibid., 2:143–145 and 162–163; and Historische Abtheilung des Generalstabes, ed., "Die Formation der freiwilligen Jäger-Detachements bei der preußischen Armee im Jahre 1813," pts. 1–3, in *BHMW* (Berlin, 1845 and 1847).
[40] Müsebeck, *Gaben*, 112; and Generalstab, *Heer*, 2:448–551.

1815, it is estimated that there were 60,000 volunteers in Germany overall, for by 1813, as the front advanced, volunteer units had also been formed outside of Prussia. The best known among them were the Hanseatic Legion and the Banner of Saxon Volunteers.[41] The most famous Prussian volunteer formation was the Lützow Free Corps, which had 1,033 men in March 1813 and grew to 3,666 in August 1813. Seven additional large free corps units emerged in the Prussian army, but none of them attained the same significance.[42]

The degree of mobilization of volunteers also differed greatly from one region of Prussia to the other, with a tendency to mirror developments in the militia. The overwhelming majority of volunteers (36,462) came from the four East Elbian military governorates, 11,790 from the Kurmark (including Magdeburg east of the Elbe), 7,807 from Silesia, 4,293 from the Neumark, 3,844 from East Prussia, 3,304 from Pomerania, 3,062 from West Prussia, 1,919 from Lithuania, and 444 from Posen. Another 7,490 volunteers came from the military governorate between the Elbe and the Weser and 5,419 from that between the Weser and the Rhine.[43]

The chief indicator of the degree of mobilization is not, however, the absolute number of volunteers, but rather what proportion of male inhabitants between 18 and 45 they represented. In this respect, the Kurmark and Neumark had the highest rates of mobilization, at 9 and 8 percent, respectively. In West and East Prussia, volunteers made up 6 percent of the eligible male population, in Pomerania 4 percent and in Lithuania and Silesia 3 percent. As in the case of the militia, urban/rural differences are striking here. The degree of mobilization was consistently far higher in the cities than in the countryside, with the highest rates in the large university and garrison towns. In Königsberg and Potsdam, 30 percent of all men between the ages of 18 and 45 volunteered for military service, in Breslau 18 percent and in Berlin and Stettin 9 percent. Even in Prussia's middle-sized and small towns the figures were surprisingly high. Thus, in Frankfurt an der Oder, Marienwerder and Stolp, the proportion was 21 percent, in Elbing 13 percent and in Landsberg 10 percent.[44]

---

[41] See Brandt, "Einstellungen," 213; Aaslestadt, *Place*, 273–284; and Marcus von Salisch, "Das Beispiel Sachsen: Militärreformen deutscher Mittelstaaten," in *Reform, Reorganisation, Transformation: Zum Wandel deutscher Streitkräfte von den preußischen Heeresreformen bis zur Transformation der Bundeswehr*, ed. Karl-Heinz Lutz et al. (Munich, 2010), 89–106, 105.

[42] See Generalstab, *Heer*, 2:207–217 and 454–455; see also Lützow, *Freikorps*; Fritz von Jagwitz, *Geschichte des Lützowschen Freikorps: Nach archivalischen Quellen bearbeitet* (Berlin, 1892); and Fritz Lange, ed., *Die Lützower – Erinnerungen, Berichte, Dokumente* (Berlin, 1953). On the other seven volunteer units, see Generalstab, *Heer*, 2:215–234 and 542–547.

[43] Müsebeck, *Gaben*, 109–112.

[44] Ibid.

The proportion of Jewish men who volunteered also seems to have been highest in the largest cities. Of the 444 Jewish volunteers recorded in the years 1813–14, more than half came from the Kurmark, with Berlin and Potsdam as centers. Their actual numbers were probably higher, since many were not identified as "Jewish" because they did not actively practice their religion during the war. The rabbis of urban communities in particular had given them permission for this.[45] In the larger cities, the well-to-do and educated Jewish population also appears to have matched the Christians in the area of wartime charity work.[46] By fulfilling their patriotic duty in the war, the enlightened male elite of the Jewish communities in particular hoped to attain full recognition as "citizens of the state" and equal access to state office and military positions, which remained closed to them even after the Emancipation Edict of 1812.[47]

Young men under 25 were the backbone of the volunteers' movement, and mobilization was highest among urban youth. That is the conclusion of Rudolf Ibbeken, who analyzed the muster rolls of 25,361 Prussian volunteers in the wars of 1813–15. According to his survey, the composition by occupation was as follows: Forty-one percent were artisans, 10 percent commercial clerks and merchants, 8 percent middle and lower civil servants, secretaries and former soldiers, 7 percent school and university students, and 5 percent higher civil servants. Most of these men resided in towns and cities. Fifteen percent were farmers, estate managers, gamekeepers and foresters, and 14 percent were day laborers and farmhands, who mostly came from the countryside. Seventy percent of the volunteers in Ibbeken's survey came from cities and small towns. His differentiation by "estates" (*Stände*) makes the social composition even more visible: Twelve percent of the volunteers in his survey belonged to the educated estates (including school and university students), 74 percent to the upper- and lower- middle classes in town and countryside and 15 percent to the lower peasantry.[48]

While Ibbeken's findings counter the national myth that it was largely academically trained young men who volunteered, educated men were nonetheless overrepresented among the volunteers, and members of the rural lower classes were substantially underrepresented.[49] Everywhere, not only in Prussia, mobilization appears to have been very marked among the pupils in the upper levels of academic secondary schools (*Gymnasium*) and university students. More than 50 percent of students at North German universities volunteered for military service.[50] The decree of 3 February 1813

[45] Fischer, *Judentum*, 47–53.
[46] See ibid., 26–29, 37–41 and 47.
[47] See ibid., 32–63.
[48] Ibbeken, *Preußen*, 447.
[49] Ibid., 442–450.
[50] Ibid., 405–408; and Erich Kuske, "Die Beteiligung der höheren Schulen Preußens an der Erhebung im Jahre 1813," *PrJb* 154 (1913): 437–450.

and subsequent addenda – which promised posts and advancement in the Prussian state service only to those 17-to-24-year-old men who had served at least one year in the military – encouraged educated young men to volunteer.[51] Nevertheless, the volunteers' movement is rightly considered to be an indicator of a broader patriotic-national mobilization especially of young men, since the prospect of a career in the civil service helps to explain the mobilization of educated youth, but not of the young urban artisans who made up an extraordinarily large proportion of volunteers when compared to the overall weight of the trades within society.

The social composition of volunteers also explains why only 40 percent of them were able to provide their own equipment.[52] The rest were outfitted by donations from a public dedicated to supplying clothing and weapons for volunteers. Beginning in mid-February 1813, appeals from the Prussian central government, military and civilian governors and local administrations, but also the Protestant state church and Jewish communities, were widely published in the press.[53] Young men who wished to volunteer also requested assistance directly through newspaper advertisements. The *Berlinische Nachrichten* of 20 March 1813, for example, printed the following advertisement under the heading "Request":

> Entrust, my dearest fatherland
> Weapons to my youthful hand!
> Which I may color with blood of foe,
> And distinguish myself as of old:
> To show with heart, mind and deed,
> That I am of the Prussian seed.[54]

It was not enough to provide the initial uniform and equipment for the volunteers, however. Since the decree of 3 February 1813 tersely stipulated that volunteers had to be able to supply their own clothing and horses, it was left to them to ensure their equipment and mounts for the duration of the war. This caused substantial problems because, with the advance of the front, volunteers were increasingly cut off from support from home and their equipment deteriorated. As a result, they frequently found themselves

[51] See Generalstab, *Heer*, 2:381–389, esp. 143–162 and 205–234; Ibbeken, *Preußen*, 393–439.

[52] See Müsebeck, *Gaben*, 112.

[53] In March 1813 alone the two larger newspapers in Berlin published "Aufruf an unsere Mitbürger der National-Repräsentation v. 13.2.1813," *BN* and *VZ*, no. 28, 6 March 1813; "Aufruf an die hiesigen Einwohner von Ober-Bürgermeister Büsching, Berlin 20.3.1813," *VZ*, no. 35, 23 March 1813 and *BN*, no. 38, 30 March 1813; "Bitte um Spenden für das Lützowsche Freicorps v. Zivil-Gouverneur Sack und Direktor Bornemann," *VZ*, no. 38, 30 March 1813; and "Bekanntmachung, daß der König die Bevölkerung zu noch mehr patriotischen Opfern ermahnt v. Militär-Gouverneur L'Estocq u. Zivil-Gouverneur Sack," *VZ*, no. 38, 30 March 1813. See also Fischer, *Judentum*, 37–41.

[54] "Bitte," *BN*, no. 34, 20 March 1813.

in a worse situation than the notoriously miserably outfitted militia. The sources contain numerous accounts of volunteers falling ill by the hundreds for lack of coats and shoes, or of walking their feet bloody so that they had to be sent to a field hospital. From autumn 1813, the army leadership and the government repeatedly attempted to solve this problem, which made a mockery of the high symbolic importance that was assigned to volunteers in the public discussion. Since the lower ranks of the military regarded the volunteer units as poorly trained and undisciplined but privileged, they contributed little to solving the problem and often counteracted commands from their superiors.[55] The situation was further aggravated by the increasing loss of eloquent spokesmen in their ranks who could have made this problem public. Most of the propertied and educated volunteers who distinguished themselves through military ability and zeal became officers soon after the war began and were transferred to the militia to compensate for the high death rate among its younger line officers. Those who remained behind were largely young volunteers from the middle and lower social classes – who, when faced with hardship and diminishing supplies, like militiamen did not stop at "informal requisitioning," which established line officers, in turn, considered to be yet another indicator of deficient discipline.[56]

In the wake of the poor treatment of volunteers, which sat ill with the promises of the royal appeals, disgruntlement and dissatisfaction spread to such an extent that Aulic Councilor Carl Heun, whose responsibilities at Prussian headquarters included the administration of public donations for the volunteers, wrote in a letter of 2 March 1814 to Prime Minister Hardenberg:

The indifferent treatment the young men experience from all sides has caused the king's appeal [...] to fade away to such an extent at the moment that were His Majesty to issue another such appeal today, not a single man would *voluntarily* take up arms. [...] [For they are] despised by their superior officers and, with regard to their provisions and clothing, everywhere come last after the common soldiers [...]. They go without shoes, without coats, dressed in mere rags, and their haggard appearance makes a mockery of the great promises made to them and the nation.[57] (Emphasis in the original)

Other reports have a similar thrust. It is remarkable that the poor provisions, clothing and equipment of the volunteers as well as the disdain for them shown by many line officers, while leading to disgruntlement and resentment, does not seem to have diminished their perseverance. Their unusually low rate of desertion, which ranged from 1–5 percent for the four

[55] See Hermann Klaje, "Über die Bekleidungsnöte der Freiwilligen Jäger von 1813/14," *FBPG* 36 (1924): 87–97.
[56] Ibid., 90–91; Heinrich Ulmann, "Die Detachements der freiwilligen Jäger in den Befreiungskriegen," *Historische Vierteljahresschrift* 10 (1907): 483–505.
[57] Quoted in Klaje, "Bekleidungsnöte," 93.

army corps, at least suggests that. The Lützow Free Corps was a notable exception, with a desertion rate of 24 percent in the infantry and 9 percent in the cavalry, as opposed to only 1 and 6 percent, respectively, among the volunteer detachments of the infantry and cavalry more generally.[58] The most likely reasons were the large size of the unit as well as the extreme regional and social differences in its composition, which were far more marked than in other volunteer units. This led to substantial internal tensions and a lack of the cohesion that otherwise prevented desertion. As the first and most famous rifle detachment, the Lützowers recruited many renegades from other German territorial states. Two groups of them seem to have been especially prone to desertion: on the one hand, war-weary volunteers who had already fought for Napoleon for many years, and who used the unit to escape the military altogether as soon as it reached their home region; and on the other, inexperienced young volunteers with particularly high expectations that quickly ran up against the realities of war, especially in the infantry where everyday life was anything but heroic.[59]

The initial enthusiasm especially of educated volunteers is evident not just in volunteers' poetry, but also in letters, diaries and war memoirs. Willibald Alexis, who volunteered in 1815 as a 17-year-old Berlin schoolboy, offered a particularly memorable description of their mood. Since his memoirs are distinguished by a critical and ironic distance, they are probably a relatively credible source. He stresses that in 1815 the youngest volunteers, who had been too young to fight in 1813, were those who continued to dwell on the ideals of 1813:

We still dreamt, were still intoxicated; we felt nothing as yet of the painful aftermath. The rousing speeches of our teachers, the lingering sounds of the learned warlike eloquence of Fichte, Schleiermacher and Arndt resounding from every lectern, the songs of Körner and Schenkendorf, the tales of the older boys who had bled and triumphed along in 1813 and 1814, all of this kept the thrill alive. We wallowed in Fouqué's Nordic sagas, in his thoroughgoing neo-Francophobia. The ideas of the gymnastic movement [*Turner*] were powerful, even outside the Hasenheide [the site of Berlin's gymnastics grounds]. [...] Jahn's Germanomania was no phantom for us, but a truth, and we still had great hope for the realization of our ideas of German folkdom, although when it came to the question of how, we were at odds with others as well as ourselves.[60]

In his memoirs, Alexis emphasizes that this idealism had been far stronger among the first generation of educated volunteers in 1813. Thus, for him, the songs of Theodor Körner "best symbolized the mood of those days."[61] Other autobiographical documents suggest that next to patriotic enthusiasm

[58] Ibbeken, *Preußen*, 450.
[59] See Brandt, "Einstellungen," 224–227; and Ibbeken, *Preußen*, 426–427.
[60] Alexis, *Jugend*, 64.
[61] Ibid., 67–68.

and adventurousness, educated young men had two main motivations for signing up for military service: the hope of a civil service post after the war and pressure from youthful peer groups. Among schoolboys and university students, those who refused to go to war were simply branded as cowards.[62]

Alexis claimed that the enthusiasm and the hopes with which many educated young men went off to war in 1813 were so great that the experience of real war initially made little impact.[63] Their consistently poor treatment by members of the regular military and the increasing mood of political restoration from the winter of 1813–14 were the main reasons that many of the volunteers of 1813 did not heed the king's second call. If they did go to war again in 1815, it was generally only in the privileged position of an officer, from which they expected advantages for their civilian careers after the war. According to Alexis, the second generation of volunteers nevertheless went off to war with nearly the same enthusiasm as the first. "The discordances" in the war experiences of the first generation of volunteers and the "incursions" of political developments had not escaped the attention of "observant young men" in the winter of 1814 and the spring of 1815, but they had largely been "far too loyal" to "apply the word tyranny, which they thoroughly detested, […] to anyone but the French emperor Napoleon." Their "natural love of liberty" had been identified "with hatred of the French." Persuaded "of the renewed necessity of popular uprising, of the divine mission," the youngest in particular had enthusiastically volunteered, eager to prove themselves. The second generation of volunteers, however, had been brought down to earth even more quickly than the first, since their treatment in the military was even worse. In the war of 1815, the Prussian government depended neither on the volunteers nor on the militia, whose mobilization merely served as a "symbol of the general will" to "continue the storm and stress of '13."[64] Alexis accordingly describes in detail the humiliating, disheartening and depressing war experiences that he and

---

[62] See, for example, the letters that Friedrich Förster exchanged with his friends between December 1812 and June 1813, in "Erinnerungen aus dem Befreiungskriege: In Briefen gesammelt von Friedrich Förster," in *Deutsche Pandora: Gedenkbuch zeitgenössischer Zustände und Schriftsteller*, ed. Gustwav Schwab, 2 vols. (Stuttgart, 1840), 1:3–88, esp. 7–13 and 19; see also Friedrich C. Lietzmann, "Preußischer freiwilliger Jäger im Ersten Leibhusaren Regiment," in *Freiwilliger Jäger bei den Totenkopfhusaren. Siebzehn Jahre Leutnant im Blücherhusaren-Regiment: Erzählungen aus Kolbergs Ruhmestagen, aus dem deutschen Befreiungskrieg, aus kleiner pommerscher Garnison und von der Grenzwacht gegen den polnischen Aufstand 1831*, ed. Karl Lietzmann (Berlin, 1909), 22–23 and 48; as well as Heinrich Luden, *Rückblicke in mein Leben: Aus dem Nachlasse von Heinrich Luden* (Jena, 1847), 215; Agnes and Wilhelm Perthes, *Aus der Franzosenzeit in Hamburg: Erlebnisse* (Hamburg, 1910), 17; and Friedrich Ludwig von Mühlenfels, "Ein Lützower Reiter," *Die Grenzboten* 20.4 (1861): 481–500.

[63] Alexis, *Jugend*, 67–68.

[64] Ibid., 65–67 and 74.

many other volunteers underwent in 1815. Not only had the officers and soldiers of the line clearly shown them that they were "not real soldiers" and thus were completely superfluous in this war, but they were also drilled like "common soldiers."[65] Thus, after a few months of military service, most of the volunteers of 1815 had been "inoculated" with a massive and lasting repugnance "for continued existence as a soldier."[66]

Willibald Alexis was not the only one to be thoroughly disabused of his illusions about the military, war and the state.[67] The wars of 1813–15 had provided him and many other young middle-class men with an experiential basis for their blanket opposition to a standing army and belief in the necessity of a pure "national defense force." Their war experience informed their later position in all debates on the structure of the Prussian military. They supported the idea of universal conscription and a militia.[68] At the same time, most memoirs published by volunteers stressed the significance of their wartime engagement for the liberation of Germany, thus helping to secure a central place for the volunteers' movement in the collective memory of these wars as "Wars of Liberty."[69]

[65] Ibid., 74–240.
[66] Ibid., 238.
[67] See chapter 14 in the fourth part.
[68] On these debates, which culminated between 1859 and 1866, see Walter, *Heeresreformen*.
[69] See chapter 14 in the fourth part.

9

War Charity: Patriotic Women's Associations

"Heroic Maidens and Women of a Great Era," is the title of a brochure in the popular series "When Germany Awoke: The People and Events of the Wars of Liberation," which appeared in 1913 to commemorate the one-hundredth anniversary of the wars of 1813–15.[1] To be sure, the centenary mainly honored the "heroic deeds" of the "brave national warriors" – the volunteers and militiamen who had gone to battle. The observance also paid homage, however, to the "great sacrifices" made by "German women" during these wars. By 1913 it was generally acknowledged that wars fought with conscript armies could be conducted most successfully when they were accompanied by a general mobilization of civilian and military society. This implied that the broad support of women was also necessary for victory. In order to convey this insight to women and girls in the bellicose era on the eve of the First World War, authors of brochures that addressed female readers regularly referred to the "heroic age" of hundred years before, in which, in their interpretation, patriotic consciousness had "awakened" in men and women alike, and members of the "female sex" had actively committed themselves to the fatherland for the first time. The pamphlet noted accordingly that

The incomparable awakening of German woman by the wars of subjugation and liberation, the unanimous gathering together of German women's will to co-operate and sacrifice for their downtrodden fatherland, was preceded by a miserable era of national indifference and the affected aping of French manners among German women. [...] That Germany's women could not yet participate in patriotic life before the Wars of Liberation is understandable in the light of the circumstances prevailing

---

[1] Otto Karstädt, *Heldenmädchen und -Frauen aus großer Zeit* (Hamburg, 1913). This chapter is based on Karen Hagemann, "Female Patriots: Women, War and the Nation in the Period of the Prussian-German Anti-Napoleonic Wars," *G&H* 16 (2004): 396–424; and idem, *Muth*, 416–426. See also Rita Huber-Sperl, "Organized Women and the Strong State: The Beginnings of Female Associational Activity in Germany, 1810–1840," *JWH* 13.4 (2002): 81–105; Quataert, *Staging*, 21–53; and Reder, *Frauenbewegung*.

in those days. The gradual development of events put a slow and belated end to these slumbers, these unexploited female powers, and one by one assigned women tasks to perform in the service of their fatherland. The Wars of Liberation produced this unleashing of female powers with sudden élan in the springtime of nations of 1813.[2]

The brochure cultivates at length the myth of the patriotic "uprising" of a German nation "degenerated" by "Frenchification," which had only come to recognize its "decadence" and "dishonor" after the "divine judgment" of the debacle of 1806–07. As shining examples of the patriotism of this period, it presents "German heroines" of all ages who had displayed a special commitment to the "good of the fatherland." The portraits include women from all social strata who had worked for the nation in a wide variety of ways: by consciously rejecting all French influences in culture, language and dress and by performing their "female duties" in the household and the family in keeping with "German manners"; by strengthening the will to fight of their conscript husbands, sons, sweethearts and brothers; by collecting monetary and material donations to equip, clothe and feed the "national warriors"; by supporting the penniless wives and children of soldiers; by nursing the sick and wounded; and by providing relief for disabled veterans, war widows and orphans.[3] Other commemorative writings for female readers that appeared before the First World War and recalled the "German heroines from the period of the Wars of Liberation" also assessed their activities in a thoroughly positive light.[4]

A hundred years previously, however, the new phenomenon of women's active patriotic involvement had been very controversial in public perception. In the following chapter, I therefore analyze not just the content and forms of female patriotism, particularly charitable war work by the patriotic women's associations, but also how it was perceived by the public in the period during and after the wars of 1813–15.

UNIVERSAL CONSCRIPTION AND WAR CHARITY

The fatherland is in peril! Its defense requires a rapid expansion of the army without cost to the state coffers. Trusting in the love of his subjects, the father of our country himself has expressed this and called for volunteers through his minister of state. [...] Those who are prevented by bodily infirmity or circumstances of employment will grieve at not being able to share this danger and honor. The appeal, however, offers them, too, room to express their patriotic sentiments. They can acquire the same merits as combatants by acting in the same spirit and donating that portion of their possessions to the fatherland that the latter needs and contributing now to

[2] Karstädt, *Heldenmädchen*, 7.
[3] Ibid., 7–10.
[4] See, for example, Otto W. von Horn, *Vier deutsche Heldinnen aus der Zeit der Befreiungskriege: Ein Büchlein für die deutsche Jugend und das Volk* (Wiesbaden, 1897).

the outfitting of poorer volunteers, in order to place them in a position to fulfill their high calling sooner and better.[5]

With this appeal, the National Representation (*Nationalrepräsentation*), the elected all-Prussian assembly of the estates, addressed their "fellow citizens" on 13 February 1813, more than a month before Prussia officially declared war on France. Members of the assembly called on their compatriots to offer material support for the war in order to ease the financial burden on the state. The appeal was necessary because the Prussian state was virtually bankrupt in 1813. It was therefore only the first of a series of similar calls, which were published widely in the daily newspapers.

After the declaration of war on France, the civilian population in Prussia responded to the appeals for donations with remarkable alacrity. A likely reason for this willingness was the fact that almost every family had to send a young man off to war for the first time. Thus, providing them with proper clothing and weapons became a personal concern of many of the men and women who stayed at home. This new type of wartime charity quickly developed into the most important form of patriotic commitment by civilian society. It appears to have enjoyed the support of broad social strata and both sexes. Apart from the moneyed and educated elite in town and country, the urban middle classes and to some extent the lower classes were also included, as is evident from the extensive coverage in local newspapers.[6] Lists of donations, which were published regularly, mention men and women of the most varied, mainly urban, population groups, including even day laborers and maidservants. The press also reported on generous donations from the Jewish communities, especially in the larger cities.[7] According to official reports, in the war years 1813–15 the civilian population of the monarchy collected a total of 10.3 million taler, 4.7 million of which came from "associations, enterprises and collections" and 1.9 million from "payments to public offices and treasuries and church offerings." This large sum was raised as a "voluntary gift." The remainder consisted mainly of payments and contributions demanded by the provincial administrations to finance the clothing, equipment and upkeep of the militia troops.[8] Together this was an important contribution to funding the wars of 1813–15, which cost the Prussian state 61.1 million taler in addition to the usual government

5 "Aufruf an unsere Mitbürger der Nationalrepräsentanten, Berlin, 13 February 1813," repr. in Müsebeck, *Gaben*, 132.
6 "Aufruf an unsere Mitbürger"; Friedrich Andreae, "Die freiwilligen Leistungen von 1813," *Zeitschrift des Vereins für Geschichte Schlesiens* 47 (1913): 150–197; Ernst Gurlt, "Die freiwilligen Leistungen der preußischen Nation in den Kriegsjahren 1813–1815: National-Denkmal oder summarische Darstellung der patriotischen Handlungen und Opfer der Preußischen Nation während der Jahre 1813, 1814, 1815 bearbeitet auf Befehl König Friedrich Wilhelms III. von der Königl. General-Ordens-Commission," *Zeitschrift für preußische Geschichte und Landeskunde* 9 (1872): 645–696.
7 Fischer, *Judentum*, 39.
8 Müsebeck, *Gaben*, 112.

spending in peacetime.[9] This contribution was particularly noteworthy because of the economic crisis the population had faced in the years after the defeat of 1806.

The significant regional variations in the willingness to donate for the war can be explained largely in terms of differing economic situations, as well as varying degrees of patriotic-national mobilization. They resemble the differences in mobilization for the militia and the volunteers' movement. In Protestant regions, per capita donations were consistently higher than in Catholic areas, and in the relatively prosperous larger cities they exceeded the average for rural regions of the same provinces, whose population was generally much poorer. Men donated money more often than women, simply because of the distribution and legal regulation of property within marriage and the family.[10] The regional differences in material war support, however, also reflected the distribution of the patriotic women's organizations within Prussia, because they contributed greatly to the collection of goods and money for militiamen and volunteers as well as war victims.

PATRIOTIC WOMEN'S ASSOCIATIONS

After the declaration of war on France, women increasingly became active in large numbers in the field of wartime charity.[11] Their commitment received official support in an "Appeal to the Women of the Prussian State" published on 23 March 1813 by twelve princesses of the house of Hohenzollern under the leadership of Princess Marianne of Prussia, the sister-in-law of King Friedrich Wilhelm III. The appeal asserted:

We women, too, must participate, and must help to promote victory. We, too, must unite with the men and boys to save our fatherland. Thus let us found an association with the name of Women's Association for the Good of the Fatherland. [...] This association will accept as donations not merely cash money, but any valuable spare trinket. – The symbol of fidelity, the wedding ring, shining adornments for the ears, costly decorations for the neck. Monthly contributions, material, linen cloth, spun wool and yarn will be gladly accepted, and even the gratis working of these raw materials will be regarded as an offering. These offerings serve to arm, clothe and equip the defenders who need it, and if the rich benevolence of women puts us in a position to do yet more, then the wounded will also be nursed, healed and returned to the grateful fatherland.[12]

With this appeal, which was published widely in the press, the female members of the royal family seized the initiative and called on women to found a patriotic association. Its primary goal was to collect money and

---

[9] Wehler, *Gesellschaftsgeschichte*, 1:435.
[10] Müsebeck, *Gaben*, 109–110.
[11] Reder, *Frauenbewegung*, 43–44.
[12] "Aufruf an die Frauen im Preußischen Staat," repr., among other places, in *VZ*, no. 39, 23 March 1813.

material for the "defenders of the fatherland." Anything above and beyond that would be used for nursing care. The call, which referred directly to the king's well-known appeal "To My People," aimed to integrate women into the valorous *Volk* family of the Prussian nation through wartime charity.[13]

Upper-middle-class and aristocratic women in particular answered the princesses' call in great numbers. In Berlin, only a few days after the appeal was published, they founded the Women's Association for the Good of the Fatherland the princesses had promoted.[14] All over Prussia, women from the educated elite followed this example and founded similar associations in the spring and summer of 1813. The scope of these women's initiatives expanded steadily during the war. They began by collecting money and material to outfit the volunteers and militias and busied themselves making flags and banners, which they handed out to the new troops in public flag consecrations.[15] Soon, however, they also began to organize nursing care for wounded and sick soldiers and set up a rapidly growing number of hospital associations.[16] Later, women also established relief efforts for disabled soldiers and for the penniless families of "warriors," particularly widows and orphans. They created special associations devoted solely to this purpose. One of the first was the Female Charitable Association, which began work in Berlin in July 1813.[17]

During the war years 1813–15, women founded patriotic associations in at least 414 Prussian towns. This represents 72 percent of the 573 documented women's associations in the German-speaking region. Over the course of the war, associations were also initiated in other German regions, mostly in territories close to the front, first in eastern and later in northern and central Germany, and finally in the western regions, reflecting the emphasis on helping to equip the men in newly founded militia and volunteer units on the one hand, and caring for the injured and ill soldiers on the other. Since the second campaign of 1815 largely took place on French territory, the western Rhineland regions were especially involved in medical care. This led to the establishment of a correspondingly high number of female hospital associations.[18]

Berlin was the center of patriotic women's activities. Its importance extended far beyond Prussia's borders. Not only did the city possess an unusual concentration of women's associations, they were also remarkably specialized. Of the 27 Berlin women's and girls' associations, eleven tended the wounded and the sick, six were so-called girls' and daughters' associations,

[13] See chapter 4 and 7 in the second part; and Hagemann, "*Volk* Family."
[14] Hagemann, *Muth*, 416–426; and Reder, *Frauenbewegung*, 52–57.
[15] Hagemann, *Muth*, 462–471.
[16] See ibid., 416–426; and Reder, *Frauenbewegung*, 68–81 and 371–381.
[17] Heinrich Gräfe, *Nachrichten von wohltätigen Frauenvereinen in Deutschland – Ein Beitrag zur Sittengeschichte des 19. Jahrhunderts* (Kassel, 1844), 12–13; and Reder, *Frauenbewegung*, 90–103.
[18] See Gurlt, "Leistungen," 346 and 382–386; and Reder, *Frauenbewegung*, 504.

five mainly collected donations of money and material for various purposes, two were devoted exclusively to relief for soldiers' widows and orphans and one was organized by domestic servants.[19] Other centers of female wartime charity were Breslau with five, Bremen with four, and Frankfurt am Main, Hamburg and Leipzig with three patriotic women's associations each. The remaining larger cities had at most two and frequently, as in most middle-sized and small towns, only one association.[20] The sizes of these associations varied greatly. Smaller groups had around ten, and larger ones like the Berlin Women's Association for the Good of the Fatherland, about 100 activists. In Brünn, Darmstadt and Munich the largest associations comprised more than 400 members. In most associations, leadership was in the hands of women from the nobility and the upper middle class. Men – generally their husbands and fathers – frequently assisted in the management of financial affairs, in particular. The organizations also incorporated women from the urban middle and lower classes into their practical activities, the latter often for a small wage, however. Because they had to work for a living they were not able to volunteer without compensation.[21]

Unlike the male national movement, where the members of the two most active groups – the *Turner* and the *Burschenschaften* – were mostly young men, women of all ages participated in the patriotic women's associations. Age and marital status, however, appear to have greatly influenced the form their activities took. Some women's and girls' associations had mainly married and widowed women of all ages and their female relatives as members. Nursing the sick and wounded quickly developed into one of their main fields of activity. Other organizations were composed primarily of unmarried young women. These so-called girls' and daughters' associations concentrated on raising money first for the militia and the volunteers and later for sick and wounded soldiers by producing and selling "female handicrafts" at bazaars and charity functions. They also embroidered flags for the new militia and volunteer units. Both activities were considered to be "seemly" for young and unmarried women.[22]

The extent and significance of women's wartime charity becomes particularly evident in their two most important fields of endeavor: collecting donations and caring for the sick and wounded. Women succeeded in raising and collecting large sums of money. The Berlin Women's Association for the Good of the Fatherland alone, for example, amassed a total of some 90,000 taler in 1813.[23] The Prussian women's associations raised 450,000 taler

[19] See the detailed account of patriotic women's activities in Berlin in Reder, *Frauenbewegung*, 41–116.
[20] See the list of the 573 patriotic women's associations in ibid., 489–503.
[21] Hagemann, *Muth*, 418–419.
[22] Ibid., 418–427. See chapter 10 in the third part.
[23] Paul Seidel, "Eine Erinnerung an den ersten Frauen-Verein 1813," *Hohenzollern Jahrbuch* 18 (1914): 237–240, 239.

that year.[24] This was nearly 5 percent of the funds collected by the Prussian population during the war years 1813–15. This sum is quite impressive, especially since it takes into account neither the many donations that women made to other collections by local governments and churches nor the extensive contributions of goods and services.[25] Even women of the lower classes participated to a remarkable degree in patriotic-national donation campaigns. One oft-reported example was the house-to-house collection conducted by female servants in the Hanseatic cities of Bremen, Hamburg and Lübeck in 1813. They yielded the formidable sum of 5,000 taler to outfit the volunteers of the Hanseatic Legion.[26] Considering that the average income of a worker was no more than eight taler a month, and female servants and day laborers earned even less,[27] this is an impressive result, especially if we keep in mind that women legally had no control over household income, which made it more difficult for them to donate. We also need to remember that women of all social strata had already experienced severe material hardship before the wars of 1813–15, which continued during wartime. They had to support their families on their own, since their fathers, brothers or husbands had been conscripted and the paltry official relief payments hardly sufficed for survival.[28]

Apart from raising and collecting donations in cash and in kind, the main field of activity of patriotic women's organizations was caring for sick and wounded soldiers. The magnitude of this new form of organized wartime nursing was unprecedented. Press accounts convey the impression that public hospitals would have provided far worse treatment for the large numbers of sick and wounded without women's support. Military medical care had by no means kept up with the development of mobile mass armies. Without organized female assistance, Prussia, for example, would have needed a military medical corps three times as large as it had for an army of 128,000 soldiers at the beginning of the war. During the course of the war, with growing numbers of troops, the ratio became even more unfavorable.[29] In March 1813 the Prussian army had equipment for three main military hospitals (each for 1,200 sick and wounded) and six smaller transportable hospitals (each for 200 sick and wounded), which together could accommodate 4,800 men at best; 179 trained military surgeons worked for the army, 46 in the main military hospitals and 133 in the transportable hospitals. This was absolutely inadequate for the size of

---

[24] Müsebeck, *Gaben*, 112.

[25] Generalstab, *Heer*, 1:542–545.

[26] Gräfe, *Nachrichten*, 8.

[27] Generalstab, *Heer*, 1:542–544.

[28] We know virtually nothing about women's actual working and living conditions at the time of the wars of 1813–15. The degree of hardship many suffered is evident from the reports of charitable associations. See Reder, *Frauenbewegung*, 95.

[29] See Generalstab, *Heer*, 2:203–204 and 457; and ibid., 1:342–347.

the army, and indicates how important the private care was that the local women's associations and the communities provided in cooperation with the military hospital administration.[30]

In the patriotic women's organizations, female patriots of the aristocracy and upper middle class in Prussia and elsewhere in Germany used the new institution of the bourgeois association – until then mainly the province of men – to become active in an organized form with high public visibility. They actually created their own "patriotic public sphere," as Jean H. Quataert has labeled it.[31] How can we explain this expansion of the "female sphere" and the extensive wartime charity work by girls and women of the educated strata? What motivated these women?

One major factor was surely patriotic-national propaganda, which mobilized women similarly to men, as indicated by the autobiographical accounts, though few in number, that were published by educated women and the extensive participation of girls and women in the many patriotic-national festivals and rituals during the wars.[32] The discourse gave women the rhetoric they needed to legitimate why they, too, – in this "emergency of the nation" – wanted to become active in the public sphere and support the "struggle for liberation" with their "female patriotism." But more personal motives, which were inextricably linked with their patriotism, inspired them as well. The new form of mass warfare, especially universal conscription, affected girls and women in new ways too. The ties between the military and civil society became much closer, at least during wartime. Fathers, brothers, fiancés, husbands and sons of military age had either volunteered or been conscripted or could expect to be called up at any time. Women were thus left to worry about equipping, feeding, nursing or burying and mourning "their warriors."[33] According to the handful of female autobiographical accounts and the many published reports of women's associations in the press, important motives for their involvement were – apart from patriotism – pity, humanitarianism and the desire to extend their own scope of action. Women hoped that the mental and material support they offered militiamen and volunteers from their home region during the war would help them to fight, persevere and return alive. They trusted that the medical care they gave to soldiers from other regions would be matched by similar aid for their own loved ones elsewhere. At the same time, these activities helped to distract them from worries and fears for their fathers, husbands and sons at the front. Moreover, wartime charity work opened new spheres of activity and experience that

---

[30] Generalstab, *Heer*, 1:347 and 2:342–347 and 2:457.

[31] Quataert, *Staging*, 6–8.

[32] See Helmina von Chézy, *Unvergessenes: Denkwürdigkeiten aus dem Leben von Helmina von Chézy – Von ihr selbst erzählt*, ed. Bertha Borngräber, 2 vols. (Leipzig, 1858); and Ferdinand Wolf, ed., *Denkwürdigkeiten aus meinem Leben von Caroline von Pichler*, 4 vols. (Vienna, 1844); and chapter 10 in the third part as well as chapter 14 in the fourth part.

[33] Andreae, "Leistungen," 160–161.

were previously closed to upper-middle-class women in particular. First of all, they now had the opportunity to participate in larger numbers in joint activities outside the home and to organize in associations as men did.[34] They experienced their own organizational skills, independent from men, often for the first time. They did this so successfully that the German-national press in particular held them up as models to motivate educated men to become more active, too. Thus, for instance, an article in the *Deutsche Blätter*, which appeared in the early summer of 1815, urged those men "who remained tied up" by other duties at home and who could not take up arms to follow women's example and found "German aid associations."[35]

PUBLIC PERCEPTIONS OF FEMALE PATRIOTISM

During the wars of 1813–15, many newspapers and journals lauded women's "active patriotism" as "female heroism." They interpreted it as proof that the "holy impulse of love for the fatherland" had gripped broad segments of the population.[36] The daily papers reported at length on women's patriotic activities, and held up especially "courageous ladies" as shining examples. One of these women was Caroline Weiß, wife of the town physician of Neumarkt in Silesia, who had volunteered at the beginning of the war to serve as battalion surgeon to the Neumarkt militia. The press reported that, when the battalion doctor himself fell ill with typhoid fever, she had left her children in the care of relatives, hurried to his side and nursed him back to health in the midst of battle.[37] She was praised as a model of "heroic loyalty to her husband." Her story was adopted so widely because it meshed neatly with reigning notions of the gender order.

As long as women proved their patriotism within the limits of the sphere assigned to them as caring spouses, housewives and mothers, their contributions were universally accepted and valued. The chief ways that a woman should express her war support in the valorous *Volk* family were as a self–sacrificing "heroic mother," "soldier's wife," "heroic sister," "warrior's bride" or "sweetheart" who sent her son, husband or fiancé off to war, boosted their fighting spirit and ensured that her "warrior" was well equipped; or as a "magnanimous nurse" who cared for sick and wounded

---

[34] Chézy, *Unvergessenes*, 2:71–75; "Brief von Rahel Levin in Prag an Varnhagen, 30. Juli 1813," in *Briefwechsel zwischen Varnhagen und Rahel (Aus dem Nachlaß Varnhagens v. E.)*, ed. Ludmilla Assing, 6 vols. (Leipzig, 1874–76; repr. Bern, 1973), 3:14; "Brief von Rahel Levin in Prag vom 4. Oktober 1813 und Varnhagen," in ibid., 3:171–172; "Brief von Rahel Levin in Prag vom 12. Oktober 1813 und Varnhagen," in ibid., 3:173–175; and "Vermischte Nachrichten: Frauenverein Oels," *PF*, 22 Nov. 1813, 87.

[35] "Deutsche Hülfsvereine," *DB* 2.14 (1815): 209–214.

[36] "Weiblicher Heroismus," *SP*, no. 2, Feb. 1814, 165–170.

[37] Ibid.; *Preußischer Patriotenspiegel: Enthaltend treffliche Charaktergemälde und schöne Züge von braven Männern und edlen Frauen des preußischen Landes während des letzten Krieges gegen die Franzosen*, 2 vols. (Quedlinburg and Leipzig, 1817, 2nd edn.), 2:96–104.

soldiers, preferably in her own home.[38] In the exceptional circumstances of the "War of Liberation," they were even allowed to extend these roles into the "patriotic public sphere." Much as in Revolutionary France, where with the introduction of the *levée en masse* in August 1793 women were expected to become "republican mothers," in Prussia during the wars of 1813–15 they were expected to become "patriotic mothers."[39] The organized nursing of sick and wounded soldiers, in particular, was thus accepted and acknowledged as an appropriate area of female endeavor. A song that a "wounded warrior" dedicated "respectfully and gratefully to the women's association of Breslau," published in March 1814 in the military newspaper *Preußische Feldzeitung*, stated accordingly:

> Our women long not
> for murderous melee, nor savage warrior vengeance,
> Yet zeal for the good cause
> Dwells in their gentle breast.
>
> A band of noble women,
> Calms the warrior's pain with mother love
> Oh, let us build them a lasting monument
> In gratitude-filled hearts![40]

The acceptance of organized forms of female patriotism in the public arena beyond medical care, such as involvement in a patriotic women's association or the dedication of a military banner, was, however, generally less unanimous, since they were harder to reconcile with prevailing ideas about the gender order than individual forms of "patriotic motherliness." Certainly, in Prussia, the princesses of the royal family themselves had called on women to organize wartime charity work in women's patriotic associations. Their engagement found support above all in the high government and military circles that were responsible for organizing the war and for ensuring that it enjoyed sufficient support – especially financial and organizational – at home. Broad segments of the patriotic-national press likewise welcomed the

---

[38] Anonymous, *Frauensteuer*, 56. For more, see Hagemann, *Muth*, 374–382; and idem, "Heldenmütter, Kriegerbräute und Amazonen: Entwürfe 'patriotischer Weiblichkeit' in Preußen zur Zeit der Freiheitskriege," in *Militär und bürgerliche Gesellschaft im 19. und 20. Jahrhundert*, ed. Ute Frevert (Stuttgart, 1997), 174–200.

[39] On the concept of the "republican mother," which was first introduced by Linda K. Kerber for the period of the American Revolution, see her "The Republican Mother: Women and the Enlightenment – An American Perspective," *American Quarterly* 28.2 (1976): 187–205, and *Intellectual History of Women: Essays by Linda K. Kerber* (Chapel Hill, NC, 1997), 41–62; for France, see Applewhite and Levy, "Women"; and for Britain, Colley, *Britons*, 237–282.

[40] "Dem Frauen-Verein zu Breslau hochachtungsvoll und dankbar gewidmet," *PF*, no. 69, 27 March 1814; see also "Zum Geburtstage an die redliche Frau von den geheilten kranken und verwundeten Kriegern, die sie versorgt, gepflegt und erquickt hat, Br., den 3ten März 1816," supplement to *SPZ*, no. 33, 16 March 1816.

activities of the women's associations and promoted their work by printing appeals and reports. From the beginning, though, there was also resistance, expressed less in published opinion than in daily practice at the local level. Men in the lower echelons of the military and civilian administration, in particular, resented the women's associations that were active in war relief as competitors. This resentment is evident in various local conflicts over areas of responsibility and rights of control in the fields of nursing care or relief for widows and orphans.[41]

Regardless of these differences, the press emphasized over and over that female involvement in the public sphere could be tolerated only because the "fatherland is in peril." With this stereotypically repeated phrase, contemporaries attempted to reconcile the demands that the new form of "people's war" made on civilian society with the prevailing ideas of a bourgeois gender order that referred women to the private sphere. There was, accordingly, a broad consensus that the "separate spheres" of the two sexes should be reestablished as quickly as possible after the war. An article in the *Deutsche Blätter* of January 1814 entitled "A Few Words on the Relationship of German Women to Present Events in the World" offered the characteristic argument:

Destined for the smaller circle of domestic life, women are excluded from the business of state and from public fame. [...] Be that as it may, there are moments when women, too, may not be refused a lively participation in public affairs, moments when the interests of all humanity hang in the balance, and when they, too, as an important segment of humanity, are called upon to be more than idle spectators. And verily! The present is just such a moment! For the great struggle that shakes Europe and grips the most hidden private life in its mighty movements serves no mere political end. The independence of peoples, national honor, the faith and manners of our forefathers, these are the sacred goods for which we fight, and which the one sex must hold just as dear as the other.[42]

When the "fatherland was in peril" – during wartime – women and men alike were expected to demonstrate unconditional patriotism. As part of the *Volk* family, women could legitimately participate in patriotic relief efforts because the exceptional conditions of a society at war demanded it.[43] After the wars, however, they had to relinquish all public activities outside the home and support the demobilization of society by healing the physical and mental wounds of their returning "warriors" and by "re-civilizing" them.

This was an expectation placed not just on the mothers and wives of soldiers, but also on young unmarried women. After the war, they were to wed only those men who had proven their ability to protect "home and

---

[41] Reder, *Frauenbewegung*, 452–476.

[42] "Einige Worte über das Verhältnis der deutschen Frauen zu den jetzigen Weltbegebenheiten I," *DB* 2.74 (1814): 311–315.

[43] See Hagemann, "*Volk* Family," 179–205; and chapter 7 in the second part.

hearth" and thus their masculinity by participating in battle. The stereotypical phrase was that "German maidens" must not marry cowards.[44] If they were already engaged, they must honor their promise of marriage even if their fiancés returned as invalids incapable of fulfilling their duties as family breadwinners. In such cases it was no disgrace for a woman to support her family, for he remained a hero and a real man, having demonstrated his masculinity in battle. The poem "The Prussian Lass to her Beloved," which appeared in the *Zeitung für die elegante Welt* in June 1814, describes this demand as follows:

> Gladly shall I keep my vow:
> Do thy duty for God and fatherland,
> At the altar I'll give you my hand,
> Be thou crippled or even deformed.
>
> Canst thou not support thy loyal wife
> She shall feed thee all thy life.
> Happily we do without,
> but never abandon what our heart desired.[45]

Like other poems, this one was not only intended to remind women of their specific postwar duties, but also served to assure homecoming wounded and disabled soldiers that they would be returning to the safety of a family, surrounded by female love and care.[46]

Unlike the men who went off to fight, women could expect no recompense for supporting the war effort and for their selfless activities in wartime und postwar charity. There were only very occasional calls for their commitment to be honored on a par with military service, for example in the article "On a German Domestic Affair and Question of Honor," which appeared in the *Schlesische Provinzialblätter* in March 1815. "Recent history offers an outstanding example of a patriotism that gripped almost the entire female sex, and Germany, our liberated fatherland, must honor the sacrifices that its worthy daughters made for this liberation no less than the heroism of its sons."[47] The overwhelming message the press conveyed to women who were active during and after the war was that their most important "reward"

[44] See, for example, Jacobs, *Deutschlands Ehre*.

[45] "Das Preußische Mädchen an ihren Geliebten," *ZfeW*, no. 108, 2 June 1814.

[46] Clemens Brentano also explicitly assigned women this task, for example in his play "Viktoria und ihre Geschwister, mit fliegenden Fahnen und brennender Lunte: Ein klingendes Spiel," which he wrote at the end of 1813 but only published in 1815. The proceeds were dedicated to the "Women's Associations of the Free Cities of Frankfurt, Bremen, Hamburg and Lübeck for charitable ends." Printed in *Clemens Brentano's Gesammelte Schriften*, ed. Christian Brentano, vol. 7: *Comödien* (Frankfurt/M., 1852), 279–466; see also Achim Hölter, *Die Invaliden: Die vergessene Geschichte der Kriegskrüppel in der europäischen Literatur bis zum 19. Jahrhundert* (Stuttgart, 1995), 368–371.

[47] "Ueber eine deutsche Ehren- und Hausangelegenheit, ein Wort vielleicht zu seiner Zeit," *SP*, no. 3 (March 1815): 238–253.

was the knowledge that they had done their duty. A poem that appeared on 16 March 1816 in the *Berlinische Nachrichten*, which was dedicated to an "honest woman by the sick and wounded warriors, now healed," whom "she had cared for, nursed and revived," accordingly stressed:

> Thou shalt find the reward in thy own breast,
> filled with the consciousness of noble deeds fulfilled,
> and civic virtue will weave thee a wreath
> of oak leaves and branches evergreen,
> Which salute thy glory more than ribbon and star.[48]

Soon after the war, a process of suppressing and forgetting active female patriotism began. The press mentioned the achievements of the patriotic women's organizations ever less frequently. One of the few publications that tried to remedy this development was the sole important women's newspaper in existence after the war, the *Allgemeine deutsche Frauen-Zeitung*, which appeared between 1816 and 1818. It regularly printed extensive accounts honoring and recalling women's patriotic wartime activities.[49] In September 1818, the paper published a vigorous defense of the patriotic activities of the women's associations against their detractors. All of the accusations that this series of three articles sought to refute revolved around a single point: Women's patriotic involvement had overstepped the boundary between the sexes and with it the limits of decency and morality. Women had been so presumptuous as to claim the masculine right to act in the public arena, doing so out of "petty passions" – "vanity" and a "desire for glory." This, patriotic women's detractors asserted, was demonstrated by the continuation of their involvement after the wars had ended. It was now high time to end all public activities by women.[50] With such arguments the male leadership in politics and the military, supported by the press, attempted to stabilize the gender order of postwar society. Parallel to the process of suppressing and forgetting active female patriotism, the disbanding of the patriotic women's associations began. Most patriotic women's associations ended their work in 1815–16. Only one in ten survived, mainly as general charitable associations.[51] In Berlin the only important association to continue its work for a substantial period after the war – until 1844 – was the Female Charitable Association, which remained dedicated to poor relief.[52]

---

[48] "Zum Geburtstage an die redliche Frau," *BN*, supplement to no. 33, 16 March 1816.

[49] See, for example, "Lobrede auf die Frauen unserer Zeit," *AFZ*, 20 March 1816.

[50] "Schutzschrift der Frauen-Vereine," pts. 1–3, *AFZ*, 2 Sept. 1818, 5 Sept. 1818 and 9 Sept. 1818.

[51] See Gräfe, *Nachrichten*, 187–317, for Prussia, see 266–283; Reder, *Frauenbewegung*, esp. 384–402; and Huber-Sperl, "Organized Women," 89–99.

[52] Hagemann, *Muth*, 424–425.

Nevertheless, through their engagement, the women who founded the first patriotic women's associations between 1813 and 1815 in Prussia and other parts of Germany established a lasting pattern of patriotic-national female activism that could be transferred from war to peacetime. Members of later patriotic-national women's groups acknowledged this achievement, referring to the tradition of the patriotic women's associations of 1813–15. The Patriotic Women's Association founded in 1867, for instance, stated that it sought to "continue what the associations of 1813 began." It vowed to "perform volunteer nursing like our valiant predecessors from the great epoch of the German awakening." In order to be ready, it aimed "to make extensive preparations for war during peacetime."[53]

The history of the patriotic women's associations is remarkable from two perspectives. It not only shows that wars conducted as "national wars" with conscript armies made it necessary from the very beginning to mobilize the largest possible number of both soldiers and civilians, but also reveals the close links between the beginnings of patriotic women's activism and the phenomenon of the "national war." The exceptional situation created by such a war opened up a new sphere of patriotic public activity for women, initially primarily for those of the upper middle class and aristocracy. To put it another way, the organized opportunity for participation in the public arena open to women during the wars was mainly a product of the new form of mass warfare legitimated by national ideology that required broad civilian support and therefore encouraged patriotic-national activism by broader social strata than ever before. In retrospect, the forms of German women's patriotic activism developed during the period of the wars of 1813–15, as well as the ideological terms in which they were legitimated, prove to have been highly influential. Images of the self-sacrificing "heroic mother," the "soldier's wife" and the "warrior's sweetheart" as well as the "magnanimous nurse" outlined the fields of endeavor in the valorous *Volk* family that would be assigned to German women and girls in later national wars up to the Second World War.

[53] Karstädt, *Heldenmädchen*, 90–91; on the history of the "Vaterländischer Frauenverein" and its remembrance of the tradition of the "Wars of Liberation," see Quataert, *Staging*, 133–292; Angelika Schaser, "Women in a Nation of Men: The Politics of the League of German Women's Associations (BDF) in Imperial Germany, 1894–1914," in Blom et al., *Gendered Nations*, 249–268, esp. 258–260.

10

De/Mobilizing Society: Patriotic-National Celebrations and Rituals

In his 1810 book *German Folkdom*, Friedrich Ludwig Jahn presents his extensive suggestions for the formation of a German "folk culture" under the heading "folk sensibility" (*Volksgefühl*).[1] For him, the "language of signs" spoken by "festivities, ceremonies and customs," was a "language of the heart," a "need of man, who recognizes the spiritual more purely in a mediating symbol." This language comes "to the aid of memory," because it creates a "lasting effect of constant realization."[2] Jahn perfectly understood the importance of emotions for the cultural construction of a nation, and the central role that ceremonies, rituals and symbols played in this process. He and many other patriots therefore intensively discussed the development of a patriotic-national festival culture in the context of the debate over the best forms of mobilization for war that began after the defeat of 1806–07.

The suggestions they made for this patriotic-national festival culture were a mix of old traditions and new ideas.[3] Early modern European monarchies had used ceremonies and rituals to display and increase their political power and prestige. The king's coronation, his birthday or important battlefield victories were typically celebrated with grand festivals. Military parades in splendid dress uniforms became a part of these ceremonies when early modern states introduced standing armies and the drilling of soldiers became commonplace. Churches were often used for state-ordered services of intercession and thanksgiving during and after wars, and eighteenth-century Prussia and Germany were no exception in this regard.[4] In the

---

[1] Jahn, *Volksthum*, 323–368.

[2] Ibid., 337–338 and 342.

[3] See, for example, Jahn, *Volksthum*, 337–360. Jahn was well aware of the debates and the French example. See also Manfred Hettling and Paul Nolte, eds., *Bürgerliche Feste: Symbolische Formen politischen Handelns im 19. Jahrhundert* (Göttingen, 1993), 8–36.

[4] See Uwe Schultz, *Das Fest: Kulturgeschichte von der Antike bis zur Gegenwart* (Munich, 1988), 140–243; J. R. Mulryne et al., eds., *Europa Triumphans: Court and Civic Festivals in Early Modern Europe* (Aldershot, 2004); Karin Friedrich, ed., *Festive Culture in Germany*

1770s and 1780s, however, a novel discourse emerged in Central Europe and elsewhere. Enlightened reformers proposed a refashioning of the public festival culture, which they now understood as part of "national culture." They believed that such celebrations could be used to foster patriotism and a feeling of national belonging among the population.[5] Revolutionary France was the first state to demonstrate vividly the potential of a state-organized festival culture for national mobilization in the early 1790s, and in the following years it became a model for others, even its enemies.[6]

The suggestions for promoting a national spirit, self-sacrifice and the willingness to defend one's country with the aid of festivals, rituals and symbols that Jahn and other patriots presented before and during the wars of 1813–15 were adopted on a wide scale. The National Festival of the Germans, held for the first time on 18 and 19 October 1814 to commemorate the decisive victory over Napoleon in the Battle of Nations at Leipzig, was only the largest and best-known national festival. Historians consider it to be the "matrix of German national festivals in the nineteenth century."[7] This festival is well studied, but many smaller patriotic celebrations have gone unnoticed. In this chapter I explore some of these smaller celebrations and rituals held throughout Germany. The focus is first on induction ceremonies for volunteers and militiamen and flag consecrations for their units. Then I examine thanksgiving and victory celebrations. All these ceremonies helped to promote patriotism and self-sacrifice. Afterwards, I explore peace festivals and festivities marking the homecoming of militiamen and volunteers, which played an important role in their symbolic reintegration into the community of "peaceful and law-abiding citizens" and the cultural demobilization of society after the war had ended. In Prussia, the government or the military mandated many of these festivals and rituals; several others were initiated independently on a local level by municipalities, the clergy and the citizenry, or spontaneously celebrated by the population. Patriotic-national festival culture was particularly well developed in the Prussian monarchy, but similar ceremonies and festivities were organized in other German territorial states as well, especially in the north and west.[8]

---

and *Europe from the Sixteenth to the Twentieth Century* (Lewiston, NY, 2000); and idem and Sara Smart, eds., *The Cultivation of the Monarchy and the Rise of Berlin: Brandenburg-Prussia 1700* (Aldershot, 2010).

[5] See Paul Münch, "Fêtes pour le peuple, rien par le peuple: Öffentliche Feste im Programm der Aufklärung," in Düding et al., *Festkultur*, 25–45.

[6] See Mona Ozouf, *La Fête révolutionnaire, 1789–1799* (Paris, 1976).

[7] Düding, "Das deutsche Nationalfest"; see also idem, "Deutsche Nationalfeste im 19. Jahrhundert: Erscheinungsbild und politische Funktion," *Archiv für Kulturgeschichte* 69 (1987): 371–388.

[8] Hagemann, *Muth*, 457–508; Katherine Aaslestad, "Remembering and Forgetting: The Local and the Nation in Hamburg's Commemorations of the Wars of Liberation," *CEH* 38.3 (2005): 384–416; and Planert, *Mythos*, 622–625.

Patriotic-national festival culture will be analyzed as both a collective practice and a medium of the political discourse of the time. Three questions frame my analysis, which takes the form of "thick description"[9]: first, how did the festival culture represent the imagined nation; second, how did these representations attempt to mold patriotic-national emotions, especially the feeling of belonging and community; and third, what importance did these emotions have for the formation of the collective memory of the wars of 1813–15? The theoretical and methodological reflections of cultural historians – who since the mid-1990s have paid increasing attention to the significance of emotions for the formation of a national political culture and national identity – are helpful for this analysis.[10] They have studied what genuinely constitutes "national sensibility" and how such cultural practices and representations as festivals, rituals and symbols could be used to produce, heighten, direct and synchronize it. The scholarship demonstrates that celebrations, rituals and symbols do more than simply help to form collective identities by combining textual, visual and material language with cultural practices and allowing for the active participation of individuals and groups; they also shape collective memories.[11] They have the potential to work in this way because of their intermediality, which ensures the successful construction of emotionally charged collective memories, and their potential to be transferred from one situation to another.[12] It is therefore no coincidence that festivities, ceremonies, rituals and symbols play a pivotal role in the "public policy of memory" of states and their military institutions. Uniforms, medals and flags are important patriotic, national and military symbols, and are inextricably connected with the rituals and festivities in which they are used. They are a central part of patriotic-national as well as military culture. Their concrete meanings, however, can only be understood in a specific historical context, since like other cultural signs they are constantly being reconstructed, although they can retain fairly consistent connotations over long periods of time.[13]

What most of this scholarship tends to overlook, however, is that the form and content of festivities, ceremonies, rituals and symbols are frequently not

[9] See Clifford Geertz, *Thick Description: Toward an Interpretive Theory of Culture* (New York, 1973); and Michael Maurer, ed., *Das Fest: Beiträge zu seiner Theorie und Systematik* (Cologne, 2004), 19–54.

[10] One of the first publications on nation and emotion was François et al., *Nation*.

[11] On the state of research, see Maurer, *Fest*; and Birgit Aschmann, "Vom Nutzen und Nachteil der Emotionen in der Geschichte: Eine Einführung," in *Gefühl und Kalkül: Der Einfluss von Emotionen auf die Politik des 19. und 20. Jahrhunderts*, ed. idem (Stuttgart, 2005), 9–32.

[12] Maurer, *Fest*, 114–115; and Astrid Erll, "Literature, Film, and the Mediality of Cultural Memory," in Erll and Nünning, *Companion*, 389–399.

[13] Erik Meyer, "Memory and Politics," in *Cultural Memory Studies: An International and Interdisciplinary Handbook*, ed. Astrid Erll and Ansgar Nünning (Berlin, 2008), 173–180; and Sabine Behrenbeck, *Der Kult um die toten Helden: Nationalsozialistische Mythen, Riten und Symbole 1923 bis 1945* (Cologne, 1996), 57–64.

merely organized along class lines, but also highly gendered. Gender images proved to be crucial not only in the discursive construction of patriotic-national ideologies and collective identities, but also in the creation of a national or military culture, in the mobilization for war, the demobilization after war and the commemoration of war.[14] Class and gender differences will therefore be major aspects of the following analysis.[15]

INDUCTION CEREMONIES FOR VOLUNTEERS AND MILITIAMEN

Even before the introduction of universal conscription, Prussian patriots had discussed how an induction ritual for conscripts could be used to encourage the idea of arming the people and to create unity and comradeship among men from very different social strata. The proposals Ernst Moritz Arndt offered in his February 1813 pamphlet *What Are the Reserves and the Militia?* proved to be most influential for the form taken by this ritual. In this very widely disseminated text, Arndt recommends that an induction ceremony be organized for the militia in each of Prussia's provincial districts:

Once the young men of a district are assembled, a solemn worship service will be held and it will be explained to the youths what war more generally and what war for the fatherland and against the French means, and that they are a far better and nobler people than the French, and thus must not suffer the latter to remain their masters; they will be told and admonished that their own land was once fortunate and glorious, and that it will become so again by their virtue and honesty; they will be reminded that dying for the fatherland is high praise in Heaven and on earth, and speeches, prayers and sacred and military songs will ignite loyalty, glory and virtue in their hearts.[16]

At the end of the ceremony the young men would swear a "precious and stalwart oath." To intensify the community-creating emotions, Arndt advised that this oath be taken "in a large company," so "that several hundred or thousand swear at the same time." On this occasion the militia's flags would also be consecrated "with Christian prayer and earnest devotion."[17] The

---

[14] See Silke Wenk, "Gendered Representations of the Nation's Past and Future," in Blom et al., *Gendered Nations*, 63–67. For gendered studies on cultural representations of the German nation in the nineteenth century, see Wagner, "Germania"; and Brandt, *Germania*, 106–343. An excellent study for France is Joan B. Landes, *Visualizing the Nation: Gender, Representation, and Revolution in Eighteenth-Century France* (Ithaca, NY, 2001).

[15] The following is based on Karen Hagemann, "Celebrating War and Nation: The Gender Order of Patriotic Ceremonies and Festivities in the Time of Prussia's Wars against Napoleon, 1813–1815," in Hagemann et al., *Gender, War and Politics*, 264–306; and Hagemann, *Muth*, 427–508.

[16] Arndt, "Landsturm," 13.

[17] Ibid., 13–14.

rhetoric Arndt suggested was very typical of the time, as was the Christian symbolism he proposed for the induction ceremony.

Contemporary press reports suggest that the organizers of most induction ceremonies – the local authorities, the military and the Protestant churches – followed Arndt's recommendations. One of the first and best-documented ceremonies was the induction of the Lützowers, which took place near Breslau on 28 March 1813. The *Preussische Correspondent* gives a vivid description:

At twilight, the assembled corps arrived at the church in Rogau, which was brightly illuminated by candles and torchlight. Martial music welcomed them. The choir struck up a heart-lifting chorale penned especially for the occasion by Körner, and Luther's powerful hymn 'A Mighty Fortress is our God!' With concise words spoken from the steps of the altar, the pastor reminded the assembled company of the duties of the warrior, the dangers of war, admonishing each to fulfil the former loyally and face the latter with courage. The soldiers then shouted as in one voice: 'We swear it!' and the pastor knelt down before God, loudly calling upon Him to 'Save the fatherland' and 'Lead the warriors to victory or death!' The warriors then raised their hands to Heaven and swore steadfast loyalty unto death to God, king and fatherland. The quiet, devout emotion of all those assembled poured forth in rivers of tears.[18]

The account portrays the ceremony, which involved a thousand volunteers, as a regional-patriotic event in which the soldiers vowed to fight for "God, king and fatherland." Only the reference to Theodor Körner explicitly indicates the ceremony's German-national orientation, which reflected the composition of the unit. In his "Song for the Solemn Consecration of the Royal Prussian Free Corps," which was part of the ceremony, Körner describes the war against Napoleon as the "German people's sanctified struggle for freedom."[19] Autobiographical recollections of the ceremony more strongly emphasize its German-national character. At the same time, these texts document the gender dimension of a ceremony that constituted an initiation ritual in which young men were transformed into soldiers. The oath was correspondingly taken not just at the altar, and thus before God, but also on the swords of the officers, the symbols par excellence of martial masculinity. Battle-tested sword-bearers and experienced soldiers administered the oath to the fledgling warriors and introduced them to their new role.[20] The degree to which sacred, patriotic-national, military and gender elements mingled and reinforced one another in the ceremony by arousing or heightening powerful emotions among the participants is evident in a

[18] "Schreiben aus Breslau v. 29ten März 1813," *PC*, no. 2, 3 April 1813.
[19] Theodor Körner, "Lied zur feierlichen Einsegnung des Königl. Preußischen Freicorps," in idem, *Zwölf freie deutsche Gedichte: Nebst einem Anhang* ([Leipzig], 1813), 5–6.
[20] See "Körner an Henriette v. Pereira in Wien, 30 March 1813," in *Theodor Körners Briefwechsel mit den Seinen*, ed. Augusta Weldler-Steinberg (Leipzig, 1910), 231–232.

letter Körner wrote on 30 March 1813 to his friend Henriette von Pereira in Vienna:

> After the singing of a song of my own composition, the local pastor gave a powerful and moving sermon, leaving not a dry eye. At last he had us swear the oath. [...] We swore. Thereupon he fell to his knees and begged God's blessing for his warriors. By the Almighty, it was a moment when the consecration of the dead trembled aflame in every breast, when every heart beat heroically.[21]

The induction of the Lützow volunteers was not the only ceremony to have such an emotional effect. Other accounts also describe the company as so moved that they were "overcome" by their feelings and wept copiously. In this Romantic period, men were still permitted and indeed expected to develop strong feelings for their country and could display them publicly without embarrassment.[22] Christian rhetoric and symbolism played an important role in fueling the emotions of the ceremony. Religion, too, was not yet viewed as primarily feminine.[23]

Most of the induction ceremonies – which became common for volunteers and militias, first in the old Prussian territories and shortly thereafter in the liberated northern and western regions of Germany – proceeded along similar lines. Organized by the provincial district administration and the military in cooperation with local church parishes, the ceremonies typically began with the militia inductees marching up to the church. The ringing of the church bells announced the ceremony itself, which took place either on the square in front of the church or inside, before the altar. Framed by patriotic-religious songs, the sermon and the communal oath were the main focus. The ceremonies were public and seem to have generated great interest everywhere. When the induction took place in the unit's home district, which was the rule for the militia, it was attended not just by the immediate family but also by an extensive network of kin and friends. The local authorities and clergy were always represented, and the program invariably featured a parade by the town's citizen guard.[24]

The ceremonies for volunteers and militias differed mainly in three respects: the militia ceremonies were far more rooted in the regional community; their political orientation was regional-patriotic, not German-national like most volunteer ceremonies; and the recruits frequently lacked

---

[21] Ibid., 232.

[22] See Hagemann, "German Heroes," 127–130; Martina Kessel, "The 'Whole Man': The Longing for a Masculine World in Nineteenth-Century Germany," *G&H* 15 (2003): 1–31; and Trepp, "Emotional Side."

[23] Hagemann, *Muth*, 143–148. See also Ann Taylor Allen, "Religion and Gender in Modern German History: A Historiographical Perspective," in Hagemann and Quataert, *Gendering*, 190–207.

[24] See, for example, "Reichenbach, den 22. April 1813," *SP*, no. 4, April 1813, 389–390.

the enthusiasm of the volunteers.[25] Accounts of the militia induction ceremonies rarely mention enthusiasm for war. Instead, they frequently stress the "quiet and earnest" mood of the militiamen who were taking the oath.[26] This may well have reflected the fact that many of them served only reluctantly. The military leadership, local authorities and clergy thus used the induction ceremonies to remind militia recruits in no uncertain terms of "men's sacred duty to defend the fatherland."[27]

The induction ceremonies for new recruits developed into an important military ritual. In its regional-patriotic version, the ritual persisted after the wars for all new conscripts of the Prussian army and later, with a more German-national and monarchic orientation, in the German Empire. The ceremonies continued to serve the purpose of attuning conscripts to military service, helping to create comradeship among soldiers and communicating the idea of "heroic death for the fatherland" to the young men.

FLAG CONSECRATIONS

The actors in the induction ceremonies were exclusively male. As a rule, women attended the events as mere spectators. Even in the symbolic repertoire of these ceremonies, they had no place. The only exceptions were those associated with flag consecrations. In these rituals women played a central part as flag embroiderers.[28] This is evident from a report in the *Deutsche Blätter* that describes an induction ceremony for 950 volunteers held on 25 January 1814 in Düsseldorf. The town was the capital of the newly created general governorate between Weser and Rhine. Under the direction of the governor-general, the event, with "many thousands" of participants, took place before and inside the city's largest church. After the swearing of the oath at the end of the usual ritual, "young female citizens of Elberfeld," a nearby town, presented the flag and banner they had made for the volunteers. The governor-general "introduced the standard- and flag-bearers to the noble donors from whose hands they received this symbol of public spirit," then a Catholic priest and two Protestant ministers jointly consecrated the flag.[29] During the war, cooperative efforts by Protestant and Catholic clergy were typical in regions with a large Catholic population, such as the Rhineland or Silesia. Propaganda stressed the common ground among German Christians to create unity.[30]

---

[25] Ibid.
[26] Ibid., 390.
[27] Ibid., 389–390.
[28] Reder, *Frauenbewegung*, 425–427.
[29] "Brief aus Düsseldorf vom 25. Januar 1814," *DB* 2.85 (Feb. 1814): 497–499.
[30] Hagemann, *Muth*, 143–148.

In 1813–14 presentations of the flag by girls and women took place not just in Prussia but also throughout central, northern and western Germany. Usually, members of the local patriotic women's organization initiated the embroidering of a flag. The younger members of these associations in particular were eager to support their volunteering brothers, fiancés and friends with an embroidered flag.[31] A song written by a Dresden association of "skilled embroideresses from the upper ranks of the citizenry" illuminates their motives. This patriotic women's association "embroidered flags for the militia as well as the volunteers' banner" and presented them in solemn flag consecration ceremonies in various Saxon towns.[32] The song, dedicated to the Banner of the Saxon Volunteers, begins

> What you have kept so long enclosed in silent hearts,
> Is now fulfilled! – The laurels have sprouted!
> The free banner of the Saxons waves!
> Receive it from your sisters, all you dear ones,
> With utmost ardor, as it passes
> From our hands to yours![33]

The flag embroiderers here portray themselves as "sisters" alongside their fighting "brothers." In so doing, they remain within the highly gendered imagery of the nation as a valorous *Volk* family, in which girls and young women were assigned the role of the "hero's sister" and "warrior's bride."[34] When they handed over the flag, they publicly demonstrated their willing acceptance of this role, but they expected their "brothers" and "sweethearts" to do their complementary patriotic duty as volunteers. The flag was meant to fire them on and "guide" their "youthful steps | To great and daring manly deeds" that would prove them to be capable protectors and thus good future husbands.[35] With the flag, the young women symbolically accompanied the "heroic lads," remained united with them in spirit, spurred them on to battle and inspired them to defend the flag to their last drop of blood.

It was primarily women and girls of the middle classes who embroidered flags for the newly formed volunteer and militia units and presented them in the context of consecration ceremonies.[36] Through this activity they could express their solidarity with the war's patriotic-national aims. At the same time, by claiming a place at the center of the induction ceremonies, they also symbolically asserted a central role in the "valorous fatherland." The work of embroidery and the public presentation of the flag were unmistakably

---

[31] Ibid., 466–467.

[32] "Sachsens Töchter an den Banner der freiwilligen Sachsen bei der Aushändigung einer Fahne (Aus Dresden, im Februar 1814)," *DB* 2.86 (Feb. 1814): 505–508.

[33] Ibid., 507.

[34] Ehrenberg, *Charakter*, 11–12; see also Hagemann, "*Volk* Family."

[35] "Sachsens Töchter," 507.

[36] See Reder, *Frauenbewegung*, 425–427.

associated with the message that women considered themselves to be part of the "nation at arms," attentively observed national affairs and the progress of the war and played their part in victory.

The significance of the embroidering, presentation and consecration of the flags and banners derived from their function as political and military symbols. Into the nineteenth century, flags, along with signal instruments, were the most important means of leading the infantry and cavalry during combat. They served as rallying points for the troops and were deployed as identifiers and directional signs. On the battlefield they communicated orders and enabled soldiers to organize their lines in the heat of a skirmish. In addition to their purely utilitarian value, flags possessed a symbolic power that reflected their importance in crisis situations as emblems that could encourage wavering troops to attack. A flag thus represented not simply a unit's identity but chiefly its "spirit" and glory. Regimental flags, which usually incorporated the insignia of the state, were granted only by the monarch as sovereign and supreme military commander. The act of bestowing a flag was at once an expression of his military and political sovereignty and an acknowledgment of extraordinary military achievements, first and foremost courage and unbending loyalty. Every regiment of the Prussian standing army possessed at least one traditional flag, which in peacetime was kept in the quarters of the regimental commander. All members of the regiment took an oath to follow this flag during battle no matter what happened. The honor of a troop unit was tightly linked with the fate of its flag. To be chosen as flag-bearer was thus considered a special distinction and entailed serious responsibility, for the loss of the regimental flag was deemed to be a disgrace to the entire regiment.[37]

Only when viewed against this background does the political nature of the act of women and girls presenting a flag to newly formed volunteer and militia units become clear. In so doing, they not only assumed a role reserved for the monarch but also, by handing over a flag to the volunteers and militiamen before they had proven themselves in battle, placed untried units on the same footing as the experienced and trusted troops of the standing army. From the viewpoint of the government and the military, this act represented a double sacrilege. The Prussian king thus sought as early as April 1813 to squelch the quickly spreading custom of dedicating flags to militia and volunteer units by banning it.[38] When this measure failed, he reinforced the prohibition on 11 May 1813 with a royal cabinet order:

[37] Walter Transfeldt and Karl Hermann Freiherr von Brand, *Wort und Brauch im deutschen Heer: Geschichtliche und sprachkundliche Betrachtungen über Gebräuche, Begriffe und Bezeichnungen des deutschen Heeres in Vergangenheit und Gegenwart* (Hamburg, 1967, 6th edn.), 214–216.

[38] "Allgemeine Kabinettsorder. An den Staatsrat Graf zu Dohna-Wundlacken, Breslau, 8.4.1813," in *Geschichte der Königlich Preußischen Fahnen und Standarten seit dem Jahre 1807*, ed. Königl. Kriegsministerium, 2 vols. (Berlin, 1889 and 1890), 2:24–26.

I cannot grant the petition to provide the militia with flags. [...] In days to come I shall award flags to such militia brigades as cover themselves with glory through courage and determination in the face of the foe; I deem the subject to be too sacred, however, to permit ladies to give flags to the militia. This privilege must be reserved solely for the government, and you are thus instructed to reject all relevant requests in accordance with this view of the matter.[39]

In order, however, to recognize and honor the "loyal disposition" that women expressed in the flags they embroidered, the king simultaneously authorized the preservation of all military flags in the churches "as mementoes of the universal enthusiasm for the good cause."[40]

The ban on presenting flags to individual troop units did not prevent patriotic-minded women and girls from continuing to dedicate embroidered flags. It apparently seemed to them no less honorable to have their flags preserved in the local church as a memorial to the attainment of "national independence and autonomy." When the presentation and consecration of a flag occurred separately from an induction ceremony, the female flag donors even became the center of attention. Walking with the town's citizen guard and local notables in the parade of honor, they carried the flag to the church and held it during the act of consecration at the altar.[41]

Since the middle-class public clearly could not imagine a military formation without a flag, and since volunteers and militiamen felt that a newly established unit without its own flag would be inferior to the standing army, the king announced in the same royal cabinet order of 11 May 1813 that, when the war ended, he would recognize those militia brigades that had distinguished themselves by granting them a flag. Because he nevertheless received repeated petitions to grant a flag, he reiterated this pledge in his "Army Order for the Four Army Corps" of 1 October 1813.[42] The pressure to recognize the militias' "bravery" with a flag during the war was so powerful that only one month after the first French surrender on 30 May 1814, when the war of 1813–14 officially ended, the king issued an order to grant flags to all new militia units, "with the exception of those that have either not faced the enemy or only participated in blockades or have not taken part in decisive battles."[43] The manufacture of flags and their accoutrements proved so time-intensive, however, that it was not until September 1815, two months after the end of the second war, that militia regiments officially received their flags.

[39] "Allgemeine Kabinettsorder. An das Militair-Gouvernement von Schlesien, Bautzen, 11.5.1813," in ibid., 2:25–27.

[40] Ibid., 1:15.

[41] See, for example, "Ehrendenkmal zu Grünberg," *SP*, no. 2, Feb. 1814, 163–165.

[42] "Armee-Befehl für die vier Armeekorps, Teplitz 1.10.1813," *AB*, no. 45, 22 Oct. 1813.

[43] "Allgemeine Kabinettsorder. An den Staats- und Kriegsminister v. Boyen, Paris 3. Juni 1814," in Kriegsministerium, *Geschichte*, 2:29–30; this cabinet order was also widely published in the press.

Typical of the postwar flag-consecration ceremonies was the program of the Second Silesian Militia infantry regiment in Glewitz, described in the 27 March 1816 issue of the *Schlesische Privilegierte Zeitung*. First, the flag was nailed to a flagpole in the market square before a large audience that included "the most respected inhabitants of the town." This task was performed "by the officer corps and the troops chosen for this duty from each rank and company." Afterward, the military and civil authorities dined together at a local inn, "while breakfast was also distributed among the remaining troops on the market square." The regiment's "unforgettable day" – as the article stresses – ended with a ball "in which the notables of the town cheerfully participated."[44]

The official awarding of a flag was an outstanding event for a militia unit. With it, the king acknowledged the bravery and loyalty of the regiment. Since, after the Anti-Napoleonic Wars, the patriotic-minded elites of urban and rural Prussia continued to regard the militia as a form of "arming the people," the act of consecrating the flag was, at least in the first postwar years, less a military celebration than a patriotic-national event in which the men of a specific region demonstrated not only their devotion to king and fatherland but also their fighting capacity and valor. This changed, however. Like the induction ceremonies for militiamen, flag consecrations continued to be important military rituals in the nineteenth-century Prussian and German armies, but they developed into purely military events. Never again would women have a prominent place in this ritual. Because the government and military administration needed the broad support of the civilian population to fight a war based on the newly introduced universal conscription, they had to make compromises in 1813–14 and respond to public opinion. This was no longer necessary after the victory over Napoleon and the political restoration.

THANKSGIVING AND VICTORY CELEBRATIONS

In Berlin, the "Wars of Liberation" began as a celebration on 11 March 1813. When Russian troops under General Ludwig Adolph Peter von Sayn-Wittgenstein marched into the city, men, women and children of all ages and classes thronged the streets, cheering as they went to welcome the approaching army. Church bells rang out everywhere, and in the evening the entire city was illuminated, without the usual orders from the municipal government. Berliners remained outdoors far into the night, generously distributing food and drink to their Russian "liberators" and enjoying the festive atmosphere.[45]

---

[44] "Glewitz, den 7. März 1816," *SPZ*, supplement to no. 38, 27 March 1816.
[45] "Der Triumpf-Einzug des Grafen von Wittgenstein in Berlin: Anders erzählt als in den Berliner Zeitungen," *RT* 1.4 (1813): 79–84.

This rousing welcome was the prelude to a whole series of spontaneous celebrations during the wars of 1813–15. Most importantly, the great victories at Leipzig in October 1813 and at Waterloo in June 1815, as well as the first and second capitulations of the French in May 1814 and July 1815, drove people in town and countryside out into the streets and squares to share first their hopes and later their relief, gratitude and joy.[46] Usually they celebrated not just the victory of their own army but that of the whole coalition, because they were aware that only by fighting together had the allies been able to defeat Napoleon's army. One example of the many spontaneous victory celebrations in the countryside is depicted in a letter of 20 April 2014 by Marie Helene von Kügelgen, wife of the history and portrait painter Gerhard von Kügelgen, who taught at the Dresden Academy of Arts. Together with her husband and children she had left French-occupied Dresden in the spring of 1813 and found refuge during the war in the small Altenburg village of Hummelshain. In the letter, written to her parents and siblings, she describes the reaction to the news of victory:

When news of the peace reached us, the entire village longed to offer shared thanks to God in church, but unfortunately the pastor had traveled to a neighboring town and the schoolmaster was not there. […] In the evening, however, all the villagers gathered, carrying small lanterns, under the two great linden trees before the house of v. Ziegesar [the local forestry official]. His huntsmen played the melodies of the songs of thanksgiving very finely, and young and old sang from their hearts. Never has anything touched me more. […] In the meantime, the pastor had arrived and now suddenly stood among his flock, who reverently gathered close around him, and under the twinkling stars he recited a prayer of thanksgiving. Now all the people processed to the highest point of a field, which is surrounded by woods and full of echoes, and here sang their Te Deum, and after each verse a salvo was shot and the reverberations rang wonderfully round the woods, like majestic thunder. Ah, all of Europe rejoices with us.[47]

This description resembles many others and shows the pronounced need people felt to thank God for the victories achieved and to give thanks for the peace. The religiosity of many seems to have been so strong that there was a profound and general feeling that, as the clergymen preached from the pulpits, victory over the French had been possible only with God's help. Clearly, even well beyond the narrow circle of patriots, perceptions and experience corresponded to the propagated image of the struggle for liberation from Napoleon as a "holy war."

The thanksgiving and victory celebrations ordered by the Prussian government after great victories and after the peace treaties of 1814 and 1815,

---

[46] See, for example, "Friedensfeier in Bremen am 26.6.1814," *TG*, no. 135, 8 July 1814.

[47] "Marie von Kügelgen, Hummelshain, 20.4.1814," in *Ein Lebensbild in Briefen: Marie Helene von Kügelgen, geb. von Zöge von Manteuffel*, ed. Anna and Emma von Kügelgen (Stuttgart, 1900, 2nd. edn.), 198–199.

which were announced in the newspapers, thus met a public need.[48] At all of the thanksgiving services, which were modeled on the traditional ceremony developed during the eighteenth century, a long ringing of church bells was followed by a sermon of thanksgiving; then the *Te Deum* was sung and a collection taken up for the "wounded defenders of the fatherland." The state-sanctioned religious service was usually embedded in a civilian ceremony and, on many occasions, a military celebration as well. These events were often preceded by a parade of the town's citizen guards or the marksmen's guild, and culminated in an evening banquet and ball for the local elite and neighborhood dances for the rest of the community. Contemporary press reports from cities and towns in Prussia and other parts of northern and western Germany confirm this unvarying program of thanksgiving and victory celebrations. Even the tiniest villages did their best to mount suitable festivities.[49] In Prussian ceremonies, with their strongly regional-patriotic orientation, the religious and monarchic aspects were in the foreground. They were to offer proper thanks for divine aid while strengthening the faithful's piety, trust in God and spirit of self-sacrifice, but also to celebrate the leaders of state and army, in Prussia especially Friedrich Wilhelm III as the victorious father of the country. The military parades by local garrison troops and citizen guards represented manly valor far from the front. Even in his absence, the Prussian king, as the "heroic general and beloved father of his country," was always honored with hurrahs, songs and poems. Furthermore, they reminded the congregations that it was their task to help to heal the wounds of the wars with charitable donations. Collections to benefit the victims of the war were ordered to demonstrate the communal nature of war relief.[50]

Everywhere the same people – local authorities and church leaders – organized thanksgiving and victory celebrations. Their prominent role in these events demonstrated their position of power in the social hierarchy. In garrison towns the local military leadership was also involved. Thus, the visible actors were always men. Women were present mainly as spectators in the streets, as members of the church choirs and congregations or as participants in the evening balls or community dances. The patriotic women's associations were frequently active in preparing the festivities, however. They arranged the decoration of streets, squares and halls, and supervised the preparation of festival banquets. In addition, they were often responsible for collecting donations for sick, wounded and disabled soldiers or for war

[48] See, for example, "Bekanntmachung wegen der glorreichen Einnahme der Festungen Stettin, Torgau und Wittenberg, Berlin 18.1.1814, vom Departemet für den Kultus und öffentlichen Unterricht im Ministerio des Innern, gez. v. Schuckman. n," *VZ* , no. 8, 18 Jan. 1814) and no. 99, 14 Aug. 1814.
[49] See for example "Silberberg, vom 28. April," *SPZ*, no. 53, 4 May 1814; and "Siegesfeiern zu Ostrave und Plukau am 8. Juli," *SP*, no. 7, July 1815, 69–73.
[50] See also chapter 9 in this part.

widows and orphans. Yet the official programs of such ceremonies never mentioned these important contributions by women.

Whereas the spontaneous thanksgiving and victory celebrations included the entire population and represented an image of the nation as a community of the people that encompassed all social strata and both sexes, the official ceremonies presented Prussia and the other territorial states as monarchical states with the king at the top. They reflected the hierarchical, male-dominated structure of the state, its administration, army and churches. It is therefore not surprising that the rituals and symbols of the official thanksgiving and victory celebrations helped shape the monarchic tradition of similar ceremonies held in Prussia and other German states during and after the wars between 1866 and 1871 that led to German unification.[51]

PEACE FESTIVALS AND THE HOMECOMING OF VOLUNTEERS AND MILITIAMEN

The spontaneous festivities organized to celebrate the peace and welcome homecoming volunteer detachments and militia regiments more closely resembled unplanned thanksgiving and victory celebrations, and assumed the character of a *Volksfest*, a popular fair or festival.[52] The mothers and fathers, wives and sweethearts, children and neighbors of the returning soldiers welcomed their "liberators and heroes" home from the front. In these events women and men played equally significant roles, which indicates the complementary importance of the home front. The peace and welcome festivities were not ordered by the state but initiated by the municipalities. There was no model of earlier celebrations for the organizers to use, and the programs were consequently far less ritualized.[53]

The festivities that were held in and around the Prussian capital of Berlin to mark the return of the first volunteer corps on 5 July 1814 were one widely reported example. The events began with several squadrons of the municipal militia riding out to meet the returning units at the village of Schöneberg, half an hour's ride from the city, where they formed an honor guard. Berliners followed their example and left the city to stand along the road where their sons, brothers, husbands and friends would soon be marching.[54] The "motley throng" took the homecoming soldiers into their midst and joined the columns.[55] "Nearly all of the fair sex, without distinction of estate," bore flowers and wreaths "with which they strewed the path and adorned the

[51] See Jakob Vogel, *Nationen im Gleichschritt: Der Kult der Nation in Waffen in Deutschland und Frankreich, 1871–1914* (Göttingen, 1997), 42–91.

[52] "Berlin, den 5ten Juli," *VZ*, no. 80, 5 May 1814.

[53] "Berlin, vom 5. Juli," *SPZ*, no. 80, 9 July 1814.

[54] Ibid.

[55] "Berlin, den 5ten Juli," *VZ*, no. 80.

volunteer troops." Groups of white-clad young girls had "set themselves up in a semi-circle" in the road to throw wreathes of oak and laurel leaves over the troops as they marched by.[56] In the village of Schöneberg, where garlands were suspended over the streets, as they were along the entire route to and in Berlin, the princes, generals and majors as well as the commander of the city militia awaited the volunteers and placed themselves at the head of the procession. A company of the marksmen's guild had taken up position at the festively decorated Potsdam Gate, which marked the entrance to Berlin. A deputation from the municipal government welcomed the detachment there. One member gave a solemn speech and thanked the returning soldiers "in the name of the city and the fatherland." More than a hundred "daughters of Berlin" from every social stratum, all "dressed in white garments with roses in their streaming hair," completed the delegation and "presented the young warriors with flowers, wreaths and poems." A choir sang "Hail to Thee in Victor's Crown," and "the dense throng of spectators joined in and shouted one 'Hail to the King' after another."[57] Then began the solemn entry into the capital, in the "strictest military order," which the relatives of the members of the volunteer unit soon disrupted. Everyone was jumbled together, "overcome with joy and happiness."[58] The streets were full of people waving scarves from their windows and tossing flowers down onto the passing troops. In the evening the "young heroes" were invited to a performance at the *Schauspielhaus*, the main local theater, followed by a "peace banquet" sponsored by the municipal government and town councilors and attended by the "city's highest military and civilian authorities." Berliners spontaneously illuminated their windows.[59]

Press accounts suggest that everywhere in Prussia and other regions of northern and western Germany, the reception of the volunteers and militiamen who began returning home in July 1814 turned into joyful celebrations. Such rejoicing was, however, largely reserved for volunteers and militiamen – the ordinary male citizens who had fought "to defend their fatherland." One finds scarcely any press reports of similarly enthusiastic homecomings for regular army units. The most notable exception was the celebration marking the "Solemn Entry of His Majesty the King and the Berlin Royal Guards" on 7 August 1814. The centerpiece of this official event, in which the royal guards were welcomed as representatives of the entire army of the line, was a large and brilliant military parade, which demonstrated the might of the army and the king as its commander-in-chief.[60] After the second war in

[56] "Berlin, vom 5. Juli," *SPZ*, no. 80.
[57] "Berlin, den 5ten Juli," *VZ*, no. 80.
[58] "Berlin, vom 5. Juli," *BN*, no. 80, 5 July 1814.
[59] "Berlin, den 5ten Juli," *VZ*, no. 80.
[60] See "Feierlicher Einzug Sr. Maj. des Königs und der königlichen Garden zu Berlin am 7ten August," pts. 1–2, *ZfeW*, nos. 163 and 164, 19 and 28 Aug. 1814.

1815, the newspapers only sporadically reported on larger ceremonies to welcome the volunteers and militiamen who returned in the autumn and winter of that year. They simply noted that the approaching troops were warmly received everywhere.[61] This striking difference between 1814 and 1815 may be attributed first of all to the fact that the second, shorter, military campaign was largely conducted with troops of the line. In addition, the general development of political restoration had caused patriotic enthusiasm to wane significantly since autumn 1814.

Wherever homecoming celebrations were held in 1814 or 1815, a central component was a large group of young girls, dressed in the white "national costume" and crowned with flowers, who presented the returning soldiers with bouquets and oak or laurel wreaths as well as poems. To dress in the white, "modestly" tailored "German gown" was one of the few ways in which girls and young women could actively participate in patriotic-national festivities and become a visible part of the public sphere. By wearing their "national costume," they could publicly demonstrate their patriotism and support for the "War of Liberation."[62] The ritual surrender of wreaths by girls dressed in white dramatized the image – widely propagated in poetry and paintings of the time – of the "German maiden" who wove a wreath of German oak leaves for the victorious returning "heroic lad" and bestowed it on him publicly as a symbol of his valor.[63] The message associated with this ritual was that the fiancée, as an "honorable German girl," had "kept herself chaste and modest" and would now fulfill her promise, made at the beginning of the war, to give her hand in marriage only to a man who had proved himself a "protector and defender of home and fatherland" and thus a suitable husband.[64]

The young women who participated in these festivities were well aware of the symbolism of their public appearance. At the same time, it had a very personal significance for many of them, such as Agnes Perthes, the eldest daughter of the well-known Hamburg publisher and bookseller Friedrich Perthes. In her 1864 memoirs she describes her emotions at the entry of the Hanseatic Legion on 30 June 1814 in Hamburg.[65] Then 16 years old, she was among the white-clad maidens who welcomed the homecoming

[61] See, for example, "Auszug aus einem Schreiben," *VZ*, supplement to no. 15, 3 Jan. 1816.

[62] See Hagemann, *Muth*, 437–446.

[63] See for example the 1815 oil painting "The Wreath-Maker" by Georg Friedrich Kersting (Figure 2 at the beginning of the book).

[64] See, for example, "Der heimkehrenden Königsbergschen Landwehr und den sie begleitenden Waffengefährten," *BN*, no. 109, 10 Sept. 1814.

[65] "Hamburg, den 1ten Juli," *VZ*, no. 82, 9 July 1814. See also Hagemann, "Reconstructing"; and Katherine Aaslestad, "Patriotism in Practice: War and Gender Roles in Republican Hamburg, 1750–1815," in Hagemann et al., *Gender, War and Politics*, 227–246.

volunteers, eagerly anticipating the return of her fiancé, her cousin Wilhelm Perthes:[66]

Many young girls gathered at our house and made no secret of their plans to hand a laurel wreath to this one or that one. [...]. All at once – hark, hark – the sounds of the Hanseatic march rang in our ears. This had an electrifying effect on all of the girls. Beet-red [they ran] into the streets, struggled through the ranks, handed over the wreath, pressed hands and saw dear, kindly eyes and ran away again! The officers could scarcely keep order to prevent the entire procession from disintegrating; it had to hold until the town hall.[67]

Agnes Perthes was overjoyed to find her beloved safe and sound. The symbolic presentation of a laurel wreath to "her" returning hero gave her a public opportunity to express her feelings in a seemly manner. The rejoicing of mothers, wives and sweethearts at the happy reunion with their men, however, did not always correspond to the mood of the men themselves, whose joy was mixed with the pain of separation from their fellow soldiers and fears for the future. Wilhelm Perthes wrote about the same event in his 1844 memoirs, which were based on diaries he kept during the wars:

The occasion for taking up arms was achieved and nothing further could bind me to the soldier's trade, although it was painful to part from friends and comrades who had honestly shared good days and bad. The battalion and company had been my home for the duration of my service in the field. The separation would have been more difficult still, by the way, had it occurred when all of us still stood together, but when we marched into Hamburg we began at once to dissolve and scatter in all directions.[68]

The civilian chaos of the joyful welcome, created mainly by the women and girls, thus helped to disperse the male community of the military.

The celebrations to welcome volunteers and militiamen were accompanied by the clear message from authorities and loved ones that those returning home should integrate as quickly as possible into civilian society. This message was expressed with particular clarity in "Song for the Returning Defenders of the Fatherland," written by the popular poet Matthias Claudius to mark the homecoming of the Hanseatic Legion. The song was soon reprinted in newspapers and disseminated all over Germany.[69] What made it so popular, apart from the theme, was the fact that it could be sung to the melody of the extremely well-liked horseman's song "Up, Comrades, Up, to

[66] On Perthes, see Heinrich Pallmann, "Perthes, Wilhelm," *ADB* 25 (1887): 401–402

[67] Perthes, *Franzosenzeit*, 89–90; for more on the Perthes family, see Hagemann, "Reconstructing."

[68] Perthes, *Franzosenzeit*, 45.

[69] Ibid., 90; Matthias Claudius, "Lied für die heimkehrenden Vaterlandsvertheidiger," *DB* 5.182 (Sept. 1814): 126–127; on Claudius, see Urban Roedl, "Claudius, Matthias," *NDB* 3 (1957): 266–267.

Horse, to Horse" by Friedrich Schiller, one of the best-known German poets
of his era. Claudius's song begins:

> Come, comrades, and *dismount* your horse!
> Lay down your armor now!
> In your own home, at your own hearth
> There's no need for arrow and bow.
>
> War is good only in times of need,
> Good only for the sake of peace.
> Truly blessed will those be
> Who earn their bread through industry.
>
> Something else then comes to the fore:
> Happiness as in days of yore.
> Only domestic bliss is true,
> And so again we return to you. [...]
>
> We all return, hand in hand,
> Light-hearted and content to our land;
> Each man into the rank and trade
> That destiny his life has made.[70] (Emphasis in the original)

These verses reminded the homecoming volunteers and militiamen of their
civic duties and called on them to return to the rules and standards of peacetime society, represented by Claudius as an extended family in which each
man performs the work assigned to him by destiny. From the perspective of
civilian society, an important postwar task was the "demilitarization" and
"civilization" of the hegemonic image of valorous masculinity. The volunteers and militiamen had to become peaceful burghers (*Bürger*) once again,
to appreciate domesticity and accept their generational and social rank. As
citizens (*Staatsbürger*), however, they must remain willing to take up arms
whenever necessary, but their foremost duties now were to devote themselves to their obligations as (future) fathers and family breadwinners and
to demonstrate their patriotism through active dedication to the common
good. The often presumptuous mores and attitudes associated with military service had to be set aside and modest civilian behavior adopted once
again.

Claudius's poem concisely summarizes the message conveyed by the
homecoming celebrations for volunteers and militiamen. The festivities
expressed symbolically the men's inevitable social and cultural demobilization. The homeland integrated its returning "warriors" into peacetime society. Particular political concepts of the state and the nation were
irrelevant to this transformation. What mattered most was to remind the
"defenders of the fatherland" through the symbolic order of the festivities

---

[70] Ibid.

that it was time to bid farewell to the military's exclusively male "band of brothers" and reintegrate into the gender-mixed *Volk* family of peacetime. The course taken by the homecoming celebrations signaled the incompatibility between a strictly regulated military order and civilian life. The undisciplined behavior of civilians, especially female relatives, prevented the troops from entering the city in marching order, the symbol par excellence of military discipline. This does not mean that they lacked respect for the military achievements of the returning men. Many may also have shared the expectation that every man would display combat-readiness and, if necessary, defend home and country. In peacetime, however, it was more important for a man to be a caring paterfamilias, a patriotic citizen and a good Prussian or German, who willingly performed his collective and individual manly duties and cultivated an appreciation of his local *Heimat*, the territorial state in which he lived, and the German nation.[71] The parallel message to women was that they should now return to their own domestic and familial duties and assist in the cultural demilitarization of the returning "warriors" in their "cozy homes." They must therefore give up all public activities, especially their work in the patriotic women's associations.[72]

During and after the wars of 1813–15, public ceremonies and rituals became an important part of political and military culture in Prussia and large areas of northern and western Germany.[73] They served two main purposes: During the wars their major function was to promote combat-readiness and patriotism and create unity beyond all differences within the nation, and after the wars they fostered cultural demobilization, especially the demilitarization of the returning volunteers and militiamen, who had to be reintegrated into civilian society. Public festivities and ceremonies were so important for both purposes because they were able to facilitate a collective emotional experience that incorporated broad segments of the population well beyond the readership of the daily papers. By deploying music and poems as well as rituals and symbols, they affected the emotions, which were far more crucial to the molding of patriotic-national bonds and cultural demobilization than intellectual arguments.[74]

Much like the critical examination of the public discourse, a "thick description" of the patriotic-national festivities and ceremonies and their symbolic elements demonstrates that contemporary visions of the state and nation were always shaped by the interplay between gender, class and familial status. The festival culture reflected and visualized the public discourse

---

[71] On postwar masculinities, see Hagemann, "German Heroes"; and Karin Breuer, "Competing Masculinities: Fraternities, Gender and Nationality in the German Confederation, 1815–30," *G&H* 20 (2008): 270–287.

[72] See Hagemann, "Female Patriots."

[73] See Aaslestad, "Remembering"; and Brophy, *Popular Culture*, 105–170.

[74] Hagemann, *Muth*, 105–158.

on nation and war in the print media, but far more than this discourse it emphasized the inclusionary dimensions. Patriotic-national festivities and ceremonies not only lent concrete form to gendered visions of the state and the nation and to the roles assigned to various social groups, generations and both sexes within those visions, but they also allowed participants to experience these visions physically and mentally. The state was presented in these festivities and ceremonies either as an absolutist paternalist monarchy with the splendid sovereign at its helm; a military "community" with the monarch as the "father" and supreme commander of the male fraternity of the army; or as a "band of brothers" composed of citizen-soldiers with the king as primus inter pares. These different representations vividly reflected and transmitted the competing absolutist, enlightened-conservative and generally regional-patriotic or early-liberal and often German-national ideas of the day and the political orders they advocated. At the same time, despite all of these political differences, the nation was consistently envisioned in the ceremonies and rituals as a *Volk* family. This latter representation created unity beyond all political differences within the nation and, at the same time, a seemingly "natural" hierarchical social and gender order that integrated each subject in a class-, gender- and age-specific way and assigned to each group distinct patriotic duties that differed in war- and peacetime. Thus, the symbolic order of festival culture and the roles that individual social groups and both sexes played in the festivities and ceremonies were crucial because they indicated the position in society that was deemed to be appropriate.[75] In this way, the symbolic order simultaneously generated and mirrored the social and gender order of wartime and postwar society.

In these complex ways, festivities and ceremonies not only formed individual perceptions of war, state and nation as well as collective identities, but also shaped collective memory in a process that had already begun during the wars of 1813–15. Historical studies of political and military culture in Germany during the long nineteenth century show that, with their rituals and symbols developed during and after the wars of 1813–15, the many smaller festivals and ceremonies – and not just the National Festival of the Germans – provided a matrix for patriotic-national and military festivities in later decades. Some of the most important and enduring ceremonies, rituals and symbols of political and military culture were created to honor surviving and fallen war heroes. Of particular importance here was the Iron Cross, a medal introduced in Prussia in 1813, and the related cult of death for the fatherland.

---

[75] See Hettling and Nolte, *Feste*, 8–36.

11

Honoring and Commemorating War Heroes: The Cult of Death for the Fatherland

On 22 February 1813, just a month before the official declaration of war on France, Friedrich Wilhelm III ordered the introduction of a "Prussian National Cockade" as an "outward sign" of the "universal expression of loyal patriotism" by all citizens of the state. All honorable men over the age of 20 who lived in Prussia were to wear the black and white cockade on their hats. Any man who refused to do his military service, prevented his male relations from doing so or brought shame upon himself through "cowardice before the enemy" forfeited the honor of wearing the national cockade. He was also threatened with loss of citizenship and exclusion from all state and municipal offices.[1] The model for the new national insignia in Prussia was the blue, white and red cockade of Revolutionary France. Educated contemporaries interpreted the Prussian cockade as a "serious and manly" countermodel. Unlike France, where at least in the early phase of the revolution women were also permitted to wear the national cockade, in Prussia it was reserved for men. The surviving accounts are unanimous in depicting the public reaction to this decree as extremely enthusiastic.[2] Educated male contemporaries regarded the symbol as a "national insignia" in the colors of the "Prussian nation," representing patriotism and a masculine willingness to defend the country.[3] It seems to have been especially important for contemporaries that *all men* – king and subjects, noblemen and peasants – were to wear the national cockade. Officers and soldiers were required to affix it to their headgear alongside the Prussian eagle. After

[1] "Verordnung wegen des Tragens der Preußischen National-Kokarde v. 22.2.1813," in *VZ* and *BN*, no. 25, 27 Feb. 1813.
[2] See, for example, "Brief eines Freundes an Friedrich Förster, Berlin, März 1813," in *Deutsche Pandora*, 1:21–22; and Boyen, *Erinnerungen*, 2:538.
[3] "National-Kokarde," *SP*, no. 3, March 1813, 235–244.

the wars against Napoleon, the Prussian army retained the black and white cockade as a national emblem.[4]

The Prussian national cockade, so popular in its day, has now been forgotten. It went out of date – but not the Iron Cross, the first German medal for bravery in combat that could be awarded to any man, regardless of his social rank. It was introduced by the Prussian monarch in March 1813 parallel to universal conscription and is still considered to be the most important German medal of all. This was once again evident in March 2008, when the German *Bundeswehr* – 53 years after its foundation – for the first time awarded a decoration "for special gallantry and extraordinary service in combat" to soldiers who had distinguished themselves during war service. The introduction of this military medal reflected the desire of the *Bundeswehr*, which has taken part in international military interventions since the 1990s, to be able once again to decorate soldiers who have demonstrated valor in combat.[5] With this new medal, the *Bundeswehr* leadership sought to revive the tradition of the Iron Cross that had – with minor stylistic changes – been awarded to soldiers and officers in all Prussian and German wars between 1813 and 1945. The recent introduction of a military decoration similar to the Iron Cross unleashed an intense debate in the German media, political parties and social organizations about the medal's traditions. Some rejected the Iron Cross because of its misuse during the Third Reich, which led to its ban after 1945, while others considered the Iron Cross to be "wholly unencumbered." They stressed the medal's roots in the "tradition of the German Wars of Liberation," of which Germans could be justifiably proud even today. Therefore, they argued, the tradition of the Iron Cross was worthy of preservation.[6] This discussion demonstrates both the enduring significance of the Iron Cross and the role of national memories and their symbolic representations in contemporary politics.

From the beginning, the Iron Cross played an extraordinary role in military culture and the changing "memory politics" that shaped the national commemoration of the Anti-Napoleonic Wars during the nineteenth and twentieth centuries.[7] In this chapter, I first examine the motivations behind the inauguration of the Iron Cross and the associated rituals and ceremonies that commemorated surviving and fallen war heroes, and then explore the changing meanings attached to the Iron Cross and the associated politics of memory up to the First World War, emphasizing which aspects of the original symbolism disappeared and what remained.[8]

[4] Hans-Peter Stein, *Symbole und Zeremoniell in deutschen Streitkräften vom 18. Jahrhundert bis zum 20. Jahrhundert* (Herford, 1984), 51.
[5] See Kai Biermann, "Bundeswehr: Heißes Eisen," *ZEIT Online* (10 March 2008), <http://www.zeit.de/online/2008/11/eisernes-kreuzl> (Accessed 14 April 2009).
[6] Ibid.
[7] Meyer, "Memory and Politics," 176.
[8] The following is based on Karen Hagemann, "National Symbols and the Politics of Memory: The Prussian Iron Cross of 1813, its Cultural Context and its Aftermath," in Forrest et al.,

MANLY HONOR AND MILITARY MEDALS

On 10 March 1813, only two weeks after the introduction of the national cockade, Friedrich Wilhelm III signed the document establishing the Iron Cross, which was published in the newspapers on 17 March, one day after the declaration of war on France. On the same day the monarch announced the introduction of universal conscription and the organization of a militia.[9] The Iron Cross, which was reserved for Prussian and to be bestowed only during wartime. Existing medals and decorations like the Order of the Black and Red Eagle or the *Pour le Mérite* were suspended until the end of the war in order not to violate the principle of equality. Before 1813, noncommissioned officers and enlisted men in Prussia, as in other German states, could only be awarded a "medal of merit" first and second class.[10]

The Iron Cross, modeled on the *Légion d'Honneur* introduced by Napoleon in 1802,[11] was not a general order of merit, but was intended solely as a "decoration for gallantry" during the war. Its introduction was part of the extensive reorganization of the Prussian military promoted by the army reformers after the dramatic defeat of 1806–07. As part of this reorganization they also discussed necessary changes to military culture. The system of military honors was one area that they wanted to reform. One of the first articles that forcefully argued for this aim appeared in November 1808 in the journal *Minerva*. Its function seems to have been to publicize the view of Prussian military reformers who sought to make "honor and patriotism" *the* chief combat motivation for all soldiers and officers and therefore aimed to recognize even simple conscripts as "men of honor."[12] The anonymous author contended that, should universal conscription be

---

War Memories, 215–244. See also Kurt-Gerhard Klietmann, *Deutsche Auszeichnungen: Eine Geschichte der Ehrenzeichen und Medaillen, Erinnerungs- und Verdienstabzeichen des Deutsches Reiches, der deutschen Staaten sowie staatlicher Dienststellen, Organisationen, Verbände usw. vom 18.–20. Jahrhundert*, 3 vols. (Berlin, 1957, 1971 and 1972); Werner O. Hütte, "Die Geschichte des Eisernen Kreuzes und seine Bedeutung für das preußische und deutsche Auszeichnungswesen von 1813 bis zur Gegenwart" (Phil. Diss., University of Bonn, 1968); Donald Abenheim, *Reforging the Iron Cross: The Search for Tradition in the West German Armed Forces* (Princeton, NJ, 1988); Jörg Nimmergut, *Das Eiserne Kreuz 1813–1939* (Lüdenscheid, 1990); and Ralph Winkle, *Der Dank des Vaterlandes: Eine Symbolgeschichte des Eisernen Kreuzes 1914 bis 1936* (Essen, 2007).

[9] "Urkunde über die Stiftung des eisernen Kreuzes v. 10.3.1813," *VZ*, no. 35, 23 March 1813; and *BN*, no. 20, 16 Feb. 1815.

[10] Stein, *Symbole*, 51–57.

[11] Pierre and Bastien Miquel, *Deux siècles de Légion d'honneur* (Paris, 2002); and Anne de Chefdebien and Bertrand Galimard de Flavigny, *La Légion d'honneur: Un ordre au service de la nation* (Paris, 2002).

[12] See Hagemann, *Muth*, 304–339.

instituted, all soldiers must have equal claims to promotion and to the bestowal of "medals of honor." He justified his position in the following terms: "Experience has taught us that the soldier of today must no longer be treated as a purely mechanical being if he is to accomplish great and excellent things, but that one must instead influence his mind and make claims upon his sense of honor in order to spur him on to heroic deeds."[13]

The idea of a decoration open to all soldiers met with broad approval in military reform circles. The king himself supported it, as is evident from his marginal notes on the "Plan in Preparation for the National Uprising," which Gneisenau presented to the monarch in August 1811 and which contained the recommendation to establish a "universal medal."[14] This idea was put into practice in the weeks before the war began. Friedrich Wilhelm III provided the following explanation in the deed of foundation:

In the present great catastrophe, in which the fortunes of the fatherland hang in the balance, the powerful sentiment that elevates the nation to such heights deserves to be honored in a very particular way. [...] For that reason we have resolved to distinguish in a particular guise any merits gained in the war now breaking out, either in actual combat with the foe, or in the field or at home, but in connection with this great struggle for freedom and independence, and no longer to bestow this particular distinction after this war.[15]

The Iron Cross was available in two classes, which were awarded sequentially (that is, one had to have received the second class before being awarded the first), and also in the form of a "Grand Cross" given exclusively to commanding officers for victory in decisive battles or for the capture or protracted defense of a fortress. The document also describes the form of the Iron Cross in some detail:

Both classes have an identical black cast-iron cross edged in silver, the front without inscription, the back with Our initials F. W. and the crown at the top, three oak leaves in the middle and the date 1813 beneath, and both classes are worn in the buttonhole from a black ribbon edged in white where the wearer has distinguished himself in combat with the foe, and from a white ribbon edged in black where this was not the case.[16]

The new medal had no material value, which, educated contemporaries noted, fittingly reflected the "age of iron." The monarch bestowed it personally as *the* sign of royal recognition for the utmost fulfillment of duty to the fatherland. Because this was also possible at the home front, the Prussian monarchy

13 "Hoffnungen und Wünsche eines preußischen Patrioten," *Minerva* 4 (Nov. 1808): 193–203, 196.
14 Neidhardt von Gneisenau, "Plan zur Vorbereitung eines Volksaufstandes, mit Kommentaren von Friedrich Wilhelm III.," in Georg Heinrich Pertz, *Das Leben des Feldmarschalls Grafen Neidhardt v. Gneisenau*, 4 vols. (Berlin, 1864, 1865, 1869 and 1880), 2:112–130, 128.
15 "Urkunde über die Stiftung des eisernen Kreuzes von 10.3.1813," VZ, no. 35, 23 March 1813.
16 Ibid.

not only introduced an Iron Cross for civilian service by men, but further-more established a female counterpart to the Iron Cross, the *Luisenorden*, on 8 August 1814, the king's birthday, in memory of his wife Queen Luise who had died in July 1810. It was to be awarded to women who had distin-guished themselves in patriotic charity, especially in nursing soldiers.[17] The fact that the Prussian monarchy introduced a civilian and female counterpart to the military medal indicates recognition of the importance of the support of the home front for the war of 1813–14. The system of newly introduced decorations represents the idea of a valorous *Volk* family, which is simultan-eously inclusive and internally differentiated. The Iron Cross was theoretic-ally available to everybody and at the same time represented clear hierarchies between the service of soldiers and civilians and men and women.

Recipients of the Iron Cross were regularly announced in the press. The soldiers and officers learned of the decorations and honors through the *Preußische Feldzeitung*, the newspaper produced for the army by Prussian headquarters.[18] During the wars of 1813–15 the Grand Cross was awarded six times, the Iron Cross First Class 635 times and Second Class 16,070 times for military merit. The king bestowed the Iron Cross First Class twice for civilian service during wartime, and the Second Class 374 times. In addition, 166 women received the *Luisenorden*. The Iron Cross was awarded to a large number of noncommissioned officers and soldiers (approximately 1 in 20 received an Iron Cross), but some 24 percent of the medal holders were officers. The decorated noncombatants were mainly government ministers and high-ranking civil servants as well as many doc-tors in the military medical corps. The women were almost exclusively leading noble and upper-middle-class members of patriotic women's asso-ciations.[19] Since the number of military medals to be produced had been limited to 9,000, by the spring of 1814 not all men marked out for this distinction could be given a cross. For that reason, it was stipulated that the Iron Cross Second Class should be "passed down" within units –that is, that recognized men who had not yet received a medal would take over a decoration from a dead "cross holder" in their unit. The last of the 6,928 men who were "eligible to inherit" received the Iron Cross between 1834 and 1839.[20]

The public responded favorably to the introduction of the Iron Cross. Public attention focused primarily on the military decoration; the non-combatant version and the *Luisenorden* played only minor roles.[21] The

---

[17] "Urkunde über die Stiftung des Luisenordens v. 3.8.1814," *BN*, no. 101, 23 Aug. 1814.

[18] Hagemann, *Muth*, 155–157.

[19] Transfeldt and von Brand, *Wort*, 210; Nimmergut, *Kreuz*, 46–47 and 109; and Reder, *Frauenbewegung*, 49–51.

[20] Transfeldt and von Brand, *Wort*, 210.

[21] Boyen, *Erinnerungen*, 2:543.

symbolism of the military medal was much discussed in newspaper and magazine articles, poems and sermons. Two lines of interpretation vied with each other for public favor – one monarchical and regional-patriotic, the other early-liberal and German-national, which reflects the divide in the public discourse on war and nation at the time. According to the first interpretation, which was propagated mainly by the Prussian government, the military and the Protestant churches, the Iron Cross was presented as a military honor open to any man of valor, and was bestowed personally by the king as a sign of his recognition of military gallantry, great love for the throne and the Prussian fatherland, and strong Christian faith. A typical example of this interpretation is the sermon "On the Meaning and Significance of the Iron Cross," preached by the Prussian army chaplain Christian Wilhelm Spieker after the bestowal of the medal upon members of the corps that had besieged Magdeburg in the spring of 1814.[22] He praised the Iron Cross as a medal that was awarded only "to the bravest in the army" as "public testament" to their glorious fight "for king and fatherland." For him it was a symbol, first, "of a pious Christian faith"; second, "of faithful love for a respected and virtuous king"; third, "of the sacred love of liberty and fatherland"; and fourth, "of a manly and gallant spirit."[23] The other surviving military sermons have a similar tone, as do the many songs and poems that were disseminated for similar events. These texts repeatedly interpret the Iron Cross as a key symbol in the patriotic-national cult of heroism centered on the Christian myth of heroic death for the fatherland.

In the second, early-liberal and German-national version, in contrast, the Iron Cross was interpreted as a distinction honoring not just services "to the crown and the person of the monarch" but also "services to the state" and to the "German fatherland."[24] A characteristic example of this interpretation is the article "The Iron Cross" by Heinrich Luden, published in the journal *Nemesis* in January 1814. The author describes the Iron Cross in this article as a "republican-monarchical distinction." He begins by noting that it is the "first aspiration of noble natures" to "be sufficient unto themselves" and that the "knowledge of having contributed decisively to the salvation, welfare, greatness or glory of the fatherland" is the "greatest joy for mortals and the most splendid reward." Thus, an "upright man will never fail to do what duty and honor demand of him." In fact, any distinction conferred by medals and insignia is superfluous for him. They are important instead for the community, for prince, people and state. For that reason, in both ancient and modern times all peoples have sought to distinguish those men "who performed important services for the commonweal in war or peace through intelligence, bravery and boldness." By recognizing them, the community

[22] On Spieker, "Spieker, Christian Wilhelm," *ADB* 35 (1893): 162.
[23] Spieker, *Gebete*, 186–187, 190, 194, 197–198, 200 and 202.
[24] Heinrich Luden, "Das eiserne Kreuz," *Nemesis* 1.1 (1814): 39–53, 46.

appropriates their heroic acts. At the same time, such recognition shows the individual man who has behaved with greatness that he is not alone. He will feel "himself to be a member of a whole" and increasingly direct his efforts to this whole. The idea of recognition and enduring fame in the community would spur him on to glorious deeds.[25] Against the backdrop of these reflections, the Iron Cross appeared to Luden as the symbol par excellence of the Anti-Napoleonic "freedom struggle" (*Freiheitskampf*):

If one looks first at the material, the *iron* suggests the terrible rod over our heads, but also the means that God has given Man to protect himself from servitude and overcome tyrants. If one looks at the form, the cross recalls the misery we have suffered, but also the holiness of the cause for which we have taken up the sword. The front is without any inscription or sign: the Iron Cross speaks for itself. On the reverse, however, the Crown first links the cause of the commonweal to the throne, then, with the initials F. W., the person of the king emerges, whose high-mindedness did not hesitate to venture Throne and Crown for the honor of the commonweal and the happiness of his subjects; here the *Oak Branch* points to German manners, German spirit and German steadfastness.[26] (Emphasis in the original)

In this German-national interpretation, which was disseminated mainly in the early-liberal press, the Iron Cross was considered to be a symbol of the greatest love of liberty and an expression of energetic masculine commitment to the German fatherland.[27] It differed from the more influential regional-patriotic interpretation in two important respects: the regional frame of reference (Prussia or Germany) and the primary motivation behind heroism (love of king and the territorial state or love of liberty and Germany). Christian rhetoric was also far more prominent in the regional-patriotic version, which promoted the interpretation of the struggle as a "holy war."

The high esteem for the Iron Cross, as expressed in sermons, songs, poems and the press, appears to have been shared by many men who went to war in 1813–15, as is evident in their letters, diaries, memoirs and drawings.[28] So many soldiers and officers were eager to gain military honors that on 24 December 1813 the Prussian king introduced a military commemorative medal as an "insignia of honor" and promised it to *all* men who had fought in the field or before a fortress and had "loyally performed their duty." The commemorative medal was to be cast after the war from melted-down enemy guns.[29] In order to prevent its unauthorized wearing, commanders

---

[25] Ibid., 39–41.

[26] Ibid., 50.

[27] See, for example, "Das Eiserne Kreuz," *DB* 2.89 (Jan. 1815): 560–562.

[28] See, for example, "Karl Friedrich Eichhorn an seine Frau, Loopik bei Utrecht, 4.12.1813," in Karl Friedrich Eichhorn, *Briefe, und zwei an ihn gerichtete Schreiben zur Säcularfeier seines Geburtstages*, ed. Hugo Loersch (Bonn, 1881), 28–29 and 79–80; and "Meldung," *RM*, no. 105, 20 Aug. 1814.

[29] "Friedrich Wilhelm III., An Mein Kriegsheer, 24.12.1813," *PC*, no. 15, 28 Jan. 1814.

had to issue the proper holders with so-called ownership documents and keep records of their names. Any man who was subject to dishonorable punishment forfeited his commemorative medal. Medals were distributed after the war as part of the official church celebrations in the soldiers' home parishes.[30] Every participant in the war could use these insignia of honor, which were also awarded for the wars of 1815, to prove himself a "valiant" man who had done his duty for his country. The success of this universal recognition of participation in combat motivated other rulers, among them Emperor Franz I of Austria, to introduce similar commemorative medals.[31]

HONORING AND COMMEMORATING WAR HEROES

Most Prussian soldiers and officers and many civilians welcomed the introduction of the Iron Cross and the commemorative medal and celebrated their public bestowal. For the state, the military and the church, both medals were inextricably linked with rituals and celebrations that would mark military and patriotic festival culture up to the First World War and beyond. It was in the context of these celebrations and rituals, centered on the veneration and commemoration of heroes, that the Iron Cross developed its lasting influence and became firmly entrenched in national memory.

On 5 May 1813, Friedrich Wilhelm III issued a decree on the "Endowment of a Permanent Monument" for soldiers who had fallen "in the struggle for independence and the fatherland." It stipulated that "every warrior who died for the fatherland during an act of heroism" and who, "according to the unanimous accounts of his superiors and comrades would have been awarded the Order of the Iron Cross," was to be honored at state expense in the regimental church with a "simple plaque, adorned at the top with an enlarged cross of the Order." More generally, commemorative plaques were to be erected at municipal expense in the churches "for all those who died on the field of honor." They would bear the inscription "From this parish there died for king and country," followed by the names of all the fallen soldiers of the parish, "beginning with those who received, or who would have been worthy to receive, the Iron Cross." Finally, a "memorial ceremony" should be held after the war to commemorate all the "warriors" who had died a "hero's death," during which "the names of the fallen were to be read out by the pastor" and "remarkable and praiseworthy events from their lives or deaths imparted to the congregation for their emulation." After this memorial ceremony, the pastors and chairmen of the parish councils were to give a public account of what had been done and would be done in the future

[30] Generalstab, *Heer*, 3:62–65.
[31] Johann Stolzer and Christian Steeb, *Österreichs Orden: Vom Mittelalter bis zur Gegenwart* (Graz, 1996).

for the "widows and orphans left behind by the fallen."[32] With this decree Friedrich Wilhelm III established a broad program for the patriotic-national cult of heroism, whose central symbol was the Iron Cross. This program was implemented after the wars in three celebrations mandated by the state: the "Festival of Thanksgiving for the Peace" (*Friedens-Dank-Fest*) of 18 January 1816, the "Memorial Ceremony" (*Todtenfeier*) of 4 July 1816, and local ceremonies held to mark the erection of the memorial plaques for the "fallen."

The Festival of Thanksgiving for the Peace had to take place throughout Prussia in conjunction with the coronation and medal-giving celebration (*Krönungs– und Ordensfest*) traditionally observed on 18 January.[33] With this date, the government signaled the observance of a genuinely Prussian festival that centered on the king as a victorious and heroic military leader and on the "heroes" honored with the Iron Cross.[34] This celebration was organized by the government authorities, the army and the church. The extensive press coverage indicates that its central elements were the same everywhere.[35] At their core was a service of worship with a *Te Deum*, announced the evening before with a long ringing of the bells. The service began with bells and ended with cannon salutes. The church services were prefaced or concluded by a military parade as well as a ceremonial procession of all decorated soldiers, in which the oak- or laurel-crowned holders of the Iron Cross assumed a place of honor. In addition, the erection of local war memorials was often an important part of these ceremonies. The government reported on this in March 1816: "In order to remind our descendants of the significance of these days through some monument, large or small, in many towns young oaks were planted, flags hung or an Iron Cross erected on the market square or hill, and these memorials were consecrated with appropriate ceremonies."[36] The three main functions of these ceremonies were to offer symbolic thanks for God's blessing, to honor the returning war heroes and to promote a lasting commemoration of the "heroic era" of the wars. Recalling the sacrifices and achievements of friends, neighbors and family members gave concrete expression to the associated appeal to citizens' future willingness to make sacrifices and defend the fatherland. What their fathers, brothers and neighbors had accomplished, sons, too, could emulate. This was the key message not just of the local war memorials but

---

[32] "Verordnung, Dresden, 5.5.1813," *PC*, no. 37, 4 June 1813.

[33] "Berlin, den 2ten Januar," *VZ*, no. 1, 2 Jan.1816.

[34] "Bericht der Westpreußischen Regierung," *VZ*, supplement to no. 28, 5 March 1816.

[35] See, for example, "Berlin, den 20ten Januar 1816," *VZ*, no. 9, 20 Jan. 1816; and *SPZ*, no. 11, 24 Jan. 1816.

[36] "Der 18te Oktober 1815 und der 18te Januar 1816," *AB*, no. 13, 29 March 1816, 124. On the history of the monuments to 1813–15, see Lürz, *Kriegerdenkmäler*, vol. 1; and Stefan-Ludwig Hoffmann, "Sakraler Monumentalismus um 1900: Das Leipziger Völkerschlachtdenkmal," in Koselleck and Jeismann, *Kriegerdenkmäler*, 105–131.

also of the many songs, poems and speeches that were part of the standard program of the services of thanksgiving. In this way, commemoration linked the individual with the local community and the local community with the nation and its future.

The Prussian government chose the anniversary of the French capitulation, 4 July 1814, as the date for the first "Memorial Ceremony" in 1816. The Department of Public Worship and Education announced this ceremony in a circular reminding clerics of their duty to mention the names of the fallen soldiers of their parish, and to report as far as possible on their lives and deaths in the field. The "memorial plaques" for all fallen soldiers of the parish were supposed to be installed in the local church soon after, if not during, the ceremonies.[37] A few days before the memorial services, it was announced in the major Prussian newspapers that all business must cease on the eve of the ceremony, and that on the morning of 4 July church bells were to be rung. It was also stipulated that the funeral service was to be combined with a collection "in all churches for the unfortunate widows and orphans of the fallen warriors." Even the liturgy, the texts of homilies and the prayers were laid down in detail. The churches, especially the chancels, were to be draped in black and illuminated by candles, and the altars adorned simply. Recommended decorations were the Iron Cross, laurel and oak wreaths and military insignia – particularly flags, helmets and swords.[38]

The "Memorial Ceremony" was conducted and perceived as a collective funeral service for the fallen soldiers, militiamen and volunteers of the "Prussian nation." It was everywhere extremely well attended. Most people appeared in mourning dress to convey their grief or their gratitude for the great sacrifices made by the fallen and their families.[39] The new ceremony created an emotionally effective form of national mourning and commemoration that corresponded to the universalized cult of heroism. For the first time, *all* fallen soldiers were included and individually commemorated regardless of social status and military rank. This cult surrounding ordinary fallen soldiers set Prussia apart at the time. In the first half of the nineteenth century, most other states, such as Britain, still made little attempt to commemorate the common man in celebrations and rituals, cemeteries or war graves, cenotaphs in state capitals, or war memorials on village greens. Such monuments and statues as there were celebrated battles, victories and commanders. And while the French revolutionaries lavished praise on acts of exceptional courage and selflessness, holding them up as examples to others,

---

[37] Erich Foerster, *Die Entstehung der Preußischen Landeskirche unter der Regierung König Friedrich Wilhelms des Dritten nach den Quellen erzählt: Ein Beitrag der Kirchenbildung im deutschen Protestantismus*, 3 vols. (Tübingen, 1905 and 1907), 1:328.

[38] "Anzeige v. 24.6.1816," *Kgl. Preußischen Staats-, Kriegs- und Friedens-Zeitung*, 24 June 1816.

[39] "Berlin, vom 6. July," *SPZ*, no. 81, 10 July 1816; and "Hammerstein, den 4ten Juli 1816," *VZ*, supplement to no. 84, 13 July 1816.

the bodies of the dead were still stripped on the battlefield and buried – as they were in all other European armies of the period – in communal graves near where they had fallen. Of course, Prussia did the same, but unlike the other European states, it also remembered each fallen soldier individually in his parish.[40] The question of *why* Prussia began to commemorate even ordinary individual soldiers earlier than other countries is difficult to answer. One reason might be that the need to mobilize as many men for war as possible and to obtain active war support from society at large was so great in 1813 that the government had to implement ceremonies and rituals that recognized these efforts in order to ensure that support. After the wars it probably became quickly evident how well they served the various purposes of the state and the military.

The erection of memorial plaques to *all* "fallen warriors" in the churches began throughout the kingdom in July 1816. The main function of these local ceremonies was to preserve "the memory of the high courage that the nation displayed in the great struggle for freedom and autonomy" among soldiers of the line and militiamen, and to fortify their readiness to fight in the future.[41] The character of the local memorial celebrations was accordingly more overtly military. They regularly began with a deployment of the local army units, whose members assembled before the church in order of rank and medal class. Then the commander gave a short address to his men and read out the names of the soldiers who had been decorated with the Iron Cross as well as those of the "fallen warriors, who, according to the testimony of their comrades in arms, would have deserved the same distinction." This was generally followed by a religious service during which the medal-holders were assigned a place of honor before the altar. Aside from the living heroes, the sermons focused on those who had died undecorated in the war and whose names were to be listed on the memorial plaques after those of the "fallen holders of the Cross." The pastors usually emphasized that these men had died as "Christian martyrs" for God and country, thus attaining the immortal glory of heroes. The best way to honor their memory, they insisted, was for each young man to strive to follow their example. After the sermon the memorial plaques were affixed to the walls and consecrated by the clergy. The ceremony ended with the obligatory collection for the victims of war and a parade.[42] Long after the wars were over, rituals, ceremonies and commemorations continued to revolve around the war heroes.

[40] See Holger Hoock, "Monumental Memories: State Commemoration of the Napoleonic Wars in Early Nineteenth-Century Britain," in Forrest et al., *War Memories*, 193–214; and Eveline G. Bouwers, *Public Pantheons in Revolutionary Europe: Comparing Cultures of Remembrance, c. 1790–1840* (Basingstoke, 2012).
[41] "Berlin, den 14ten Dezember," *VZ*, no. 151, 17 Dec. 1816.
[42] Ibid.

THE IRON CROSS IN NINETEENTH-CENTURY
CULTURE

With the Iron Cross, the commemorative medal and the related ceremonies
and rituals, the state, churches and military in Prussia created the means of
honoring and remembering heroes that reflected the needs of an army based
on universal conscription.[43] When it was introduced, the cult of heroism had
to be nationalized and democratized. The rituals and ceremonies that were
developed between 1813 and 1816 became an enduring component of the
political and military culture first of Prussia and later of Imperial Germany.[44]
At their heart were the Iron Cross and the cult of living and dead heroes,
which glorified death in war as a sacrifice for the nation. During the wars
of 1813–15, this cult of heroism helped to arouse a patriotic-national willingness to fight and sacrifice. After the wars it was used to help the families
and friends of fallen soldiers deal with their grief, offering acknowledgment
of their sacrifice and commemorating the heroism of their loved ones. An
afterlife in the national memory would render the fallen immortal. The cult
of heroism was also accorded a central role in cultural nation-building in
Prussia and, more generally, throughout Germany. National continuity was
to be created by recalling the sacrifices and heroic deeds of past generations
and presenting them to future ones as models and inspiration.[45]

Over the course of the nineteenth century, the memory of the wars against
Napoleon assumed the function of creating unity and continuity and became
associated with the cult of heroism. What united people across political and
increasingly even regional lines was the perception of this era as a "heroic
epoch," albeit within two competing political interpretations. In monarchical, regional-patriotic memory, the conflict continued to be referred to as
the "Wars of Liberation," and in the German-national and liberal interpretation it was known as the "Wars of Liberty."[46] While the first interpretation was genuinely Prussian up to 1871, and afterward evolved into a
conservative-monarchic German one; from the beginning the second offered
points of reference for the creation of an identity that extended well beyond
the Kingdom of Prussia, especially for democrats and liberals. It allowed
people elsewhere to relate their regionally specific and often quite different
memories of the wars to the German cause and at the same time to emphasize their own memories independent of Prussia, because this interpretation
could accommodate both regional patriotism and German nationalism.[47]

---

[43] Generalstab, *Heer*, 2:458–551, esp. 548–551.

[44] See Hagemann, *Muth*, 457–508.

[45] Hagemann, "German Heroes."

[46] See chapter 6 in the second part.

[47] See Aaslestadt, "Remembering"; Planert, *Mythos*, 632–641; and Bouwers, *Pantheons*,
161–212.

These competing memories of the wars against Napoleon, and with them of the Iron Cross, were kept alive in Prussia and Germany by means of a whole series of media and cultural practices. Early on, songs and poems – thousands of which were already produced and disseminated during the wars – played a central role.[48] After the wars they were reprinted time and again in songbooks and volumes of poetry and cultivated as part of the rapidly growing movement of choral associations.[49] Among the most often reprinted poems celebrating the medal was "The Iron Cross," written in 1813 by Max von Schenkendorf, a Prussian official and war volunteer. It remained part of the school curriculum until the First World War.[50] Schools in general were accorded a central role in the cultivation of memories of the war years of 1813–15. Schoolbooks told the stories of the heroes of the "Wars of Liberation" and reproduced songs and poems by the most popular poets of those wars such as Arndt, Körner and Schenkendorf.[51] The authors of a multiplicity of memoirs and historical novels also tried to keep these memories alive. The first war memoirs were published during and immediately after the conflict.[52] The first novel bearing the title *The Iron Cross*, by forestry official Karl Gottlob Kramer, appeared as early as 1815 and influenced many subsequent "historic tales," for Kramer was one of the most widely read novelists of his day.[53] An increasing number of plays also told the story of the Iron Cross.[54]

---

[48] The most frequently reprinted poem in praise of the Iron Cross was Theodor Heinrich Friedrich, "Das Eiserne Kreuz," in his *Gedichte* (Berlin, 1816), 26–30. See also chapter 4 in the second part.

[49] Klenke, *Mann*; idem, "Zwischen nationalkriegerischem Gemeinschaftsideal und bürgerlich-ziviler Modernität: Zum Vereinsnationalismus der Sänger, Schützen und Turner im Deutschen Kaiserreich," *GWU* 45 (1994): 207–223; and idem, "Ein 'Schwur für's deutsche Vaterland: Zum Nationalismus der deutschen Sängerbewegung zwischen Paulskirchenparlament und Reichsgründung," in *Liberalismus, Parlamentarismus und Demokratie*, ed. Michael Epkenhans et al. (Göttingen, 1994), 67–107.

[50] See the reprint in Anonymous, ed., *Das Eiserne Kreuz im Spiegel deutscher Dichtung: 1813, 1870, 1914* (Leipzig, 1915), 5–6; Carl Rossow, *Bilder und Lieder vom Eisernen Kreuz 1813/14, 1870/71, 1914/16: Ein Gang von Deutschlands Erwachen durch Deutschlands Einheit zu Deutschlands Weltsendung!* (Leipzig, 1916), 42–44; and Heinrich Heidenreich, *Das Eiserne Kreuz in Geschichte und Dichtung (Beiheft der Blätter für die Fortbildung des Lehrers und der Lehrerin*, vol. 8 (Berlin, 1914). These three volumes give a representative overview of the most popular poetry about the Iron Cross. On the importance of Schenkendorf in Prussian schools, see also Reinhard Zellmann, "Das Eiserne Kreuz: Eine Präparation," *Deutsche Blätter für erziehenden Unterricht* 41 (1913–14): 465–468; and idem, *Präparationen zu vaterländischen Dichtungen* (Langensalza, 1913), 101–108.

[51] Zellmann, *Präparationen*; see also Akaltin, *Die Befreiungskriege*.

[52] See the fourth part.

[53] Carl Gottlob Kramer, *Das Eiserne Kreuz: Ein kriegerischer Halb-Roman aus den Jahren 1812, 1813 und 1814* (Hamburg, 1815); and Christoph Hildebrandt, *Der achtzehnte October oder das Eiserne Kreuz: Ein Roman* (Quedlinburg, 1816). See also the fourth part.

[54] See, for example, Wolfgang Fricke, *Das Eiserne Kreuz: Ein Drama in 3 Aufz.* (Berlin, 1870); Emil von Schlack, *Das Eiserne Kreuz oder Ahnen und Enkel vor Paris: Militairisches Festspiel*

A wealth of commemorative books and brochures too proved influential. In 1847–48 the first journal bearing the title *Das Eiserne Kreuz* appeared in Prussia, presenting readers with "a monument, built from the history of Prussia and the German liberation struggle of 1813–1815, in memory of the heroes of liberty," and offered for sale "to benefit infirm and needy Prussian veterans of those years." Its editor Alexander Mallwitz, a journalist and former volunteer, sought to spread the German-national interpretation of the wars of 1813–15 and of the Iron Cross, and supported the Revolution of 1848, which he regarded as a continuation within Germany of the fight for freedom that had been thwarted by the postwar restoration. Mallwitz had to abandon his undertaking in October 1848, however, for lack of subscribers. In this revolutionary time, educated readers were more interested in the exciting present and future than in the heroic past.[55]

Military associations also played their part in processing memories of the wars of 1813–15. Veterans' and volunteers' associations, as well as "war graves associations" and "garrison and militia support associations" cultivated memories of the wars in their meetings and ceremonies. At least in Prussia, the majority of these associations appear not to have been formed until the 1830s and 1840s. They were largely pro-monarchy and pro-state, and the cult of living and fallen heroes and the symbol of the Iron Cross played a central role in their culture.[56]

In Prussia, the regional-patriotic, monarchic interpretation of the Iron Cross and the wars of 1813–15 dominated the culture and politics of memory in the first half of the nineteenth century. This interpretation was actively promoted by the Prussian dynasty, especially under Friedrich Wilhelm IV, who ascended the throne in 1840. The period of the wars against Napoleon had strongly influenced the childhood and youth of the monarch and his siblings. Honoring the surviving heroes of those wars was a matter of genuine concern to him. On 3 August 1841, the birthday of his late father, the founder of the medal, the young king set up the Senior Foundation to improve the economic situation of the Iron Cross-decorated veterans of 1813–15, who remained poorly provided for. All surviving "Cross holders" received a modest "gratuity" (*Ehrensold*).[57] Wilhelm I, who followed his elder brother and became king of Prussia in 1861 and German emperor in 1871, continued this tradition. He ordered that all surviving veterans of the wars of 1813–15 – of whom around 60,000 (about a quarter of all those who had served) were still alive – should receive a second commemorative medal, which was to remain in the possession of their families, at the great jubilee

in zwei Bildern aus der deutschen Kriegsgeschichte (Berlin, 1885); and Benno Rödel, *Das eiserne Kreuz oder Weihnachtssegen: Festspiel in drei Abteilungen* (Munich, 1898).
[55] See *Das Eiserne Kreuz*, nos. 1–24 (Jan. 1847 – Dec. 1848), 1:2–3 and 24:113–120.
[56] Trox, *Konservatismus*, 35–61, 45.
[57] Hütte, "Geschichte," 47.

celebrated in Prussia on 17 March 1863. No monetary award was attached to it, however.[58]

The intense work devoted to constructing the public memory of the wars against Napoleon meant that by the first half of the nineteenth century, the Iron Cross had already become the central symbol of the wars of 1813–15 in Prussia. In order not to "dishonor" these memories, Wilhelm I refused to revive the medal for the wars against Denmark and Austria in 1864 and 1866. He did not believe that these wars lived up to the "heroic era" of 1813–15. For him, only the confrontation with France in 1870–71, which evoked memories of the Anti-Napoleonic Wars, justified reintroducing the Iron Cross. In his declaration of war of 19 July 1870, he presented France to the public as an aggressor that once again threatened the very existence of Prussia and Germany. The state propaganda and patriotic literature of 1870–71 repeatedly drew parallels with the events of 1806–15 and invoked the need for unity, patriotism and valor.[59]

In a statute backdated to 19 July 1870, Wilhelm I of Prussia announced the reintroduction of the Iron Cross for the duration of the war. The preamble explicitly established a connection to the "Wars of Liberation," but did not restrict the medal to Prussia:

In the light of the grave situation of our fatherland, and in grateful recollection of the heroic deeds of our forefathers in the great years of the Wars of Liberation, it is our intent to revive, in all its significance, the Iron Cross medal endowed by our father who now rests in God. The Iron Cross shall be granted without distinction of rank or estate.[60]

The rest of the text is largely identical to the document of 1813. The Iron Cross itself looked the same, with the exception of the king's initials and the date. The purpose of the struggle was different, however: it was conducted "for the honor and autonomy of the dear fatherland," with the latter no longer conceived of as Prussia, but Germany. In 1813 the fight had been for "liberty and autonomy."[61] Other key differences were that the Iron Cross was no longer awarded to Prussian citizens alone and that other decorations were not suspended, in recognition of the altered political and military circumstances. The medal was now to be a symbol of German territorial unity and the "German fight against France."

[58] Theodor von Troschke, *Das eiserne Kreuz* (Berlin, 1872, 3rd edn.), 7.
[59] See Frank Becker, *Bilder von Krieg und Nation: Die Einigungskriege in der bürgerlichen Öffentlichkeit Deutschlands, 1864–1913* (Munich, 2001); and Alexander Seyfarth, *Die Heimatfront 1870/71: Wirtschaft und Gesellschaft im deutsch-französischen Krieg* (Paderborn, 2007), 265–381. For the history of the war, see François Roth, *La Guerre de 1870* (Paris, 1990); and Geoffrey Wawro, *The Franco-Prussian War: The German Conquest of France in 1870–1871* (New York, 2003).
[60] Troschke, *Kreuz*, 12.
[61] Ibid.

This corresponded to political developments. The new imperial German state was already established during the Franco-German War. In response to this war, the South German states – the Grand Duchy of Baden and the kingdoms of Bavaria and Württemberg – joined the North German Confederation founded in 1866, paving the way for imperial unification. The protracted negotiations culminated in the coronation of Emperor Wilhelm I on 18 January 1871 at Versailles. The constitution of Imperial Germany had already been enacted on 1 January.[62]

By July 1871 the newly established Federal Decorations Commission of Imperial Germany had decided to bestow a total of 44,488 medals of distinction: Eight Grand Crosses, 1,230 Iron Crosses First Class and 40,200 Iron Crosses Second Class to combatants and 2,050 medals to noncombatants. Once again, some 24 percent of decorations were awarded to officers. Male civilians and women could be recognized for their wartime service with equivalent distinctions similar to those bestowed in 1813–15.[63] The certificates awarded to those who were decorated show that Wilhelm I, who had endowed the Iron Cross while still king of Prussia, continued to present the medal in this capacity even after he became emperor. The Decorations Commission, however, conducted the distribution, and stipulated that the Iron Cross was to take precedence over the decorations awarded by the individual states and must be worn in premier position on the medal bar. Many Prussians and supporters of Prussia in the new empire proudly followed these instructions and wore the Iron Cross as part of their military dress uniform or on their coat lapels. Others rejected such symbolic subjugation to the kingdom of Prussia. The stipulation led to disaffection, particularly among the decorated officers of the kingdoms of Baden, Bavaria, Saxony and Württemberg. Thus, they not infrequently wore the medals of valor from their own states before the Iron Cross.[64] No such controversy surrounded the commemorative war medal that Emperor Wilhelm I created on 20 May 1871 for all participants in the battles and sieges of the Wars of Unification.[65]

The politics of memory pursued by the imperial government and the military leadership sought to create an inextricable link between victory over France and the Iron Cross. Thus, Emperor Wilhelm I also decorated regiments with the symbol. All flags and banners that had been "under fire" were assigned an Iron Cross to be displayed on their flagstaffs. Regiments that had already been awarded the Iron Cross in 1813–15 now received an additional streamer bearing the symbol.[66] Once again, the state and the military

---

[62] On German unification and the empire, see Volker R. Berghahn, *Imperial Germany, 1871–1918: Economy, Society, Culture, and Politics* (New York, 2005).
[63] Nimmergut, *Kreuz*, 109.
[64] Ibid., 98–99.
[65] Ibid., 103–104.
[66] Ibid.

used the rituals and celebrations for the veneration and commemoration of heroes that accompanied the bestowal of the Iron Cross – in which soldiers, officers and regiments were honored and the fallen remembered – to bolster the idea of national unity. It was a celebration of the "nation in arms" that built on the repertoire already developed in Prussia during and after the wars of 1813–15.[67]

The national day marking victory over France became *Sedantag*, which was observed every year on 2 September. It commemorated the Battle of Sedan on 2 September 1870, in which Prussian, Bavarian and Saxon troops had won a decisive victory over the French and the Prussians had captured Emperor Napoleon III. The first celebration in 1873 saw the consecration not only of the Victory Column in Berlin, which displayed the Iron Cross at the end of the goddess's bayonet guard, but also of local war memorials throughout Germany.[68] Both the military and national components of the foundation of the empire were emphasized in nearly every official celebration.[69] These included the festival programs and speeches in schools, which everywhere marked *Sedantag*.[70] There was nevertheless significant resistance to these celebrations and to the Protestant-Prussian military interpretation of the founding of the empire that they symbolized. Opposition came, for varying reasons, mainly from the South German states, the Catholic Church and the Social Democrats.[71]

This resistance could not, however, prevent an overall militarization, deliberalization and nationalization of the public interpretation of the Iron Cross in Imperial Germany, which was directly related to the memory of the wars of 1870–71. The imperial government and the military leadership tried to portray the medal as *the* German war decoration par excellence. To strengthen this interpretation, on 18 August 1895, the twenty-fifth anniversary of the victory of 1871, the new emperor, Wilhelm II, awarded "battle bars" (*Gefechtsstangen*) to be worn to the left of the Iron Cross, symbolizing the battle for which the holder had won his Cross.[72]

---

[67] See Annette Maas, "Der Kult der toten Krieger: Frankreich und Deutschland nach 1870/71," in François et al., *Nation*, 215–231; Vogel, *Nationen*; and idem, "Rituals of the 'Nations in Arms': Military Festivals in Germany and France (1871–1914)," in Friedrich, *Culture*, 245–264.

[68] Reinhard Alings, *Die Berliner Siegessäule: Vom Geschichtsbild zum Bild der Geschichte* (Berlin, 2000).

[69] Fritz Schellack, *Nationalfeiertage in Deutschland von 1871 bis 1945* (Frankfurt/M., 1990), 67–132.

[70] Rüdiger Wulf, " 'Hurra, heut ist ein froher Tag, des Kaisers Wiegenfest!': Schulfeiern zum Kaisergeburtstag und zum Sedantag des Kaiserreichs," in *"Furchtbar dräute der Erbfeind!": Vaterländische Erziehung in den Schulen des Kaiserreichs 1871–1918*, ed. Jochen Löher and Rüdiger Wulf (Dortmund, 1998), 57–95.

[71] Schellack, *Nationalfeiertage*, 86–91; Vogel, *Nationen*, 213–226 and 270–275.

[72] Nimmergut, *Kreuz*, 103–105.

While the German-national quality of the Iron Cross was now in the foreground of public perception, the liberal political interpretation that had originally been associated with it continued to wane in importance, a process that had been underway since at least 1848–49. This development is also evident in the poems, songs and novels that treat the subject during and after the Wars of Unification. There was no longer any talk here of liberty within Germany.[73] As a military medal, the Iron Cross had come to symbolize masculine strength, courage and honor, and this was the message it assumed in everyday material culture. This trend became even more marked during the centenary celebrations of 1913–14, establishing a nationalist and militarist interpretation that would pass seamlessly into the propaganda of the First and Second World Wars.[74] This German-national militarist interpretation meshed perfectly with the myth of the "Wars of Liberation" as the heroic period of German history in which the "national spirit awakened," a myth that became increasingly popular in the nineteenth century and stood at the center of the dominant cultural memories of the time of the Anti-Napoleonic Wars before 1914.

The recent German debate about the reintroduction of a medal for "military valor" based on the Iron Cross perpetuates a tradition that began in the years during and after the wars against Napoleon in 1813–15. From its inception, the medal was deployed in memory politics. Two interpretations of the new medal competed for public support: a monarchical, at first regional-patriotic Prussian and later Prussian-German one, and an early-liberal, German-national one. Whatever their political differences, both shared a high esteem for military heroism as a sign of "true" manliness. This combination of political open-endedness and an acceptance of the core military values associated with the Iron Cross meant that, under the conditions of universal conscription, the medal could develop into the ultimate award for military valor in modern German history. In every subsequent war, the breadth of interpretation present from the outset enabled the government and military to develop a reading of the medal adapted to their policies, one that took up existing traditions while emphasizing elements specific to the needs of the moment.

The enduring influence of the Iron Cross was considerably increased by the development of a repertoire of rituals and ceremonies to venerate and commemorate heroes that played on the emotions and created community. This invention of a tradition of the cult of heroism offered a framework that could be and was deployed in future wars. It was effective precisely because

[73] Rossow, *Bilder*, 40–89. See also Becker, *Bilder*, 201–376.
[74] Siemann, "Krieg und Frieden"; Hoffmann, "Mythos"; Kirstin Schäfer, "Die Völkerschlacht," in *Deutsche Erinnerungsorte*, ed. Étienne François and Hagen Schulze (Munich, 2001), 1:187–201. On perceptions of the Iron Cross before, during and after World War I, see Winkle, *Dank*; Hütte, "Geschichte," 72–125; and Nimmergut, *Kreuz*, 135–223.

of its long tradition, which linked the present to the past and the future, even if it was routinely reinterpreted to reflect contemporary interests. Its symbolic potency was strengthened by continual references in sermons, songs, poems, novels and other textual forms, as well as through patriotic and military associational culture. This intermediality of the culture of memory had a particularly lasting effect, and helped to ensure that the Iron Cross would be reintroduced in every one of the major wars in which Prussia or Germany was subsequently involved. Every war saw a degree of reinterpretation, to be sure, but the central idea remained: that this was a medal for military valor, which was open to soldiers of all ranks and social classes.

Conclusion

The collective practices and the political culture of the period of the wars of 1813–15 and the postwar era with their movements, associations, festivals, rituals and symbols, developed in Prussia and other parts of Germany, were not only instrumental in their time, but also had a lasting influence on monarchical, nationalist and military culture until the First World War. During the wars of 1813–15 they significantly helped to mobilize patriotic-national sentiments and with them war support, albeit with substantial regional variations, as indicated by the different levels of mobilization for the militia and the volunteers' movement, for wartime charity and patriotic women's associations, and for the patriotic-national and military festivals, rituals and symbols introduced. After the wars, associations, celebrations, rituals and symbols organized the commemoration of the fallen soldiers and other war victims and supported the process of cultural demobilization more generally, including the integration of the returning militiamen and volunteers into civilian life. Just as the patriotic-national discourse of the wars of 1813–15 and the postwar era yielded a template for nationalist rhetoric in the following century, so too did the patriotic-national associations, festivals, rituals and symbols of the period provide a blueprint for monarchical, nationalist and military culture up to the First World War, as the history of the Iron Cross demonstrates. Hence, both the patterns of political thinking and the collective practices and cultural representation developed during and after the period of the struggle against Napoleon were important carriers of the collective memories of the Anti-Napoleonic Wars. These memories reflected to a surprising extent the old political and regional battles of the war and postwar period, at least until German unification in 1871. Popular literary media were another important carrier of collective memories. The most influential among them were the history books, autobiographical accounts and novels that are studied in the next two parts.

PART FOUR

LITERARY MARKET, HISTORY AND WAR MEMORIES

This book takes us back to the time when the German people learned to conceive of itself as a single entity, when the Germans' new national sentiment emerged, the time whence comes the political unity we enjoy today: to the year 1813, then to 1848 and 1870; and there have doubtless been changes and conflicts, and some contradictions and unfinished business remain, but ever since 1813 the German people has harbored thoughts of unification and inner consolidation: it has awakened.[1]

These words introduce an extensive two-volume work entitled *The Time of the French in the German Lands, 1806–1815,* a collection of lavishly illustrated eyewitness accounts and documents from the period of the "Wars of Liberation." The Leipzig firm of R. Voigtländer published the first edition in 1908. Its editor Friedrich Schulze had studied literature and art history in Jena and Leipzig. From 1910 he was on the staff of the newly founded Leipzig Museum, where he became director in 1918. Schulze was one of the many authors who published commemorative works to mark the centenary of the Anti-Napoleonic Wars of 1806–15. His work was extraordinarily widely read, reprinted several times, and can be found even today in many libraries. It was among the numerous richly illustrated, glossy publications that middle-class Germans displayed in their living rooms as a mark of their education and patriotism.[2]

The profile of the author is quite typical of the many writers, completely forgotten today, who produced commemorative texts on the period of the Anti-Napoleonic Wars. Most of them were men of noble or middle-class origin who had studied at academic secondary schools or universities, worked in the civil or military service or earned their living as publishers, journalists

---

[1] Friedrich Schulze, ed., *Die Franzosenzeit in deutschen Landen, 1806–1815: In Wort und Bild der Mitlebenden,* 2 vols. (Leipzig, 1908), 1:xiii; on Schulze, see Akaltin, *Befreiungskriege,* 80.

[2] Its popularity was exceeded only by Hermann Müller-Bohn, *Die deutschen Befreiungskriege: Deutschlands Geschichte von 1805–1815,* ed. Paul Kittel, 2 vols. (Berlin, 1901); on Müller-Bohn, see Akaltin, *Befreiungskriege,* 75.

or writers. Many similar texts on the period of the Napoleonic Empire were published in other European countries. In his *Bibliography of the Age of Napoleon*, which appeared from 1908 to 1912 with the respected military publisher Mittler & Sohn in Berlin, the historian Friedrich M. Kircheisen counted a total of 200,000 articles and books, including translations, in Germany, Europe and abroad. From among these, he selected 8,000 titles for his two-volume bibliography that he considered to be "necessary for an understanding of the Napoleonic epoch." He included only texts that met his standards of scholarly historiography and biography, whose value as sources he recognized or which he deemed to be part of the literary canon.[3] For that reason, the bibliography completely ignored thousands of popular texts, among them commemorative brochures, autobiographies, war memoirs, biographies and novels.

Academic history on the period of the Napoleonic Empire, too, has long ignored these popular texts, as has literary scholarship, which for decades has focused on the high literary canon of acknowledged significance and shown little interest in even those novels that were bestsellers in their day. This middlebrow literature – novels of the recent past and historical novels written for readers of broad social strata, all generations and both sexes – were mostly distributed via the growing number of lending libraries. Other popular reading matter in these libraries included autobiographies, war memoirs and biographies as well as history books written for a wide audience. Here, too, works on the Napoleonic era in Germany and Europe were much in demand.[4] In interplay with other textual and visual media of memory, as well as monuments, rituals and symbols like the Iron Cross, this reading matter helped to shape the collective memory of this period and the Anti-Napoleonic Wars during the long nineteenth century.

The most important literary media of memory – academic, military and popular historiography, autobiographies, war memoirs and novels – published between 1815 and 1914 and their role in memory production is the focus of analysis in the following two parts. This fourth part begins with an overview of the conditions of literary production, focusing on changes in political culture and censorship policy, the literary market and the reading public, since their interplay did much to shape the literary production of memory – far more than most scholars realize.[5] Then I seek to explain the changing perception of time, which led to the striking growth of general interest in the past, but especially in the history of the Anti-Napoleonic Wars after 1815, outlining contemporary historiography as a central medium of

3 Friedrich Kircheisen, *Bibliographie des Napoleonischen Zeitalters einschliesslich der Vereinigten Staaten von Nordamerika*, 2 vols. (Berlin, 1908); on Kircheisen, see Akaltin, *Befreiungskriege*, 70.
4 Martino, *Leihbibliothek*, 135–548.
5 See also Forrest et al., "Introduction: Memories."

memory construction, which produced the master narratives that influenced other media. The emphasis here is on the most influential publications of popular, academic and military history that found a wider audience. Finally, one of the two single most important media of popular literary memory – published autobiographies and war memoirs – will be introduced in more detail. The fifth part explores novels of the recent past and historical novels as the other important popular literary media of memory. The central questions for both parts are: Who produced these literary media of memory? Which factors influenced memory production in these media? Which key narratives competed with one another in them? And how and why did they change over time and influence collective memories of the Prussian and German struggle against Napoleon?

Politics, Market and Media: The Development of a Culture-Consuming National Public

Germany changed dramatically over the hundred years between the end of the Napoleonic Wars and the beginning of World War I. No area of the economy, society, politics or culture remained unaffected. Processes such as industrialization, population growth and urbanization transformed the face of the countryside and cities alike and led to rising social mobility, but they also caused new problems. The steam engine and other new technologies revolutionized craft and industrial production, and the railway system connected businesses and people in different regions. Long before unification, the German economy and society had begun to coalesce.[1] The literary market also became increasingly national. More and more people were able to read. At the beginning of the twentieth century, Germany had one of the highest literacy rates in the world, nearly 100 percent.[2] Technological changes in paper manufacturing and the printing industry allowed for the production of cheap illustrated reading matter. Books, newspapers and magazines became mass commodities, sources of profit, but also of unease. The conservative elites in state and society feared the spread of "subversive" liberal, democratic and socialist literature to broader strata of the population.[3] As before, the response of governments was political suppression of the opposition and censorship. But the forms of communication control were adapted to the new social and political circumstances.[4]

---

[1] Thomas Nipperdey, *Germany from Napoleon to Bismarck, 1800–1866* (Princeton, NJ, 1996), 85–236; idem, *Deutsche Geschichte, 1866–1918*, 2 vols. (Munich, 1990), 1:192–395; and Volker R. Berghahn, *Imperial Germany, 1871–1918: Economy, Society, Culture, and Politics* (New York, 2005), 1–120.

[2] Jürgen Osterhammel, *Die Verwandlung der Welt: Eine Geschichte des 19. Jahrhunderts* (Munich, 2009), 1118.

[3] Lyons, *History*, 153–154.

[4] Wolfram Siemann, "Von der offenen zur mittelbaren Kontrolle: Der Wandel in der deutschen Preßgesetzgebung und Zensurpraxis des 19. Jahrhunderts," *in "Unmoralisch an sich …": Zensur im 18. und 19. Jahrhundert*, ed. Herbert G. Göpfert and Erdmann Weyrauch

In this chapter, I first describe the changes in political culture and communication control, which were one important factor that influenced the production of collective memories. Then I explore the transformation of the literary market, which played a crucial role as well, and finally I look at the development of the reading public over the long nineteenth century. My main argument is that the process of constructing nationally shared – albeit contested – collective memories of the Anti-Napoleonic Wars would have been impossible without the evolution of a culture-consuming national public. And, conversely, that the emergence of nationally shared memories in literature contributed to the making of a national reading public.

CHANGES IN POLITICAL CULTURE AND COMMUNICATION CONTROL

Mass reading had been a social and political problem for the conservative elites ever since the first reading revolution of the late eighteenth century, because they viewed increased reading among broader strata of the population as dangerous. The first decades after 1815 were marked by postwar restoration. The Carlsbad Decrees of September 1819 led to the political persecution of supporters of the national-liberal opposition as well as to increased censorship. The police system of preventive censorship that was re-implemented in the German Confederation along with these decrees would have far-reaching consequences for book, magazine and newspaper production. Censorship interventions could be introduced not only by the federal state within whose borders the publishing or printing house was domiciled, but also by any member state of the German Confederation if its government found it to be appropriate, as well as by the press commission of the Federal Assembly. In this way, particularly reactionary states such as Austria and Prussia could enforce their censorship policies in more liberal states such as Saxony and Württemberg as well.[5]

The reactionary powers of the Metternich era, however, were unable to suppress oppositional literature completely during the restoration period. The July Revolution of 1830 in France reignited the movement for national unification and political liberation, which was fed by political and social discontent and reemerged during the *Vormärz*, the period preceding the Democratic Revolution of 1848–49. The Hambach Festival of May 1832 became its powerful early symbol. In the 1830s and 1840s, an increasing number of younger

---

(Wiesbaden, 1988), 293–308.; and Andreas Graf and Wolfram Siermann, "Verbote, Normierungen und Normierungsversuche," in *Geschichte des Deutschen Buchhandels im 19. und 20. Jahrhundert*, ed. Georg Jäger et al., 2 vols. (Frankfurt/M., 2001), 1:87–121.

[5] For the regulations, see chapter 4 in the second part; see also Huber, *Verfassungsgeschichte*, pt. 1, 732–734; Siemann, *Staatenbund*, 332–333; idem, "Kontrolle"; and Schneider, "Pressefreiheit," 243–274.

authors – among them Ludwig Börne, Heinrich Heine and Karl Gutzkow[6] – voiced opposition to the reactionary restoration regime, but also distanced themselves from the literature of Romanticism and the Germanomania of the period of the wars of 1813–15. These writers of "Young Germany" called for poetry and literature to intervene actively in contemporary politics.[7] After they began using the gaps in their work that were the result of the cuts of the censor to protest against censorship, in 1837 the Prussian government even prohibited the censors from marking their interventions in any way. The other German states soon followed suit.[8] The conflict over censorship intensified increasingly in the 1830s and 1840s. Alongside political texts, the censors focused on *belles lettres* that targeted a broad audience.[9] The Austrian censors were particularly severe in this respect, banning one-third of the novels permitted elsewhere in Germany in the 1840s.[10]

Authors dealt with censorship as they had in the past. On the one hand, they made use of the differing censorship practices in the German states. Texts especially critical of Prussia, for example, came out in Leipzig. Authors who criticized Austria and were not allowed there published in Berlin. Once a book was printed it crossed all borders, if necessary illegally. Humor and irony were another strategy, which was especially popular with the writers of Young Germany. After Friedrich Wilhelm IV followed his father onto the Prussian throne in June 1840, hopes for change were high. At first, the situation indeed improved slightly. The new Prussian king toned down the state's reactionary policies, easing press censorship and promising to enact a constitution. But it was only under the pressure of the Revolution of 1848 that the Federal Assembly of the German Confederation revoked the Carlsbad Decrees on 2 April 1848. The governments of the individual states followed in subsequent months by abolishing preventive censorship.[11]

The Revolution of 1848 had started in Paris in February. Demonstrations and riots quickly spread on the European continent. The main causes of the rebellion in the German states were demands for national unity, a constitution and greater civil and political rights. Working-class supporters were also fighting to improve their living and working conditions. On 18 May 1848 the National Assembly in Frankfurt am Main, the first democratically

---

[6] See Fritz Martini, "Börne, Ludwig," *NDB* 2 (1955): 404–406; Eberhard Galley, "Heine, Heinrich," *NDB* 8 (1969): 286–291; and Wilmont Haacke, "Gutzkow, Karl Ferdinand," *NDB* 7 (1966): 354–357.

[7] Todd Kontje, ed., *A Companion to German Realism, 1848–1900* (Rochester, NY, 2002), 1. see Helmut Koopmann, *Das Junge Deutschland: Eine Einführung* (Darmstadt, 1993).

[8] Huber, *Verfassungsgeschichte*, pt. 1, 732–734; and Siemann, "Kontrolle."

[9] Wittmann, *Geschichte*, 226–230 and 244–247.

[10] Kurt and Günter Mühlberger, "Gewinner und Verlierer: Der historische Roman und sein Beitrag zum Literatursystem der Restaurationszeit, 1815–1848/49," *IASL* 21.1 (1996): 91–123, 109–110.

[11] Nipperdey, *Germany*, 350–355.

elected German national parliament, assembled for the first time and began work on a national constitution. It was resolved and proclaimed on 27 December 1848 and went into effect immediately, thereby introducing freedom of opinion and the press alongside other fundamental rights of the German people.[12]

But the high hopes for national unification, a single German constitution, equal political rights for all men and a free press were to be dashed once again. The revolutionaries were defeated everywhere by the conservative monarchical powers and their militaries, but they also failed because of political differences and a lack of popular support.[13] The negotiations at the Frankfurt National Assembly glaringly indicated the major divides: moderate liberals argued against radical democrats, advocates of a *Großdeutschland* under Austrian leadership fought against the defenders of a *Kleindeutschland* led by Prussia, and Catholics distrusted Protestants.[14]

The achievements of the revolutionaries of 1848 were reversed in all German states after 1849. The "outcome of the revolution was," however, as Thomas Nipperdey has emphasized, "not only its failure. The revolution had created a national public, over and above all the elites, and a national democratic nation." It had "abolished the major elements of feudal society. Despite the failure, the age became more civilian. And indeed, Prussia's transition to a constitutional state fits into this context."[15] Friedrich Wilhelm IV had dissolved the new Prussian National Assembly, which had begun work on a constitution for the monarchy in May 1848, as soon as he regained political control, but he was forced to introduce a constitution of his own in December 1848. This monarchist constitution maintained the ultimate authority of the king and instituted a bicameral legislature with a *Herrenhaus* (house of peers) and a *Landtag* (lower house). The elections to the latter were based on a three-class franchise, in which representation was proportional to the amount of taxes paid.[16] The king and the newly elected legislature continued to negotiate this first Prussian constitution until February 1850, when it was finally adopted. It remained in force until November 1918.[17]

Officially, press freedom continued to exist for a time in the postrevolutionary era. Not until August 1851 was the new national constitution rescinded by a decision of the revived Federal Assembly of the German Confederation. In addition, between 1849 and 1852 the individual states enacted new press laws, which, while formally guaranteeing freedom of

[12] Graf and Siemann, "Verbote," 88.

[13] See Jonathan Sperber, *The European Revolutions, 1848–1851* (Cambridge, 2005); and Wolfram Siemann, *The German Revolution of 1848–49* (London, 1998).

[14] Nipperdey, *Germany*, 323–355 and 527–598; and Sheehan, *History*, 588–729.

[15] Nipperdey, *Germany*, 595.

[16] Ibid., 604–609.

[17] Ibid., 599–715.

the press and affirming the abolition of preventive censorship, nonetheless allowed for intense communication control through a bundle of new measures. The new Federal Press Law of July 1854 then formulated universally binding guidelines. It replaced the old "police system" with preventive censorship by a "judicial system." Now, after a work was printed, it was up to the courts to decide whether the author should be punished or the book confiscated. "Juridification thus turned into criminalization, a more subtle and yet effective form of communication control."[18] The new control mechanisms included security deposits and the revocation of commercial concessions; exclusion from postal distribution; stamp taxes; bans on foreign publications; intensive control of peddling; and, above all, the joint criminal liability of all persons involved in the production and distribution of books. Whereas previously the censor had been responsible for censorship, it was now up to authors, publishers and booksellers to decide whether the police and courts might deem a printed work to be "seditious," "immoral" or "inimical to religion." In order to prevent a judicial ban and thus significant economic losses, they had to internalize the censorship norms.[19]

In the first decade after 1848–49 the state exerted strong pressure on authors and the press that only diminished gradually over time. Many supporters of the national-liberal opposition in Prussia and elsewhere in the German states adapted their political agenda to this *Nachmärz* era of a "second restoration."[20] They now promoted *realpolitik* and increasingly focused on the aim of national unification under Prussian leadership. The literature produced in this period reflects this change, with "German Realism" dominating until 1900. The authors of this literary movement – the best known among contemporaries were Berthold Auerbach, Gustav Freytag and Friedrich Spielhagen[21] – distanced themselves from Romanticism, Young Germany and *Vormärz* literature and called for a "realistic" literature that fostered national unity under the aegis of *realpolitik*.[22] Their writings show an "increased awareness that one is living in an era of unpredictable and accelerating historical change,"[23] a perception of the times that had first become dominant in the era of the French Revolution and the Napoleonic Wars, and that remained prevalent throughout the nineteenth century.

---

[18] Wittmann, *Geschichte*, 257.

[19] Graf and Siemann, "Verbote."

[20] Wehler, *Gesellschaftsgeschichte*, 3:196–251.

[21] Fritz Martini, "Auerbach, Berthold," *NDB* 1 (1953): 434–435; Fritz Martini, "Freytag, Gustav," *NDB* 5 (1961): 425–427; and Jeffrey L. Sammons, "Spielhagen, Friedrich," *NDB* 24 (2010): 686–688.

[22] For more on "literary realism," see chapter 15 in the fifth part.

[23] Kontje, *Companion*, 3–4.

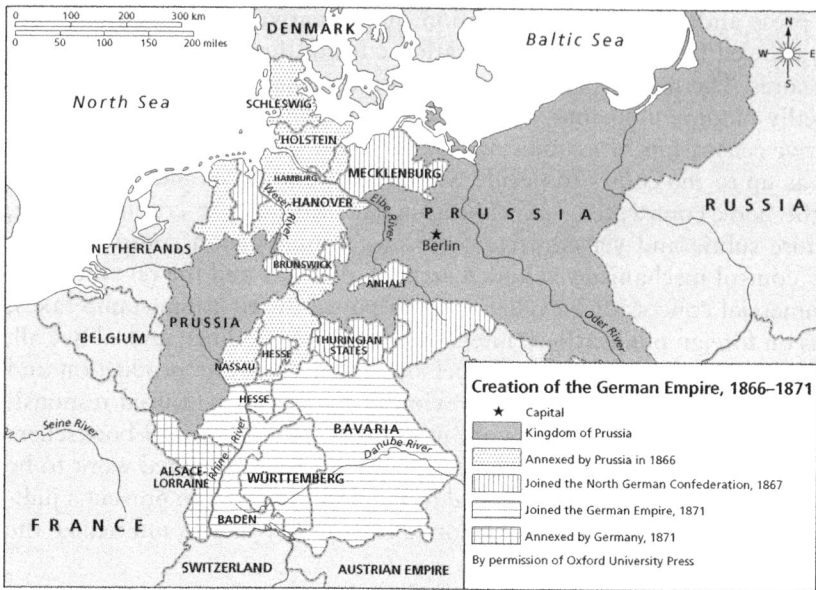

MAP 4. Creation of the German Empire, 1866–71.

In the early 1860s a "revolution from above" set in, pursued by the Prussian government.[24] In the "New Era," contemporaries witnessed a booming economy, political liberalization expressed in the revival of political parties, trade unions and associations, and the first steps toward national unification with the founding in 1866–67 of the North German Confederation (*Norddeutscher Bund*), a union of 22 independent states with nearly 30 million inhabitants. On 18 January 1871 the German nation was finally united in a federal nation-state and established as a constitutional monarchy based on a three-class voting system. This "unification by blood and iron" rather than constitutional reform followed the First Schleswig War from 1848 to 1851 and the Wars of Unification fought between 1864 and 1871 (the Second Schleswig War of 1864, the Austro-Prussian War of 1866 and the Franco-German War of 1870–71) (see Map 4). The creation of the German Empire under Prussian leadership, with its 25 federal states that now included Alsace-Lorraine, was a victory for the supporters of *Kleindeutschland*. Austria would remain outside the German Empire, which became the most populous and urbanized state in continental Europe. From a population of 41 million in 1871 it grew to 65 million in 1910.[25]

---

[24] Wehler, *Gesellschaftsgeschichte*, 3:251–376.
[25] Ibid., 3:7–37 and 493–546, esp. 494 and 512.

The Imperial Press Act of May 1874 was part of the "revolution from above" in the 1860s and 1870s. It put an end not just to compulsory security deposits and concessions, but also to stamp taxes and threatened exclusion from postal sales, which greatly increased legal certainty. Censorship conflicts arose repeatedly nevertheless. It has been estimated that more than 10,000 newspapers and books were banned in the period between 1850 and 1932, with Prussia and Saxony at the top as centers of the book trade. Two main thrusts emerge: the struggle against "seditious" democratic and socialist texts and the fight against what was known as *Schund und Schmutz* – texts that were perceived as lurid and obscene, especially those sold by peddlers.[26]

The first chancellor of the German Empire, Otto von Bismarck, devoted much of his attention to the cause of national unity under the ideological aegis of *Borussianismus* (Prussianism). His aim was to forge the political culture accordingly. He opposed conservative Catholic politics, especially the powers of the Vatican under Pope Pius IX, in the *Kulturkampf*, fought against *Schund und Schmutz*, and tried to combat the rise of the working-class movement – represented by the Social Democratic Workers Party and the trade unions – with a mixture of social reforms and political repression. The Anti-Socialist Laws, a series of acts passed by the German *Reichstag*, the national parliament, between 1878 and 1890, did not ban the party itself, but rather any socialist or social democratic organization or activity, including socialist newspapers.[27] The *Kulturkampf*, the Anti-Socialist Laws and their aftermath, increasing racial anti-Semitism, militarism and national chauvinism were combined with imperialist dreams that culminated in a bellicose colonialist policy that dominated the political culture of the German Empire up to World War I.[28]

The transformation of the political culture and communication control had a largely indirect effect on the production of memories of the Anti-Napoleonic Wars. It strongly informed the selection of themes and the coming and going fashions of the history of the Napoleonic era, led to internalized self-censorship and prevented the Marxist interpretation of the "Wars of Liberty" from gaining any influence beyond the labor movement. The laws of the market, however, proved as important, if not more

[26] Siemann, "Kontrolle"; and idem, "Ideenschmuggel," 105–106.

[27] Wehler, *Gesellschaftsgeschichte*, 3:892–914; see Michael B. Gross, *The War against Catholicism: Liberalism and the Anti-Catholic Imagination in Nineteenth-Century Germany* (Ann Arbor, MI, 2004); and Horst Bartel, *Das Sozialistengesetz, 1878–1890: Illustrierte Geschichte des Kampfes der Arbeiterklasse gegen das Ausnahmegesetz* (Berlin, 1980).

[28] Marcel Stoetzler, *The State, the Nation, and the Jews: Liberalism and the Antisemitism Dispute in Bismarck's Germany* (Lincoln, NE, 2008); Wolfram Wette, *Militarismus in Deutschland: Geschichte einer kriegerischen Kultur* (Darmstadt, 2008), 35–100; and Hull, *Destruction*.

influential, especially for the production of the popular literary media of memory such as autobiographies, war memoirs and novels.[29]

THE TRANSFORMATION OF THE LITERARY MARKET

The German literary market boomed in the century between 1815 and 1914. Before World War I, more books were published in Germany than anywhere else in the world: 31,281 titles in 1910, compared to 29,057 in Russia, 13,470 in the United States, 12,615 in France and 10,804 in Britain.[30] The expansion proceeded in phases. By the early nineteenth century, the first major period of innovation and growth was finished. In 1805 production reached a high point of 4,181 new book and periodical titles. After the significant decline in literary production during the war years 1806–15, this level was not attained again until 1821. The pace of growth in literary production accelerated once more starting in the late 1820s. The second marked growth phase occurred in the 1840s. There was a new high point in 1843, with 14,039 new titles. The literature that appeared on the occasion of the twenty-fifth anniversary of the wars of 1813–15 contributed to this boom.

Before and during the Revolution of 1848, parallel to the prevailing economic stagnation, political unrest and civil war, literary production again dropped dramatically, reaching a nadir in 1849 with 8,197 titles. The decline affected *belles lettres* in particular. As had already occurred during the Anti-Napoleonic Wars, newspapers and magazines became the preferred reading matter in these turbulent times. In the postrevolutionary era of the second restoration, the number of new books and periodicals stagnated. It was only in the 1860s that it gradually increased. One reason was the second boom of literature produced to mark the fiftieth anniversary of the wars of 1813–15. This boom received added impetus from the "Year of the Classics" in 1867, when a resolution of the Federal Council (*Bundesrat*) of the North German Confederation permitted the reprinting of the works of all classic German authors who had died before 1837. The introduction of freedom of profession (*Gewerbefreiheit*) in the North German Confederation in 1869, which applied to all of Imperial Germany from 1871, gave the boom another boost. In 1868 new production of literature once again attained the level of 10,563. Unlike the Anti-Napoleonic Wars and the Revolution of 1848–49, the Wars of Unification did not lead to a collapse in publishing figures. Instead, the era saw the beginning of a third period of growth in the literary market that would last for several decades. In 1881, 15,1941 new titles were

[29] Wittmann, *Geschichte*, 325.
[30] Barbara Kastner, "Statistik und Topographie des Verlagswesens," in Jäger, *Geschichte*, 2:300–367, 362.

published, surpassing 1843 levels for the first time. By 1913 the number of new titles had grown to 34,871.[31]

The boom in the literary market involved different fields and genres to widely varying degrees. Until the mid-1850s, theological and religious publications made up the largest percentage of new titles, but their proportion of the total dropped relatively steadily from 29 percent at the beginning of the nineteenth century to 8 percent in 1910. They were replaced by works on jurisprudence, politics and statecraft, "educational works," including school textbooks and children's literature, and *belles lettres*.[32] This reflects four trends: secularization; professionalization in all sectors of the workforce – not only academia, the civil service and the army; the scientification of all areas of life; and, as an important precondition for all of these changes, the growing importance of education.

Belles lettres, especially novels, contributed significantly to the increase in new publications. During the first period of restoration after the Napoleonic Wars, the proportion of *belles lettres* rose to 11 percent in 1828. But in the following two decades it dropped again, reaching a low point of 4 percent in 1846. The second restoration period after 1848–49 again witnessed a rapid and significant rise in the proportion of *belles lettres*, reaching 10 percent of new titles in 1855.[33] In the two restoration periods, many educated readers seem to have chosen novel-reading as a form of escapism, often turning to a better past portrayed in nostalgic historical novels, which were driving the boom. Up to 1870, however, production of *belles lettres* stagnated and increased only slowly in the following decades; in 1910 it reached 13 percent.[34] Next to *belles lettres*, "educational works" were on the rise, growing continuously from 11 to 16 percent of book production between 1855 and 1910, and displacing theological and religious publications from the top spot among new titles by 1880. Here, too, novels written for children and adolescents became increasingly important. At the same time, nonfiction in various fields gained increasing significance in the second half of the nineteenth century. As part of this trend, historical literature reached 4 percent of the total in 1910 and military studies 2 percent.[35]

31 Reinhard Wittmann, *Buchmarkt und Lektüre im 18. und 19. Jahrhundert: Beiträge zum literarischen Leben, 1750–1880* (Tübingen, 1982), 115–119; and Kastner, "Statistik," 300–301. Both use the "Systematic Overview of the Literary Products of the German Book Trade" (*Übersicht der literarischen Erzeugnisse des deutschen Buchhandels*), which the firm of J. C. Hinrichs published annually in the book trade publication *Börsenblatt für den Buchhandel*, as a source. The *Börsenblatt* appeared from 1834; figures for earlier years are based on the annual book fair catalogues. See Wittmann, *Geschichte*, 220–222.

32 Wittmann, *Geschichte*, 258–260.

33 Ibid., 219–220 and 258–260.

34 Kastner, "Statistik," 323; and Wittmann, *Geschichte*, 295–296.

35 Kastner, "Statistik," 302–347 and 323; Goldfriedrich, *Geschichte*, 4:202–203; and Wittmann, *Geschichte*, 229–230; on the popularization of knowledge, see Andreas W. Daum,

Until the regulation of copyright in the 1870s and 1880s, a substantial portion of the new novels published were translations of foreign titles: up to 30 percent in the 1850s and 1860s. These translations included fiction from such renowned authors as Charles Dickens, Alexandre Dumas, George Sand, Sir Walter Scott, Leo Tolstoy and Emile Zola.[36] Some of these titles, such as Dumas's *The Count of Monte Cristo* (first published in French in 1845–46) and Tolstoy's *War and Peace* (first published in Russian in 1865–67), presented competing narratives of the Napoleonic Wars. One especially successful series of foreign novels was *Franck's Belletristisches Ausland* (1843–65) with no fewer than 3,618 volumes. For publishers of mass-market fiction it was generally a good deal cheaper to hire a translator than to pay the fees demanded by respected German authors. Translations were also very popular among the reading public, as is evident from the borrowing records of the lending libraries.[37] It was only in June 1870 that the North German Confederation enacted a "Statute concerning authors' rights to works of literature, illustrations, musical compositions, and dramatic works," which the new empire adopted unaltered in April 1871. In 1886 the first multilateral, international copyright agreement – the Berne Convention – transformed the many separate pacts concerning unauthorized reprints and translations between the individual German states and foreign countries into binding international agreements. This juridification would have a lasting effect on the literary market. German novels now became competitive and dominated the market.[38]

The booming literary market was evident not just in new titles, but also in the development of the German book trade as such, which gives us information about the distribution of reading matter. The number of firms in all areas of book production listed in the *Address Book of the German Book Trade* rose from 519 companies in 163 towns in 1820 to 1,340 in 385 towns in 1840. With 113 and 108 bookshops, respectively, in 1840, Leipzig and Berlin continued to be the centers of bookselling, followed by Vienna with 52, Frankfurt am Main with 35, Stuttgart with 30, Nuremberg with 26, Dresden with 25, and Hamburg and Munich with 22 bookshops each.[39] The book trade expanded further in the decades that followed. In 1875 the *Address Book of the German Book Trade* listed 4,614 firms, which had risen to 7,474 by 1890 and reached 12,412 in 1913. From the 1820s on,

Wissenschaftspopularisierung im 19. Jahrhundert: Bürgerliche Kultur, naturwissenschaftliche Bildung und die deutsche Öffentlichkeit, 1848–1914 (Munich, 1998).

[36] Eggert, *Studien*, 27; and Martin Vogel, "Recht im Buchwesen: Die Entwicklung des Urheberrechts," in Jäger, *Geschichte*, 1:122–138.

[37] Wittmann, *Geschichte*, 238–239; idem., *Buchmarkt*, 124–125; Martino, *Leihbibliothek*, 275–288 and 404–417; and Norbert Bachleitner, "'Übersetzungfabriken': Das deutsche Übersetzungswesen in der ersten Hälfte des 19. Jahrhunderts," *IASL* 14.1 (1989): 1–49.

[38] Wittmann, *Geschichte*, 258–260; and Vogel, "Recht," 128–134.

[39] Wittmann, *Geschichte*, 220; and Goldfriedrich, *Geschichte*, 4:460–463.

the greater part of the companies were retail bookshops, which made up 61 percent of firms in 1890, while 22 percent were pure publishing enterprises, and 16 percent sold popular literature through peddlers (colportage). The respective proportions of these three sectors remained constant over the decades, but there was a growing specialization within the three branches of the book trade.[40] Leipzig and Berlin remained the centers of the book trade up until the First World War, but from the 1860s on Berlin replaced Leipzig at the top. The relative significance of the other places of publication changed little, except for the growing importance of Munich as a publishing center in the second half of the nineteenth century.[41]

The number of publishing houses increased from 668 to 1,665 between 1865 and 1890. Of these, however, 450 specialized in the production and sale of scores, music supplies and musicology literature, 398 concentrated on the production and sale of art prints and art history literature and 195 also traded in secondhand books. The production of books, journals, newspapers and other reading material was controlled by 622 publishing houses.[42] Within this group there was increasing specialization over the long nineteenth century. Publishers concentrated on the production of academic books, judicial or medical literature, military studies, dictionaries and encyclopedias, advice books, religious literature, schoolbooks and children's and youth literature, *belles lettres* (especially novels) and newspapers and journals.[43] In addition, the most successful publishing houses in the centers of the book trade – in particular Berlin and Leipzig – became much larger, and more capital-intensive. Family enterprises still dominated, but from the 1870s the largest publishing houses were transformed into capital companies, a trend that was particularly marked in newspaper and magazine publishing.[44] But as I will show in the fifth part, in the production of novels, too, a very small number of publishing houses controlled the market of the German Empire. Small local publishing houses continued to exist, of course, with a varied range of publishing products and in association with printing businesses.[45] In the end, it was the publishers, driven by political and commercial interests, who decided what was published and promoted on the literary market. This also applies to the production of literary memories of the period of the Napoleonic Wars.

[40] Goldfriedrich, *Geschichte*, 4:491–493. On the various branches of the book trade, see Jäger, *Geschichte*, 1:339–643 and 2:7–367.
[41] Wittmann, *Geschichte*, 296; and Dieter Langewiesche, "Entwicklungsbedingungen im Kaiserreich," in Jäger, *Geschichte*, 1:42–86, 65. On the development of modes of distribution in the book trade, see Jäger, *Geschichte*, 2:523–699.
[42] Goldfriedrich, *Geschichte*, 491–493.
[43] Jäger, *Geschichte*, 1:339–645, and 2:5–367.
[44] Ibid., 1:197–325.
[45] Ibid., 1:326–338.

This development of an increasingly national literary market was influenced by the complex interplay of multiple factors, including a number of economic ones alongside political transformations: greater ease of transportation through improvements in roads and the expansion of the railways, which helped to connect the various widely dispersed German regions; the introduction of freedom of profession; and the disappearance of tolls and customs duties. A very important step toward a national literary market was the creation of the German Customs Union (*Deutsche Zollverein*) in 1834. Its foundation was laid by a variety of custom unions among the German states since 1818. In 1866, the year of the founding of the North German Confederation, the *Zollverein* included most of the German states, with the exception of Austria. The *Zollverein* facilitated the nation-wide distribution of literature and at the same time contributed to the exclusion of Austria from the German literary market.[46]

In addition, industrialization enabled and fostered the development of a national mass literary market. It made the production of printed works significantly faster and cheaper. In 1840 there were more than 1,100 steam-powered rotary presses in operation in Prussia alone. Bookbinding was mechanized, cheap paper made from wood pulp was manufactured in continuous sheets, and book and picture printing improved significantly. These changes allowed for the inexpensive mass production of books, magazines, newspapers and other printed matter. This process contributed to the commercialization and nationalization of the literary market. Successful publishing houses needed more and more capital. To amortize their investments they had to sell increasingly large numbers of products to a national readership. This, in turn, influenced their selection of books to publish, which also affected literary memory production.[47]

Another consequence of the technological innovations in the printing industry was a significant change in the offerings of the book trade, which also had far-reaching consequences for the literary production of memory. In the first half of the nineteenth century, the number of volumes and pages of novels grew substantially. The multivolume novel established itself gradually in the 1820s and became popular among the owners of lending libraries, since it ensured that borrowers would come back for more. It was not until the 1860s that there was an increasing return to the single-volume

---

[46] Monika Estermann and Georg Jäger, "Geschichtliche Grundlagen und Entwicklungen des Buchhandels im Deutschen Reich bis 1871," in Jäger, *Geschichte*, 1:17–41; Langewiesche "Entwicklungsbedingungen"; and Wittmann, *Geschichte*, 220–225. On the history of the *Zollverein*, see Richard H. Tilly, *Vom Zollverein zum Industriestaat: Die wirtschaftlich-soziale Entwicklung Deutschlands 1834 bis 1914* (Munich, 1990).

[47] Peter Naumann, "Industrielle Buchproduktion," in Jäger, *Geschichte*, 1:170–181; and Georg Jäger, "Vom Familienunternehmen zur Aktiengesellschaft – Besitzverhältnisse und Gesellschaftsform im Verlagswesen," in ibid., 1:197–215.

novel.[48] Most of the authors who published historical novels in the decades before the founding of the German Empire also wrote works in several volumes. One of the most successful publishers of such novels was Otto Janke, who had founded his firm in Berlin in 1850.[49]

Technological innovations in printing also made it possible to publish high print runs of cheap novel series, which became increasingly popular among publishers from the 1820s because, much like serialized novels, they helped to ensure sales. Complete series were generally sold by subscription to a fixed number of volumes for a relatively low price and published in mass editions. The volumes of open series were also sold separately. The prototype here was *Reclams Universalbibliothek*, which the Leipzig publishing house of Phil. Reclam jun. (founded in 1828) launched in the "Classics Year" of 1867 as an inexpensive collected edition of all "classic German authors." The series soon expanded into a broad and popular mix of edification and entertainment, which sought to make German and foreign literature available to everyone at a price of 2 groschen, which was hard to beat. The usual edition size at the time was 1,000 copies at most, but *Reclams Universalbibliothek* easily reached 5,000 or more.[50] Many series specialized in a particular reading public, a specific region, genre or theme, which was generally directly addressed in the series title. Especially in the decade before the centenary of the wars of 1813–15, several series were published that specialized in memory texts on the period of the Anti-Napoleonic Wars.[51]

The extraordinary expansion of the press during the nineteenth century, too, was only possible because of the technological innovations in printing. Periodicals increasingly competed with books. This is evident in the ratio of book to periodical titles, which was 1:14 in 1826, 1:8 in 1867, 1:6 in 1890 and 1:4 in 1914. Of the 34,801 new titles published that year, 6,689 were periodicals. In 1860 the number of periodicals had been only 316, a figure that rose to 4,933 in 1900. At that point, according to *Sperling's Address Book of the German Periodicals and Outstanding Political Daily Papers*, 11 percent were devoted to "jurisprudence and statecraft, politics, the commonweal and statistics" (595 titles; 15 with a print run greater than 1,000), 9 percent were "general-interest magazines" (*Unterhaltungszeitschriften*) (479 titles; 53 with a print run greater than 1,000), 6 percent were "literary magazines, reviews, and academic journals" (313 titles; 7 with a print run greater than 1,000), and 2 percent were magazines on "the military and military science" (112 titles; 7 with print runs larger than 1,000). All of

[48] Kurt Habitzel and Günter Mühlberger, "Die Leihbibliotheksforschung in Deutschland, Österreich und der Schweiz: Ergebnisse und Perspektiven," *IASL* 22.2 (1997): 66–108, 113–117.

[49] Karl Friedrich Pfau, "Janke, Otto," *ADB* (1905): 631.

[50] Wittmann, *Geschichte*, 244 and 268–269; on Reclam, see "Phil. Recam jun. Verlag, Leipzig 1828," in Reinhard Würffel, *Lexikon Deutscher Verlage von A–Z* (Berlin, 2000), 684–690.

[51] Estermann and Jäger, "Grundlagen," 1:20–21.

these were involved in the publication of texts that recalled the Napoleonic Wars and of reviews that critiqued these texts. Berlin and Leipzig were, and remained throughout the nineteenth century, the clear centers of periodical production followed at some distance by Vienna and Munich, with the concentration in Berlin in particular increasing after the foundation of the empire. Around 1900, more than one-quarter of all German periodicals appeared in Berlin.[52]

Four groups of periodicals were especially important in shaping the culture of memory: journals on history, politics and military history; literary magazines; reviews and academic journals; and general-interest magazines. The significance of these four groups within the literary market changed tremendously over the course of the nineteenth century, however. During the restoration period and the *Vormärz,* literary-cultural magazines such as Cotta's *Morgenblatt für Gebildete Stände* (1807–65) dominated.[53] Beyond their literary and entertainment value, they also served as "journalistic forums for bourgeois communication," since censorship significantly hindered the publication of political-historical journals. The influence of the latter, which had been substantial between 1806 and 1815, only rose again for a brief time before and during the Revolution of 1848–49 because of the abolition of censorship. As in 1813–15, hundreds of new periodicals of this type were founded, which then quickly folded in the postrevolutionary restoration.[54] The literary-cultural and political-historical journals established by committed journalists who generally served as both editor and publisher, which had shaped the periodicals market since the Enlightenment, lost their influence in the second half of the century. In the rapidly commercializing periodicals market, most magazines and journals were put out by publishers who delegated the editorial work to journalists specifically hired for the purpose. This promoted the professionalization of journalism beyond the daily newspapers.[55]

In the 1850s a new type of periodical, the general-interest family magazine, began to assert itself alongside a rapidly growing number of professional, associational and company journals as well as (popular) science publications.[56] The prototype was the extraordinarily successful *Gartenlaube* (1853–1944), which the Leipzig publisher Ernst Keil launched with a print run of 5,000, and which reached its highest circulation of 382,000 in the 1870s. The *Gartenlaube* presented the typical mix of liberal faith in progress,

[52] Georg Jäger, "Das Zeitschriftenwesen," in idem., *Geschichte*, 2:368–389, 368–371 and 376.

[53] In 1837 the title was changed to *Morgenblatt für gebildete Leser.*

[54] Wittmann, *Geschichte*, 226–247 and 277–279.

[55] Christian Göbel, *Der vertraute Feind: Pressekritik in der Literatur des 19. und frühen 20. Jahrhundert* (Würzburg, 2011), 25–26.

[56] Jäger, "Das Zeitschriftenwesen"; and Andreas Graf and Susanne Pellatz, "Familien- und Unterhaltungszeitschriften," in Jäger, *Geschichte*, 2:409–522.

monarchical nationalism, education and entertainment that appealed to the middle classes.[57] A whole series of other family magazines pursued similar aims, all of them with significantly smaller print runs. One example is the Christian conservative competitor *Daheim* (1864–1943), published in Bielefeld by August Klasing, which attained a maximum circulation of 80,000 in the 1870s.[58]

The more ambitious cultural, literary and political magazines that targeted an educated middle- and upper-class readership had a far lower average circulation. In its heyday, the *Morgenblatt für Gebildete Stände* had a print run of 2,500. The *Blätter für literarische Unterhaltung* (1826–96) – founded in 1818 by Kotzebue and continued after his murder by Friedrich Arnold Brockhaus and his sons – never exceeded a circulation of 1,000 to 2,000 copies. This Leipzig literary magazine, alongside the *Morgenblatt*, whose supplement *Literatur-Blatt* (1817–49) was devoted exclusively to book reviews, became an institution of literary criticism. Even *Die Grenzboten* (1841–1922) – founded in 1841 and published from 1843 on in Leipzig – did not achieve a higher circulation in its prime. Its editors included Julian Schmidt (1848–61) and Gustav Freytag (1848–61 and 1867–70), who turned the magazine into a mouthpiece of the national-liberal bourgeoisie and the most influential organ of programmatic realism in literature. Only *Westermanns Illustrierte Deutsche Monatshefte* (1856–1987), launched in Braunschweig by the publisher Georg Westermann, attained a significantly higher circulation of 12,000 copies. With its broader range of topics, which included the natural sciences, however, it also appealed to a wider public.[59]

These and many other periodicals as well as the newspaper culture pages attracted readers with their announcements of forthcoming titles, reviews of the latest academic and literary publications and serialized advance publication of novels. Reviews were of particular importance for the success of a novel. Using the examples of the *Allgemeine Literatur-Zeitung* (1785–1850) – which appeared first in Jena and from 1803 in Halle and Leipzig – and the *Literatur-Blatt*, Kurt Habitzle and Günter Mühlberger have shown how pivotal reviews were for the dissemination of historical novels. Books that were not reviewed did not appear in the catalogues of the lending libraries. The most successful ones were overwhelmingly those that had earned critical praise. Even negative reviews proved better for the dissemination of a book than absolute silence. The main indicator of attention to a book in

57 Graf and Pellatz, "Familien- und Unterhaltungszeitschriften," 2:435–437; "Ernst Keil Verlag, Leipzig, 1845–1938," in Würffel, *Lexikon*, 419–421; see also Kirsten Belgum, *Popularizing the Nation: Audience, Representation, and the Production of Identity in "Die Gartenlaube," 1853–1900* (Lincoln, NE, 1998).

58 Graf and Pellatz, "Familien- und Unterhaltungszeitschriften," 2:427–429; and "Klasing & Co GmbH Verlag," in Würffel, *Lexikon*, 430–431.

59 Akaltin, *Die Befreiungskriege*, 235–244; Graf and Pellatz, "Familien- und Unterhaltungszeitschriften," 2:433–434; and "Georg Westermann Verlag, Braunschweig, 1838," in Würffel, *Lexikon*, 975–976.

the literary public sphere was the length of reviews. For example, more than two-thirds of the most successful historical novels that became bestsellers with the lending libraries had been reviewed at length after publication.[60] Serialized preprints were crucial too for a novel's success. Many cultural and literary magazines also printed serialized novels to attract readers. Afterwards these novels frequently appeared in book form. Few authors, even established ones, could dispense with this source of income and advertisement.[61] From the 1860s, specialized novel magazines were also established to satisfy the hunger of the reading public. The first and most widely read of these was Janke's *Deutsche Roman-Zeitung* (1864–1944), which appeared weekly and in its heyday had a print run of 15,000 copies.[62]

As the nineteenth century wore on, readers of the newspaper culture sections, too, increasingly expected light reading, mainly short stories and serialized novellas and novels.[63] Printing such works contributed significantly to demand and thus to rising newspaper circulation figures. This in turn increased the demand for literature, especially light fiction, since the number of newspapers and their circulation also expanded significantly between 1815 and 1915. In 1912, 3,500 newspapers with a total circulation of 25.5 million were being published in Imperial Germany. Big city newspapers run by publishers represented the lion's share; Berlin's *Vossische Zeitung*, for example, had a circulation of 43,000 and the *Berliner Tageblatt* 230,000 before the First World War. In the second half of the nineteenth century, newspapers of this type increasingly competed with papers put out by the political parties – the most successful of which was *Vorwärts*, the central organ of the Social Democrats founded in 1876, which attained a circulation of 154,000 in 1914 – and illustrated weeklies such as Ullstein's *Berliner Illustrierte Zeitung*, which was founded in 1891 and reached a circulation of one million in 1914. It was sold not by subscription, but rather for the first time by street vendors at the extraordinarily cheap price of 10 pfennigs.[64] All of these papers published serialized novels, several of them historical novels on the Napoleonic Wars.

At the end of the nineteenth century, readers, above all female ones, could not get enough of novels, which led to their industrial mass production and

[60] Kurt Habitzel and Günter Mühlberger, "Gewinner und Verlierer: Der historische Roman und sein Beitrag zum Literatursystem der Restaurationszeit (1815–1848/49)," *IASL* 21.1 (1996): 91–123, 99–101; see Christian Göbel, *Der vertraute Feind: Pressekritik in der Literatur des 19. und frühen 20. Jahrhundert* (Würzburg, 2011)., 49–78.

[61] Eggert, *Studien*, 45–52; and Graf and Pellatz, "Familien- und Unterhaltungszeitschriften."

[62] Rudolf Schmidt, *Deutsche Buchhändler: Deutsche Buchdrucker*, 6 vols. (Berlin, 1905), 3:510–514.

[63] Norbert Bachleitner, *Kleine Geschichte des deutschen Feuilletonromans* (Tübingen, 1999).

[64] Goldfriedrich, *Geschichte*, 4:578; Stöber, *Pressegeschichte*, 146–150; and Graf and Pellatz, "Familien- und Unterhaltungszeitschriften," 2:422–423.

ever cheaper paperback series.[65] Before 1914 alone, 25–30 million of these booklets had been sold. These slim volumes with their lurid cover illustrations were 32–64 pages long and cost no more than 10–25 pfennigs.[66] This further increased the chasm between highbrow literature (*Kulturbuch*) and the lowbrow popular fiction (*Massenbuch*) that was sold in train station and department store bookshops, as well as by stationers, tobacconists and peddlers.[67] Jürgen Habermas has therefore interpreted the transformation of the literary market during the nineteenth century, which was driven by industrialization and commercialization, as a transformation from a "culture-debating" (*kulturräsonierend*) to a "culture-consuming" national public.[68]

For all those who hoped to make a living from their writing, this development, which Habermas views negatively from an Enlightenment perspective, nevertheless meant a considerable improvement in their opportunities to work, as well as increasingly necessary specialization and professionalization. Writers whom the literary public accepted into the canon of high literature, the female authors of middlebrow literature, writers of fiction for mass consumption, children's book authors, military writers, political journalists and daily newspaper editors now all competed with one another in the literary market. As a rule, only those who wrote what the market expected were successful with their contemporaries and thus found their way into print.[69]

Among the beneficiaries of this development were female authors, whose proportion among the producers of *belles lettres* rose significantly over the nineteenth century, from about 5 percent at the beginning of the century to 15 percent in the 1820s and 1830s. Around 1900, their share was 20 percent. Women writers conquered the literary market along with the expansion of novel production from the 1820s.[70] Since publishing houses and lending libraries, if they hoped to be successful, had to meet the needs of the large female readership, which preferred the novel to all other genres, they needed novels that also appealed to women readers. Publishers employed women writers to serve this market, since they were often in a better position to do so than their male colleagues.[71]

[65] Lyons, *History*, 156–167.
[66] Wittmann, *Geschichte*, 325.
[67] Ibid., 295–328.
[68] Habermas, *Transformation*, 158–175.
[69] Wehler, *Gesellschaftsgeschichte*, 3:1235–1236.
[70] See Norbert Otto Eke and Dagmar Olasz-Eke, *Bibliographie, der deutsche Roman 1815–1830: Standortnachweise, Rezensionen, Forschungsüberblick* (Munich, 1994), 25–27; and Bland and Müller-Adams, *Frauen*, 14–19.
[71] See Caroline Bland and Elisa Müller-Adams, eds., *Schwellenüberschreitungen: Politik in der Literatur von deutschsprachigen Frauen, 1780–1918* (Bielefeld, 2007), 9–20.

A GROWING READERSHIP

Apart from the political, economic and technological preconditions for expanding the German literary market, it was above all the rapid advance of literacy in the nineteenth century – largely as a consequence of the growth of the educational system – that made this boom possible.[72] Industrialization was the most important factor promoting the expansion of public education, which occurred unevenly in different regions and between the city and the countryside. It led to a quickly rising demand in the trades, industry, commerce and administration for a workforce capable of reading and writing. The military, too, with its system of universal male conscription, needed recruits who had mastered the fundamental skills of reading, writing and arithmetic.[73] Because the literacy rate was generally much higher in towns and cities, urbanization also advanced its rise. Between 1871 and 1910, the proportion of the population in the German Empire living in towns of more than 2,000 inhabitants increased from 36 to 60 percent. On the eve of the First World War, every fifth German lived in a city of 100,000 or more residents.[74]

Estimates of the extent of literacy vary for the entire nineteenth century. Rudolf Schenda assumes that, in 1840, up to 40 percent of the population in the German-speaking region could read.[75] By 1871 this proportion had supposedly risen to approximately 88 percent. The differences between regions, town and countryside, age cohorts, genders, and confessions as well as ethnic groups remained substantial, however. Thus in 1871 approximately 18 percent of Catholics were illiterate, but only about 12 percent of Protestants. In West Prussia, a largely agricultural region with a high proportion of Catholic Polish and Kashubian inhabitants, some 33 percent of men and 40 percent of women could neither read nor write in 1871. In that same year, in contrast, only 1 percent of men and 3 percent of women in Berlin were illiterate. By World War I, these differences evened out and the literacy rate in the German Empire had reached nearly 100 percent.[76] This does not mean that the entire population was actually in a position truly to "comprehend printed texts"; even after 1900, some 20–25 percent lacked this skill.[77]

For broad segments of the literate population, lack of time and places to read as well as lack of funds to buy or borrow reading materials remained

---

[72] In 1846 the percentage of children who attended school in Prussia ranged from 73 percent in the province of West Prussia to 95 percent in the province of Saxony. Winnige, "Alphabetisierung," 53.

[73] Wittmann, *Geschichte*, 322–323.

[74] Wehler, *Gesellschaftsgeschichte*, 3:7–37 and 493–546, esp. 494 and 512.

[75] Schenda, *Volk*, 444–445.

[76] Langewiesche, "Entwicklungsbedingungen," 63–69.

[77] Wittmann, *Geschichte*, 323.

the main obstacles. Despite a general improvement in living conditions, even in 1900 the overwhelming majority was still considered to be of "modest means," and could afford at most a newspaper subscription.[78] Large print runs, cheap forms of publication and sale by peddlers did little to change this. Around 1900 the middle classes still represented no more than 15 percent of the population. Of them, 5 percent belonged to the so-called educated elite, the upper-middle class with money and an academic education (among men). The rest consisted of members of the old and new lower-middle classes, including craftsmen.[79]

Apart from the aristocracy, these middle classes continued to represent the majority of readers, book buyers and newspaper and periodical subscribers. The increase in readership was mainly among the lower-middle classes. Even most middle-class and petty bourgeois readers, however, rarely bought literary texts or subscribed to magazines, apart from those that featured light family entertainment. Those who wished to read novels, autobiographies, biographies, works of history or the more serious periodicals visited the nearest lending library, where novels were especially popular, chief among them historical novels, love stories and tales of adventure as well as detective novels, which made up 80 to 90 percent of the overall titles borrowed. Biographies and memoirs were also favorites among borrowers.[80]

According to the *Address Book of the Book Trade*, there were 617 commercial lending libraries in the German-speaking region in 1865, a figure that rose to 1,056 in 1880 and to 3,000 in 1903. Since many provincial firms were not members of the German Book Trade Association (*Börsenverein des Deutschen Buchhandels*), scholars have estimated that the actual figure was double that. In addition, a growing number of public libraries were established in villages, towns and cities by church parishes, adult education associations and later also municipalities beginning in the 1830s and 1840s. The figures rose significantly, particularly from the 1870s on. After the lifting of the Anti-Socialist Laws, the Social Democratic Party and trade unions also opened workers' libraries all over the country. In 1914 a total of 1,147 workers' libraries existed in 748 towns.[81]

In his extensive study of German lending libraries, Alberto Martino estimates that the average proportion of the population who were regular users of all types of libraries was 6 percent in the 1880s, but increased manyfold in the two decades that followed. Library use reflected the growth of the reading population. It spread first in the old and new middle classes, then in the petty bourgeoisie and later in the skilled and organized working class. Even in Berlin, where 81 trade union libraries existed in 1906, unskilled and

---

[78] Ibid., 250–256, 285–294 and 322–328.
[79] Ibid., 68; and Wehler, *Gesellschaftsgeschichte*, 3:712–772.
[80] Wittmann, *Geschichte*, 255.
[81] Ibid., 275–277 and 327–328; and Martino, *Leihbibliothek*, 289–308, esp. 303–308.

semiskilled workers never represented more than one-quarter of all library users.[82] Despite these qualifications, Martyn Lyons concludes in his comparative history of reading that "The half-century between the 1880s and the 1930s was the golden age of the book." The "first generation which acceded to mass literacy was also the last to see the book unchallenged as a communications medium."[83] For the broad mass of the population, especially women and workers, it was only the formation of a national culture-consuming public that gave them access to books, magazines and newspapers, and it was only with this access that the influence of literary memories of the era of the Napoleonic Wars could flourish.

Politics, the market and the media all influenced the construction of collective memories of the Anti-Napoleonic Wars in German Central Europe. Without the development of a culture-consuming national public and the successful use of literary media such as popular history books and autobiographies as well as war memoirs and novels, the wide dissemination of literary war memories would have been impossible. As I will show in more detail later in this fourth part as well as in the fifth part, the specific media of memory, their potential audience and their chances on the literary market and in the lending libraries influenced the production of these war memories during the nineteenth century far more than has been recognized thus far. Certainly, transformations in political culture and with them changing censorship practices were important as well, and they were partly reflected by the booms in memory production, but the twenty-fifth, fiftieth and one-hundredth anniversaries of the Anti-Napoleonic Wars were far more crucial for these booms. Without the public's growing interest in the history of this period, however, all of the other factors that influenced memory production would have been irrelevant. Thus we need first to explain this interest and to explore the role of academic, military and popular histories.

[82] Martino, *Leihbibliothek.*
[83] Lyons, *History*, 153.

13

Inventing History: Nostalgia, Historiography and Memory

It is a dangerous time, this time of transition, which will probably not be over in half a century. Often, it appears to lift us, to shoot us to the stars and beyond with hopes, designs and prospects, and then dash us deep into the dust, and indeed sometimes into the mud, to remind us of all things human and mundane.[1]

Ernst Moritz Arndt wrote these words in May 1817 to his friend Councilor of War Johann Georg Scheffner in Königsberg. Like many of his contemporaries, he sensed that he was living in a period of transition and rapid transformation. The experience of the French Revolution and the Napoleonic Wars had changed the perception of time in many ways, leading to a "memory crisis" that educated contemporaries responded to in large numbers by turning toward history. The intensity of the renewed "historical impulse" since the early nineteenth century expressed the powerful perception of a "deprivation of the past."[2] In the German-speaking region this development became evident not just in the political journalism and Romantic literature of the time,[3] but also in the writings of early historicism,[4] which turned with heightened interest to the German past, including the most recent events. The first accounts of the history of the wars of 1813–15 and the "time of the French" appeared soon after it was over. In subsequent decades, this historical impulse

---

[1] "Arndt an Scheffner, Berlin 22.5.1817," in *Briefe und Aktenstücke zur Geschichte Preußens unter Friedrich Wilhelm III. vorzugsweise aus dem Nachlass von F. A. von Stägemann*, ed. Franz Rühl, 3 vols. (Leipzig, 1899–1902), 2:124–126.

[2] Richard Terdiman, *Present Past: Modernity and the Memory Crisis* (Ithaca, NY, 1993), 32; see also Koselleck, *Futures*; Fritzsche, *Stranded*; idem, "Specters of History: On Nostalgia, Exile, and Modernity," *AHR* 106 (2001): 1587–1618; and Becker, "Zeiterfahrungen."

[3] Dennis F. Mahoney, ed., *The Literature of German Romanticism* (Rochester, NY, 2004); and Nicholas Saul, ed., *The Cambridge Companion to German Romanticism* (Cambridge, 2009).

[4] Daniel Fulda, *Wissenschaft aus Kunst: Die Entstehung der modernen deutschen Geschichtsschreibung, 1760–1860* (Berlin, 1996), 267–295; and Wolfgang Hardtwig, *Geschichtskultur und Wissenschaft* (Munich, 1990), 58–102.

expressed itself in the development of history into a professional academic discipline and the accompanying triumph of historicism,[5] the founding of a variety of archaeological and historical societies as well as local historical and museum associations,[6] in the culture of monuments[7] and not least in the first boom in autobiographies and war memoirs and the growing treatment of subjects from history in other literary texts such as biographies and novels.[8] The development of this history boom suggests that – apart from a number of more general factors that led to a discovery of the past and a growing interest in historical topics among the broader public – the period of the Napoleonic Wars itself was such a formative experience for contemporaries and subsequent generations that it required intensive processing in individual and collective memory beyond the national politics of memory pursued by the state, the military and churches.

In this chapter I first discuss the various factors that led to this turn toward the past and intensive processing of memories of the Napoleonic Wars and then sketch the development of German-language academic, military and popular historiography on the wars with a focus on the most widespread and influential texts, since the master narratives of historiography did not merely shape the basic lines of the historical narrative in the popular literary media of memory, but were themselves part of those media.

REVOLUTION, WAR AND THE RISE OF HISTORY

In 1979, in his seminal *Futures Past: On the Semantic of Historical Time*, Reinhard Koselleck already pointed to the transformation of the understanding of *time* in the epoch of the French Revolution and the Napoleonic Wars.[9] Since then, historians have studied this phenomenon extensively.

---

[5] See Fulda, *Wissenschaft*, 296–446; Hardtwig, *Geschichtskultur*, 58–160; and idem, "Die Verwissenschaftlichung der neueren Geschichtsschreibung," in *Geschichte: Ein Grundkurs*, ed. Hans-Jürgen Goertz (Reinbek, 2007), 245–260.

[6] Susan A. Crane, *Collecting and Historical Consciousness in Early Nineteenth-Century Germany* (Ithaca, NY, 2000); and Georg Kunz, *Verortete Geschichte: Regionales Geschichtsbewusstsein in den deutschen Historischen Vereinen des 19. Jahrhunderts* (Göttingen, 2000).

[7] Ulrich Schlie, *Die Nation erinnert sich: Die Denkmäler der Deutschen* (Munich, 2002), 7–70; and Wolfgang Hardtwig, *Politische Kultur der Moderne: Ausgewählte Aufsätze* (Göttingen, 2011), 17–64.

[8] See Norbert Otto Eke and Hartmut Steinecke, eds., *Geschichten aus (der) Geschichte: Zum Stand des historischen Erzählens im Deutschland der frühen Restaurationszeit* (Munich, 1994); eidem, *Bibliographie*, 9–50; and Michael Meyer, "Die Entstehung des historischen Romans in Deutschland und seine Stellung zwischen Geschichtsschreibung und Dichtung: Die Polemik um eine 'Zwittergattung' (1785–1845)" (Phil. Diss., University of Munich, 1973); for Europe more generally, see Brian R. Hamnett, *The Historical Novel in Nineteenth-Century Europe: Representations of Reality in History and Fiction* (Oxford, 2011).

[9] Koselleck, *Futures*, 43–57; German edition: *Vergangene Zukunft: Zur Semantik geschichtlicher Zeiten* (Frankfurt/M., 1979).

They all emphasize "fundamental breaks in the Western consciousness of time, which in turn structured the way Europeans viewed their place in history, their connections with the past, and their ability to fashion themselves as active political subjects."[10] Before the French Revolution, history was perceived as comparatively static; past and present were believed to be in balance with one another. Even the Enlightenment, with its concept of "historical progress" moving "society toward the completion of a rational plan or universal scheme" did nothing to change this. "Both the retrograde aspects of the past and the rational endeavors of the present provided unmistakable evidence for progress unfolding." It was therefore unnecessary to scrutinize temporal differences between the past, the present and the future.[11]

The events of the French Revolution, however, quickly and radically rendered this understanding of time obsolete. Contemporaries recognized that after the revolution, which was perceived as a violent rupture, there was no way back to the past. At the same time, they acknowledged that this break, and with it the present, was in many ways a product of the past. They were at once cut off from and shaped by the past – no revolution without the ancien régime. What was perceived as especially new and ineluctable about the revolution "was its authorization of so many new historical subjects," its "explicitly ideological nature," its "rejection of the past, and its celebration of the people and the nation."[12] The perception of the French Revolution as an irrevocable break with the past made it what Koselleck has called a *geschichtsphilosophischer Perspektivbegriff*:[13] "The revolution was transformed for everyone into a historicophilosophical concept, based on a perspective which displayed a constant and steady direction" toward the future.[14] Subsequently, the difference between the space of experience (*Erfahrungsraum*) and the horizon of expectations (*Erwartungshorizont*) grew. Previously unimaginable changes, not just in politics but also in society and the economy, suddenly became possible – even for social groups such as slaves, workers and women who seemed to have played no role as historical agents in the past. This expanding horizon of expectations unleashed a utopian potential that produced an open notion of progress – that is, the hope that, despite short-term setbacks, the economy, society and politics would change for the better in the long term. This faith in progress strongly influenced the thinking of the liberal middle classes, in particular, in the nineteenth century.[15] At the time of the French Revolution and the

[10] Peter Fritzsche, "Specters of History: On Nostalgia, Exile, and Modernity," *AHR* 106.5 (2001): 1587–1618, 1589; and idem, *Stranded*; and James Chandler, *England in 1819: The Politics of Literary Culture and the Case of Romantic Historicism* (Chicago, 1998).

[11] Fritzsche, "Specters," 1590.

[12] Ibid., 1597.

[13] Koselleck, *Zukunft*, 78.

[14] Koselleck, *Futures*, 51.

[15] Ibid., 43–57; see also Becker, "Zeiterfahrungen."

Napoleonic Wars, this faith was accompanied by the sense that progress was accelerating in the present, which seemed to further reinforce the feeling of contemporaries that they had to leave the past irrevocably behind them. This in turn led to the "memory crisis" discussed by Richard Terdiman and, frequently but not always, to a sense of nostalgia – "the deep feelings of dispossession" elicited by the past.[16] A remark made by Joseph Görres in a letter of February 1811 to his publisher friend Friedrich Perthes is typical of this mix of feelings:

Our time retains nothing that remains the same: just as the leisurely old way of making books has ceased among scholars, the merchants have also been chased from the quiet seats in their counting houses. Those who cannot survive on their previous acquisitions must climb down from the sedan chair and onto their horses; the infantry must be provided with mounts, for time itself is fleeing in a chariot.[17]

As Peter Fritzsche has shown, a similar nostalgic state of mind can be found in the letters, diaries and memoirs of many educated contemporaries.[18] The sense of living at a time of accelerated change, which differed fundamentally from the irretrievable past, went hand in hand with the quite emancipatory insight that history is made by ordinary mortals, not just rulers and generals, and is thus subject to change, and that at the same time the specific conditions of an era shape the people who live in it to a great degree.[19] "The ability of contemporaries to conceive of themselves as historical products of specific periods opened the way for them to think of themselves as active agents of history. This new way of thinking, which recognized individuals as subjects of history and afforded them autonomy and agency, was associated with the consciousness of generation-specific experiences of the present and thus also of the past and the future.[20] As a consequence of this development, from the end of the eighteenth century on, along with changing perceptions of time, interest in the political events of the present and their history grew markedly among increasingly broad strata of the population. One aspect of this "authorization of new historical subjects was the self-recognition and self-positioning of the subject in the new histories," which led to the boom in autobiographies and memoirs as well as historical novels.[21]

The Revolutionary and Napoleonic Wars, which affected millions of people across Europe and beyond, significantly intensified these altered perceptions of time. The mass experience of these wars by soldiers and civilians over the long period of 23 years made the present something that

---

[16] Fritzsche, "Specters," 1589; and Terdiman, *Past*, 66–71.
[17] "Görres an Perthes, Koblenz Februar 1811," in Joseph von Görres, *Gesammelte Schriften*, ed. Marie Görres, 8 vols. (Munich, 1854–74), 8:166–170, 169.
[18] Fritzsche, *Stranded*.
[19] Böning, *Revolution*.
[20] Peter Fritzsche, "The Case of Memory," *JMH* 73 (2001): 87–117, 96.
[21] Fritzsche, "Specters," 1598.

affected everyone in their everyday lives, was shared by all and touched the inhabitants of even the tiniest villages in the remotest corners of Europe, especially during the Napoleonic Wars. The exceedingly high military and civilian casualties, which surpassed anything seen before, and "the extreme violence that characterized the period"[22] as well as its legitimation by a bellicist and nationalist ideology distinguished the wars between 1792 and 1815 from all previous ones. Their mutually recognizable experience thus created a common historical field that people shared; it turned them into "contemporaries" – beyond all other differences – and further fostered their interest in the present.[23]

The feeling of *Zeitgenossenschaft* (contemporaneity in the sense of being a contemporary of others), a term often used in writings of the time, was significantly intensified by the movement of large crowds – soldiers, sailors, refugees, exiles and prisoners of war from many different lands – across vast stretches of the European continent and the adjacent seas. Sooner or later, troops marching through, requisitions, occupation, billeting, the accommodation of prisoners of war and the need to care for sick and wounded soldiers, both one's own and those of the enemy, affected many regions. These experiences made for high politics and military affairs that affected everyone. Simultaneously, they created a variety of occasions for forced encounters with "foreigners," which allowed people to experience collective identity as well as alterity. This is one reason why military memoirs relating war experiences in foreign regions, such as the Iberian Peninsula and Eastern Europe, became so popular after 1815.[24] Even simple soldiers and civilians who had never been far from home recognized, frequently for the first time, what the people of their home region and nation shared despite their internal social and religious differences, and what distinguished them from other, "alien" peoples. Fostered by the nationalization of the political discourse, this made it possible to see unity on the level of the territorial state and the nation, and at the same time to recognize distinctions within this unity.

The national rhetoric used to legitimize wars, which also served the purpose of patriotic mobilization, was an important additional factor that influenced the altered perceptions of time and people and the increasing interest in the past. As I showed in the second part, the German-speaking region witnessed a massive nationalization of the political discourse after 1806, which was expressed not only in contemporary political writing but also in sermons, poems and songs as well as fiction. Romantic authors such as Achim von

[22] Philip G. Dwyer, "'It Still Makes Me Shudder': Memories of Massacres and Atrocities during the Revolutionary and Napoleonic Wars," *WiH* 16 (2009): 381–405, 385; and Philip G. Dwyer and Lyndall Ryan, eds., *Massacre in the Old and New Worlds, c. 1780–1820*, special issue of the *Journal of Genocide Research* 15.2 (2013).

[23] Fritzsche, *Stranded*, 205.

[24] See chapter 14 in this part.

Arnim, Clemens Brentano, Caroline and Friedrich de la Motte Fouqué and Friedrich Schlegel shared the patriotism of Arndt, Brockhaus, Fichte, Görres and Jahn.[25] In their common striving to create national unity by constructing a German cultural nation, they deployed history, or rather a mythologized national past, alongside language, custom and the Christian religion. They rediscovered the distant Germanic past and the Middle Ages and with them the art and architecture of those epochs. At the same time, an awareness of and interest in the history of the individual regions and not just of the nation grew, as expressed in the founding of countless local and regional historical and archaeological societies during the first half of the century. The regions were increasingly perceived as an important part of the nation.[26]

Educated contemporaries seem to have hoped that looking backward in history, often through the rosy lens of nostalgia, would offer orientation for the present and the future. The historian Heinrich Luden accordingly wrote in his 1810 *On the Study of National History*, "The present passes quickly by; the future is unknown to us; only the past stands firmly anchored in history and responds to our questions."[27] The reverse of all this looking backward, which lay in the discovery of their own history, was the hope of a better future. Consequently, the adherents of German nationalism linked their active support for the struggle for liberation from Napoleonic rule with aspirations toward national unity and more political liberties. In 1813–15 they still believed the promises of their princes. Even less radically minded contemporaries shared their hopes for reforms and, albeit in a politically far more moderate manner, for increased civil and political rights.[28]

During the restoration period, however, these expectations were so thoroughly and permanently disappointed that the widespread faith in monarchical government was severely shaken, and not just among radical proponents of the German national idea. After 1815 – and the literature often ignores this – even moderate patriots and indeed conservatives like the Brandenburg *Junker* Friedrich August Ludwig von der Marwitz experienced this fundamental loss of faith. Looking back from the 1830s, he noted in his posthumously published memoirs:

Scarcely anyone spoke of freedom and constitutions anymore. Not just here, but in nearly every land in Europe, the ministries boasted of their wisdom. They alone had vanquished the enemy with their splendid combinations and brought about the present happy (!!) circumstances. If someone objected that the abused people's strength and love of liberty had also played their part, this was either denied out-right or it was admitted that the peoples had behaved so well out of love for their

[25] Walter Pape, ed., *Arnim und die Berliner Romantik: Kunst, Literatur und Politik* (Tübingen, 2001).

[26] Brandt, *Germania*; Edith Höltenschmidt, *Die Mittelalter-Rezeption der Brüder Schlegel* (Paderborn, 2000); Crane, *Collecting*; and Kunz, *Geschichte*.

[27] Heinrich Luden, *Über das Studium der vaterländischen Geschichte* (Jena, 1810), 13.

[28] Fritzsche, "Case," 96.

rightful monarchs! Too little of this love had been apparent, however, for neither beforehand nor afterwards did these monarchs conduct themselves in such a way as to be deserving of love.[29]

For Marwitz, the conduct of the princes and their governments – who in the restoration period denigrated the wartime achievements of the people and broke the promises they had made – ran the risk of protracted social conflict between monarchs and nobility on the one hand, and citizens on the other. In his view, this behavior had caused a fundamental loss of faith in the existing order and increased the risk of violent upheaval.

Marwitz's retrospective assessment appears to have been quite accurate. The editor of the first edition of Marwitz's memoirs, published in 1852 by the conservative Prussian diplomat and historian Marcus von Niebuhr, perceived it as so dangerous, following the defeated Democratic Revolution of 1848–49, that he deleted it.[30] We only find it in the second, more complete 1908 edition by the Berlin historian Friedrich Meusel. It took nearly a century for academic historians to accept Marwitz's observation that the men of the nobility and the middle classes who, for a wide variety of reasons, had supported the wars of 1813–15 with their pens or swords, shared a single experience: Many of them had acted autonomously and collectively for the first time, and felt their power as historical subjects, which is why they found the "collective experience" of 1813 so impressive and important. They had trusted the promises of their rulers to grant them greater political rights and a constitution after the "universal people's war" – no matter that their political visions had diverged. Irrespective of all political differences, they cultivated the myth of the "popular uprising" of 1813 so assiduously after 1815 in order to recall these promises. The myth and the hopes associated with it contrasted sharply with actual developments in the following decades. This tension between expectation and experience promoted political dissatisfaction in the long term and was processed repeatedly in a large number of memory texts, including not just autobiographies and war memoirs but also academic histories and literary works. Up until unification in 1871, many of them functioned as reminders of the political promises made by princes, as some authors explicitly stated in their publications.[31]

[29] Friedrich August Ludwig von der Marwitz, *Ein märkischer Edelmann im Zeitalter der Befreiungskriege*, ed. Friedrich Meusel, 2 vols. (Berlin, 1908–13), 1:588–589; on Marwitz, see Karl Erich Born, "Marwitz, Ludwig von der," *NDB* 16 (1990): 318–320; and Ewald Frie, *Friedrich August Ludwig von der Marwitz 1777–1837: Biographien eines Preussen* (Paderborn, 2001).

[30] Marcus von Niebuhr, ed., *Aus dem Nachlasse Friedrich August Ludwig's von der Marwitz auf Friedrichsdorf*, vol. 1: *Lebensbeschreibung* (Berlin, 1852). The ultraconservative editor altered this first edition so dramatically that his interventions were criticized by more liberal contemporaries; see "Historische Denkwürdigkeiten von drei preußischen Generalen," *Blätter für literarische Unterhaltung*, no. 35, 1852, 817–825, 817.

[31] See the following section and chapter 14.

The memory texts written in the decades following the wars also processed experiences of adventure and freedom, of new and remarkable impressions as well as the traumas of violence, captivity, injury, loss and death.[32] Since the wars of the period between 1792 and 1815 involved middle-class men on a much broader scale than ever before, these men, who were literate, expressed their experiences in autobiographies and war memoirs, of which we have many more in German than from any previous war. They regarded their experiences as so dramatic and significant that they appeared worth preserving for family and friends or even a wider public. Middle-class readers, in turn, wanted to know whether their experiences were similar to those of their contemporaries and also to hear about completely different adventures. For that reason, they read the memoirs not only of famous but also of unknown authors, as well as accounts of unfamiliar regions such as Eastern Europe or the Iberian Peninsula and translations of works relating the experiences of people from other lands.[33] Authors and readers shared an interest in recollections that tried to rescue from oblivion their own experiences and roles in the great events of the Napoleonic Wars. The producers of various literary forms worked together here and their texts were mutually reinforcing, referring to one another explicitly or implicitly.

The quickly growing number of autobiographies, war memoirs, historical biographies, novels and history books on the period of the Napoleonic Wars published in the decades after 1815 all over Europe clearly indicates the reading public's increasing interest in the recent past. What arose was a mutually reinforcing web of recollection of this past in the different media of memory. The producers of these recollections were not free to present history however they saw fit. Following reader expectations, even the authors of autobiographical accounts, biographies and novels had to stick to the basic outlines of historical events, especially when the eyewitnesses were still alive, which was the case into the 1870s. Literary scholars have pointed out that well into the second half of the nineteenth century, the writers of historical novels, for example, sought to reproduce their settings "with factual precision and the exact reconstruction of a historical milieu." Their references to historiography as the basis of their narratives had the function of "establishing a claim to truth and authenticity," a claim repeated

[32] See Fritzsche, *Stranded*, 168; idem, "Specters"; Philip G. Dwyer, "Public Remembering, Private Reminiscing: French Military Memoirs and the Revolutionary and Napoleonic Wars," *French Historical Studies* 33 (2010): 231–258; Harari, "Military Memoirs"; and idem, *The Ultimate Experience: Battlefield Revelations and the Making of Modern War Culture, 1450–2000* (Basingstoke, 2008), 190–193.

[33] On the British experience, see Gavin Daly, *The British Soldier in the Peninsular War: Encounters with Spain and Portugal, 1808–1814* (Basingstoke, 2013). On the experiences of the Russian War of 1812, see Zamoyski, *Moscow*; and Murken, *Bayerische Soldaten*.

again and again in the prefaces.[34] The same was necessary for the authors of autobiographies and war memoirs. Thus an important precondition for the glut of such literary memory texts was the rapid emergence of academic, military and popular historiography on the Napoleonic Wars.[35]

THE WARS OF 1813–15 IN NINETEENTH-CENTURY HISTORIOGRAPHY

The first historical accounts of the Napoleonic Wars appeared immediately after the last battles were fought in the various theaters. In the nascent web of recollections, the boundaries between the different types of historical narratives – in autobiographies, war memoirs, novels, history books and other media – were often quite fluid, especially in the first postwar decades, when the fields of academic and military history were still in the making. Theorists of early historicism recognized this. For instance, in his influential lecture "On the Historian's Task," presented at Berlin's Royal Academy of Sciences in 1820, Wilhelm von Humboldt, an acknowledged authority, posited a kinship between the historian and the poet in their shared emphasis on representation and dependence on imagination. He began his lecture by asserting, "The historian's task is to present what actually happened. The more purely and completely he achieves this, the more perfectly has he solved his problem. [...] An event, however, is only partially visible in the world of the senses; the rest has to be added by intuition, inference and guesswork." He then continued, comparing poets and historians:

Differently from the poet, but in a way similar to him, he [the historian] must work the collected fragments into a whole. [...] For if the historian [...] can only reveal the truth of an event by presentation, by filling in and connecting the disjointed fragments of direct observation, he can do so, like the poet, only through imagination.[36]

Leopold von Ranke, Johann Gustav Droysen and Heinrich von Treitschke, the doyens of German historicism, also set great store by vivid and memorable narrative, which becomes apparent when reading their texts, but they distinguished more strictly and systematically between various forms

[34] Gabriele Sieweke, *Der Romancier als Historiker: Untersuchungen zum Verhältnis von Literatur und Geschichte in der englischen Historiographie des 19. Jahrhunderts* (Frankfurt/M., 1994), 4 and 10.

[35] To explore in more detail the complex relationship between literature and historiography, see Wolfgang Hardtwig, "Formen der Geschichtsschreibung: Varianten des historischen Erzählens," in Goertz, *Geschichte*, 218–237; Hardtwig, *Geschichtskultur*, 92–102; and Fulda, *Wissenschaft*, esp. 299–343.

[36] Wilhelm von Humboldt, "Über die Aufgabe des Geschichtsschreibers (1820–21)," in *Wilhelm von Humboldt's Gesammelte Werke*, 7 vols. (Berlin, 1841–52), 1:1–25; Engl.: "On the Historian's Task," *History and Theory* 6 (1967): 57–71, 57–58. On Humboldt, see Gerhard Masur and Hans Arens, "Humboldt, Wilhelm," *NDB* 10 (1974): 43–51.

of representation. Droysen even developed a theory of representation that consciously went beyond Humboldt and Ranke, differentiating between narrative, didactic and discursive forms.[37] Aside from efforts to maintain a lively writing style and artful narrative, in the decades after the wars of 1813–15 many historians also shared with the authors of autobiographies and war memoirs, novels and other memory texts a commitment to keeping the memory of this period alive.

The first histories of the wars of 1813–15 appeared during the conflict and immediately after it ended. Their authors sought to inform readers in detail about recent events in the various regions of the German-speaking world and Europe, and at the same time hoped to establish their own "proper" understanding of these events. Already these early historical accounts thus reflected the intense conflict over interpretational sovereignty that had begun during the wars. Up to World War I the question of whether the wars of 1813–15 had been "Wars of Liberation" or "Wars of Liberty" remained controversial among historians, even if the monarchic-conservative inter-pretation gained dominance during the time of the German Empire. From the beginning, academic and military historians and the authors of popular histories competed for readers. Despite the differences in their analyses and interpretations of the period between 1806 and 1815, they shared two mas-ter narratives. The first was the myth of the downfall and renewed rise of Germany in these years, and the second, related, one was the perception of the wars of 1813–15 as the culmination of this rise. As the final act of heroic liberation, the events of 1813–15 stood at the center of most histories of the period. The dispute over the interpretation of the period was also settled in other media of memory. As the nineteenth century wore on, however, professional historians increasingly insisted on the hegemony of academic historiography in the process of historical writing and memory production. Only they, so they said, were qualified by their university training to write "truthful" history and decide this dispute.

Early Popular and Academic Historiography

A harbinger of the many works on the Russian campaign of 1812 and the wars of 1813–15 that would be published in the following decades was the brief study *The Retreat of the French from Russia* by the Prussian offi-cer Ernst von Pfuel, which appeared in Berlin in 1813. The text depicts in graphic scenes the dramatic retreat of the French army from Russia and describes the shortcomings of the French leadership. It was printed that same year in English, French and Swedish as well. Pfuel was a patriot and

---

[37] See Hardtwig, "Formen," 221–223; on Ranke, see Leonard Krieger, "Elements of Early Historicism: Experience, Theory, and History in Ranke," *History and Theory* 14.4 (1975): 1–14.

strong supporter of the Prussian military reformers. In 1809 he had left the Prussian military service and joined the Austrian army to fight against Napoleon. In 1812 he joined the Russian army. When he returned to the Prussian military service in 1814, he was soon promoted to the rank of general. In 1867, one year after Pfuel's death, historian Friedrich Förster, a former Lützower, republished the text together with his own fond recollections of his old friend.[38]

More publications followed soon after the war. One of the earliest appeared in 1816 under the title *The War of Liberation in Germany in 1813* and was penned by the Leipzig private scholar, historian and philosopher Johann Adam Bergk, who proposed a staunchly German-national, early-liberal interpretation of the wars, which is presumably why he had his text published anonymously (by Baumgärtner in Leipzig) during the ensuing political restoration.[39] That same year, Brockhaus published *Russia's and Germany's Wars of Liberation from French Domination under Napoleon Buonaparte in the Years 1812–1815* by the theologian and historian Carl Venturini, which offers an interpretation of the wars similar to Bergk's. This account stresses the achievements of the people and criticizes the incipient restoration. For that reason, it was banned in Prussia in 1819, which did more to encourage than hinder further editions. As in the case of Bergk, Venturini's German-national and early-liberal views hampered his career in the civil service during the restoration era, and he had to earn his living as a pastor in Braunschweig.[40] In his announcement of the work, Venturini explains why he nevertheless felt compelled to write it:

Many and varied things have been said and written about a worthy national monument to the great and unforgettable events that rescued and restored German liberty. One of the most worthy, and also the most efficacious, means of ensuring that the sacred sense of German liberty and autonomy does not expire is doubtless a history of the war [...] from which we can rightly expect the reconquest of our human dignity, our national worth and our national virtue! Such a history – portrayed powerfully with dignity and truth and in a German spirit – will and must be a source of sacred self-awareness, true national wisdom and strong civic virtue for all

---

[38] Ernst von Pfuel, *Der Rückzug der Franzosen aus Rußland* (Berlin, 1813); and Friedrich Förster, ed., *Der Rückzug der Franzosen aus Rußland: Aus dem Nachlasse des verstorbenen königlich preußischen Generals der Infanterie Ernst von Pfuel* (Berlin, 1867); on Pfuel, see Bärbel Holtz, "Pfuel, Ernst Heinrich Adolf von," *NDB* 20 (2001): 362–363.

[39] [Johann Adam Bergk], *Der Befreiungskrieg in Teutschland im Jahr 1813* (Leipzig, 1816). For a brief overview of the development of the historiography, see Berding, "Problem"; on Bergk, see Arthur Richter, "Bergk, Johan Adam," *ADB* 2 (1975): 289.

[40] Carl Venturini, *Russlands und Deutschlands Befreiungskriege von der Franzosen-Herrschaft unter Napoleon Buonaparte in den Jahren 1812–1815*, 4 vols. (Leipzig, 1816); on Venturini, see Horst-Rüdiger Jarck and Günter Scheel, eds., *Braunschweigisches Biographisches Lexikon: 19. und 20. Jahrhundert* (Hannover, 1996), 178.

classes, indeed a bond of unity between prince and people, such as we have, alas, not possessed up to now.[41]

This line of argument is quite typical of many authors of historical accounts of the wars of 1813–15 in the first half of the nineteenth century. They sought to bolster national pride by keeping alive memories of the struggle for freedom, which for them had been directed both outward and inward and supported by "all classes of the population." As they saw it, the victory over Napoleon had succeeded only because of the alliance between people and monarch. Their memory construction thus reflected their political agenda during the wars and their own "steadfast and virile action" to realize it by pen and sword. According to Venturini, society should commemorate above all the heroic acts of "youths and men," thereby spurring future generations on to similar deeds. In this vein he wrote:

We love and seek to emulate the heroes who rescued the fatherland; we honor and esteem the fatherland for the sake of the heroes it bestowed upon us. And this and this alone is the true source of the mighty feeling of national honor and genuine national pride, which protects a people's autonomy more powerfully than all the declamations on glory and patriotism. To write such a history of the war in the years 1812, 1813, 1814 and 1815; to provide the nation with a work that gives German men and youths strength, counsel, comfort and enthusiasm, is my intention.[42]

We encounter very similar phrasing in the preface to the ten-volume *Universal History: From the Inception of Historical Knowledge to Our Days* by early-liberal Freiburg history professor Karl von Rotteck, which appeared between 1812 and 1827. The final two volumes treated the most recent events.[43] The work was reprinted a number of times into the second half of the nineteenth century. In 1832–33 Herder in Freiburg was already publishing the "eighth expanded and newly revised original edition." By 1868 it had gone through 25 editions with 100,000 copies. Rotteck deliberately used the term "Wars of Liberty" to set his work apart from the monarchic-conservative interpretation of the wars of 1813–15. For him, too, these wars were, accordingly, an "uprising of the people" enraptured and mobilized by "dreams of liberty."[44]

As in the accounts by Bergk and Venturini, in Rotteck's narrative "the people" consisted exclusively of (middle- and upper-class) youths and men. Women are absent from most historical representations of the Anti-Napoleonic Wars that appeared in the long nineteenth century; academic, military and popular historiography did not differ in this. Women's active support for the war, among other things in the patriotic women's associations,

---

[41] Venturini, *Russlands*, xvii–xx.
[42] Ibid.
[43] Rotteck, *Geschichte*, 10:vii.
[44] Ibid., 9:422–428; and Eggert, *Studien*, 53.

is ignored or, as was later the case in Heinrich von Treitschke's five-volume *German History of the Nineteenth Century* (1879–94), mentioned at best in passing as evidence of "universal" support for the war.[45]

These findings reflect the highly gendered understanding of history among academic historians, which was strongly shaped by the dominant notion of gender-specific spheres. It assigned men the "public space" of the economy, politics and war and women the "private space" of family and household. In this sphere, suited to their particular "nature," women were perceived as ahistorical, divorced from the events of their time. For that reason, their memories appeared to possess no historical relevance. The construction of a highly gendered "fixed canon" of subjects appropriate for historiography that focused on politics and war was reinforced the believe of male historians that only they were able to study history in a scholarly manner. For the developing profession of academic history, "objectivity" no longer "relied exclusively on the causality of past events and on the chain of argument"; it was "affected by the subjectivity of the historian." To defend "history against arbitrary interpretations" they introduced the historicist methodology: "Historical truth consequently had to be verified in terms of objective evidence, which mostly meant written documents."[46] Women could not meet these standards, however, because they had no access to academic education. Studying history at a university became the precondition for any "proper" historiography. The result was that not only women, but also men without professional academic training and even historians with a different methodological approach to historiography were excluded from academic history writing. Women could only produce memory texts outside of academia and for a broader public, particularly by writing novels and literature for young people. Here, as we will see in the fifth part, their narratives competed with and complemented male recollections.[47]

Into the 1840s, to the extent permitted by censorship, the dominant portrayal of the wars of 1813–15 in the rapidly evolving historiography was as "people's wars" and "Wars of Liberty," fought by "German men," thus challenging the monarchic-conservative interpretation propagated by governments and parts of the military.[48] Even the young Johann Gustav Droysen

[45] Treitschke, *Geschichte*, 1:431–432; on Treitschke, see Georg Iggers, "Heinrich von Treitschke," in Wehler, *Historiker*, 2:66–80.

[46] Angelika Epple, "Questioning the Canon: Popular Historiography by Women in Britain and Germany (1750–1850)," in Paletschek, *Popular Historiographies*, 21–33, 25–26.

[47] On the gender-specific character of academic historiography, see Epple, "Questioning the Canon"; Bonnie G. Smith, *The Gender of History: Men, Women, and Historical Practice* (Cambridge, MA, 1998); Epple and Schaser, *Gendering Historiography*; and Angelika Epple, *Empfindsame Geschichtsschreibung: Eine Geschlechtergeschichte der Historiographie zwischen Aufklärung und Historismus* (Cologne, 2003).

[48] See Friedrich Christoph Förster, *Von der Begeisterung des preussischen Volkes i. J. 1813, als Vertheidigung unsres Glaubens* (Berlin, 1816); Friedrich Kohlrausch, *Die Teutschen Freiheits-Kriege von 1813, 1814 und 1815* (Elberfeld, 1821); Carl von Weiss [Karl von Müffling], *Beiträge zur Kriegsgeschichte der Jahre 1813 und 1814: Die Feldzüge der schlesischen*

adopted a similar position in his *Lectures on the Wars of Liberty*, published in Kiel in 1846.[49] The majority of the first generation of authors of historical accounts of these wars (unlike Droysen, who was born in 1808) had actively supported the wars or fought in them personally, most of them as volunteers, which explains their attitude toward the wars and their critique of restoration policy. A typical example is Carl Friedrich Friccus, a Prussian jurist who had fought as a volunteer and commander of a Königsberg militia battalion and returned to the judicial service after 1815. In 1837 he became the first auditor-general of the Prussian army, the head of the military judicial administration. In 1843 Friccus published *History of the War in the Years 1813 and 1814*, in which he particularly stressed the achievements of the Prussian militia, which conservatives had repeatedly questioned after 1815, although the army leadership had officially recognized them early on in the wars.[50]

From the 1840s on, however, this first generation of historians of the wars of 1813–15, who had actively supported them with the pen or the sword, was increasingly being replaced by academically trained scholars who taught in one of the emerging history departments (*Historische Seminare*) that most universities had established by the 1870s. Notwithstanding all of their differences, what the first and second generations of historians of the period of the Napoleonic Wars shared was a passion for the "German question." During the first half of the nineteenth century, most of the historians of the wars of 1813–15 were already advocating a Protestant *kleindeutsch* position that propagated a unified Germany without Austria under Prussian leadership. Despite the course of restoration, which had been pushed by Austria but with the active support of Prussia, they regarded the Prussian monarchy as the only force capable of uniting the German states and leading them into a nation-state. And yet, from early on, there were opposing voices. Whereas Friccus's book, for example, offered a critical portrayal of Austria's involvement in the war and emphasized Prussian achievements, Austrian author Johann Sporschill's *The German Wars of Liberty in the Years 1813, 14, 15* shared the former's German-national and early-liberal position, albeit in a more moderate version, but passionately advocated a *großdeutsch* solution to the national question – a united Germany that included Austria – and insisted on the part played by the German people as

Armee, 2 vols. (Berlin, 1824); Friedrich Richter, *Geschichte des deutschen Freiheitskrieges: Vom Jahre 1813–1815*, 4 vols. (Berlin, 1843); and Barthold Georg Niebuhr, *Geschichte des Zeitalters der Revolution: Vorlesungen an der Universität zu Bonn im Sommer 1829*, 2 vols. (Hamburg, 1845), vol. 2.

[49] Droysen, *Vorlesungen*; on Droysen, see Jörn Rüsen, "Johann Gustav Droysen," in Wehler, *Historiker*, 2:7–23.

[50] Carl Friedrich Friccus, *Geschichte des Kriegs in den Jahren 1813 und 1814, mit besonderer Rücksicht auf Ostpreußen und das Königsberger Landwehrbataillon* (Altenburg, 1843); on Friccus, see Akaltin, *Befreiungskriege*, 65.

a whole, not just the inhabitants of Prussia, in liberation from Napoleon's "foreign rule." Sporschill stressed Austria's role in this struggle. His nine-volume account appeared for the first time in 1838–39 on the occasion of the twenty-fifth anniversary of the wars and had gone through six editions by 1845–56. Sporschill, who grew up in Brünn (present-day Brno) and studied law and politics in Vienna, was an extraordinarily successful historical journalist and author who reached an audience throughout the German-speaking lands, with the vigorous support of his Braunschweig publisher Westermann.[51] In this way, the debates over the interpretation of the wars of 1813–15 in the historiography of the restoration period anticipated the conflicts over the "German question" in the Frankfurt National Assembly in 1848–49.[52]

Of course, monarchic-conservative authors also contributed to the early historiography on the wars of 1813–15. One of them was the Leipzig professor of *Staatswissenschaft* Friedrich von Bülau, whose *History of Germany from 1806–1830* was published by Perthes in Hamburg in 1842. But in the first half of the nineteenth century their influence in popular and academic historiography was still limited. In the first postwar decades it was mainly Prussian military historians – generals and officers – who promoted a more monarchic-conservative narrative of the wars.

The Emerging Military Historiography

The professional military historiography that emerged in the wake of the increasing professionalization of the armed forces, a process that had begun in Prussia with the military reforms of 1807 to 1813, became a major bastion of such an interpretation. The Department of War History of the General Staff of the Prussian Army, established in 1815 under the leadership of Colonel Otto August Rühle von Lilienstern, gained great influence. Its work focused on two themes: the wars of the "great" Prussian king and military leader Friedrich II and the campaigns of the wars of 1813–15. One of its first publications was the four-volume account of *The War in Germany and France During the Years 1813 and 1814* by Prussian Major Carl Baron von Plotho, who had participated in the campaigns of those years at the king's headquarters and was promoted to the rank of lieutenant colonel in 1816. Plotho's work, published by Amelang in Berlin, described the campaigns in detail, and was a great success outside Prussia as well, since he sought to provide a balanced account of events and suitably acknowledged

---

[51] Johann Sporschill, *Die Freiheitskriege der Deutschen in den Jahren 1813, 14, 15*, 9 vols. (Braunschweig, 1845–46, 6th edn.; 1st edn. 1838–39); on Sporschill, see Akaltin, *Befreiungskriege*, 80–81.

[52] Friedrich von Bülau, *Geschichte Deutschlands von 1806–1830* (Hamburg, 1842); on Bülau, see Mörikofer, "Bülau, Friedrich von," *ADB* 3 (1876): 512–513.

the allies' role in the victory. The volumes were reprinted the next year.[53] Plotho's aim was to write a "systematically presented" "contemporary history" (*Tagesgeschichte*). He described his approach as follows:

In keeping with the purpose and necessities, the treatment of the subject matter is limited to a simple narrative, based upon genuine documents. It shall thus not be a historical work; I feel called neither to criticize the documents, beyond their authenticity, nor to provide a critique of the events themselves. […] To be sure, much is already known of this subject from war reports, newspapers, magazines and many other books, and the recollection of these glorious years remains fresh in all our memories; – yet these accounts are missing a good deal that is noteworthy, and it is only beyond our own lives, upon our graves, that history arises.[54]

Plotho explained to his readers that he would primarily present "genuine military facts," based upon a plethora of material, which he had "taken great pains to collect from the hands of individual friends of good will." Readers appear to have appreciated his efforts. In 1836, his portrayal was still praised as a "most excellent source" in the *Militair-Conversations Lexikon*, a military encyclopedia published by "several German officers" in Leipzig.[55]

A second early publication put out by the Department of War History of the General Staff of the Prussian Army that would exert a lasting influence on military historiography was the five-volume *Plan of the Battles and Skirmishes Fought by the Prussian Army in the Campaigns of 1813, 14 and 15: Written under Commission from the Highest Authorities and Supplied with the Necessary Historical Elucidations*, which was published by Reimer in Berlin between 1821 and 1825 and reprinted in 1831.[56] This publication concentrates far more than Plotho had on the successes of the Prussian army, above all its professional units. The achievements of volunteers and militia, though mentioned, are given short shrift. It represents the move to a more Prussian-centered conservative interpretation of the wars of 1813–15 in the Prussian military during the restoration. This move was also apparent in the third influential Prussian account published in the 1820s, General Karl Baron von Müffling's *On the War History of the Years 1813 and 1814: The Campaigns of the Silesian Army under Field Marshal Blücher from the End of the Ceasefire to the Conquest of Paris*, which appeared in 1824 with E. S. Mittler in Berlin and was reprinted in 1827. Müffling, chief of the

[53] Carl von Plotho, *Der Krieg in Deutschland und Frankreich in den Jahren 1813 und 1814*, 4 vols. (Berlin, 1817); on Plotho, see Akaltin, *Befreingskriege*, 79.

[54] Ibid., 1:iii–v.

[55] "Militair-Literatur," *Militair-Conversations Lexikon*, vol. 5 (Leipzig, 1836): 413.

[56] August Wagner, *Plane der Schlachten und Treffen, welche von der preussischen Armee in den Feldzügen der Jahre 1813, 14 und 15 geliefert worden: Unter Allerhöchster Genehmigung entworfen, und mit den nöthigen historischen Erläuterungen versehen*, 5 vols. (Berlin, 1821–25).

Prussian General Staff since 1820, ignores volunteers and militia altogether in his narrative. For him, it was the policies of monarchs and generals – above all the Prussians at Allied Headquarters – that had brought about the victory.[57] The campaigns of 1813–15 were also a central theme in the *Militair-Wochenblatt*, which was published by the Department of War History of the General Staff of the Prussian Army beginning in 1816 with the approval of King Friedrich-Wilhelm III. Rühle von Lilienstern became editor-in-chief of this first official military journal of the Prussian army. His coeditor was General Karl von Decker, who was also responsible for the *Militair-Literaturzeitung*, launched in 1820 as the literary supplement to the *Militair-Wochenblatt*. After the unification in 1871 the latter became the official journal of the German General Staff and appeared until 1919. The *Militair-Wochenblatt*, which was published by E. S. Mittler in Berlin, quickly developed into *the* leading German military journal.[58] From 1843 the supplement, *Beihefte zum Militär-Wochenblatt*, became a venue for the publication of longer studies based on material in the Prussian War Archive. Here, too, the period of the Napoleonic Wars was a central topic. Most works were written by officers of the Department of War History for their peers and focused on the detailed study of campaigns and battles or questions of military organization and leadership.[59] But the *Beihefte* also published longer biographies of leading generals of the period.[60] Through the *Militär-Wochenblatt* and the *Beihefte* the Prussian General Staff hoped to influence the "spirit" of officers efficiently and lastingly as well as to educate them for their profession.

Apart from the *Militair-Wochenblatt*, the most influential German-language military journals that published articles on the period of the Napoleonic Wars were the *Allgemeine Militär-Zeitung* and the *Österreichische Militärische Zeitschrift*. The *AMZ* was issued between 1826 and 1902 by "a society of German officers and military officials"

---

[57] Karl von Müffling, *Zur Kriegsgeschichte der Jahre 1813 und 1814: Die Feldzüge der schlesischen Armee unter dem Feldmarschall Blücher von der Beendigung des Waffenstillstandes bis zur Eroberung von Paris* (Berlin, 1824); on Müffling, see Joachim Niemeyer, "Müffling, Karl," *NDB* 18 (1997): 266–267.

[58] Reinhard Brühl, *Militärgeschichte und Kriegspolitik: Zur Militärgeschichtsschreibung des preußisch-deutschen Generalstabes 1816–1945* (Berlin, 1973), 57–72.

[59] Early examples are "Die Formation der freiwilligen Jäger-Detachements bei der preußischen Armee im Jahre 1813," in *BHMW* (Sept.–Oct. 1845; Nov –Dec. 1845: 481–515, and Jan.–Feb. 1847); [R. K. von Scherbening], "Die Reorganisation der Preußischen Armee nach dem Tilsiter Frieden," pt. 1: "Die Jahre 1806 bis 1808 mit einem Beitrag zur frühen Geschichte des Generalstabs," in *BHMW* (Oct. 1854–June 1855, May–Dec. 1856 and July–Dec. 1862); and idem., "Die Reorganisation der Preußischen Armee nach dem Tilsiter Frieden," pt. 2: "Die Jahre 1809 bis 1812," in *BHMW* (Aug. 1865–Oct. 1866).

[60] For example, "General-Lieutenant Rühle v. Lilienstern: Ein biographisches Denkmal," in *BHMW* (Oct.–Dec. 1847); or "Gneisenau," in *BHMW* (Jan.–Apr. 1856).

based in Leipzig and Darmstadt. They published this nationwide, more liberal military journal with the aim of inspiring open debate on all military issues. To that end they printed all articles anonymously, so that the authors would feel freer to express their views. The third important military journal, the *Österreichische Militärische Zeitschrift*, which still appears today in Vienna, was far more conservative. It was founded in 1808 by Major Moritz Gomez de Parientos, the then-director of the Austrian War Archive.[61]

Prussian military historiography on the Napoleonic Wars was challenged early on by dissenting narratives written by officers and generals from the armies of the states of the former Confederation of the Rhine, who were eager to defend the military honor of these armies and their units. One of the first was by the Saxon officer and member of the General Staff, Otto Baron von Odeleben, *Napoleon's Campaign in Saxony*, published in 1816 by Arnold in Dresden. The text went through at least two more editions up to 1840.[62] Also widely read was *The Campaign at the Niederelbe in the Years 1813 and 1814* by Danish Major Count Danneskiold-Løvendal, representative of the Danish forces at the headquarters of French Marshal Davout. This report was published by A. F. J. Schmidt in Kiel in 1818 and focuses on the fighting around Hamburg, trying to paint an "impartial" picture of this conflict and the city at its center.[63] The third early publication was written by Wilhelm Krieg von Hochfelden, who bore the titles of Grand Ducal Badensian Major, Knight of the Grand Ducal Badensian Carl Friedrich Order of Military Merit and Knight of the Royal French Legion of Honor, as he stated proudly on the cover of his study, which had the long title *Historical Account of All the Incidents and Military Engagements Involving the Grand Ducal Badensian Troops in Spain from the End of 1808 to the End of 1813 in Connection with the Significant Occurrences around the Division of the Confederation of the Rhine within the French Army*. The main aim of this text, too – published in 1823 by Herder in Freiburg – was to defend the honor of his army and inform readers of its heroism during the campaign in Spain, from which only 7,000 of the original 10,000 men had returned. Like many other works of this type, the text emphasizes that the army and its leader, the grand duke of Baden, were "forced" by Napoleon to fight in the Grande Armée. The attached list of 325 subscribers clearly

[61] Karl Flöring, "Zur Geschichte der Allgemeinen Militärzeitung, 1826–1902," *MGM* 18.2 (1975): 11–31; and Horst Pleiner, "Die Österreichische Militärische Zeitschrift: Ein historischer Rückblick von den Anfängen bis zur Gegenwart," *Österreichische Militärische Zeitschrift* 46 (2008): 39–63.

[62] Otto Freiherr von Odeleben, *Napoleons Feldzug in Sachsen im Jahr 1813: Eine treue Skizze dieses Krieges, des französischen Kaisers und seiner Umgebungen, entworfen von einem Augenzeugen in Napoleons Hauptquartier* (Dresden, 1816); on Odeleben, see Bernhard von Poten, "Odeleben, Ernst Otto," *ADB* 24 (1887): 145–146.

[63] Danneskiold Løvendal, *Der Feldzug an der Niederelbe in den Jahren 1813 und 1814: Von einem Augenzeugen übersetzt aus dem Dänischen* (Kiel, 1818).

indicates the audience for this kind of book: upper- and middle-class men who had served in the ducal army or had lost relatives in the war.[64] Such military history books, but also many eyewitness accounts by men who had belonged to the armed forces of the Confederation of the Rhine, which will be analyzed in the next chapter, sought to counterbalance the dominant military narrative of the victorious Prussian army, especially in the restoration and *Vormärz* era. Grappling with the fact that, for a shorter or longer period, they had belonged to a defeated power that ended up on the "wrong side" of history, their obvious aim was to reclaim the military honor of their army or unit and with it their own manly honor as officers.

Popular National-Liberal Historiography after 1848–49

After the failed Democratic Revolution of 1848–49, the next boom in historiography on the wars of 1813–15 came in the run-up to their fiftieth anniversary. The authors of the most successful works by far for a broad public were Heinrich Beitzke and Friedrich Förster. Their books were published in multivolume editions, with, respectively, Duncker & Humblodt in 1854–55 and Hempel in 1856–61, both Berlin publishing houses. Beitzke and Förster had fought in the wars as volunteers. Beitzke had served as a major in the Prussian army until 1845, after which he worked as a freelance writer. Förster had studied theology in Jena before the wars, then taught history at the Engineering and Artillery College in Berlin, but was dismissed during the persecution of the so-called demagogues. He did not obtain another post until 1829, when he was rehabilitated and received an appointment at the Royal Museum in Berlin, with the title of court councilor (*Hofrat*). Both men had already made names for themselves as historical authors before the 1850s. Förster's three volumes were part of his extremely successful series *Prussia's Heroes in War and Peace: A History of Prussia from the Great Elector to the End of the Wars of Liberty, in the Biographies of Its Great Men*, which he had begun in 1846 and continued until his death in 1868.[65] Even in old age both men held on to their German-national and liberal-democratic opinions, and in their historical accounts written in the run-up to the fiftieth anniversary of the wars they sought to recall the achievements of

[64] Wilhelm Krieg von Hochfelden, *Geschichtliche Darstellung sämmtlicher Begebenheiten und Kriegsvorfälle der Großherzoglich Badischen Truppen in Spanien von Ende 1808 bis Ende 1813 in Verbindung der allgemeinen bedeutenden Ereignisse der Rheinischen Bundes Division in der französischen Gesamtarmee* (Freiburg, 1823), 1–12; on Krieg, see W., "Krieg, Georg Heinrich," *ADB* 17 (1883): 162–163.

[65] Heinrich Beitzke, *Geschichte der Deutschen Freiheitskriege in den Jahren 1813 und 1814*, 3 vols. (Berlin, 1854–55); on Beitzke, see Franz Xaver von Wegele, "Beitzke, Heinrich," *ADB* 2 (1875): 295–296; Friedrich Christoph Förster, *Geschichte der Befreiungskriege 1813, 1814, 1815*, 3 vols. (Berlin, 1856–61); on Förster, see Ernst Förster, "Förster, Friedrich Christoph," *ADB* 7 (1877): 185–189.

the volunteer and militia units and the broad support of "the people" – but above all of the patriotic-minded middle classes – for the wars, in the hope of "resurrecting" the "spirit of liberty and patriotism."[66] At the same time, after the failed Revolution of 1848–49, they wanted to preserve collective memory of the promises made by monarchs during the wars of 1813–15 to unify Germany in a nation-state with a uniform constitution. Their publications propagated a *kleindeutsch* solution to the national question and also criticized the hesitant stance of the states of the Confederation of the Rhine in 1813. Beitzke even accused the Confederation's princes of having repudiated "German interests."[67]

Many reviewers recognized and welcomed Beitzke's and Förster's intentions and interpretations. Robert Prutz, for example, wrote the following in his 1855 review of Beitzke in his own "journal for literature, art and public life," the *Deutsches Museum*:

Any future development of our fatherland, to the extent that it is to be a boon and a blessing, will always have to take the Prussian uprising as its point of departure, and German unity as its objective. Never were we closer to that goal, never was the old misconception that the German nation is incapable of a unified and lasting political uprising more splendidly disproved than in those wars of liberation; modern history has nothing to compare with it [...]. Therefore the memory of these wars should and must never be extinguished among us; the fire lit upon the altar is so pure and sacred that even today there is no better spot than here for our young people to swear their oaths of loyalty and patriotism.[68]

In his day, Prutz was a well-known political poet and democratic writer, who served as a nontenured professor of literature in Halle from 1849 to 1859. In his extensive review of Beitzke, he went on to explain that, thus far, no work had existed that could assist "the wider public in reaching a proper understanding and an impartial assessment of that unforgettable epoch." "Popular writings" had suffered not simply from a "great imprecision in their details," but also from the "narrowmindedness and obtrusiveness of their purported patriotism, which, when viewed in the cold light of day, was nothing but blatant adulation" for the monarchs and their armies. The "strictly scientific, that is, military, literature" had "for many years produced some quite worthy works on the history of the wars of liberty, joined most recently by numerous historical contributions, in biographies and memoirs." Little of this was suitable for the "broad public," however, because the style in which it was written was too difficult to understand. Like other reviewers, Prutz especially praised the quality of Beitzke's work:

---

[66] Friedrich Christoph Förster, "Abschiedsgruß," in Förster, *Geschichte*, vol. 1.
[67] Beitzke, *Geschichte*, 1:25.
[68] Robert Prutz, "Literatur und Kunst," *Deutsches Museum*, no. 3, 1 Jan. 1855, 104–106; on Prutz, see Edda Bergmann, "Prutz, Robert Eduard," *NDB* 20 (2001): 748–749.

The author, once a military man himself, and personally raised on the memories of that great time, spent ten years in all working on this book, carefully studying even the most far-flung sources, which lends the entire history a new, critically corrected and permanent form. More important to us still [...] is his political and moral standpoint: he is a patriot in the purest and noblest sense of the word, devoted to the greatness and unity of the nation.[69]

The Leipzig editor, publisher and politician Otto Wigand came to quite similar conclusions about Beitzke's work that same year in his *Jahrbücher für Wissenschaft und Kunst*.[70] Beitzke's three-volume *History of the German Wars of Liberty in the Years 1813 and 1814*, which had been reprinted three times by 1864, made him so popular that he was elected to the Prussian House of Deputies as a Liberal in 1858 and reelected in 1862 as a deputy of the newly founded German Progress Party.

The Historical Mainstream and Its Prussianism

The middle-class reading public clearly enjoyed Beitzke's and Förster's accounts, which they found to be uplifting. Their great success in the lending libraries cannot be explained otherwise. They bolstered the masculine self-image of liberal-national citizens following the failed Revolution of 1848–49. The founders of academic historiography, doyens of historicism and Prussianism such as Leopold von Ranke, Heinrich von Sybel, Johann Gustav Droysen and Heinrich von Treitschke, in contrast, criticized these works as insufficiently scholarly and overly partisan.[71] Prutz's review of Beitzke defends him against this critique, stressing the author's many years of research and intense work with original sources. The argument over the academic quality of these two extremely successful history books aimed at a popular audience was at bottom a conflict over the political interpretation of the wars, since in retrospect the quality of Beitzke's and Förster's work was neither better nor worse than that of Ranke, Sybel, Droysen or Treitschke. The main difference was that, unlike Beitzke and Förster, these four men held professorships of history at major German universities: Ranke in Berlin from 1834 to 1871; Sybel in Marburg from 1845 to 1856, and then in Munich until 1861 and thereafter in Bonn; Droysen in Kiel from 1840, in Jena from 1851 and in Berlin from 1859; and Treitschke in Kiel from 1866, moving to Heidelberg in 1867 and succeeding Ranke in Berlin in 1873. In their positions, all four exerted a lasting influence on the historical profession

---

[69] Prutz, "Literatur und Kunst"; see also idem, "Literatur und Kunst," *Deutsches Museum*, no. 25, 21 June 1855, 913–915.

[70] "Deutsche Freiheitskriege," *Jahrbücher für Wissenschaft und Kunst*, ed. Otto Wigand (Leipzig, 1855), 4:99–107.

[71] On Ranke, see Helmut Berding, "Leopold von Ranke," in Wehler, *Historiker*, 1:7–23; on Sybel, see Helmut Seier, "Heinrich von Sybel," in Wehler, *Historiker*, 1:24–38.

of their day, including its professional commissions and academic journals. Ranke, for instance, was editor of the *Historisch-politische Zeitschrift* from 1833 to 1836, while Treitschke edited the *Preußische Jahrbücher* from 1858 and Sybel founded the *Historische Zeitschrift* in 1859.[72] His successors were Treitschke (1895–96) and Friedrich Meinecke (1896–1935), who became professor of history in Strasbourg in 1901, moved to Freiburg in 1906 and returned in 1914 to Berlin, where he had written his habilitation thesis, thus qualifying for a professorship.[73]

To be sure, these academic historians shared with authors like Beitzke and Förster an aspiration to recognize the overall course of history and shape the future accordingly; in other words, they, too, hoped to draw lessons from the past for the future. Their interpretation of the past, however, was informed by Prussianism (also labeled Borussianism), which for Wolfgang Hardtwig was characterized by the fact "that it reconciled the basic convictions and traits of liberalism with the power-political, military and bureaucratic traditions of Prussia, thereby bringing the active energy, conscientiousness, political passion and political faith of large segments of the liberal middle classes into the new German Empire."[74] In short, the Borussian historians believed in the need for a constitutional monarchy and the power of a German Empire under Prussian leadership. In this way, Prussianism weakened the conflict between the old ideals of unity and liberty and offered a coherent ideological foundation for Prussia's and Imperial Germany's striving for power.

Accordingly, the Borussian portrayal and interpretation of the period from 1806 to 1815 also viewed the wars of 1813–15 as the rebirth of the Prussian and German nation. However, this approach attributed the success of the "Wars of Liberation" solely to the actions of princes and statesmen and their armies, while stressing Prussia's outstanding role in national liberation. For historians such as Droysen and Treitschke, in 1813 the Prussian king had called and his people had responded – followed, quite reluctantly, by the other German monarchs.[75] Treitschke represented an especially extreme version of this position, proceeding from his axiom "that the conscious will of active men makes history, not the mysterious mindless force of public opinion," let alone the hoi polloi.[76] The Borussian reading of the wars of 1813–15 was far better suited to the Bismarck era, with its national unification through "blood and iron" than was old-style liberalism, which had inextricably linked the internal with the external struggle for liberty.

---

[72] See Hardtwig, *Geschichtskultur*, 103–160.
[73] On Meinecke, see Schulin, "Friedrich Meinecke."
[74] Hardtwig, *Geschichtskultur*, 160.
[75] Berding, "Freiheitskriege," 684–685.
[76] Heinrich von Treitschke, *Politik: Vorlesungen gehalten an der Universität zu Berlin von Heinrich von Treitschke*, 2 vols. (Leipzig, 1898–99), 2:60.

Droysen's *History of Prussian Politics*, which was published from 1868 to 1886 but ended with the eighteenth century because he died before finishing it, became one of the first academic standard works of Prussian history to propagate the Borussian-*kleindeutsch* notion of history.[77] Heinrich von Treitschke's *German History in the Nineteenth Century*, which appeared from 1879 to 1894, was, as one of the most frequently borrowed academic works in the lending libraries, similarly influential.[78] The two historians were the most important protagonists of the "Hohenzollern legend," which claimed that the German mission of the Hohenzollern dynasty had created a unified nation-state.[79] In his account of the "War of Liberation," for example, Treitschke wrote,

In its first and difficult half, the German War of Liberation was a struggle by Prussia against the three-quarters of the German nation ruled by France. Like the inception of the modern states, the reestablishment of national independence proceeded from the North alone. The new political and moral ideals of a youth up in arms bore the stamp of North German cultivation; the old Germanic god to whom they prayed was the God of the Protestants.[80]

The country had changed utterly by 1879, the year when the first volume of Treitschke's *German History in the Nineteenth Century*, which ended with the May 1814 Treaty of Paris, was published. German unity had been achieved with the wars of unification under Prussian leadership. The first successful years under Imperial Chancellor Bismarck had passed. The middle classes had adapted and now increasingly shared the dominant interpretation of German history among academic historians. At least that is what the reviews would appear to indicate. In 1879 Friedrich von Weech, chamberlain, historian and archive director in the Grand Duchy of Baden, for example, wrote in his review of Treitschke in the "weekly for literature, art and public life" *Die Gegenwart*, "It was no longer a matter now of showing the German people the pathology of their political situation; instead, the phase of the Confederation era [between 1815 and 1866] had become an episode in the history of the German nation." In view of the "splendid success of Prussian arms in 1866," the "national upsurge of 1870" and the "newly tested heroism of all German armies, which had [won] the victory," as well as, finally, the "founding of the new German Empire," German history appeared in a wholly different light than it had when Treitschke had begun writing his work in 1866. The South German reviewer praises

[77] Johann Gustav Droysen, *Geschichte der Preußischen Politik*, 3 vols. (Leipzig, 1868–86); and idem, *Das Leben des Feldmarschalls Grafen York von Wartenburg* (Berlin, 1851).
[78] Martino, *Leibibliothek*, 633.
[79] Stefan Berger, "Prussia in History and Historiography from the Eighteenth to the Nineteenth Century," in *The Rise of Prussia, 1700–1830*, ed. Philip G. Dwyer (Harlow, 2000), 27–44, 39.
[80] Treitschke, *Deutsche Geschichte*, pt. 1 (Berlin, 1886), 434.

everything about Treitschke's book: the "extraordinarily fine portrayal" of the national rising of 1813, with its "great men, who prepared and led the sacred fight for the fatherland," the "clearly organized" and "vividly executed" accounts of battles, but above all the fact that Treitschke was writing "his German history *for Germans*," "*as a German patriot for German patriots*." (Emphasis in the original)[81]

In his 1906 work *The Age of the German Uprising, 1795–1815*, Friedrich Meinecke still propounds this Borussian-*kleindeutsch* interpretation of the era of the Anti-Napoleonic Wars in a politically moderate form, expressly acknowledging the achievements of the Prussian reforms, which he deemed to be prerequisites for the "uprising" of 1813. In his extensive appreciation of the reformers, he stresses the differences and disharmonies among them, which had led to the ultimately "dissatisfying" outcome of the "age of the uprising," if one compared "what people hoped for with what they achieved." At the same time, he also emphasizes that it was only thanks to "their flight to the highest heights" and their striving "to attempt the impossible and fly beyond the actual state" that now, nearly a century later, the "state is no longer a cold oppressive force" and the "nation is no longer a crude, nativist concept," and "both instead provide spiritual light and warmth and breathing space for the free individual soul."[82] Naturally, Meinecke was thinking primarily of middle-class men here, which was so obvious to him and his readers that it literally went without saying.

Critics of Prussianism

Such Prussianism certainly dominated the production of historical research and writing at universities in Imperial Germany, as well as most works produced for a broader public, such as those by the previously mentioned Friedrich Schulze, which were published in the decade before World War I. But some critical voices in academia continued to pursue a more liberal-democratic interpretation of the wars of 1813–15. One of them was Max Lehmann, who began teaching at the Berlin Military Academy and became a member of the Prussian Academy in 1887. He was appointed professor of history in Marburg one year later, in Leipzig in 1892 and in Göttingen in 1893.[83] Lehmann published various studies of the period of the Anti-Napoleonic Wars. Particularly influential among them were his works on *Scharnhorst*, which appeared in 1886–87, and on *Freiherr von Stein*,

[81] Friedrich von Weech, "Heinrich von Treitschke: 'Deutsche Geschichte im neunzehnten Jahrhundert'. Erster Theil. 'Bis zum Pariser Frieden' (1879)," repr. in *Deutschsprachige Literaturkritik, 1870–1914: Eine Dokumentation*, pt. 1, 1870–1889, ed. Helmut Kreuzer (Frankfurt/M., 2006), 368–372; on Weech, see Peter P. Albert, "Weech, Friedrich von," *Beilage zur Allgemeinen Zeitung*, no. 270, 1905, 349–351.

[82] Meinecke, *Zeitalter*, 133.

[83] See Rüdiger vom Bruch, "Lehmann, Max," *NDB* 14 (1985): 88–90.

which came out in 1902–05.[84] His "Address to Celebrate the Memory of 1813," given at the University of Göttingen on 3 February 1913, was also widely noted. The lecture was published that same year in the *Preußische Jahrbücher* under the title "Uprising of 1813." Like other historians before him, he stressed that this "uprising" was the work not of the king and his advisors, but of the "reformers and patriots" in the administration and army and the population they had activated. Had the Prussian government already "declared war on Napoleon in December 1812, not one man of the army that crossed the Neman in the summer would have reached the Rhine. But Prussia's government did not find the strength for such a decision." He also emphasized the importance of Russia and later also Austria within the anti-Napoleonic coalition of 1813.[85]

The editor of the *Preußische Jahrbücher*, Hans Delbrück, shared Max Lehmann's critical stance. Delbrück, who began studying history in Heidelberg and Bonn in 1868 and earned his doctorate in 1873 under Sybel, became an untenured professor of history at Berlin University in 1885 and a tenured one in 1895 and thus a successor to Heinrich Treitschke. From 1883 on he was the editor of the *Preußische Jahrbücher* alongside Treitschke, and from 1889 the sole editor-in-chief, a position he held until 1919. Unresolvable tensions with Treitschke led to this shift at the helm. Delbrück was one of the first modern military historians who aimed to incorporate military history into history more generally. Like his role model Carl von Clausewitz, he emphasized the close relationship between war and politics. This break with the tradition of leaving the history of war in the narrower sense to military men met with resistance among both fellow historians and officers. The innovative approach of the liberal-conservative historian, who was not afraid to publicly criticize Imperial Germany's increasingly aggressive militarism and nationalism, also shaped his scholarship on the period of the Anti-Napoleonic Wars, including his two-volume *Life of Field Marshal Count Neidhardt von Gneisenau*, which appeared in 1880–81.[86] His aloofness from the Borussian historical mainstream and its interpretation of the period of the wars of 1813–15 is also evident in his review "Recent Works on 1813," which he published in the *Preußische Jahrbücher* in 1914. This essay analyzes the historical works that came out on the occasion of the centenary celebrations in 1913. Delbrück criticized their overly positive depiction of the role of Friedrich Wilhelm III and their denial of the wars' character as a "people's uprising." Citing Max Lehmann,

---

[84] See Lehmann, *Freiherr vom Stein*; and idem, *Scharnhorst*.

[85] Max Lehmann, *Die Erhebung von 1813: Rede zur Feier des Gedächtnisses von 1813 am 3. Februar 1913 im Namen der Georg-August-Universität gehalten* (Göttingen, 1913), 4–5.

[86] Hans Delbrück, *Das Leben des Feldmarschalls Grafen Neidhardt von Gneisenau*, 2 vols. (Berlin, 1880–81); on Delbrück, see Andreas Hillgruber, "Hans Delbrück," in Wehler, *Historiker*, 4:40–52.

he stressed that the king had "only entered the struggle for liberty against his innermost inclinations, under the strongest possible pressure, indeed virtual coercion."[87] His article also underlines the necessity – in opposition to *kleindeutsch* historiography – of reassessing the role of Austria:

It has been clear to me for some time, and has gradually become clearer still, that the part played by Austria in the Wars of Liberty (I prefer this older expression to the now usual 'Wars of Liberation') has been improperly underestimated by historians and is still underestimated today.[88]

He attributed this above all to the rivalry between Austria and Prussia, which continued through the greater part of the nineteenth century:

Since the growing power of the national idea in Germany meant that the majority of the most talented historians sought salvation in Prussia, while the public mind in Austria was being heavily policed, the Prussian tendency firmly gained the upper hand in the history of the Wars of Liberty as well.[89]

For Delbrück, a new, "broadly conceived, systematic work" had put an end to this tendency. It was put out by the Department of War History of the General Staff under the leadership of Rudolf von Friedrich with the title *The Prussian Army of the Wars of Liberation*. Mittler & Sohn published the first volume on 1813 in 1912. According to Delbrück, the three-volume project was based on "the most careful archival research" and avoided partisanship.[90] In his view, the parallel work from the Imperial and Royal War Archive in Vienna was proceeding with equal thoroughness.[91]

  In fact, even in retrospect, the military history research published since unification by the General Staff's Department of War History proves to have been more balanced and sophisticated than the ideologically shaped work of academic historians such as Droysen und Treitschke. This applies to the acknowledgment of the military achievements not just of coalition partners, but even of the enemy. A century after the wars, professional officers could appreciate Napoleon's achievements as a military leader, as well as those of his generals and soldiers, much better than many academic historians. This had not always been the case, however. Into the 1840s and 1850s, most historical accounts by (former) military men, especially the Prussians among them, also painted Napoleon as a "tyrant bent on domination" and the "archenemy of Europe."[92] Only a few authors, such as Friccus and Beitzke, recognized even at that time the successful modernization of the French army, the fighting spirit of its soldiers and the military leadership

---

[87] Hans Delbrück, "Neues über 1813," *PrJb* 157 (July–Sept. 1914): 34–69, 35–36.
[88] Ibid., 37.
[89] Ibid., 38.
[90] Ibid., 34.
[91] Ibid., 37.
[92] See [Bergk], *Befreiungskrieg*; Weiss, *Beiträge*; and Venturini, *Russlands*.

skills of Napoleon.[93] In the 1860s and 1870s, Sybel and Treitschke were still propagating an extremely negative image of Napoleon.[94] Historians' assessments of Napoleon changed only over the course of the later nineteenth century, but above all after the turn of the century. That is why Walter Zelle, a doctor and freelance historian, explicitly stressed in his 1903 *History of the Wars of Liberty, 1812–1815* that

> gone are the times when every German historian deemed it necessary to add friendly epithets such as 'Corsican tyranny,' 'crude presumption,' 'insatiable greed,' 'unscrupulous self-interest' and the like to any description of Napoleon I, as a sort of excuse whenever he allowed himself to make positive mention of any of the emperor's warlike or peaceful deeds.[95]

Zelle, too, emphasized that it was mainly military historians who initiated a change here. Their primary interest in the history of war was practical: they wanted to learn from past military successes and errors and to train succeeding generations of officers accordingly. For that reason, they had no interest in misconstruing the causes of Napoleon's long-term military successes as well as his defeat.

As this analysis of the development of the popular, academic and military historiography on the Anti-Napoleonic Wars up to the First World War has shown, it followed the commemorative booms on the twenty-fifth, fiftieth and hundredth anniversaries. The number of history books on the topic increased markedly overall in the course of the nineteenth century. As a consequence, the quantity of works published in the two decades before 1914 exceeded the production of preceding years many times over. This can be attributed only partly to interest in the subject as such. We must also take into account the expansion and professionalization of academic and military historiography and journals in the field as well as the increase in the number of state archives in the various German states, which significantly promoted the publication of lengthy individual primary sources and extensive source editions. More general factors were the changing political culture, which reflected contemporary events, and the expansion of literary production overall.

It remains remarkable nonetheless how intensively the German historical profession in the long nineteenth century – an exclusively male guild, clearly dominated by Protestants – treated the 1806–15 period, which, despite many differences of detail, they unanimously defined as a national foundation period, and how strongly their competing interpretations were molded by ideology, consistently influenced by the political aims of their day. This

---

[93] See Friccus, *Geschichte*; and Beitzke, *Geschichte*.

[94] See Treitschke, *Deutsche Geschichte*, pt. 1; and Heinrich von Sybel, *Die Erhebung Europas gegen Napoleon I* (Munich, 1860); see also Akaltin, *Befreiungskriege*, 87–107.

[95] Akaltin, *Befreiungskriege*, 91.

applies to both supporters of the monarchic-conservative interpretation of the wars of 1813–15 as "Wars of Liberation" and their national-liberal and democratic-liberal opponents who, like their German-national and early-liberal predecessors in 1813, continued to refer to the conflicts as "Wars of Liberty." Academic historiography set out the scholarly depiction and interpretation of the era of the Anti-Napoleonic Wars that the authors of autobiographies and war memoirs would have to take into account. Historians insisted on their mastery and emphasized the difference between their own academic and other forms of historical writing. Referring to memoirs, Leopold von Ranke, for example, wrote in the preface to his 1877 edition of the *Memorabilia of Chancellor of State Prince von Hardenberg up to the Year 1806*:

What, then, is the difference between memoirs and history? In the first, the memories of the author dominate, and their business is to explain his personal circumstances. The historian, in contrast, must take care not to be carried away by these memories. For it is a peculiarity of the personal that it frequently cannot be verified: the impressions conveyed to the actor by friends or foes are always at play.[96]

In this assessment, the founder of modern source-based history was responding to the increasing number of autobiographies and war memoirs on the period of the Napoleonic Wars, mainly by male authors, that were first published in the decades after the wars and often republished in an edited version years later, by trying to create a clear hierarchy of the "accuracy" of historical narratives in different media of memory.

---

[96] Leopold von Ranke, "Vorrede," in *Denkwürdigkeiten des Staatskanzlers Fürsten von Hardenberg bis zum Jahre 1806*, ed. idem (Leipzig, 1877), 1:v-xii, x.

14

Remembering the Past: The Napoleonic Wars in Autobiographies and War Memoirs

The decades after the Napoleonic Wars witnessed the publication of a veritable flood of autobiographies and war memoirs in Germany as in many other European countries.[1] The sheer number of these texts differentiates this postwar period from all earlier ones. And yet it was also the distinct quality of these accounts that set them apart from previous texts, as David A. Bell emphasizes:

Up until the late eighteenth century, only a relatively few military figures (virtually all officers) composed military memoirs. These men almost never included reflections on their interior lives and had little concern for the flavor and color of particular events. They celebrated deeds that fit stereotyped images of noble valor, making the writing flat and tedious to modern sensibilities. The post-Napoleonic accounts broke dramatically with this tradition, in their vastly greater numbers, their concern for realism, and their frankly personal style.[2]

Emerging Romantic notions of the self inspired the autobiographies and war memoirs not just of middle-class men who joined the army as volunteers; even texts by many noblemen who served during the wars as professional officers or generals reflect the trend to greater realism and the psychologization of autobiographical accounts. This confirms the shift to a more "modern regime of selfhood" based on interiority and innate qualities.[3]

The dramatic historical experiences of revolution, war and crisis that many educated contemporaries underwent in the decades of the late eighteenth and

---

[1] Because of the hybrid nature of many texts in this corpus, it can be quite difficult to distinguish precisely between autobiographies and memoirs. I will speak of *autobiographies* when referring to texts that portray a longer period in a person's life and of *war memoirs* when the narrative focuses on shorter or longer experiences in wartime.

[2] Bell, *Total War*, 312; see also Harari, *Experience*, 199–212.

[3] Harari, *Experience*. However, this rise of the "modern self" and with it of autobiographical writing did not occur evenly across Germany and Europe from the late eighteenth century on. See Harari, "Military Memoirs."

early nineteenth centuries promoted a turn toward historical self-reflection and with it autobiographical writing. Literary fashions too, especially those texts that were intensely discussed among the literary public, strongly influenced these new types of writings.[4] Of considerable impact were, first and foremost, the more self-reflective autobiographies by well-known authors, such as Johann Wolfgang von Goethe's *From My Life: Poetry and Truth* (the first three volumes were published in 1811–14 and the fourth and final one a year after his death in 1833).[5] The more emotional and self-reflective style of autobiographical writing that came into vogue after the Napoleonic Wars was also informed by two new forms of the novel, which focused on the psychological and moral growth of the protagonist from youth to adulthood: the psychological novel and the *bildungsroman*. Karl Philipp Moritz's *Anton Reiser* (published in four parts between 1785 and 1790), and Goethe's *Wilhelm Meister's Apprenticeship* (published in six volumes, 1795–96) were particularly influential here.[6] Both literary genres had been gaining popularity in educated circles since the late eighteenth century and clearly influenced the writing of autobiographical accounts by educated middle- and upper-class authors, who now focused more than previously on their personal and professional development and subjective experiences in the context of the time.

The popular picaresque novel was another literary genre that influenced memoirs on the Napoleonic Wars, especially those by authors from the lower military ranks. In a realistic and often humorous style, these works related the adventures of a hero, usually of a lower social class, who survives on his luck and wits.[7] The fashionable travelogue, a genre that informed readers about foreign countries and people, also became quite influential. Several accounts by ordinary soldiers, corporals and lower-ranking officers read like

[4] See Frederic S. Steussy, *Eighteenth-Century German Autobiography: The Emergence of Individuality* (New York, 1996), esp. 1–32; and Sabine Groppe, *Das Ich am Ende des Schreibens: Autobiographisches Erzählen im 18. und frühen 19. Jahrhundert* (Würzburg, 1990), esp. 1–44.

[5] Johann Wolfgang von Goethe, *Aus meinem Leben: Dichtung und Wahrheit*, 3 vols. (Stuttgart, 1811–14); Engl.: *From My Life: Poetry and Truth*, trans. Robert R. Heitner, ed. Thomas P. Saine and Jeffrey L. Sammons, 2 vols., *Goethe's Collected Works*, vols. 4–5 (New York, 1987).

[6] See Karl Philipp Moritz, *Anton Reiser*, 4 vols. (Berlin, 1785–90); Engl.: *Anton Reiser: A Psychological Novel*, trans. Ritchie Robinson (Harmondsworth, 1997); on Moritz, see Albert Meier, "Moritz, Carl Philipp," *NDB* 18 (1997): 149–152; Johann Wolfgang von Goethe, *Goethes neue Schriften*, vols. 3–6: *Wilhelm Meisters Lehrjahre: Ein Roman* (Berlin, 1795–96); Engl.: *Wilhelm Meister's Apprenticeship*, trans. and ed. Eric A. Blackall and Victor Lange, *Goethe's Collected Works*, vol. 9 (New York, 1989); and Tobias Boes, *Formative Fictions: Nationalism, Cosmopolitanism, and the Bildungsroman* (Ithaca, NY, 2012).

[7] On the history of this traditional genre, see Alexander Blackburn, *The Myth of the Picaro: Continuity and Transformation of the Picaresque Novel, 1554–1954* (Chapel Hill, NC, 1979).

adventure stories and war travelogues.[8] Finally, the tradition of conventional military memoirs also retained its importance. These texts focused mainly on military affairs; described the mobilization for war; recounted battles in great detail, mostly from a bird's-eye view; analyzed the causes of victories and defeats and compared national armies, their leaders and soldiers. One central aim of these conventional military memoirs was to educate younger generations of officers in the history of the military and war.[9]

Apart from these literary fashions and conventions, which frequently shaped autobiographical writing in an eclectic mix, a number of other factors also affected the composition and publication of autobiographies and war memoirs recalling the time of the Napoleonic Wars. They included the development of the literary market, especially its commercialization, the professionalization of academic history and archives, booms in political commemoration and regional cultures of memory. In this chapter I take a closer look at how these factors influenced the production of autobiographical memoirs. First I examine the corpus of German-language autobiographies and war memoirs published up to World War I and the social profile of the authors. Then I explore the narratives of the influential texts published by military men and civilians before 1875, because they reflect the communicative memory of contemporaries. Many of these texts were published by the authors themselves or on their behalf shortly after they died. The main criteria for their selection were the total number of editions and their estimated circulation, the number of reviews and their presence in lending libraries up to 1914.

AUTOBIOGRAPHIES AND WAR MEMOIRS AS MEDIA OF MEMORY

Thousands of autobiographical texts recalling the Napoleonic Wars were probably published in the German-speaking region over the course of the nineteenth century in the form of books and magazine and newspaper articles: autobiographies, war memoirs, correspondence and diaries, but also shorter sketches and text fragments. For this study, I examined 369 autobiographies and war memoirs that appeared between 1815 and 1915, mainly in book form.[10] This sample reveals first of all that the production

---

[8] On travel accounts in this period, see Bernhard Struck, *Nicht West – nicht Ost: Frankreich und Polen in der Wahrnehmung deutscher Reisender zwischen 1750 und 1850* (Göttingen, 2006).

[9] On the varieties and transformation of this genre, see Dwyer, "Public Remembering"; Harari, "Military Memoirs," and *Ultimate Experience*.

[10] I built up a Filemaker database that includes a total of 596 German-language autobiographical accounts on the period of the Anti-Napoleonic Wars published to date: 369 of these texts written by 204 authors were published before 1915; 269 of these were first editions published before 1915 and 160 were first editions published before 1875. In the case of

of autobiographical accounts, like the historiography of the Napoleonic Wars, largely followed the memory booms of the twenty-fifth, fiftieth and one-hundredth anniversaries and also steadily increased, reflecting the more general expansion of the literary market. The rise in the number of published autobiographies and war memoirs was facilitated from the mid-nineteenth century on by a growing number of new editions and reprints of already published texts, a trend that peaked in the decade before World War I. Of the 369 texts, 10 percent were published in the jubilee years 1831–40 (38; 22 of them in the years 1838–40 alone), 15 percent in the jubilee years 1856–65 (54; 30 of them in the years 1862–64 alone) and 30 percent in the jubilee years 1906–15 (109; 51 of them in the years 1911–13 alone). Thus, 54 percent (201) of all texts came out during the three jubilee periods.

Closer scrutiny was devoted to 269 first editions, many of them later published by other companies as reprints or new editions. This selection not only confirms the developmental booms, but makes them more evident above all for the twenty-fifth and fiftieth anniversaries. Of the 269 first editions, 23 percent (61) appeared between 1830 and 1849 alone and 25 percent (66) between 1850 and 1869.[11] The main places of publication for these works correspond to the general trends in the literary market. Leipzig and Berlin, followed by Stuttgart, Hanover, Vienna and Munich, were also the leading publishing centers for autobiographical books. In the second half of the nineteenth century, especially in the decade before the First World War, a growing number of smaller local publishing houses also brought out autobiographical accounts of the Napoleonic Wars. The most important publishing companies were E. S. Mittler and Alexander Duncker

---

multivolume editions published over a period of two years or more, I have counted only the year of the first volume's publication and merely recorded the other years in the database. For all texts published before 1915, I tried to gather as much information on the authors and the texts themselves as possible. I also endeavored to identify the number of editions and searched for contemporary reviews of the texts in journals and magazines, which I integrated into the database. I accessed 71 texts as complete PDFs and 150 as complete copies. For biographical information, I used the *Deutsche Biographie*: http://www.deutsche-biographie.de/projekt.html, which incorporates the *Allgemeine Deutsche Biographie*, 56 vols. (Leipzig, 1875–1912) and the *Neue Deutsche Biographie*, 24 vols. (Berlin, 1953–2013). In addition, I utilized the following sources: Heinrich Gross, *Deutschlands Dichterinnen und Schriftstellerinnen: Eine literarhistorische Skizze* (Vienna, 1882, 2nd edn.); Carl Herloßsohn, ed., *Damen Conversations Lexikon*, 10 vols. (Leipzig, 1834–38); Ernst Heinrich Kneschke, ed., *Neues Allgemeines Deutsches Adels-Lexicon*, 9 vols. (Leipzig, 1859–70); *Brockhaus Conversationslexikon*, 16 vols. (Leizpig, 1882–87, 13th edn.); Lina Morgenstern, *Die Frauen des 19. Jahrhunderts: Biographische und culturhistorische Zeit- und Charactergemälde* (Berlin, 1891); and Sophie Pataky, *Lexikon deutscher Frauen der Feder*, 2 vols. (Berlin, 1898).

[11] A further 7 percent (19) appeared up to 1829, 14 percent (37) between 1870 and 1889, 16 percent (43) between 1890 and 1909 (31 after 1900 alone), and 14 percent (38) between 1910 and 1915.

in Berlin, as well as Brockhaus, Arnold and Reclam in Leipzig. Later, Robert Lutz Verlag in Stuttgart, founded in 1885, which built up its own *Library of Memoirs*, and Gutenberg Verlag in Hamburg, founded in 1904, which published the *Library of Worthy Memoirs*, quickly gained in importance. In the decade before the First World War, Georg Wiegand Verlag in Leipzig – which specialized, among other things, in "youth and popular literature," published the very widely distributed series *From Yellowed Parchments: A Series of Diaries, Letters and Reports from the Napoleonic Epoch* and successfully reprinted highly abridged and edited texts in pocket form at very reasonable prices – contributed to the popularization of memoirs.

This was a general trend that began in Wilhelmine Germany. An increasing number of autobiographical memoirs, which in the 1830s and 1840s and the 1850s and 1860s had first appeared in several volumes because of their great length, now appeared in much abridged and revised "popular editions" for the broad reading public. The editors radically cut any passages they deemed unsuitable, unimportant or problematic. A typical example is *Forester Fleck's Wartime Journey and Captivity in Russia, 1812–1814*, published in 1845 by Gerstenberg Verlag in Hildesheim, which vividly recounts the wartime experiences of an ordinary soldier and his time as a prisoner of war in Russia. The memoirs of Fleck – who came from Hildesheim, was forced to take part in the Russian campaign as a soldier of the Kingdom of Westphalia and found a position as a forester in the Hanoverian service in 1814 – were published by the same company in 1907 in a new edition prepared by local historian August Tecklenburg and reprinted three times up to 1912. In his preface, Tecklenburg praises the work as

a valuable recollection and urgent admonition of the era now a century past, which, while a witness to German disgrace, was also a time when the ideas of German unity and national rebirth were emerging and falling on fertile ground. We harvested the fruits in the years 1870 and 1871 and continue to do so today.[12]

Tecklenburg hoped to revive this memory "and render it accessible once again for our people and youth." Since in his opinion an "unaltered reprint" "no longer sufficed" for the "demands" of his time, he modernized the "expression and style," removed descriptions of countries and people "which scarcely apply anymore," reorganized the text in a "practical" manner and provided a "historical introduction." He hoped that the revised text would bolster the self-sacrifice and patriotism of male youth for the next war and instruct them in the old idea of heroic death for the fatherland.[13]

[12] August Tecklenburg, ed., *Förster Flecks Kriegsfahrt und Gefangenschaft in Rußland 1812–1814: Beschreibung meiner Leiden und Schicksale während Napoleons Feldzug und meiner Gefangenschaft in Rußland* (Hildesheim, 1907), iv. Further editions were: Vienna, 1908; Berlin and Leipzig, 1910; and Cologne, 1912.

[13] Ibid., v.

The text lent itself to such a nationalist interpretation because Fleck himself had articulated anti-French and German-national sentiments in his book.[14]

Alongside a rapidly growing number of similarly heavily revised texts for "the people and youth," there was also a rise in the publication of scholarly editions for the educated public, which sought to be faithful to the originals. They were commissioned by professional historians and archivists on behalf of local historical societies or state and municipal archives. A typical instance is the first edition of the *Memoirs of Baron Hermann von Gaffron-Kunern*, published by Ferdinand Hirth in Breslau in 1913 as a "Memorial Publication of the Society for the History of Silesia on the Centenary of the Wars of Liberation." The recollections of Gaffron-Kunern, completed in 1862, focus on the years 1806–15, when he was a young man in Silesia. He describes the terrible effects of the Prussian defeat of 1806 on his life, his family and his home region, and his experiences as a volunteer and lieutenant with the Silesian Cuirassiers between 1813 and 1815.[15] The editor was the Breslau historian Friedrich Andreae, who published the memoirs "in their entirety," as he emphasized, merely removing the occasional repetition.[16] These two examples illustrate the overall trend toward a growing differentiation, professionalization and popularization of autobiographical memory production on the Napoleonic Wars during the German Empire.[17]

Apart from memory booms around anniversaries, the professionalization of academic historiography and the commercialization and expansion of the literary market, the authors of autobiographical texts themselves and the perceptions of publishers and reviewers also influenced memory production. Only authors who believed that they had experienced something significant or had something important to say published their recollections during their lifetimes. Only memoirs by authors whose memories were perceived as valuable and worthy by subsequent generations were published posthumously. The typical editors of such texts – family members, friends, regimental comrades, local historians, archivists and academic historians – however, pursued a variety of interests in publishing. Some wanted to keep family memories alive, while others sought to save the family's reputation or restore the honor of the deceased, present their interpretation of the regional or national history of the Napoleonic Wars, or revise the dominant interpretation of a well-known military officer or statesman. The publishers also

[14] Ibid., 1–2.
[15] "Herman von Gaffron-Kunern," in *Neues Allgemeines Deutsches Adels-Lexicon* (1861), 3:425–426.
[16] Friedrich Andreae, ed., *Denkwürdigkeiten des Freiherrn Hermann von Gaffron-Kunern: Festgabe des Vereins fur Geschichte Schlesiens zur Jahrhundertfeier der Befreiungskriege* (Breslau, 1913), viii and xv.
[17] This trend is also evident in comparable memory media such as biographical texts, which include such diverse formats as scholarly biographies, popular texts "for youth and the people" and biographical novels.

pursued very diverse political or commercial aims in choosing their authors. To that extent the profile of the authors of published autobiographical texts is extremely illuminating for an analysis of memory production.

Of the authors of the 269 autobiographies and war memoirs in the study that were published for the first time between 1815 and 1915, 254 were men and 15 were women (6 percent).[18] Unlike works of history, at least a few of these texts were thus by women, but with two exceptions, all were published posthumously.[19] Publishing autobiographical recollections of the time of the Napoleonic Wars was a male affair: It was mainly men who believed their experiences were worth reading about,[20] and primarily the memoirs of men that were deemed interesting by editors and publishers, especially when their authors had fought in the wars or had supported them through political action. The strikingly small number of memoirs published by women – like the writing and publishing of history books – reflects the dichotomous gender images of the period, in which men were assigned the historically relevant public sphere of politics and war, and women the seemingly natural and thus timeless private sphere of family and household. Their memoirs were therefore considered to be uninteresting. Of course educated women also kept diaries and noted down their recollections, but as a rule these texts were not published.[21]

Who were these men and women whose autobiographical recollections of the Napoleonic War era were considered interesting enough to print? I was able to gather more detailed information on the ages, social origins and education levels of 152 men and 15 women whose autobiographies and war memoirs were published before World War I. Two-thirds of them were born between 1775 and 1795 – that is, they belonged to the age groups who actively experienced the war as young or middle-aged adults. These were also the age cohorts with the highest degree of military mobilization, which also included most patriots and reformers not just in Prussia but in

---

[18] The following social profile naturally does not reflect all those who wrote autobiographical accounts of the wars. The number of unpublished texts was probably far greater, as indicated by the unpublished manuscripts held in archives; see Murken, *Bayerische Soldaten*, 10–17.

[19] See Regula Engel, *Lebensbeschreibung der Wittwe des Obrist Florian Engel von Langwies, in Bündten, geborner Egli von Fluntern, bey Zürich [...]* (Zurich, 1821); on the history of this original text, see Claudia Ulbrich, "Deutungen von Krieg in den Lebenserinnerungen der Regula Engel," in *Krieg und Umbruch um 1800: Das französisch dominierte Mitteleuropa auf dem Weg in eine neue Zeit*, ed. Ute Planert (Paderborn, 2008), 297–314. The second text was Auguste Vater, *Was wir Erlebten im Oktober 1813: Denkschrift für den Verein zur Feier des 19. Oktobers in Leipzig* (Leipzig, 1845).

[20] Among the male authors whose works appeared as first editions before 1875, only ca. 11 percent of autobiographical texts by civilians and ca. 38 percent by military men were published posthumously.

[21] See Hagemann, "Reconstructing"; and Heike Steinhorst, "Autobiographisches und fiktionales Schreiben von Frauen um 1800," in *Schwellenüberschreitungen*, ed. Bland and Müller-Adams, 117–133.

other parts of Germany too.[22] The remainder overwhelmingly belonged to the age groups born either before 1775 or more rarely after 1795. Of the men whose memory texts were published, 49 percent were from the nobility; 16 percent from the educated middle class; 7 percent, mainly craftsmen, from the lower middle class and 6 percent from the wealthy bourgeoisie. Accordingly, 43 percent had studied at university, 16 percent at a military academy and 13 percent had at least attended secondary school without going on to higher education. Of the women, 69 percent were noble and 23 percent were from the upper middle class. In keeping with their origins, they had been privately educated by governesses or tutors.

Of the 216 authors whose profession in later life is known, 46 percent remained in the military after the war (of 100, 16 were ordinary soldiers, 52 were officers, 10 were noncommissioned officers and 22 were generals), 14 percent held higher positions in state service (of 31, 8 were teachers, 7 were clergymen and 6 were civil servants), 8 percent (18) earned their living as professional writers and 8 percent (17) held higher political positions – that is, were government ministers, senior officials or diplomats. Of the 15 female authors, most were married; only two had remained single and one was divorced. Three had made their names as authors and one as an artist; one had worked as a school headmistress.

The published autobiographical accounts of the Napoleonic Wars, and with them communicative memory, were dominated from the beginning by men of the educated middle and upper classes, especially those who had fought in the wars as officers and generals or had been otherwise actively involved as politicians, diplomats, pastors and journalists. A significant proportion of even the men who worked in civilian occupations after 1815 had fought in the wars of 1813–15, often as volunteers. The social profile of the published memoirs by women was more selective still. It was above all texts by well-known women of the aristocracy and the upper-middle class who had made their names in the literary world that were considered interesting enough to be worth publishing.[23] This attitude on the part of editors and publishers only changed in the final decade before the First World War, with the increased publication of local memoirs on the occasion of the centenary celebrations.[24]

In what follows, I will take a closer look at the corpus of autobiographical accounts that appeared for the first time up to 1875, since it was mainly these texts – a significant portion of which were either published or

[22] See Hagemann, *Muth*, 158–203.

[23] Exceptions are Vater, *Was wir Erlebten*; and Marianne Prell, *Erinnerungen aus der Franzosenzeit in Hamburg: Für Kinder erzählt* (Hamburg, 1863).

[24] Examples are Perthes, *Franzosenzeit*; Caesar Amsinck, "Elisabeth Dorothea Mollers Tagebuch aus der Belagerung Hamburgs in den Jahren 1813 und 1814," *Zeitschrift des Vereins für Hamburgische Geschichte* 11 (1903): 184–226; and W. Ad. Schultze, "Frau Professor Radspiller's Tagebuch aus Hamburg's Franzosenzeit," in ibid., 227–258.

authorized for posthumous publication by those who wrote them – that at once reflected and shaped communicative memory. I will begin with texts by men who had fought in the wars between 1806 and 1815, and then examine those by civilians, both male and female, who described their experiences of the time.

MILITARY WAR STORIES

Military service and war were dominant experiences for many German men who were young adults in the first two decades of the nineteenth century. Their published autobiographical accounts show a broad variety of responses. Some clearly embraced having been in the military and fought in the wars. Regardless of their regional origins, war memoirs written by German-speaking professional officers who had served the various powers during the period of the Napoleonic Wars – Austria, Britain, France, Prussia and Russia – reveal a strong professional identity and powerful aspirations toward honor, glory and military career advancement. If they had fought in the Grande Armée, these officers and generals spoke of the "wars waged by Napoleon" or Napoleonic Wars. It was mainly officers who had fought on the side of the anti-Napoleonic coalition who recalled their struggle as the "Anti-Napoleonic Wars."[25] Memoirs by others, especially volunteers from the different German regions, in contrast, emphasized that they had enlisted and fought out of a need to "defend their German fatherland" against the French. Their writing underlined patriotic or nationalist motivations, but also pointed to other motives such as adventurousness or peer pressure at school and university. Everyday life in the military, however, rarely lived up to the romantic notions of manly heroism harbored by many volunteers during the wars of 1813–15, and in their memoirs quite a few of them expressly stated how happy they had been to return to their civilian occupations after the war, even if they did miss the comradeship of their unit. These volunteers mainly spoke of "Anti-Napoleonic Wars" and remembered the wars of 1813–15 often as "Wars of Liberty."[26] The few published memoirs

[25] See, for example, Alfred Freiherr von Wolzogen, ed., *Memoiren des Königlich Preußischen Generals der Infanterie Ludwig Freiherrn von Wolzogen: Aus dessen Nachlass unter Beifügung officieller militärischer Denkschriften* (Leipzig, 1851); Clotilde François von Schwartzkoppen, ed., *Karl von François: Ein deutsches Soldatenleben: nach hinterlassenen Memoiren* (Schwerin, 1873); and Mathilde Quednow, ed., *Denkwürdigkeiten aus dem Leben des Generals der Infanterie von Hüser* (Berlin, 1877).

[26] See, for example, Archibald Graf von Keyerling, *Aus der Kriegszeit: Erinnerungen von Archibald Grafen von Keyserling*, 2 vols. (Berlin, 1847–55); Georg Friedrich Bärsch, *Erinnerungen aus meinem vielbewegten Leben: Als Manuscript für meine Freunde* (Aachen, 1856); Ludwig von Hoffmann, *Erinnerungen eines alten Soldaten und ehemaligen Freiwilligen aus den Kriegsjahren 1813 und 1814* (Berlin, 1863); and Adolf Heilborn, ed., *Willibald Alexis: Als Kriegsfreiwilliger nach Frankreich 1815: Blätter aus meinen Erinnerungen* (Berlin, 1915).

by military doctors, in particular, vividly describe the destructive physical and mental effects of war and the poor medical treatment of soldiers. These recollections repeatedly point out that the military administrations of the various powers were quite clearly unable to secure proper medical care for the huge numbers of sick and wounded soldiers engendered by the new mass armies.[27] Their realistic texts, together with the comparatively small number of war memoirs written by conscripted soldiers and noncommissioned officers, give us the clearest sense of everyday life in wartime and what war looked like from below. Depending on their military affiliation and political standpoint, they spoke of "Napoleonic Wars" or "Wars against Napoleon."[28]

The analysis of the 129 German-language military memoirs dealing with the period of the Napoleonic Wars that appeared before 1875, two-thirds of them self-published, provides more information about the social profile of the authors and the central themes of their texts. The interplay between the time of publication, the regional origin, the military rank of the author and the thematic focus of his text, in particular, tells us about regional and group-specific memory booms and competing narratives. The publication dates of this text corpus confirm the significance of memory booms around the anniversary years of the wars of 1813–15. Of the 129 texts, 9 percent appeared between 1813 and 1825, 17 percent between 1826 and 1835, 16 percent between 1836 and 1845, 22 percent between 1846 and 1855, 26 percent between 1856 and 1865 and fewer than 10 percent between 1866 and 1875. As to the regional origins of authors, it is striking that 50 percent of all texts were penned by authors who fought between 1806 and 1813 in the armies of the states of the Confederation of the Rhine, above all the kingdoms of Westphalia (12 percent), Württemberg (11 percent) and Saxony (11 percent). Forty percent of the authors had belonged primarily to the Prussian army between 1806 and 1815, and only 7 percent to the Austrian army.[29] These regional origins were quite unevenly distributed

---

[27] See, for example, *Wenzel Krimer, Erinnerungen eines alten Lützower Jägers, 1795–1819*, 2 vols. (Stuttgart, 1833); Wilhelm Meier, *Erinnerungen aus den Feldzügen 1806 bis 1815: Aus den hinterlassenen Papieren eines Militärarztes* (Karlsruhe, 1854); E. von Stockmar, ed., *Denkwürdigkeiten aus den Papieren des Freiherrn Christian Friedrich von Stockmar* (Braunschweig, 1872); and Paul Holzhausen, ed., *Mit Napoleon in Rußland: Erinnerungen von Heinrich von Roos* (Stuttgart, 1910).

[28] See, for example, August Böck, *Leben und Schicksale des ehemaligen Musikmeisters im Königl. Preuß. 24sten Infanterie-Regiment August Böck, vormaliger Trompeter im Schill'schen Corps* (Halle, 1832); Franz Bersling, *Der böhmische Veteran: Franz Bersling's Leben, Reisen und Kriegsfahrten in allen fünf Welttheilen* (Schweidnitz, 1840); [Christian Ludwig Marter], *Fünf Marter-Jahre: Schicksale eines deutschen Soldaten in Spanien und Sicilien* (Weimar, 1834); and Wilhelm Mente, *Von der Pieke auf: Erinnerungen an eine neun und vierzigjährige Dienstzeit in der Königlich Preußischen Artillerie* (Berlin, 1861).

[29] These figures only count the army to which the author had belonged for the longest period between 1806 and 1815 and with which he clearly identifies in the text; the temporary

among the military ranks. Of the 129 military men in the sample, 27 had reached the rank of general by the end of the war in 1815 (56 percent from Prussia), 42 had become professional officers (26 percent from Prussia) and 9 noncommissioned officers (11 percent from Prussia). Twenty men had fought as ordinary soldiers (only 20 percent from Prussia). Three had served as military doctors in one of the armies of the Confederation of the Rhine. Twenty-seven had fought as volunteers, 85 percent of them from Prussia and North Germany. Fourteen had joined the King's German Legion, which fought against Napoleon under the English flag from 1803 to 1816. Most of them came from the Prussian territories that fell to Saxony and the newly established Kingdom of Westphalia after the Peace of Tilsit in July 1807, which had cut Prussia in half.[30] Former Lützowers penned six accounts. Thus, the authors who had belonged to the armies of the Confederation of the Rhine included a clearly higher percentage of men from the lower ranks of the military. Generals, officers and volunteers, in contrast, predominated among the authors of Prussian memoirs.

This striking regional and social diversity of autobiographical memoirs by military men published up to 1875 is also evident in the thematic range of the texts, which reflects their varying war experiences in the years 1806–15. Sixty-seven of the texts describe the 1812 Russian campaign. Of these, two-thirds (45) were written by members of one of the armies of the Confederation of the Rhine. Twenty-three of the works also treat the dramatic experience of Russian captivity. Twenty-six describe war experiences on the Iberian Peninsula between 1809 and 1814. These, too, were largely written by officers and soldiers of the armies of the Confederation of the Rhine. Only six of them had fought with the British in Portugal and Spain as members of the King's German Legion. Sixty-three texts focus mainly on the war of 1813–14 with battles on German soil, especially the Battle of the Nations at Leipzig, the crossing of the Rhine, the conquest of France and the entry into Paris. Here, nearly two-thirds (37) were the work of Prussian authors. The experiences of the war of 1806–07, too, and above all the dramatic defeat of the Prussian-Saxon army, were also a central theme treated in 23 texts. All of the authors who dealt with this topic came from Prussia (15) or Saxony (8). A few works also describe participating in Schill's 1809 campaign (4) or the fight for the Tyrol that same year (3). The close relationship between regional origins, time of publication and thematic focus is striking and will be explored more in the following.

---

switches common in this period, above all of Prussian officers to the British, Austrian and Russian armies, could not be taken into account.
[30] For more, see Jasper Heinzen, "Transnational Affinities and Invented Traditions: The Napoleonic Wars in British and Hanoverian Memory, 1815–1915," *English Historical Review* 127 (2012): 1404–1434; and Mark Wishon, *German Forces and the British Army: Interactions and Perceptions, 1742–1813* (Basingstoke, 2013), 165–195.

Memoirs by Authors from the Armies of the
Confederation of the Rhine

Authors who had fought with the troops of the Confederation of the Rhine or avoided serving under Napoleon by fleeing and joining the King's German Legion frequently not only published their own memoirs, but also did so relatively early. Nearly half of all texts by military men from the former states of the Confederation of the Rhine, but only one-third of those by former members of the Prussian army, were published before 1845. Here, as in works of military history, the Confederation of the Rhine authors clearly felt a strong need for legitimation. In the postwar period, men who from a Prussian and German-national perspective had fought on the wrong side–the side of the French "oppressors" and historic "losers" – appear to have felt compelled to defend their own military honor and that of their regiments by emphasizing their soldierly achievements, which led them to take up their pens. In their memoirs, they countered the national code of honor with a professional one. To be sure, quite a few of them emphasized that they had already felt German and hated the French even before their territorial state joined the coalition against Napoleon in the autumn of 1813. At the same time, it is striking how often they praise Napoleon's brilliant achievements as a military leader and the organizational efficiency of his army.

This observation is confirmed by Julia Murken, who analyzes many of these texts in detail in her study of the Russian campaign. She points out that the memoirs typically emphasize heroic deeds, bravery, courage, a code of honor and masculinity. At the same time, she notes, many of the texts claim Francophobe sentiments. To what degree the latter was a postwar rhetorical strategy that primarily served the purpose of integration into the victorious German national community is apparent from comparison with surviving letters from the war years written by German soldiers and officers of the Grande Armée. They are often entirely devoid of references to Germany, and disparaging remarks regarding their French allies are few and far between; on the contrary, many of these letters seem more laudatory than critical of Napoleon and the French.[31] This respect for Napoleon and his long-victorious Grande Armée, but also the marked regional-state patriotism that readily went along with it, also comes through in the memoirs of soldiers and officers of the armies of the former Confederation of the Rhine.

A typical example of this early type of text was written by the former Saxon Major General Karl Wilhelm Ferdinand von Funck and published one year after his death in 1829 under the title *Memoirs from the Campaign of the Saxon Corps under General Count Reynier in 1812*.[32] Funck, born

---

[31] See Murken, *Soldaten*, 161–196.

[32] Karl Wilhelm Ferdinand von Funck, *Erinnerungen aus dem Feldzuge des sächsischen Corps unter dem General Grafen Reynier im Jahr 1812: Aus den Papieren des verstorbenen Generalleutnants von Funck* (Dresden, 1829). The complete memoirs appeared

in 1761, entered the Saxon Garde du Corps as an officer in 1780, became adjutant general to the Saxon king in 1807 and commanded the 21st Division of the Grande Armée during the Russian campaign of 1812. Since Funck had supported the Saxon king until his arrest by the Allies after the Battle of the Nations in October 1813, he was at first dismissed by the new Russian commander-in-chief of the Saxon troops in January 1814. After returning to the throne, the Saxon king rescinded this decision in May 1815.[33] Funck's prominent position alone ensured that his portrayal of the Russian campaign soon became well known in military circles. His main aim was to defend the military achievements and sacrifices of the Saxon army and its leadership. Similar memoirs of the Spanish and Russian campaigns were written by a whole series of generals and officers of the Confederation of the Rhine in the first decades after the war.[34] Some of these works were also reviewed in the leading military journals, but the reviews were often not very positive. Thus, for example, a reviewer in the *Militär-Wochenblatt* wrote of Funck's *Memoirs*

To judge by the many corrections that this work contains, it appears as if General v. Funk [sic] was in part not always properly informed, and in part wrote some things down in a fit of ill-temper and discontent. [...] It is, alas, the habit of all who pursue honor to think always first of their own intentions and desires and when necessary to sacrifice all other considerations to them.[35]

The review alerts us to Funck's desperate attempts to defend the honor of the Saxon king and his army – against all criticism. Such a negative review in a Prussian journal probably did little to hinder the dissemination of the text in Saxony and other former member states of the Confederation of the Rhine, but it clearly indicates the continuing tensions between Prussian and Saxon army leaders.

---

only a century later: Artur Brabant, ed., *Im Banne Napoleons: Aus den Erinnerungen des sächsischen Generalleutnants und Generaladjutanten des Königs Ferdinand von Funck* (Dresden, 1928).

33 On Funck, see Heinrich Theodor Flathe, "Funck, Karl Wilhelm Ferdinand," *ADB* 8 (1878): 200–201; on Saxony, see Jens Eschert, " 'Mit der Zeit gescheitert': Friedrich August I. von Sachsen und die Völkerschlacht," in *Verlierer der Geschichte: Von der Antike bis zur Moderne*, ed. Sabine Graul and Marian Nebelin (Berlin, 2008), 289–308.

34 Examples are Georg Muhl, ed., *Denkwürdigkeiten aus dem Leben des Freiherrn C. R. von Schäffer, großherzoglich badischen General-Lieutenants und Präsidenten des Kriegs-Ministeriums* (Pforzheim, 1840); Wilhelm Grafen von Bismarck, *Aufzeichnungen des Generallieutenants Friedrich Wilhelm Grafen von Bismark* (Karlsruhe, 1847); Franz Ludwig August von Meerheim, *Erlebnisse eines Veteranen der großen Armee während des Feldzuges in Rußland 1812* (Dresden, 1860); and Philipp Ruder von Diersburg, ed., *Denkwürdigkeiten des Markgrafen Wilhelm von Baden aus den Feldzügen von 1809 bis 1815: Nach dessen hinterlassenen eigenhändigen Aufzeichnungen* (Karlsruhe, 1864).

35 "Berichtigung der Schrift (des Generals v. Funk)," *MW* 17. 829 (1832): 4720.

The generally quite conventional war memoirs by generals and officers of the Confederation of the Rhine told readers very little of the adventures and everyday hardships of soldiers and officers in Spain or Russia. In order to learn more they had to resort to the works of ordinary soldiers, above all non-commissioned officers. They described quite vividly the bivouacs, marches and battles, billeting and foraging, the drill and the chicaneries of their superiors, hunger and disease, injuries and death as well as captivity.[36] They also offered observations on the countries and peoples they encountered – Spaniards and Portuguese, Poles, Russians, Cossacks and Jews – frequently stressing the "barbarism" of these "alien peoples" and thereby also the "civilized nature" of their own regional or German culture.[37] These generally shorter texts were often printed by local publishers or even self-published. They recalled the fate of those native sons of the town or region who had fallen in or returned from Spain and Russia, and thereby also acquainted literate locals with their frequently traumatic war experiences, which helped authors and readers alike to process them. At the same time, these accounts often bolstered national stereotypes, especially prejudices against Southern and Eastern Europeans.

One of the earliest texts of this type was the *Description of the Fate and Sufferings of the Former Corporal Büttner, Now Duty Sub-Collector in Nennsling, During His 19-Month-Long Captivity in Russia in the Years 1812 and 1813*, which was self-published in 1828. Büttner was conscripted into the Bavarian army in 1809 at the age of 20 and, as he emphasizes in his preface, had followed the royal call to join the Russian campaign in 1812 "with true joy and a burning desire to fight for God, king and fatherland." His text then depicts not just the sobering everyday reality of war and the hardships of captivity, but also his harsh lot as a 27-year-old disabled veteran. Only in 1820, after six years of bitter poverty, was he able to secure a post in the Bavarian civil service, which allowed him to support his young family.[38] An account published in Nuremberg in 1834 under the title *The Curious Fate of the Nuremberg Sergeant Joseph Schrafel in the War against Tyrol in 1809, the Campaign against Russia in 1812 and Captivity from 1812 to 1814*, had a quite similar tenor, and was already reprinted a year later and afterward appeared in several more editions. Like many other

---

[36] For more, see Mayer, *Soldaten*; and Murken, *Soldaten*.

[37] An interesting exception here is Jakob Meyer, *Erzählung der Schicksale und Kriegsabenteuer des ehemaligen westfälischen Artillerie-Wachtmeisters Jakob Meyer aus Dransfeld während der Feldzüge in Spanien und Russland* (Dransfeld, 1836). The author was Jewish or, as he referred to himself, an "Israelite." The text was reprinted twice in 1837 and 1838.

[38] Büttner, *Beschreibung der Schicksale und Leiden des ehemaligen Korporals Büttner, jetzt Aufschlag-Untereinnehmer in Nennsling, während seiner 19-monatlichen Gefangenschaft in Russland, in den Jahren 1812 und 1813: Von ihm selbst geschrieben* (Nennsling, 1828), 91–95; see also Theodor Daniel Goethe, *Aus dem Leben eines sächsischen Husaren und aus dessen Feldzügen 1809, 1812 und 1813 in Polen und Russland* (Leipzig, 1853).

authors, Schrafel, also a fiery Bavarian patriot, emphasized in his preface that his family and friends had persuaded him to recount his war experiences to his "dear fellow citizens" with the "strictest veracity."[39] Such texts by obscure authors from small publishing companies were generally not reviewed in national periodicals, but at most noted in the local press. Their readers were mainly locals. A few of these texts, like Schrafel's, however, were republished on the occasion of the centenary celebrations, when the local historical society discovered the past of their region a hundred years before and with it the stories of the local everyday heroes and heroines of that past.

War Memoirs of Prussian Authors

Prussian military men, not just generals and officers but also noncommissioned officers and common soldiers who had participated in the wars of 1806–07 and 1812–15 and found themselves on the winning side of German history, seem to have felt far less personal pressure to publish their recollections. Published texts by generals and officers were generally written late in life and, as they noted with great regularity in their prefaces, were intended above all for their families and friends. It is also striking that many authors of published texts had either been close to Prussian military reform circles in the period 1806–13 and wrote in defense of this political and military legacy against conservative critics,[40] or had voluntarily left the Prussian service for a time during those turbulent years and joined the British, Austrian or Russian army to fight against Napoleon, returning to Prussian service in 1813 or later. Both groups of men appear to have felt a stronger need to justify their actions publicly and therefore to write. Thus former military reformers penned their memoirs in order to defend their legacy against conservative critics, while those officers who had left Prussia in its years of crisis felt compelled to justify their decision. Moreover, they usually had more interesting recollections of their service in other armies and their experiences in foreign lands, which, much like the works of the memoirists from the Confederation of the Rhine, seem to have met with keen interest among readers and hence publishers.[41] Nevertheless, even these authors frequently insisted that their memoirs only be published posthumously. Accordingly, the overwhelming proportion of Prussian memory texts did not appear

---

[39] Joseph Schrafel, "Vorwort," in *Des Nürnberger Feldwebels Joseph Schrafel merkwürdige Schicksale im Kriege gegen Tirol 1809, im Feldzug gegen Rußland 1812 und in der Gefangenschaft 1812–1814* (Nuremberg, 1834). The text was reprinted in 1834, 1835 and 1913.

[40] Quednow, *Denkwürdigkeiten.*

[41] Wolzogen, *Memoiren*; and Heinrich von Brandt, ed., *Aus dem Leben des Generals der Infanterie z.D. Dr. Heinrich von Brandt. Aus den Tagebüchern und Aufzeichnungen seines verstorbenen Vaters zusammengestellt* (Berlin, 1868).

until the fiftieth anniversary of the wars of 1813–15 or later. Most of them offered a review of the author's own life and military career, in which the era of 1806 to 1815 was accorded a central role.[42]

Among the earliest publications of this kind were the *Recollections of My Life* by Count Wilhelm Ludwig Victor Henckel von Donnersmarck, which were published in Zerbst in 1846.[43] Born in 1775, Donnersmarck joined a Prussian dragoon regiment in 1789, held the rank of *Rittmeister* in the Garde du Corps in 1803 and participated as a major in the 1806–07 campaign. In 1810 he became aide-de-camp to King Friedrich Wilhelm III; in the wars of 1813–15 he fought as a colonel, rising afterward to the rank of lieutenant general. He left the military in 1820. Donnersmarck published his memoirs himself, dedicating them to "His Royal Highness the Prince of Prussia," who provided a very friendly preface.[44] In his own foreword, Donnersmarck explains that the urging of many friends and relatives, but also a need for "self-scrutiny and self-reflection" typical of his mature years had driven him to write his memoirs. His gratitude to his benefactor King Friedrich Wilhelm III, who had died a few years before, encouraged him to publish them himself. In writing his memoirs, he sought to "rescue from oblivion" his experiences with and under the king between 1806 and 1815, since these had been "such remarkable years," the likes of which "occur only rarely in world history." Donnersmarck emphasized his obligation to "the truth." He therefore limited himself to portraying those events that he had experienced personally. At the same time, he stressed that, out of respect for those who were still alive or had only recently died, he had exercised "restraint in the description of specific individuals who intervened in the history of the war."[45]

The decidedly conservative Prussian-monarchical interpretation of the era of the Napoleonic Wars in Donnersmarck's *Recollections* met with a generally positive response in Prussian court and military circles.[46] This notwithstanding, the work sparked a series of "declarations" in the *Militär-Wochenblatt* in which members of the military complained that former superiors, relatives or they themselves had been portrayed or quoted inaccurately. Donnersmarck responded by stating "that he had had not the

[42] One example is Menno Burg, *Geschichte meines Dienstlebens: Zum Besten einer milden Stiftung nach seinem Tode herausgegeben* (Berlin, 1854). This text by a Jewish volunteer, who after the war became the only Jewish officer to serve in the Prussian army before 1914, is an extremely interesting document about his experiences in the artillery. It was published again in 1916.

[43] Wilhelm Ludwig Victor Graf Henckel von Donnersmarck, *Erinnerungen aus meinem Leben* (Zerbst, 1846; 2nd edn. Leipzig, 1913).

[44] On Donnersmarck, see Ferdinand Freiherr von Meerheimb, "Henckel von Donnersmarck, Victor Amadeus Graf," *ADB* 11 (1880): 732–734.

[45] Donnersmarck, *Erinnerungen*, vii–x.

[46] "Rezensionen zu drei geschichtlichen Werken," *ALZ* 2, no. 185, 1847, 328–329.

slightest intention of hurting or insulting anyone." He called upon his critics to make public "objections" of any kind "without previous notification by letter" and to provide "evidence of the contrary" of his assertions.[47] This silenced them, but Donnersmarck's unpleasant experiences with honor-obsessed colleagues may have motivated other Prussian military men not to publish their memoirs during their lifetimes, leaving this task instead to their survivors.

This also applied to the *Memoirs of the Royal Prussian Infantry General Baron Ludwig von Wolzogen*, which his son Baron Alfred von Wolzogen brought out with the Leipzig publishing house of Wigand in 1851, six years after his death, "from his papers, with the addition of official military memoranda." The work was republished in 1908 in an edition revised and heavily abridged "for school and household."[48] Wolzogen, born in 1773, began his *Memoirs* with a brief account of his childhood and youth in Württemberg. The main part of the book concentrates on his military service, from his entry into the Prussian army in 1794 until his retirement in 1836. Here, too, the focus is on the years 1805–15. Wolzogen traced his turbulent military career: from 1805 to 1807 he served with the army of Württemberg, and then until 1814 with the Russians. He participated in the Russian campaign of 1812 and the 1813–14 campaigns in Germany and France as a colonel on the Russian general staff. After a brief stint as chief of the general staff for the duke of Saxony-Weimar in 1814–15, he returned to the Prussian service in 1815 with the rank of major-general. In 1818 Friedrich Wilhelm III appointed him permanent plenipotentiary in the Military Commission of the German Confederation.[49]

As a reviewer in the literary magazine *Blätter für literarische Unterhaltung* noted, Wolzogen's *Memoirs* were marked, "in contrast to countless other autobiographies [...] by one of the rarest qualities, to wit, the strictest reticence in speaking of himself." The text is praised for its interesting and factual information on military and wartime history, but at the same time criticized because "no one who knows nothing of the author but what is to be found in the book can gain any impression of his person." A military autobiography worth reading must provide information about the life and deeds of an interesting if not well-known man, including his personal development and "educational path," seasoned with at least a soupçon of

---

[47] "Erklärungen," *MW*, no. 50, 12 Dec. 1846, 213–214; no. 4, 23 Jan. 1847, 14–16; no. 17, 24 April 1847, 74.

[48] Wolzogen, *Memoiren*. The memoirs appeared in 1908 in a much-abridged edition: Ernst Keller, ed., *Memoiren des königlich preußischen Generals der Infanterie Ludwig Freiherrn von Wolzogen* (Frankfurt/M., 1908).

[49] On Wolzogen, see Bernhard von Poten, "Wolzogen, Justus Adolf Philipp Wilhelm Ludwig," *ADB* 44 (1898): 206–208; also Alexander Mikaberidze, *The Russian Officer Corps in the Revolutionary and Napoleonic Wars, 1792–1815* (Spellmount, 2005), 447–448.

"uncommon adventure."[50] Here, the reviewer clearly defines his expectations of a successful military autobiography. But most memoirs by Prussian generals and officers published in the 1850s and 1860s – usually a few years after their deaths – will have disappointed him. They had a similar, strictly military historical character and were most likely read mainly in military circles.[51]

More to the taste of a broad readership were war memoirs like those of Prussian Lieutenant General Karl von François, born in 1785, which his daughter Clotilde von Schwartzkoppen published in Schwerin in 1871 under the title *Karl von François: A German Soldier's Life. According to His Memoirs*. That, at least, is what the many reprints of the work seem to indicate. The text was already reprinted in Leipzig in 1873, and appeared in a second augmented edition in Berlin in 1889, which was reprinted in 1910.[52] Because of his eventful life and highly entertaining writing style, François's recollections read more like a military adventure novel. He had served in the Prussian army from 1803 to 1807, but was forced to seek a new employer when the size of the army was halved, and joined the Württembergian forces. There he was sentenced to death for insubordination in 1808, but reprieved at the last minute before the firing squad and sentenced to imprisonment. After fleeing he joined Ferdinand von Schill's *Freikorps* as an officer in 1809, experienced the defeat of Schill's rebellion by the Napoleonic army and ended up in French captivity. After his release he joined the Russian service in 1812, attained the rank of cavalry captain in the general staff and participated in the 1812–14 campaigns in Russia, Germany and France. He returned to Prussian service in 1815 and rose to the rank of lieutenant general.[53]

A reviewer of the 1889 edition in the *Blätter für literarische Unterhaltung* noted, "It is extremely gratifying to see the above mentioned book appear in a second edition, for, as thrilling as the destiny of its hero may be, it nevertheless also offers not merely entertaining but also genuinely uplifting reading" – not least because of the author's marked hatred of the French and strong Prussian-German patriotism, which was very much in keeping with the monarchic-conservative interpretation of the "Wars of Liberation" that dominated Borussian historical writing in those days.[54] Other reviewers

50 "Historische Denkwürdigkeiten." The following very positive review makes similar comments: "V. Wolzogen's Memoiren," *Heidelberger Jahrbücher der Literatur* 45 (1852) 17:258–272 and 18:273–272.
51 Eduard Freiherr von Müffling, ed., *Friedrich Karl Ferdinand Freiherr von Müffling: Aus meinem Leben* (Berlin, 1851).
52 Schwartzkoppen, *François*.
53 On François, see Friedrich Wilhelm Schaafhausen, "François, Kurt Karl Bruno von" *NDB* 5 (1961): 333–334.
54 "Karl von François: Ein Soldatenleben," *BLU*, no. 29, 1889, 461–462.

were also full of praise. The *Jahrbücher für deutsche Armee und Marine*, for example, wrote, "seldom have we encountered a military memoir that gripped us to such a degree from start to finish."[55] Readers apparently felt the same way.

Published recollections of the Anti-Napoleonic Wars by Prussian soldiers and noncommissioned officers were rare and far less popular with the mainly educated male readers who were interested in military autobiographies and memoirs. One of the few such texts was Wilhelm Mente's *From the Bottom Up: Recollections of Forty-Nine Years of Service in the Royal Prussian Artillery*. Mente, who began his military service in 1805 at the age of 13, retired with the rank of colonel. His memoirs, written in 1860, appeared one year later with Alexander Duncker's Berlin publishing house. The author's stated aim was not just "to describe the early conditions in and the nature of the army in such a way that it enables the younger generation to compare past and present." He expressly wished to portray the life of common soldiers in the wars of 1806 to 1814 in order to recall their achievements.[56] The book, which has much to offer today's historians, met with little interest among contemporaries, at least among book reviewers. The brutal everyday life in the old Prussian army seemed too well known and the changes that the Prussian army reforms of 1806 to 1813 had also brought for ordinary soldiers and noncommissioned officers were not considered to be particularly fascinating 50 years later.

Volunteers' Memoirs

Far more popular, at least among the educated middle-class reading public, were the many memory texts by volunteers of the 1813–15 wars, especially when they were penned by such well-known contemporaries as philosophy professor Wilhelm Traugott Krug, poet and author Friedrich de la Motte Fouqué, professor of natural philosophy Henrich Steffens, writers August Varnhagen von Ense and Willibald Alexis or history professor Heinrich Luden.[57] Many of these texts appeared on the occasion of the twenty-fifth

---

[55] "Karl von François," *Jahrbücher für die deutsche Armee und Marine* 72 (1889): 244–245.

[56] Mente, *Pieke*, 1–2; see also Böck, *Leben*.

[57] Wilhelm Traugott Krug, *Krug's Lebensreise in sechs Stazionen, von ihm selbst beschrieben: Neue verbesserte und vermehrte Ausgabe* (Leipzig, 1842); Friedrich de la Motte Fouqué, *Lebensgeschichte des Barons Friedrich de la Motte-Fouqué: Aufgezeichnet durch ihn selbst* (Halle, 1840); Karl August Varnhagen von Ense, *Denkwürdigkeiten des eigenen Lebens*, 3 vols. (Leipzig, 1843); Willibald Alexis, "Als Kriegsfreiwilliger in Frankreich 1815: Blätter aus meinen Erinnerungen," in *Penelope: Taschenbuch für das Jahr 1844, 1845 and 1846*, ed. Karl Gottfried Theodor Winkler, 3 vols. (Leipzig, 1844–46); Heinrich Steffens, *Was ich erlebte 1802–1814: Knechtschaft und Freiheit*, 10 vols. (Breslau, 1840–45); and Heinrich Luden, *Rückblicke in mein Leben: Aus dem Nachlasse von Heinrich Luden* (Jena, 1847).

anniversary of the "Wars of Liberty." The fiftieth anniversary inspired a second wave of publications. [58]

One of the main functions of most volunteers' memoirs, especially those written by educated middle-class authors, was to recall the "uplifting time" of the "German rising" or "people's war" and to demand that rulers and governments live up to the promises of political liberties they had made at the time. This remained an important aim in the run-up to the March Revolution of 1848 and became even more significant after its failure. A few authors distanced themselves in old age from the pathos of their youth and the political naiveté that had made them believe the promises of princes in 1813, and some criticized the fanatical excess of the era, which had expressed itself in hatred of the French and affectedly Germanic language and costume, but none fundamentally distanced themselves from the old, still unachieved political aims of unity and liberty. Even if the tone of the memoirs, which frequently extended over several volumes and embedded the portrayal of the years 1806–15 in the story of an entire life or a broader picture of the time of the Napoleonic Wars, was ironic or humorous, this did not mean that the authors fundamentally questioned their old political ideals. It was more a strategy to deal with political disappointment and censorship.

Among the earliest texts of this type was *Krug's Life Journey in Six Stations, Described by Himself*, which first appeared in 1825 in Leipzig. Shortly before his death in 1842, Wilhelm Traugott Krug published a "new, improved and augmented" edition.[59] Krug, born in 1770, had studied philosophy and theology in Wittenberg, Jena and Göttingen, earned a doctorate and habilitation and had his first posts as a professor in 1805 in Königsberg and 1809 in Leipzig, where he served as rector of the university in 1813–14. He had fought against Napoleonic rule in the *Tugendbund* (League of Virtue) and other patriotic associations since 1808 and, having frequently encouraged the students of his university to fight, joined the newly established Banner of Saxon Volunteers after the Battle of the Nations in October 1813 and went to war.[60] His wartime experiences were, however, not particularly heroic and he recounted them in an ironic tone. What especially irked him was the "eternal sameness and pettiness of service, the military pedantry," "chicaneries" and "miserable treatment by superiors." He was also repelled by being forced as a soldier to "live at the expense of others" if he wished to survive:

[58] For examples, see Karl Georg von Raumer, *Erinnerungen aus den Jahren 1813 und 1814* (Stuttgart, 1850); Bärsch, *Erinnerungen*; Christian Wilhelm Harnisch, *Mein Lebensmorgen: Nachgelassene Schrift von Wilhelm Harnisch: Zur Geschichte der Jahre 1784–1822* (Berlin, 1865); Hoffmann, *Erinnerungen*; and Hermann Kletke, ed., *Kunst und Leben: Aus Friedrich Försters Nachlaß* (Berlin, 1873).

[59] Krug, *Lebensreise*.

[60] On Krug, see Friedbert Holz, "Krug, Wilhelm Traugott," *NDB* 13 (1982): 114–115.

To be sure one lives quite cheaply, but it is also terrible to have to enter another's house so frequently with the awareness of being an unwelcome guest. [...] And when one sees traces of poverty and suffering wherever one looks, which are sometimes the result of the burdens of previous billeting, one would have to be utterly heartless not to be pained by the sight. One's feelings become gradually deadened, but I have never been able to suppress them completely.[61]

For that reason he warned "any man not drawn by duty or an irresistible penchant for the soldier's estate from entering it. It is naught but glittering misery, whether in peacetime or war. It is naught but an eternal alternation between slavery and detachment, blind obedience and an overbearing attitude. Only a higher purpose, enthusiasm for an ideal," as occurred in the years 1813–15, "can render such a life bearable for an educated man."[62] After the war, Krug, like other volunteers, supported the retention of universal conscription in wartime and opposed a standing army, based on his own negative experiences. In view of the unpatriotic stance of the Saxon king, he did not criticize the partition of the kingdom in 1815. In this he differed markedly from other Saxon political authors of his day.[63] In retrospect, it appeared to Krug, as to many of his contemporaries, that 1813 had been by far the "most remarkable year" of his life. "For it was a great and difficult year, for my humble self as well as for entire peoples and states."[64]

Krug's critical attitude toward the military and war was shared by other volunteers after the wars of 1813–15. Willibald Alexis, for example, published his "As a Military Volunteer in France in 1815: Pages from My Recollections," in Karl Gottfried Theodor Winkler's *Penelope: Taschenbuch für das Jahr 1844* and in the following issues up to 1846. Alexis was descended from a Huguenot refugee family; his father had held a high position in the war department in Berlin. Alexis had served as a volunteer in the Prussian army in 1815. After returning from the war, he studied law in Berlin and Breslau and entered the legal profession, but soon embarked on a career as a writer and journalist in Berlin. His historical novels proved to be especially popular. His war memoirs, like Krug's, were not heroic, but realistic and ironic. He, too, however, continued to uphold the old liberal ideals of the "Wars of Liberty" as much as ever.[65]

Other former volunteers such as Henrich Steffens and his fellow professor Karl von Raumer described the period of the Anti-Napoleonic Wars

[61] Krug, *Lebensreise*, 168–170.
[62] Ibid., 170–171.
[63] See Bernhard Lange, *Die öffentliche Meinung in Sachsen von 1813 bis zur Rückkehr des Königs 1815* (Gotha, 1912).
[64] Ibid., 208.
[65] Alexis, "Als Kriegsfreiwilliger." The text was reprinted in 1915 and 1916 by Reclam in Leipzig. On Alexis, see Walter Heynen, "Alexis, Willibald," *NDB* 1 (1953): 197–198.

with a good deal less critical distance in their memoirs.[66] In the preface to his *Recollections of the Years 1813 and 1814*, which appeared for the first time in 1850, for instance, Karl Georg von Raumer noted:

I gratefully acknowledge it as divine grace that I had the undeserved good fortune during the war to experience at close quarters the greatest of great men. [...] Wise posterity will seek out as sacred relics every notice that treats the events of the past, and will not be indifferent even to the life of an individual, insignificant man, since it surely reflects more or less the greater life of contemporary existence.[67]

Raumer, born in 1783, studied law in Göttingen and Halle, but then switched to mineralogy. In 1811 he was working as a mining official (*Bergrat*) at the department of mines in Breslau and a professor of mineralogy at the university there. He fought in the wars of 1813–14 as a volunteer, serving as adjutant to Lieutenant General August Neidhardt von Gneisenau, the chief of staff to Field Marshal Blücher. As he proudly noted, Raumer retired from the military with the Iron Cross.[68] In 1819 he transferred to the University of Halle and the department of mines there, where he stayed until 1823. In 1827 he went to Erlangen as professor of natural history. Raumer wrote his memoirs in 1849–50, "the saddest period, when the honor that Germany regained in the Wars of Liberty was disgracefully defiled, and we earned the scorn and derision of other peoples." A "profound pain consumed" him in those years. In order to "revive and refresh" himself, he turned his "gaze longingly back to those splendid years of 1813 and 14." He closed his memoirs with words of encouragement for his fellow national-liberal middle-class contemporaries, who had also been disappointed by the crushing of the Democratic Revolution of 1848–49:

Then the hope arose within me: God will not utterly abandon my poor fatherland now. Just as he awakened heroes and hosts after the seven disgraceful years following the Battle of Jena, now that we have acknowledged and atoned with sacred earnestness for the sins of the miserably wasted long years of peace, which we spent in a sort of trance, may he provide the fatherland with new heroes and hosts and, after new victories, bestow upon us an honorable peacetime in unity and, through unity, a power that fears only God but not men.[69]

This message was well received by his educated contemporaries. Reviewers warmly recommended the book,[70] which was published in 1866, one year

---

[66] Steffens, *Was ich erlebte*; Raumer, *Erinnerungen*; on Steffens, see Otto Liebmann "Steffens, Henrich," *ADB* 35 (1893): 555–558; and on Raumer, Wilhelm von Gümbel, "Raumer, Karl von," *ADB* 27 (1888): 420–423.

[67] Steffens, *Was ich erlebte*, vi–viii; Luden, *Rückblicke* is quite similar.

[68] Raumer, *Erinnerungen*, 112–113.

[69] Ibid., 146.

[70] See, for example, "Erinnerungen aus den Jahren 1813 und 1814," *BLU*, no. 3, 3 Jan. 1851, 11.

after the author's death, under the title *Karl von Raumer's Life Told by Himself*, and went through two further editions before World War I.[71]

A similar tenor prevails in numerous other autobiographical texts by early-liberal Prussian and German patriots who had fought in the wars of 1813–15 and sought, on the occasion of the fiftieth anniversary, to recall both their achievements and their unattained political aims. In communicative memory their texts had to compete with three sources of recollections: on the one hand, the many memoirs by soldiers, officers and generals from the Confederation of the Rhine states, who rarely addressed political issues and instead stressed military achievements and sacrifice; and, on the other, the mainly monarchist, conservative, patriotic-national memoirs of Prussian generals and officers who described the wars of 1813–15 as "Wars of Liberation," largely in the vein of a conventional history of war, but sometimes also as entertaining literary memoir, similarly ignoring the struggle for increased political liberties associated with military mobilization. At the same time, the memoirs by early-liberal Prussian and German patriots challenged Prussian academic historiography with its Borussianism, which was becoming increasingly influential after 1848–49. The variety of conflicting narratives in the communicative memory of the men who had been active as soldiers, officers and generals in the period of the Napoleonic Wars also vied with the narratives of civilians who described this period in their autobiographies and war memoirs.

CIVILIAN WAR NARRATIVES

Up to the founding of the German Empire, the communicative memory of the Napoleonic Wars as reflected in published autobiographical memory texts was shaped by the accounts of those who had participated actively in these wars as soldiers, officers and generals as well as volunteers. In the sample I studied, their 129 texts were juxtaposed with only 31 autobiographical accounts by civilians – 27 men and 5 women – that appeared for the first time up to 1875 and dealt in greater detail with the war years between 1806 and 1815.[72] Only one-sixth of accounts by civilians were war memoirs in the strict sense of the word – these texts recorded experiences during the war years 1806–07 and 1813–15 – compared to half of the published recollections of military men. The overwhelming majority of the autobiographical texts by civilians cover broader periods of their lives. Like many officers, civilians described the years 1806–15 in their memoirs as one, albeit very significant, period of their lives. More clearly among civilians than military men, the memory booms reflected the anniversaries of the wars of 1813–15;

---

[71] The following further editions appeared: Stuttgart, 1866; Leipzig, 1912; and Wiesbaden, 1913.

[72] The only authors who counted as civilians were those who did no military service during the war years.

in comparison to military memoirs, however, a far higher proportion had already appeared at the time of the twenty-fifth anniversary. Just 7 percent were published between 1815 and 1825 and 3 percent between 1826 and 1835, while 29 percent came out between 1836 and 1845. Twenty-three percent each appeared in the periods 1846–55 and 1856–65, and only 16 percent between 1866 and 1875.

While the authors of military memoirs were mainly of noble origin, most authors of civilian memoirs came from the educated middle classes. These men were in state service as higher civil servants, diplomats, professors, teachers and pastors or worked as medical doctors or lawyers. Many had been politically active from 1806 to 1815 and had supported the fight for liberation with their writings, or they came from regions in which the civilian population had been especially strongly affected by the wars. In publishing their recollections, they wished to record their own life achievements and their roles in the war years 1806–15, felt compelled to defend their activities at the time or simply wanted to highlight the suffering and sacrifices of their fellow citizens as a result of the wars. Accordingly, nearly all of the male authors saw to the first publication of their memoirs during their lifetimes. Only six of the texts appeared posthumously, and three of these were written by women. Like the autobiographical accounts by former military men, the largest proportion of civilian authors (48 percent) came from the Confederation of the Rhine, above all the kingdoms of Saxony (19 percent) and Westphalia (10 percent). Thirty-nine percent of the authors were from Prussia and 13 percent from Austria.

The comparatively high percentage of Saxon authors reflects the significance of memories of the Battle of the Nations. A whole series of texts published over several decades vividly depicts the dramatic effects of the spring and autumn campaign of 1813 on Saxony, above all on the civilian population of Leipzig and its environs. By recalling these sacrifices for the liberation of Germany, Saxon authors sought integration into the national community and claimed a place in the German nation's collective memory of the wars of 1813–15.[73] One example are the recollections *What We*

---

[73] See, for example, Wilhelm Adolf Lindau, *Darstellung der Ereignisse in Dresden im Jahre 1813 von einem Augenzeugen* (Dresden, 1816); Vater, *Was wir Erlebten*; Ludwig Schlosser, *Erlebnisse eines sächsischen Landpredigers in den Kriegsjahren von 1806 bis 1815* (Leipzig, 1846); Friedrich Gottlob Nagel, *Kriegsbilder aus der Heimath, hauptsächlich aus Halberstadt, Magdeburg und der Umgegend: Zur Erinnerung an die denkwürdigen Jahre von 1806 bis 1815* (Halberstadt, 1848); Johann Carl Groß, *Erinnerungen aus den Kriegsjahren: Zum Besten der Pestalozzistiftungen in Leipzig und Dresden* (Leipzig, 1850); and Ludwig Hussell, *Leipzigs Schreckenstage während der Völkerschlacht: Nach eignen Erlebnissen und Anschauungen dargestellt* (Leipzig, 1863). On the consequences of the Battle of Leipzig for the civilian population, see Hagemann, "Desperation." Other memoirs by civilians portray the effects of the war on everyday life. See, for example, Ignaz August, *Erinnerungen aus Hannover und Hamburg aus den Jahren 1803–1813: Von einem Zeitgenossen* (Leipzig,

Experienced in October 1813, which appeared in 1845 as a *Memorandum of the Association for the Celebration of 19 October in Leipzig*. They were penned by Auguste Vater. The pastor's daughter had been 16 years old in 1813. In her brief text she relates how she, her parents and five siblings experienced the Battle of the Nations in a small village near Leipzig. The family had been forced to flee together with other local people. The village itself, like many surrounding Leipzig, was largely destroyed in the fighting. The family was fortunate to find at least the foundation walls of their house still standing when they returned home. Others lost everything they owned. Vater claims in her account that her family made this sacrifice with "calm submission" as the price of liberation "from the French yoke."[74] The conclusion neatly summarizes the overall theme of her account:

Despite all the horrors and tribulations of that remarkable year, we still look back with pleasure, and among a long series of life experiences we would not want to do without it. [...] Anyone who appreciates the greatness of the inner uprising of an entire people, the beauty of such universal energy directed at the noblest possessions of humankind, must be glad to have lived through that time.[75]

To be sure, Vater qualifies this patriotic outlook with a remark that not all of the hopes placed in the fight for liberation had been fulfilled, but excuses this with the "human imperfection and weakness to which monarchs, like others, are subject," causing them to leave unfinished "some things they have begun."[76] The tenor of the text, which was only distributed locally, suited the *Vormärz* period preceding the Revolution of 1848, in which the urban middle classes reintensified the struggle they had begun in 1813–15 for national unity, a constitution, and the civil rights and liberties it guaranteed. Interestingly, no reviewer commented on the fact that this text was written by a woman.

The only memoirs written by civilians focusing on the Anti-Napoleonic Wars to reach a broader public in the 1830s and 1840s were those by authors who were known throughout the German-speaking region. They included Friedrich Ludwig Jahn and Ernst Moritz Arndt, who published their recollections on the occasion of the twenty-fifth anniversary of the wars of 1813–15.[77] Their central motivation for publishing, they said, was

---

1843); and Ludwig Hänselmann, ed., *Treue Bauern in Nöthen der Fremdherrschaft: Erinnerungen Heinrich Oppermanns aus Ölper* (Braunschweig, 1903, 1st edn. 1855).

[74] Vater, *Was wir Erlebten*, quoted from a reprint in Thomas Nabert, ed., *Zeugen des Schreckens: Erlebnisberichte aus der Völkerschlachtzeit in und um Leipzig* (Leipzig, 2012), 13–56, 52.

[75] Ibid., 56.

[76] Ibid.

[77] Karl Schöppach, ed., *Denknisse eines Deutschen oder Fahrten des Alten im Bart* (Schleusingen, 1835); Ernst Moritz Arndt, *Erinnerungen aus dem äußeren Leben* (Leipzig, 1840); also Karl Müchler, *Doppelflucht um den Verfolgungen der Franzosen zu entgehen. Bruchstücke aus den Erinnerungen meines Lebens* (Cottbus, 1841).

a fear that the "great era" or the "German rising" might fall into oblivion, a theme one finds in many texts of the period,[78] among others a review in the *Blätter für literarische Unterhaltung* of Arndt's *Memoirs of My Outer Life*, published by Weidemann in Leipzig in 1840:

The pace of life is so fast nowadays that a quarter-century suffices to make us forget the greatest moment in our history. Scarcely anyone thinks anymore of the struggle against Napoleonic domination, of the time of foreign oppression; and to the current generation, the men who in those days of sublime self-defense carried the banner of the noble idea of the fatherland appear almost like the fragments of a dark chivalric past. The direction of the present is so very universal, encompassing all of humanity, that sometimes a mighty admonition is necessary that the homeland too makes its special claims upon us, and makes them as strongly and as urgently as ever.[79]

The author of this unusually long, four-part review therefore warmly recommended Arndt's memoirs to his readers as a book "for our times," which Germany urgently needed.[80] Even today, he wrote, Arndt remains a model "in sentiment and deed":

What powers of description! What truth and vividness in his depictions! Persons, circumstances, the entire history of those days of struggle are there, alive and gripping, and revolve around the modest, decent man, the bard of battles and victories! The book provides a profound glimpse into circumstances that are almost beginning to disappear from the view of today's generation.[81]

In fact, Arndt's *Memoirs*, which he completed the year they were published, offer instructive insights into how he perceived his own life and work in retrospect, above all the years 1805 to 1819. Arndt, who was born in 1769 on the Baltic island of Rügen, had earned his habilitation at the University of Greifswald in history and philosophy in 1800, and since then had mainly worked as a writer. He was one of the leading German-national and early-liberal political authors of his day. In 1818 he was appointed professor of history in Bonn, but was dismissed in 1826 during the so-called persecution of the demagogues. It was only in 1840 that the new Prussian King Friedrich Wilhelm IV rehabilitated him, even appointing him as rector of the University of Bonn in 1841. In 1848–49 Arndt was a member of the National Assembly in Frankfurt. After its failure, the disillusioned Arndt withdrew from politics.[82] Arndt's *Memoirs*, which he wrote before his rehabilitation, were also penned as a defense against persistent attacks on his

---

[78] "Geleitwort," in Arndt, *Erinnerungen*; see also "Avisbrief," in Karl Immermann, *Memorabilien*, 3 vols. (Hamburg, 1840–43).

[79] "Ernst Moritz Arndt," *BLU*, no. 295, 21 Oct. 1840, 1189–1191, 1189; no. 296, 22 Oct. 1840, 1193–1196; no. 297, 23 Oct. 1840, 1197–1199; and no. 298, 24 Oct. 1840, 1201–1202.

[80] Ibid., no. 295, 1189.

[81] Ibid., no. 298, 1202.

[82] On Arndt, see Gustav Freytag, "Arndt, Ernst Moritz," *ADB* 1 (1875): 541–548.

person, his work and his German-national opinions. As in his texts from the "time of the uprising," one accordingly finds German chauvinism and hatred of the French openly expressed. This fit well into the context of the Rhine crisis of 1840, a diplomatic conflict between the French kingdom and the German Confederation instigated by French claims to the territories west of the Rhine that unleashed a new wave of German nationalism.[83] This led to a return to the German-national rhetoric of the wars of 1813–15, which Arndt had been instrumental in developing.[84]

When Friedrich Ludwig Jahn's memoirs, edited by the young historian Karl Schöppach and published by a small Schleusingen publishing house, had appeared five years earlier under the title *Recollections of a German, or Travels of the Old Man with a Beard*, the response had been far more critical; on the one hand because of the different times, and on the other because of Jahn's far more controversial personality.[85] Jahn, born in 1778, had studied German and history but never earned a university degree. He made his living as a teacher and political writer. He was best known as the author of *German Folkdom*, initiator of the gymnastic movement and organizer of the Lützow Free Corps. Jahn, too, was charged in 1819 as part of the persecution of the demagogues but acquitted in 1825 and rehabilitated in 1840 by Friedrich Wilhelm IV, who in 1842 also lifted the ban on gymnastics enacted by his father. In 1848 Jahn also joined the National Assembly in Frankfurt, where he however supported the conservative monarchist forces.

Jahn's German chauvinism and radical anti-French nationalism were considered to be outmoded, above all by the literati of Young Germany who set the tone in the national literary scene in the mid-1830s. Their model, after the July Revolution of 1830, was the more liberal France, which for Jahn and his followers remained the "hereditary enemy" par excellence.[86] A review by Karl Gutzkow, published in 1839 in his literary journal *Beiträge zur Geschichte der neuesten Literatur*, begins as follows, and is typical of the stance of the Young Germans:

The recently published *Recollections of a German* could also be called the Reminiscences of an Unpolished Fellow, or of a Bear, or Memoirs of a Bruiser. In short, they are anecdotes or *tall tales* from the life of the old gymnast and eternal

---

[83] Wolf D. Gruner, "Der Deutsche Bund, die deutschen Verfassungsstaaten und die Rheinkrise von 1840: Überlegung zur deutschen Dimension einer europäischen Krise," *Zeitschrift für bayerische Landesgeschichte* 53 (1990): 51–78.

[84] See "Erinnerungen aus dem äußeren Leben," *Repertorium der gesammten deutschen Literatur* 24 (1840): 552–553; and "Deutschland und Frankreich," *Beilage zum Berliner politischen Wochenblatt*, no. 47, 21 Nov. 1840, 253–254.

[85] See Wilhelm A. Meiningen, *Zur Erinnerung an Karl Schöppach* (Meiningen, 1844). Jahn's memoirs were only reprinted as part of his collected works (Hof, 1884 and Leipzig, 1906). On Jahn reception, see Sprenger, *Jahnrezeption*.

[86] Schöppach, *Denknisse*, v.

schoolboy *Jahn*. The old man cannot keep quiet. He still wants to be part of things.[87] (Emphasis in the original.)

Gutzkow then spends the next six pages ridiculing Jahn's life and work. The main target of his biting scorn was Jahn's Germanomania, with its ancient Germanic dress and insistence on a German language purged of all foreign elements. Other reviewers also found little to praise in Jahn's eccentric *Recollections* and rejected his German chauvinism, even if, unlike Gutzkow, they at least acknowledged Jahn's importance at the time of the Anti-Napoleonic Wars. The only activities deemed worthy of appreciation and positive remembrance were his achievements as founder of the gymnastic movement.[88]

Arndt's *Memoirs* were received quite differently in 1840, during the Rhine crisis, not least because his German nationalism and persistent warnings against France's "appetite for conquest" suddenly seemed extremely relevant again.[89] By 1840 at the latest, both belonged to the standard rhetorical repertoire of many German-national liberals – at least in times of crisis and war. Arndt's songs and poems of the years 1812–15, which were reprinted over and over again in song anthologies and school textbooks and belonged to the canon of schools, universities and clubs in Wilhelmine Germany, retained their popularity up to World War I.[90] His *Memoirs* also seem to have been popular reading matter. They were probably the most widely published political memoirs on the period of the Napoleonic Wars; at least eleven editions were printed up to 1915 by five different companies, including a paperback in *Reclams Universal-Bibliothek* in 1891.[91]

The success of Arndt's *Memoirs* was exceeded only by accounts of the period produced expressly for entertainment value. Wilhelm von Kügelgen's *Memoirs of Youth by an Old Man*, published in 1870, became *the* best-seller under Wilhelmine Germany's autobiographies, going through at least 27 editions with nine publishers. It also appeared as a Reclam paperback in 1898.[92] Like the *Memorabilia* published in 1840–43 by the dramatist

[87] See "Jahn," *Beiträge zur Geschichte der neuesten Literatur* 2 (1839): 107–114, 107.

[88] "Denknisse eines Deutschen," *Blätter für literarische Unterhaltung* 174 (1835): 719; and "Rückblick auf Jahn und seine Zeit," *Allgemeine Zeitung München* 145 (24 May 1840): 1156.

[89] "Ernst Moritz Arndt," *BLU*, no. 297, 1198.

[90] See Walter Erhart und Arne Koch, eds., *Ernst Moritz Arndt (1769–1860): Deutscher Nationalismus – Europa – transatlantische Perspektiven* (Tübingen, 2007); and Thomas Vordermayer, "Die Rezeption Ernst Moritz Arndts in Deutschland 1909/10 – 1919/20 – 1934/35," *Vierteljahrshefte für Zeitgeschichte* 58.4 (2010): 483–508.

[91] Arndt, *Erinnerungen*. Editions: Leipzig, 1842, 1891, 1892, 1898, 1908, 1909 and 1910; Berlin, 1912; Cologne, 1913; Munich, 1913; and Hanover, 1915. The autobiography was also published in Russian translation in 1871 and in English in 1879.

[92] Wilhelm Kügelgen, *Jugenderinnerungen eines alten Mannes* (Berlin, 1870). Editions: Berlin, 1870, 1871, 1881, 1882, 1883, 1903, 1904, 1912 and 1913; Bielefeld and Leipzig, 1913 and 1914; Leipzig, 1898, 1903, 1905 and 1911; Düsseldorf, 1907, 1910, and 1914; Munich,

and writer Karl Immermann[93] or the 1861 memoir *Of My Life* by the poet and writer Ludwig Rellstab,[94] *Memoirs of Youth* by the well-known painter Kügelgen depict the "time of the French" from the perspective of childhood or adolescence. Immermann was born in 1796, Rellstab in 1799 and Kügelgen in 1802. This point of view allowed all three authors to assume a humorous distance from the period they were recalling without having to fundamentally question the patriotic aims and ideals that their parents had also supported at the time. They looked back nostalgically "at the good old days." Kügelgen's *Memoirs of Youth*, which were brought out posthumously by the journalist and publisher Philipp von Nathusius, became one of the favorite books of middle-class Germans in the Wilhelmine era. The preface to the 1911 Munich edition accordingly notes that

these "Memoirs of Youth" have long since become the inalienable property of the nation. Countless people of all walks of life have wandered with the old man through the alien and vivid country of his youth. – All have been gripped by the power and simplicity of his character, and refreshed by the joyful grace of his heart.[95]

Kügelgen, son of the portrait and history painter Gerhard von Kügelgen and his wife Helene Marie Zöge von Manteuffel, spent his early childhood in Dresden with his younger brothers, attended the *Gymnasium* in Bernburg on the Saale and studied at the Academy of Art in Dresden. His memoirs end with the murder of his father in the course of a robbery in 1820. In 1830 Kügelgen became court painter at the summer residence of Anhalt-Bernburg in Ballenstedt, where he spent the rest of his life with his wife and their six children.[96]

Apart from the writing style, what made his extraordinarily entertaining one-volume *Memoirs of Youth* so attractive for middle-class readers, both male and female, was their focus on his parental home and the family's wide circle of friends, which served as the center of early Romanticism in Dresden. This circle included Caspar David Friedrich, Georg Friedrich Kersting, Christian Gottfried Körner and his son Theodor as well as Friedrich Schiller.[97] Kügelgen vividly depicts the influence of politics and

---

1910 and 1912; Stuttgart, 1899, 1900, 1903 and 1915; Vienna, 1910; and Wolfenbüttel, 1912 and 1913.

93 Immermann, *Memorabilien*; on Immermann, see Benno von Wiese, "Immermann, Karl," *NDB* 10 (1974): 159–163.

94 Ludwig Rellstab, *Aus meinem Leben*, 2 vols. (Berlin, 1861); on Rellstab, see Gertrud Maria Rösch, "Rellstab, Heinrich Friedrich Ludwig," *NDB* 21 (2003): 407–408.

95 "Vorwort," in Wilhelm von Kügelgen, *Jugenderinnerungen eines alten Mannes, 1802–1820* (Munich, 1911).

96 On Kügelgen, see Adalbert Elschenbroich, "Kügelgen, Wilhelm," *NDB* 13 (1982): 185–186.

97 On Körner, see Fritz Jonas, "Christian Gottfried Körner," *ADB* 16 (1882): 708–712.

war on family life and their friends. A reviewer in the *Blätter für literarische Unterhaltung* accordingly noted in 1870:

Kügelgen [...] recounts the course of his youthful years with such grace and fine self-observation that a breath of 'Poetry and Truth' surrounds the reading of these notes. To be sure, the turbulent first two decades of the century, with their great political upheavals, are but a faint and distant rustling in the pages upon which a highly gifted man has recorded the history of his youth: it is mainly the family's quiet haven in which all events occur, and it is only as through a veil that the mighty major and state actions of the Napoleonic era pass by. But we are compensated by a thousand insights into the everyday life of the Kügelgen family.[98]

In an interesting way, Kügelgen at once recalled the period of the Anti-Napoleonic Wars and contributed to the process of forgetting. The wars themselves merely serve as the historical backdrop to a narrative in which the family takes center stage. But it is precisely this shift of focus onto family and friends that made the text attractive for a female audience, which was rarely catered to in military and political memoirs. His mild-mannered political approach also seems to have been greatly appreciated by female readers in particular. Kügelgen presents a moderate national-liberal and monarchist interpretation of the years 1806 to 1813, which seems to have corresponded to the mood of female middle-class readers in Wilhelmine Germany.[99] Rejecting Germanomania and Francophobia, he seeks to mediate in the "war of viewpoints and opinions," which he deemed to be dangerous to the "life of state and church."[100]

Female Autobiographies

Apart from Kügelgen's *Memoirs of Youth*, it was probably mainly the few published autobiographies by women that dealt more intensively with the period of the Napoleonic Wars which spoke to female readers. However, of the six texts that appeared in first editions before 1875, only two seem to have attracted any attention on the national literary market: the memoirs of the well-known writers Caroline von Pichler and Helmina von Chézy.[101] *Memorabilities of My Life*, by Pichler, who was born in 1769 and made a name for herself as the author of novels, short stories, plays and poetry,

[98] "Jugenderinnerungen," *BLU*, no. 4, 20 Jan. 1870, 53–54; and "Jugenderinnerungen," *Wissenschaftliche Beilage der Leipziger Zeitung*, no. 33, 23 April 1874, 208.
[99] Kügelgen, *Jugenderinnerungen*, 129–132.
[100] Ibid., 206. In keeping with this, he, as a Saxon, offers a balanced, impartial assessment of the partition of the Saxon kingdom in 1815 and the role of Prussia, which had acquired the northern regions of Saxony; see ibid., 217–220.
[101] On Pichler's *Denkwürdigkeiten*, see Wolf, *Denkwürdigkeiten*; on Pichler, see Stefan Jordan, "Pichler, Caroline, geboren von Greiner," *NDB* 20 (2001): 411–412; see also Chézy, *Unvergessenes*.

caused a stir not only because they had been written by an "honorable, decent woman," and "gifted and noble authoress," but also because she was Austrian. For, as the Austrian magazine *Österreichische Blätter für Literatur und Kunst* remarked, "Memoirs from Austria are as rare as white ravens."[102] In 1796 Pichler had married the wealthy Viennese court official Andreas Pichler, who supported her literary ambitions. The happy couple, who had one daughter, liked to entertain and their salon became a center of the literary and artistic world in Vienna that was known well beyond the city. Guests included Ludwig van Beethoven, Franz Grillparzer, Theodor Körner, Friedrich Schlegel and Franz Schubert, among others.[103]

Pichler's substantial four-volume *Memorabilities* were published one year after her death by a friend, the court librarian Ferdinand Wolf. They clearly followed the literary model of a *bildungsroman*. "The actual purpose" of this work, she wrote in the introduction, was to show "how I became what I was, through which influences, environment, instruction, errors and obstacles my mind and temperament took the direction that is now peculiar to them."[104] Thus nobody should expect to read about "noteworthy events, strange fates or outstanding points in the general history of the fatherland." In fact, her *Memorabilities* treat her family and friends as well as her own literary career at great length, all the while sketching a vivid picture of social and cultural life in Vienna. She shows, among other things, how Austrian patriotism and a marked distaste for Napoleon during the war years 1809 and 1813–15 were expressed in the art and literature of the time. In general, however, Pichler treats the politics and wars of the Napoleonic era in her autobiography mainly as a historical setting for the development of her own life and work.[105]

Reviewers responded quite differently to Pichler's *Memorabilities*. The *Österreichische Blätter für Literatur und Kunst* praised them as a "dignified and chaste" recollection of "Austria's heroic age,"[106] while *Die Grenzboten* described them as "honorable" and "well-meaning" but mediocre. Pichler, the reviewer wrote, was a "zealous Austrian and loyal subject," who in her memoirs remained true to the "sphere of her sex and rank," judging "the world of the state and the highest echelons of society only to the extent" that they impinged upon or reflected "this sphere," which made for uninspired reading. Between the lines one can already read the misogynist attitude of the editors of *Die Grenzboten* toward female writers, which they shared

---

[102] "Notizen," *Die Grenzboten* 3.1 (1844): 665–670.
[103] On Grillparzer, see Gerhart Baumann, "Grillparzer, Franz Seraphicus," *NDB* 7 (1966): 69–75.
[104] Wolf, *Denkwürdigkeiten*, 1:4.
[105] Ibid., 1:380–433; 2:1–87.
[106] "Memorien-Literatur," *Österreichische Blätter für Literatur und Kunst* 54 (5 May 1846): 417–420.

with other literary critics. The reviewer believed that women should not write memoirs, because they had nothing interesting to say.[107]

This attitude was expressed even more clearly in the reviews of Helmina von Chézy's two-volume memoirs, which were published by Brockhaus in Leipzig under the title *Unforgotten: Memorabilities from a Life* in 1858, two years after the author's death. They met with a chilly reception among male reviewers. Chézy, born in 1783, offered a much larger target for attack than Caroline von Pichler because of her extremely unusual way of life, which overstepped the "spheres of her sex." Chézy had made her authorial debut in 1797, when she was just 14 years old. Her first marriage in 1799 ended in divorce a year later. In 1800 Chézy traveled on her own to Paris, where she worked as a correspondent for several German newspapers and for a time also published her own magazine. There she married the Orientalist Antoine-Léonard de Chézy in 1805, and the couple had two sons. After five years she was divorced again and returned with her children to Germany, where she lived in Darmstadt, Cologne, Dresden and Munich, among other places, before settling in Geneva, Switzerland.[108] She tried to support herself and her sons by writing – a very difficult undertaking. Her experiences as a writer and the resistance she encountered were accordingly a central theme in her memoirs.[109]

The other central theme of her *Memorabilities* was her patriotic activities in the years 1812–17. She describes in detail supporting the struggle for liberation from "the Napoleonic yoke" in word and deed, emphasizing at the same time that she had always rejected the excessive hatred of the French that had led to cruel conduct during the wars, such as the inhumane treatment of prisoners of war and the sick and wounded soldiers of the Grande Armée.[110] She had become engaged in military nursing to help these and other soldiers. In the years 1814–16 she was involved, among other things, in the local women's associations that were active in the military hospitals of Cologne and Naumur.[111] The care provided to sick and wounded soldiers, above all militiamen and volunteers, that Chézy experienced there was so inadequate that in 1816 she publicly criticized the desolate conditions and the corruption that were rife in the Prussian-managed military hospitals. As a result she was charged with slandering the Commission for the Assessment of War Wounded (*Invaliden-Prüfungs-Kommission*), but was acquitted by a Berlin court in 1817. This conflict, which was broadly discussed in the contemporary press, assumes a central place in the *Memorabilities*.

---

[107] "Notizen. Denkwürdigkeiten aus meinem Leben," *Die Grenzboten* 3:1 (1844): 665–667.
[108] On Chézy, see Hyacinth Holland, "Chézy, Wilhelmine von," *ADB* 4 (1876): 119–122.
[109] Chézy, *Unvergessenes*, 1:261, 332, 372–373; and 2:12.
[110] Ibid., 2:69–77 and 82–84.
[111] Ibid., 2:107–132.

Chézy sought in her recollections to defend herself against all of the accusations made against her,[112] above all the allegation that "the way she had treated the matter of the military hospital had been unwomanly," and that she had set out to attract public attention. She parried this criticism with the assertion that it had been necessary, since, apart from one doctor she knew, "no man had stepped forward" to "uncover abuses with strength and courage and bring the truth before the public forum."[113] At the same time, she sought in her *Memorabilities* to commemorate the achievements of the many women who, like her, had tended to the wounded, sick and disabled soldiers of the wars of 1813–15 as members of the patriotic women's associations, making many sacrifices in the process. She also emphasized that other patriotically minded women, too, had come into conflict with military doctors and inspectors, since the poor treatment of ailing soldiers, militiamen and volunteers and the deficient assistance for disabled veterans revealed the low value placed on them by the state and the military administration. This was not merely a question of "justice and humanitarianism," but also of politics, for "how can we expect a warrior to go into battle willingly and joyfully if he must fear that he will emerge as a cripple and invalid from the military hospitals" because proper care was not available.[114]

Chézy's unusual way of life and her willingness to overstep society's gender boundaries in her words and actions attracted the contempt not only of many male contemporaries, but even years later of most literary critics as well. They simply panned the *Memorabilities*, which Chézy had dictated toward the end of her life to her great-niece Berta Borngräber, who also published them. For example, the author of an 1859 review in *Die Grenzboten* entitled "Female Writers," asked:

And what might be the reason for the prejudice against women writers? – [...] First of all, there is something unwholesome and disorderly about 'the specific literary life'; a focus on the personal in the individual and a confusion of this with the objects that man, accustomed to and created for all manner of struggle, can more readily cope with than woman, who often overcomes these difficulties only at the expense of her womanly nature. – And then woman lacks that observation of reality (let us call it historical) that is available only to those who participate in it actively: She is dependent upon either opening her own heart, or copying her wholly external observations.[115]

Karl Gutzkow was not much kinder to her in his review entitled "Conversations at the Domestic Hearth" published in 1858 in the magazine *Unterhaltungen am häuslichen Herd*.[116] For these authors, women existed

---

[112] Ibid., 2:132–180.
[113] Ibid., 2:141.
[114] Ibid., 2:178–180.
[115] "Schriftstellerinnen," *Die Grenzboten* 18.1 (Leipzig, 1850): 161–181, 174–175.
[116] "Helmina von Chézy," *Unterhaltungen am häuslichen Herd*, NF, 4.22 (1858): 350–352.

outside of history, which they equated with war and politics. If women wrote about such subjects, as Chézy did, they could only do so by appropriating male experience, that is, copying or "daguerrotyping" them. Women's memoirs thus could never be substantive or "true." Women were simply denied the competence to judge the events of their times.[117] Most male historians, literary critics and publishers seem to have shared this attitude, which meant that the published autobiographical memory of the time of the Napoleonic Wars in Germany and Austria up to 1914 was dominated by men.[118]

[117] "Schriftstellerinnen," 175.
[118] See also "Deutsche Memoiren-Literatur," *Wissenschaftliche Beilage der Leipziger Zeitung,* no. 50, 23 June 1859, 218–220.

Conclusion

A closer analysis of the development of the literary market, the popular, military and academic historiography on the period of the Napoleonic Wars and the publication of autobiographies and war memoirs treating this era up to the First World War reveals remarkably clear trends in the production of memories of the Anti-Napoleonic Wars. It shows the increasing influence of the expanding literary market and with it the creation of a culture-consuming national public. It points to the growing authority of the master narratives produced by a professionalizing academic historiography, but also demonstrates that these master narratives were always challenged by the counter-narratives of academic, military and popular historians – even though the multiplicity of interpretations accepted in academia declined and a pro-Prussian, monarchic-conservative or national-liberal interpretation of the period of the Anti-Napoleonic Wars gained ascendancy in Imperial German historiography. Furthermore, this analysis demonstrates that throughout the nineteenth century, the master narratives of historians competed with the far more diverse recollections of the era in published autobiographies and war memoirs. These memory texts reveal the broadest diversity of interpretations, because the majority of them were not written by Prussian supporters of the struggle against Napoleon, but by soldiers, officers and generals who had fought in the Napoleonic army up to 1813.

For both historiography and autobiographical accounts, the importance of the twenty-fifth, fiftieth and one-hundredth anniversaries of the wars as occasions for writing and publishing is striking. Political events such as the Rhine crisis, the failure of the Revolution of 1848–49, the Wars of German Unification and the founding of the German Empire clearly left their mark on the narratives and their reception. While the commercialization of the literary market and the growing readership had more influence on the production of autobiographical memory, both contributed especially to the boom in edited reprints of autobiographical accounts of the Anti-Napoleonic Wars occasioned by the hundredth anniversary.

Before the establishment of the German Empire, Prussian texts of a national-liberal or monarchic-conservative stamp clearly did not dominate memory construction. This applies for both historiography and autobiographical texts. What is particularly striking for this period is, rather, the strong presence of texts from the states of the Confederation of the Rhine, which seek to inscribe the sacrifices and achievements of their army, their regiments or their region on the regional and national memory. Up to 1914, the autobiographical accounts were, moreover, undoubtedly shaped by authors who had fought in the Napoleonic Wars as professional military men – generals, officers and noncommissioned officers – as well as volunteers. They focus on wartime adventures in foreign lands; soldierly bravery and sacrifice; military, territorial-state and national honor; and heroism. It is mainly the memory texts by volunteers and well-known German-national patriots like Arndt that refer to the political dimension of the "struggle for liberty" in 1813–15 and call on rulers and governments to make good the political promises they had given during the "Wars of Liberty." These texts were politically significant above all before the founding of the German Empire – and they competed from the beginning with academic and popular history books. In Wilhelmine Germany, autobiographies such as Arndt's were still reprinted and quite successful. But memoirs like Kügelgen's, which told of the time of the Napoleonic Wars in the form of a gripping family saga, or abridged editions of memoirs for "youth and the people" that dramatically rewrote older texts according to the dominant master narratives were more likely to capture the imagination of the reading public. With the development of a culture-consuming national public, autobiographical accounts, as long as they were written in a pleasing style and confirmed their beliefs, were able to reach the broader strata of middle-class readers eager for "patriotic" entertainment. Historical novels also appealed to the new taste, and they would become *the* central popular vehicle of memory of the "time of the French."

PART FIVE

NOVELS, MEMORY AND POLITICS

In the decades following the Napoleonic Wars, history books, autobiographical accounts and novels evolved into three at once complementary and competing media in the production of memory about these wars, which would shape collective memory for a long time to come. They all reflected the "emergence of history" – the formation of a new postrevolutionary and postwar historical consciousness that began to develop in the first half of the nineteenth century.[1] The conditions in which they arose were influenced by a mixture of differing and shared factors. Changing political circumstances affected all the media of memory. The creation of all three types of texts was also subject to the structural transformation of the literary market. However, this applied less to history books, which tended to serve a relatively small and specialized market segment, than to autobiographies and war memoirs and especially to novels intended for a wide audience. While historians were increasingly expected to meet the expectations of a professionalizing discipline, which narrowed the accepted forms of historical writing, and memoirists who hoped for success could only operate within a framework constructed as "true" by historians and eyewitnesses, novelists had greater latitude. Their interpretation of the period of the wars from 1806 to 1815 simply had to strike the reader as credible and plausible. In order to create this impression, novelists had to acknowledge the historical master narratives and the basic, accepted historical facts, but in general they could interpret the era more freely, a possibility that increased with the temporal distance to the remembered events. Even more than history books and autobiographical recollections, novels could therefore be used to comment on present-day society, culture and politics. In writing about the past, novelists remarked upon and criticized or affirmed the society and politics of their own day. These authors were driven by their political ideals, but many others primarily tried to serve the market by choosing topics that would

[1] For more, see chapter 14 in the fourth part.

sell. Most novelists wrote to earn a living. Those who were freelance writers depended far more than most authors of history books and autobiographies on the market, because for many of the latter writing was not their main source of income.

Hundreds of novels set in the Napoleonic era were published between 1815 and 1914, initially as novels of the recent past, which appeared in the first two decades after the war and confronted well-remembered events, and thereafter as historical novels.[2] Most of these texts are forgotten today, since only the works of a few authors have entered the literary canon and remain familiar. They include Theodor Fontane with his four-volume *Before the Storm: A Novel of the Winter of 1812/13*, published in 1878 by Hertz in Berlin, and his novella *Schach von Wuthenow: A Tale from the Era of the Gensdarmes Regiment*, published in 1883 by Friedrich in Leipzig. Fontane has been the subject of numerous studies by literary scholars over the past decades.[3] His predecessors, however – novelists such as Caroline de la Motte Fouqué,[4] Caroline Pichler,[5] Ludwig Rellstab[6] or Willibald Alexis[7] – have been forgotten. Even far more successful contemporaries – such as

---

[2] The transitions between the two genres are fluid, and they will be examined together here. On the novel of the recent past in the late eighteenth and nineteenth century, see Göttsche, *Zeit*, esp. 65–433; on the historical novel, see Aust, *Roman*; Eggert, *Studien*; and Eke and Olasz-Eke, *Bibliographie*.

[3] Theodor Fontane, *Vor dem Sturm: Roman aus dem Winter 1812 auf 13* (Berlin, 1878), Engl.: *Before the Storm: A Novel of the Winter of 1812–13*, trans. R. J. Hollingdale (Oxford, 1985); and idem, *Schach von Wuthenow: Erzählung aus der Zeit des Regiments Gensdarmes* (Berlin, 1883), Engl.: *A Man of Honor*, trans. E. M. Valk (New York, 1975). On his oeuvre and the research on Fontane, see Wolfgang Rasch, *Theodor Fontane Bibliographie: Werk und Forschung*, 3 vols. (Berlin, 2006); on Fontane, see Kurt Schreinert, "Fontane, Henri Théodore," *NDB* 5 (1961): 289–293; and more extensively, Wolfgang Hädecke, *Theodor Fontane: Biographie* (Munich, 1998); and Helga Bemmann, *Theodor Fontane: Ein preussischer Dichter* (Berlin, 1998).

[4] Caroline de La Motte Fouqué, *Edmund's Wege und Irrwege: Ein Roman aus der Vergangenheit* (Berlin, 1815). On Fouqué and this novel, see Baumgartner, *Public Voices*, 144–251; and Elisa Müller-Adams, *"Dass die Frau zur Frau redete": Das Werk der Caroline de la Motte Fouqué als Beispiel für weibliche Literaturproduktion der frühen Restaurationszeit* (St. Ingbert, 2003), 307–333.

[5] Caroline Pichler, *Frauenwürde* (Leipzig, 1818).

[6] Ludwig Rellstab, *1812: Ein historischer Roman*, 4 vols. (Leipzig, 1834).

[7] Willibald Alexis, *Ruhe ist die erste Bürgerpflicht oder Vor 50 Jahren: Vaterländischer Roman*, 5 vols. (Berlin, 1852); and idem, *Isegrimm: Vaterländischer Roman*, 3 vols. (Berlin, 1854); on Alexis and his novels, see Wolfgang Beutin, *Königtum und Adel in den historischen Romanen von Willibald Alexis* (Berlin, 1966); idem, "Melpomenes Dolch und Klios noch schärferer Griffel: Die Brandenburg-preußischen ('vaterländischen') Romane von Willibald Alexis," in *Willibald Alexis (1798–1871): Ein Autor des Vor- und Nachmärz*, ed. Wolfgang Beutin and Peter Stein (Bielefeld, 2000), 177–194; and Caroline Hobi, *Willibald Alexis – 'Ruhe ist die erste Bürgerpflicht': Eine erzähltheoretische Analyse und Interpretation* (Bern, 2007).

Gustav Freytag[8], Friedrich Spielhagen[9] or Herman Sudermann[10] – were long ignored by the mainstream of literary history after 1945. Clara Mundt, who published under the pseudonym Louise Mühlbach and was the most widely read German author of historical novels in the second half of the nineteenth century, has also fallen into obscurity.[11] Her works were huge hits at the lending libraries, far ahead of all the other authors mentioned above.[12] Only in recent decades have Germanists rediscovered her texts, along with those of other authors of this middlebrow literature.[13]

In this fifth part I take a closer look at novels that treated the period of the Napoleonic Wars and were published between 1815 and 1914. In the first chapter of this part, the novel of the recent past and the historical novel are introduced as central media of memory. I begin by sketching the debate on the form and function of the historical novel, then I examine the corpus of texts, specific memory booms, the factors that influenced them, and the social profiles of the authors. In the second and third chapters of this part, I locate especially influential texts that appeared between 1815 and 1914 and shaped collective memory within the boom periods and analyze them with particular attention to their central memory narratives and reception. Like the autobiographies, the main selection criteria for these texts were the total number of editions they reached and their estimated circulation,

[8] Gustav Freytag, *Die Ahnen*, 6 vols. (Leipzig, 1873–81), vol. 6: *Aus einer kleinen Stadt* (1880); on Freytag, see Fritz Martini, "Freytag, Gustav," *NDB* 5 (1961): 425–427; on his novels, Claus Holz, *Flucht aus der Wirklichkeit: "Die Ahnen" von Gustav Freytag – Untersuchungen zum realistischen historischen Roman der Gründerzeit 1872–1880* (Frankfurt/M., 1983); Lynne Tatlock, "'In the Heart of the Heart of the Country': Regional Histories as National History in Gustav Freytag's *Die Ahnen* (1872–80)," in *A Companion to German Realism, 1848–1900*, ed. Todd Kontje (Rochester, NY, 2002), 85–109; and Larry L. Ping, *Gustav Freytag and the Prussian Gospel: Novels, Liberalism and History* (Oxford, 2006).

[9] Friedrich Spielhagen, *Noblesse oblige* (Leipzig, 1882). On Spielhagen and his novels, see Jeffrey L. Sammons, "Spielhagen, Friedrich," *NDB* 24 (2010): 686–688; idem, *Friedrich Spielhagen: Novelist of Germany's False Dawn* (Tübingen, 2004); idem, "Fighting Napoleon – Loving the French: Friedrich Spielhagen, *Noblesse oblige* (1888)," in Maierhofer, *Women*, 247–264; Christa Müller-Donges, *Das Novellenwerk Friedrich Spielhagens in seiner Entwicklung zwischen 1851 und 1899* (Marburg, 1970); and Henrike Lamers, *Held oder Welt?: Zum Romanwerk Friedrich Spielhagens* (Bonn, 1991).

[10] Hermann Sudermann, *Der Katzensteg* (Stuttgart, 1889); on Sudermann, see Jessica Stegemann, "Sudermann, Hermann," *NDB* 25 (2013): 669–670; and Günter Heintz, "Kompromiß und Wirkung: Kritische Anmerkungen zu Hermann Studermanns Der Katzensteg," in *Hermann Sudermann: Werk und Wirkung*, ed. Walter T. Rix (Würzburg, 1980), 201–214.

[11] Louise Mühlbach, *Napoleon in Deutschland*, 16 vols. (Berlin, 1858); on Mühlbach and her novels, see Lydia Schieth, "Mühlbach, Louise," *NDB* 18 (1997): 269–270; Cornelia Tönnesen, *Die Vormärz-Autorin Luise Mühlbach: Vom sozialkritischen Frühwerk zum historischen Roman* (Neuss, 1997); Peterson, *History*, 166–181; and idem, "Mühlbach, Ranke, and the Truth of Historical Fiction," in Kontje, *Companion*, 53–84.

[12] Martino, *Leihbibliothek*, 406–416.

[13] Peterson, *History*; and Lynne Tatlock, ed., *Publishing Culture and the "Reading Nation": German Book History in the Long Nineteenth Century* (Rochester, NY, 2010).

the number of reviews and their presence in lending libraries up to 1914, because these are all indicators of their success and with it their influence on collective memory construction. The focus lies on novels published up to the late 1880s, since not only did the production of historical novels on the era of the Napoleonic Wars decline sharply after the founding of the German Empire, but the competition between differing political interpretations of the period also largely ceased. Novels increasingly came to reflect a national-conservative reading of the period. Democratic and liberal authors appear to have stopped writing about the epoch. In the years that followed, the interpretation of the era was reshaped more and more by the myth of the wars of 1813–15 as the German nation's natal hour, in which the German people rediscovered their own power and strength.

15

Re-Creating the Past: The Time of the Anti-Napoleonic Wars in Novels

The question, occasionally raised, of whether the historical novel is entitled to a place in the literary realm is essentially pointless. There can scarcely be any doubt that it belongs to a lower art form than those branches of literature that allow for and promote free creativity, any more than that it is always an awkward undertaking to introduce imagination into accounts that properly belong to scholarship. On the other hand, however, one cannot deny that historiography is not wholly adequate to the task of keeping hold of a great past.[1]

This assertion opens an article entitled "Patriotic Novels" that appeared in the most important national-liberal cultural journal, *Die Grenzboten*, in 1852, penned by one of its two editors, presumably Julius Schmidt. The essay intensively elucidates the function of the historical novel and its relationship to historiography on the one hand and prose literature on the other. The author – who interestingly enough equates the historical novel with the "patriotic novel," that is, assumes that it mainly treats the writer's own national history – recognizes the importance of the genre but regards it as a "lower art form." For him, the historical novel's main task was "to recreate for us, based on earlier research, the manners of the past era in all respects." Only such an approach, he believed, could produce works "that arouse in the imagination and sentiments anything approaching the impression engendered by free creation."[2] The author of this contribution was clearly convinced that the chief object of novels was to address the imagination and emotions.

Not just *Die Grenzboten*, but also other cultural and literary magazines intensely discussed the form and function of the historical novel that became popular in the 1820s. From that time, novelists and literary critics negotiated the new genre's position in the literary world.[3] Today, Benedikte Naubert is

---

[1] "Der vaterländische Roman," *GB* 11.3 (1852): 481–489, 481.
[2] Ibid.
[3] On the discussion, see Meyer, "Die Entstehung," 95–188; and Eggert, *Studien*, 53–88 and 148–194.

considered the founder of the historical novel that emerged in German in the late eighteenth century. Up to her death in 1819, she published more than 50 such works, most of them anonymously, many of which were translated into English and French. Her books influenced the Scottish author Sir Walter Scott, whose *Waverley* (1814) and subsequent novels made the genre so popular across Europe that it experienced its first literary heyday in the 1820s and 1830s.[4]

The literary debate on the form and function of the historical novel was also fed by criticism from historians. The professionalization of history was an essential precondition for the growing flood of historical novels over the century, since historians provided their authors with the information they needed. The public expected historical fiction to be "authentic" and to reflect historical events accurately, which is why knowledge of history was indispensable for novelists.[5] At the same time, the professionalization of history, especially the triumph of historicism, meant that academic history sought to distance itself systematically from fictional historical narratives in novels by questioning their veracity.[6] It was on this difficult terrain that the authors of novels of the recent past and historical fiction set during the time of the Napoleonic Wars had to operate and decide what objectives they were pursuing in their writing. I will explore this terrain through the example of one of the most successful authors, Louise Mühlbach, before examining the novel as a medium of memory in more detail.

HISTORICAL NOVELS, HISTORY AND LITERATURE

In the preface to her 17-volume novel cycle *Germany in Storm and Stress*, published by Constenoble in Jena in 1867–68, Louise Mühlbach explains the function of the historical novel in detail to her readers. Its chief aim, she notes, is

> to illustrate history, to render it popular; to move the great figures, like the great facts, that reveal themselves in history books to the scholar, the individual of higher learning, from the silence of the study to the marketplace of life, and to make what had previously been the province of the learned the common property of all.[7]

That, at least, was her understanding of the profession of the historical novelist, which she had chosen "not with frivolity and vain arrogance," but

---

[4] Meyer, "Die Entstehung," 46–94; Eggert, *Studien*, 25–28; Aust, *Roman*, 52–85; Eke and Olasz-Eke, *Bibliographie*, 9–50; and Habitzel and Mühlberger, "Gewinner."

[5] Petersen, *History*, 29–32.

[6] Meyer, "Die Entstehung," 35–45; and Peterson, "Mühlbach," esp. 62–80; see also chapter 13 in the fourth part.

[7] Louise Mühlbach, *Deutschland in Sturm und Drang: Historischer Roman. Erste Abtheilung: Der alte Fritz und die neue Zeit*, 4 vols. (Jena, 1867), v–xv, viii.

"suffused with the grandeur" of this task.[8] This mission led to the production of some 290 volumes, including edited reprints and various translations, which made her one of the most widely read nineteenth-century German authors of historical novels. Louise Mühlbach, born Clara Müller in 1814, grew up in the small Prussian town of Neubrandenburg. Her father, a lawyer, was able and willing to give his daughter a very good private education. In 1839 she married the Young German writer Theodor Mundt, who supported her literary ambitions. The couple had two children and ran a hospitable house in Berlin. Their salon welcomed the literary elite of the city and many of its visitors. Both were active supporters of the Democratic Revolution of 1848–49.[9]

Beginning in the late 1830s, Louise Mühlbach published novellas, novels and travel accounts. Only death in 1873 brought an end to her creative output. In the run-up to the Revolution of 1848–49, she mainly concentrated on social novels centered around female protagonists fighting for their own identities as women and for their independence. Taking up the emancipatory ideas of the Young Germany movement, she confronted the present in a critical spirit. These novels were not very successful, however.[10] Only after 1850, when she began to concentrate on novels about eighteenth- and nineteenth-century German and European history, did her work meet with broad interest.[11] Her historical fiction focuses on the lives and times of outstanding personalities like Prussian Kings Friedrich II and Friedrich-Wilhelm III, Queen Luise of Prussia, Austrian Emperor Joseph II and Field Marshal Archduke Johann, Napoleon Bonaparte and his first wife Joséphine de Beauharnais as well as his second wife Marie-Louise of Austria, or Hortense de Beauharnais, stepdaughter of Napoleon I and briefly queen of Holland. Louise Mühlbach continued to be strongly interested in female characters, and for that reason was especially attracted to exploring well-known women in history and their spheres of action. Quite realistically, she did not seriously challenge the boundaries of the dominant model of the middle-class gender order that assigned men and women complementary roles in "the public" and "the private sphere" based on their assumed "natural differences" – at least not for the ordinary female characters in her novels. Her leading heroines, however, like Queen Luise of Prussia or Joséphine de Beauharnais, had far more room to maneuver. As queens, empresses and princesses they had leeway to transgress the norms of this model. At the same time, Mühlbach showed that as women, they were nevertheless

---

[8] Ibid., vii.

[9] Tönnesen, *Vormärz-Autorin*, 2; and Schieth, "Mühlbach, Louise"; on her reception in the United States, see Lieselotte E. Kurth-Voigt and William H. McClain, "Louise Mühlbach's Historical Novels: The American Reception," *IASL* 6.1 (1981): 52–77.

[10] Tönnesen, *Vormärz-Autorin*, 113–189.

[11] Förster, *Königin Luise-Mythos*, 62–67.

bound by these norms, although not to the same extent as the majority of middle- and upper-class women.[12]

As Mühlbach never tired of reminding readers, her historical fiction was always based on intensive study of a wide range of sources, from historical accounts and biographies to published letters and diaries. She therefore regarded the rejection of her work by "learned historians" and "men of science" as a challenge and set out to defend the genre of historical fiction and with it her reputation as a writer in the extensive preface already cited at the beginning of this section. In this text, she criticizes the "scholars" for simply condemning the historical novel and the facts "marshaled therein as incorrect or unhistorical" without considering its most important prerequisite and main function.[13] While any serious historical novel must be based on a "thorough study of history," it nevertheless differs fundamentally from historiography:

The rigorous historian deals only in facts; following the strictest outward truth, he may write down and record only those matters that occurred outwardly. He depicts the battles of peoples, the struggles of nations, the great deeds of heroes, the deeds of princes, he presents *accomplished facts*. To plumb the innermost essence of these accomplished facts, to discover the motives from which they sprang, and to bring these to light in their fine inner workings, that is the task of the historical novel. – The scholar shows the outer face, the mighty shape of history; the historical novel should show you the *heart* of history, and render humanly precious matters that seemed very distant.[14] (Emphases in the original.)

Thus, for her, historical fiction does not compete with historiography, but rather complements it in two ways. Based on a solid grounding in history and the imagination of the author, the historical novel could, on the one hand, delineate the variety of motives of historical figures that stood at the "heart" of their actions. It could, for instance, show and explain exemplary forms of male and female patriotism and self-sacrifice in the past with the aim of inspiring present and future generations to act accordingly. On the other hand, the historical novel, much like a history painting, could attempt to illuminate the emotional "mainsprings" and the specific "spirit" of history and in this way help to bring history to life.[15] Both functions were closely connected for Mühlbach, who clearly understood the power of emotion in history and in learning from history. At the same time, her definition of the functions of the historical novel ingeniously deploys the dominant notions of the gender order to assert her place as an author of historical novels. These notions banished women from politics, war and the writing of history, denying them rationality but attributing to them all the more emotion. This

[12] Eggert, *Studien*, 69–78; and Peterson, *History*, 166–181.
[13] Mühlbach, *Deutschland*, 1:v.
[14] Ibid., ix.
[15] Ibid., xi.

predestined women to be experts in the "inner workings" and the "heart of history," and thus also made them best placed to write historical fiction that centered on these subjects.

With her historical biographical novels – which focus more on the individual and his or her role in the community, include the private sphere and report on the emotional lives of her protagonists – Mühlbach hoped to reach population groups not addressed by other historical media. By "privatizing"[16] and emotionalizing history and memory, she must also have appealed strongly to female readers, which was important for commercial success because women of the middle and upper classes, and in the second half of the nineteenth century increasingly of the lower-middle class as well, were the main readers of novels. In a sense, the historical novels in lending libraries were history books for women.[17]

Neither for Mühlbach nor for many other authors was the attempt to popularize history through the historical novel an end in itself. Quite a few of them also saw their novels as commentaries on the present, which served the purposes of moral and political education and the formation of cultural identity. Thus, after the failed Revolution of 1848–49, it was a central political objective for those writers who increasingly published historical novels in the *Nachmärz* period to keep alive the national-liberal ideas of the "Wars of Liberty" and the *Vormärz*.[18] Louise Mühlbach accordingly told her old friend Prince Hermann von Pückler-Muskau in a letter of 1864 that

I have set myself the same aim in all of my historical works: to awaken among the German people a knowledge of German history and a patriotic consciousness, to make them feel passionately about German honor and to acquaint them with their heroes.[19]

The motivations of other historical novelists in the 1850s and 1860s were similar, even if they may have looked down on the "prolific scribbler" Mühlbach, who avowedly wrote for an audience of literary consumers rather than literary critics. Many of them probably hoped that they and their works would enter the national canon of high culture and thus cultural memory, but in fact they, too, like Mühlbach, wrote middlebrow literature, whose readership Brent O. Peterson describes as follows:

Their primary readers were neither the critics and professors who shaped the canon nor the unwashed masses who preferred what the British call 'penny dreadfuls.' Rather the audience for middlebrow literature ranged from university graduates, down through the ranks of the army, the bureaucracy, and the professional classes, and on to families of craftsmen and merchants. These books' readership ended in

[16] Eggert, *Studien*, 72.
[17] Ibid., 37.
[18] Tönnesen, *Vormärz-Autorin*, 210–214.
[19] Ibid., 212.

libraries for the working classes, where Social Democratic Party activists pushed the same notion of *Bildung* (education *and* culture) that united the middle and upper reaches of society.[20]

The readers of middlebrow literature, both male and female, indeed expected both edification and entertainment from their reading matter. Books should address not just the mind, but also the heart.

A significant portion of the historical novels that appeared between 1815 and 1914, and not just those by Mühlbach, may be considered middlebrow literature. A remarkable percentage of them, as we will see, treated the period of the Anti-Napoleonic Wars.[21] Since these novels reached a readership of literary consumers to a greater extent than even popular history books or autobiographies and war memoirs, they contributed decisively to popularizing the collective memories of these wars. Along with songs and poetry, they addressed the emotions more strongly than other literary media of memory, which contributed greatly to their wide dissemination, since in order to take root in the long term, memories must not only be thought but above all felt and emotionally relived.[22]

NOVELS OF THE RECENT PAST AND HISTORICAL NOVELS AS MEDIA OF MEMORY

The historical novel, which nineteenth-century historians and literary critics alike often viewed skeptically, questioning its artistic value, was a favorite genre among readers up to the First World War and beyond.[23] Publishing figures and lending library records as well as the reactions of literary critics confirm this. In their extensive Innsbruck research project on historical fiction, Kurt Habitzel and Günter Mühlberger located 3,341 German-language historical novels alone for the century between 1815 and 1914, about 412 (12 percent) of which treat the period of the Napoleonic Wars.[24] Their broad definition of "historical novels" encompasses "works of prose fiction of at least 150 pages, set for the most part in a time before the author's birth."[25] The present study also includes novels of the recent past (*Zeitromane*), which reflect contemporary history. This is necessary if we wish to understand the novelistic creation of memories of the Napoleonic past, which, much like historiography and memoir production, began immediately after the wars

[20] Peterson, *History*, 23.

[21] See Eggert, *Studien*, 90–91.

[22] See Confino, "Collective Memory," 1390; and Bob Uttl et al., eds., *Memory and Emotion: Interdisciplinary Perspectives* (Oxford, 2006), esp. 1–12.

[23] Eggert, *Studien*, 7.

[24] See http://www.uibk.ac.at/germanistik/histrom/. In all this database contains about 6,300 entries for the period 1780–1945, of which approximately 570 treat the period of the Napoleonic Wars.

[25] Mühlberger and Habitzel, "German Historical Novel," 5–6.

of 1813–15.[26] In the framework of this study, 195 novels on the Napoleonic era written between 1815 and 1914 were analyzed more closely.[27]

Booms in the publication of historical novels do not coincide with that of autobiographies and war memoirs. Of the 195 novels, a substantial 11 percent had already appeared between 1815 and 1829. Seventeen percent were published between 1830 and 1849, 43 percent between 1850 and 1869, 12 percent between 1870 and 1889 and 19 percent after 1890, 6 percent of them between 1910 and 1914 alone. In the case of historical novels, too, these figures suggest the significance of the three major anniversaries of the wars of 1813–15 for production and publication. A total of 47 percent of all texts appeared in the jubilee years, but the proportion was significantly lower than that of autobiographies and war memoirs, which amounted to 54 percent. For historical novels, the clear temporal focus was the fiftieth anniversary, while for autobiographical texts it was the centenary: only 5 percent of the novels examined appeared during the anniversary years 1831–40 (12, 5 of them from 1838–40), 30 percent in the anniversary years 1856–65 (59, 21 of them from 1862–64) and 11 percent in the anniversary years 1906–15 (21, 7 of them from 1911–13). The production of novels clearly depended less on the demand created by jubilees than did the publication of history books and memoirs. Their composition and publication were much more contingent on the literary market than those of history books, autobiographies and war memoirs. Because most novelists needed to sell their texts, they had to respond to the demands of their readers. As a result, literary fashion and changing political culture influenced their writing more strongly; at the same time, they could also respond more freely to both in their novels – within the limits set by censorship.

The figures only partly reflect the development of the historical novel as such, increased production of which did not begin until the mid-1820s, spurred by the enthusiastic reception of Scott's novels. This first peak continued into the mid-1830s. Production then fell precipitously in the mid-1840s, as it had for *belles lettres* more generally in the years before, during and immediately after the Revolution of 1848–49. This decline persisted until the mid-1850s. A second boom phase followed, lasting until the late 1860s. Thereafter, publication figures fell again, but remained at a much higher level. Only after 1900, above all between 1910 und 1915, did production again rise substantially.

[26] Göttsche, *Zeit*, 20–21.

[27] These 195 titles were included in the Filemaker database. In the case of multivolume editions published over a period of two years or more, I have counted only the year of the first volume's publication and only recorded the other years in the database. For all novels, I tried to gather as much information on the authors and the texts themselves as possible. I also tried to identify the number of editions and searched for contemporary reviews of the novels in journals and magazines, which are integrated into the database. I accessed 113 novels as complete PDFs and 25 as books. I used the same sources for biographical and bibliographical information as I did for the autobiographies and war memoirs. See note 10 in chapter 14.

Historical novels were particularly in demand during the two periods of political restoration: after the wars of 1813–15, but especially following the failed Revolution of 1848–49. They seem to have been an important literary site for processing experiences of war, revolution and restoration.

In the historical novel, educated citizens, both male and female, found their own history as authors and as readers. They could express the desire for their own traditional world and in imagination create the individual and collective identity they aspired to. They were aided in this by the fact that the historical novel did *not*, as a rule, treat those protagonists who were the heroes of the historiography of their day – the statesmen and generals, the men who, according to historicist scholars like Ranke and Treitschke, "make history" – but rather the "middling heroes." This latter term, coined by Georg Lukács in his pathbreaking 1955 study *The Historical Novel*, refers to the central figure of historical fiction, who bridges the gap between present and past, but also between the world of the reader and that of the novel.[28] This "merely correct and never heroic 'hero'" comes into conflict with his past or present, is driven by them and displays the same human yearnings and weaknesses, but also mindsets and virtues as the mostly middle-class readership. This "middling hero" belongs to various communities – the family, the village, the town, the region, the state or the nation – and, like many contemporaries in "the extraordinary times" of upheaval, struggles with his multiple identities. In other words, the historical novel "draws upon the life of the people, rendering visible their conditions and needs," as an 1854 review in Cotta's *Morgenblatt für gebildete Leser* put it.[29] In the historical novel, history and memory become at once a commentary on the present and a vision of the future. The author could operate simultaneously on several temporal planes – narrative time (the time of the narrator), narrated time (the period in which the action of the novel itself is set), and the fictional experience of time (the time that the reader projects onto the text) – thereby linking past, present and future and exploring alternatives for action.[30]

Fritz Martini accordingly explains the boom of historical novels in the second restoration period as follows: "Bourgeois self-awareness, which saw itself rebuffed by political life and found all the greater opportunities to evolve in the realms of culture and civilization," sought to understand itself "as the representative of a development reaching far back into the past, the bearer of its very own, historically evolved worldview."[31] Much as

---

[28] Georg Lukács, *Probleme des Realismus*, vol. 3: *Der historische Roman* (Neuwied, 1971), 40. Engl.: *The Historical Novel*, trans. Hannah and Stanley Mitchell (Harmondsworth, 1981), 33.

[29] "Neueste Romanliteratur," *Morgenblatt für gebildete Leser* 48.2 (1854): 1195–1197, 1196.

[30] Peterson, *History*, 9; and Göttsche, *Zeit*, 39.

[31] Fritz Martini, *Deutsche Literatur im Bürgerlichen Realismus, 1848–1998* (Stuttgart, 1962), 28.

in historiography and autobiography, memory of the Napoleonic War era seems to have been an important component of this retrospective search for an understanding of the course of the past, a place in history and the construction of identity, particularly before the founding of the German Empire. One indicator is the extraordinarily large proportion of texts on the Anti-Napoleonic Wars, especially during the second heyday of the historical novel. The highest figures were 17 percent in 1855, 20 percent in 1860 and 18 percent in 1865. This is consistent with Hartmut Eggert's findings. He concludes that nearly half of all historical novels published before 1875 treated the eighteenth and early nineteenth century, while thereafter authors turned more frequently to earlier historical epochs, especially antiquity, the Germanic period, the Middle Ages and the Thirty Years' War. Interest in the most recent past as a subject for historical fiction waned considerably after the founding of the German Empire, and as a result the proportion of historical novels on the Anti-Napoleonic Wars dropped dramatically as a share of overall production,[32] ranging from 6–9 percent in the 1880s and 1890s. In the context of the centenary celebrations it then rose to more than 10 percent after 1900, and even surpassed 15 percent again in 1915.

The success of historical fiction treating the era of the Napoleonic Wars, like that of novels more generally, depended on a series of factors. Apart from literary fashion and the author's talent, the publishing company was most important. Just ten publishers printed more than half of all historical novels.[33] The main places of publication for the works considered here reflect the influence of these major publishing firms that dominated the market for historical fiction between 1815 and 1914. They were Leipzig (64 titles), where Brockhaus, Kollmann and Hirzel were especially influential, Berlin (30 titles), where Janke dominated, Vienna (10 titles), where Kober & Markgraf controlled the market and Jena (5 titles) with Constenoble. Other significant places of publication were Breslau, Dresden, Hamburg and Stuttgart, where Cotta was the main figure.[34] The companies did most of their business in regions belonging to the German Customs Union founded in 1834, which Austria never joined. This was a significant obstacle to the distribution of literature by Austrian authors in the German market unless their publishers were domiciled in the territory of the Customs Union.

Historical novels published by large and prestigious companies and written by well-known authors did best on the market and thus in the lending libraries.[35] These were also the novels that received more extensive reviews in literary and cultural magazines and newspaper arts sections, which meant more attention from readers and library proprietors and increased demand

[32] Eggert, *Studien*, 90–91 and 209.
[33] Ibid., 40.
[34] On Brockhaus, see Würffel, *Lexikon*, 115–117; and on Janke, ibid., 397–398.
[35] Eggert, *Studien*, 39–42; and Habitzel and Mühlberger, "Gewinner," 110–113.

in the lending libraries.[36] For that reason, edition size, the number and length of reviews as well as library borrowing figures are good indicators of the success of a novel and thus presumably also of the influence of its memory narrative. The majority of historical novels were reviewed, if at all, in the feuilleton of the regional newspapers where they were published. Most of these reviews were no more than short announcements of the book's publication. Apart from reviews, another means of creating attention and making novels better known was to publish them in installments in newspapers. In the second half of the nineteenth century, 19 percent of all historical novels were serialized in this form before their book publication – in the heyday of historical novel production, the 1860s, the figure was even 24 percent.[37]

Despite all attempts by authors and publishers to attract attention, 90–95 percent of historical novels never had a second printing, and the first edition usually consisted of only 1,000 to 1,200 copies.[38] Only the most famous authors of historical novels set in the Napoleonic War period achieved larger edition sizes; they included Willibald Alexis, Theodor Fontane, Louise von François,[39] Gustav Freytag, Georg Hesekiel,[40] Louise Mühlbach, Ludwig Rellstab, Friedrich Spielhagen, Paul Schreckenbach[41] and Paul Sperl.[42] The most successful historical novel of all was probably *Cat's Bridge* by Hermann Sudermann. Published by Cotta in 1890, it had gone through 95 editions by World War I and was translated into English, Finnish, French, Japanese, Lithuanian and Swedish. The historical context (i.e., the narrated time) had very little importance anymore for the plot, however. This is also why the naturalist novel was so successful abroad as well. It treated topics of concern to the global zeitgeist.[43]

An author's regional origins, in contrast, had little influence over his or her success. Since the founding of the German Customs Union, novels had

[36] Habitzel and Mühlberger, "Gewinner," 98–101.

[37] Eggert, *Studien*, 45–46.

[38] Ibid., 27 and 31.

[39] On François, see Adalbert Elschenbroich, "François, Marie Louise," *NDB* 5 (1961): 334–225.

[40] On Hesekiel, see Otto Neuendorff, "Hesekiel, Johann George Ludwig," *NDB* 8 (1969): 744–745; and idem, *George Hesekiel* (Berlin, 1932).

[41] On Schreckenbach, see Ingrid Bigler, "Schreckenbach, Paul (Friedrich Immanuel)," in *Deutsches Literatur-Lexikon: Biographisch-bibliographisches Handbuch* (Munich, 1996), 16:258–259.

[42] On Sperl, see Helene Hoffmann, *August Sperl und seine Quellen in der ersten Schaffensperiode seines Lebens, eine literarhistorische Untersuchung auf Grund seines Familienarchivs, sowie mündlicher und schriftlicher Mitteilungen seiner Angehörigen, Verwandten und Freunde* (Laßleben, 1935).

[43] Sudermann, *Katzensteg*. Editions: Stuttgart, 1889, 1892, 1894, 1895, 1898, 50th edn.: 1902, 1904, 1907, 1910; 95th. edn.: 1914. The first English translation had a different title: *Regina or the Sins of the Fathers*, trans. Beatrice Marshall (Chicago, 1894); other early translations came out in French (Paris, 1900); Finnish (Helsinki, 1809); Lithuanian (Brooklyn, 1909); and Swedish (Stockholm, 1917).

become a product of the national literary market. Among the historical novels, too, the largest proportion of authors – more than 40 percent – came from Prussia. Fewer than 10 percent were Austrian. The homes of the remaining authors were scattered across the German-speaking region. Those who hoped to be successful had to pursue their writing careers professionally, making and maintaining contacts with renowned publishers wholly independent of their regional origin. In general, according to Habitzel and Mühlberger, "the degree of professionalization and success were mutually reinforcing." Accordingly, half of all successful and bestselling novels were published by professional writers, who had not just the talent and experience but also the right connections. Most of the authors who published more than one historical novel on the era of the Napoleonic Wars – 37 percent of the 123 authors examined – belonged to this group.[44]

The social profile of historical novelists who wrote about the years 1806–15 differed markedly from that of authors of history books and memoirs with respect to gender, age, social class and position. Of the 195 historical novels studied, 47 were written by women. A total of 123 authors wrote these 195 books, 93 men and 30 women. The proportion of historical novels penned by women and the proportion of women among the authors was thus 24 percent. The latter rose significantly in the course of the nineteenth century. It was 23 percent on average before 1871, and 29 percent thereafter. These figures mirror the general trend toward more female writers as the nineteenth century went on. The percentage of women was far higher among historical novelists, however, than among novelists more generally, where it was about 20 percent in 1900. Since historical fiction did not enjoy the same literary prestige as the "proper" novel, which literary critics regarded as a higher art form, it seems to have been easier for women to break into the genre.[45]

To be sure, a significant proportion of the authors of the novels that interest us here were born before, during or immediately after the Napoleonic era; 23 percent before 1800, 35 percent between 1800 and 1820 and 43 percent thereafter. Since writing historical novels was not, however, tied to personal experience, the proportion of younger age cohorts was a good deal higher than was the case for autobiographies and war memoirs. That makes it all the more remarkable how many authors of historical novels experienced the years 1806–15 either as adults, youths or children or were born in the first postwar decade when communicative memories were still very much present. Surely one of their motivations for writing, much like the memoirists, was to process the dramatic impressions of the years of war and crisis.

It is striking that most of the authors of historical fiction on the Napoleonic Wars were of middle-class origin, far more than was the case for memoir writers. Some 24 percent were from the aristocracy, 54 percent from the

[44] Habitzel and Mühlberger, "Gewinner," 104.
[45] Ibid., 104–106; Eggert, *Studien*, 37–38; and Bland and Müller-Adams, *Frauen*, esp. 9–25.

upper-middle classes and 22 percent from lower-middle-class strata. More than two-thirds had been to university. Fifty-one percent earned their livings as writers and journalists, 11 percent as teachers, 10 percent as military officers, 7 percent as clergymen and 5 percent as higher civil servants. Among the female authors, 36 percent were from the aristocracy, 47 percent from the upper-middle class and 17 percent from lower-middle-class strata. The proportion of aristocrats was consistently higher among the women than the men. Noble birth seems to have given women the social prestige and self-confidence as well as the relative material independence and education they needed to try their luck as authors. A far larger number of the women than men were single. While 56 percent of the female authors were married, the proportion of widows was notable at 28 percent. Twelve percent were unmarried and 4 percent divorced. More than three-quarters (77 percent) of the female authors supported themselves by writing. They were viewed accordingly by their contemporaries and listed in the biographical dictionaries of their day as professional writers.

Among the most successful female authors of historical fiction on the Napoleonic era were Caroline de la Motte Fouqué, Caroline Pichler and Fanny Lewald[46] alongside Louise von François and Louise Mühlbach.[47] All five had well-known publishers. Their books were extremely popular in the lending libraries.[48] Most women writers had to make do with smaller publishers, which greatly limited the distribution of their works. The publisher with the most female authors on his list in the second half of the nineteenth century was Otto Janke in Berlin.[49] There is every indication that historical novels by women were on average "neither especially successful, nor particularly unsuccessful."[50] With few exceptions, however, their works were less likely to be reprinted, and none of them made it into the cultural heritage canon, which had little to do with the quality of their novels and everything to do with the completely male-dominated guild of literary

[46] On Lewald, see Renate Möhrmann, "Lewald, Fanny," *NDB* 14 (1985): 409–410; Christina Ujma, ed., *Fanny Lewald (1811–1889): Studien zu einer großen europäischen Schriftstellerin und Intellektuellen* (Bielefeld, 2011); and Margaret E. Ward, *Fanny Lewald: Between Rebellion and Renunciation* (New York, 2006).
[47] On François, see Thomas C. Fox, *Louise von François and Die letzte Reckenburgerin: A Feminist Reading* (New York, 1988); idem, "A Women's Post: Gender and Nation in Historical Fiction by Louise François," in Kontje, *Companion*, 109–132; Uta Scheidemann, *Die Wunschbiographien der Louise von François: Dichtung und Prosaische Lebenswirklichkeit im 19. Jahrhundert* (Frankfurt/M., 1993); and Caroline Bland, "The Triumph of Moderation? The 'Wars of Liberation' in the Writing of Louise von François," in Maierhofer, *Women*, 223–246.
[48] Martino, *Leihbibliothek*, 404–413.
[49] Eggert, *Studien*, 40–41.
[50] This is suggested, among other things, by the fact that the proportion of texts written by women corresponded to their proportion among novelists whose works appeared in the lending libraries; see Eggert, *Studien*, 105.

scholarship and its criteria. Except for Louise Mühlbach, women were also not among the extremely prolific authors of historical fiction on the period of the Napoleonic Wars. They had to grasp all of the possibilities of the expanding and increasingly commercialized literary market and diversify in order to earn a living from writing.

Their historical novels frequently appear to have been more successful in appealing to women, since they tended to address female life spheres in history. Commercial publishers like Janke, who targeted a mass public, were well aware of this and had to cater to the interests of a female readership.[51] Even male novelists who strove for commercial success had to keep the female audience in mind, unlike the overwhelmingly male authors of history books, autobiographies and war memoirs, which were mainly written for a male readership. This is one reason why historical fiction on the period of the Anti-Napoleonic Wars focuses far more strongly on society, the family and social relations. Female protagonists are the equals of the main male characters, or even the center of the plot. The novels usually spend less time describing military action and with it the heroism of soldiers, officers, militiamen and volunteers, concentrating instead on the varied war experiences of the civilian population back home and the interactions between military and civilian society. For that reason, historical fiction is full of representations of female patriotism that are lacking in so many history books and memoirs. This appealed to the growing female readership particularly from the middle classes, for whom historical fiction was probably a key source of collective memories of the Napoleonic era.

The next two chapters take a closer look at how these memories were fashioned between 1815 and 1914, using the examples of especially successful and influential novels and focusing on their central narratives.

---

[51] See Bland and Müller-Adams, *Frauen*, 9–25.

16

Hopefulness and Disappointment: Novels of the Restoration Era and the *Vormärz*

The publication of novels dealing with the years 1806–15, like memory production more generally, began immediately after the wars. Yet the proportion of novels of the recent past was still comparatively small when measured against total novel production in the period 1815–20; during the first five postwar years, no more than about 6 percent of all novels of the recent past addressed these wars.[1] None of these early novels, whose most famous authors included Karl Gottlob Kramer,[2] Caroline de la Motte Fouqué and Caroline Pichler, were reprinted frequently or entered the literary canon, but all of them were very popular among lending-library readers, and their authors were among the libraries' most successful between 1815 and 1848. Kramer and Pichler retained this status until the end of the nineteenth century.[3] With the exception of Ludwig Rellstab, the authors whose novels appeared from the 1820s to the 1840s did not achieve the large number of new editions and translations that some of the bestsellers in the second half of the century did. Writers such as Willibald Alexis, who began his career in the early 1820s, Friedrich de la Motte Fouqué and Karl Ludwig Häberlin, alias H. E R. Belani, were very well known among contemporary readers, as suggested by the borrowing records of the lending libraries. Their audience was socially far more circumscribed than in the second half of the century, though, consisting largely of the educated classes.

HOPES AND CONCERNS FOR THE FUTURE

Most early postwar novels presented the years from 1806 to 1815 as a sea change, which they described, depending on their worldviews, as a

---

[1] Göttsche, *Zeit*, 304.
[2] Kramer, *Das Eiserne Kreuz*; on Kramer, see Jakob Franck, "Kramer, Karl Gottlob," *ADB* 4 (1876): 558–559.
[3] See Martino, *Leihbibliothek*, 276–288 and 404–408. For more on these early novels, see Göttsche, *Zeit*, 304–334.

threat to the traditional order, a new beginning or, ambivalently, as both simultaneously. In the novels, this upheaval also dramatically affects relations in the interior space of society – associations, sociability, circles of friends and the family. At the same time, most novels depict the great significance of the family for the cultural demobilization of society, the restoration of the social order and the reintegration into civilian life of the militiamen and volunteers who had fought in the wars of 1813–15. Marriage is usually the reward for the veterans' happy homecoming and successful adaptation to peacetime life. Just as the moral and social order endangered by the "time of the French" was restored by the wars of 1813–15 and the victory over Napoleon, the (gender) order of the private sphere, which had been threatened by the wars, was reestablished by the reuniting of existing or the founding of new families. The marriage with which nearly all of the studied novels end holds out the promise of a future not just for the younger generation, but symbolically for the entirety of postwar society. The early novels already hint at the political conflicts of the war years, which quickly intensified in the postwar period, but accord them no great importance before 1819. On the whole, the mood of the novels is still optimistic.

Among the earliest novels of the recent past to treat these topics were Caroline de la Motte Fouqué's *Edmund's Ventures and Vagaries: A Novel of the Most Recent Past*, published in three volumes in 1815 by Fleischer in Leipzig, and Caroline Pichler's *Female Dignity*, published in three volumes in 1818 by Liebeskind in Leipzig and Anton Pichler in Vienna.[4] Both novels were reviewed extensively in various literary periodicals, but only Caroline Pichler's text went through seven more editions, all of them in the 1820s.[5]

Caroline de la Motte Fouqué was born in 1773 as the daughter of the Brandenburg estate owner Philipp von Briest. In 1803, after the death of her first husband, she married Friedrich Baron de la Motte Fouqué, who had already made his name as a writer. Their estate Nennhausen in the Mark Brandenburg was the center of a Romantic literary circle whose members included Adelbert von Chamisso, Joseph von Eichendorff, Karl August Varnhagen von Ense, Rahel Levin-Varnhagen von Ense, August Wilhelm Schlegel and E. T. A. Hoffmann.[6] Caroline de la Motte Fouqué's novel of the recent past, *Edmund's Ventures and Vagaries,* offers a critical account and reflections on the period just ended as well as representative forms of the zeitgeist. The novel poses the central question of whether the wars of 1813–15 had indeed created national unity and what this meant

4 Caroline de la Motte Fouqué, *Edmund's Wege und Irrwege: Ein Roman aus der Vergangenheit* (Berlin, 1815); and Pichler, *Frauenwürde.*

5 Eke and Olasz-Eke, *Bibliographie*, 111–112 and 251–252; Pichler, *Frauenwürde.* Editions: Leipzig and Vienna, 1820, 1821, 1826, 1828; Reutlingen, 1820; Stuttgart, 1821, 1828.

6 See Arno Schmidt, "Fouqué, Friedrich Heinrich Karl Baron de la Motte-Fouqué," *NDB* 5 (1961): 306–307.

for the social and gender order. The action of the novel takes place between 1805 and 1814, and brings together the fate of young Count Edmund and the political events of the Napoleonic epoch. In the course of the novel Edmund, an aimless and disoriented student, must abandon his aristocratic, cosmopolitan and idle life, and grows, through various wrong turns, into a man full of patriotism who dedicates himself to the fatherland and fights as a volunteer in the wars of 1813–15. With the victory over Napoleon, Edmund's return home and the honor of being asked to serve as a political adviser to his king, nothing stands in the way of his marriage to his beloved Agnes von Nordheim, his equal in patriotic sentiment and conduct. In the novel, the wars of 1813–15 and the patriotic enthusiasm and self-sacrifice associated with them heal the "selfish and strife-torn" German society of the years 1805–12.[7] Just as, on the individual level, the war and the attendant self-sacrifice turn melancholy, inwardly torn boys into soldiers and genuine, valorous men with equally patriotic and active women at their side. The war also cures the sick and fragmented fatherland, which was no longer conscious of itself. The future of the German nation is based on cooperation between the reform-minded monarch and the "people," which in the novel, in keeping with the contemporary discourse, means the educated middle and the noble upper classes.[8]

Following the political discourse of the time, which combined national and religious rhetoric, the wars of 1813–15 themselves are portrayed in the novel as a struggle of good against evil. Napoleon is the demon who needs to be fought and vanquished.[9] Edmund and his friends go off to a "holy war" armed with "cross and sword"; they set forth on a "pilgrimage to the tomb of redemption, of liberty."[10] While a few scenes of Fouqué's novel juxtapose the mythic glorification of war as a "people's war" and a struggle for liberty with the horrors of battle, the latter are immediately patriotically glorified and portrayed as a necessary "blood sacrifice," offering liberation from old debts.[11] Here too, the language of the novel reflects the political rhetoric of the portrayed era. With the war and the victory, the "wheel of fate" had turned, "the onerous old debt was settled, the exuberant admonishers paid. A newborn people breathed free."[12]

---

[7] Motte-Fouqué, *Edmunds Wege*, 3:172 and 178; for more on the novel, see Göttsche, *Zeit*, 373–389; Müller-Adams, *Dass die Frau*, 306–333; Baumgartner, *Public Voices*, 144–151; Todd Kontje, *Women, the Novel, and the German Nation, 1771–1871: Domestic Fiction in the Fatherland* (Cambridge, 1998), 98–107; and Hartmut Vollmer, *Der deutschsprachige Roman, 1815–1820: Bestand, Entwicklung, Gattungen, Rolle und Bedeutung in der Literatur und in der Zeit* (Munich, 1993), 62–68.

[8] See Motte Fouqué, *Edmund's Wege*, 3:172, 175 and 200.

[9] Ibid., 1:112.

[10] Ibid., 3:176.

[11] Ibid., 3:191, 155 and 217.

[12] Ibid., 3:211.

Reviewers responded ambivalently to *Edmund's Ventures and Vagaries*. Some criticized the hopes, expressed in the novel, that the wars of 1813–15 would prove to be significant for a national rebirth as "simple-hearted" and pointed to the beginning political restoration. Others attacked the novel's setting in mainly aristocratic circles and thereby its concentration on a social stratum whose members did not have to work for a living. The plot of the novel seemed to be not realistic for them. The reviewer in the *Leipziger Literaturzeitung*, for example, wrote that Fouqué did not really portray the wars as people's wars, because she ignored the role of the middle class, and that the novel still represented the old "caste spirit." This would not win over middle-class readers who were proud of their contributions to the war and the victory.[13]

Critics looked more kindly on Caroline Pichler's multi-perspective epistolary novel *Female Dignity*, which depicts the years 1810–14 in an imaginary state of the Confederation of the Rhine and treats quite similar issues as Fouqué. Pichler was the most famous Austrian novelist of her day, but most male literary critics regarded her merely as the author of "women's books."[14] Here, too, an aristocratic hero becomes a man by participating in the wars of 1813–15. "A married couple from the provinces, Ludwig and Leonore von Fahrnau, young and wealthy, noble, domestic and faithful, travel to a spa where their quiet happiness is undermined."[15] Ludwig has a dishonorable affair and leaves his estate, wife and children. Leonore, however, asserts her female dignity and all by herself shepherds the estate through wartime. Her female virtue is contrasted with Ludwig's superficial and seductive mistress "Rosalie von ***." When the novel ends, not only has the fatherland's lost honor been restored by its "liberation," but Ludwig emerges from the fighting a reformed man, able to reconstitute his lost manly honor by the blood he has willingly sacrificed. Filled with remorse, he returns to his wife, who magnanimously forgives him. The couple takes refuge on their estate and in private family life. Although in this novel, too, the old social and gender order is restored after the war, unlike in Fouqué's work, the upper-class postwar man who aspires to the new middle-class values is offered no public sphere of action. All that remains to him is a retreat to the private sphere. Furthermore, in contrast to Fouqué, the nation here is represented more explicitly through both a male and a female protagonist, and the "dignity" of the latter is the permanent quality on which the fate of the family and with it nation ultimately depends.[16]

[13] "Edmunds Wege und Irrwege," *Leipziger Literatur-Zeitung* (7 Oct. 1816): 1980–1983, 1982; more positive reviews are "Edmunds Wege und Irrwege," *Intelligenzblatt der Zeitung für die elegante Welt* (21 May 1816): unpag.; and "Edmunds Wege und Irrwege," *Deutsches Unterhaltungsblatt für gebildete Leser aus allen Ständen* (11 Sept. 1816): 290.

[14] See "Frauenwürde, ein Roman von Carol. Pichler," *Literarisches Wochenblatt*, 2.37 (1818): 303–304; "Pichler, Carolina, sämmtliche Werke," *Literarischer Anzeiger* 44 (1819): 347–349; and "Sämmtliche Werke von Caroline Pichler," *Jahrbücher der Literatur* 6 (1819): 79–86.

[15] "Frauenwürde, ein Roman," 303.

[16] On Pichler's novel, see Baumgartner, *Public Voices*, 147–150; and Göttsche, *Zeit*, 463–464; on her ideas about the gender order, see Lucia Lauková, "Die emanzipierte

Reviewers loved Pichler's novel and its "dignified" image of women.[17] Only her friend Therese Huber, editor-in-chief of the publisher Cotta's paper *Morgenblatt für gebildete Stände*, clearly recognized how circumscribed the male protagonist's sphere of influence was. In a letter of September 1820 to Pichler she comments, "Ludwig [is] alas most trenchantly [authentic] – do you not feel quite keenly what a pitiful thing we portray when we depict an excellent German?"[18] In her response of December 1820 Pichler stresses that the novel reads differently in the present than she had originally intended. Because of the course "of world events" – by which she probably meant the restoration and the 1819 Carlsbad Decrees – "participation in the great struggle of the nations [...] no longer [appears] in such a pure light."[19]

RESTORATION AND POLITICAL DISILLUSIONMENT

Pichler, like Fouqué and many other patriotic-minded authors of the time, soon abandoned her optimistic interpretation of the postwar political situation in the wake of the rapidly escalating restoration. In the novels on the Napoleonic era and the postwar years that she and other authors published in the 1820s, political participation in society is no longer possible for protagonists, and even the integration of returning veterans proves to be difficult.[20] Moreover, after the Carlsbad Decrees and the subsequent persecution of the so-called demagogues, the political tensions between early liberalism, German nationalism and restoration politics played an increasing role in novels of the recent past – in most cases implicitly, since intensified censorship made it harder to discuss these conflicts openly.[21]

Willibald Alexis, Friedrich de la Motte Fouqué and Karl Ludwig Häberlin were among the most successful and well-known authors of the 1820s, and their novels on the Napoleonic period reflect the growing political tensions of the first postwar decade in exemplary fashion.[22] They, too, were highly popular in the lending libraries of their day, but their works went through at most two new editions.[23] Among the first authors to take up the social and political problems of the restoration period was Willibald Alexis

---

Emanzipationsgegnerin: Caroline Pichlers theoretische Schriften," *New German Review* 24 (2009–10): 95–111.

[17] See "Frauenwürde, ein Roman."

[18] "Th. Huber an K. Pichler, 28. Sept. 1820," in *Schriftstellerinnen und Schwesterseelen: Der Briefwechsel zwischen Therese Huber (1764–1829) und Karoline Pichler (1769–1843)*, ed. Brigitte Leuschner (Marburg, 1995), 63–65, 64.

[19] "K. Pichler an Th. Huber, Wien, 20. und 23. Dez. 1820," in ibid., 68–70, 69.

[20] Also, Baumgartner, *Public Voices*, 222.

[21] Göttsche, *Zeit*, 390.

[22] On Häberlin, see Ludwig Ferdinand Spehr, "Häberlin, Karl Ludwig," *ADB* 10 (1879): 279–280.

[23] Martino, *Leihbibliothek*, 276–288.

in his novella *The Outlaws*, which was published in 1825 by Duncker & Humblodt in Berlin and extensively reviewed, but reprinted only once.[24] The novella, which encompasses the years 1809 to 1823, focuses on the experiences of the young rifleman "Theodor von ***," who is living in a small town on the Elbe in the Altmark province of Prussia. In the spring of 1809, in a fit of patriotism and adventurousness, he joins the passing Free Corps of Ferdinand von Schill, who was busy trying to move the inhabitants of Prussia and the rest of North Germany to rise up against Napoleon under the slogan "Better a horrible end than horror without end. Long live the King!"[25] Theodor participates in what is described in the novel as the Free Corps's utterly hopeless campaign and its devastating defeat. He is able to avoid French pursuit on a small Baltic island near Rügen, where he survives the war of 1813–15 in quiet seclusion, without even being aware of events, is discovered in his hermitage by old friends in 1819, taken home and reunited with his former beloved Agnes, who is still mourning his presumed death. But they are not (yet) married, because Theodor feels like a stranger in his own land and believes he is not a full-fledged man. The fact that he, as a robust "youth," had not fought "in the great Wars of Liberation" was a stigma in a military-obsessed postwar Prussia.[26] Theodor observes that even those "who had once been considered the most cowardly and weak" appear by "their own accounts to have been heroes" in the recent wars. The early heroism of Schill's undertaking, in contrast, "was mostly [...] quite forgotten" in restoration Prussia.[27] Those who remembered regarded involvement in Schill's campaign as a pointless sacrifice. Theodor therefore decides to leave Germany. Only after a two-year cure in Nice, where he encounters Agnes and her father, shared travels and a final test of his mettle can Theodor feel like a man again and be happy. On a sea voyage they are attacked by pirates. Theodor helps to save the ship, vanquish the pirates and free their galley slaves. Among them he finds an old friend from Schill's corps, whom the French had made a galley slave and then sold to pirates. With this heroic act Theodor succeeds in restoring his manly honor. Now he can finally marry Agnes and plan a happy return home. His liberated friend, however, sets off to fight for Greek independence, since there is no longer any place in the homeland for radical freedom fighters.[28]

In the novella, Alexis criticizes not just Schill's senseless adventure and his men's blind, fanatical hatred of the French,[29] but also the imperial violence

---

[24] Willibald Alexis, *Die Geächteten: Novelle* (Berlin, 1824); "Die Geächteten," *Der Gesellschafter: Blätter für Geist und Herz* 104 (1 July 1815): 520; and "Berlin, b. Duncker & Humblodt," *ALZ*, no. 14, 1826, col. 412; see also Eke and Olasz-Eke, *Bibliographie*, 145.

[25] Alexis, *Geächteten*, 8–9.

[26] Ibid., 326.

[27] Ibid., 327.

[28] Ibid., 352.

[29] Ibid., 6.

of the French, who lawlessly kill their opponents or make them galley slaves, and the exaggerated Prussian patriotism and militarism of the postwar era. A central theme of the work is the question of what in recent history is worth remembering as heroic, and Alexis arrives at an ambivalent answer. Ultimately, it is human beings and their honorable conduct. The male hero can only live and marry happily in postwar society after he has restored his masculine honor. This public act is the precondition for his happiness, which he and his beloved find not in the nation, but in the private familial sphere. Those who wish to continue to fight for liberty honorably and manfully after the wars of 1813–15 have to leave Germany and do so elsewhere, for example in Greece. This conclusion of Alexis's novella is well suited to the restoration and Biedermeier era. The great hopes for the future of the war years were not forgotten, but rather were withdrawn and nurtured in private in a spirit of resigned nostalgia. Middle-class men and women found a modus vivendi with the restoration. Reviewers were displeased with the ambivalence of Alexis's novella, the very aspect that makes it so interesting for readers today.[30]

Although other authors of the 1820s were less ambiguous in their interpretation of the recent past, much to the delight of critics, and presented the wars of 1813–15 as a positive counterpoint to the restoration, these texts, too, clearly disassociated themselves from the fanaticism of the years 1806 to 1819. Novels of the recent past consistently addressed the problems of extreme Francophobia and Germanomania. One instance is Friedrich de la Motte Fouqué's novel *The Refugié or Home and Abroad* of 1824, published by Henning in Gotha. In this patriotic work, Fouqué remains true to his old Romantic interpretation of the "Wars of Liberation" and contrasts the myth of manly heroism among Prussian volunteers and militiamen, who fought a "holy war" to liberate the fatherland, with the rather unheroic present.[31]

Karl Ludwig Häberlin's novel *The Demagogues*, brought out in two volumes by Wienbrack in Leipzig in 1829 under the pseudonym H. E. R. Belani, offers a more radical critique of the present.[32] Häberlin came from Erlangen in Franconia and was a lawyer and very successful novelist for the broad public. In *The Demagogues* he tells the story of the radicalism of the patriotic student associations, the *Burschenschaften*, between 1815 and 1820, focusing on the roots of "political fanaticism," which the novel traces back to the French Revolution.[33] The protagonist, Herrmann, comes

---

[30] "Die Geächteten"; and "Berlin, b. Duncker & Humblodt"; on the novel, see Göttsche, *Zeit*, 445–451; and Peterson, *History*, 90–94.

[31] Friedrich Baron de La Motte Fouqué, *Der Refugié oder Heimat und Fremde: Ein Roman aus der neueren Zeit* (Gotha, 1824); on the novel, see Eke and Olasz-Eke, *Bibliographie*, 115; and Göttsche, *Zeit*, 438–445.

[32] H. E. R. Belani (Karl Ludwig Häberlin), *Die Demagogen: Novelle aus der Geschichte unserer Zeit*, 2 vols. (Leipzig, 1829).

[33] Ibid., 2:133.

from a middle-class family and is orphaned at an early age. His name signals that he stands for the German man as such, alluding as it does to the hero Arminius or "Hermann der Cherusker," the liberator of Germania from Roman rule described by Tacitus. As a pupil in Berlin in 1811, Hermann participates in the gymnastics movement, then studies in Königsberg, where he volunteers for military service in the spring of 1813, remaining in the army until 1815. He fights in the decisive battles of Leipzig and Waterloo, and is gravely wounded in the latter. After the war he returns to university and with his school friend Arnold joins the *Burschenschaften,* the avant-garde of the German-national opposition to postwar restoration, to continue the fight for Germany's inner freedom that for him and his comrades had started with the "Wars of Liberty" in 1813. While Arnold supports the radicalism of the student movement and joins in the book burning at the Wartburg Festival of 1817, Hermann increasingly rejects this fanaticism. Nevertheless, both men fall victim to the persecution of the demagogues. Hermann is exonerated but sees no future in Germany and emigrates to America, the "land of liberty," where he finally marries and finds wealth and happiness. At the heart of the novel, whose plot, in conformity with contemporary reader taste, is peppered with all manner of amorous and other adventures, is the "moral disaster of the sudden transformation of radical political idealism into terrorist fanaticism."[34] Häberlin criticizes not just this fanaticism, though, but the impossibility of even moderate liberalism in restoration Germany.[35]

This novel met with outraged disapproval among supporters of the German-national movement and conservative literary critics alike. The German nationalists disliked the condemnation of their Germanomania and fanaticism and the conservatives disapproved of the criticism of their restoration politics. One of the most critical reviews was published by Wolfgang Menzel, editor-in-chief since 1825 of the *Literatur-Blatt* of the *Morgenblatt für gebildete Stände.* Menzel, himself a former *Burschenschaftler,* had fled to Switzerland in 1820 to escape the persecution of the demagogues, only returning to Germany in 1824. He adopted increasingly conservative positions and became the harshest critic of the writers of Young Germany. In 1830 he wrote in the *Literatur-Blatt* about Häberlin's novel: "The author of *The Demagogues* is himself a demagogue. Who deserves this honorific title more than those besmirchers of the novel who flatter the crudest fantasy and basest sentiments of the lowest but also the most numerous public."[36] In his review the conservative Menzel distances himself not just from the political tenor of the novel, but also its lurid style. For him the critique of the restoration era expressed in the novel was especially dangerous, because

---

34 Göttsche, *Zeit,* 455.
35 On the novel, see ibid., 452–462.
36 Wolfgang Menzel, "Romane, 10) Die Demagogen," *LB,* no. 25, 5 March 1830, 97–98, 97.

its author reached a broad audience with his captivating texts. He feared the "subversive influence" of a growing group of extremely prolific authors who, like Häberlin, began to publish one historical novel after another under various pseudonyms, thus ushering in the first heyday of historical fiction in the mid-1820s, which continued into the 1830s. Only a fraction of these novels, however, dealt with the era of the Napoleonic Wars and its aftermath; most focused on earlier periods.[37] The writers of Young Germany, who became increasingly influential in the 1830s, on the other hand, were mainly interested in the present and the future.

THE POLITICS OF FORGETTING AND REMEMBERING

Novel writing in the 1830s and 1840s was dominated by the authors of Young Germany and the *Vormärz*. They preferred to treat the social and political issues of the immediate present in their texts. According to them, the novel should primarily be a "mirror of its time," concentrating on a critical portrayal of their own mental and moral reality.[38] As a consequence, after the July Revolution of 1830 in France there was an initial marked decline, especially among the younger generation, in interest in the years 1806–19, which were now relegated to the past once and for all. Only in the early 1840s, in the context of the twenty-fifth anniversary of the wars of 1813–15, were more novels published that were set during that period.

The best-known and most successful authors of the younger generation to address the Anti-Napoleonic Wars included Ludwig Rellstab with his four-volume *1812: A Historical Novel* published by Brockhaus in 1834. It went through ten new editions up to 1914 and was translated into Danish, English, Dutch, Polish and Russian.[39] The novel remained successful in the lending libraries into the late nineteenth century.[40] Rellstab was born in 1799 as the son of the Berlin musician Johann Karl Rellstab and earned his living as a journalist, writer and noted music critic, especially for the Berlin *Vossische Zeitung*.[41] He begins his voluminous novel with a "Dedication. To the Princes and Peoples of Europe" in which he explains why the work focuses on the year 1812 and elucidates its objectives. He writes:

Just as the year 1789 gave birth to and generated all the great ideas that now shape our world, the year 1812, which lends its name to the present work, must be regarded

[37] On Häberlin's many novels, see Eke and Olasz-Eke, *Bibliographie*, 142–143.

[38] Theodor Mundt, quoted in Göttsche, *Zeit*, 506, see also 506–572.

[39] Rellstab, *1812*. Editions: Leipzig, 1836, 1843–44, 1854, 1858, 1860, 1892, 1900, 1912; Berlin, 1912; and Philadelphia, 1857; transl. into Danish (Copenhagen, 1835–35), Dutch (Amsterdam, 1838), English (New York, 1838, and London, 1849), Polish (Warsaw, 1912) and Russian (n.p., 1912), and reprinted in these languages as well.

[40] Martino, *Leihbibliothek*, 285 and 404–413.

[41] Rösch, "Rellstab."

as the natal year, or better, as the year of conception of today's political relations in Europe [...]. Never has a destiny been more horrible, never has a similar nemesis been visited upon individual pride in the face of all-powerful providence. All the hells swallowed the conqueror's army; out of the bounding flames of burning cities they were cast down, like Dante's damned, into the more horrific suffering of icy abysses of eternal numbness.[42]

For Rellstab the downfall of Napoleon's army in Russia had been the precondition for the successful liberation struggle of the nations in 1813–14. "Who does not thrill with holy enthusiasm when he thinks of those days? Days of awakening, of uplifting struggle, of the most sumptuous promises!" The dedication ends with the rhetorical question of whether these promises had been fulfilled, and the appeal: "Remember the promising dawn of the year 1812! Think of the hopes that illuminated the two subsequent years of holy struggle! [...] You came to know what a people is! Forget it not!"[43]

More clearly than in any of the novels on the Napoleonic Wars published between 1815 and then, Rellstab calls on the princes to keep their promises of national unity and political freedom, and at once implicitly entices and threatens them with the power of the people, which made a good deal of sense four years after the July Revolution in France and two years after the Hambach Festival. However, he articulates this political program more in the dedication than in the novel itself. The story focuses on Ludwig Rosen, "a young German,"[44] who after his studies in Heidelberg and an educational voyage to Italy in the spring of 1812 returns to Dresden, in his Saxon home region, to stand by his mother and his sister Marie during Napoleon's expected war against Russia, in which Saxony as France's ally would have to fight. On his return journey, Ludwig meets, under mysterious circumstances, not just his future fiancée, Bianca, but also the Polish count and colonel Stephan Rasinki and his companions, Count Boleslaw and Count Jaromir, with whom he becomes friends.[45] In Dresden, he is also reunited with his old friend Bernhard, a young painter. The happiness of their reunion is brief, however, for soon the French wrongly accuse Ludwig of high treason. His friends help him to flee.[46] Together with Bernhard he disappears into Count Rasinski's newly founded Free Corps, with which he participates in the Russian campaign, experiences the great fire of Moscow and, beset by all manner of complications, suffers through the retreat of the Napoleonic army.[47] On their way back, the friends must, among other

[42] Ludwig Rellstab, *1812*, in idem, *Gesammelte Schriften: Neue Ausgabe*, vols. 1–4 (Leipzig, 1860), 1:xiv.

[43] Ibid., 1:xiv.

[44] Ibid., 1:3.

[45] Ibid., 1:77–78.

[46] Ibid., 1:162–179.

[47] Ibid., vols. 2, 3 and 4:1–144.

things, free Bianca (whose life Ludwig had already saved once before during the journey from Italy), as well as Marie, who had been forced by French persecution to take refuge with Count Rasinki's wife in Warsaw. All four manage to make their way together to Königsberg. Bianca and Bernhard, who was raised by foster parents, discover that they are siblings of noble birth. And Ludwig and Marie also finally learn from their dying mother the secret of their noble origins.[48] In Königsberg in February 1813 the two friends hear of the Prussian king's call for volunteers and enthusiastically join the Prussian army. Bianca and Marie, themselves fervent patriots, support their resolve. Bernhard and Ludwig see their voluntary involvement in the struggle for liberation as atonement for fighting on Napoleon's side during the Russian campaign. The only drop of bitterness for them is the knowledge that their friend and repeated savior, Count Rasinki, would still be fighting on the side of the French for the liberty of his Polish homeland. The novel ends with Rasinski's death at the Battle of Leipzig and Bernhard and Ludwig fighting on until 1815, returning home unharmed and being happily reunited with and marrying their fiancées Bianca and Marie as a reward for their manly deeds.[49]

Critical responses to the novel differed widely. In September 1834 the *Allgemeine Literaturzeitung* published a harsh and sarcastic review: "According to the title and the dedication 'To the Princes and Peoples of Europe' one might with right expect one of the greatest novels ever written, or rather never written; it is, however, merely a long and not a great work." The author should not have chosen "insignificant persons" as "the chief players in these events of world history."[50] Other reviewers were kinder. They praised the precise characterization of the protagonists and the realistic depictions of the Russian campaign and the great fire of Moscow.[51] In fact, the beginning and end of the novel in particular are marked by declarations of German nationalism and an admonition to the princes to finally deliver the promised political liberties. The main action then includes, alongside the heroes' diverse adventures and vagaries, an account of the sacrifices and sufferings of the soldiers of various nationalities during the war in Russia. What is remarkable about the novel is that the friends and heroes respect one another across social and national boundaries, and remain friends until the end, even though they have to fight against each other in 1813. Napoleon is also not portrayed as an absolute villain, as he was in many other works of the time.[52] Ludwig long vacillates between admiration for the emperor, who he hoped would finally introduce the needed reforms in Germany, and rejection of his

[48] Ibid., 2:283–292.
[49] Ibid., 4:293–314.
[50] "Leipzig, b. Brockhaus," *ALZ*, no. 161, 1834, cols. 70–71.
[51] "1812, ein Historischer Roman," *LB*, no. 34, 1 April 1836, 135–136.
[52] See Rellstab, *1812*, 1:114–115.

imperial policies. Moreover, Rellstab's perspective is, by his own admission, "German." The narrator not only explicitly introduces Ludwig Rosen, at first described as a middle-class student, whose origins are however later revealed to be noble, as a "German," but Ludwig also introduces himself as such to other characters.[53] The novel's protagonists easily cross social boundaries, which play no role in their relationships. Regional differences, too, have little significance. More important is their awareness of national identity. Unity and fighting for the "fatherland" are the highest values of all, which they also accord to those from other nations like the Poles and the Russians. All of this probably contributed to the novel's success, as well as to its translation; *1812* was the first and for a long time the only German novel on the Napoleonic Wars to appear in many other languages.[54]

A number of other novels on the years 1806–15 appeared up to the Revolution of 1848–49, but none were as successful as *1812*. Most were written by now long-forgotten authors such as August Leibrock[55] or Ferdinand Stolle,[56] who were favorites in the lending libraries of their day.[57] An exception is Fanny Lewald, whose work has been rediscovered by literary scholars in the last decade. She was one of the most successful female authors of her generation.[58] Lewald was born in Königsberg in 1811, the daughter of a Jewish merchant who permitted his three children to convert to Protestantism. Lewald received a very good private school education and began her writing career in the early 1840s. Her first novel came out in 1843. *Prince Louis Ferdinand*, which appeared in three volumes with Max & Comp. in Breslau in 1849 and was reprinted ten years later by Hoffmann & Comp. in Berlin, treats the situation in Prussia in the years 1805–06.[59] The novel, which did well with the contemporary public, shows "Prussia in 1806 with an indolent king, an incompetent government, a thoroughly corrupt society and a wastrel prince."[60] With *Prince Louis Ferdinand*

---

53 Rellstab, *1812*, 1:78.

54 On the novel, see Peterson, *History*, 95–96.

55 August Leibrock, *Die schwarzen Husaren: Kriegerischer Halbroman aus dem Jahre 1809* (Leipzig, 1841). On the productive novelist, see Paul Zimmermann, "Leibrock, Johann Ludwig August," *ADB* 51 (1906): 623–625.

56 Ferdinand Stolle, *1813: Ein historischer Roman* (Leipzig, 1838); idem, *Elba und Waterloo: Ein historischer Roman. Fortsetzung von 1813* (Leipzig, 1838); idem, *Der neue Cäsar: Ein Seitenstück zu "1813" und "Elba und Waterloo"* (Leipzig, 1841); and idem, *Boulogne und Austerlitz: Historischer Roman* (Tabor, 1848); on this popular writer, see Ludwig Fränkel, "Stolle, Ludwig Ferdinand," *ADB* 36 (1893): 786–788.

57 Martino, *Leihbibliothek*, 286 and 404–410.

58 See Ujma, *Fanny Lewald*; and Ward, *Fanny Lewald*.

59 Fanny Lewald, *Prinz Louis Ferdinand* (Breslau, 1849); on the novel, see Peterson, *History*, 151–157; on her presence in libraries, see Martino, *Leihbibliothek*, 405–416. See also her *Die Familie Darner: Roman* (Berlin, 1887), which focuses on the capture and liberation of Königsberg between 1803 and 1813.

60 Peterson, *History*, 157.

Lewald ushered in a wave of novels in the following decades that explored more intensively the causes of the Prussian-Saxon defeat of 1806 and the preconditions for the success of the German "national rising" in the years 1813–15. Interest in the topic not coincidentally came at the time of another defeat of the national-liberal middle classes. It expresses the strong desire to complete at last the work begun in 1813–15 by unifying Germany: the struggle for political unity and liberty.

17

Critique, Desire and Glory: Novels of the *Nachmärz* and the German Empire

The failure of the Revolution of 1848–49 was a watershed moment not only for politics and society, but also for literary production. The second half of the nineteenth century became the golden age of "literary realism" in Germany. The literary historian Julian Schmidt and his colleague, the writer Gustav Freytag, were instrumental in developing the program for this movement in their joint literary and cultural journal *Die Grenzboten*. According to them, authors should only describe "reality," all the while "awakening and nourishing a sense of the beautiful and the sublime." As they saw it, "Poetic realism will lead to pleasing works of art when it also seeks out the positive side of reality, when it is combined with the joy of life." They rejected the socially critical novels of Young Germany and the *Vormärz* as ugly and unpoetic, along with the mysticism of Romantic literature or the "cookie cutter writers" of historical fiction.[1] They expected historical novels written in the spirit of literary realism to treat the author's own national history:

The present must cast its light onto the past, so that the past appears to us as the present; not so that we recognize our present sentiments and reflections in it, but rather so that we understand the inner connection between the apparently alien point of view and our present one.[2]

In order to offer "a picture [of history] that is vivid and comprehensible down to the slightest detail," the author of a historical novel will however "need to accommodate to the conditions of history: he will base his picture

---

[1] "Der neueste Englische Roman und das Prinzip des Realismus," *GB* 15.4 (1856): 466–474, 473–474; see also "Die Märzpoeten," ibid. 9.1 (1850): 5–13; "Die Reaction in der deutschen Poesie," ibid. 10.1 (1851): 17–25; and "Der vaterländische Roman," 483. Fore more see also Michael Thormann, "Der programmatische Realismus der Grenzboten im Kontext von liberaler Politik, Philosophie und Geschichtsschreibung," *IASL* 18.1 (2009): 37–68; and Kontje, *Companion.*

[2] "Der vaterländische Roman," 486.

on provincial history." At the same time, the novel must be set during a period of this regional history "to which general historical interest is attached." Only in this way can a provincial novel become a national one that appeals to an audience beyond a single region and attains national and international recognition.[3] This ideal notion of realism within literary theory was faced with a practice in which the term increasingly evolved into a "catchword, a term of approbation" for the combination of literature with history and politics. Particularly since the beginning of the "New Era" in the 1860s, "realism" was used more generally to refer to a national-liberal program of literature and politics that focused on building the nation under *kleindeutsch* Prussian auspices.[4]

The triumph of realism by this definition is also evident in the historical novels on the Anti-Napoleonic Wars that appeared between the 1850s and 1880s, with the foundation of the German Empire in 1871 as a key turning point. Based on the number of editions, edition sizes and borrowing from the lending libraries,[5] the most important authors in the 1850s and 1860s, *the* boom years for historical fiction before 1914, were Willibald Alexis, Eduard Breier,[6] Louise von François, George Hesekiel,[7] Karl von Holtei,[8] Louise Mühlbach and Levin Schücking.[9] In the decades after the founding of the empire, when the production of historical novels on the Napoleonic era was clearly on the wane, the most successful authors were Gustav Freytag, Theodor Fontane, Friedrich Spielhagen and Hermann Sudermann, whose works were extraordinarily popular even in labor movement lending

---

3   Ibid., 484.

4   Thormann, "Der programmatische Realismus."

5   Martino, *Leihbibliothek*, 404–416.

6   Eduard Breier, *1809: Historischer Roman*, 3 vols. (Vienna, 1847); idem, *Der Congreß zu Wien: Historischer Roman*, 4 vols. (Vienna, 1854); and idem, *1805 oder: Die Franzosen zum ersten Mal in Wien*, 2 vols. (Vienna, 1864). On Breier, an Austrian-Jewish journalist and very prolific novelist, see: http://www.jewishencyclopedia.com/articles/3676-breier-eduard.

7   George Hesekiel, *Vor Jena: Nach den Aufzeichnungen eines Königl. Offiziers vom Regiment Gensd'arms*, 2 vols. (Berlin, 1859); idem, *Von Jena nach Königsberg: Roman*, 3 vols. (Berlin, 1860); idem, *Bis nach Hohen-Zieritz: Roman*, 3 vols. (Berlin, 1861); and idem, *Stille vor dem Sturm*, 3 vols. (Berlin 1862); see also idem, *Krummensee: Historischer Roman*, 6 vols. (Berlin, 1861); and idem, *Vier Junker: Historischer Roman*, 3 vols. (Berlin, 1865). All these novels focus on the years 1806–15.

8   Karl Holtei, *Christian Lammfell: Roman* (Breslau, 1853); on Holtei, see Joachim Wilcke, "Holtei, Carl von," *NDB* 9 (1972): 553–554; and Christian Andree, ed., *Karl von Holtei (1798–1880): Ein schlesischer Dichter zwischen Biedermeier und Realismus* (Würzburg, 2005).

9   Levin Schücking, *Die Rheider Burg: Roman*, 2 vols. (Prague, 1859); idem, *Ein Staatsgeheimnis: Roman*, 3 vols. (Leipzig, 1859); and idem, *Aus der Franzosenzeit* (Wien, 1863). On this very popular and prolific journalist and novelist, see Walter Gödden, "Schücking, Christoph Bernhard Levin," *NDB* 23 (2007): 630–631; and Johannes Hagemann, *Levin Schücking: Der Dichter und sein Werk* (Emsdetten/Westf., 1959).

libraries.[10] The only other authors to achieve similar mass printings were those like Paul Schreckenbach[11] and August Sperl,[12] whose novels on the Napoleonic Wars appeared on the occasion of the centenary celebrations on the eve of the First World War.

For all of these authors, the national question was a central theme in their novels on the years 1806–15. In the *Nachmärz* period they particularly addressed the obstacles to national unity, which is what made the subject of the causes of defeat, national rising and victory so central. After the founding of the empire the old question of what constituted the German nation and how to define its borders arose once again. A key problem now treated in many of the novels using the example of the Anti-Napoleonic War era was that of unity and difference within the nation. They asked how national unity was possible despite the many regional, confessional, political and social differences. Depending on their political convictions, the authors arrived at quite diverse answers, ranging from extremely conservative to democratic positions. Hesekiel and Spielhagen represented the two poles of the spectrum.[13]

The usual focus on a specific region within the German nation as the concrete setting for the novel's action, which was also propounded by theorists of historical fiction, not only rendered the story more vivid, but also highlighted regional differences while at the same time marking them as an important characteristic of the nation. In the novels, regional diversity became a sort of fixed component of German national identity. Accordingly, the novels are set in very different parts of the German-speaking region: from Hamburg and North Germany (Spielhagen), the Mark Brandenburg and Berlin (Alexis, Fontane and Hesekiel), Saxony (François), the Rhineland or Westphalia (Schücking and Schreckenbach), and Franconia (Sperl) to East Prussia (Sudermann), Silesia (Freytag) and Austria, especially Vienna (Mühlbach and Breier). The authors combine regional history with the history of the German people. The credibility of fictional "middling heroes" in the foreground of the novel is reinforced by genuine, widely known historical figures in the background. Even the focus on the German periphery was no obstacle to success if it was used to explore themes of universal significance; on the contrary, it allowed writers to bring issues to a head and

[10] See Martino, *Leihbibliothek*, 410–416 and 444–448.

[11] Paul Schreckenbach, *Der böse Baron von Krosigk: Roman aus der Zeit deutscher Schmach und Erhebung* (Leipzig, 1907).

[12] August Sperl, *Burschen heraus! Roman aus der Zeit unserer tiefsten Erniedrigung* (Munich, 1913).

[13] On Hesekiel, see Peterson, *History*, 184–188; on Spielhagen, see Jeffrey L. Sammons, "Friedrich Spielhagen: The Demon of Theory and the Decline of Reputation," in Kontje, *Companion*, 133–158, esp. 146–149; and Volker Neuhaus, "Friedrich Spielhagen – Critic of Bismarck's Empire," in *1870/71–1989/90: German Unifications and the Change of Literary Discourse*, ed. Walter Pape (Berlin, 1993), 135–143.

contrast "backwardness" with "modernity."[14] It is striking more generally that in the novels set in the Anti-Napoleonic War era published after 1850, the significance of region changed. As the wars of 1813–15 receded further into the past, but above all after the founding of the empire, region became politically less important in the novels. Increasingly, the region is primarily defined as a social and cultural "homeland" (*Heimat*) within "Germany." The nation becomes the central political frame of reference.[15] In this way, the historical novels of the *Nachmärz* and Wilhelmine period studied here contributed to internal nation-building.

At the same time, the novels address the boundaries of the nation. They reflect on whether Jews and Polish migrants should belong to the German nation, and how to conceptualize relations with the French, Polish and Russian nations. In this, too, the novels differed markedly. Attitudes toward Jews ranged from strong economic and political anti-Semitism in the work of Hesekiel,[16] to more culturally based anti-Semitism in that of Freytag and ambivalence in Fontane's texts,[17] to philo-Semitism in Spielhagen and Mühlbach, both of whom presented minor Jewish characters in their novels who are fiery German patriots.[18] The depiction of other nationalities also differs from novel to novel. Portrayals of Poles and Russians are frequently highly ambivalent.[19] Apart from the stereotypical negative image of "the French" that goes back to the wars of 1813–15, as in Hesekiel and François,

---

[14] See Peterson, *History*, 199–265; and Tatlock, "In the Heart of the Heart."

[15] See, for example, Gustav Freytag, *Bilder aus der deutschen Vergangenheit*, 4 vols. (Leipzig, 1859–67); and Hermann Sudermann, *Der Katzensteg* (Stuttgart, 1903, 55th edn.), 1–5; on the theme of *Heimat*, region and nation in German literature more generally, see Lynne Tatlock, "Regional Histories as National Histories: Gustav Freytag's *Bilder aus der deutschen Vergangenheit* (1859–1867)," in *Searching for Common Ground: Diskurse zur deutschen Identität, 1750–1871*, ed. Nicholas Vazsonyi (Cologne, 2000), 161–178; and Celia Applegate, "The Mediated Nation: Regions, Readers and the German Past," in *Saxony in German History: Culture, Society, and Politics, 1830–1933*, ed. James Retallack (Ann Arbor, MI, 2000), 33–50.

[16] See Peterson, *History*, 184–188.

[17] See Martin Gubser, *Literarischer Antisemitismus: Untersuchungen zu Gustav Freytag und anderen bürgerlichen Schriftstellern des 19. Jahrhunderts* (Göttingen, 1998), 264–270; Peter Schumann, "Theodor Fontane und die Juden," *GWU* 49.9 (1998): 530–543; Bernd Balzer, "'Zugegeben, daß es besser wäre sie fehlten, oder wären anders, wie sie sind': Der selbstverständliche Antisemitismus Fontanes," in *Theodor Fontane, am Ende des Jahrhunderts*, ed. Hanna Delf von Wolzogen and Helmuth Nürnberger, 3 vols. (Würzburg, 2000), 1:197–210; and Hannah Burdekin, *The Ambivalent Author: Five German Writers and their Jewish Characters, 1848–1914* (Oxford, 2002), 17–86 and 199–247.

[18] Examples include Samuel Hirsch in Spielhagen, *Noblesse oblige*, 44–53, or Marianne Maier and Fanny Itzig in Louise Mühlbach, *Napoleon in Deutschland*, pt. 1: *Rastatt und Jena*, 4 vols. (Berlin, 1858), 1:102–105 and 301; see also Peterson, *History*, 168–169.

[19] On Freytag's mostly negative, sometimes ambivalent perceptions of Poland, see Isabela Surynt, *Das "ferne," "unheimliche" Land: Gustav Freytags Polen* (Dresden, 2004), esp. 159–342. Fontane was more positive and nuanced; see his *Vor dem Sturm: Roman aus dem Winter 1812 auf 13*, 4 vols. (Frankfurt/M., 1986).

one also finds exemplary French characters in the novels, for example those of Alexis, Mühlbach and Spielhagen, or at least ambiguous ones, as in Freytag.[20] A comparison of the corpus reveals two striking tendencies. On the one hand, novels written quickly to cater to mass tastes offered more stereotypical portrayals of other nationalities; this was especially true of youth literature on the Napoleonic Wars, which became increasingly popular in Wilhelmine Germany.[21] On the other hand, novels published in the final decades before the First World War and generally written for an audience of literary consumers were a good deal more nationalistic and thus more clichéd in their representation of national differences. They depicted the French as the "hereditary enemy" and their portrayal of Jews and Poles was informed by anti-Semitic and anti-Slavic stereotypes.[22]

One important aspect of the topic of nation-building in the novels on the Anti-Napoleonic Wars published up to the late 1880s was the relationship between the different social strata, generations and sexes within the nation. These texts consistently refer back, in two ways, to the image of the nation as a *Volk* family, which had already developed during the period of the Wars against Napoleon. First, the question of who belongs to or must be excluded from the nation, and in what ways, is frequently depicted using the example of marital and family conflicts, which form the center of the plot. These conflicts are embedded in a specific local and regional community, enabling the authors to include not just both sexes and all generations but also various social strata, and to integrate ethnic and confessional differences. Second, the nation itself is imagined as a *Volk* family, which allows all differences – and the hierarchies in the nation connoted by them – to appear "natural," and thereby also harmonizes them. While women, as part of this *Volk* family, assume an important role in the novels as complements to the male protagonists, they are accorded little latitude for action even in works by female novelists. They could and should become active outside the private sphere only in extraordinary emergencies in the family, the local community or the nation. The period of the Anti-Napoleonic Wars was, as already in the rhetoric of that era, depicted as such a time of national emergency. Female war support was now generally expected in the novels and accordingly depicted in a positive light. One example is the portrayal of female activism

---

[20] For example, Louis von Bovillard in Alexis, *Ruhe*; Captain Dessalle in Freytag, *Aus einer kleinen Stadt*; and Marquis Hypolit d'Hericourt in Spielhagen, *Noblesse oblige*.

[21] An extraordinarily popular example is Clementine Helm, *Das vierblättrige Kleeblatt: Eine Erzählung aus dem Freiheitskriege für junge Mädchen* (Bielefeld, 1878), which continued to be reprinted into the 1950s; on Helm, see Hermann Arthur Lier, "Beyrich, Clementine," *ADB* 46 (1902): 535–536. For a more general account, see Reiner Wild, ed., *Geschichte der deutschen Kinder- und Jugendliteratur* (Stuttgart, 2008, 3rd edn.), esp. 148–152 and 228–240; and Gisela Wilkending, ed., *Mädchenliteratur der Kaiserzeit: Zwischen weiblicher Identifizierung und Grenzüberschreitung* (Stuttgart, 2003), esp. 219–280.

[22] See Schreckenbach, *Baron von Krosigk*; and Sperl, *Burschen*.

in the patriotic women's associations. But when the emergency of the wars was over, women were expected to marry or, if already married, to return to their duties in the family, which was depicted as the foundation of state and nation. The novels by Freytag and Schreckenbach offer two examples of this message.[23] Even where female protagonists do overstep the limits imposed on their sex temporarily or in the long term, for example by successfully managing an estate as in the novels of François and Spielhagen, in the end they are generally reintegrated into the dominant middle-class gender order, which also meant the restoration of the social order, because the gender order was at its heart.[24] In other cases they even had to die, as in Sudermann's novel, since there was no place for them in marriage, family or the village community.[25]

In the historical fiction of the second half of the nineteenth century, memories of the Anti-Napoleonic Wars served the present and above all the future ever more clearly. The fewer authors had actually been witnesses to the period and the more they learned of the remembered time solely from history books and other media of memory, the less important the remembered time itself became. Increasingly, writers deployed the period from 1806 to 1815 in their novels either as a relatively unspecific historical background to the plot, which explored contemporary themes, as did Sudermann, who was primarily interested in processing the question of generational- and gender-specific guilt and atonement as well as honor and duty and the relationship between nature and convention in relations between the sexes.[26] Or, like Schreckenbach and Sperl, they recalled the time with the aim of patriotic-national mobilization above all of young men for a new war.

A comparative analysis of the historical novels on the Anti-Napoleonic Wars that appeared in the *Nachmärz* and Wilhelmine Germany therefore affirms the trend already evident in the memoir literature: Above all in the final decades before the First World War, the memory texts increasingly produced for the literature-consuming public – "youth and the people" – sought to spread the national founding myth of the defeat, rising and unification of the German nation between 1806 and 1815, and linked 1813 with 1871. Meanwhile, the "time of the French" was addressed ever more often in new novels by authors of conservative and nationalist views. Their texts, however, continued to compete in the literary market and cultural memory

[23] See Minchen von Buskow in Gustav Freytag, *Die Ahnen: Roman*, pts. 4–6 (Leipzig, n.d.), 583–845, 765–767 and 785–788.

[24] See Louise von François, *Die letzte Reckenburgerin* (Berlin, 1871; repr. Berlin, n.d.), 286–293; and Spielhagen, *Noblesse oblige*, 333–339.

[25] See the fate of Regine Hackelberg, who sacrifices herself for Boleslav von Schraden and dies at the end at the hands of her own drunkard father in Hermann Sudermann, *Der Katzensteg: Roman* (Berlin, n.d.), 315–322.

[26] On Sudermann, see Heintz, "Kompromiß."

with the more ambivalent and nuanced novels of earlier generations of writers that had originally appeared in the 1850s and 1860s and remained successful, at least in the lending libraries.

ANALYZING THE PRESENT THROUGH THE PAST

In the 1850s and 1860s, Willibald Alexis was the most respected author of historical fiction on the period of the Napoleonic Wars. He had experienced the time as a young man and, as he expressly emphasized, saw himself as its "historian."[27] His most significant novel on the period, *Keeping Calm Is the Citizen's First Duty or 50 Years Ago*, appeared in five volumes with Barthol in Berlin in 1852, and was already published in an abridged "popular edition" by Janke in 1861. By 1913 the book had gone through 15 new editions.[28] The sequel, *Isegrimm: Patriotic Novel from the Age of Hardship and Liberation*, which the same company published in three volumes in 1854, was sold by Janke in a "popular edition" beginning in 1871 and reprinted eight times.[29] Alexis, long stamped by literary scholars as "patriotic" and a "glorifier of Prussia," has been rediscovered and reassessed only in recent decades. Nowadays, scholars acknowledge the innovative character of these two novels, which subject Prussian, and thereby German society and politics to comprehensive criticism.[30] After the failed Revolution of 1848–49, such a fundamental critique, revealing the problems of the present through the past, seemed more necessary than ever to Alexis.[31]

In *Keeping Calm*, Willibald Alexis presents a sweeping study of Prussia in the years 1805–06, at the center of which is the capital, Berlin. Alexis weaves all classes, generations and spheres of society into a complicated web of plots and subplots. He explains this approach as follows in the preface:

When a work of literature undertakes to portray a bygone time in its broad outlines, it becomes clear and comprehensible only when it illustrates both civic and family life, and customs in palace and hovel alike. Only by looking boldly at the social circumstances of those days can we understand the state of moral disorder and decay that facilitated Prussia's defeat and preceded its national rising.[32]

[27] Alexis, "Nachwort," in idem, *Isegrimm*, 3:358–360.
[28] Alexis, *Ruhe*; Editions: Berlin, 1861, 1870, 1872, 1874, 1881, 1898, 1900, 1901, 1903–04, 1910, 1913; Halle, 1900; and Leipzig, 1900, 1910, 1913.
[29] Alexis, *Isegrimm*. Editions: Berlin, 1871, 1881, 1999, 1904, 1910, 1911; Halle, 1903; and Leipzig, 1912 (abridged edition).
[30] On the development of this research, see Wolfgang Gast, *Der deutsche Geschichtsroman im 19. Jahrhundert: Willibald Alexis – Untersuchungen zur Technik seiner "vaterländischen Romane"* (Freiburg/Br., 1972), 1–13; Beutin, *Königtum*, 101–155; idem, "Melpomenes"; Eggert, *Studien*, 56–59 and 150–164; and Hobi, *Willibald Alexis*, 19–27.
[31] See Beutin, "Melpomenes," 182–183; and Gast, *Geschichtsroman*, 55–59.
[32] Alexis, *Ruhe*, 1:vi.

Alexis dissects the desolate state of Prussia with an acid pen. He expects help neither from the nobility nor the court, the government or the military, indeed not even from the king and his consort, Queen Luise, whom other novels, for example Mühlberg's, glorify as a patriotic martyr to Prussia. For Alexis, the only hope lies in the reformist patriots around Stein, elements of the common people and youth.[33] *Keeping Calm* focuses on *Geheimrätin* Lupinius, married to Privy Council (*Geheimrat*) Lupinius, and the spy Baron von Wandel, both of whom are unmasked at the end as poisoners and arrested. Other central characters are her widowed brother-in-law, a privy councilor too, and his nursemaid Charlotte, whom he loves and marries at the end, as well as Adelheid Alltag, the patriotic daughter of a middle-class councilor of war, who is taken up by *Geheimrätin* Lupinius and later serves as a lady-in-waiting to Queen Luise. Adelheid has two suitors: Louis von Bovillard, the son of the French ambassador, who fights on the French side and falls in battle in November 1806, and Walter van Asten, the patriotic son of a rich merchant and war profiteer, who works first as Adelheid's private tutor and then as a reformer in the Prussian state service under Minister of State Baron von Stein. Although Adelheid marries Bovillard, following his rival's death Van Asten has hopes of winning her over after all, for with their youth and patriotism the two would make an ideal German couple. The novel ends with the announcement of the Prussian defeat via Minister Schulenburg's well-known poster – "The king has lost a battle. His Majesty and his brothers, their Royal Highnesses, are alive and unharmed. Keeping calm is the citizen's first duty!"[34] – and the royal family's flight from Berlin. The novel's ironic undertone clearly suggests that the citizen's duty after the defeat is anything *but* keeping calm, since what state and society need in order to regenerate themselves is patriotic engagement.

Although most book critics were respectful in their reviews of the famous author's novel and recommended it to readers, they nevertheless had problems with its considerable length and unaccustomed form, with no outstanding personalities as protagonists, clearly structured narrative or happy ending.[35] They were also troubled by the ironic tone, the ambivalence of value judgments and the political tendency. According to the review in the *Blätter für literarische Unterhaltung*, for example, "It is one great soggy moral morass." To this reviewer, nothing was sufficiently true, clear or unambiguous. He found the harsh criticism of Prussia, which did not even stop at the court and the royal family, bewildering in the extreme:

Willibald Alexis is known to us from previous years as a specifically Prussian patriot. […] Whatever has happened to this author that he has suddenly been gripped by the

---

[33] Ibid., 4:329–384, esp. 374–379.
[34] Ibid., 4:357.
[35] See Robert Prutz, "Willibald Alexis," *Deutsches Museum*, no. 1, 1852, 945–946 and no. 2, 471–471; and "Willibald Alexis," *BLU*, no. 24, 11 June 1853, 558–566.

very opposite? [...] Where is the lenient judgement, indeed, where is the historical truth? [...] The author's assessment of political circumstances is exceedingly harsh and caustic.[36]

Like some others, the reviewers from *Die Grenzboten* had nothing negative to say about this political tendency, but they would have preferred a more positive general attitude with more exemplary characters and a more stringent, reader-friendly plotline.[37] Such reviews did not, however, prevent the public from making *Keeping Calm*, like its sequel *Isegrimm*, a success in the lending libraries.[38] The ironic tone of both novels seems to have corresponded to the zeitgeist of educated contemporaries who were trying to come to terms with the defeat of the Revolution of 1848–49 and its social and political causes.

Isegrimm centers on the story of the noble family von Quarbitz auf Ilitz during the French occupation of Prussia. The main action ends in 1809, but the story of the family continues up to 1848–49 in order to illustrate the long-term effects of war and crisis on Prussian society. The novel is set on the country estate of the von Quarbitz auf Ilitz family somewhere in the Mittelmark region between the Elbe and Oder rivers. This estate and its environs represent Prussian agrarian society more generally. Although the plot concentrates on Wolf von Quarbitz auf Ilitz, known as Isegrimm, along with his two sons and three daughters – who all end up happily married, if not necessarily within their class and to the satisfaction of their father – in this novel, too, it is ultimately social and political circumstances, this time in the countryside, that are the focus. The picture Alexis paints of the future of the nobility and the Prussian agrarian society they dominated is not very hopeful either. In his view, the only future for the nobility is to overcome caste thinking and open up to the middle classes, as Isegrimm's youngest daughter Amalie, a fervent Prussian patriot, does. Against her father's wishes, after the wars of 1813–15 Amalie marries Albert Mauritz, the young local pastor, who had fought as a volunteer and returns as an officer decorated with the Iron Cross. Amalie, Mauritz and their children represent hope for the future of the German nation.[39] The novel ends with the crushing of the Revolution of 1848 and the deaths of Isegrimm and Mauritz. Amalie tries to comfort her two sons following the death of their father:

As a Christian, he [Mauritz] often preached to us that there will come a resurrection for peoples as well [...] Therefore, children, walk bravely into the sad times before you, doubly sad ones for young men, where the proud thoughts and noble enthusiasm for ideas that lifted your father above himself and the daily round meet with hostility and indeed infamy. [...] You, no, you will not despair under slavishness and

[36] "Willibald Alexis," *BLU*, no. 24, 11 June 1853, 559.
[37] "Ein neuer Roman von Willibald Alexis," *GB* 11.2 (1852): 94–97.
[38] Martino, *Leihbibliothek*, 418–432.
[39] See Alexis, *Isegrimm*; on the novel, see Peterson, *History*, 219–223.

hypocrisy, you will not be subdued by evil times, but will triumph with good if you remain free, strong and true![40]

This ending is an obvious appeal to contemporaries to uphold the liberal and democratic principles of the Revolution of 1848–49, despite its defeat. In the afterword to the novel Alexis explains to his readers why he did not close the book with the positive image of the national rising of 1813–15 and the "rebirth of the fatherland." In the history of this heroic time, evil had overcome good. In order to help the good to break through, it was necessary to recognize, name and combat what was evil.[41]

Critics responded more positively to *Isegrimm*, which appeared to them "in many and significant respects to be more successful and better," although they again disapproved of the novel's negative mood, since the proponents of literary realism in particular expected historical fiction to be patriotically uplifting and edifying.[42] At the same time, however, they were forced to acknowledge, as the reviewer in the *Blätter für literarische Unterhaltung* did, that "in this sad tableau," Alexis had "very effectively" portrayed "the sleep of any genuine patriotic feeling," the "thoroughgoing selfishness," the "rivalry between the estates and classes, and especially the complete apathy of the lower classes and the utter lack of ideas of the upper classes."[43]

The fiction of Louise Mühlbach and George Hesekiel conveyed far more "uplifting" memories of the Anti-Napoleonic Wars. Mühlbach's novel *Napoleon in Germany* was published by Janke in 16 volumes from 1858–59, and reprinted three times up to 1914.[44] In keeping with her aspiration to write biographical historical novels that would improve the people's knowledge of German history and awaken their patriotic consciousness, the series focuses on popular heroes of Prussian history between 1806 and 1815 such as General Blücher and Queen Luise. The first eight volumes revolve around the Prussian queen, who, in keeping with the widespread myth that arose even before her death, is portrayed as an affectionate mother to her people and a Prussian martyr. The Prussian nation of 1806–15 in Mühlbach's works is a *Volk* family headed by caring, attentive parents. In the novel, Queen Luise spurs on the patriotic struggle to liberate Prussia and Germany and ultimately dies of sorrow because of the disgrace of the German debacle.[45]

[40] Alexis, *Isegrimm*, 3:358.
[41] Ibid., 3:358–360.
[42] "W. Alexis' neuester brandenburgischer Roman," *BLU* 1 (1854): 604–607, 604; and "Isegrimm, Roman von Willibald Alexis," *GB* 13.1 (1854): 321–328.
[43] "W. Alexis' neuester brandenburgischer Roman," 605.
[44] Mühlbach, *Napoleon in Deutschland*, pt. 1: *Rastatt und Jena*, 4 vols. (Berlin, 1858); pt. 2: *Napoleon und Königin Louise*, 4 vols. (Berlin, 1858); pt. 3: *Napoleon und Blücher*, 4 vols. (Berlin, 1858); and pt. 4: *Napoleon und der Wiener Congreß*, 4 vols. (Berlin, 1859). Other editions were Berlin, 1860, 1861–68 and 1868; the work was translated into Dutch (Deventer, 1861) and English (New York, 1867) and reprinted in English several times.
[45] Mühlbach, *Napoleon in Deutschland*, 1:212.

Thus, the queen is not merely the representative of Prussia, but also of Germany, and a model of female patriotism as such. She is glorified as the ideal German woman. What is interesting about Mühlbach's portrayal is that this ideal image expands the scope accorded to women by the bourgeois gender order. The queen intervenes in politics, a realm generally reserved for men, and claims the right to public action. But unlike normal middle-class women, she can and is permitted to do so in her function as queen. At the same time she is presented as a caring mother to her own children and the Prussian and German nation, which embeds her in the dominant model of the gender order.[46] Like Alexis, Mühlbach also emphasizes the positive influence in the state and the military of reformers and patriots, whose work, in her interpretation, ultimately led to the successful national rising of Prussia and Germany. In so doing, she stresses that Queen Luise had actively supported their efforts. Unlike Alexis, however, Mühlbach avoids any explicit criticism of political conditions in her own time. This and her non-partisan patriotism were important preconditons for her broad success.[47] Even though Louise Mühlbach was *the* most popular female lending library author of the 1850s to 1880s, most literary critics simply ignored her novels. They were worth a brief notice at best in the literary and cultural magazines. She faced the same prejudices against female writers as her less successful colleagues.[48]

Like Mühlbach, Georg Hesekiel intended his cycle of "Patriotic Novels" set during the era of the Napoleonic Wars to promote Prussian patriotism. He offered his interpretation of the years 1805–12 in *Before Jena* (1859), *From Jena to Königsberg* (1861), *As Far as Hohenziritz* (1861) and *Calm Before the Storm* (1862), each of which appeared in three volumes. Like Mühlbach, his publisher was Janke in Berlin. Hesekiel, born in 1809, studied history and philosophy and worked as a journalist and author. From 1848 on he was an editor at the conservative newspaper *Neue Preußische Zeitung* – better known as the *Kreuzzeitung* – in Berlin, where Fontane also worked until 1870.[49] In his novels, Hesekiel explains the reasons for Prussia's defeat in 1806 quite differently than Alexis did. He particularly emphasizes the corrupting influence of money on Prussian society, which had even reached the countryside. As a result, old Prussian virtues such as hard work, thrift and a sense of order and duty as well as courage and honor had been lost. His novels have a strong anti-Semitic tendency, portraying Jews as usurers and war profiteers who have corroded the intellectual and cultural life of the era with their greed and cosmopolitanism.[50] The reviewers discussed Hesekiel's

[46] Förster, *Königin Luise-Mythos*, 67–72.

[47] On the novel, see Peterson, *History*, 166–171.

[48] For example, "Notizen," *Deutsches Museum* 9 (1859): 415.

[49] Neuendorff, *George Hesekiel*, 5–46.

[50] Hesekiel, *Vor Jena*; idem, *Von Jena nach Königsberg*; idem, *Bis nach Hohen-Zieritz*; and idem, *Stille vor dem Sturm*. On the novels, see Peterson, *History*, 184–188; and Neuendorff, *George Hesekiel*, 117–127.

novels quite extensively and respectfully, but criticized what the *Blätter für literarische Unterhaltung* called his "predilection for the ancien régime" and the "privileged classes of society," which are the setting for most of his novels. In the end, according to his critics, the reader does not truly understand what caused the defeat of 1806 and facilitated the national rising of 1813, since the author dares not criticize political conditions in those days for fear of "liberal views."[51]

Louise von François portrays the Napoleonic era in a similarly Prussian monarchist spirit as Hesekiel, but from a far more liberal basic stance, in her novel *The Last von Reckenburg*, which first appeared in Janke's *Deutsche Romanzeitung* in 1870 and one year later as a book with the same publisher. The work went through ten editions up to 1914, appearing as a paperback in Reclams Universalbibliothek in 1911.[52] François uses the historical context of the plot, which spans the period from the 1790s to the 1830s, primarily to address the problems of her own time. In her novel, the period is mainly a backdrop. She seems to have chosen this time primarily because of its rapid and dramatic changes, which had challenged the old order and offered new opportunities for nations, regions, local communities, families and individuals, much like the 1860s and 1870s. In addition, this time period had forced contemporaries to deal with the same question of how to define and form a nation.

François was born into a Prussian Huguenot family in 1817, lost her father Major Friedrich von François early and had to earn her living by writing. She took care of her mother until her death and never married. As she wrote, the novel reflects her own experiences.[53] The main part is narrated in retrospect by Eberhardine von Reckenburg, the only daughter of impoverished aristocrats, who as a young woman is brought to live with her aunt, the elderly Countess von Reckenburg, at the family manor house and manages the estate very successfully after her death. Eberhardine proves to be an able reformer of both agriculture and social life on the estate. In managing the estate, following the guiding principles of honor, duty and right, she reveals a character connoted as masculine in the novel.[54] Eberhardine

---

[51] "Georg Hesekiel," *BLU* no. 14, 1 April 1860, 253–257; see also "Hesekiel, George, Stille vor dem Sturm," *BLU*, no. 12, 1863, 216–217.

[52] François, *Reckenburgerin*. Editions: Berlin, 1871, 1872, 1873, 1878, 1888, 1895, 1900, 1904, 1909; and Leipzig, 1911. The first English translation was published by Gardener in 1888; there were also translations into Danish and Dutch. See Barbara Burns, *The Prose Fiction of Louise von François (1817–1892)* (Oxford, 2006), 11–16. Her second novel on this period was *Frau Erdmuthens Zwillingssöhne: Roman aus dem Zeitalter der Befreiungskriege*, 2 vols. (Berlin, 1872), which, however, is not included here because it is only available in a Nazi-era edition of 1944. Eggert, *Studien*, 40–41.

[53] On her biography, see Fox, *Louise von François*, 13–56; Scheidemann, *Wunschbiographien*, 11–88; and Burns, *Prose Fiction*, 11–16.

[54] François, *Reckenburgerin*, 166–167 and 278–279.

remains the last Reckenburg, since for complicated reasons involving shame, responsibility, duty and loyalty she is unable to marry.[55] In the end, she turns the estate over to her foster daughter Hardine and her new husband, the young estate manager Ludwig Nordheim.[56] Hardine's father, August Müller, had been born the illegitimate son of Eberhardine's friend, the tavern keeper's daughter Dorothea Müller. Since Dorothea did not want to reveal her situation to society and her future husband – the ambitious young physician Faber – August Müller is raised with Eberhardine's help by foster parents and never meets his mother. When the gravely ill, widowed veteran August returns from the wars of 1813–15 and, together with little Hardine, goes off in search of his mother, he wrongly believes that he has found her in Eberhardine. Since he is near death, he begs her to take care of his little girl.[57] Eberhardine's sense of duty turns to love, which transforms the old woman from an austere, severe matron into a warmhearted, maternal woman. This has a positive effect on life on the estate, which is now ruled not just by law and order, but also by happiness and joy.[58]

In this novel, according to Caroline Bland, François exercises "quiet criticism of her society's gender role expectations."[59] For Bland, François uses the work to call into question women's limited scope of action at the time. In fact, the novel shows that women can be men's equals in intelligence, ability and sense of duty, as we see with the old Countess Reckenburg and Eberhardine. What feminist literary scholars overlook, however, is the novel's ambivalence. At the same time it stresses that women cannot be truly happy without marital love and above all without motherhood, for "Nature suppressed always takes her revenge," as the female narrator emphasizes at the end. This becomes evident in both Eberhardine's and Dorothea's destinies. Eberhardine is only happy when she takes in a child and has the opportunity to express her maternal feelings. Dorothea dies unhappy because she married a man she did not love and repudiated her own child.[60]

The novel also probes the possibilities and limits of social mobility and underlines the necessity for the aristocracy to open up to the middle classes. By allowing the noble family of Reckenburg to die out, and placing the future of their estate in the hands of a young middle-class couple – the

[55] Ibid., 53–251.

[56] Ibid., 288–290.

[57] Ibid., 1–50.

[58] Ibid., 265–289. On François and the novel, see also Fox, *Louise von François*, 69–157; and "A Women's Post," 117–122; Bland, "Triumph," 223–246; and Burns, *Prose Fiction*, 85–98.

[59] Caroline Bland, "The End of 'Noblesse oblige' in German Realism? Social Mobility and Social Obligation in the Writing of Louise von François," *German Life and Letters* 66.2 (2013): 137–155, 151; see also Fox, *Louise von François*, 34–43.

[60] François, *Reckenburgerin*, 254, 274–277 and 285–291. I believe that scholars have not paid adequate attention to the novel's ending. See, for example, Burns, *Prose Fiction*, 87.

estate manager Ludwig Nordheim and his wife Hardine, who is described as the very epitome of the caring and hardworking bourgeois housewife – François emphasizes that the future of society and the economy lies not with the aristocracy, but with the middle classes and their productive labor.[61] Another central, closely related theme is that of duty. In all areas of her life, Eberhardine acts primarily out of a sense of duty. The novel presents even her patriotism as a duty rather than a passion: a duty of the individual to serve community and nation, a duty that men and women alike must perform when necessary. Accordingly, the narrator Eberhardine speaks only briefly of her extensive patriotic activities before and during the wars of 1813–15, for which she was awarded the medal of the *Luisenorden*; it seems to her to be a self-evident service for the fatherland, which is not worth discussing at length.[62] Thus for François, the nation is primarily defined positively, as a shared undertaking of men and women, the nobility and the middle classes, to shape the future of the country, its economy and society in a productive manner.[63]

Unlike Mühlbach, François enjoyed the recognition of fellow writers, but only as a female exception, and only after Gustav Freytag, writing in 1872 in the magazine *Im neuen Reich*, praised her book as one of "the best German novels to be published in recent decades." For Freytag, François was "despite the French-sounding name a German female soul, which the reader will come to love through her book."[64] The message of the novel fit well into the national-liberal program of the middle classes in the founding period of the empire, at a time when they were once again claiming the right to participation.

BUILDING A UNIFIED NATION

Gustav Freytag may also have praised Louise von François so highly because he approved of not just her "genuine poetic work" but also her ideas on the nation and the significance of marriage and the family as the foundation of a productive and happy national order.[65] Since the problem of internal nation-building was increasingly on the political agenda after the founding of the German Empire in 1871, it also seems to have been taken up by those writers who were still publishing historical fiction on the Anti-Napoleonic

[61] Burns, *Prose Fiction*, 92–94.
[62] Ibid., 45, 99–100 and 238.
[63] Bland, "Triumph," 241. This is also evident in Louise von François, *Geschichte der preussischen Befreiungskriege in den Jahren 1813 bis 1815* (Berlin, 1874).
[64] Gustav Freytag, "Ein Roman von Luise von François," *Im neuen Reich* 2, no. 8, 1872, 295–300, 295; see also "Die letzte Reckenburgerin," *BLU*, no. 24, 1872, 375–376. On the history of her reception, see Fox, *Louise von François*, 158–209.
[65] See Gustav Freytag, "*Erinnerungen aus meinem Leben*," in *Gesammelte Werke* (Leipzig, 1887), 1:253–256.

Wars. Among the most successful of these authors in the 1870s and 1880s were Gustav Freytag, Theodor Fontane and Friedrich Spielhagen, all three of whom belonged to the generation of "Forty-Eighters" who had actively supported the Democratic Revolution of 1848–49. In general, however, now that the national task of the 1813 rising had been fulfilled with *kleindeutsch* unification under Prussian leadership, the production of novels on this time period dropped sharply.

Gustav Freytag's novel *From a Small Town* was the sixth volume in his series *The Ancestors*, which was published by Hirzel in Leipzig between 1872 and 1880 and went through 24 editions up to 1913, but was never translated into English or any other foreign language before 1914.[66] Freytag was born in 1816 into an Upper Silesian family of medical doctors. After studying philology and cultural history in Breslau and Berlin he began a career as a journalist and writer in the 1840s. Like Fontane and Spielhagen, he supported the Democratic Revolution of 1848–49. His first major success was the six-volume novel series *Debit and Credit*, which appeared in 1855, also with Hirzel. Between 1859 and 1867, the same company published his four-volume social and cultural history *Pictures from the German Past*, which presents German history using selected primary sources and also contains three sections on recent history with the programmatic titles "From the Time of Destruction" (1789–1806), "The National Rising" (1807–15) and "Sickness and Healing" (1816–48).[67] The series was one of the most successful historical works in the lending libraries, because unlike the publications of academic historians, it shows how historical change affected the various strata of the population.[68] For Freytag, working on *Pictures* was important preparation for the novel series *The Ancestors* and its final volume *From a Small Town*.[69] In his memoirs, Freytag admits that he had also "blithely and generously drawn upon" impressions from his own youth for this volume.[70]

The novel is set in a small Silesian town and its rural environs during the years 1805–15. The story closes with a look at prospects for the development of the next generation, ending with the Revolution of 1848–49. The protagonists of the main section of the novel are the young Dr. Ernst König and his

---

[66] Freytag, *Aus einer kleinen Stadt*. Leipzig, 2nd–4th edn.: 1881–1882; 5th–6th edn.: 1885–1888; 7th–8th edn.: 1889–1892; Editions; 9th–13th edn.: 1894–1900; 14th–20th edn.: 1900–1909; Berlin, 1900; and Heilbronn, 1914.

[67] On Freytag's biography, see Ping, *Gustav Freytag*, esp. 21–64.

[68] Freytag, *Bilder*, vol. 4: *Aus neuer Zeit* (Leipzig, 1867); Martino, *Leihbibliothek*, 421; see also Martin Nissen, "Populäre Geschichtsschreibung im 19. Jahrhundert: Gustav Freytag und seine 'Bilder aus der deutschen Vergangenheit,'" *Archiv für Kulturgeschichte* 89.2 (2007): 395–425; and Larry L. Ping, "Gustav Freytag's *Bilder aus der deutschen Vergangenheit* and the Meaning of German History," *German Studies Review* 32.3 (2009): 549–568.

[69] Freytag, *Aus einer kleinen Stadt*.

[70] Freytag, "*Erinnerungen*," 250.

future wife Henriette, daughter of an older country pastor, the tax collector Köhler and his intended Minchen von Buskow, and König's adversary, the Frenchman Captain Dessalle. Ernst König returns to his hometown in 1805 to practice medicine. He falls in love with Henriette, but Prussia's defeat in 1806 and the subsequent French occupation of the region put a damper for the time being on any hopes for marriage and the future. Captain Dessalle saves Henriette and her parents from the plundering Bavarian soldiers of the Napoleonic army by pretending that she is his fiancée and sealing it with a ring. All involved feel that they are bound by this betrothal.[71] Ernst can only marry Henriette after he has proven his manliness as a patriot by demonstrating that he actively supports preparations for a national rising against the French and going off to the wars of 1813–14 as a volunteer in a Hussar regiment. Desalle and König meet on the battlefield. Desalle is captured, but König spares him, and after the young doctor has magnanimously saved the wounded man's life, the latter finally sets Henriette free.[72] Back home, patriotism is also awakening. The tax collector Köhler, who is too old to fight, organizes arms and equipment for the volunteers and militia, as well as war relief and nursing. Here he collaborates closely with Minchen, Henriette and others who have founded a patriotic women's association.[73] After the war Köhler and Minchen also become a happy couple.

Freytag's novel compactly recounts the German-national myth of the rising of the Prussian and German people, which, guided by patriots and reformers, was successful chiefly because of communal, age- and gender-specific patriotic action and universal self-sacrifice. The body of the novel accordingly ends not only with a double wedding, but also with the following commentary by the narrator:

Rejoice and dance […], for with hundreds of thousands of your fellows you have vanquished the evil foe and lifted the fatherland up out of degradation. In these years of defeat and national rising, the best part of the nation has been with you, the ordinary people, not the rulers, whose pride and will were all too weak, and not with the highly educated and cultivated, whose lamps flickered uncertainly and who, even after the peace, still do not know where the fatherland begins and ends.[74]

For Freytag, the wars of 1813–15 were and always would be "the people's Wars of Liberty," and the novel's afterword on developments up to 1848 shows that, like many liberals, he felt cheated of the political liberties that governments had promised in 1813.[75] His interpretation of the "time of the French" was simpler and plainer than that offered by Alexis and Fontane,

[71] Gustav Freytag, *Werke*, vol. 2: *Die Ahnen*, pt. 6: *Aus einer kleinen Stadt* (Leipzig, n.d.), 585–850, 629–641.
[72] Ibid., 770–783.
[73] Ibid., 762–769.
[74] Ibid., 790.
[75] See also Ping, *Gustav Freytag*, 332–335; and Holz, *Flucht*, 114–174.

and less ambivalent. This made him *the* favorite author of the national-liberal middle classes in Imperial Germany. He offered uplifting reassurance for adults and edifying reading for youth. That is why his series of novels was also so popular with reviewers, even if they were not wholly uncritical.[76]

Far less known to the broader public than Freytag was Theodor Fontane when he published his first novel, *Before the Storm: A Novel of the Winter of 1812/13*, in 1878. It was first serialized in the family magazine *Daheim* and then appeared in four volumes with Hertz in Berlin.[77] Fontane was born in 1819 to a family of Huguenot apothecaries in the Brandenburg town of Neuruppin. He initially followed his father into the profession, only deciding to live from his writing in 1849. In the early years, he made his name mainly with poetry and travel accounts as well as theater reviews in Berlin,[78] and only began to write fiction later. *Before the Storm* went through 16 editions by 1913 and appeared that same year in an abridged version for the schools. It was translated into English in the year it came out and was published by Oxford University Press.[79] The novella *Schach von Wuthenow: A Tale from the Era of the Gensdarmes Regiment*, which appeared with Friedrich in Leipzig in 1883, achieved six editions.[80]

Before the Storm is a wide-ranging portrait of Prussian society before the wars of 1813–15. The novel is set in the Oderbruch region of Brandenburg, west of the cities of Frankfurt/Oder and Küstrin, and in Berlin. The novel begins on Christmas Eve 1812 and ends in March 1813 with the Prussian king's declaration of war. The "hero of the piece" is Lewin von Vitzewitz, who arrives home from Berlin, where he is studying, to spend Christmas with family and friends.[81] His father Berndt von Vitzewitz, sister Renate and her friend Marie Kniehase anxiously await him on their estate, Hohen-Vietz. Marie, a foundling raised by the local justice of the peace, was educated together with Renate.[82] These four, their extensive circle of family and friends and the village community around Hohen-Vietz and the neighboring manor house of Guse – whose chatelaine is Berndt von Vitzewitz's older sister, Countess Amalie – are the focus of the novel. All of them are looking forward to Christmas, but also nervously awaiting news from the

76 For an example, see Otto Brahm, "Der Schlußband von Freytag's 'Ahnen,'" *Deutsche Rundschau* 26 (1881): 315–317; and Adolf von Gottschall, "Der Schlußband von Freytag's 'Ahnen,'" *BLU* no. 3, 20 Jan. 1881, 35–38.

77 Fontane, *Vor dem Sturm*, vol. 1: *Hohen-Vietz*; vol. 2: *Schloß Guse*; vol. 3: *Alt-Berlin*; and vol. 4: *Wieder in Hohen-Vietz*.

78 On Fontane's biography, see Hädecke, *Theodor Fontane*.

79 Fontane, *Vor dem Sturm*. Editions: Berlin, 1878, 1890–91, 1898, 1900, 1905–12, 1913–15; Stuttgart, 1904–05, 1907–09 and 1912–13 (13th–16th edn.); and Munich, 1913 (abridged edition for the schools); first English translation (New York, 1911).

80 Fontane, *Schach von Wuthenow*. Editions: Leipzig, 1883; Berlin, 1890–94, 1901, 1905, 1908 and 1911.

81 Fontane, *Vor dem Sturm* (1986), 1:1–14.

82 Ibid., 1:76–83.

east, where the Napoleonic army has been beaten for the first time and forced to make an ignominious retreat. The first harbingers of the dramatic defeat in Russia are French refugees. In this situation, Berndt von Vitzewitz, a retired officer and a widower, is moved to take action against the French as quickly as possible, partly from patriotic and partly from personal motives, because the French occupation has caused the death of his wife. For that reason alone he fervently hates the French.[83] While sharing Berndt's rejection of Napoleon, although far less passionately, his sister Amalie nevertheless continues in the Friderician tradition of cultivating French culture and language at Guse.[84] Lewin does not share his father's hatred either; his patriotism is of a more moderate and pragmatic nature. He recognizes that important reforms to the state, military and society were instituted under Napoleon, or rather under pressure from his rule.[85] Lewin's best friend Tubal Ladalinski, a cousin of Polish origin who studies with him in Berlin, and Tubal's sister Kathinka also have mixed feelings. Lewin hopes to marry her, but she runs away with Count Bninski, a Pole, and moves with him to Paris, since the two of them regard Napoleonic rule as the only hope for Polish independence. This disappoints not just Lewin, but also her father, Privy Councilor Alexander von Ladalinski, who lives in Berlin and has made Prussia his fatherland.[86] Around these figures Fontane groups an entire cosmos of original and eccentric characters, such as Major General von Bamme auf Quirlsdorf,[87] the poet Hansen-Grell, Justice of the Peace Kniehase,[88] Pastor Seidentopf, Councilor of Justice Turgany,[89] Doctor Faulstich[90] and Hoppenmarieken, a "dwarf" who earns her keep as a messenger and is allowed to live on the estate.[91] With this network of major and minor characters Fontane paints a portrait of society that includes all strata and both sexes. The male originals and mavericks are juxtaposed with strong female characters. The nation is thus portrayed as a colorful cosmos of diversity in which the sexes, generations and social strata complement and enrich one another through their differences.

The plot itself is far less complex. In light of the retreat of the defeated French army through the region and the growing patriotism of the population, which hopes for a counterstrike, Berndt von Vitzewitz and his old friend Major-General von Bamme are planning to form a local militia on the East Prussian model, which Bamme will command. This militia is supposed

[83] Ibid., 1:28–36.
[84] Ibid., 2:8–32.
[85] Ibid., 1:1–14.
[86] Ibid., 3:27–39.
[87] Ibid., 2:20–32.
[88] Ibid., 1:69–72.
[89] Ibid., 1: 89–101.
[90] Ibid., 2:74–82.
[91] Ibid., 1:62–69.

to conduct an assault on the French at Frankfurt/Oder. Vitzewitz and Bamme believe that in this extraordinary situation they must place loyalty to the fatherland above allegiance to the king. They hope that their action will serve as a signal for a general uprising. In order to carry out their plans, they cooperate with the Russian flying parties that have arrived in the region. The assault fails miserably, however, since the preparations are insufficient and the promised Russian assistance never materializes. Lewin, who disapproves of the enterprise from the outset but takes part out of loyalty to his father, is taken prisoner by the French and threatened with a firing squad. For that reason Vitzewitz, his friends and some men from the village organize to free Lewin. Tubal is mortally wounded in the process.[92] The story closes with an afterword in the form of an entry from Renate's diary, recounting Lewin's return from the wars of 1813–15 in which he had fought as a volunteer. She describes his manlier appearance now and tells of his marriage to Marie, whom he has learned to love, and ends with her own plans. She intends to remain single and join a *Fräuleinstift*, a convent for Protestant gentlewomen, where she will devote herself "to quiet works of mercy."[93]

As he told his publisher Wilhelm Hertz in 1866, Fontane's declared objective in this "poly-perspectival novel" (*Vielheitsroman*)[94] was

to present, without murders or fires or stories of great passion [...] a large number of figures from the Mark Brandenburg (i.e. *German-Wendish*, for herein lies their peculiarity) from the winter of [18]12 to 13. Figures such as they existed in those days and as they, by and large, still exist today. I was not interested in conflicts, but rather in showing how the great consciousness born in those days came upon the most various people and how it affected them.[95](Emphasis in the original.)

His intention was to entertain the reader with "lovable figures" and, "where possible, ultimately to gain his love."[96] In the view of most present-day readers, he succeeds admirably. At the time, however, this approach was still very unaccustomed, and the book met with substantial misgivings among reviewers and gained a following only slowly.[97] The fact that *Before the Storm* does not join in the universal paeans to recent German unity under the auspices of Prussianism and militarism – unlike Fontane's colleague Gustav Freytag's

---

[92] Ibid., 4:193–200.
[93] Ibid., 4:223–226. On the novel, see Walter Müller-Seidel, *Theodor Fontane: Soziale Romankunst in Deutschland* (Stuttgart, 1975), 111–132; Gordon A. Craig, *Theodor Fontane: Literature and History in the Bismarck Reich* (New York, 1999), 155–171; and Bernd Witte, "Ein preußisches Wintermärchen: Thedor Fontanes erster Roman *Vor dem Sturm*," in Wolzogen, *Theodor Fontane*, 1:143–156.
[94] "Fontane an Paul Heyse, 9. Dez. 1878," quoted in Charlotte Jolles, *Theodor Fontane* (Stuttgart, 1993), 39.
[95] Quoted in Edda Ziegler and Gotthard Erler, *Theodor Fontane: Lebensraum und Phantasiewelt – Eine Biographie* (Berlin, 1996), 181.
[96] Ibid.
[97] Jolles, *Theodor Fontane*, 39–44; and Witte, "Wintermärchen," 146–148.

From a Small Town a short while later – doubtless also played its part. Fontane's aim instead was to keep alive the enlightened spirit of humanity and tolerance, to which he believed the new German Empire should remain true.[98] Loyalty is thus a central theme in the novel: loyalty to one's principles and tried-and-true traditions; loyalty in love, marriage and the family; loyalty to one's homeland, king and people. The question Fontane poses in the novel is which form of loyalty should enjoy priority: loyalty to the people or to the king, to one's own principles or to one's father?[99]

Another central theme is the understanding of patriotism and nationalism, with which he simultaneously questions the founding myth of the German Empire that viewed 1871 as the continuation and completion of the national rising of 1813. Through the many characters in the novel, Fontane explores the different versions of patriotism and nationalism not just in the winter of 1812–13, but also in the newly founded empire. The protagonists' conversations and debates in the novel and their actions, which he portrays with gentle irony, make it clear that, for Fontane, mercy, humanity and upright convictions were worth more than zealous nationalism, hatred of the French and military heroism.[100] According to the novel:

All stay-at-homes prate continually of 'sacrifice in the field'; old seasoned soldiers, however, who know from the experience of fifty battles what a strange and uncertain thing courage is, and on the other hand how small a degree of excitation suffices to produce the heroic deed of the ordinary stamp, all these keep a very cool head with regard to acts of bravery and have as a rule long since ceased to see anything especially glorious about them.[101]

In such reflections Fontane not only criticizes the propagandistic glorification of military heroism and masculine self-sacrifice after the Wars of Unification, but also challenges the excessive nationalism of his time, especially the idea of absolutely distinct and separate national identities. In the novel, the idea appears absurd in the light of the very mixed history of the Oderbruch region and the German-Polish clan. For Fontane, national identity and patriotism are matters of choice.[102]

Reviewers responded reticently to this complex and ambivalent novel, with its humorous and ironic undertone, which was as out of place in the

[98] See Hugo Aust, "'…und das Lachen verging mir.' Theodor Fontane und der Nationalismus," in Wolzogen, *Theodor Fontane*, 1:241–254; and Gudrun Loster-Schneider, *Der Erzähler Fontane: Seine politischen Positionen in den Jahren 1864–1898 und ihre ästhetische Vermittlung* (Tübingen, 1986), 55–66.

[99] Michael Gratzke, *Blut und Feuer: Heldentum Bei Lessing, Kleist, Fontane, Jünger und Heiner Müller* (Würzburg, 2011), 104.

[100] Ibid., 93–108; and Loster-Schneider, *Der Erzähler*, 41–66.

[101] Fontane, *Vor dem Sturm* (1986), 2:28. The English translation of this passage is from Fontane, *Before the Storm*, 144.

[102] Fontane, *Vor dem Sturm* (1986), 2:95–101; see also Müller-Seidel, *Theodor Fontane*, 117–120.

political landscape of early Imperial Germany as the novella *Schach von Wuthenow: A Tale from the Era of the Gensdarmes Regiment*, in which Fontane addresses the causes of the Prussian defeat of 1806 as critically as he does the national rising of 1813 in *Before the Storm*.[103] The reviewer in the *Deutsche Rundschau* found *Before the Storm* to be lacking in "outward coherence," but praised the "overall impression of the book" as "refreshing." The book was more "a sequence of pictures of the times and manners, a gallery of family portraits" than a novel.[104] *Die Grenzboten* similarly criticized the absence of a "main storyline, the silhouette of the narrative," but nevertheless considered the book to be a successful historical novel with a positive tendency.[105] The *Blätter für literarische Unterhaltung* judged the work more harshly. The subject was "brittle and difficult" and the text "convoluted" and devoid of a dramatic arc.[106] Readers appear to have taken a similar view, at least at first, since the book did not do very well in the lending libraries compared to Freytag in the 1880s. Fontane was long popular mainly in Berlin and Prussia, but this changed in the two decades before the First World War. He also became very sought after in libraries run by the Social Democrats and the free trade unions.[107]

Friedrich Spielhagen's novel *Noblesse oblige*, published in 1888 by Stackmann in Leipzig, takes a similarly critical approach to Imperial Germany as Fontane's *Before the Storm*. Spielhagen had been exceedingly popular with readers since the 1860s. After Louise Mühlberg, and well ahead of Freytag, Hesekiel and Fontane, he was among the most successful authors in the lending libraries of the Wilhelmine era. *Noblesse oblige* went through 12 editions by 1908 and appeared as a "popular edition" in 1910; it was also published as part of the edition of Spielhagen's collected novels, which was printed 19 times up to the First World War.[108] Spielhagen was born in 1829 and grew up in a family of civil servants first in Magdeburg, and later in Stralsund. After studying law and philology in Bonn, Berlin and Greifswald he worked mainly as a teacher. It was not until the late 1850s that he published his first novella and began to live from his writing. In the 1860s he became quite successful with his socially critical novels of the recent past written for a wide readership. Spielhagen's colleagues regarded

[103] See Müller-Seidel, *Theodor Fontane*, 132–151; and Walter P. Guenther, *Preussischer Gehorsam: Theodor Fontanes Novelle "Schach von Wuthenow" – Text und Deutung* (Munich, 1981), 179–273. For a list of all reviews, see Rasch, *Theodor Fontane*, 3:1857–1858.

[104] "Theodor Fontanes 'Vor dem Sturm,'" *Deutsche Rundschau* 18 (1879): 317–319, 317.

[105] "Theodor Fontane," *GB* 4.2 (1882): 538–546, 542.

[106] "Theodor Fontane: 'Vor dem Sturm,'" *BLU*, no. 9, 1879, 131–132. For a list of all reviews, see Rasch, *Theodor Fontane*, 3:1821–1823.

[107] Martino, *Leihbibliothek*, 453 and 543–544.

[108] Spielhagen, *Noblesse oblige*; the text was also translated into Russian (St Petersburg, 1896); on its success in lending libraries, see Martino, *Leihbibliothek*, 412–413 and 444–448.

him as a favorite author among women.[109] In the early 1880s, however, his work became the target of a wave of criticism from more conservative journalists and writers who denounced him as the author of "tendentious, partisan novels" and a "liberal politicizing and moralizing partisan writer."[110] Victor Klemperer defended him against these accusations in a 1913 article in *Die Grenzboten*, writing that Spielhagen had always "striven for objectivity, showing bad liberals and good conservatives, and as a proper writer above all showed people, that is, creatures, in which good and evil were strangely mixed. He never championed a person, but only a cause."[111] In fact, as an "unwavering Forty-Eighter," Spielhagen remained true to his democratic opinions throughout his life, which led to growing political friction with his more conservative colleagues in the antidemocratic political climate of the Bismarck era. Spielhagen's works were increasingly controversial among literary critics, but this did not stop readers from loving his novels.[112]

Noblesse oblige is the only historical novel by Spielhagen, who actually rejected the genre. In this work, like Fontane, he indirectly addresses the dogmatic nationalism and overt anti-French invective of the first two decades after the Franco-Prussian War of 1870–71. The novel is set in French-occupied Hamburg and its North German environs. The action begins in October 1812 and ends with liberation from the French occupation in May 1814. This scenario allows Spielhagen to describe in detail the effects of the French occupation on the economy, society and politics, the suffering of the Hamburg population and the efforts of patriots to liberate the city. His portrayal adheres very closely to accounts in historical works on Hamburg during the "time of the French."[113] This approach also permits him to closely interweave public and private life. The novel focuses on Minna Warburg, the patriotic daughter of the respected but debt-ridden merchant and senator Warburg, and her large circle of family and friends. They include old Warburg, who tries by every means, including the betrayal of his own daughter, to save his bankrupt business; his son Georg, a fervent German-national patriot who fights as a volunteer against the detested French, is taken prisoner and only released on bond; and Minna's younger sister Johanna, who wants to marry her Swedish fiancé Oskar, son of a business partner, but needs the money for a proper trousseau. Others who play important roles are Minna's one true love, her fiancé the French officer Marquis Hypolit Drouot d'Hericourt, who participates in the Russian campaign and then in battles in Germany; and not least the wealthy merchant

[109] Sammons, *Friedrich Spielhagen*, 46–47.
[110] Victor Klemperer, "Friedrich Spielhagen," *GB* 71.1 (1912): 238–242, 242.
[111] Ibid., 239–240.
[112] Klemperer, "Friedrich Spielhagen," 241–242; see also Sammons, "Friedrich Spielhagen," 147, and *Friedrich Spielhagen*, 40–51.
[113] See Aaslestad, "Paying for War;" and idem, "Remembering."

Theodor Billow, who is in love with Minna and offers to save the family finances and thereby solve all their problems in return for her hand in marriage. This cast of characters sets up the two major conflicts for Minna. On the one hand, she must choose between her own love, which would make her happy but cause her family's downfall, and the possibility, by wedding a man she does not love, of saving her father's company from bankruptcy and allowing her sister to marry. On the other, the brutal occupation of Hamburg by General Davout confronts her with the question of how to reconcile her love for a Frenchman with her passionate patriotism and love for her nationalist brother, who opposes their relationship. At first, Minna tries to have it both ways. She actively supports the work of the circle around the well-known Hamburg patriot Friedrich Perthes for the liberation of Hamburg and the liberty of the German fatherland. After the first attempt to liberate the city fails, when the French return and the situation becomes increasingly dramatic, old Warburg's financial problems also worsen. He systematically seeks to undermine Minna's relationship with d'Hericourt, keeping his letters from her, and presses her to marry Billow, which she ultimately agrees to do. Yet the relationship, and with it the novel, does not end happily. While Hamburg is finally liberated after its long hardships, the war has a dramatic aftermath. Not only is the family's property in Hamburg largely destroyed, but the family relationships also suffer greatly. Minna has lost her baby. Her tension-filled marriage with Billow ends with his death, and Minna, like Eberhardine, becomes a successful estate owner at Warnesoe Manor, which she inherits from Billow. But she still cannot marry her true love, since d'Hericourt dies in the attempt to save Billow.[114]

The novel is fascinating and unusual, not just because, like *The Last von Reckenburg*, it focuses on a strong and self-confident woman, but also because it very precisely describes her limited opportunities for action, which were not much better in 1888 than in 1813, and integrates them into the social conflicts. In *Noblesse oblige*, much as in his other novels, Spielhagen reveals a sensitive understanding of women's constricted social circumstances and the limits placed on strong women like Minna in particular. This was greatly appreciated by his female readership, which included, by their own admission, such well-known middle-class feminists as Hedwig Dohm and Helene Lange and pacifists like Berta von Suttner.[115] Minna is not merely described as an active patriot, but in the postwar period also as a just, intelligent, socially conscious and reform-oriented estate owner who is dedicated in every respect to the common good and has a great regard for ordinary people. Spielhagen is articulating a social critique here, since

[114] Friedrich Spielhagen, *Noblesse oblige* (Berlin, n.d.), 324–330.
[115] *Friedrich Spielhagen: Dem Meister des deutschen Romans zu seinem 70. Geburtstage von Freunden und Jüngern gewidmet* (Leipzig, 1889), 35, 53–54 and 70.

it is a commoner, not the landed aristocracy, who reforms conditions in the countryside.[116]

Spielhagen's liberal-democratic views are also evident in his treatment of the novel's second major theme: the nation, patriotism and war. The book offers a vivid portrayal of the dramatic effects of the wars more generally, but especially of Davout's despotic rule in Hamburg, which after Leipzig suffered more than any other German city in 1813–14. This is his explanation for contemporaries' hatred of the French. At the same time, however, he also criticizes the blind fanaticism, for example, of Georg, who places nationality above humanity, an error he ultimately ends up acknowledging.[117] The novel describes in very positive terms the commitment of the German patriots, whose thinking and actions he thus recommends to posterity as a worthy tradition. This characterizes the nation as a matter for all of the people, for which women too can and should work, parallel and complementary to men.[118] However, he also stresses the decency, dignity and sense of honor of the Frenchman Hypolit, whom even Georg will describe at the end as "the noblest of men,"[119] as well as the highly developed humanity and patriotism of the Jewish banker Samuel Hirsch.[120] His negative characterizations are mainly reserved for profiteers and opportunists like Billow and Warburg, who lack any principles and look only to their own advantage. The novel ends with a clear statement against war in any form, which is highly unusual for a novel set during the Anti-Napoleonic Wars, closing with the following excerpt from a letter by Hypolit, written to Minna in September 1814 from the burning city of Moscow:

It is a dreadful barbarism to which we have forced our enemies, through which they in turn forced us to commit atrocities that would never have happened otherwise. Oh, my beloved friend, my heart stops when I think of this pernicious circle, which coils itself around millennia of history! Will there never come a time when Man will fully enjoy the privilege of being ennobled above all creatures through the gift of reason; will freely and cheerfully live up to the duties that flow from this highest form of nobility; will be allowed to be human, without inhumanity being demanded of him in the name of familial love, welfare, the fatherland, national honor?[121]

The novel's antiwar ending is a plea for humanity. At a time of heightened public national chauvinism, imperialism and militarism, in which those who thought differently – like the Social Democrats – were persecuted by Bismarck's government, Spielhagen revealed himself as one of "the most democratic writers in German literature" of his period.[122] As a result, his

---

[116] Spielhagen, *Noblesse oblige* (Berlin, n.d.), 331–333.
[117] Ibid., 330.
[118] Ibid., 121–125.
[119] Ibid.
[120] Ibid., 38–39.
[121] Ibid., 339.
[122] Sammons, "Friedrich Spielhagen," 147.

novel had a hard time gaining recognition from the national-conservative literary critics of his day.[123] Like-minded colleagues, in contrast, commended the book "as thoroughly praiseworthy."[124] It also found its way into the lending libraries and to readers.

Friedrich Spielhagen's *Noblesse oblige* was one of the last successful novels in Imperial Germany set in the period of the Anti-Napoleonic Wars that remembered this time in a more critical way. What followed was largely nationalist mythmaking in novel form and texts quickly dashed off for the commercialized book market. Most novels written from the late 1880s on interpreted the time quite unambiguously and helped to spread and reinforce the national myth of the period of 1806–15 as a "heroic era" in German history when, following the national debacle of Jena and Auerstedt, unity, patriotism and a will to sacrifice had led to Prussia's and Germany's "national rising" and finally to victory. It was particularly novels for "youth and the people," as publishers' advertisements called them, that conveyed this myth with a strong monarchic-conservative or nationalist undertone. Only now, in the last two decades before the First World War, did the interpretation of the wars of 1813–15 as "Wars of Liberation," and with it the Borussian master narrative of academic historiography, assert itself in fiction as well.

Typical examples of this type of nationalist novel set at the time of the Anti-Napoleonic Wars and written for an increasingly commercialized book market are the bestsellers by Paul Schreckenbach, August Sperl and Emmy von Winterfeld-Warnow. They continued to imagine the German nation as a *Volk* family with the royal family at its helm and exhorted women and men alike to display self-sacrifice and patriotism, albeit in gender-specific ways. The notion of heroic death for the nation was inscribed into this nationalism with the myth of young military volunteers who had gladly sacrificed their lives on the altar of the fatherland. Patriotic women were depicted in a complementary manner as the heroic mothers of militiamen and volunteers or cheerful war brides who sent their fiancés off to battle. In these historical novels women actively supported the struggle for the liberation of the nation through war charities or as voluntary nurses.

Paul Schreckenbach's *The Infamous Baron von Krosigk: A Novel of the Time of Germany's Disgrace and National Rising* was published by Staackmann in Leipzig in 1907. It went through nine editions up to 1914 and had sold 53,000 copies by 1926.[125] Schreckenbach, born in 1866 in Neumark, a town near Weimar, had studied theology and history, and had

[123] Joseph Necker, "Friedrich Spielhagen: 'Noblesse oblige' (1888)," *GB* 47.2 (1888): 224–228.

[124] Konrad Teleman, "'Noblese oblige,'" *Das Magazin für die Literatur des In- und Auslandes* 57.24 (1888): 376–379; and "Friedrich Spielhagen, 'Noblesse oblige,'" *Deutsche Literaturzeitung* 9 (1888): 48.

[125] See Schreckenbach, *Baron von Krosigk*; and Bigler, "Schreckenbach, Paul."

worked since 1896 as a Protestant pastor in a small village near Torgau in northwestern Saxony. He made his name as an author of well-researched historical novels written for a broad audience, which was what critics mainly praised in their short reviews.[126] *The Infamous Baron von Krosigk* tells the story of a real historical figure, Baron Heinrich Ferdinand von Krosigk (1778–1813), Prussian estate owner and former major from the Saalekreis region in Saxony-Anhalt, and his struggle against Jérôme Bonaparte, king of the newly founded Kingdom of Westphalia, and his French occupation forces. During his own time von Krosigk was already infamous for his steadfast and witty resistance against the French occupiers, who called him *le mauvais Baron*. The novel, which covers the period between 1806 and 1813, describes not only his struggle, but also the support of his wife, Friederike von Schurff, his family, friends and neighbors. The novel ends with von Krosigk's heroic death at the Battle of Leipzig in October 1813 and his return to his estate in a large funeral procession in which the entire population of the region participates and honors him as their "protector" against French tyranny. Friederike von Schurff heroically accepts his death and opens the rooms of her estate for the care of wounded and sick soldiers, supported by the women of the municipality.[127] The subtitle of the novel already suggests its nationalist tone. Male steadfastness, conscientiousness, honor and heroism, especially the willingness to die for the fatherland, are core traits of German men that the author praises. The French foe, in contrast, is depicted as "lustful," "degenerate" and "dishonorable."[128]

Quite similar, but a bit more nuanced, is the tone of August Sperl's *Students Out! A Novel of the Time of Our Deepest Degradation*, which focuses on the story of volunteers from the *Burschenschaften*, the patriotic student organizations, between 1806 and 1813. It is set in the small capital of a southwest German electoral principality that is occupied by the French and becomes part of the Confederation of the Rhine. The novel, which appeared in 1913 and was published by Beck in Munich, describes the changing attitudes of a population that increasingly resented and resisted the French, as well as the role of the *Burschenschaften* as the avant-garde of this resistance. It was suitable reading for anybody with hopes of a new volunteer movement in August 1914. It went through seven editions up to 1917 and had sold 26,000 copies by 1925. Sperl was born in Fürth in 1862. After studying philology and history he worked as an archivist in various Bavarian archives. He, too, became known as the author of well-researched historical novels, popular with readers but not literary critics.[129]

---

[126] See "Der böse Baron von Krosigk," *Leipziger Zeitung*, no. 50, 14 December 1907, 223.

[127] Schreckenbach, *Baron von Krosigk*, 306–307.

[128] Ibid., 191.

[129] Sperl, *Burschen*; and Hoffmann, *August Sperl*. See the brief review in *Das literarische Echo* 16.6 (15 December 1913): 427–428.

The female complement to the "truly German heroes" in Schreckenbach's and Sperl's novels were strong courageous "German women," female patriots who shared the heroes' love of fatherland and were, when needed, always "willing to sacrifice their domestic happiness on the altar of higher duty," in particular in the national emergency of war.[130] Emmy von Winterfeld-Warnow's *German Women in Difficult Times: Novel from the Years 1806–1812*, published in 1901 by Otto Janke in Berlin presents a similar ideal of female patriotism as the novels written by Schreckenbach and Sperl. Her novel sold for 4 marks in paperback, a price that still greatly exceeded the annual fee for lending libraries, which in small towns was no higher than 50 pfennigs (100 pfennigs equal 1 mark).[131] Winterfeld-Warnow was born in Bremen in 1861. Her father, a lawyer, died early, but her mother was nevertheless able to finance a good school education for her daughter. In 1888 Winterfeld-Warnow married the wealthy Prussian estate owner Hans von Winterfeld, who encouraged her to follow her passion and write. *German Women in Difficult Times* was her first novel, which already reached a second edition after only one year. The text also describes women as ardent supporters of the Anti-Napoleonic struggle for the "liberation of the fatherland." It depicts shining instances of "individual women" who "were priestesses of patriotism and led the way with action and by example; German women whose hearts have always beaten in burning love for their country, even in the times of deepest shame."[132] Much like the main male protagonists in the novels by Schreckenbach and Sperl, Winterfeld-Warnow's central female protagonists are intended to function as role models for patriotic behavior in the next national war, which women were expected to support in their own gender-specific way. Educated readers and discerning literary critics and librarians looked down on this kind of literature, treating popular "women's novels" like *German Women in Difficult Times* in particular with condescension. The following scathing review, for example, appeared in 1902 in the *Blätter für Volksbibliotheken und Lesehallen*, a supplement to the *Zentralblatt für Bibliothekswesen*, the central journal for libraries and librarians:

This patriotic tale will be a welcome offering for undemanding readers, especially more mature youth. It is by no means of any literary value; any interest arises solely from the simple but affectionately narrated episodes from the time of the gradual awakening of German heroic might with so many outstanding female figures.[133]

---

[130] Schreckenbach, *Baron von Krosigk*, 224.

[131] See "Berichte über Bibliotheken einzelner Städte," *Blätter für Volksbibliotheken und Lesehallen* 3.11/12 (1902): 187–193.

[132] Emmy von Winterfeld, *Deutsche Frauen in schwerer Zeit: Roman aus den Jahren 1806–1812 nach alten Familienpapieren und Überlieferungen* (Berlin, 1901), 292; on Winterfeld-Warnow, see Wilhelm Lührs, ed., *Bremische Biographie, 1912–1962* (Bremen, 1969), 563.

[133] "Winterfeld-Warnow, E. v., Deutsche Frauen in schwerer Zeit," *Blätter für Volksbibliotheken und Lesehallen* 3.11/12 (1902): 210.

Such novels received a short nod at best in the newspaper feuilletons and no mention at all in the well-known cultural and literary journals, but they were very popular among the rapidly growing number of "women and girls" from broader circles of "the people" who preferred "light fiction," which was why the lending libraries bought them.[134]

Although such monarchic-conservative and national bestsellers dominated the production of *new* novels recalling the period of the Anti-Napoleonic Wars that came on the market in the decade before the First World War, their narratives were still contested by older, more ambivalent and critical novels on the time. It is impossible to stress strongly enough that novels by authors such as Alexis, Fontane, Freytag, Lewald, Mühlberg, Rellstab and Spielhagen continued to be very successful in the lending libraries–up to 1914. They even attracted new strata of readers in the growing number of libraries maintained by the trade unions and the Social Democratic Party. Thus, the recollection of the period of the Anti-Napoleonic Wars remained contested in the main media of popular literary memory – the novel – until the First World War.

---

[134] "Berichte über Bibliotheken einzelner Städte," *Blätter für Volksbibliotheken und Lesehallen* 3.11/12 (1902): 192.

Conclusion

The many conflicts and debates over the "legacy" of the era of the Anti-Napoleonic Wars, their proper commemoration and their significance for present-day society and politics – as expressed not just in autobiographies and war memoirs but also in novels of the recent past and historical fiction – are quite fascinating in light of the assumption among historians, which persisted so long after 1945, that the monarchic-conservative and nationalistic interpretations had been the dominant readings of the Anti-Napoleonic Wars in nineteenth-century collective memory since the restoration period. The same is true of the obvious importance of the gender dimension in these memories, which has been completely ignored by historians until recently. In memories of this period and in their appropriation for the present – as at the remembered time itself – gender images and gender relations assumed a central significance in the continuing imagination of the nation as a *Volk* family, an imagination in which the collective memories of the period of the Anti-Napoleonic Wars played a crucial role.

Because West German historians writing after 1945 based their interpretation of collective memories of the period from 1806 to 1815 on works by their earlier counterparts – the recognized academic historians of Imperial Germany – and did not deign to descend into the depths of middlebrow literature with its numerous novels of the recent past, works of historical fiction, autobiographies, war memoirs and the like, they de facto simply continued the master narratives of the leading Wilhelmine historians. They overlooked the continuous competition and conflict in public memory production, influenced not only by regional, social, generational, ethnic, religious and political as well as gender differences, but also by the literary market, different media of memory and last but not least the changing political culture.

In a paradoxical way, historians were still bound to the master narratives of their Wilhelmine forefathers, when, with critical intent, they so radically challenged their predecessors' interpretations as to call into question the very idea that an early patriotic-national movement had existed before and during the wars of 1813–15, even in North Germany and Prussia. As a result, they failed to recognize the liberal potential that was *also* inherent in the patriotism of the wars of 1813–15. They were at once "Wars of Liberation" and "Wars of Liberty," and this is reflected in the long and hotly contested collective literary memory of those events in the nineteenth century.

EPILOGUE

HISTORICIZING WAR AND MEMORY,
2013–1813–1913

On 20 October 2013 a great battle took place on the outskirts of Leipzig. On a battlefield measuring 500,000 square meters, 6,000 men from 26 countries (women were allowed only as camp followers on the edges of the battlefield) donned their colorful period uniforms, cleaned their old muskets, loaded them with blanks and brought their cannon into position to reenact, with much thunder and gun smoke, the so-called Battle of the Nations of 16–19 October 1813. The event organizer, the *Verband Jahrfeier Völkerschlacht b. Leipzig 1813 e.V.* (Association to Commemorate the 1813 Battle of the Nations at Leipzig), repeatedly emphasized to the public and the press – 350 journalists from home and abroad observed the spectacle – that the reenacted scenario was historically accurate and had been developed and checked by a military history commission. The combat demonstration by the infantry, cavalry and artillery lasted several hours. A total of 35,000 spectators were admitted, but the same number had to be turned away because the crowd that gathered to watch the spectacle surpassed all expectations.[1]

The reenactment was the spectacular close to a commemorative week in Leipzig and environs recalling the Battle of the Nations and the consecration 100 years later of the monument erected to it. Numerous events surrounding the double anniversary took place throughout the year under the slogan "Leipzig 1813–1913–2013 – A Landmark of European History," organized by the city of Leipzig, especially the museums and city archive, in cooperation with the *Verband Jahrfeier Völkerschlacht b. Leipzig 1813 e.V.* and financed by private sponsors and the tourism industry.[2] The public commemoration in 2013 focused on military combat (in the reenactment), the history of memory of the battle and the "Wars of Liberation" and

---

[1] See the website of the "Verband Jahrfeier Völkerschlacht b. Leipzig 1813 e.V.": http://www
.leipzig1813.com/en/home.html; and "Kartoffelschnaps und Kriegsgeschrei," *Der Tagesspiegel*, 21 October 2013.

[2] See http://www.voelkerschlacht-jubilaeum.de/en/home.html.

the associated national myths and legends (in the exhibition at the Leipzig City Museum, *Helden nach Maß* or Heroes Made to Measure),[3] and the hardship and suffering of the civilian population (in the massive panorama "Leipzig 1813 – Amidst the Confusion of the Battle of the Nations" by artist Yadgar Asisi in Leipzig's *Gasometer*).[4] These topics were also picked up by the regional public television station *Mitteldeutscher Rundfunk* (MDR). It accompanied the commemorations with extensive reporting and a variety of documentaries. The much discussed "highlight" was a daily 45-minute "live" report on the events of the battle during the primetime *MDR Top News* program from 16–19 October. Well-known newsreaders and reporters described the progress of the battle and its consequences for soldiers and civilians and explained the political context as if it were all happening in the present. Reenacted historical scenes "documented" the events.[5] This unusual format, as well as the reenactment, were intended "to bring history alive" and make it interesting for the younger generation in particular.[6]

That is also the aim of a historical novel commissioned by the *Verband Jahrfeier Völkerschlacht b. Leipzig 1813 e.V.* on the occasion of the commemorative year. They approached writer Sabine Ebert, who has made a name for herself as the author of extremely popular historical "women's novels" that center on female main characters. Her book *1813 – Fire of War* made a timely appearance on 14 March 2013, 200 years after the beginning of the commemorated wars, and was presented at a reading in Leipzig's symbolic Nikolaikirche before an audience of 2,000. Like her colleague Louise Mühlbach 150 years earlier, Ebert stresses that *1813*, like all of her other historical novels, is based on intense study of primary sources and secondary literature. On her website she states that her book "by no means [recounts] only bloody battles, but also [describes] how the civilian population experienced this time and what was going on in secret diplomacy and how war destroys souls and individuals maintain their humanity. It is no battle epic, but a book against war."[7] She deliberately disassociates her depiction from the heroic national legends and myths that had long marked memories of the Battle of the Nations and the year 1813 in Germany.

---

3 See http://www.stadtgeschichtliches-museum-leipzig.de/site_deutsch/ausstellungen/Helden. php; Rodekamp, *Helden*; and Andreas Platthaus, "Keine Daten und Schlachtordnungen!" *Frankfurter Allgemeine Zeitung*, 17 October 2013.
4 See http://www.asisi.de/index.php?id=7#asisi_index_id_58; and Andreas Platthaus, "Im Schatten der Völkerschlacht von Leipzig," *Frankfurter Allgemeine Zeitung*, 12 Aug. 2013.
5 See http://www.mdr.de/voelkerschlacht/topnews/verteilseite3010.html and http://www .mdr.de/voelkerschlacht/index.html, as well as Markus Ehrenberg, "Breaking News: Völkerschlacht – live beim MDR," *Der Tagesspiegel*, 13 October 2013.
6 Michael Kothe, main organizer of the reenactment of the Battle of the Nations, in "Umgang mit 200 Jahren Völkerschlacht," *Friedrich Ebert Stiftung im Studio* 3; see http://www.info-tv-leipzig.de/mixed/allgemeines/umgang-mit-200-jahren-voelkerschlacht/.
7 See http://www.sabine-ebert.de/; and Ebert, *1813*.

The tenor of all official events for the double anniversary was also antiwar and pro-international understanding in Europe. This was expressed particularly clearly by Martin Schulz, the Social Democratic president of the European Parliament, in his address "Leipzig 1813 – 1913 – 2013: Anniversary of the Battle of the Nations and the Monument to the Battle of the Nations" on the occasion of the renovated monument's reopening on 18 October 2013. He pointed out that the monument nowadays is perceived first and foremost as a place to commemorate the dead, which recalls the more than 100,000 men from many European countries who lost their lives in the battle. At the same time, he interpreted the Battle of the Nations itself and the wars of 1813–15 as well as the consecration ceremony for the Monument to the Battle of the Nations a century later as "harbingers of what was to come." Here, "nationalism" had already shown "its second, ugly face."[8] This pacifist and antinationalist interpretation of the Battle of Leipzig and the monument to it is new in official commemoration. It reflects the changes in West German society after 1945, for which peace and international understanding had become declared guiding values. Until well into the twentieth century, this central site of memory for German history had been associated, in one way or another, with nationalism and often also with militarism. But in a city and a federal state that had belonged to the former GDR until 1989, it also replaced the master narrative of East German historians, who interpreted the wars of 1813–15 as "people's wars" that proved victorious only in the "brotherhood in arms" with Russia. The aim of this GDR narrative was to provide an identity-creating tradition for the new "people's state" and "German-Soviet friendship."[9]

Using the history of recollections of the Battle of the Nations, which because of its dimensions and significance occupied a special place in the national memory, I would like in this conclusion to summarize and discuss the interplay of factors that shaped the contested memories of Germany's and Prussia's wars against Napoleon and their transformations. Since collective memory represents at once the past, the present and the future, and must accordingly always be historicized and contextualized, I also begin the following overview with the event itself. The dramatic experience of this

8 "Leipzig 1813–1913–2013: Jubiläum Völkerschlacht und Völkerschlachtdenkmal – Rede Von Martin Schulz, Präsident des Europäischen Parlaments," http://www.europarl.europa.eu/the-president/en/press/press_release_speeches/speeches/sp-2013/sp-2013-october/html/leipzig-1813–1913–2013-jubilaum-v-lkerschlacht-und-v-lkerschlachtdenkmal--rede-von-martin-schulz-prasident-des-europaischen-parlaments.

9 Uwe Puschner, "18. Oktober 1813: 'Möchten die Deutschen nur alle und immer dieses Tages gedenken!' – Die Leipziger Völkerschlacht," in *Erinnerungstage: Wendepunkte der Geschichte von der Antike bis zur Gegenwart*, ed. Étienne François and Uwe Puschner (Munich, 2010), 145–162, 158–162; and Steffen Poser, "Zur Rezeptionsgeschichte des Völkerschlachtdenkmals zwischen 1914 und 1989," in Keller and Schmid, *Vom Kult*, 78–104, 92–102.

battle, like that of the Anti-Napoleonic Wars more generally, was a central factor that exerted a lasting influence on memory. Contemporary events and the discourses of the remembered time formed the framework for communicative memory in particular.

EXPERIENCE, MEDIA, POLITICS AND MEMORY CONSTRUCTION

Between 16 and 19 October 1813 a total of more than 171,000 men under Napoleon's supreme command, including many soldiers of his remaining German allies Baden and Saxony, faced more than 300,000 Coalition forces under the command of the Austrian field marshal Prince Schwarzenberg.[10] A substantial segment of Europe's armed forces – more than 470,000 soldiers from 12 countries – had massed in Saxony in the heart of Central Europe.[11] That made the battle the largest in history before the First World War. The liberation of Germany, which had officially begun on 16 March 1813 with the declaration of war by the Prussian-Russian coalition, was certainly not decided by this battle, and it did not bring an end to the War of the Sixth Coalition. It would be six months before Napoleon was deposed in April 1814 – but the Battle of Leipzig did represent Napoleon's second dramatic defeat, after the Russian campaign of 1812. After Leipzig, the remains of his army, 60,000 men, had to retreat to the Rhine to defend France's frontiers. The Napoleonic army, victorious for so long, never recovered from this debacle.[12]

At least 110,000 soldiers died during the four-day battle, for which the groundwork had already been laid since August 1813 with protracted fighting in North and Central Germany involving heavy losses. Never again on German soil were so many soldiers killed within such a short time. The Coalition estimated their total losses at 54,000, and the Napoleonic army's at 66,000 men.[13] It took more than two weeks for the French prisoners of war and conscripted Saxon civilians deployed for the task to transport the wounded and remove the bodies from the battlefields around Leipzig. The figures for the number of soldiers left wounded and sick after the battle vary widely. In Leipzig alone, a city of about 35,000 inhabitants, the estimate is at least 38,000 and in neighboring Halle an additional 5,000. Whatever the

---

[10] Robert Naumann, *Die Völkerschlacht bei Leipzig: Nebst Nachrichten von Zeitgenossen und Augenzeugen über dieselbe* (Leipzig, 1863), 5–7. See also Platthaus, "Völkerschlacht"; Poser, *Völkerschlacht*; and Hagemann, "Unimaginable Horror."

[11] In total, the Grande Armée was around 440,000 strong and the Coalition Field Army around 510,000 strong. Karl-Heinz Börner, "Die Völkerschlacht bei Leipzig 1813 – Bedeutung und Wirkung," *Militärgeschichte* 4 (1988): 323–326.

[12] Leggiere, *Napoleon*, 276; and David Chandler, *The Campaigns of Napoleon* (New York, 1966), 936.

[13] Leggiere, *Napoleon*, 276.

precise figure, it fell rapidly because of the high mortality rate. Every day 600–800 died.[14] Fifty-four large private and public buildings were turned into military hospitals in which over 800 men and women worked as doctors and nursing staff.

The enormous number of sick and wounded soldiers brought epidemics like typhus and dysentery back to the city and the region, which had already been suffering since the march-through of soldiers returning from Russia in the spring of 1813. Increasing numbers of inhabitants fell ill, an average of 700 to 800 per week in the last three months of 1813. The mortality rate was especially high among doctors and nurses, nearly 50 percent of whom became infected and died. In 1813 about 13,500 inhabitants of Leipzig contracted epidemic typhus – more than one-third of the population – of whom 2,700 (20 percent) died.[15] By June 1814 a further 1,000 people had fallen victim to the epidemic, which claimed the lives of one-tenth of the urban and surrounding rural population.[16] The epidemic was able to spread so widely not least because even months after the battle the population was still suffering the "greatest hardship and most extreme want," leaving children and old people in particular in a weakened condition.[17]

Overall, at least 60 villages in the region had been substantially destroyed. Twenty of them had suffered heavy bombardment during the fighting and had been burnt virtually to the ground. Materials for rebuilding were in short supply because for months the soldiers of the huge armies had been requisitioning anything they could get their hands on, especially in the countryside. For the population it mattered little whether they were "friend" or "foe." It was almost a year before the most obvious traces of the fighting had been removed and the majority of the tens of thousands of refugees forced to flee their homes and farms could return. Most fields and gardens in the region had been destroyed beyond all recognition. Crops and livestock had been decimated. Seeds were in scarce supply. When the fields were tilled again for the first time in the spring the epidemic broke out again because the farmers found thousands of decaying corpses that had been hastily buried during battle. Reconstruction took years, especially in the villages surrounding Leipzig that had suffered most from the battle. The city itself, in contrast, where the destruction had been more limited, recovered relatively quickly from the trauma of battle and war.[18]

[14] Julius v. Pflugk-Harttung, *Leipzig 1813: Aus den Akten des Kriegsarchiv, des Geheimen Staatsarchivs Berlin, Staatsarchivs in Breslau und des Ministeriums der auswärtigen Angelegenheiten in London* (Gotha, 1913), 426; Gerhard Graf, *Die Völkerschlacht bei Leipzig in zeitgenössischen Berichten* (Berlin, 1988), 138; and Naumann, *Völkerschlacht*, 138 and 421–423.

[15] Naumann, *Völkerschlacht*, 423–424 and 429–430.

[16] Graf, *Völkerschlacht*, 138.

[17] Naumann, *Völkerschlacht*, 153.

[18] Hagemann, "Unimaginable Horror."

These dramatic civilian experiences of war, which other embattled cities and their environs went through in 1813 (if not to the same degree), and the terrible events endured by many soldiers, continued to influence the contested shaping of memories of the wars against Napoleon over the course of the nineteenth century. The quickly growing number of autobiographies, war memoirs, historical biographies, novels and history books on these wars published in the first decades after 1815 clearly indicate the interest of authors and readers in recollections that sought to rescue from oblivion their own experiences and roles in the great events of the Napoleonic Wars. Their experiences were processed and the associated political, economic or social claims expressed above all in communicative memory. As a result most of these texts only made it into the "archive," "the passively stored memory that preserves the past past," but not into the "canon," "the actively circulated memory that keeps the past present," which is not built up anew by every generation; "on the contrary, it outlives the generations who have to encounter and reinterpret it anew according to their time." Aleida Assmann, one of the most prolific and influential theorists of cultural memory, has suggested this differentiation between archive and canon, which helps us to understand the complicated process of forgetting and remembering in collective memory.[19] For her, canon and archive are in specific ways "anchored in institutions that are not closed against each other but allow for mutual influx and reshuffling," which "accounts for the dynamics within cultural memory and keeps it open for change and negotiations," which also explains the multiple use of recollections in collective memory and the booms in remembrance and forgetting that we also can observe with respect to the Anti-Napoleonic Wars.[20]

The dramatic war experiences of ordinary people – civilians, soldiers and officers – clearly led to the memory boom in the first decades after the Napoleonic Wars and were one important factor that informed communicative memory, far beyond the most affected regions. But these experiences of violence and death were more and more lost in the canon of the cultural memory of the Napoleonic Wars. Here, the heroic national narratives increasingly dominated. As long as historians of the era only focus on the canon of the collective memories of these wars and do not pay closer attention to archive and with it the dimension of violence; as long as they do not take into account the varied regional experiences of war and accept that the new forms of warfare had far-reaching consequences for civilians and soldiers alike, they cannot hope to grasp the modern character of these first "total wars"[21] or to understand why these wars, and with them events such

---

[19] Aleida Assmann, "Canon and Archive," in Erll and Nünning, *Companion*, 97–107; and Assmann, *Cultural Memory*.

[20] Assmann, "Canon and Archive," 100–103.

[21] Bell, *War*.

as the Battle of Leipzig, occupied such a significant place in popular regional, national and European commemoration during the nineteenth century.

The specific and often very violent experiences of war were, however, but one important factor that shaped memories. The competing political interpretations of the wars of 1813–15 were also highly significant. As this study has shown, central patterns of argumentation and concepts in the patriotic and national discourse developed during the turbulent period of the Anti-Napoleonic Wars would be drawn upon repeatedly throughout the long nineteenth century. This also applies to the understanding of key terms such as *Nation* and *Volk* or patriotism and citizenship, which were contested from the beginning, as well as to new, quite controversial ideas about the military and war and their relationship to politics. Central questions that were debated during and after the wars of 1813–15 more intensively than before included, on the one hand, what constituted the German nation, who belonged to it and under what conditions, and what duties and rights were associated with this affiliation; and on the other, whether these wars were "Wars of Liberation," "Wars of Liberty" or "people's wars." The competing interpretations of the historical events that evolved within the debate over these key terms formed the political framework for the contested construction of national memory of the wars of 1813–15 in the German Confederation and German Empire, and with it recollections of the Battle of Leipzig.

The conservative Prussian-dominated master narrative spoke of "Wars of Liberation" fought by "subjects" who had followed their king's call and, led by his generals, fought for liberation. Saxony and other states of the former Confederation of the Rhine ruled by monarchs as well as Austria shared a monarchic-conservative interpretation of the wars, but downplayed the role of Prussia and emphasized regional patriotism. The liberal German-national master narrative, in contrast, spoke of "Wars of Liberty" in which "the German people," in a "free, autonomous movement," had conducted a "struggle for outward and inward liberty."[22] A third interpretation that had gained influence since the *Vormärz* challenged both master narratives, but was and remained a minority position until 1914. Democrats and Marxists interpreted the wars of 1813–15 as "people's wars"; however, unlike the German-national and liberal readings, their interpretation featured the autonomous agency of the "popular masses," including the urban and rural poor.[23] Franz Mehring, a Social Democratic historian and journalist, for example, argued in 1913 in his *1813 to 1819: From Kalisch to Karlsbad*, that 1813 had not yet been a "struggle of the 'peoples.' " Only in a few regions, such as Spain and the Tyrol in 1809 and Prussia and northern Germany in 1813, had "mass movements" emerged in the sense of a

---

[22] See chapter 10 in the third part and chapter 13 in the fourth part.
[23] See Engels, "Ernst Moritz Arndt"; and Mehring, "Zur deutschen Geschichte."

"people's war," and they had mainly been directed "against the foreigner and despot" Napoleon. Particularly in Prussia, however, the high degree of mobilization for the militia and volunteer units had been an "exceedingly rare achievement." It was impossible to attain "such high troop figures, no matter how mighty the means of recruitment," "if the population does not rush to arms with the greatest enthusiasm."[24] The present study does of course not share all elements of this interpretation, but it argues similarly that above all in 1813, the Prussian monarchy was able to launch the war and prosecute it successfully only because of the active support of large portions of the Prussian population, both men and women, especially in the cities, and one major reason for this support was the devastating experience of French occupation in 1806–08 and the continuing oppression and exploitation up to 1812.[25]

The debate over the name and meaning of the wars of 1813–15, which revolved around the role of "the people" or the "nation," and the political claims derived from it, retained its politically explosive potential primarily up to the founding of the German Empire, as I have also shown. The legacy of these wars was used, on the one hand, to legitimate German-national desires for unification as well as liberal and democratic demands for increased political rights. On the other, it served to justify Prussia's leadership role in the future of the newly founded German Empire. While the conflict surrounding the issue of "Wars of Liberation" versus "Wars of Liberty" continued to influence the construction of collective memory even after German unification by "blood and iron" in 1871, which culminated in a German nation-state without Austria, the conservative-monarchic narrative became increasingly dominant and also shaped recollections of the Battle of Leipzig.[26] This Borussian master narrative continued, however, to compete with the German-national and liberal-democratic interpretations, as the analysis of academic, popular and military historiography, the construction of memory in published autobiography and war memoirs as well as novels of the recent past and historical novels has shown; but the influence of competing narratives receded steadily from the 1880s onward. The transformation of political culture and the growing influence of academic historiography, which in Imperial Germany was dominated by Prussianism and increasingly claimed sole interpretational sovereignty, were decisive here.[27]

The widely varying political and military situation in the different regions of Continental Europe between 1792 and 1815 was a further important

---

[24] Franz Mehring, *1813 bis 1819: Von Kalisch nach Karlsbad* (Stuttgart, 1913, 2nd edn.), 104-105.

[25] See the first part as well as chapter 8 and 9 in the third part.

[26] See chapter 12 and 13 in the fourth part.

[27] See chapter 9 and 10 in the third part and part five.

factor that influenced memory construction. One example of long-term influence is the conflict over Saxony. After the Battle of Leipzig the Coalition put Saxony under Russian and then Prussian administration and temporarily deposed the Saxon King Friedrich August I, who had stuck by Napoleon to the end. This experience left a lasting impression on the collective memory of the Saxon monarchy. The fate of Saxony would become one of the main issues discussed at the Congress of Vienna in 1814 and 1815. In the end, Friedrich August I was restored to the throne, but lost 40 percent of his territory to Prussia. Saxony became one of the 39 members of the German Confederation.[28] Because of this postwar development, memories of the war were highly conflicted in Saxony, even more so than in most other territories belonging to the Confederation of the Rhine. Like all former states of the Confederation, the Saxon monarchy had to confront its time as Napoleon's ally in its memory construction. However, unlike all the other states that changed sides – at least quite late in the game, in most cases shortly before the decisive Battle of the Nations, when Napoleon's defeat had become likely – Saxony remained on Napoleon's side until the final defeat in Leipzig. In addition, more conservative supporters of Friedrich August I and his early-liberal and German-national opponents, many of whom had fought in 1813 as volunteers against Napoleon and their own king, competed in the process of memory construction in Saxony.

The Saxon case and the comparison with Prussia are interesting not just because of the specific interplay among the abovementioned factors in constructing collective memory, but because they also allow us to tease out the different roles and significance of the literary media of memory and their interactions as well as the influence of the changing political culture. The analysis of the contemporary press and autobiographical memories suggests that most Saxons, like the inhabitants of Prussia and other German regions, welcomed the victory over Napoleon at the Battle of Leipzig as well as the Coalition's triumph in April 1814. Prussia's role as a German driving force in this struggle was universally recognized.[29] After the partition of Saxony, however, a strongly anti-Prussian tone emerged, at least in the local press. Regional historiography, which, as we have seen, arose in Saxony and other German states immediately after the war, also sought to portray the kingdom as a victim not just of Napoleon and the wars, but also of Prussia.[30] This interpretation cannot, however, be found in many published autobiographies by Saxon authors, which represent about one-tenth of all the autobiographical texts published before 1875 studied here. Works written by civilians reported above all on the events surrounding the Battle of the Nations and their effects on the population, while military men depicted the

---

[28] See Lange, *Die öffentliche Meinung*.
[29] See, for example, Vater, *Was wir Erlebten*, 52.
[30] Töppel, *Die Sachsen*, 308–317; and Köpping, *Sachsen*.

devastating Russian campaign and emphasized the heroism, military honor and self-sacrifice of Saxon soldiers and officers. Saxon volunteers, in contrast, much like their former comrades-in-arms in Prussia, emphasized their German-national and early-liberal beliefs and commemorated the wars of 1813–15 as "Wars of Liberty."[31]

The production of communicative memory, which, as I have shown, was intensively shaped by the boom in published autobiographical texts, was dominated overall by memoirs written by men, especially generals, officers and noncommissioned officers as well as volunteers, and also politicians and civil servants. On the whole, memory production began far earlier in the states of the former Confederation of the Rhine than in Prussia, apparently because people there felt a far greater need for individual and collective self-justification following the victory over Napoleon – their former ally. A broad wave of autobiographical publications by Prussian authors, which made up two-fifths of all texts, peaked around the fiftieth anniversary of the wars of 1813–15. These texts were mainly penned by officers, statesmen and patriots and stressed the outstanding role played by Prussia in the "struggle for liberation," or by former volunteers defending the idea that the "Wars of Liberty" had been fought not just for liberation from the external enemy but also for inner freedom. Women were rare among the authors of history books and published autobiographies about the Anti-Napoleonic Wars. Their significant role during the wars of 1813–15 was generally ignored in both histories and autobiographical memory texts.[32]

The main genres of published works to recall their active support for the war, for example in the patriotic women's associations, were novels of the recent past and historical novels. Women also represented a significantly higher proportion of their authors and readers. The companies that published novels had to serve their female audience if they hoped to be successful, and they therefore accepted far more female authors particularly for so-called women's novels. The influence of the market on memory production is clear here, especially the rise of a national book market for a mass reading public, whose members drew their reading matter mainly from the lending libraries and in which women from the middle and lower middle classes and later workers represented a growing proportion. This influence is also evident in the treatment of regional political differences, which play a relatively minor part in the historical novels. While the texts were set throughout the German-speaking region, their authors were generally professional writers and thus far more dependent on the market than those of history books or autobiographies, who usually had other professions, so they had to offer topics and stories that appealed to a national market. A key function of the novels set during the Anti-Napoleonic Wars was

[31] See chapter 14 in the fourth part.
[32] See ibid.

to imagine the nation and – through the invariably deployed construct of the "*Volk* family," which had already played a central role in the patriotic-national discourse of the remembered time itself – to define not just national belonging, but at the same time also hierarchies in the nation, and to determine the rights and duties of individuals according to their social position, age, family status and sex in a seemingly "natural" way.[33]

Patriotic and national festivals, rituals and symbols also fulfilled this task of at once creating national unity and differentiating within the nation. As we have seen, the period of the Anti-Napoleonic Wars saw the emergence of the national repertoire of ceremonies, rituals and symbols in political and military culture that would be deployed throughout the long nineteenth century, with specific forms and interpretations adapted to the concrete events of the time. One instance is the Iron Cross, a military decoration newly introduced in 1813 (as well as its female counterpart, the *Luisenorden*), and the ceremonies and rituals for commemorating heroes, which were developed during the wars of 1813–15 and continued up to 1914. Another is the many festivities dedicated to mobilization for war and demobilization. The history of the commemorative ceremonies as well as the culture of monuments recalling the Leipzig Battle of the Nations is a third one. The commemoration of this battle is an especially good example of the changing national memories of the wars of 1813–15 because of the battle's central place in the national political culture. The development of the memories about it reflect the discussed lines of conflict in memory production and illustrate the continuing importance of anniversaries, which persists to this day: the twenty-fifth, fiftieth and one-hundredth anniversaries of the wars of 1813–15, like the bicentennial, were boom periods – at least in Germany – for the production of national memories.[34]

CHANGING NATIONAL MEMORIES

The anniversary of the Battle of Leipzig was celebrated for the first time on 18 and 19 October 1814 as the National Festival of the Germans. The suggestion for this celebration, which came from a circle of German-national patriots around the popular poet and journalist Ernst Moritz Arndt, was associated from the beginning with the idea of building a national monument.[35] While the idea of the National Festival was taken up widely in the German-speaking region in 1814, decades would pass before the planned monument was finally realized.[36] Commemorative ceremonies were also held in the following two Octobers. As part of the politics of restoration, the authorities

[33] See part five.
[34] See chapter 9 and 10 in the third part and chapter 13 and 14 in the fourth part.
[35] Arndt, *Ein Wort*.
[36] See Hoffmann, *Des Teutschen Volkes*.

increasingly suppressed the "National Festivals of the Germans" held everywhere to recall the "people's participation" in the "War of Liberty," however,
since their German-national and early liberal tendencies were deemed inop-
portune.[37] Historians consider the National Festival with services of thanksgiving, festival processions, gymnastics demonstrations, bonfires with torch
relays and a wealth of patriotic speeches and songs to be a "matrix of the
nineteenth-century German national festivals." With its ceremonies and symbolism, it also provided the model for later festivities to mark the twenty-
fifth, fiftieth and one-hundredth anniversaries of the Battle of Leipzig.[38]

The twenty-fifth anniversary was observed mainly on the regional level.
Veterans of the wars of 1813–15, who since the 1830s, mainly in Prussia,
had increasingly formed their own organizations, especially the so-called
Garrison and Militia Support Associations, became important sponsors
of the festivities.[39] Alongside them the Associations to Commemorate the
Leipzig Battle of the Nations, founded in 1814, continued to exist in some
places, one was Leipzig, or were reactivated. In 1838, in the context of
regional celebrations for the twenty-fifth anniversary, the Leipzig Association
to Commemorate the 19th of October initiated the erection of local monuments at key memorial sites of the battle in Leipzig and its environs. The
association's stated goal was to recall the great sacrifices made by the region
and to emphasize its contribution to the national history of liberation with
local memorials to outstanding military men and patriots as well as local
battle sites. The association organized all of the consecration ceremonies for
the first eight monuments, which were erected between 1845 and 1863, in
conjunction with the local authorities, the Lutheran Church and local associations – here, too, taking up the tradition of 1813–15.[40]

On the occasion of the fiftieth anniversary the association erected 44
additional "landmarks" on the battlefield. The initiative for this came from
the Leipzig legal scholar, writer and local historian Theodor Apel, who also
financed it because he hoped that "our future grandchildren may someday
visit the landmarks as the last that bear witness, on the battlefields of Leipzig,
to struggle and war, that is, to the terrible mischief for which mankind mis-
uses the powers granted by God."[41] In all, well over 100 memorials – monuments, boulders, solitary graves, plaques and the "Apel stones" – to the days
of October 1813 were erected in Leipzig and its surroundings in the nineteenth century.[42] The 1863 anniversary was celebrated throughout Germany,
especially among the national-liberal middle classes. Leipzig was *the* central

---

[37] See Hagemann, *Muth*, 481–497.
[38] See Düding, "Nationalfest."
[39] Trox, *Konservatismus*, 55–62.
[40] Hartleb, *1813: Das Zeitalter*, 36–39.
[41] Steffen Poser, *Denkmale zur Völkerschlacht*, ed. Stadtgeschichtliches Museum Leipzig
    (Leipzig, 2013), 106.
[42] Ibid., 8.

commemorative site of a great national celebration mounted by the German cities, notably Berlin and Leipzig, with the acquiescence of the Saxon government. After the failed Revolution of 1848–49, this celebration represented a clear statement of political will on the part of the national-liberal middle classes, with which they underlined the unmet demands of 1813 for unity and liberty – much like the very popular histories of the "Wars of Liberty" from this time and the many historical novels, which in this heyday of the genre recalled the "struggle for unity and liberty" of the years 1813–15. The organizers of the national commemorative celebration in Leipzig accordingly also very deliberately resorted to the ceremonial forms, images, symbols and rhetoric of the "Wars of Liberty," and integrated the *Burschenschaften* as well as the gymnastic and choral associations into the festival program, groups that had already played an active part in fashioning the National Festival of the Germans in 1814. Songs from the "Wars of Liberty" naturally also formed part of the festivities. As in 1813, songs by Arndt and Körner were especially popular among the participants. The central procession in Leipzig assigned a prominent position to the surviving veterans of 1813–15, without regard to military or social rank, which was meant to symbolize their equal status as "comrades, warriors and victors in Germany's greatest battle."[43] A special place in the festival procession was also reserved for the white-clad "maidens of honor," daughters of the Leipzig bourgeoisie. As in the poetry and pictures of the years 1813–15, they represented the "priestesses of victory, joy and hope" and thus, as had been the case in the patriotic-national celebrations during the wars of 1813–15, these "German maidens" embodied the future of the German nation.[44] Some 20,000 people in all took part in the festival procession proper; the estimated number of spectators was about 100,000. At the close of the festivities the idea of a national monument was taken up again, and the foundation stone was laid just outside the city. It would be another 50 years, however, before the memorial was inaugurated.[45]

The 1913 jubilee celebrations were very different from those of 1863. It was only after the Wars of Unification, in the newly founded German Empire, that recollections of the Anti-Napoleonic Wars increasingly disappeared from communicative memory and became part of cultural memory. Their significance in national memory was overlaid by, or associated with, the Wars of Unification. More than 40 years after the 1871 founding of the empire, the focus was on the German-national myth of the Battle of the Nations as the "German people's natal hour," which had unleashed the "noblest forces" of "folkdom, of the German *Volk* consciousness." This

[43] Hoffmann, "Sakraler Monumentalismus"; idem, "Mythos und Geschichte: Leipziger Gedenkfeiern der Völkerschlacht im 19. und frühen 20. Jahrhundert," in François et al., *Nation*, 111–132, 119; and Puschner, "18. Oktober 1813," 154–156.

[44] Hoffmann, "Mythos," 119.

[45] Ibid., 118.

myth had become increasingly influential since the founding of the empire, which broad segments of the national-liberal middle classes, in particular, interpreted as the "execution" of 1813. It found expression in the monumental architecture of the memorial to the Battle of the Nations in Leipzig. The erection of this monument was initiated in 1894 by the League of German Patriots. Construction was almost wholly financed by donations, and for that reason could not begin until 1898. Even today, the 91-meter-high colossus is the tallest monument in Europe.[46]

Like the entire collective memory of the Anti-Napoleonic Wars, the monument linked past, present and future, and this is also expressed in the architecture itself. On the one hand, the monument was designed to honor the fallen German warriors of the Battle of the Nations (the many dead of other nations who fought on both sides were not commemorated). Death in the past was meant to lend a sacred character to the idea of the nation in the present. On the other, it was to serve as a reminder to coming generations. The monument's lower story contains a crypt supported by eight columns, which is open at the top and guarded by two colossal mourning warriors. The crypt leads to the upper story, the temple-like Hall of Fame of the German People, featuring four gigantic sculptural groups symbolizing the supposedly specific German national virtues: self-sacrifice, courage, strength of belief and the power of the people. These virtues were expected of all Germans, male and female, in the present and the future.[47]

Six hundred thousand people had already visited the site during construction. The national monument was consecrated on 18 October 1913 with a gigantic procession and in the presence of Emperor Wilhelm II. The 100,000 participants included 45,000 gymnasts from every corner of the empire who had come to Leipzig in "messenger relays" and some 3,000 professors and students in their *Burschenschaft* uniforms, as well as members of veterans', choral, gymnastic and shooting associations from all over Germany, whose donations had contributed significantly to funding construction.[48] Not everyone joined the national hymns of praise to the memorial, however. In the Social Democratic milieu it was known disparagingly as "the rock-pile." During the week of the consecration, the Social Democratic Party held large protest rallies in Leipzig against the "nationalist lies about history" that the monument embodied and the prevailing general bellicose mood in national-conservative circles. It warned with the protest against the dangers of a new war.[49] The Free German Youth

---

[46] Peter Hutter, "Zur Baugeschichte des Völkerschlachtdenkmals in Leipzig," in Keller and Schmid, *Vom Kult*, 42–61.

[47] Hoffmann, "Mythos," 124–125.

[48] Ibid.

[49] Marc von Lüpke, "Völkerschlachtdenkmal in Leipzig: Pyramide der Patrioten," *Spiegel Online*, 17 December 2013; and Heidi Mühlenberg, "Die Leipziger Löwenjagd und das Völkerschlachtdenkmal," *MDR Fernsehen*, 3 October 2013.

movement also organized a counter-event, which took place on 11 and 12 October 1913 on the Hoher Meißner, a mountain in Hesse. Two to three thousand boys and girls mainly from middle- and upper-class backgrounds took part in this Festival of Youth directed against the authorities of the Wilhelmine Empire and their militarism.[50]

Such protests could not halt the machinery of nationalist spectacle, however. Among the "noblest forces" lauded in speeches and the press on the occasion of the inauguration ceremony of 19 October 1913 was the willingness to sacrifice oneself unconditionally for the nation. This quality was in great demand again on the eve of the First World War. The festivities of 1913 conveyed an image of war calculated to prepare people mentally for a great new battle of the nations and praised war as a catalyst for national unity and renewal. This image of war met with broad approval even in national-liberal educated middle-class circles. Thus, in the chapter on "The German Risings of 1813, 1848, 1870 and 1914" in his 1914 work *The German Rising of 1914*, which appeared shortly after the war began, the Berlin historian Friedrich Meinecke consciously refers to the war tradition of 1813–15. He stresses that "death for the fatherland, that ancient sacrifice […] has assumed a new and eternal significance" and signifies "a sacred spring for all of Germany."

In the years before we were apparently incurably divided and often quite wearied and disheartened by our unfortunate class and religious hatreds and the threats to our spiritual life. Now at one stroke we are lifted above all barriers, a single, mighty, and deep-breathing community of the people, unto life and death.[51]

For him and many other educated, national-liberal men of the middle classes who welcomed the new war in 1914, this closed the circle to the wars of 1813–15. In fact, the First World War initiated a new round in the production of heroic recollections in cultural memory, in which the history of the Anti-Napoleonic Wars and the Battle of the Nations were once again deployed for present-day purposes. Important stages in this process were its cooptation by the national-conservative right, with nationalist-*völkisch* and militarist intent, during the Weimar Republic and then by the Nazi Party during the Third Reich.[52] In the last decades before World War I, the sufferings of soldiers and the civilian population during the Anti-Napoleonic Wars and the massive battle at Leipzig, along with the liberal and democratic tradition of interpretation, were increasingly sinking into oblivion in cultural memory. It was forgotten in the "archive" of collective memory. In the "canon" a heroic and nationalist master narrative dominated until 1945.

---

[50] "Jugend in Aufruhr," *MDR Figaro*, 1 October 2013; and Winfried Mogge and Jürgen Reulecke, *Hoher Meißner 1913 – Der Erste Freideutsche Jugendtag in Dokumenten, Deutungen und Bildern* (Cologne, 1988).

[51] Meinecke, *Zeitalter*, 28–29.

[52] Puschner, "18. Oktober 1813," 158–162; and Poser, "Zur Rezeptionsgeschichte," 78–104.

FORGETTING AND REMEMBERING

Aleida Assman's distinction between "canon" and "archive" helps us to understand the complicated process of forgetting and remembering in cultural memory. Her emphasis on the complex interplay between several factors in this process, especially the role of institutions and different media and their specific modes of transmission, explains the mechanisms of forgetting and remembering.[53] The history of memories of the Anti-Napoleonic Wars in Prussia and Germany and of the central battle at Leipzig affirms the complex interactions among a number of factors in the construction of collective memories and their transformation. The specific experiences, politics and political culture, the (literary) market and the respective function and mode of operation of individual media of memory such as history books and commemorative volumes, biographies, autobiographies and war memoirs, songs and poems as well as novels were of particular importance in the case explored here.

This study, however, also points to the central influence of class and gender differences on the construction of memory – an aspect long neglected in the scholarship on memory. Not just the discourses on the nation and war at the time of the Anti-Napoleonic Wars themselves, but also the construction of memories of those wars, were organized along class lines and were highly gendered. Class and gender marked not only the identity of the agents and institutions that produced memories and their political influence as well as access to different media of memory and the market, but also the media of memory utilized and the constructed memories themselves.[54] For different social strata and both sexes, various literary media were influential in the discourse of the time of the Anti-Napoleonic Wars themselves, as well as in the construction of collective memories, and the process of remembering and forgetting. History books, autobiographies and war memoirs largely targeted men, especially men of the educated strata. They told the stories of male heroes in war and politics – male-connoted areas of "the public." It was mainly historical novels that reached female readers and later also workers in large numbers. Fittingly, they addressed the home front at war, spoke about the family, and reflected upon the question of who, in which positions and roles, belonged to the aspired to and later realized German nation. The image of the nation as a "valorous *Volk* family" in which each individual was assigned duties and rights in keeping with his or her age, class and gender proved especially durable. This model of the national gender and social order during wartime, which evolved in the discourse of the

[53] Assmann, "Canon and Archive;" and idem, *Cultural Memory*.
[54] See Hirsch and Smith, "Feminism and Cultural Memory"; Assmann, "Geschlecht"; and Schraut and Paletschek, "Introduction: Gender and Memory Culture."

time of the Anti-Napoleonic Wars, appeared repeatedly in the nationalist and militarist propaganda of the two World Wars.[55]

Historians also long forgot the transnational or European dimension of recollections of the time of the Napoleonic Wars, which was stylized as the founding era of the nation in many other countries in Europe, just as it was in the German Confederation and Imperial Germany.[56] Sooner or later, depending on the specific political culture, the developmental stage of academic historiography and the literary market, a stronger interest in history, especially the recent past, emerged everywhere.[57] The central contents of and booms in memory differ greatly in the various countries. The media of memory, in contrast, and their specific modes of transmission, are similar. During the course of the nineteenth century, the historical novel became one of the most important literary media of memory for broad segments of the population in many European countries. It helped to make history vivid and emotional, and brought the past into the present and the future.[58] Facilitated by technical advances in book production and the expanding literary markets, historical novels crossed national borders, but only when the story or at least the message was transnational. In this way they offered alternative perspectives and interpretations for remembering the Napoleonic era that challenged national narratives. An important reason for the wide dissemination of translations, which in the 1850s and 1860s comprised up to one-third of all novels on the German market, was that they were far cheaper than German novels, whose authors had to be paid appropriately. The influence of translations fell significantly from the early 1870s onward, when authors' and publishing rights were regulated on the international level for the first time. This development supported the "nationalization" of cultural memories.[59]

In the twentieth century, alongside the novel, the new mass medium of film took over the function of bringing memories to a broad public and crossed national boundaries in the process. The spread of cinema in the 1920s went hand in hand with a further Europeanization of memories of the wars between 1792 and 1815, since most films were produced for an international audience. At the same time, however, there were strong national

[55] See, for example, Andrea Süchting-Hänger, *Das "Gewissen der Nation": Nationales Engagement und politisches Handeln konservativer Frauenorganisationen 1900 bis 1937* (Düsseldorf, 2002), esp. 90–12; and Karen Hagemann and Stefanie Schüler-Springorum, eds., *Home/Front: The Military, War, and Gender in Twentieth-Century Germany* (Oxford, 2002).

[56] See Flacke, *Mythen*.

[57] See chapter 13 in the fourth part.

[58] See Hamnett, *Historical Novel*; and Lars Peters, *Romances of War: Die Erinnerung an die Revolutions- und Napoleonischen Kriege in Großbritannien und Irland, 1815–1945* (Paderborn, 2012).

[59] See chapter 12 in the fourth part as well as part five.

differences in filmic memory. A nationalist politics of memory is especially evident in the film production of Weimar and Nazi Germany. Films on the Napoleonic era, which was mythologized as a "period of national uprising," were quite clearly used to process the defeat of 1918.[60]

The European transfer of memories of the era of the Revolutionary and Napoleonic Wars was particularly successful where novels and films offered intersections and congruities between various national memories. Because this only applied to a small proportion of works, the memories remained largely tied to the framework of national reception. Many novels and films simply lacked the requisite transnational connections. Moreover, after a while the need for European topoi of memory appears to have been satisfied. In general, the formation of national master narratives on recollections of the Napoleonic Wars had apparently been largely completed with the transition from communicative to cultural memory in the 1860s and 1870s. Afterward, few new topoi emerged, and the circulating topoi were merely repeated, extended, advanced, completed and updated. These adaptations were mainly oriented toward the respective contemporary interests and expressed specific national memory constellations and booms. They therefore say far more about the time in which they were produced than they do about the remembered time.

In retrospect, a regional and temporal framework becomes visible in which a European landscape of memories of the Napoleonic Wars and with them an image of Europe constituted itself in the long term. This landscape of memory was shaped above all by *concrete places and spaces* (Trafalgar, Austerlitz, Madrid/Spain/Iberian Peninsula, Tyrol, Berezina/Moscow/ Russia, Leipzig/Paris/Elba, Waterloo/St Helena) as well as their *anniversaries* and the divergent but also shared memories related to them. In addition, a *basic repertoire of heroes and antiheroes* arose that was familiar in all European countries. The figure of Napoleon Bonaparte clearly dominated here. Leading military men like the Britons General Wellington and Admiral Nelson, the Prussian General von Blücher, the Austrian Field Marshal Schwarzenberg or the Russian General Kutuzov were also of universal significance. Statesmen and monarchs such as the Austrian Minister von Metternich or the Russian Tsar Alexander I rounded out the picture. Only a few female figures played a central role in European memory. Among them were Joséphine de Beauharnais, Napoleon's first wife, and Queen Luise of Prussia. There were also central *collective European topoi*, such as the "time of the French," "Spanish guerilla warfare," the "Russian campaign" or the "Cossacks."[61]

---

[60] See Koller, *Historienkino*.
[61] These are the core findings of the DFG-funded German research group *Nations, Borders and Identities: Memories of the Revolutionary and Napoleonic Wars in Europe, 1792–1945*,

Nowadays too, spaces, heroes and anniversaries form the European memories of the Napoleonic Wars and their last chapter, the successful struggle against Napoleon in 1813–15. For fans of the Emperor and military buffs, battlegrounds, campaigns, uniforms and weapons are still at the forefront of their remembrance, as the popularity of the reenactments at central battle sites of the Napoleonic Wars and the many military history books on the period written for a broad audience demonstrate. Napoleon is still among the major historical figures who fascinate historians and readers alike, as the large number of new biographical studies indicate. But his interpretation changed; historians depict him more ambivalently and critically, as a great military leader, political reformer and ruthless imperialist.[62] The main national myths and legends of the time still have their place in national memories, but they are now also critically deconstructed. Today's memories, colored by antinationalist and antiwar sentiment, accentuate the transnational, European and even global dimension of the Napoleonic Wars and emphasize the need for international understanding, as the celebration of the bicentenary of the wars of 1813–15 in Germany demonstrates.

These and many other past and current memories of the period share a common denominator: The more complex the mnemonic potential of these places, persons, groups, events and ideas, the greater their significance in the European landscape of memory, as is evident from the many events and publications of the past decade in various European countries marking the anniversaries of 1805, 1806, 1809, 1812 and 1813, and as the bicentennial celebrations for the Battle of Waterloo in 2015 will doubtless show again. The power of the anniversaries that shape remembrance, however, makes it likely that once the current series of anniversary years is over the media, and with them the public, will soon lose interest in the period of the Anti-Napoleonic Wars once again, only to enthusiastically embrace the next jubilee of another historical event. Nowadays, market interests seem to determine the production of history and memory more than ever before.

which Étienne François and I directed; for the findings, see Forrest et al., *War Memories*; Peters, *Romances*; Kirsten Buchinger, *Napoléomanie* (Berlin, 2013); and Koller, *Historienkino*.

[62] See most recently, Philip Dwyer, *Napoleon: The Path to Power* (New Haven, CT, 2008); idem., *Citizen Emperor: Napoleon in Power* (New Haven, CT, 2013); Alan Forrest, *Napoleon* (London, 2011); Volker Hunecke, *Napoleon: Das Scheitern eines guten Diktators* (Paderborn, 2011); and Johannes Willms, *Napoleon* (Munich, 2005).

Bibliography

Introduction

In the following bibliography I only list cited titles of importance. For my research I explored many more sources, especially primary documents. I combined quantitative and qualitative methods by building up large data-files with Filemaker on the different primary source groups, which include a variety of information on the authors, the text, its different editions and its reception. For the analysis of the political discourse of the time I built up three Filemaker databases, the first with 61 newspapers and historical-political, military and theological journals and magazines, mostly published between 1800 and 1830; the second with 91 editions of sermons and the third with 310 editions and collections of patriotic poetry, with 2,885 poems and songs published between 1806 and 1820. I was able to collect more precise biographical information for 374 men and 12 women who produced this "topical literature" (*Tagesliteratur*). For the analysis of the collective memory I built up two Filemaker databases. The first includes 369 German-language autobiographical accounts on the period of the Napoleonic Wars written by 204 authors (only 15 of them women) that were published before 1915; 269 of these were first editions published before 1915 and 160 were first editions published before 1875. The second includes 195 German-language novels of the recent past and historical novels published between 1815 and 1915. A total of 123 authors wrote these 195 novels, 93 men and 30 women. For the texts in both databases, I tried to gather as much information on the authors and the texts themselves as possible too. I also attempted to identify the number of editions and searched for contemporary reviews of the texts in journals and magazines, which are integrated into the database.

Primary Works

Encyclopedias

Allgemeine Deutsche Biographie, ed. Historische Kommission bei der Bayerischen Akademie der Wissenschaften, 56 vols. (Leipzig, 1875–1912).

Brockhaus Conversations-Lexicon oder Encyclopädisches Handwörterbuch für gebildete Stände, 10 vols. (Altenburg and Leipzig, 1814–19).

Brockhaus Conversationslexikon, 16 vols. (Leipzig, 1882–87, 13th edn).

Gross, Heinrich, *Deutschlands Dichterinnen und Schriftstellerinnen: Eine literarhistorische Skizze* (Vienna, 1882, 2nd. edn.).

Herloßsohn, Carl, ed., *Damen Conversations Lexikon*, 10 vols. (Leipzig, 1834–38).

Hübener, Johann, ed., *Reales Staats-Zeitungs- und Conversations-Lexicon: Neue verbesserte u. stark vermehrte Ausgabe* (Leipzig, 1782, repr. 1789).

Jablonskie, Johann Theodor, ed., *Allgemeines Lexicon der Künste und Wissenschaften*, von neuem durchg., verb. u. stark verm. v. Johann Joachim Schwaben (Königsberg and Leipzig, 1767).

Jarck, Horst-Rüdiger and Günter Scheel, eds., *Braunschweigisches Biographisches Lexikon: 19. und 20. Jahrhundert* (Hannover, 1996).

Kneschke, Ernst Heinrich, ed., *Neues Allgemeines Deutsches Adels-Lexicon*, 9 vols. (Leipzig, 1859–70).

Krünitz, Johann Georg, ed., *Oeconomische Encyclopädie oder allgemeines System der Staats-Stadt-Haus- und Landwirthschaft in alphabetischer Ordnung*, 242 vols. (Berlin, 1773–1858).

Lühe, Hans Eggert Willibald von der (ed.), *Militair-Conversations Lexikon*, 9 vols. (Leipzig, 1833–41).

Morgenstern, Lina, *Die Frauen des 19. Jahrhunderts: Biographische und culturhistorische Zeit- und Charactergemälde* (Berlin, 1891).

Neue Deutschen Biographie, ed. Historische Kommission bei der Bayerischen Akademie der Wissenschaften, 24 vols. (Berlin, 1953–2013).

Pataky, Sophie, *Lexikon deutscher Frauen der Feder*, 2 vols. (Berlin, 1898).

Zedler, Johann Heinrich, ed., *Grosses vollständiges Universal-Lexicon aller Wissenschaften und Künste*, 64 vols. and 4 suppl. vols. (Halle and Leipzig, 1732–54, repr. Graz 1961–64).

Newspapers and Journals

Allgemeine deutsche Frauen-Zeitung, ed. Friedrich Keyser and Dr J. M. Laubling, publ. Friedrich Keyser, vols. 1–3 (Erfurt, 1816–18).

Allgemeine Literatur-Zeitung, founded by Christian Gottfried Schütz and Christoph Martin Wieland, publ. Friedrich Justin Bertuch, vols. 1–34 (Halle, 1815–49).

Allgemeine Militär-Zeitung, ed. by an "association of German officers and military administrators" (Leipzig and Darmstadt, 1826–1902).

Amts-Blatt der königlich kurmärkischen Regierung, vols. 1–3 (Potsdam, 1811–16).

Berliner Abendblätter, ed. Heinrich von Kleist, publ. Julius Eduard Hitzig, vols. 1–2 (Berlin, 1810–11, repr. Darmstadt 1959).

Berlinische Nachrichten von Staats- und gelehrten Sachen, ed. and publ. Johann Karl Philipp Spener (Berlin, 1806–20).

Blätter für literarische Unterhaltung, publ. Friedrich Arnold Brockhaus and Heinrich Brockhaus, vols. 1–70 (Leipzig, 1826–96).

Das Eiserne Kreuz, ed. and publ. Alexander Mallwitz, nos. 1–24 (Belzig, Jan. 1847 – Dec. 1848).

Das literarische Echo, ed. Josef Ettlinger and Ernst Heilborn, publ. Deutsche Verlagsanstalt, vol. 1–16 (Stuttgart, 1898–1914).

Das neue Deutschland: Enthaltend größtentheils freimütige Berichte zur Geschichte der Bedrückung und der Wiederbefreiung Deutschlands, ed. and publ. Johann Christian Gädicke, vols. 1–2 (Berlin, 1813–14).

Denkwürdigkeiten für die Kriegskunst und Kriegsgeschichte, ed. Rühle von Linienstern, publ. Georg Andreas Reimer, nos. 1–6 (Berlin, 1817–20).

Der Freimüthige oder Unterhaltungsblatt für gebildete, unbefangene Leser, ed. Friedrich August Kuhn, publ. Johann Daniel Sander, vols. 1–13 (Berlin, 1803–16).

Der Preussische Correspondent, ed. Barthold Georg Niebuhr, Friedrich Schleiermacher, Achim von Arnim and Friedrich Rühs, publ. Georg Andreas Reimer, vols. 1–2 (Berlin, 1813–14).

Der Wächter, eine Zeitschrift in zwanglosen Heften, ed. Ernst Moritz Arndt, publ. Heinrich Rommerskirchen, vols. 1–3 (Cologne, 1815–16).

Deutsche Blätter, ed. and publ. Friedrich Arnold Brockhaus, vols. 1–6 (Leipzig and Altenburg, 1813–15) and NS vols. 1–2 (1815).

Deutsche Rundschau, ed. Julius Rodenberg and Bruno Hake, publ. Gebrüder Paetel Verlag, vol. 1–40 (Berlin, 1874–1914).

Deutsches Literaturblatt, ed. Ludolf Wienbarg, vols. 1–3 (Hamburg, 1840–42).

Deutsches Museum, ed. Friedrich Schlegel, publ. Camesinische Buchhandlung, vols. 1–2 (Vienna, 1812–13).

Deutsches Museum: Zeitschrift für Literatur, Kunst und öffentliches Leben, ed. Robert Prutz, Wilhelm Wolfsohn and Karl Frenzel, publ. J. C. Hinrichs (1851–52) and F. A. Brockhaus (1851–67), vol. 1–16 (Leipzig, 1851–67).

Deutschlands Triumph oder das entjochte Europa, ed. J. G. Wilhelm Scheerer, publ. G. Heyn, vol. 1 (Berlin, 1814).

Die Biene oder neue kleine Schriften: Eine Quartalsschrift, ed. August von Kotzebue, publ. Friedrich Nicolovius, vols. 1–3 (Königsberg, 1808–10).

Die Grenzboten [subtitle since 1842: *Eine deutsche Revue*, since 1844: *Eine deutsche Revue für Politik und Literatur* and since 1871: *Zeitschrift für Politik, Literatur und Kunst*], ed. Ignaz Kuranda, Gustav Freytag, Julian Schmidt and Georg Cleinow, publ. Herbig, vols. 1–81 (Berlin and Leipzig, 1841–1922).

Die Musen: Eine norddeutsche Zeitschrift, ed. Friedrich Baron de la Motte Fouqué and Wilhelm Neumann, publ. C. Salfeld (vol. 1) and Julius Eduard Hitzig (vols. 2–4), vols. 1–4 (Berlin, 1812–14, repr. Nendeln, 1971).

Forschungen zur brandenburgischen und preußischen Geschichte, ed. Reinhold Koser (1888–91), Albert Naudé (1892–97), Otto Hinze (1898–1913), vols. 1–44, publ. Duncker & Humblot (vols. 1–34) and Oldenbourg (since vol. 25) (Berlin and Leipzig, 1888–1922, Munich, 1923–33).

Freimüthige Blätter für Deutsche, in Beziehung auf Krieg, Politik und Staatswesen: Eine Zeitschrift in zwanglosen Heften [since 1816: *Freimüthige literarische Blätter*] ed. Friedrich von Cölln, publ. Karl Friedrich Wilhelm Duncker and

Wilhelm von Humblot, since no. 9 (1816): Friedrich August Maurer, nos. 1–36 (Berlin, 1815–18).

Gemeinnütziges Magazin für Prediger auf dem Lande und in kleinen Städten, ed. Raymund Dapp, publ. Friedrich Nicolai, vols. 1–8 (Berlin and Stettin, 1804–16).

Historische Vierteljahresschrift, ed. E. Brandenburg, publ. W. B. von Baensch, vols. 1–15 (Leipzig and Dresden, 1897–1914).

Historische Zeitschrift, ed. Heinrich von Sybel, Heinrich von Treitschke and Friedrich Meinecke, publ. Cottasche Buchhandlung and Oldenbourg, vols. 1–55 (Munich, 1859–1914).

Hohenzollern Jahrbuch: Forschungen und Abbildungen zur Geschichte der Hohenzollern in Brandenburg-Preußen, ed. Paul Seidel, publ. Giesecke & Devrient, vols. 1–18 (Berlin and Leipzig, 1897–1914).

Jahrbücher der preußischen Monarchie unter der Regierung Friedrich Wilhelms III, ed. Friedrich Schlegel, publ. Johan Friedrich Unger, vols. 1–4 (Berlin 1798–1801).

Janus: Ruinen und Blüthen, bei Deutschlands Wiederauferstehung 1814, ed. G. A. Wundermann (alias: Hermann Germanus), publ. Gottfried Andreas Joachim, vols. 1–2 (Vienna, St Petersburg and Berlin [Leipzig], 1814).

Journal für Prediger [since vol. 21: *Neues Journal für Prediger*], ed. Carl August Kümmel, vols. 50–59 (Halle, 1806–16).

Kieler Blätter, ed. and publ. Gesellschaft Kieler Professoren, vols. 1–5 (Kiel, 1815–19).

Leuchtkugeln: Ein Journal in zwanglosen Heften, ed. Karl Nicolai, publ. Gottfried Basse, vols. 1–4 (Quedlinburg, 1815–1816).

Magazin für Prediger, ed. Josias Friedrich Christian Löffler, publ. Friedrich Frommann, vols. 1–8 (Jena, 1803–16).

Militär-Wochenblatt, ed. until 1847 by Johann Jacob Otto August Rühle von Lilienstern and Karl von Decker, publ. Ernst Siegfried Mittler, vols. 1–102 (Berlin, 1816–1914).

Minerva: Ein Journal historischen und politischen Inhalts, first ed. by Johann Wilhelm Archenholz (Hamburg, 1792–1808), vols. 14–66 (Hamburg and Jena, 1806–58).

Nemesis: Zeitschrift für Politik und Geschichte, ed. Heinrich Luden, publ. Justin Friedrich Bertuch, vols. 1–12 (Weimar, 1814–18).

Neue Fakkeln: Ein Journal in zwanglosen Heften, ed. Karl Nicolai, publ. Gottfried Basse, vols. 1–6 (Quedlinburg, 1813–15).

Neuestes Magazin von Fest-, Gelegenheits- und andern Predigten und kleinen Amtsreden, ed. Gottfried August Ludwig Hanstein, Rulemann Friedrich Eylert and Johann Heinrich Bernhard Dräseke, publ. Wilhelm Heinrichshofen, vols. 1–4 (Magdeburg, 1816–20).

Politische Flugblätter, ed. August von Kotzebue, publ. Friedrich Nicolovius, vols. 1–2 (Königsberg, 1814–16).

Preußische Feldzeitung, ed. Carl Heun et al. on behalf oft the Prussian headquarter, Berlin among other places, nos. 1–72 (Berlin, 1813–14, repr. Potsdam, 1940).

Preußische Jahrbücher, ed. Rudolf Haym, Heinrich von Treitschke, Hans Delbrück and Walther Schotte, publ. Georg Reimer, vols. 1–75 (Berlin, 1858–1933).

Rheinischer Merkur, ed. Johann Joseph von Görres, publ. Pauli, vol. 1, and Hriot, vols. 2–4 (Koblenz, 1814–16, repr. Bern, 1971).

Russisch-Deutsches Volks-Blatt, ed. August von Kotzebue on behalf general count Wittgenstein, nos. 1–10 (Berlin, 1813, repr. Berlin, 1953).

Rußlands Triumpf 1812 oder das erwachte Europa, 2nd edn.: *Das erwachte Europa*, eds. Karl Müchler and Ernst Adolph Heinrich von Pfuel, publ. Achenwall und Compagnie, vols. 1–2 (Berlin, 1814–15).

Schlesische Privilegierte Zeitung, ed. and publ. Johann Gottlieb Korn (Breslau, 1812–16).

Schlesische Provinzialblätter, ed. Karl Konrad Streit and Friedrich A. Zimmermann, publ. Wilhelm Gottlieb Korn, vols. 56–64 (Breslau, 1812–16).

Tageblatt der Geschichte, ed. Ernst Moritz Arndt and Friedrich Lange, publ. Georg Andreas Reimer, nos. 1–254 (Berlin, 1815).

Teutsche Blätter [für das Jahr 1814] *welche nach dem hohen Armeebefehl in Freyburg fortgesetzt wurden. Erste Abtheilung, Kriegs- und politische Nachrichten, oder die neuesten offiziellen Armee-Nachrichten vom Einmarsch der verbündeten Armeen in die Schweiz bis zum Rückzug derselben aus Frankreich nach dem Frieden von Paris. Zweyte Abtheilung, Patriotische Erhebungen, welche den Zweck haben, auf den öffentlichen Geist in Teutschland den großen Zweck der hohen Alliierten gemäß wohlthätig einzuwirken, und von dieser Epoche eine würdige Schilderung zu liefern*, ed. Karl von Rotteck, publ. Bartholomäus Herder, nos. 1–76 (Freiburg/Br. and Konstanz, 1814).

Vaterländisches Museum, ed. and publ. Friedrich Perthes, vols. 1–2 (Hamburg, 1810–11).

Vossische Zeitung: Königlich-privilegierte Berlinische Zeitung vonStaats- und Gelehrten Sachen, ed. and publ. Christian Friedrich Lessing (Berlin, 1806–20).

Westermann's Illustrierte deutsche Monatshefte, ed. Adolf Glaser, publ. Georg Westermann, vols. 1–68 (Braunschweig, 1856–1914).

Wetterfahnen. Freimüthige Blätter für Fürsten und Volk: Zeitschrift in zwanglosen Heften, ed. Karl Nicolai, publ. Gottfried Basse, nos. 1–3 (Quedlinburg, 1816–17).

Zeitschrift des Vereins für die Geschichte Schlesien, ed. Colmar Grünhagen, vols. 1–59 (Breslau, 1855–1914).

Zeitschrift für die neueste Geschichte, die Staaten- und Völkerkunde, ed. Christian Friedrich Rühs and Samuel Heinrich Spiker, publ. Georg Andreas Reimer, vols. 1–4 (Berlin, 1814–16).

Zeitung aus dem Feldlager, ed. Karl August Varnhagen von Ense on behalf general count Wittgenstein, nos. 1–5 (Bremen among other places, Sept. 1813 – Jan. 1814).

Zeitung für die elegante Welt: Mode, Unterhaltung, Kunst, Theater, first ed. by Johann Gottlieb Karl Spazier, publ. Leopold Voß, vols. 1–58 (Berlin and Leipzig, 1801–59).

Autobiographical Documents

Alexis, Willibald, "Als Kriegsfreiwilliger in Frankreich 1815: Blätter aus meinen Erinnerungen," in *Penelope: Taschenbuch für das Jahr 1844, 1845 and 1846*, ed. Karl Gottfried Theodor Winkler, 3 vols. (Leipzig, 1844–46).

Eine Jugend in Preußen: Erinnerungen (repr. Berlin, 1991).

Amsinck, Caesar, "Elisabeth Dorothea Mollers Tagebuch aus der Belagerung Hamburgs in den Jahren 1813 und 1814," *Zeitschrift des Vereins für Hamburgische Geschichte* 11 (1903): 184–226.

Andreae, Friedrich, ed., *Denkwürdigkeiten des Freiherrn Hermann von Gaffron-Kunern. Festgabe des Vereins für Geschichte Schlesiens zur Jahrhundertfeier der Befreiungskriege* (Breslau, 1913).

Arndt, Ernst Moritz, *Erinnerungen aus dem äußeren Leben* (Leipzig, 1840).

Assing, Ludmilla, ed., *Briefwechsel zwischen Varnhagen und Rahel* (Aus dem Nachlaß Varnhagens v. E.), 6 vols. (Leipzig, 1874–76; repr. Bern, 1973).

Bärsch, Georg Friedrich, *Erinnerungen aus meinem vielbewegten Leben: Als Manuscript für meine Freunde* (Aachen, 1856).

Beguelin, Heinrich and Amalie von, *Denkwürdigkeiten aus den Jahren, 1807–13, nebst Briefen von Gneisenau und Hardenberg,* ed. Adolf Ernst (Berlin, 1892).

Bersling, Franz, *Der böhmische Veteran: Franz Bersling's Leben, Reisen und Kriegsfahrten in allen fünf Welttheilen* (Schweidnitz, 1840).

Bismark, Wilhelm Grafen von, *Aufzeichnungen des Generallieutnants Friedrich Wilhelm Grafen von Bismark* (Karlsruhe, 1847).

Böck, August, *Leben und Schicksale des ehemaligen Musikmeisters im Königl. Preuß. 24sten Infanterie-Regiment August Böck, vormaliger Trompeter im Schill'schen Corps* (Halle, 1832).

Borngräber, Bertha, ed., *Helmina von Chézy: Unvergessenes: Denkwürdigkeiten aus dem Leben von Helmina von Chézy. Von ihr selbst erzählt,* 2 vols. (Leipzig, 1858).

Bourgogne, Adrien-Jean-Baptiste-François, *1812–13: Kriegserlebnisse v. F. Bourgogne, Sergeant d. französischen Kaisergarde.* Volksausgabe (Stuttgart, 1900).

Brabant, Artur, ed., *Im Banne Napoleons: Aus den Erinnerungen des sächsischen Generalleutnants und Generaladjutanten des Königs Ferdinand von Funck* (Dresden, 1928).

Brandt, Heinrich von, ed., *Aus dem Leben des Generals der Infanterie z.D. Dr. Heinrich von Brandt. Aus den Tagebüchern und Aufzeichnungen seines verstorbenen Vaters zusammengestellt* (Berlin, 1868).

Brockhaus, Heinrich Eduard, ed., *Brockhaus, Friedrich Arnold, Sein Leben und Wirken nach Briefen und anderen Aufzeichnungen,* 3 vols. (Leipzig 1872, 1876 and 1881).

Burg, Menno, *Geschichte meines Dienstlebens: Zum Besten einer milden Stiftung nach seinem Tode herausgegeben* (Berlin, 1854).

Büttner, *Beschreibung der Schicksale und Leiden des ehemaligen Korporals Büttner, jetzt Aufschlag-Untereinnehmer in Nennsling, während seiner 19-monatlichen Gefangenschaft in Russland, in den Jahren 1812 und 1813. Von ihm selbst geschrieben* (Nennsling, 1828).

Coignet, Jean-Roch, *Von Marengo bis Waterloo: Memoiren des Sekundärllieutnants Capitaine Coignet* (Stuttgart, 1910).

Diersburg, Philipp Ruder von, ed., *Denkwürdigkeiten des Markgrafen Wilhelm von Baden aus den Feldzügen von 1809 bis 1815: Nach dessen hinterlassenen eigenhändigen Aufzeichnungen* (Karlsruhe, 1864).

Donnersmarck, Wilhelm Ludwig Victor Graf Henckel von, *Erinnerungen aus meinem Leben* (Zerbst, 1846).

Eichhorn, Karl Friedrich, *Briefe, und zwei an ihn gerichtete Schreiben zur Säcularfeier seines Geburtstages*, ed. Hugo Loersch (Bonn, 1881).

Engel, Regula, *Lebensbeschreibung der Wittwe des Obrist Florian Engel von Langwies, in Bündten, geborner Egli von Fluntern, bey Zürich: enthaltend: die Geschichte ihres Herkommens, Jugendschicksale, Verheurathung, und weitläufigen Reisen im Gefolge der französischen Armeen durch ganz Frankreich, die Niederlande, Italien, Spanien, Portugall, die Oesterreichischen und Preussischen Staaten, Deutschland, und besonders auch der Expedition in Egypten, und einer spätern Reise nach Amerika* (Zurich, 1821).

Fouqué, Friedrich Baron de la Motte, *Lebensgeschichte des Barons Friedrich de la Motte-Fouque: Aufgezeichnet durch ihn selbst* (Halle, 1840).

Freytag, Gustav, *Erinnerungen aus meinem Leben*, in *Gesammelte Werke*, vol. 1 (Leipzig, 1887).

Funck, Karl Wilhelm Ferdinand von, *Erinnerungen aus dem Feldzuge des sächsischen Corps unter dem General Grafen Reynier im Jahr 1812: Aus den Papieren des verstorbenen Generalleutnants von Funck* (Dresden, 1829).

Goethe, Johann Wolfgang von, *Aus meinem Leben: Dichtung und Wahrheit*, 3 vols. (Stuttgart and Tübingen, 1811–14). Engl.: *From My Life: Poetry and Truth*, trans. Robert R. Heitner, ed. Thomas P. Saine and Jeffrey L. Sammons, 2 vols., in *Goethe's Collected Works*, vols. 4–5 (New York, 1987).

Goethe, Theodor Daniel, *Aus dem Leben eines sächsischen Husaren und aus dessen Feldzügen 1809, 1812 und 1813 in Polen und Russland* (Leipzig, 1853).

Heilborn, Adolf, ed., *Willibald Alexis. Als Kriegsfreiwilliger nach Frankreich 1815: Blätter aus meinen Erinnerungen* (Berlin, 1915).

Henrich, Steffens, *Was ich erlebte*, ed. Willi A. Koch (Leipzig, 1938, abridged edn.).

Hoffmann, Ludwig von, *Erinnerungen eines alten Soldaten und ehemaligen Freiwilligen aus den Kriegsjahren 1813 und 1814* (Berlin, 1863).

Holzhausen, Paul, ed., *Mit Napoleon in Rußland: Erinnerungen von Heinrich von Roos* (Stuttgart, 1910).

Hüser, Johann von, *Denkwürdigkeiten aus dem Leben des Generals der Infanterie von Hüser größtenteils nach dessen hinterlassenen Papieren* (Berlin, 1877).

Keller, Ernst, ed., *Memoiren des königlich preußischen Generals der Infanterie Ludwig Freiherrn von Wolzogen* (Frankfurt/M., 1908).

Keyerling, Archibald Graf von, *Aus der Kriegszeit: Erinnerungen von Archibald Grafen von Keyserling*, 2 vols. (Berlin, 1847–55).

Kletke, Hermann, ed., *Kunst und Leben: Aus Friedrich Försters Nachlaß* (Berlin, 1873).

Kleßmann, Eckart, ed., *Deutschland unter Napoleon in Augenzeugenberichten* (Düsseldorf, 1965).

Köhler, Karl August, *1813–14: Tagebuchblätter eines Feldgeistlichen, des Dr. K. A. Köhler, Prediger der Brigade des Generalmajors Dobschütz*, ed. Kadettenhauspfarrer Jäkel (Berlin-Lichterfelde, 1912).

Krimer, Wenzel, *Erinnerungen eines alten Lützower Jägers, 1795–1819*, 2 vols. (Stuttgart, 1833).

Krollmann, Christian Anton, ed., *Landwehrbriefe 1813: Ein Denkmal der Erinnerung an den Burggrafen Ludwig zu Dohna-Schlobitten* (Danzig, 1913).

Krug, Wilhelm Traugott, *Krug's Lebensreise in sechs Stazionen, von ihm selbst beschrieben: Neue verbesserte und vermehrte Ausgabe* (Leipzig, 1842).

Kügelgen, Anna and Emma von, eds., *Ein Lebensbild in Briefen: Marie Helene von Kügelgen, geb. von Zöge von Manteuffel* (Stuttgart, 1900, 2nd. edn.).

Kügelgen, Wilhelm, *Jugenderinnerungen eines alten Mannes* (Berlin, 1870 and Munich, 1911).

Lange, Fritz, ed., *Die Lützower – Erinnerungen, Berichte, Dokumente* (Berlin, 1953).

Leuschner, Brigitte, ed., *Schriftstellerinnen und Schwesterseelen: Der Briefwechsel zwischen Therese Huber (1764–1829) und Karoline Pichler (1769–1843)* (Marburg, 1995).

Lietzmann, Karl, ed., *Freiwilliger Jäger bei den Totenkopfhusaren: Siebzehn Jahre Leutnant im Blücherhusaren-Regiment. Erzählungen aus Kolbergs Ruhmestagen, aus dem deutschen Befreiungskrieg, aus kleiner pommerscher Garnison und von der Grenzwacht gegen den polnischen Aufstand 1831* (Berlin, 1909).

Linnebach, Karl, ed., *Gerhardt von Scharnhorst: Briefe*, vol. 1: *Privatbriefe*, (Munich, 1914).

ed., *Carl und Marie von Clausewitz: Ein Lebensbild in Briefen und Tagebuchblättern* (Berlin, 1917, 2nd edn.).

Luden, Heinrich, *Rückblicke in mein Leben: Aus dem Nachlasse von Heinrich Luden* (Jena, 1847).

Marbot, Jean-Baptiste Antoine Marcellin, *Memoirs of Baron de Marbot: Late Lieutenant General in the French Army* (London, 1894).

[Marter, Christian Ludwig], *Fünf Marter-Jahre: Schicksale eines deutschen Soldaten in Spanien und Sicilien* (Weimar, 1834).

Marwitz, Friedrich August Ludwig von der, *Ein märkischer Edelmann im Zeitalter der Befreiungskriege*, ed. Friedrich Meusel, 2 vols. (Berlin, 1908–13).

Meerheim, Franz Ludwig August von, *Erlebnisse eines Veteranen der großen Armee während des Feldzuges in Rußland 1812* (Dresden, 1860).

Meier, Wilhelm, *Erinnerungen aus den Feldzügen 1806 bis 1815: Aus den hinterlassenen Papieren eines Militärarztes* (Karlsruhe, 1854).

Mente, W.[ilhelm], *Von der Pieke auf: Erinnerungen an eine neun und vierzigjährige Dienstzeit in der Königlich Preußischen Artillerie* (Berlin, 1861).

Meyer, Jakob, *Erzählung der Schicksale und Kriegsabenteuer des ehemaligen westfälischen Artillerie-Wachtmeisters Jakob Meyer aus Dransfeld während der Feldzüge in Spanien und Russland* (Dransfeld, 1836).

Müchler, Karl, *Doppelflucht um den Verfolgungen der Franzosen zu entgehen: Bruchstücke aus den Erinnerungen meines Lebens* (Cottbus, 1841).

Müffling, Eduard Freiherr von, ed., *Friedrich Karl Ferdinand Freiherr von Müffling: Aus meinem Leben* (Berlin, 1851).

Muhl, Georg, ed., *Denkwürdigkeiten aus dem Leben des Freiherrn C. R. von Schäffer, großherzoglich badischen General-Lieutenants und Präsidenten des Kriegs-Ministeriums* (Pforzheim, 1840).

Mühlenfels, Friedrich Ludwig von, "Ein Lützower Reiter," *GB* 20.4 (1861): 481–500.

Nabert, Thomas, ed., *Zeugen des Schreckens: Erlebnisberichte aus der Völkerschlachtzeit in und um Leipzig* (Leipzig, 2012).

Niebuhr, Barthold Georg, *Die Briefe, 1776–1816*, ed. Dietrich Gerhard and William Norvin, 2 vols. (Berlin 1926–29).

Niebuhr, Marcus von, ed., *Aus dem Nachlasse Friedrich August Ludwig's von der Marwitz auf Friedrichsdorf*, vol .1: *Lebensbeschreibung* (Berlin, 1852).

Perthes, Agnes and Wilhelm, *Aus der Franzosenzeit in Hamburg: Erlebnisse* (Hamburg, 1910).

Prell, Marianne, *Erinnerungen aus der Franzosenzeit in Hamburg: Für Kinder erzählt* (Hamburg, 1863).

Quednow, Mathilde, ed., *Denkwürdigkeiten aus dem Leben des Generals der Infanterie von Hüser* (Berlin, 1877).

Ranke, Leopold von, ed., *Denkwürdigkeiten des Staatskanzlers Fürsten von Hardenberg bis zum Jahre 1806* (Leipzig, 1877).

Raumer, Karl Georg von, *Erinnerungen aus den Jahren 1813 und 1814* (Stuttgart, 1850).

Rellstab, Ludwig, *Aus meinem Leben*, 2 vols. (Berlin, 1861).

Rühle von Lilienstern, Johann Jakob Otto August, *Bericht eines Augenzeugen von dem Feldzug der während den Monaten September und Oktober 1806 unter dem Kommando des Fürsten zu Hohenlohe-Ingelfingen gestandenen königlich-preußischen und kurfürstlich sächsischen Truppen* (Tübingen, 1807).

Schlosser, Wilhelm Gottlob, *Erlebnisse eines sächsischen Landpredigers in den Kriegsjahren 1806–1815* (Wiesbaden, 1914).

Schmidt, Dorothea, ed., *Erinnerungen aus dem Leben des Generalfeldmarschalls Hermann von Boyen*, 2 vols. (Berlin, 1990).

Schoeps, Hans Joachim, ed., *Aus den Jahren preußischer Not und Erneuerung: Tagebücher und Briefe der Gebrüder Gerlach und ihres Kreises, 1805–1820* (Berlin, 1963).

Schöppach, Karl, ed., *Denknisse eines Deutschen oder Fahrten des Alten im Bart* (Schleusingen, 1835).

Schrafel, Joseph, *Des Nürnberger Feldwebels Joseph Schrafel merkwürdige Schicksale im Kriege gegen Tirol 1809, im Feldzug gegen Rußland 1812 und in der Gefangenschaft 1812–1814* (Nuremberg, 1834).

Schultze, W.Ad., "Frau Professor Radspiller's Tagebuch aus Hamburg's Franzosenzeit," *Zeitschrift des Vereins für Hamburgische Geschichte* 11 (1903): 227–258.

Schwartzkoppen, Clotilde von, ed., *Karl von François: Ein deutsches Soldatenleben. Nach hinterlassenen Memoiren* (Schwerin, 1873).

Steffens, Heinrich, *Was ich erlebte 1802–1814: Knechtschaft und Freiheit*, 10 vols. (Breslau, 1840–45).

Stockmar, E. von, ed., *Denkwürdigkeiten aus den Papieren des Freiherrn Christian Friedrich von Stockmar* (Braunschweig, 1872).

Tecklenburg, August, ed., *Förster Flecks Kriegsfahrt und Gefangenschaft in Rußland 1812–1814: Beschreibung meiner Leiden und Schicksale während Napoleons Feldzug und meiner Gefangenschaft in Rußland* (Hildesheim, 1907).

Varnhagen von Ense, Karl August, *Denkwürdigkeiten des eigenen Lebens*, 3 vols. (Leipzig 1843).

Denkwürdigkeiten des eignen Lebens, ed. Joachim Kühn, 2 vols. (repr. Berlin 1922–23).

Vater, Auguste, *Was wir erlebten im Oktober 1813: Denkschrift für den Verein zur Feier des 19. Octobers in Leipzig* (Leipzig, 1845).

Weldler-Steinberg, Augusta, ed., *Theodor Körners Briefwechsel mit den Seinen* (Leipzig, 1910).

Wolf, Ferdinand, ed., *Denkwürdigkeiten aus meinem Leben von Caroline von Pichler*, 4 vols. (Vienna, 1844).

Wolzogen, Alfred Freiherrn von, ed., *Memoiren des Königlich Preussischen Generals der Infanterie Ludwig Freiherrn von Wolzogen: Aus dessen Nachlass unter Beifügung officieller militärischer Denkschriften* (Leipzig, 1851).

Novels

Alexis, Willibald, *Die Geächteten: Novelle* (Berlin, 1824).

Isegrimm: Vaterländischer Roman, 3 vols. (Berlin, 1854).

Ruhe ist die erste Bürgerpflicht oder Vor 50 Jahren: Vaterländischer Roman, 5 vols. (Berlin, 1852).

Baczko, Ludwig von, *Die Familie Eisenberg oder die Gräuel des Kriegs* (Halle and Leipzig, 1817).

Breier, Eduard, *1805 oder: Die Franzosen zum ersten Mal in Wien*, 2 vols. (Vienna, 1864).

1809: Historischer Roman, 3 vols. (Vienna, 1847).

Der Congreß zu Wien: Historischer Roman, 4 vols. (Vienna, 1854).

Fontane, Theodor, *Schach von Wuthenow*, in *Fontanes Werke in fünf Bänden* (Berlin, 1977).

Schach von Wuthenow: Erzählung aus der Zeit des Regiments Gendarmes (Berlin, 1883).

Vor dem Sturm: Roman aus dem Winter 1812 auf 13, 4 vols. (Frankfurt/M., 1986 and Berlin, 1878).

Fouqué, Caroline de La Motte, *Edmund's Wege und Irrwege: Ein Roman aus der Vergangenheit* (Berlin, 1815).

Fouqué, Friedrich Baron de la Motte, *Der Refugié oder Heimat und Fremde: Ein Roman aus der neueren Zeit* (Gotha, 1824).

François, Louise von, *Die letzte Reckenburgerin* (Berlin, 1871).

Frau Erdmuthens Zwillingssöhne: Roman (Berlin, 1873).

Freytag, Gustav, *Die Ahnen*, 6 vols. (Leipzig, 1873–81), vol. 6: *Aus einer kleinen Stadt* (1880).

Goethe, Johann Wolfgang von, *Goethes neue Schriften*, vols. 3–6: *Wilhelm Meisters Lehrjahre: Ein Roman* (Berlin 1795–96). Engl.: *Wilhelm Meister's Apprenticeship*, trans. and ed. Eric A. Blackall and Victor Lange in *Goethe's Collected Works*, vol. 9 (New York, 1989).

Häberlin, Karl Ludwig (Pseudonym: H. E. R. Belani), *Die Demagogen: Novelle aus der Geschichte unserer Zeit*, 2 vols. (Leipzig, 1829).

Helm, Clementine, *Das vierblättrige Kleeblatt: Eine Erzählung aus dem Freiheitskriege für junge Mädchen* (Bielefeld and Leipzig, 1878).

Hesekiel, George, *Bis nach Hohen-Zieritz: Roman*, 3 vols. (Berlin, 1861).

Krummensee: Historischer Roman, 6 vols. (Berlin, 1861).

Stille vor dem Sturm: Roman, 3 vols. (Berlin, 1862).

Vier Junker: Historischer Roman, 3 vols. (Berlin, 1865).

Von Jena nach Königsberg: Roman, 3 vol. (Berlin, 1860).

Vor Jena: Nach den Aufzeichnungen eines Königl. Offizier vom Regiment Gensd'arms, 2 vols. (Berlin, 1859).

Holtei, Karl, *Christian Lammfell: Roman* (Breslau, 1853).

Kramer, Carl Gottlob, *Das Eiserne Kreuz: Ein kriegerischer Halb-Roman aus den Jahren 1812, 1813 und 1814* (Hamburg, 1815).

Leibrock, August, *Die schwarzen Husaren: Kriegerischer Halbroman aus dem Jahre 1809* (Leipzig, 1841).

Lewald, Fanny, *Die Familie Darner: Roman* (Berlin, 1887).

Prinz Louis Ferdinand (Breslau, 1849).

Moritz, Karl Philipp, *Anton Reiser*, 4 vols. (Berlin, 1785–90). Engl.: *Anton Reiser: A Psychological Novel*, trans. Ritchie Robinson (Harmondsworth, 1997).

Mühlbach, Louise, *Deutschland in Sturm und Drang: Historischer Roman*, 17 vols. (Jena, 1867–68).

Napoleon in Deutschland, 16 vols. (Berlin, 1858).

Pichler, Caroline, *Frauenwürde* (Leipzig, 1818).

Rellstab, Ludwig, *1812: Ein historischer Roman*, 4 vols. (Leipzig, 1834).

Gesammelte Schriften: Neue Ausgabe, vols. 1–4 (Leipzig, 1860).

Schreckenbach, Paul, *Der böse Baron von Krosigk: Roman aus der Zeit deutscher Schmach und Erhebung* (Leipzig, 1907, repr. Berlin, 2012).

Schücking, Levin, *Aus der Franzosenzeit* (Vienna, 1863).

Die Rheider Burg: Roman, 2 vols. (Prague, 1859).

Ein Staatsgeheimnis: Roman, 3 vols. (Leipzig, 1859).

Sperl, August, *Burschen Heraus! Roman aus der Zeit unserer tiefsten Erniedrigung* (Munich, 1913).

Spielhagen, Friedrich, *Noblesse oblige* (Leipzig, 1882).

Sudermann, Hermann, *Der Katzensteg* (Stuttgart, 1889).

Winterfeld-Warnow, Emmy von, *Deutsche Frauen in schwerer Zeit: Roman aus den Jahren 1806–1812 nach alten Familienpapieren und Überlieferungen* (Berlin, 1901).

Songs and Poems

Anonymous, *Kriegslieder der Deutschen: Erstes Dutzend* (Breslau, 1813).

Kriegslieder für die Königlich Preussischen Truppen vorzüglich den Jäger Detachements gewidmet: Beym Ausmarsch den 23. März 1813 (n.p., 1813).

Kriegslieder für die Königlich Preußischen Truppen vorzüglich den Jäger-Detachements gewidmet: Beym Ausmarsch den 23sten März 1813 (Breslau, 1813).

Lieder für Preußische Soldaten (Berlin, 1812).

Schlachtgesänge und Vaterlandslieder für deutsche Jünglinge (Berlin, 1813).

Arndt, Ernst Moritz, *Lieder für Teutsche im Jahr der Freiheit 1813* (Leipzig, 1813, repr. Berlin, 1913).

Arndt, Ernst Moritz and Theodor Körner, *Lob teutscher Helden* (Frankfurt/M., 1814).

Arnold, Robert F., ed., *Deutsche Literatur: Sammlung literarischer Kunst- und Kulturdenkmäler in Entwicklungsreihen*, vol. 2: *Fremdherrschaft und Befreiung, 1795–1815* (Leipzig, 1932).

Becker, Rudolph Zacharias, *Mildheimisches Liederbuch: Faksimiledruck nach der Ausgabe von 1815* (Stuttgart, 1971).

[Bodenburg, Christian Christoph], *Preußische Kriegslieder und einige andere Gedichte von B.: Erstes Heft* (n.p., 1813).

Ditfurth, Franz Wilhelm Freiherr von, ed. *Die Historischen Volkslieder des siebenjährigen Krieges nebst geschichtlichen und sonstigen Erläuterungen* (Berlin, 1871).

Fouqué, Friedrich Baron de la Motte, *Kriegslied für die freiwilligen Jäger im Brandenburgischen Kürassier-Regiment* ([Berlin, 1813]).

Heun, Carl, *Lied der Preussen: Der König rief, und alle, alle kamen, mit Begleitung des Forte-Piano und der Guitarre* (Hamburg, 1813).

Horner, Emil, ed., *Deutsche Literatur: Sammlung literarischer Kunst- und Kulturdenkmäler in Entwicklungsreihen*, vol. 1: *Vor dem Untergang des alten Reichs, 1756–1795* (Leipzig, 1930).

[Jahn, Friedrich Ludwig], ed., *Deutsche Wehrlieder für das Königlich-Preussische Frei-Corps herausgegeben. Erste Sammlung* (Berlin, Easter 1813).

Körner, Theodor, *Gedichte vor und im heiligen Kriege gesungen von Theodor Körner* (n.p., 1814).

Leyer und Schwert (Berlin, 1814, 2nd edn.).

Zwölf freie deutsche Gedichte: Nebst einem Anhang ([Leipzig], 1813).

Longfellow, Henry Wadsworth, *The Poets and Poetry of Europe* (Philadelphia, PA, 1845).

Sermons

Anonymous, *Dank-Gebeth welches statt der gewöhnlichen Collecta vor dem Altar in der St. Georgen Zucht- und Waisenhaus-Kirche mit der ganzen Versammlung auf den Knien, am 19. Sonntag nach Trinitatis, also am 1. Sonntag nach der dreytägigen Schlacht und Eroberung von Leipzig mit Sturm ist gehalten worden wegen Errettung der Stadt* (Leipzig, 24 October 1813).

Bertholdt, Leonhard, *Zwei Predigten am Siegesfeste und dem darauf eingefallenen gewöhnlichen allgemeinen Buß- und Bettage in der Universität zu Erlangen gehalten* (Sulzbach, 1814).

Herrosee, C. F. W., *Rede bei der Vereidigung einiger Kompagnien der Züllichauschen Landsturmmänner, gehalten in der königlichen Schloßkirche am 3ten Junius 1813* ([Züllichau, 1813]).

Mundt, G. W., *Einige Reden und Predigten bei wichtigen Veranlassungen des Krieges gehalten* (Halle and Berlin, 1816).

Nicolai, Carl Friedrich Ferdinand, *Vaterlands-Predigten im Jahre 1813 gehalten in der Kirche des Waisenhauses bei Züllichau* (Züllichau, 1814).

Offelsmeyer, Friedrich Wihelm, *Predigt in Anwesenheit der großen Hauptquartiere, zu Frankfurt in der St. Katharinenkirche am 28. November 1813* (Frankfurt/M., 1814, 3rd edn.).

Spieker, Christian Wilhelm, *Gebete, Predigten und Reden: Zur Zeit der Erhebung des Preußischen Volks gegen die Tyrannei des Auslandes, im Felde und in der Heimath gehalten* (Berlin, 1816).

Tiemann, D. Carl Ludwig Traugott, *Die Freude des Christen über die Erlösung unseres Vaterlandes. Predigt bey Wiedereröffnung der St. Georgen-Kirche zu Glaucha vor Halle am 3ten Advents-Sonntage 1813 gehalten und auf Verlangen dem Druck übergeben* (Halle, 1814).

Other Primary Sources

Abbt, Thomas, *Vom Tode für das Vaterland* (Berlin, 1761).

Allgemeines Landrecht für die Preußischen Staaten (ALR) (Berlin, 1 Juni 1794).

Andreae, Friedrich, "Die freiwilligen Leistungen von 1813," *Zeitschrift des Vereins für die Geschichte Schlesiens* 47 (1913): 150–197.

Anonymous, ed., *Das Eiserne Kreuz im Spiegel deutscher Dichtung: 1813, 1870, 1914* (Leipzig, 1915).

Anonymous, *Die Juden in Lübeck* (Frankfurt/M., 1816).

Frauensteuer an der Wiege des wiedergeborenen Vaterlandes: Von Elisabeth von F. (n.p., [1814]).

Über Juden-Reformation (Bavaria [Augsburg], 1819).

Was war der deutsche Krieger unter Napoleon? Und was ist er jetzt? ([Heidelberg], 1814).

Welche Aussichten eröffnen sich für Deutschland wenn der Rhein die künftige Gränze zwischen ihm und Frankreich bilden sollte? (Nuremberg, 1814).

Wort zu deutschen Bürgern (n.p., 1813).

Zum Angedenken der Königin Luise von Preußen: Sammlung der vollständigen und zuverlässigen Nachrichten von allen das Absterben und die Trauerfeierlichkeit dieser unvergeßlichen Fürstin bestreffenden Umständen. Nebst einer Auswahl der bei diesem Anlaß erschienenen Gedichte und Gedächtnispredigten (Berlin, 1810).

Arndt, Ernst Moritz, *Ansichten und Aussichten der Teutschen Geschichte*, pt. 1 (Leipzig, 1814).

Blick aus der Zeit auf die Zeit (Germanien [Frankfurt/M.], 1814).

Das preußische Volk und Heer im Jahr 1813 ([Leipzig], 1813).

Der Rhein, Teutschlands Strom, aber nicht Teutschlands Gränze (Leipzig, 1813).

Die Huldigungsfeier in Aachen am 15ten Mai 1815 (Aachen, 1815).

Ein Wort über die Feier der Leipziger Schlacht (Frankfurt/M., 1814).

Entwurf einer teutschen Gesellschaft (Frankfurt/M., 1814).

"Geist der Zeit, Theil I und II (1806 und 1809)," in *Arndts Werke: Auswahl in zwölf Teilen*, ed. August Lesson and Wilhelm Steffens (Berlin, n.d.), pt. 6.

Katechismus für den teutschen Kriegs- und Wehrmann, worin gelehret wird, wie ein christlicher Wehrmann seyn und mit Gott in den Streit gehen soll ([Leipzig], 1813).

Kurzer Katechismus für teutsche Soldaten, nebst einem Anhang von Liedern, (n.p. [Petersburg], 1812); reprint in Arndt, *Drei Flugschriften: Kurzer Katechismus für teutsche Soldaten—Zwei Worte über die Entstehung und Bestimmung der Teutschen Legion—Was bedeutet Landsturm und Landwehr?*, ed. Rolf Weber (Berlin, 1988).

Kurzer Katechismus für teutsche Soldaten, nebst zwei Anhängen von Liedern ([Königsberg], 1813).

Noch ein Wort über die Franzosen und über uns (n.p., 1814).

Ueber die Feier der Leipziger Schlacht (Frankfurt/M., 1815, 2nd edn.)

Ascher, Saul, *Die Germanomanie: Skizze zu einem Zeitgemälde* (Berlin, 1815).

Beitzke, Heinrich, *Geschichte der Deutschen Freiheitskriege in den Jahren 1813 und 1814*, 3 vols. (Berlin, 1854 and 1855).

[Bergk, Johann Adam], *Der Befreiungskrieg in Teutschland im Jahr 1813* (Leipzig, 1816).

"Die Formation der freiwilligen Jäger-Detachements bei der preußischen Armee im Jahre 1813," in *BHMW* (Sept.–Oct. 1845, Nov.–Dec. 1845 and Jan.–Feb. 1847).

"Entwicklung der Preußischen Kriegsartikel," in *BHMW* 7 (1890): 351–194.

Boost, [Philipp Friedrich], *Ueber die National-Ehre der Deutschen: Eine historisch-philosophische Untersuchung* (Wiesbaden, 1812).

Brentano, Clemens, "Der Philister vor, in und nach der Geschichte: Scherzhafte Abhandlung," in *Clemens Brentano's Gesammelte Schriften*, ed. Christian Brentano, vol. 5: *Der kleinen Schriften zweiter Theil* (Frankfurt/M., 1852), 371–446.

"Victoria und ihre Geschwister mit fliegenden Fahnen und brennender Lunte: Ein klingendes Spiel," in *Clemens Brentano's Gesammelte Schriften*, ed. Christian Brentano, vol. 7: *Comödien* (Frankfurt/M., 1852), 279–466.

Buchholz, Carl August, *Actenstükke, die Verbesserung des bürgerlichen Zustandes der Israeliten betreffend* (Stuttgart and Tübingen, 1815).

Über die Aufnahme der jüdischen Glaubensgenossen zum Bürgerrecht (Lübeck, 1814).

Buchholz, Friedrich, ed. *Chauffour's, des Jüngeren, Betrachtungen über die Anwendung des kaiserlichen Dekrets vom 17ten März 1808 in Betreff der Schuldforderungen der Juden* (Berlin, 1809).

Moses und Jesus, oder über das intellektuelle und moralische Verhältnis der Juden und Christen (Berlin, 1803).

Bülau, Friedrich, *Geschichte Deutschlands von 1806–1830* (Hamburg, 1842).

Burdach, Heinrich, *Ueber die endliche Erhebung Germaniens oder wie kann die Hoffnung auf eine bessere Zukunft in Erfüllung gehen?* (Berlin, 1814).

Clausewitz, Carl von, *Historical and Political Writings*, ed. and trans. Peter Paret and David Moran (Princeton, NJ, 1992).

Nachrichten über Preußen in seiner großen Katastrophe (1823–25), ed. Großer Generalstab, Abteilung für Kriegsgeschichte (Berlin, 1888).

On War, transl. Michael Howard and Peter Paret, abridged with an Introduction and Notes by Beatrice Heuser (Oxford, 2006)

Schriften – Aufsätze – Studien – Briefe: Dokumente aus dem Clausewitz-, Scharnhorst- und Gneisenau-Nachlaß sowie aus öffentlichen und privaten Sammlungen, ed. Werner Hahlweg, 2 vols. (Göttingen, 1966 and 1990).

Vom Kriege: Hinterlassenes Werk. Ungekürzter Text (Frankfurt/M., 1991).

Czygan, Paul, "Totenfeier für die Königin Luise 1810," *Altpreußische Monatsschrift* 54 (1917): 347–359.

Zur Geschichte der Tagesliteratur während der Freiheitskriege, 3 vols. (Leipzig, 1909–11).

Delbrück, Hans, *Das Leben des Feldmarschalls Grafen Neidhardt von Gneisenau*, 2 vols. (Berlin, 1880–81).

Dohm, Christian Konrad Wilhelm von, *Über die bürgerliche Verbesserung der Juden*, 2 vols. (Berlin and Stettin, 1781–83, repr. Hildesheim, 1973, 2 pts. in one vol.).

Droysen, Johann Gustav, *Das Leben des Feldmarschalls Grafen York von Wartenburg* (Berlin, 1851).

Vorlesungen über die Freiheitskriege, 2 vols. (Kiel, 1846).

Ehrenberg, Friedrich, *Das Volk und seine Fürsten: Volkswesen und Volkssinn, Reden, von Friedrich Ehrenberg, Hofprediger in Berlin* (Leipzig, 1815).

Der Charakter und die Bestimmung des Mannes (Elberfeld, 1808, 2nd edn., 1822).

Embser, [Johann Valentin], *Die Abgötterei unseres philosophischen Jahrhunderts. Erster Abgott: Ewiger Friede* (Mannheim, 1779).

Engels, Friedrich, "Ernst Moritz Arndt," in *Karl Marx and Friedrich Engels. Werke. Ergänzungsband*, pt. 2 (Berlin, 1967).

Ewald, Johann Ludwig, *Der Geist des Christentums und des ächten deutschen Volksthums, dargestellt gegen die Feinde der Israeliten* (Karlsruhe, 1817).

Der gute Jüngling, gute Gatte und Vater, oder Mittel um es zu werden: Ein Gegenstück zu der Kunst ein gutes Mädchen zu werden, 2 vols. (Frankfurt/M., 1804).

Ideen über die nöthige Organisation der Israeliten in Christlichen Staaten (Karlsruhe, 1816).

Feuerbach, Anselm, *Ueber die Unterdrückung und Wiederbefreiung Europens* (Deutschland, [1813]).

Fichte, Johann Gottlieb, *Reden an die deutsche Nation* (Berlin, 1808).

Über den Begriff des wahrhaften Krieges in Bezug auf den Krieg im Jahre 1813 (Tübingen, 1815).

Förster, Friedrich Christoph, ed., *Der Rückzug der Franzosen aus Rußland. Aus dem Nachlasse des verstorbenen königlich preußischen Generals der Infanterie Ernst von Pfuel* (Berlin, 1867).

Geschichte der Befreiungs-Kriege 1813, 1814, 1815, 3 vols. (Berlin, 1856, 1858 and 1861).

Von der Begeisterung des preussischen Volkes i. J. 1813, als Vertheidigung unsres Glaubens (Berlin, 1816).

Fouqué, Caroline de La Motte, *Ruf an die deutschen Frauen* (Berlin, 1813).

François, Louise von, *Geschichte der preussischen Befreiungskriege in den Jahren 1813 bis 1815* (Berlin, 1874).

Friccus, Carl Friedrich, *Geschichte des Kriegs in den Jahren 1813 und 1814, mit besonderer Rücksicht auf Ostpreußen und das Königsberger Landwehrbataillon* (Altenburg, 1843).

Fries, Jacob Friedrich, *Über die Gefährdung des Wohlstandes und Charakters der Deutschen durch die Juden. Eine aus den Heidelberger Jahrbüchern der Litteratur besonders abgedruckte Recension der Schrift des Professors Rühs in Berlin: "Ueber die Ansprüche der Juden an das deutsche Bürgerrecht. Zweyter verbesserter Nachdruck"* (Heidelberg, 1816).

Generalstab, Großer, Kriegsgeschichtliche Abteilung II, ed., *1806: Das Preußische Offizierkorps und die Untersuchung der Kriegsereignisse* (Berlin, 1906).

ed., *Das Preußische Heer der Befreiungskriege*, 3 vols. (Berlin, 1912–14).

Generalstabes, Historischen Abtheilung, ed., "Die Formation der freiwilligen Jäger-Detachements bei der preußischen Armee im Jahre 1813," in *BHMW* (Berlin, Sept.–Oct. 1845): 449–479, (Berlin, Nov.–Dec. 1845): 481–515, (Berlin, Jan.–Feb. 1847): 1–38.

ed., "Geschichte der Organisation der Landwehr," 1: "In dem Militair-Gouvernement zwischen Elbe und Weser," 2: "In dem Militair-Gouvernement zwischen Weser und Rhein im Jahre 1813 und 1814," in *BHMW* (Berlin, 1857).

[Gleim, Betty], *Was hat das wiedergeborne Deutschland von seinen Frauen zu fordern? Beantwortet durch eine Deutsche* (Bremen, 1814).

Gneisenau, Neidhardt von, "Über den Krieg von 1806," in *Ausgewählte militärische Schriften*, ed. Gerhard Förster and Christa Gudzent (Berlin, 1984), 50–62.

Görres, Joseph V., *Gesammelte Schriften*, ed. Marie Görres, 8 vols. (Munich, 1854–74).

Gräfe, Heinrich, *Nachrichten von wohltätigen Frauenvereinen in Deutschland – Ein Beitrag zur Sittengeschichte des 19. Jahrhunderts* (Kassel, 1844).

Granier, Herman, ed., *Berichte aus der Berliner Franzosenzeit, 1807–1809: Nach den Akten des Berliner Geheimen Staatsarchivs und des Pariser Kriegsarchivs* (Leipzig, 1913).

Grattenauer, Carl Wilhelm Friedrich, *Über die physische und moralische Verfassung der heutigen Juden: Stimme eines Kosmopoliten, Germanien* ([Leipzig], 1791).

Wider die Juden: Ein Wort der Warnungen an alle unsere christlichen Mitbürger (Berlin, 1803).

Gurlt, Ernst, "Abhandlung über den Ursprung der Sprache, welche den von der Königl. Academie der Wissenschaften für das Jahr 1770 Gesetzten Preis erhalten hat (1772)," in *Herder Werke*, vol. 1, ed. Ulrich Gaier (Frankfurt/M., 1985), 695–810.

"Briefe zur Beförderung der Humanität," in *Herder Werke*, vol. 7, ed. Dietrich Irmscher (Frankfurt/M., 1991).

"Die freiwilligen Leistungen der preußischen Nation in den Kriegsjahren 1813–1815: National-Denkmal oder summarische Darstellung der patriotischen Handlungen und Opfer der Preußischen Nation während der Jahre 1813, 1814, 1815 bearbeitet auf Befehl König Friedrich Wilhelms III. von der Königl. General-Ordens-Commission," *Zeitschrift für preußische Geschichte und Landeskunde* 9 (1872): 645–696.

Heidenreich, Heinrich, *Das Eiserne Kreuz in Geschichte und Dichtung (Beiheft der Blätter für die Fortbildung des Lehrers und der Lehrerin*, vol. 8 (Berlin, 1914).

[Helvig, Amalie von], *An Deutschlands Frauen von einer ihrer Schwestern* (Leipzig, 1814).

Hess, Michael, *Freimüthige Prüfung der Schrift des Herrn Professor Rühs, über die Ansprüche der Juden an das deutsche Bürgerrecht* (Frankfurt/M., 1816).

Hochfelden, Wilhelm Krieg von, *Geschichtliche Darstellung sämmtlicher Begebenheiten und Kriegsvorfälle der Großherzoglich Badischen Truppen in Spanien von Ende 1808 bis Ende 1813 in Verbindung der allgemeinen bedeutenden Ereignisse der Rheinischen Bundes Division in der französischen Gesamtarmee* (Freiburg, 1823).

Hoffmann, Karl, ed., *Des Teutschen Volkes feuriger Dank- und Ehrentempel oder Beschreibung wie das aus zwanzigjähriger französischer Sklaverei durch Fürsten-Eintracht und Volkskraft gerettete Teutsche Volk die Tage der entscheidenden Völker- und Rettungsschlacht bei Leipzig am 18. und 19. October zum erstenmale gefeiert hat* (Offenbach, 1815).

Horn, W. Otto von, *Vier deutsche Heldinnen aus der Zeit der Befreiungskriege: Ein Büchlein für die deutsche Jugend und das Volk* (Wiesbaden, 1897).

Huber, Ernst Rudolf, ed., *Dokumente zur deutschen Verfassungsgeschichte*, 3 vols. (Stuttgart, 1961–66).

Humboldt, Wilhelm von, *Wilhelm von Humboldt's Gesammelte Werke*, 7 vols. (Berlin, 1841–52).

Hundt-Radowsky, Hartwig von, *Judenspiegel: Ein Schand- und Sittengemälde alter und neuer Zeit* (Würzburg, 1819).

Jacobi, Georg Arnold, *Natürliche Gränzen* (Düsseldorf, 1814).

Jacobs, Friedrich, *Deutschlands Ehre: Dem Andenken der in dem heiligen Kriege gegen Frankreich gefallenen Deutschen gewidmet* (Gotha, 1814).

Deutschlands Gefahren und Hoffnungen: An Germaniens Jugend (Gotha, 1813, 2nd edn.)

Jagwitz, Fritz von, *Geschichte des Lützowschen Freikorps: Nach archivalischen Quellen bearbeitet* (Berlin, 1892).

Jahn, Friedrich Ludwig, *Deutsches Volksthum* (Lübeck, 1810).

Jörg, Johann Christian Gottfried, *Ahndungen für Deutsche bei Eröffnung des Feldzuges von 1814* (Leipzig, 1814).

Judo, Martin and Johann Isaak Freihr. von Gerning, *Ansichten und Bemerkungen über die bürgerlichen Rechts-Verhältnisse der Juden in der freyen Stadt Frankfurt a. M.* (Teutschland [Frankfurt/M.], 1816).

Karstädt, Otto, *Heldenmädchen und -Frauen aus großer Zeit* (Hamburg, 1913).

Kircheisen, Friedrich, *Bibliographie des Napoleonischen Zeitalters einschliesslich der Vereinigten Staaten von Nordamerika*, 2 vols. (Berlin, 1908–12).

Klewitz, Wilhelm Anton von, ed., *Denkmal der Preußen für ihre verewigte Königin Luise, durch weibliche Erziehungsanstalten* (Halberstadt, 1814).

Kohlrausch, Friedrich, *Deutschlands Zukunft: In sechs Reden* (Elberfeld, 1814).

Kosmann, Johann W. Andreas, *Für die Juden – Ein Wort zur Beherzigung an die Freunde der Menschheit und die wahren Verehrer Jesu* (Berlin, 1803).

Kreuzer, Helmut, ed., *Deutschsprachige Literaturkritik, 1870–1914: Eine Dokumentation*, pt. 1: 1870–1889 (Frankfurt/M., 2006).

Kriegs-Artikel für die Unter-Offiziere und gemeinen Soldaten, den 3ten August 1808 (Königsberg, 1808).

Kriegsministerium, Königl., ed., *Geschichte der Königlich Preußischen Fahnen und Standarten seit dem Jahre 1807*, 2 vols. (Berlin, 1889–90).

Kuske, Erich, "Die Beteiligung der höheren Schulen Preußens an der Erhebung im Jahre 1813," *PrJb*154 (1913): 437–450.

Laubert, Manfred, "Die schlesische Landwehr der Befreiungskriege," *Zeitschrift des Vereins für Geschichte die Schlesiens* 47 (1913): 1–21.

Lehmann, Max, *Die Erhebung von 1813: Rede zur Feier des Gedächtnisses von 1813 am 3. Februar 1913 im Namen der Georg-August-Universität gehalten* (Göttingen, 1913).

Freiherr vom Stein, 3 vols. (Leipzig, 1902–05).

Scharnhorst, 2 vols. (Leipzig, 1886–87).

Lips, Alexander, *Über die künftige Stellung der Juden in den deutschen Bundesstaaten, ein Versuch, diesen wichtigen Gegenstand endlich auf die einfachen Prinzipien des Rechts und der Politik zurückzuführen* (Erlangen, 1819).

Løvendahl-Danneskiold, *Der Feldzug an der Niederelbe in den Jahren 1813 und 1814: Von einem Augenzeugen übersetzt aus dem Dänischen* (Kiel, 1818).

Luden, Heinrich, *Über das Studium der vaterländischen Geschichte* (Jena, 1810).

Lüder, August Ferdinand, *Über die Veredelung der Menschen, besonders der Juden durch die Regierungen* (Braunschweig, 1808).

Lützow, Karl von, *Adolf Lützows Freikorps in den Jahren 1813–1814* (Berlin, 1884).

Mehring, Franz, *1813 bis 1819: Von Kalisch nach Karlsbad* (Stuttgart, 1913, 2nd edition).

"Zur deutschen Geschichte von der Zeit der Französischen Revolution bis zum Vormärz, 1789–1847," in *Gesammelte Schriften*, ed. Thomas Höhle, Hans Koch and Joseph Schleifstein, vol. 6 (Berlin, 1965).

Meinecke, Friedrich, *Die Deutschen Gesellschaften und der Hoffmannsche Bund: Ein Beitrag zur Geschichte der politischen Bewegungen in Deutschland im Zeitalter der Befreiungskriege* (Stuttgart, 1891).

Das Zeitalter der deutschen Erhebung, 1795–1815 (Leipzig, [1906], repr. Göttingen, 1957, 6th edn.).

Meiningen, Wilhelm A., *Zur Erinnerung an Karl Schöppach* (Meiningen, 1844).

Müffling, Karl Freiherr von, *Zur Kriegsgeschichte der Jahre 1813 und 1814: Die Feldzüge der schlesischen Armee unter dem Feldmarschall Blücher von der Beendigung des Waffenstillstandes bis zur Eroberung von Paris* (Berlin, 1824).

Müller, Rudolf, "Geschichte von Arndts Schrift: Was bedeutet Landsturm und Landwehr?," *Nord und Süd* 123 (1907): 224–253.

Müller-Bohn, Hermann, *Die deutschen Befreiungskriege: Deutschlands Geschichte von 1805–1815*, ed. Paul Kittel, 2 vols. (Berlin, 1901).

Müsebeck, Ernst, *Freiwillige Gaben und Opfer des preußischen Volkes in den Jahren 1813–1815: Nach der amtlichen Statistik zusammengestellt* (Leipzig, 1913).

Naumann, Robert, *Die Völkerschlacht bei Leipzig: Nebst Nachrichten von Zeitgenossen und Augenzeugen über dieselbe* (Leipzig, 1863).

Odeleben, Otto Freiherr von, *Napoleons Feldzug in Sachsen im Jahr 1813: Eine treue Skizze dieses Krieges, des französischen Kaisers und seiner Umgebungen, entworfen von einem Augenzeugen in Napoleons Hauptquartier, Otto Freiherrn von Odeleben* (Dresden, 1816).

Paalzow, Christian Ludwig, *Helm und Schild: Gespräche über das Bürgerrecht der Juden* (Berlin, 1817).

Über den Juden-Staat (de civitate Judaeorum) oder über die bürgerlichen Rechte der Juden: Eine historische Abhandlung (Berlin, 1803).

Pertz, Georg Heinrich, *Das Leben des Feldmarschalls Grafen Neidhardt v. Gneisenau*, 4 vols. (Berlin 1864–80).

Pflugk-Harttung, Julius von, "Die Aufrufe 'An mein Volk' und 'An Mein Kriegsheer,' 1813," in *Forschungen zur brandenburgischen und preußischen Geschichte* 26 (1913): 265–274.

Leipzig 1813: Aus den Akten des Kriegsarchiv, des Geheimen Staatsarchivs Berlin, Staatsarchivs in Breslau und des Ministeriums der auswärtigen Angelegenheiten in London (Gotha, 1913).

Pfuel, Ernst von, *Der Rückzug der Franzosen aus Rußland* (Berlin, 1813).

Plotho, Carl von, *Der Krieg in Deutschland und Frankreich in den Jahren 1813 und 1814*, 4 vols. (Berlin, 1817).

Pockels, Carl Friedrich, *Der Mann: Ein anthropologisches Charaktergemälde seines Geschlechts*, 4 vols. (Hannover 1805–06).

Prahl, Karl, "Die Soldatenkatechismen von E. M. Arndt," *PrJb* 153 (1913): 450–464.

Richter, Johann Lorenz Friedrich, *Vaterlandskatechismus der Teutschen aus den höheren Ständen* (Erlangen and Leipzig, 1814).

Rotteck, Karl von, *Allgemeine Geschichte: Vom Anfang der historischen Kenntnis bis auf unsere Zeiten*, 10 vols. (Braunschweig, 1851; 1st edn: Freiburg, 1812–27).

Ueber stehende Heere und Nationalmiliz (Freiburg, 1816).

Rossow, Carl, *Bilder und Lieder vom Eisernen Kreuz 1813/14, 1870/71, 1914/16: Ein Gang von Deutschlands Erwachen durch Deutschlands Einheit zu Deutschlands Weltsendung!* (Leipzig, 1916).

Rühl, Franz, ed., *Briefe und Aktenstücke zur Geschichte Preussens unter Friedrich Wilhelm III. vorzugsweise aus dem Nachlass von F. A. von Stägemann*, 3 vols. (Leipzig 1899–1902).

[Rühle von Lilienstern, Johann,] *Kriegs-Katechismus für die Landwehr* (Breslau, 1813).

Vom Kriege: Ein Fragment aus einer Reihe v. Vorlesungen über die Theorie der Kriegskunst (Frankfurt/M., 1814).

Rühle von Lilienstern, Johann Jakob Otto August, ed., *Die Deutsche Volksbewaffnung in einer Sammlung der darüber in sämmtlichen Deutschen Staaten ergangenen Verordnungen* (Berlin, 1815).

Scheel, Heinrich, ed., *Das Reformministerium Stein: Akten zur Verfassungs- und Verwaltungsgeschichte aus den Jahren 1807/1808*, 3 vols. (Berlin, 1966–68).

[Scherbening, R. K. von], "Die Reorganisation der Preußischen Armee nach dem Tilsiter Frieden," pt. 1: "Die Jahre 1806 bis 1808 mit einem Beitrag zur frühen Geschichte des Generalstabs," in *BHMW* (Oct. 1854–June 1855, May–Dec. 1856 and July–Dec. 1862).

"Die Reorganisation der Preußischen Armee nach dem Tilsiter Frieden," pt. 2: "Die Jahre 1809 bis 1812," in *BHMW* (Aug. 1865–Oct. 1866).

ed., *Die Reorganisation der Preußischen Armee nach dem Tilsiter Frieden*, 2 vols. (Berlin, 1862 and 1866) (also in *BHMW*, 1854–1866).

Schmidt-Philseldek, Konrad Georg Friedrich von, *Über das Verhältnis der jüdischen Nation zum christlichen Bürgerverein* (Wiesbaden, 1816).

Schultze, Maximilian, *Die Landwehr der Neumark von 1813 bis 1815*, 2 vols. (Landsberg, 1912 and 1914).

Schulze, Friedrich, ed., *Die Franzosenzeit in deutschen Landen, 1806–1815: In Wort und Bild der Mitlebenden*, 2 vols. (Leipzig, 1908).

Schütt, Johann Matthias, *Was giebts nach achtzehn Jahrhunderten vergeblichem Warten auf einen anderen Messias noch für gerechte Mittel, die im Lande Christi und also unter Christen Befehl stehenden Juden zu ihm zu bekehren, damit sie das jüdische Land in Segen wieder besitzen?* (Hamburg, 1819).

Schwab, Gustav, ed., *Deutsche Pandora: Gedenkbuch zeitgenössischer Zustände und Schriftsteller*, 2 vols. (Stuttgart, 1840–41).

Seidel, Paul, "Eine Erinnerung an den ersten Frauen-Verein 1813," *Hohenzollern Jahrbuch* 18 (1914): 237–240.

Spies, Hans-Bernd, ed., *Die Erhebung gegen Napoleon 1806–1814/15 (Quellen zum politischen Denken der Deutschen im 19. und 20. Jahrhundert*, vol. 2) (Darmstadt, 1981).

Sporschill, Johann, *Die Freiheitskriege der Deutschen in den Jahren 1813, 14, 15*, 9 vols. (Braunschweig, 1845–46, 6th edn.; 1st edn. 1838–39).

Stein, Heinrich Friedrich Karl Freiherr vom, *Briefe und Amtliche Schriften*, eds. Erich Botzenhart and Walther Hubatsch, 10 vols. (Stuttgart, 1957–74).

Sybel, Heinrich von, *Die Erhebung Europas gegen Napoleon I* (Munich, 1860).

Theremin, Franz, *Werke*, 4 vols. (Berlin, 1828).

Treitschke, Heinrich von, *Deutsche Geschichte im Neunzehnten Jahrhundert*, 5 vols. (Leipzig, 1879–89).

   Politik: Vorlesungen gehalten an der Universität zu Berlin von Heinrich von Treitschke, 2 vols. (Leipzig, 1898–99).

Troschke, Theodor von, *Das eiserne Kreuz* (Berlin, 1872, 3rd edn.).

Ulmann, Heinrich, "Die Detachements der freiwilligen Jäger in den Befreiungskriegen," *Historische Vierteljahresschrift* 10 (1907): 483–505.

Vaupel, Rudolph, ed., *Das Preußische Heer vom Tilsiter Frieden bis zur Befreiung, 1807–1814*, 2 vols. (Berlin, 1938).

Venturini, Carl, *Russlands und Deutschlands Befreiungskriege von der Franzosen-Herrschaft unter Napoleon Buonaparte in den Jahren 1812–1815*, 4 vols. (Leipzig, 1816).

Verordnung wegen der Militair-Strafen, Königsberg, den 3ten August 1808 (Königsberg, 1808).

Wachler, Ludwig, *Ernste Worte der Vaterlandsliebe an alle, welche Deutsche sind und bleiben wollen* (Marburg, 1813).

Wagner, August, *Plane der Schlachten und Treffen, welche von der preussischen Armee in den Feldzügen der Jahre 1813, 14 und 15 geliefert worden: Unter Allerhöchster Genehmigung entworfen, und mit den nöthigen historischen Erläuterungen versehen*, 5 vols. (Berlin, 1821–25).

Weil, Jacob, *Bemerkungen zu den Schriften der Herrn Professoren Rühs und Fries über die Juden und deren Ansprüche auf das deutsche Bürgerrecht* (n.p. [Frankfurt/M.], 1816).

Weiss, Carl von (Karl von Müffling), *Beiträge zur Kriegsgeschichte der Jahre 1813 und 1814: Die Feldzüge der schlesischen Armee*, 2 vols. (Berlin, 1824).

Wolf, Joseph and Gotthold Salomon, *Der Charakter des Judenthums* (n.p., 1817).

Zimmern, Sigmund, *Versuch einer Würdigung der Angriffe des Herrn Professor Fries auf die Juden* (Heidelberg, 1816).

Secondary Works

1813: Auf dem Schlachtfeld bei Leipzig. Ein Rundgang durch das Gemälde "Siegesmeldung" von Johann Peter Krafft, exhibition catalogue, ed. German Historical Museum Berlin (Berlin, 2013).

Aaslestad, Katherine, "Paying for War: Experiences of Napoleonic Rule in the Hanseatic Cities," *CEH* 39 (2006): 641–675.

   Place and Politics: Local Identity, Civic Culture, and German Nationalism in North Germany during the Revolutionary Era (Leiden, 2005).

   "Remembering and Forgetting: The Local and the Nation in Hamburg's Commemorations of the Wars of Liberation," *CEH* 38.3 (2005): 384–416.

Aaslestad, Katherine and Johannes Joor, eds., *Revisiting Napoleon's Continental System: Local, Regional and European Experiences* (Basingstoke, 2014).

Aaslestad, Katherine and Karen Hagemann, eds., "Collaboration, Resistance, and Reform: Experiences and Historiographies of the Napoleonic Wars in Central Europe." Special Issue of *CEH* 39.4 (2006).

Aaslestad, Katherine, Karen Hagemann and Judith Miller, eds., special issue, *EHQ* 37.4 (2007): "Gender, War and the Nation in the Period of the Revolutionary and Napoleonic Wars – European Perspectives."

Abenheim, Donald, *Reforging the Iron Cross: The Search for Tradition in the West German Armed Forces* (Princeton, NJ, 1988).

"AHR Forum: Historiographic 'Turns' in Critical Perspective," *AHR* 117.3 (2012): 688–813.

"AHR Forum: Revisiting 'Gender: A Useful Category of Historical Analysis,'" *AHR* 113.5 (2008): 1344–1430.

Akaltin, Ferdi, *Die Befreiungskriege im Geschichtsbild der Deutschen im 19. Jahrhundert* (Frankfurt/M., 1997).

Alings, Reinhard, *Die Berliner Siegessäule: Vom Geschichtsbild zum Bild der Geschichte* (Berlin, 2000).

Anderson, Benedict R., *Imagined Communities: Reflections on the Origin and Spread of Nationalism* (London, 2006).

Andree, Christian, ed., *Karl von Holtei (1798–1880): Ein schlesischer Dichter zwischen Biedermeier und Realismus* (Würzburg, 2005).

Applegate, Celia, "The Mediated Nation: Regions, Readers and the German Past," in *Saxony in German History: Culture, Society, and Politics, 1830–1933*, ed. James Retallack (Ann Arbor, MI, 2000), 33–50.

A Nation of Provincials: The German Idea of Heimat (Berkeley, CA, 1990).

Applewhite, Harriet B. and Darline G. Levy, "Women and Militant Citizenship in Revolutionary Paris," in *Rebel Daughters: Women and the French Revolution*, ed. Sara E. Melzer and Leslie W. Kabine (New York, 1992), 79–101.

Assmann, Aleida, "Canon and Archive," in *A Companion to Cultural Memory Studies*, ed. Astrid Erll and Ansgar Nünning (Berlin, 2010), 97–107.

Cultural Memory and Western Civilization: Functions, Media, Archives (New York, 2011).

Erinnerungsräume: Formen und Wandlungen des kulturellen Gedächtnisses (Munich, 1999).

"Geschlecht und kulturelles Gedächtnis," *Freiburger FrauenStudien* 19 (2006): 29–46.

Assmann, Jan and John Czaplicka, "Collective Memory and Cultural Identity," *New German Critique* 65 (1995): 125–133.

Aust, Hugo, *Der historische Roman* (Stuttgart, 1994).

"'… und das Lachen verging mir.' Theodor Fontane und der Nationalismus," in *Theodor Fontane, am Ende des Jahrhunderts*, ed. Hanna Delf von Wolzogen and Helmuth Nürnberger, 3 vols. (Würzburg, 2000), 1:241–254.

Bachleitner, Norbert, *Kleine Geschichte des deutschen Feuilletonromans* (Tübingen, 1999).

"'Übersetzungfabriken': Das deutsche Übersetzungswesen in der ersten Hälfte des 19. Jahrhunderts," in *IASL* 14.1 (1989): 1–49.

Baker, Keith Michael, *Inventing the French Revolution: Essays on French Political Culture in the Eighteenth Century* (Cambridge, 1990).

Balzer, Bernd, "'Zugegeben, daß es besser wäre sie fehlten, oder wären anders, wie sie sind': Der selbstverständliche Antisemitismus Fontanes," in *Theodor Fontane am Ende des Jahrhunderts*, ed. Hanna Delf von Wolzogen and Helmuth Nürnberger, 3 vols. (Würzburg, 2000), 1:197–210.

Bartel, Horst, *Das Sozialistengesetz: 1878–1890: Illustrierte Geschichte des Kampfes der Arbeiterklasse gegen die Ausnahmegesetze* (Berlin, 1980).

Bauer, Gerhard, Gorch Pieken and Matthias Rogg, eds., *Blutige Romantik: 200 Jahre Befreiungskriege – Essays*, exhibition catalogue (Dresden, 2013).

Baumgartner, Karin, *Public Voices: Political Discourse in the Writings of Caroline de la Motte Fouqué* (Oxford, 2009).

Beachy, Robert, *The Soul of Commerce: Credit, Property and Politics in Leipzig, 1750–1840* (Leiden, 2005).

Becker, Ernst Wolfgang, "Zeiterfahrung zwischen Revolution und Krieg: Zum Wandel des Zeitbewusstseins in der napoleonischen Ära," in *Die Erfahrung des Krieges: Erfahrungsgeschichtliche Perspektiven von der Französischen Revolution bis zum Zweiten Weltkrieg*, ed. Nikolaus Buschmann and Horst Carl (Paderborn, 2001), 76–96.

Becker, Frank, *Bilder von Krieg und Nation: Die Einigungskriege in der bürgerlichen Öffentlichkeit Deutschlands, 1864–1913* (Munich, 2001).

Behrenbeck, Sabine, *Der Kult um die toten Helden: Nationalsozialistische Mythen, Riten und Symbole 1923 bis 1945* (Cologne, 1996).

Belgum, Kirsten, *Popularizing the Nation: Audience, Representation, and the Production of Identity in* Die Gartenlaube, *1853–1900* (Lincoln, NE, 1998).

Bell, David A., *The Cult of the Nation in France: Inventing Nationalism, 1680–1800* (Cambridge, MA, 2001).

The First Total War: Napoleon's Europe and the Birth of Warfare As We Know It (Boston, 2007).

Bemmann, Helga, *Theodor Fontane: Ein preussischer Dichter* (Berlin, 1998).

Berding, Helmut, "Das geschichtliche Problem der Freiheitskriege 1813–1814," in *Historismus und moderne Geschichtswissenschaft: Europa zwischen Revolution und Restauration 1797–1815*, ed. Karl Otmar Freiherr von Aretin and Gerhard A. Ritter (Wiesbaden, 1987), 201–215.

Moderner Antisemitismus in Deutschland (Frankfurt/M., 1988).

Berger, Stefan and Chris Lorenz, eds., *The Contested Nation: Ethnicity, Class, Religion and Gender in National Histories* (Basingstoke, 2011).

Berger, Stefan, "Prussia in History and Historiography from the Eighteenth to the Nineteenth Century," in *The Rise of Prussia, 1700–1830*, ed. Philip G. Dwyer (Harlow, 2000), 27–44.

"Prussia in History and Historiography from the Nineteenth to the Twentieth Centuries," in *Modern Prussian History, 1830–1945*, ed. Philip G. Dwyer (Harlow, 2001), 21–40.

Berggren, Jan, *Bernadotterna och Helsingborg: 200 år sedan Karl XIV Johan landsteg i Helsingborg* (Helsingborg, 2010).

Berghahn, Volker R., *Imperial Germany, 1871–1918: Economy, Society, Culture, and Politics* (New York, 2005).

Bethan, Angelika, *Napoleons Königreich Westphalen: Lokale, deutsche und europäische Erinnerungen* (Paderborn, 2012).

Beutin, Wolfgang, *Königtum und Adel in den historischen Romanen von Willibald Alexis* (Berlin, 1966).

"Melpomenes Dolch und Klios noch schärferer Griffel: Die Brandenburg-preussischen ('vaterländischen') Romane von Willibald Alexis," in *Willibald Alexis (1798–1871): Ein Autor des Vor- und Nachmärz*, ed. Wolfgang Beutin and Peter Stein (Bielefeld, 2000), 177–194.

Biegel, Gerd and Christof Römer, eds., *Patriotische Flugblätter, 1800–1815 und ihr Umfeld*, exhibition catalogue (Braunschweig, 1990).

Blackburn, Alexander, *The Myth of the Picaro: Continuity and Transformation of the Picaresque Novel, 1554–1954* (Chapel Hill, NC, 1979).

Bland, Caroline, "The End of 'Noblesse Oblige' in German Realism? Social Mobility and Social Obligation in the Writing of Louise von François," *German Life and Letters* 66.2 (2013): 137–155.

ed., *Frauen in der literarischen Öffentlichkeit, 1780–1918* (Bielefeld, 2007).

Bland, Caroline and Elisa Müller-Adams, eds., *Schwellenüberschreitungen: Politik in der Literatur von deutschsprachigen Frauen 1780–1918* (Bielefeld, 2007).

Blessing, Werner K., "Umbruchkrise und Verstörung: Die Napoleonische Erschütterung und ihre sozialpsychologische Bedeutung (Bayern als Beispiel)," *Zeitschrift für Bayerische Landesgeschichte* 42 (1979): 75–106.

Blitz, Hans-Martin, *Aus Liebe zum Vaterland: Die deutsche Nation im 18. Jahrhundert* (Hamburg, 2000).

Blom, Ida, Karen Hagemann and Catherine Hall, eds., *Gendered Nations: Nationalisms and Gender Order in the Long Nineteenth Century* (Oxford, 2000).

Bödeker, Hans Erich, "Die gebildeten Stände im späten 18. und frühen 19. Jahrhundert: Zugehörigkeit und Abgrenzungen – Mentalitäten und Handlungspotentiale," in *Bildungsbürgertum im 19. Jahrhundert*, pt. 4: *Politischer Einfluß und gesellschaftliche Formation*, ed. Jürgen Kocka (Stuttgart, 1989), 21–52.

"Zur Rezeption der französischen Menschen- und Bürgerrechtserklärung von 1789/1791 in der deutschen Aufklärungsgesellschaft," in *Grund- und Freiheitsrechte im Wandel von Gesellschaft und Geschichte: Beiträge zur Geschichte der Grund- und Freiheitsrechte vom Ausgang des Mittelalters bis zur Revolution von 1848*, ed. Günter Birtsch (Göttingen, 1981), 258–286.

Boes, Tobias, *Formative Fictions: Nationalism, Cosmopolitanism, and the Bildungsroman* (Ithaca, NY, 2012).

Böning, Holger, ed., *Französische Revolution und deutsche Öffentlichkeit: Wandlungen in Presse und Alltagskultur am Ende des 18. Jahrhunderts* (Munich, 1992).

Börner, Karl-Heinz, "Die Völkerschlacht bei Leipzig 1813 – Bedeutung und Wirkung," *Militärgeschichte* 4 (1988): 323–326.

Bouwers, Eveline G., *Public Pantheons in Revolutionary Europe: Comparing Cultures of Remembrance, c. 1790–1840* (Basingstoke, 2012).

Bovekamp, Boris, *Die Zeitschrift "Minerva" und ihre Herausgeber Johann Wilhelm von Archenholz (1743–1812) und Friedrich Alexander Bran (1767–1831): Ein Beitrag zur Kompatibilität von Militär, Aufklärung und Liberalismus* (Kiel, 2009).

Brammer, Annegret H., *Judenpolitik und Judengesetzgebung in Preußen 1812 bis 1847 mit einem Ausblick auf das Gleichberechtigungsgesetz des Norddeutschen Bundes von 1869* (Berlin, 1987).

Brandt, Bettina, *Germania und ihre Söhne: Repräsentationen von Nation, Geschlecht und Politik in der Moderne* (Göttingen, 2010).

Brandt, Peter, "Die Befreiungskriege von 1813 bis 1815 in der deutschen Geschichte," in *Geschichte und Emanzipation*, ed. Michael Grüttner, Rüdiger Hachtmann and Heinz-Gerhardt Haupt (Frankfurt/M., 1999), 17–57.

"Einstellungen, Motive und Ziele von Kriegsfreiwilligen 1813–14: Das Freikorps Lützow," in *Kriegsbereitschaft und Friedensordnung in Deutschland, 1800–1814*, ed. Jost Dülffer (Münster, 1995), 211–233.

Braun, Gertrud, "Die Königsberger Zeitschriften von 1800 bis zu den Karlsbader Beschlüssen: Ein Beitrag zur Publizistik" (Phil. Diss, University of Königsberg, 1936).

Breitenborn, Konrad and Justus H. Ulbricht, eds., *Jena und Auerstedt: Ereignis und Erinnerung in europäischer, nationaler und regionaler Perspektive* (Dößel, 2006).

Breuer, Karin, "Competing Masculinities: Fraternities, Gender and Nationality in the German Confederation, 1815–30," *G&H* 20 (2008): 270–287.

Breuilly, John, *The Formation of the First German Nation-State, 1800–1871* (Basingstoke, 1996).

Brody, James, "The Politicization of Traditional Festivals in Germany, 1815–48," in *Festive Culture in Germany and Europe from the Sixteenth to the Twentieth Century*, ed. Karin Friedrich (Lewiston, NY, 2000), 73–106.

Broers, Michael, *Europe Under Napoleon, 1799–1815* (London, 1996).

Broers, Michael, Agustin Guimera and Peter Hicks, eds., *The Napoleonic Empire and the New European Political Culture* (Basingstoke, 2011).

Brophy, James M., *Popular Culture and the Public Sphere in the Rhineland, 1800–1850* (Cambridge, 2007).

Brubaker, Rogers, *Citizenship and Nationhood in France and Germany* (Cambridge, MA, 1992).

Bruer, Albert A., *Aufstieg und Untergang: Eine Geschichte der Juden in Deutschland, 1750–1918* (Cologne, 2006).

Geschichte der Juden in Preußen, 1750–1820 (Frankfurt/M., 1991).

Brühl, Reinhard, *Militärgeschichte und Kriegspolitik: Zur Militärgeschichtsschreibung des preussisch-deutschen Generalstabes 1816–1945* (Berlin, 1973).

Brunner, Otto, Werner Conze and Reinhart Koselleck, eds., *Geschichtliche Grundbegriffe: Historisches Lexikon zur politisch-sozialen Sprache in Deutschland*, 8 vols. (Stuttgart, 1972–97).

Buchinger, Kirsten, *Napoléomanie* (Berlin, 2013).

Burdekin, Hannah, *The Ambivalent Author: Five German Writers and their Jewish Characters, 1848–1914* (Oxford, 2002).

Burns, Barbara, *The Prose Fiction of Louise von François (1817–1893)* (Oxford, 2006).

Büsch, Otto, ed., *Handbuch der Preußischen Geschichte*, 3 vols. (Berlin, 1992–2009).

Military System and Social Life in Old-Regime Prussia, 1713–1807: The Beginnings of the Social Militarization of Prusso-German Society (Atlantic Highlands, NJ, 1997).

Buschmann, Nikolaus and Horst Carl, eds., *Die Erfahrung des Krieges: Erfahrungsgeschichtliche Perspektiven von der Französischen Revolution bis zum Zweiten Weltkrieg* (Paderborn, 2001).

Buschmann, Nikolaus and Dieter Langewiesche, eds., *Der Krieg in den Gründungsmythen europäischer Nationen und der USA* (Frankfurt/M., 2003).

Calhoun, Craig, ed., *Habermas and the Public Sphere* (Cambridge, MA, 1992).

Canning, Kathleen, "Feminist History after the Linguistic Turn: Historicizing Discourse and Experience," in *Gender History in Practice*, 62–100.

Gender History in Practice: Historical Perspectives on Bodies, Class, and Citizenship (Ithaca, NY, 2006).

Chandler, David, *The Campaigns of Napoleon* (New York, 1966).

Chandler, James, *England in 1819: The Politics of Literary Culture and the Case of Romantic Historicism* (Chicago, 1998).

Charters, Erica, Eve Rosenhaft and Hannah Smith, eds., *Civilians and War in Europe, 1618–1815* (Liverpool, 2012).

Chefdebien, Anne de and Bertrand Galimard de Flavigny, *La Légion d'honneur: un ordre au service de la nation* (Paris, 2002).

Chickering, Roger and Stig Förster, eds., *War in an Age of Revolution, 1775–1815* (Cambridge, 2010).

Clark, Christopher, *Iron Kingdom: The Rise and Downfall of Prussia, 1600–1947* (Cambridge MA, 2006).

"The Wars of Liberation in Prussian Memory: Reflections on the Memorialization of War in Early Nineteenth-Century Germany," *JMH* 68.3 (1996): 550–576.

Colley, Linda, *Britons: Forging the Nation, 1707–1837* (London, 2003).

Confino, Alon, "Collective Memory and Cultural History: Problems of Method," *AHR* 102 (1997): 1386–1403.

The Nation as a Local Metaphor: Württemberg, Imperial Germany, and National Memory, 1871–1918 (Chapel Hill, NC, 1997).

Connell, R. W., *Masculinities* (St. Leonards, 1995).

Cornelißen, Christoph, "Was heißt Erinnerungskultur? Begriff – Methoden – Perspektiven," *GWU* 54 (2003): 548–563.

Craig, Gordon A., *Theodor Fontane: Literature and History in the Bismarck Reich* (New York, 1999).

Crane, Susan A., *Collecting and Historical Consciousness in Early Nineteenth-Century Germany* (Ithaca, NY, 2000).

Daly, Gavin, *The British Soldier in the Peninsular War: Encounters with Spain and Portugal, 1808–1814* (Basingstoke, 2013).

Dann, Otto, "Geheime Organisierung und politisches Engagement im deutschen Bürgertum des frühen 19. Jahrhunderts: Der Tugendbund-Streit in Preußen," in *Geheime Gesellschaften*, ed. Peter Christian Ludz (Heidelberg, 1979), 399–428.

ed., *Lesegesellschaft und bürgerliche Emanzipation: Ein europäischer Vergleich* (Munich, 1981).

Dann, Otto, *Nation und Nationalismus in Deutschland, 1770–1990* (Munich, 1996, 3rd edn.).

Daum, Andreas W., *Wissenschaftspopularisierung im 19. Jahrhundert: Bürgerliche Kultur, naturwissenschaftliche Bildung und die deutsche Öffentlichkeit, 1848–1914* (Munich, 1998).

Davidoff, Leonore, Keith McClelland and Eleni Varikas, eds., *Gender and History: Retrospect and Prospect* (Oxford, 2000).

Demandt, Philipp, *Luisenkult: die Unsterblichkeit der Königin von Preussen* (Cologne, 2003).

Diethe, Carol, *Towards Emancipation: German Women Writers of the Nineteenth Century* (New York, 1998).

Dorpalen, Andreas, "The German Struggle against Napoleon: The East German View," *JMH* 41 (1969): 485–516.

Dow, James Elstone, *A Good German Conscience: The Life and Time of Ernst Moritz Arndt* (Lanham, MD, 1995).

Duchhardt, Heinz, *Mythos Stein: Vom Nachleben, von der Stilisierung und von der Instrumentalisierung des preußischen Reformers* (Göttingen, 2008).

Dudink, Stefan, Karen Hagemann and Anna Clark, eds., *Representing Masculinity: Citizenship in Modern Western Culture*, (Basingstoke, 2007).

Dudink, Stefan, Karen Hagemann and John Tosh, eds., *Masculinities in Politics and War: Gendering Modern History* (Manchester, 2004).

Düding, Dieter, "Deutsche Nationalfeste im 19. Jahrhundert: Erscheinungsbild und politische Funktion," *Archiv für Kulturgeschichte* 69 (1987): 371–388.

Organisierter gesellschaftlicher Nationalismus in Deutschland, 1808–1847: Bedeutung und Funktion der Turner- und Sänger-Vereine für die deutsche Nationalbewegung (Munich, 1984).

Düding, Dieter, Peter Friedemann and Paul Münch, eds., *Öffentliche Festkultur: Politische Feste in Deutschland von der Aufklärung bis zum Ersten Weltkrieg* (Reinbek, 1988).

Dühr, Albrecht, "Die Text- und Druckgeschichte des 'Soldaten-Katechismus' E. M. Arndts," *Zeitschrift für Bibliothekswesen und Bibliographie* 8 (1961): 337–349.

Dwyer, Philip G., *Citizen Emperor: Napoleon in Power* (New Haven, CT, 2013).

ed., *Napoleon and Europe* (Harlow, 2001).

Napoleon: The Path to Power (New Haven, CT, 2008).

"Public Remembering, Private Reminiscing: French Military Memoirs and the Revolutionary and Napoleonic Wars," *French Historical Studies* 33:2 (2010): 231–258.

Dwyer, Philip G. and Alan Forrest, eds., *Napoleon and his Empire: Europe, 1804–1814* (Basingstoke, 2007).

Dwyer, Philip G. and Lyndall Ryan, eds. *Massacre in the Old and New Worlds, c. 1780–1820*, special issue, *Journal of Genocide Research* 15.2 (2013).

Ebert, Sabine, *Kriegsfeuer: 1813* (Munich, 2013).

Echternkamp, Jörg, *Der Aufstieg des deutschen Nationalismus, 1770–1840* (Frankfurt/M., 1998).

Echternkamp, Jörg and Sven Oliver Müller, *Die Politik der Nation: deutscher Nationalismus in Krieg and Krisen, 1760–1960* (Munich, 2002).

Eggert, Hartmut, *Studien zur Wirkungsgeschichte des deutschen historischen Romans, 1850–1875* (Frankfurt/M., 1971).

Eisenhardt, Ulrich, *Die kaiserliche Aufsicht über Buchdruck, Buchhandel und Presse im Heiligen Römischen Reich deutscher Nation (1496–1806): Ein Beitrag zur Geschichte der Bücher- und Pressezensur* (Karlsruhe, 1970).

Eissenhauer, Michael, ed., *König Lustik!? Jérôme Bonaparte und der Modellstaat Königreich Westphalen*, exhibition catalogue (Kassel, 2008).

Eke, Norbert Otto and Dagmar Olasz-Eke, *Bibliographie, der deutsche Roman 1815–1830: Standortnachweise, Rezensionen, Forschungsüberblick* (Munich, 1994).

Eke, Norbert Otto and Hartmut Steinecke, eds., *Geschichten aus (der) Geschichte: Zum Stand des historischen Erzählens im Deutschland der frühen Restaurationszeit* (Munich, 1994).

Eley, Geoff and Ronald Grigor Suny, eds., *Becoming National: A Reader* (Oxford, 1996).

Engelmann, Susanne, "Der Einfluß des Volksliedes auf die Lyrik der Befreiungskriege" (Phil. Diss., University of Heidelberg, 1909).

Engelsing, Rolf, *Analphabetentum und Lektüre: Zur Sozialgeschichte des Lesens in Deutschland zwischen feudaler und industrieller Gesellschaft* (Stuttgart, 1973).

Epple, Angelika, *Empfindsame Geschichtsschreibung: Eine Geschlechtergeschichte der Historiographie zwischen Aufklärung und Historismus* (Cologne, 2003).

Epple, Angelika and Angelika Schaser, eds., *Gendering Historiography: Beyond National Canons* (Frankfurt/M., 2009).

Erb, Rainer and Werner Bergmann, *Die Nachtseite der Judenemanzipation: Der Widerstand gegen die Integration der Juden in Deutschland 1780–1860* (Berlin, 1989).

Erhart, Walter and Arne Koch, eds., *Ernst Moritz Arndt (1769–1860): Deutscher Nationalismus – Europa – transatlantische Perspektiven* (Tübingen, 2007).

Erll, Astrid and Ansgar Nünning, eds., *A Companion to Cultural Memory Studies* (Berlin, 2010).

eds., *Cultural Memory Studies: An International and Interdisciplinary Handbook* (Berlin, 2008).

eds., *Gedächtniskonzepte der Literaturwissenschaft: Theoretische Grundlegung und Anwendungsperspektiven* (Berlin, 2005).

eds., *Medien des kollektiven Gedächtnisses: Konstruktivität, Historizität, Kulturspezifität* (Berlin, 2004).

Eschert, Jens, "'Mit der Zeit gescheitert': Friedrich August I. von Sachsen und die Völkerschlacht," in *Verlierer der Geschichte. Von der Antike bis zur Moderne*, ed. Sabine Graul and Marian Nebelin (Berlin, 2008), 289–308.

Esdaile, Charles J., *Napoleon's Wars: An International History, 1803–1815* (London, 2009).

Popular Resistance in the French Wars: Patriots, Partisans and Land Pirates (Basingstoke, 2005).

"Recent Writing on Napoleon and His Wars," *The Journal of Military History* 73 (2009): 209–220.

Fahrmeir, Andreas, *Citizens and Aliens: Foreigners and the Law in Britain and the German States, 1789–1870* (Oxford, 2000).

Fasel, Peter, *Revolte und Judenmord: Hartwig von Hundt-Radowsky (1780–1835): Biografie eines Demagogen* (Berlin, 2010).

Favret, Mary, *War at a Distance: Romanticism and the Making of Modern Wartime* (Princeton, NJ, 2010).

Fehrenbach, Elisabeth, *Vom Ancien Régime zum Wiener Kongreß* (Munich, 1986, 2nd edn.).

Fesser, Gerd, *1806: die Doppelschlacht bei Jena und Auerstedt* (Jena, 2006).

1813: Die Völkerschlacht bei Leipzig (Jena, 2013).

Fiedler, Siegfried, *Kriegswesen und Kriegsführung im Zeitalter der Revolutionskriege* (Koblenz, 1988).

Fischer, Horst, *Judentum, Staat und Heer in Preußen im frühen 19. Jahrhundert: Zur Geschichte der staatlichen Judenpolitik* (Tübingen, 1968).

Flacke, Monika, ed., *Mythen der Nationen: Ein europäisches Panorama*, exhibition catalogue (Munich, 1998).

Flöring, Karl, "Zur Geschichte der Allgemeinen Militärzeitung, 1826–1902," *MGM* 18.2 (1975): 11–31.

Foerster, Erich, *Die Entstehung der Preußischen Landeskirche unter der Regierung König Friedrich Wilhelms des Dritten nach den Quellen erzählt: Ein Beitrag der Kirchenbildung im deutschen Protestantismus*, 3 vols. (Tübingen, 1905 and 1907).

Forrest, Alan, *Napoleon* (London, 2011).

Forrest, Alan, Étienne François and Karen Hagemann, eds., *War Memories: The Revolutionary and Napoleonic Wars in Modern European Culture* (Basingstoke, 2012).

Forrest, Alan, Karen Hagemann and Jane Rendall, eds., *Soldiers, Citizens and Civilians: Experiences and Perceptions of the French Wars, 1790–1820* (Basingstoke, 2009).

Forrest, Alan and Peter Wilson, eds., *The Bee and the Eagle: Napoleonic France and the End of the Holy Roman Empire*, (Basingstoke, 2008).

Förster, Birte, *Der Königin Luise-Mythos: Mediengeschichte des "Idealbilds deutscher Weiblichkeit," 1860–1960* (Göttingen, 2011).

Fox, Thomas C., *Louise von François and Die letzte Reckenburgerin: A Feminist Reading* (New York, 1988).

François, Étienne, "Alphabetisierung und Lesefähigkeit in Frankreich um 1800," in *Deutschland und Frankreich im Zeitalter der Französischen Revolution*, ed. Helmut Berding, Étienne François und Hans-Peter Ullmann (Frankfurt/M.: Suhrkamp, 1989), 407 – 425.

François, Étienne, Hannes Siegrist and Jakob Vogel, eds., *Nation und Emotion: Deutschland und Frankreich im Vergleich 19. und 20. Jahrhundert* (Göttingen, 1995).

François, Étienne and Hagen Schulze, eds., *Deutsche Erinnerungsorte*, 3 vols. (Munich, 2001).

François, Étienne and Uwe Puschner, eds., *Erinnerungstage: Wendepunkte der Geschichte von der Antike bis zur Gegenwart* (Munich, 2010).

Fregosi, Paul, *Dreams of Empire: Napoleon and the First World War, 1792–1815* (London, 1989).

Frevert, Ute, *"Mann und Weib, und Weib und Mann": Geschlechter-Differenzen in der Moderne* (Munich, 1995).

A Nation in Barracks: Modern Germany, Military Conscription and Civil Society (Oxford, 2004).

"Was haben Gefühle in der Geschichte zu suchen," *GG* 35:2 (2009): 183–208.

Frie, Ewald, *Friedrich August Ludwig von der Marwitz (1777–1837): Biographien eines Preussen* (Paderborn, 2001).

Friedrich, Karin, ed., *Festive Culture in Germany and Europe from the Sixteenth to the Twentieth Century* (Lewiston, NY, 2000).

Friedrich, Karin and Sara Smart, eds., *The Cultivation of the Monarchy and the Rise of Berlin: Brandenburg-Prussia 1700* (Aldershot, 2010).

Fritzsche, Peter, "The Case of Memory," *JMH* 73.1 (2001): 87–117.

"Specters of History: On Nostalgia, Exile, and Modernity," *AHR* 106.5 (2001): 1587–1618.

Stranded in the Present: Modern Time and the Melancholy of History (Cambridge, MA, 2004).

Frühsorge, Gotthardt, "Die Begründung der 'väterlichen Gesellschaft' in der europäischen oeconomia christiana: Zur Rolle des Vaters in der 'Hausväterliteratur' des 16. bis 18. Jahrhunderts in Deutschland," in *Das Vaterbild im Abendland I: Rom, Frühes Christentum, Mittelalter, Neuzeit, Gegenwart*, ed. Hubertus Tellenbach (Stuttgart, 1978), 110–123.

Fulda, Daniel, *Wissenschaft aus Kunst: Die Entstehung der modernen deutschen Geschichtsschreibung 1760–1860* (Berlin, 1996).

Furrer, Daniel, *Soldatenleben: Napoleons Russlandfeldzug 1812* (Paderborn, 2012).

Gärtner, Hannelore, *Georg Friedrich Kersting* (Leipzig, 1988).

Gast, Wolfgang, *Der deutsche Geschichtsroman im 19. Jahrhundert: Willibald Alexis – Untersuchungen zur Technik seiner "vaterländischen Romane"* (Freiburg/Br., 1972).

Gat, Azar, *A History of Military Thought: From the Enlightenment to the Cold War* (Oxford, 2001).

Gates, David, *The Napoleonic Wars, 1803–1815* (London, 1997).

Geertz, Clifford, *Thick Description: Toward an Interpretive Theory of Culture* (New York, 1973).

Gender-Killer, A.G., ed., *Antisemitismus und Geschlecht: von "effeminierten Juden," "maskulinisierten Jüdinnen" und anderen Geschlechterbildern* (Münster, 2005).

Genschorek, Wolfgang, *Carl Gustav Carus: Arzt, Künstler, Naturforscher* (Leipzig, 1980).

Giesen, Bernhard, *Die Intellektuellen und die deutsche Nation: Eine deutsche Achsenzeit* (Frankfurt/M., 1993).

Gisch, Heribert, "'Preßfreiheit' – 'Preßfrechheit': Zum Problem der Presseaufsicht in napoleonischer Zeit in Deutschland (1806–1818)," in *Deutsche Kommunikationskontrolle des 15.–20. Jahrhunderts*, ed. Heinz-Dietrich Fischer (Munich, 1982), 56–74.

Gleixner, Ulrike and Marion W. Gray, eds., *Gender in Transition: Discourse and Practice in German-Speaking Europe, 1750–1830* (Ann Arbor, MI, 2006).

Göbel, Christian, *Der vertraute Feind: Pressekritik in der Literatur des 19. und frühen 20. Jahrhundert* (Würzburg, 2011).

Goldfriedrich, Johann Adolf, *Geschichte des deutschen Buchhandels*, 4 vols. (Leipzig, 1886–1913, repr. Leipzig, 1970).

Gosewinkel, Dieter, *Einbürgern und Ausschließen: Die Nationalisierung der Staatsangehörigkeit vom Deutschen Bund zur Bundesrepublik Deutschland* (Göttingen, 2001).

Göttsche, Dirk, *Zeit im Roman: Literarische Zeitreflexion und die Geschichte des Zeitromans im späten 18. und im 19. Jahrhundert* (Munich, 2001).

Graf, Gerhard, *Die Völkerschlacht bei Leipzig in zeitgenössischen Berichten* (Berlin, 1988).

Gottesbild und Politik: Eine Studie zur Frömmigkeit in Preußen während der Befreiungskriege 1813–1815 (Göttingen, 1993).

Gratzke, Michael, *Blut und Feuer: Heldentum bei Lessing, Kleist, Fontane, Jünger und Heiner Müller* (Würzburg, 2011).

Gray, Marion, "Men as Citizens and Women as Wives: The Enlightenment Codification of Law and the Establishment of Separated Spheres," in *Reich oder Nation? Mitteleuropa, 1780–1815*, ed. Heinz Duchhardt and Andreas Kunz (Mainz, 1998), 279–298.

Green, Abigail, *Fatherlands: State-Building and Nationhood in Nineteenth-Century Germany* (Cambridge, 2001).

Groppe, Sabine, *Das Ich am Ende des Schreibens: Autobiographisches Erzählen im 18. und frühen 19. Jahrhundert* (Würzburg, 1990).

Gross, Michael B., *The War against Catholicism: Liberalism and the Anti-Catholic Imagination in Nineteenth-Century Germany* (Ann Arbor, MI, 2004).

Gruner, Wolf D., "Der Deutsche Bund, die deutschen Verfassungsstaaten und die Rheinkrise von 1840: Überlegung zur deutschen Dimension einer europäischen Krise," *Zeitschrift für bayerische Landesgeschichte* 53 (1990): 51–78.

Gubser, Martin, *Literarischer Antisemitismus: Untersuchungen zu Gustav Freytag und anderen bürgerlichen Schriftstellern des 19. Jahrhunderts* (Göttingen, 1998).

Gudehus, Christian, Ariane Eichenberg and Harald Welzer, eds., *Gedächtnis und Erinnerung: Ein interdisziplinäres Handbuch* (Stuttgart, 2010).

Guenther, Walter P., *Preussischer Gehorsam: Theodor Fontanes Novelle "Schach von Wuthenow" – Text und Deutung* (Munich, 1981).

Haage, Johannes R., "Heinrich Luden: Seine Persönlichkeit und seine Geschichtsauffassung" (Phil. Diss., University of Leipzig, 1930).

Habermas, Jürgen, *The Structural Transformation of the Public Sphere: An Inquiry into a Category of Bourgeois Society* (Cambridge, 1989).

Strukturwandel der Öffentlichkeit: Untersuchungen zu einer Kategorie der bürgerlichen Gesellschaft (Neuwied, 1962).

Habitzel, Kurt and Günter Mühlberger, "Gewinner und Verlierer: Der historische Roman und sein Beitrag zum Literatursystem der Restaurationszeit (1815–1848/49)," *IASL* 21.1 (1996): 91–123.

Hädecke, Wolfgang, *Theodor Fontane: Biographie* (Munich, 1998).

Hagemann, Johannes, *Levin Schücking: Der Dichter und sein Werk* (Emsdetten/Westf., 1959).

Hagemann, Karen, "Der 'Bürger' als 'Nationalkrieger': Entwürfe von Militär, Nation und Männlichkeit in der Zeit der Freiheitskriege," in *Landsknechte, Soldatenfrauen und Nationalkrieger: Militär, Krieg und Geschlechterordnung im historischen Wandel*, ed. Karen Hagemann and Ralf Pröve (Frankfurt/M., 1998), 74–102.

"Female Patriots: Women, War and the Nation in the Period of the Prussian-German Anti-Napoleonic Wars," *G&H* 16 (2004): 396–424.

"Gendered Boundaries: Civil Society, the Public/Private Divide and the Family," in *The Golden Chain: Family, Civil Society and the State*, ed. Paul Ginsborg, Jürgen Nautz and Ton Nijhuis (New York, 2012), 43–65.

"Gendered Images of the German Nation: The Romantic Painter Friedrich Kersting and the Patriotic-National Discourse during the Wars of Liberation," *Nation and Nationalism* 12:4 (2006): 653–679.

"Heldenmütter, Kriegerbräute und Amazonen: Entwürfe 'patriotischer Weiblichkeit' in Preußen zur Zeit der Freiheitskriege," in *Militär und bürgerliche Gesellschaft im 19. und 20. Jahrhundert*, ed. Ute Frevert (Stuttgart, 1997), 174–200.

"Literaturmarkt, Zensur und Meinungsmobilisierung: Die politische Presse Preußens zur Zeit der Napoleonischen Kriege," in *Agenten der Öffentlichkeit: Theater und Medien im 19. Jahrhundert*, ed. Maike Wagner (Bielefeld, 2012), 171–196.

"Mannlicher Muth und Teutsche Ehre": Nation, Militär und Geschlecht zur Zeit der Antinapoleonischen Kriege Preußens (Paderborn, 2002).

"Of 'Manly Valor' and 'German Honor': Nation, War and Masculinity in the Age of the Prussian Uprising against Napoleon," *CEH* 30.2 (1997): 187–220.

"Reconstructing 'Front' and 'Home': Gendered Experiences and Memories of the German Wars against Napoleon – A Case Study," *WiH* 16:1 (2009): 25–50.

Hagemann, Karen, Gisela Mettele and Jane Rendall, eds., *Gender, War and Politics: Transatlantic Perspectives, 1775–1830* (Basingstoke, 2010).

Hagemann, Karen and Jean H. Quataert, eds., *Gendering Modern German History: Rewriting Historiography* (New York, 2007).

Hagemann, Karen, and Stefanie Schüler-Springorum, eds., *Home/Front: The Military, War and Gender in Twentieth-Century Germany* (Oxford, 2002).

Halbwachs, Maurice, *Les cadres sociaux de la mémoire* (Paris, 1925).

Hamnett, Brian R., *The Historical Novel in Nineteenth-Century Europe: Representations of Reality in History and Fiction* (Oxford, 2011).

Hanke, Birgid, *Reformer, Demokrat, Schriftsteller – auf Fritz Reuters Spuren* (Hamburg, 2010).

Harari, Yuval Noah, "Military Memoirs: A Historical Overview of the Genre from the Middle Ages to the Late Modern Era," *WiH* 14:3 (2007): 289–309.

The Ultimate Experience. Battlefield Revelations and the Making of Modern War Culture, 1450–2000 (Basingstoke, 2008).

Hardtwig, Wolfgang, "Die Verwissenschaftlichung der neueren Geschichtsschreibung," in *Geschichte: Ein Grundkurs*, ed. Hans-Jürgen Goertz (Reinbek/Hamburg, 2007), 245–260.

"Formen der Geschichtsschreibung: Varianten des historischen Erzählens," in *Geschichte: Ein Grundkurs*, ed. Hans-Jürgen Goertz (Reinbek/Hamburg, 2007), 218–237.

Geschichtskultur und Wissenschaft (Munich, 1990).

Politische Kultur der Moderne: Ausgewählte Aufsätze (Göttingen, 2011).

Hartleb, Renate, ed., *1813: Die Zeit der Befreiungskriege und die Leipziger Völkerschlacht in Malerei, Graphik, Plastik*, exhibition catalogue (Leipzig, 1989).

Hattenhauer, Hans, *Deutsche Nationalsymbole: Zeichen und Bedeutung* (Munich, 1984).

Hausen, Karin, "Family and Role Division: The Polarisation of Sexual Stereotypes in the Nineteenth Century – An Aspect of the Dissociation of Work and Family," in *The German Family: Essays on the Social History of the Family in Nineteenth- and Twentieth-Century Germany*, ed. Richard J. Evans and W. R. Lee (London, 1981), 51–83.

Heenemann, Horst, "Die Auflagenhöhe der deutschen Zeitungen: Ihre Entwicklung und ihre Probleme" (Phil. Diss., University of Berlin, 1930).

Heintz, Günter, "Kompromiß und Wirkung: Kritische Anmerkungen zu Hermann Sudermanns *Der Katzensteg*," in *Hermann Sudermann: Werk und Wirkung*, ed. Walter T. Rix (Würzburg, 1980), 201–214.

Heinzen, Jasper, "Transnational Affinities and Invented Traditions: The Napoleonic Wars in British and Hanoverian Memory, 1815–1915," *The English Historical Review* 127 (2012): 1404–1434.

Heitzer, Heinz, *Insurrection zwischen Weser und Elbe: Volksbewegungen gegen die französische Fremdherrschaft im Königreich Westfalen, 1806–1813* (Berlin, 1959).

Henning, Friedrich-Wilhelm, *Handbuch der Wirtschafts- und Sozialgeschichte Deutschlands*, 3 vols. (Paderborn, 1991, 1996 and 2003).

Herberg-Rothe, Andreas, *Clausewitz's Puzzle: The Political Theory of War* (Oxford, 2007).

Herrmann, Hans Peter, Hans-Martin Blitz and Susanna Mossmann, *Machtphantasie Deutschland: Nationalismus, Männlichkeit und Fremdenhaß im Vaterlandsdiskurs deutscher Schriftsteller des 18. Jahrhunderts* (Frankfurt/M., 1996).

Herrmann, Ulrich, ed., *Volk – Nation – Vaterland* (Hamburg, 1996).

Hess, Jonathan M., *Germans, Jews and the Claims of Modernity* (New Haven, CT, 2002).

Hettling, Manfred and Paul Nolte, eds., *Bürgerliche Feste: Symbolische Formen politischen Handelns im 19. Jahrhundert* (Göttingen, 1993), 8–36.

Heuvel, Jon Vanden, *A German Life in the Age of Revolution: Joseph Görres, 1776–1848* (Washington, DC, 2001).

Higonnet, Margaret R., Jane Jenson, Sonya Michel and Margaret Collins Weitz, eds., *Behind the Lines: Gender and the Two World Wars* (New Haven, CT, 1987).

Hirsch, Marianne and Valerie Smith, eds., *Gender and Cultural Memory*, special issue, *Signs* 82.1 (2002).

Hobi, Caroline, *Willibald Alexis, "'Ruhe ist die erste Bürgerpflicht': Eine erzähltheoretische Analyse und Interpretation* (Bern, 2007).

Hoffmann, Helene, *August Sperl und seine Quellen in der ersten Schaffensperiode seines Lebens, eine literarhistorische Untersuchung auf Grund seines Familienarchivs, sowie mündlicher und schriftlicher Mitteilungen seiner Angehörigen, Verwandten und Freunde* (Laßleben, 1935).

Hoffmann, Lutz, "Die Konstruktion des Volkes durch seine Feinde," *Jahrbuch für Antisemitismusforschung* 2 (1993): 13–37.

Hofmann, Wolfgang, *Caspar David Friedrich* (New York, 2000).

Hofmeister-Hunger, Andrea, *Pressepolitik und Staatsreform: Die Institutionalisierung staatlicher Öffentlichkeitsarbeit bei Karl August von Hardenberg, 1792–1822* (Göttingen, 1994).

Hölscher, Lucian, *Öffentlichkeit und Geheimnis: Eine begriffsgeschichtliche Untersuchung zur Entstehung der Öffentlichkeit in der frühen Neuzeit* (Stuttgart, 1979).

Höltenschmidt, Edith, *Die Mittelalter-Rezeption der Brüder Schlegel* (Paderborn, 2000).

Hölter, Achim, *Die Invaliden: Die vergessene Geschichte der Kriegskrüppel in der europäischen Literatur bis zum 19. Jahrhundert* (Stuttgart, 1995).

Holz, Claus, *Flucht aus der Wirklichkeit: "Die Ahnen" von Gustav Freytag – Untersuchungen zum realistischen historischen Roman der Gründerzeit 1872–1880* (Frankfurt/M., 1983).

Honegger, Claudia, *Die Ordnung der Geschlechter: Die Wissenschaft vom Menschen und das Weib 1750–1850* (Frankfurt/M., 1991).

Hortzitz, Nicoline, *"Früh-Antisemitismus" in Deutschland (1789–1870/72): Strukturelle Untersuchungen zu Wortschatz, Text und Argumentation* (Tübingen, 1988).

Hubatsch, Walther, *Die Stein-Hardenbergschen Reformen* (Darmstadt, 1977).

Huber, Ernst Rudolf, *Deutsche Verfassungsgeschichte seit 1789*, 8 vols. (Stuttgart, 1957–91).

Huber-Sperl, Rita. "Organized Women and the Strong State: The Beginnings of Female Associational Activity in Germany, 1810–1840," *JWH* 13.4 (2002): 81–105.

Hubmann, Gerald, *Ethische Überzeugung und politisches Handeln: Jakob Friedrich Fries und die deutsche Tradition der Gesinnungsethik* (Heidelberg, 1997).

Hunecke, Volker, *Napoleon: Das Scheitern eines guten Diktators* (Paderborn, 2011).

Hull, Isabel V., *Absolute Destruction: Military Culture and the Practice of War in Imperial Germany* (Ithaca, NY, 2005).

Sexuality, State, and Civil Society in Germany, 1700–1815 (Ithaca, NY, 1996).

Hunt, Lynn, *Politics, Culture, and Class in the French Revolution* (Berkeley, CA, 1984).

Hütte, Werner O., "Die Geschichte des Eisernen Kreuzes und seine Bedeutung für das preußische und deutsche Auszeichnungswesen von 1813 bis zur Gegenwart" (Phil. Diss., University of Bonn, 1968).

Ibbeken, Rudolf, *Preußen 1807–1813: Staat und Volk als Idee und in Wirklichkeit* (Cologne, 1970).

Imhof, Kurt, "Vermessene Öffentlichkeit – vermessene Forschung? Vorstellung eines Projektes," in *Zwischen Konflikt und Konkordanz: Analyse von Medienereignissen in der Schweiz der Vor- und Zwischenkriegszeit*, ed. Imhof, Heinz Kleger and Gaetano Romano (Zurich, 1996), 11–60.

Jäger, Georg, Dieter Langewiesche and Wolfram Siemann, eds., *Geschichte des Deutschen Buchhandels im 19. und 20. Jahrhundert*, 2 vols. (Frankfurt/M., 2001).

James, Leighton S., *Witnessing the Revolutionary and Napoleonic Wars in German Central Europe* (Basingstoke, 2012).

Janic, Christa, "Ausgegraben: Friedrich Friesen oder Wie wird man ein deutscher Held?," *WerkstattGeschichte* 6 (1993): 22–34.

Jarausch, Konrad H. and Michael Geyer, *Shattered Past: Reconstructing German Histories* (Princeton, NJ, 2003).

Jay, Martin, *Songs of Experience: Modern American and European Variations on a Universal Theme* (Berkeley, CA, 2005).

Jeismann, Michael, *Das Vaterland der Feinde: Studien zum nationalen Feindbegriff und Selbstverständnis in Deutschland und Frankreich, 1792–1918* (Stuttgart, 1992).

Jentsch, Irene, "Zur Geschichte des Zeitungslesens in Deutschland am Ende des 18. Jahrhunderts: Mit besonderer Berücksichtigung der gesellschaftlichen Formen des Zeitungslesens" (Phil. Diss., University of Leipzig, 1937).

Jolles, Charlotte, *Theodor Fontane* (Stuttgart, 1993).

Kaiser, Gerhard, *Pietismus und Patriotismus im literarischen Deutschland: Ein Beitrag zum Problem der Säkularisation* (Wiesbaden, 1961).

Katz, Jacob, *Die Hep-Hep-Verfolgungen des Jahres 1819* (Berlin, 1994).

  From Prejudice to Destruction: Anti-Semitism, 1700–1933 (Cambridge, MA, 1980).

Keller, Katrin and Hans-Dieter Schmid, eds., *Vom Kult zur Kulisse: Das Völkerschlachtdenkmal als Gegenstand der Geschichtskultur* (Leipzig, 1995).

Kennedy, Catriona, *Narratives of War: Military and Civilian Experience in Britain and Ireland, 1793–1815* (Basingstoke, 2011).

Kerber, Linda K. *Intellectual History of Women: Essays by Linda K. Kerber* (Chapel Hill, NC, 1997).

  "The Republican Mother: Women and the Enlightenment – An American Perspective," *American Quarterly*, 28.2 (1976): 187–205.

Kessel, Martina, "The 'Whole Man': The Longing for a Masculine World in Nineteenth-Century Germany," *G&H* 15 (2003): 1–31.

Kirchner, Joachim, *Bibliographie der Zeitschriften des deutschen Sprachgebietes bis 1900*, vol. 1: *Die Zeitschriften des deutschen Sprachgebietes von den Anfängen bis 1830* (Stuttgart, 1969).

Klaje, Hermann, "Über die Bekleidungsnöte der Freiwilligen Jäger von 1813/14," *FBPG* 36 (1924): 87–97.

Klenke, Dietmar, *Der singende "deutsche Mann": Gesangvereine und deutsches Nationalbewußtsein von Napoleon bis Hitler* (Münster, 1998).

  "Ein 'Schwur für's deutsche Vaterland: Zum Nationalismus der deutschen Sängerbewegung zwischen Paulskirchenparlament und Reichsgründung," in *Liberalismus, Parlamentarismus und Demokratie*, ed. Michael Epkenhans, Martin Kottkamp and Lothar Snyders (Göttingen, 1994), 67–107.

  "Zwischen nationalkriegerischem Gemeinschaftsideal und bürgerlich-ziviler Modernität: Zum Vereinsnationalismus der Sänger, Schützen und Turner im Deutschen Kaiserreich," *GWU* 45 (1994): 207–223.

Kloosterhuis, Jürgen and Sönke Neitzel, eds., *Krise, Reformen und Militär: Preussen vor und nach der Katastrophe von 1806* (Berlin, 2009).

Knott, Sarah and Barbara Taylor, eds., *Women, Gender and Enlightenment* (Basingstoke, 2005).

Kocka, Jürgen, ed., *Bürger und Bürgerlichkeit im 19. Jahrhundert* (Göttingen, 1987).

Koller, Wolfgang, "Heroic Memories: Gendered Images of the Napoleonic Wars in German Feature Films of the Interwar Period," in *War Memories: The Revolutionary and Napoleonic Wars in Modern European Culture*, ed. Alan Forrest, Étienne François and Karen Hagemann (Basingstoke, 2012), 366–385.

Historienkino im Zeitalter der Weltkriege: Die Revolutions- und Napoleonischen Kriege in der europäischen Erinnerung (Paderborn, 2013).

König, Helmut, *Zur Geschichte der bürgerlichen Nationalerziehung in Deutschland zwischen 1807 und 1815*, 2 vols. (Berlin, 1972–73).

Kontje, Todd, ed., *A Companion to German Realism, 1848–1900* (Rochester, NY, 2002).

Women, the Novel, and the German Nation, 1771–1871: Domestic Fiction in the Fatherland (Cambridge, 1998).

Koopmann, Helmut, *Das Junge Deutschland: Eine Einführung* (Darmstadt, 1993).

Kopf, Hermann, *Karl von Rotteck, zwischen Revolution und Restauration* (Freiburg/Br., 1980).

Köpping, Reinhard, *Sachsen gegen Napoleon: Zur Geschichte der Befreiungskriege 1813–1815* (Berlin, 2001).

Koselleck, Reinhart, *Futures Past: On the Semantic of Historical Time* (New York, 2004).

Preußen zwischen Reform und Revolution: Allgemeines Landrecht, Verwaltung und soziale Bewegung von 1791 bis 1848 (Stuttgart, 1981, 3rd edn.).

Koselleck, Reinhart and Michael Jeismann, eds., *Der politische Totenkult: Kriegerdenkmäler in der Moderne* (Munich, 1994).

Kramer, Lloyd, *Nationalism in Europe and America: Politics, Cultures, and Identities Since 1775* (Chapel Hill, NC, 2011).

Kreutz, Wilhelm and Karl Scherer, eds., *Die Pfalz unter französischer Besetzung, 1918/19–1930* (Kaiserslautern, 1999).

Krieger, Leonard, "Elements of Early Historicism: Experience, Theory, and History in Ranke," *History and Theory* 14.4 (1975): 1–14.

Krimmer, Elisabeth and Patricia Anne Simpson, eds., *Enlightened War: German Theories and Cultures of Warfare from Frederick the Great to Clausewitz* (Rochester, NY, 2011).

Kuhlbrodt, Peter, "Die Französische Revolution und die Frauenrechte in Deutschland," *ZfG* 38 (1990): 405–421.

Kunisch, Johannes and Herfried Münkler, eds., *Die Wiedergeburt des Krieges aus dem Geist der Revolution: Studien zum bellizistischen Diskurs des ausgehenden 18. und beginnenden 19. Jahrhunderts* (Berlin, 1999).

Kunstverein, Rostock, ed., *Ausstellung Deutsche Romantik: Malerei und Zeichnung: 18. Oktober–15. November 1936 im Städt. Kunst- und Altertumsmuseum* (Rostock, 1936).

Kurth-Voigt, Lieselotte E. and William H. McClain, "Louise Mühlbach's Historical Novels: The American Reception," *IASL* 6.1 (1981): 52–77.

Lahrkamp, Monika, *Münster in napoleonische Zeit, 1800–1815: Administration, Wirtschaft und Gesellschaft im Zeichen von Säkularisation und Französischer Herrschaft* (Münster, 1976).

Lamers, Henrike, *Held oder Welt?: Zum Romanwerk Friedrich Spielhagens* (Bonn, 1991).

Landes, Joan B., ed. *Feminism, the Public and the Private* (Oxford, 1998).

Visualizing the Nation: Gender, Representation, and Revolution in Eighteenth-Century France (Ithaca, NY, 2001).

Women and the Public Sphere in the Age of the French Revolution (Ithaca, NY, 1988).

Lange, Bernhard, *Die öffentliche Meinung in Sachsen von 1813 bis zur Rückkehr des Königs 1815* (Gotha, 1912).

Langewiesche, Dieter and Georg Schmidt, eds., *Föderative Nation: Deutschlandkonzepte von der Reformation bis zum Ersten Weltkrieg* (Munich, 2000).

Liberalism in Germany (Princeton, NJ, 2000).

Lauková, Lucia, "Die emanzipierte Emanzipationsgegnerin: Caroline Pichlers theoretische Schriften," *New German Review* 24 (2009–10): 95–111.

Leggiere, Michael V., *The Fall of Napoleon*, vol. 1: *The Allied Invasion of France, 1813–1814* (Cambridge, 2007).

Napoleon and Berlin: Franco-Prussian War in North Germany, 1813 (Norman, OK, 2002).

Leonhard, Jörn, *Bellizismus und Nation: Kriegsdeutung und Nationsbestimmung in Europa und den Vereinigten Staaten 1750–1914* (Munich, 2008).

Levinger, Matthew, *Enlightened Nationalism: The Transformation of Prussian Political Culture, 1806–1848* (Oxford, 2000).

Lieven, Dominic, *Russia Against Napoleon: The Battle for Europe, 1807 to 1814* (London, 2009).

Lincoln, Margarette, ed., *Nelson & Napoléon* (London, 2005).

Loster-Schneider, Gudrun, *Der Erzähler Fontane: Seine politischen Positionen in den Jahren 1864–1898 und ihre ästhetische Vermittlung* (Tübingen, 1986).

Lukács, Georg, *Probleme des Realismus*, vol. 3: *Der historische Roman* (Neuwied, 1971).

Lürz, Meinhold, *Kriegerdenkmäler in Deutschland*, vol. 1: *Die Befreiungskriege* (Heidelberg, 1985).

Luys, Karin, *Die Anfänge der deutschen Nationalbewegung von 1815 bis 1819* (Münster, 1992).

Lyons, Martyn, *A History of Reading and Writing in the Western World* (Basingstoke, 2010).

Mahoney, Dennis F., ed., *The Literature of German Romanticism* (Rochester, NY, 2004).

Maierhofer, Waltraud, Gertrud M. Roesch and Caroline Bland, eds., *Women Against Napoleon: Historical and Fictional Responses to His Rise and Legacy* (Frankfurt/M., 2007).

Martini, Fritz, *Deutsche Literatur im Bürgerlichen Realismus, 1848–1998* (Stuttgart, 1962).

Martino, Alberto, *Die deutsche Leihbibliothek: Geschichte einer literarischen Institution, 1756–1914* (Wiesbaden, 1990).

Mason, Laura, *Singing the French Revolution: Popular Culture and Politics, 1787–1799* (Ithaca, NY, 1996).

Maurer, Michael, ed., *Das Fest: Beiträge zu seiner Theorie und Systematik* (Cologne, 2004).

Max, Hubert, *Wesen und Gestalt der politischen Zeitschrift: Ein Beitrag zur Geschichte des politischen Erziehungsprozesses des deutschen Volkes bis zu den Karlsbader Beschlüssen* (Essen, [1942]).

Mayer, Karl J., *Napoleons Soldaten: Alltag in der Grande Armeé* (Darmstadt, 2008).

Maynes, Mary Jo, Jennifer L. Pierce and Barbara Laslett, *Telling Stories: The Use of Personal Narratives in the Social Sciences and History* (Ithaca, NY, 2008).

Mazura, Sylvia, *Die preußische und österreichische Kriegspropaganda im Ersten und Zweiten Schlesischen Krieg* (Berlin, 1996).

Melton, James Van Horn, *The Rise of the Public in Enlightenment Europe* (Cambridge, 2001).

Melzer, Sara E. and Leslie W. Kabine, eds., *Rebel Daughters: Women and the French Revolution* (New York, 1992).

Meyer, Hans-Friedrich, "Berlinische Nachrichten von Staats- und Gelehrten Sachen, Berlin (1740–1974)," in *Deutsche Zeitungen des 17.–20. Jahrhunderts*, ed. Heinz-Dietrich Fischer (Munich, 1971), 103–114.

Meyer, Klaus, "Das 'Russisch-Deutsche Volks-Blatt' von 1813," in *Russen und Rußland aus deutscher Sicht. 19. Jahrhundert: Von der Jahrhundertwende bis zur Reichsgründung, 1800–1871*, ed. Mechthild Keller (Munich, 1992), 400–416.

Meyer, Michael A., "Die Entstehung des Historischen Romans in Deutschland und seine Stellung zwischen Geschichtsschreibung und Dichtung. Die Polemik um eine 'Zwittergattung' (1785–1845)" (Phil. Diss., University of Munich, 1973).

Meyer, Michael A. and Michael Brenner, eds., *German-Jewish History in Modern Times*, 4 vols. (New York, 1996).

Michaud, Philippe-Alain, *Aby Warburg and the Image in Motion* (New York, 2004).

Mieck, Ilja, "Preußen von 1807 bis 1850: Reformen, Restauration und Revolution," in *Handbuch der Preußischen Geschichte*, vol. 2: *Das 19. Jahrhundert und Große Themen der Geschichte Preußens*, ed. Otto Büsch, 3 vols. (Berlin, 1992), 3–292.

Militärgeschichtlichen Forschungsamt, ed., *Handbuch zur deutschen Militärgeschichte, 1648–1939*, 9 vols. (Frankfurt/M., 1964–81).

Miquel, Pierre, *Deux siècles de Légion d"honneur* (Paris, 2002).

Mogge, Winfried and Jürgen Reulecke, *Hoher Meißner 1913 – Der Erste Freideutsche Jugendtag in Dokumenten, Deutungen und Bildern* (Cologne, 1988).

Moran, Daniel, *Towards the Century of Words: Johann Cotta and the Politics of the Public Realm in Germany 1795–1832* (Berkeley, CA, 1990).

Mühlberger, Günter and Kurt Habitzel, "The German Historical Novel (1780–1945): The German Historical Novel from 1780 to 1945 – Utilising the Innsbruck Database," in *Travellers in Time and Space: The German Historical Novel*, ed. Osman Durrani and Julian Preece (Amsterdam, 2001), 5–23.

Müller, Donges, Christa, *Das Novellenwerk Friedrich Spielhagens in seiner Entwicklung zwischen 1851 und 1899* (Marburg, 1970).

Müller-Adams, Elisa, *"Dass die Frau zur Frau redete": Das Werk der Caroline de la Motte Fouqué als Beispiel für weibliche Literaturproduktion der frühen Restaurationszeit* (St. Ingbert, 2003).

Müller-Seidel, Walter, *Theodor Fontane: Soziale Romankunst in Deutschland* (Stuttgart, 1975).

Mulryne, J. R., Helen Watanabe-O'Kelly and Margaret Shewring, eds., *Europa Triumphans: Court and Civic Festivals in Early Modern Europe* (Aldershot, 2004).

Münch, Paul, "Die 'Obrigkeit im Vaterstand' – Zu Definition und Kritik des 'Landesvaters' während der frühen Neuzeit," *Daphnis* 11 (1982): 15–40.

Münchow-Pohl, Bernd von, *Zwischen Reform und Krieg: Untersuchungen zu Bewußtseinslage in Preußen* (Göttingen, 1987).

Murken, Julia, *Bayerische Soldaten im Russlandfeldzug 1812: Ihre Kriegserfahrungen und deren Umdeutungen im 19. und 20. Jahrhundert* (Munich, 2006).

Mustafa, Sam A., *The Long Ride of Major von Schill: A Journey through German History and Memory* (Lanham, MD, 2008).

Neuendorff, Otto, *George Hesekiel* (Nendeln/Liechtenstein, 1967).

Neuhaus, Volker, "Friedrich Spielhagen – Critic of Bismarck's Empire," in *1870/71–1989/90: German Unifications and the Change of Literary Discourse*, ed. Walter Pape (Berlin, 1993), 135–143.

Nienhaus, Stefan, *Geschichte der deutschen Tischgesellschaft* (Tübingen, 2003).

Nimmergut, Jörg, *Das Eiserne Kreuz 1813–1939* (Lüdenscheid, 1990).

Nipperdey, Thomas, *Deutsche Geschichte, 1866–1918*, vol. 1: *Arbeitswelt und Bürgergeist* (Munich, 1990).

Germany from Napoleon to Bismarck, 1800–1866 (Princeton, NJ, 1996).

Nissen, Martin, "Populäre Geschichtsschreibung im 19. Jahrhundert: Gustav Freytag und seine 'Bilder aus der deutschen Vergangenheit,'" *Archiv für Kulturgeschichte* 89.2 (2007): 395–425.

Nitschke, Heinz G., *Die Preußischen Militärreformen, 1807–1813: Die Tätigkeit der Militärreorganisationskommission und ihre Auswirkungen auf die preußische Armee* (Berlin 1983).

Nolte, Paul, *Staatsbildung als Gesellschaftsreform: Politische Reformen in Preußen und den süddeutschen Staaten 1800–1820* (Frankfurt/M., 1990).

Norden, Albert, "Das Volk stand auf und siegte," in *Der Befreiungskrieg 1813*, ed. Peter Hoffmann (Berlin, 1967), 1–10.

Nowak, Kurt, *Schleiermacher: Leben, Werk und Wirkung* (Göttingen, 2001).

Nye, Robert A., "Western Masculinities in War and Peace," *AHR* 112.2 (2007): 417–438.

Oesterle, Günter, "Juden, Philister und romantische Intellektuelle: Überlegungen zum Antisemitismus in der Romantik," *Athenäum: Jahrbuch für Romantik* 2 (1992): 55–89.

Osterhammel, Jürgen, *Die Verwandlung der Welt: Eine Geschichte des 19. Jahrhunderts* (Munich, 2009).

Ozouf, Mona, *La Fête révolutionnaire, 1789–1799* (Paris, 1976).

Paletschek, Sylvia, ed., *Popular Historiographies in the 19th and 20th Centuries: Cultural Meanings, Social Practices* (Oxford, 2011).

Paletschek, Sylvia and Sylvia Schraut, eds., *The Gender of Memory: Cultures of Remembrance in Nineteenth- and Twentieth-Century Europe* (Frankfurt/M., 2008).

Pape, Walter, ed., *Arnim und die Berliner Romantik: Kunst, Literatur und Politik* (Tübingen, 2001).

Paret, Peter, *Clausewitz and the State: The Man, His Theories, and His Times* (Princeton, NJ, 2007).

The Cognitive Challenge of War: Prussia 1806 (Princeton, NJ, 2009).

Yorck and the Era of Prussian Reform 1807–15 (Princeton, NJ, 1966).

Pawley, Margaret, *The Watch on the Rhine: The Military Occupation of the Rhineland, 1918–1930* (London, 2007).

Peters, Lars, *Romances of War: Die Erinnerung an die Revolutions- und Napoleonischen Kriege in Großbritannien und Irland, 1815–1945* (Paderborn, 2012).

Peterson, Brent O., *History, Fiction, and Germany: Writing the Nineteenth-Century Nation* (Detroit, MI, 2005).

Ping, Larry L., "Gustav Freytag's Bilder aus der deutschen Vergangenheit and the Meaning of German History," *German Studies Review* 32.3 (2009): 549–568.

Gustav Freytag and the Prussian Gospel: Novels, Liberalism and History (Oxford, 2006).

Planert, Ute, *Der Mythos vom Befreiungskrieg: Frankreichs Kriege und der deutsche Süden: Alltag – Wahrnehmung – Deutung, 1792–1841* (Paderborn, 2007).

ed., *Krieg und Umbruch in Mitteleuropa um 1800: Erfahrungsgeschichte(n) auf dem Weg in eine neue Zeit* (Paderborn, 2009).

Platthaus, Andreas, *1813: Die Völkerschlacht und das Ende der Alten Welt* (Berlin, 2013).

Pleiner, Horst, "Die Österreichische Militärische Zeitschrift: Ein historischer Rückblick von den Anfängen bis zur Gegenwart," *Österreichische Militärische Zeitschrift* 46 (2008): 39–63.

Porter, Roy, ed., *Rewriting the Self: Histories from the Renaissance to the Present* (London, 1997).

Portmann-Tinguely, Albert, *Romantik und Krieg: Eine Untersuchung zum Bild des Krieges bei deutschen Romantikern und "Freiheitssängern:" Adam Müller, Joseph Görres, Friedrich Schlegel, Achim von Arnim, Max von Schenkendorf und Theodor Körner* (Freiburg/Br., 1989).

Poser, Steffen, *Denkmale zur Völkerschlacht*, ed. Stadtgeschichtliches Museum Leipzig (Leipzig, 2013).

Die Völkerschlacht bei Leipzig: "In Schutt und Graus begraben," ed. Stadtgeschichtliches Museum Leipzig (Leipzig, 2013).

Prüsener, Marlies, *Lesegesellschaften im achtzehnten Jahrhundert* (Frankfurt/M., 1972).

Puschner, Marco, *Antisemitismus im Kontext der politischen Romantik: Konstruktionen des "Deutschen" und des "Jüdischen" bei Arnim, Brentano und Saul Ascher* (Tübingen, 2008).

Quataert, Jean, *Staging Philanthropy: Patriotic Women and the National Imagination in Dynastic Germany, 1813–1916* (Ann Arbor, MI, 2001).

Rasch, Wolfgang, *Theodor Fontane Bibliographie: Werk und Forschung*, 3 vols. (Berlin, 2006).

Reddy, William M., "Historical Research on the Self and Emotions," *Emotion Review* 1.4 (2009): 302–315.

The Navigation of Feeling: A Framework for the History of Emotions (Cambridge, 2001).

Reder, Dirk, *Frauenbewegung und Nation: Patriotische Frauenvereine in Deutschland im frühen 19. Jahrhundert, 1813–1830* (Cologne, 1998).

Reiber, Karl, "Die Deutschen Blätter von Brockhaus 1813–1816" (Phil. Diss., University of Cologne, 1937).

Reimer, Doris, *Passion & Kalkül: Der Verleger Georg Andreas Reimer, 1776–1842* (Berlin, 1999).

Requate, Jörg, *Journalismus als Beruf: Entstehung und Entwicklung des Journalistenberufs im 19. Jahrhundert. Deutschland im internationalen Vergleich* (Göttingen, 1995).

Ricoeur, Paul, *La mémoire, l'histoire, l'oubli* (Paris, 2000).

Rodekamp, Volker, ed., *Helden nach Maß: 200 Jahre Völkerschlacht bei Leipzig*, exhibition catalogue (Leipzig, 2013).

Rohrbacher, Stefan, *Gewalt im Biedermeier: Antijüdische Ausschreitungen in Vormärz und Revolution, 1815–1848/49* (Frankfurt/M., 1993).

Rose, Paul Lawrence, *Revolutionary Antisemitism in Germany from Kant to Wagner* (Princeton, NJ, 1990).

Roth, François, *La Guerre de 1870* (Paris, 1990).

Rowe, Michael, *From Reich to State: The Rhineland in the Revolutionary Age, 1780–1830* (Cambridge, 2003).

Rürup, Reinhard, *Emanzipation und Antisemitismus: Studien zur "Judenfrage" der bürgerlichen Gesellschaft* (Frankfurt/M., 1987, 2nd edn.).

Salisch, Marcus von, "Das Beispiel Sachsen: Militärreformen deutscher Mittelstaaten," in *Reform, Reorganisation, Transformation: Zum Wandel deutscher Streitkräfte von den preußischen Heeresreformen bis zur Transformation der Bundeswehr*, ed. Karl-Heinz Lutz, Martin Rink and Marcus von Salisch (Munich, 2010), 89–106.

Sammons, Jeffrey L., *Friedrich Spielhagen: Novelist of Germany's False Dawn* (Tübingen, 2004).

Samuels, Maurice, *The Spectacular Past: Popular History and the Novel in Nineteenth-Century France* (Ithaca, NY, 2004).

Sauder, Gerhard, "'Bürgerliche' Empfindsamkeit," in *Bürger und Bürgerlichkeit im Zeitalter der Aufklärung*, ed. Rudolf Vierhaus (Heidelberg, 1981), 149–164.

Saul, Nicholas, ed., *The Cambridge Companion to German Romanticism* (Cambridge, 2009).

Savoy, Bénédicte, ed., *Napoleon und Europa: Traum und Trauma*, exhibition catalogue (Munich, 2011).

Schäfer, Karl Heinz, "1813 – Die Freiheitskriege in der Sicht der marxistischen Geschichtsschreibung der DDR," *GWU* 21 (1970): 2–21.

   Ernst Moritz Arndt als politischer Publizist: Studien zu Publizistik, Pressepolitik und kollektivem Bewußtsein im frühen 19. Jahrhundert (Bonn, 1974).

   "Kollektivbewußtsein am Beginn des 19. Jahrhunderts, dargestellt am Beispiel der Verbreitung der Schriften Ernst Moritz Arndts," in *Presse und Geschichte: Beiträge zur historischen Kommunikationsforschung* (Munich, 1977), 137–148.

Scheel, Heinrich, ed., *Das Reformministerium Stein: Akten zur Verfassungs- und Verwaltungsgeschichte aus den Jahren 1807/1808*, 3 vols. (Berlin, 1966–68).

Scheibenberger, Karl, "Der Einfluß der Bibel und des Kirchenliedes auf die Lyrik der deutschen Befreiungskriege" (Phil. Diss., University of Frankfurt/M., 1936).

Scheidemann, Uta, *Die Wunschbiographien der Louise von François: Dichtung und prosaische Lebenswirklichkeit im 19. Jahrhundert* (Frankfurt/M., 1993).

Schellack, Fritz, *Nationalfeiertage in Deutschland von 1871 bis 1945* (Frankfurt/M., 1990).

Schenda, Rudolf, *Volk ohne Buch: Studien zur Sozialgeschichte der populären Lesestoffe, 1770–1910* (Frankfurt/M., 1970).

Schilling, René, *"Kriegshelden": Deutungsmuster heroischer Männlichkeit in Deutschland, 1813–1945* (Paderborn, 2002).

Schissler, Hanna, *Preußische Agrargesellschaft im Wandel: Wirtschaftliche, gesellschaftliche und politische Transformationsprozesse von 1763 bis 1847* (Göttingen, 1978).

"Preußische Finanzpolitik 1806–1820," in *Preußische Finanzpolitik 1806–1810: Quellen zur Verwaltung der Ministerien Stein und Altenstein*, ed. Hanna Schissler and Hans-Ulrich Wehler (Göttingen, 1984), 13–64.

Schlie, Ulrich, *Die Nation erinnert sich: Die Denkmäler der Deutschen* (Munich, 2002).

Schmidt, Dorothea, *Die preußische Landwehr: Ein Beitrag zur Geschichte der allgemeinen Wehrpflicht in Preußen zwischen 1813 und 1830* (Berlin, 1981).

Schneider, Franz, *Pressefreiheit und politische Öffentlichkeit: Studien zur politischen Geschichte Deutschlands bis 1848* (Neuwied, 1966).

Schnell, Werner, *Georg Friedrich Kersting (1785–1847): Das zeichnerische und malerische Werk mit Oeuvrekatalog* (Berlin, 1994).

Schön, Erich, *Der Verlust der Sinnlichkeit oder Die Verwandlung des Lesers: Mentalitätswandel um 1800* (Stuttgart, 1987).

Schöner, Gerhard, *Gerhard von Kügelgen: Leben und Werk* (Kiel, 1982).

Schönpflug, Daniel, *Luise von Preussen: Königin der Herzen – Eine Biographie* (Munich, 2010).

Schuck, Gerhard, *Rheinbundpatriotismus und Politische Öffentlichkeit zwischen Aufklärung und Frühliberalismus, Kontinuitätsdenken und Diskontinuitätserfahrung in den Staatsrechts- und Verfassungsdebatten der Rheinbundpublizistik* (Stuttgart, 1994).

Schulte, Regina, "The Queen – A Middle Class Tragedy: The Writing of History and the Creation of Myths in Nineteenth-Century France and Germany," *G&H* 14 (2002): 266–293.

Schultz, Hans-Dietrich, "Land – Volk – Staat: Der geographische Anteil an der 'Erfindung' der Nation," *GWU* 54 (2000): 4–16.

Schultz, Uwe, *Das Fest: Kulturgeschichte von der Antike bis zur Gegenwart* (Munich, 1988).

Schulze, Hagen, *States, Nations, and Nationalism: From the Middle Ages to the Present* (Oxford, 1996).

Schulze, Winfried, "Die Entstehung des nationalen Vorurteils: Zur Kultur der Wahrnehmung fremder Nationen in der europäischen Frühen Neuzeit," *GWU* 46 (1995): 642–665.

Schumann, Peter, "Theodor Fontane und die Juden," *Geschichte in Wissenschaft und Unterricht* 49.9 (1998): 530–543.

Scott, Joan W., "The Evidence of Experience," *Critical Inquiry* 17.4 (1991): 773–797.

"Experience," in *Feminists Theorize the Political*, ed. Judith Butler and Joan W. Scott (New York, 1992), 22–40.

Gender and the Politics of History (New York, 1989).

Seyfarth, Alexander, *Die Heimatfront 1870/71: Wirtschaft und Gesellschaft im deutsch-französischen Krieg* (Paderborn, 2007).

Sheehan, James J., *German History, 1770–1866* (Oxford, 1989).

"State and Nationality in the Napoleonic Period," in *The State of Germany: The National Idea in the Making, Unmaking and Remaking of a Modern Nation-State*, ed. John Breuilly (London, 1992), 47–59.

Shepard, Alexandra and Garthine Walker, eds., *Gender and Change: Agency, Chronology and Periodization* (Oxford, 2009).

Siemann, Wolfram, *The German Revolution of 1848–49* (London, 1998).

"Ideenschmuggel: Probleme der Meinungskontrolle und das Los deutscher Zensoren im 19. Jahrhundert," *HZ* 245 (1987): 71–106.

Vom Staatenbund zum Nationalstaat: Deutschland 1806–1871 (Munich, 1995).

"Von der offenen zur mittelbaren Kontrolle: Der Wandel in der deutschen Preßgesetzgebung und Zensurpraxis des 19. Jahrhunderts," *in "Unmoralisch an sich ...": Zensur im 18. und 19. Jahrhundert*, ed. Herbert G. Göpfert and Erdmann Weyrauch (Wiesbaden, 1988), 293–308.

Sieweke, Gabriele, *Der Romancier als Historiker: Untersuchungen zum Verhältnis von Literatur und Geschichte in der englischen Historiographie des 19. Jahrhunderts* (Frankfurt/M., 1994).

Sikora, Michael, "Desertion und nationale Mobilmachung. Militärische Verweigerung 1792–1813," *Armeen und ihre Deserteure: Vernachlässigte Kapitel einer Militärgeschichte der Neuzeit*, ed. Ulrich Broeckling and Michael Sikora (Göttingen, 1998), 112–140.

Simpson, Patricia Anne, *The Erotics of War in German Romanticism* (Lewisburg, PA, 2006).

Sinha, Mrinalini, "Gender and Nation," in *Women's History in Global Perspective*, ed. Bonnie G. Smith, 3 vols. (Urbana, IL, 2004), 1:229–312.

Smets, Josef, "Von der 'Dorfidylle' zur preußischen Nation: Sozialdisziplinierung der linksrheinischen Bevölkerung durch die Franzosen am Beispiel der allgemeinen Wehrpflicht (1802–1814)," *HZ* 262 (1996): 695–738.

Smith, Bonnie G., *The Gender of History: Men, Women, and Historical Practice* (Cambridge, MA, 1998).

Sösemann, Bernd, ed., *Gemeingeist und Bürgersinn: Die preußischen Reformen* (Berlin, 1993).

Sperber, Jonathan, *The European Revolutions, 1848–1851* (Cambridge, 2005).

Sprenger, Reinhard K., *Die Jahnrezeption in Deutschland 1871–1933: Nationale Identität und Modernisierung* (Schorndorf, 1985).

Stamm-Kuhlmann, Thomas, *König in Preußens großer Zeit: Friedrich Wilhelm III – Der Melancholiker auf dem Thron* (Berlin, 1992).

Stauber, Reinhard, "Nationalismus vor dem Nationalismus? Eine Bestandsaufnahme der Forschung zu 'Nation' und 'Nationalismus' in der Frühen Neuzeit," *GWU* 47 (1996): 139–165.

Stein, Hans-Peter, *Symbole und Zeremoniell in deutschen Streitkräften vom 18. Jahrhundert bis zum 20. Jahrhundert* (Herford, 1984).

Steinhorst, Heike, "Autobiographisches und fiktionales Schreiben von Frauen um 1800," in *Schwellenüberschreitungen: Politik in der Literatur von deutschsprachigen Frauen 1780–1918*, ed. Caroline Bland and Elisa Müller-Adams (Bielefeld, 2007), 117–133.

Steinitz, Wolfgang, *Deutsche Volkslieder demokratischen Charakters aus sechs Jahrhunderten*, 2 vols. (Berlin, 1955).

Steussy, Frederic S., *Eighteenth-Century German Autobiography: The Emergence of Individuality* (New York, 1996).

Stöber, Rudolf, *Deutsche Pressegeschichte: Einführung, Systematik, Glossar* (Konstanz, 2000).

Stoetzler, Marcel, *The State, the Nation, & the Jews: Liberalism and the Antisemitism Dispute in Bismarck's Germany* (Lincoln, NE, 2008).

Stolleis, Michael, "Untertan – Bürger – Staatsbürger: Bemerkungen zur juristischen Terminologie im späten 18. Jahrhundert," in *Bürger und Bürgerlichkeit im Zeitalter der Aufklärung*, ed. Rudolf Vierhaus (Heidelberg, 1981), 65–100.

Stolzer, Johann and Christian Steeb, *Österreichs Orden: Vom Mittelalter bis zur Gegenwart* (Graz, 1996).

Strachan, Hew, *Clausewitz's On War: A Biography* (New York, 2007).

Straube, Fritz, *Das Jahr 1813: Studien zur Geschichte und Wirkung der Befreiungskriege* (Berlin, 1963).

Struck, Bernhard, *Nicht West – nicht Ost. Frankreich und Polen in der Wahrnehmung deutscher Reisender zwischen 1750 und 1850* (Göttingen, 2006).

Stübig, Heinz, *Armee und Nation: Die pädagogisch-politischen Motive der preußischen Heeresreform, 1807–1814* (Frankfurt/M., 1971).

Stulz, Percy, *Fremdherrschaft und Befreiungskampf: Die preußische Kabinettspolitik und die Rolle der Volksmassen in den Jahren 1811 bis 1813* (Berlin, 1960).

Süchting-Hänger, Andrea, *Das "Gewissen der Nation": Nationales Engagement und politisches Handeln konservativer Frauenorganisationen 1900 bis 1937* (Düsseldorf, 2002).

Surynt, Isabela, *Das "ferne," "unheimliche" Land: Gustav Freytags Polen* (Dresden, 2004).

Tatlock, Lynne, ed., *Publishing Culture and the "Reading Nation": German Book History in the Long Nineteenth Century* (Rochester, NY, 2010).

Tchernodarov, Andrej, ed., *"Und Frieden aller Welt gebracht": Russisch-Preußischer Feldzug 1813–1814*, exhibition catalogue (Berlin, 1813).

Terdiman, Richard, *Present Past: Modernity and the Memory Crisis* (Ithaca, NY, 1993).

Thamer, Hans-Ulrich, *Die Völkerschlacht bei Leipzig: Europas Kampf gegen Napoleon* (Munich, 2013).

Thiele, Gerhard, *Gneisenau: Leben und Werk des königlich-preussischen Generalfeldmarschalls – Eine Chronik* (Potsdam, 1999).

Thoral, Marie-Cécile, *From Valmy to Waterloo: France at War, 1792–1815* (Basingstoke, 2010).

Tilly, Richard H., *Vom Zollverein zum Industriestaat: Die wirtschaftlich-soziale Entwicklung Deutschlands 1834 bis 1914* (Munich, 1990).

Tlusty, Ann B., *The Martial Ethic in Early Modern Germany: Civic Duty and the Right of Arms* (Basingstoke, 2011).

Tönnesen, Cornelia, *Die Vormärz-Autorin Luise Mühlbach: Vom sozialkritischen Frühwerk zum historischen Roman* (Neuss, 1997).

Töppel, Roman, *Die Sachsen und Napoleon: Ein Stimmungsbild 1806–1813* (Cologne, 2008).

Tosh, John, "Hegemonic Masculinity and the History of Gender," in *Masculinities in Politics and War: Gendering Modern History*, ed. Stefan Dudink, Josh Tosh and Karen Hagemann (Manchester, 2004), 41–60.

"What Should Historians Do with Masculinity? Reflections on Nineteenth-Century Britain," in idem., *Manliness and Masculinities in Nineteenth-Century Britain: Essays on Gender, Family, and Empire* (Harlow, 2004), 29–60.

Transfeldt, Walter and Karl Hermann Frhr. von Brand, *Wort und Brauch im deutschen Heer: Geschichtliche und sprachkundliche Betrachtungen über Gebräuche, Begriffe und Bezeichnungen des deutschen Heeres in Vergangenheit und Gegenwart* (Hamburg, 1967, 6th edn).

Trepp, Anne-Charlott, "The Emotional Side of Men in Late Eighteenth-Century Germany (Theory and Example)," *CEH* 27 (1994): 127–152.

Sanfte Männlichkeit und selbständige Weiblichkeit: Frauen und Männer im Hamburger Bürgertum zwischen 1770 und 1840 (Göttingen, 1996).

Treue, Wilhelm, "Preußens Wirtschaft vom Dreißigjährigen Krieg bis zum Nationalsozialismus," in *Handbuch der Preußischen Geschichte*, vol. 2: *Das 19. Jahrhundert und Große Themen der Geschichte Preußens*, ed. Otto Büsch (Berlin, 1992), 449–604.

Trox, Eckhard, *Militärischer Konservativismus: Kriegervereine und "Militärpartei" in Preußen zwischen 1815 und 1848/49* (Stuttgart, 1990).

Ueberhorst, Horst, ed., *Friedrich Ludwig Jahn: 1778/1978* (Munich, 1978).

Ufer, Peter, *Leipziger Presse 1789 bis 1815: Eine Studie zu Entwicklungstendenzen und Kommunikationsbedingungen des Zeitungs- und Zeitschriftenwesens zwischen Französischer Revolution und den Befreiungskriegen* (Münster, 2000).

Ujma, Christina, ed., *Fanny Lewald (1811–1889): Studien zu einer großen europäischen Schriftstellerin und Intellektuellen* (Bielefeld, 2011).

Uttl, Bob et al., eds., *Memory and Emotion: Interdisciplinary Perspectives* (Oxford, 2006).

Vazsonyi, Nicholas, ed., *Searching for Common Ground: Diskurs zur deutschen Identität, 1750–1870* (Cologne, 2000).

Veltzke, Veit, ed., *Für die Freiheit – Gegen Napoleon: Ferdinand von Schill, Preußen und die deutsche Nation*, exhibition catalogue (Cologne, 2009).

ed., *Napoleon: Trikolore und Kaiseradler über Rhein und Weser*, exhibition catalogue (Cologne, 2007).

Vogel, Barbara, *Allgemeine Gewerbefreiheit: Die Reformpolitik des preußischen Staatskanzlers Hardenberg, 1810–1820* (Göttingen, 1983).

"Staatsfinanzen und Gesellschaftsreform in Preußen," in *Privatkapital, Staatsfinanzen und Reformpolitik im Deutschland der napoleonischen Zeit*, ed. Helmut Berding (Ostfildern, 1981), 37–57.

Vogel, Jakob, *Nationen im Gleichschritt: Der Kult der Nation in Waffen in Deutschland und Frankreich, 1871–1914* (Göttingen, 1997).

Vollmer, Hartmut, *Der deutschsprachige Roman, 1815–1820: Bestand, Entwicklung, Gattungen, Rolle und Bedeutung in der Literatur und in der Zeit* (Munich, 1993).

Vordermayer, Thomas, "Die Rezeption Ernst Moritz Arndts in Deutschland 1909/10–1919/20–1934/35," *Vierteljahrshefte für Zeitgeschichte* 58.4 (2010): 483–508.

Wahrman, Dror, *The Making of the Modern Self: Identity And Culture In Eighteenth-Century England* (New Haven, CT, 2004).

Walter, Dierk, *Preußische Heeresreformen, 1807–1870: Militärische Innovation und der Mythos der "Roonschen Reform"* (Paderborn, 2003).

Ward, Margaret E., *Fanny Lewald: Between Rebellion and Renunciation* (New York, 2006).

Wawro, Geoffrey, *The Franco-Prussian War: The German Conquest of France in 1870–1871* (New York, 2003).

Weber, Ernst, *Lyrik der Befreiungskriege, 1812–1815: Gesellschaftspolitische Meinungs- und Willensbildung durch Literatur* (Stuttgart, 1991).

Weber, Max, *Wirtschaft und Gesellschaft: Grundriß der verstehenden Soziologie* (Tübingen, 1972, 5th edn.).

Wehler, Hans-Ulrich, *Deutsche Gesellschaftsgeschichte*, vols. 1–3 (Munich, 1987–95).

ed., *Deutsche Historiker*, 7 vols. (Göttingen, 1971–80).

Weichlein, Siegried, "Nationalismus als Theorie sozialer Ordnung," in *Geschichte zwischen Kultur und Gesellschaft: Beiträge zur Theoriedebatte*, ed. Thomas Mergel and Thomas Welskopp (Munich, 1997), 171–202.

Weissert, Gottfried, *Das Mildheimische Liederbuch: Studien zur volkspädagogischen Literatur der Aufklärung* (Tübingen, 1966).

Welke, Martin, "Zeitung und Öffentlichkeit im 18. Jahrhundert: Betrachtungen zur Reichweite und Funktion der periodischen deutschen Tagespublizistik," in *Presse und Geschichte: Beiträge zur historischen Kommunikationsforschung* (Munich, 1977), 71–99.

Weller, Christoph, "Feindbilder – zwischen politischen Absichten und wissenschaftlichen Einsichten," *Neue Politische Literatur* 54 (2009): 87–104.

Wenzel, Kay, "Befreiung oder Freiheit? Zur politischen Ausdeutung der deutschen Kriege gegen Napoleon von 1913 bis 1923," in *Griff nach der Deutungsmacht: Zur Geschichte der Geschichtspolitik in Deutschland*, ed. Heinrich August Winkler (Göttingen, 2004), 67–89.

Wette, Wolfram, *Militarismus in Deutschland: Geschichte einer kriegerischen Kultur* (Darmstadt, 2008).

Widdecke, Erich, *Geschichte der Haude- und Spenerschen Zeitung 1734 bis 1874* (Berlin, 1925).

Wild, Reiner, ed., *Geschichte der deutschen Kinder- und Jugendliteratur* (Stuttgart, 2008, 3rd edn.)

Wilkending, Gisela, ed., *Mädchenliteratur der Kaiserzeit: Zwischen weiblicher Identifizierung und Grenzüberschreitung* (Stuttgart, 2003).

Williamson, George S., "What Killed August von Kotzebue?: The Temptations of Virtue and the Political Theology of German Nationalism, 1789–1819," *JMH* 72 (2000): 890–943.

Willms, Johannes, *Napoleon* (Munich, 2005).

Wilson, Peter H., *German Armies: War and German Politics, 1648–1806* (London, 1998).

Winnige, Norbert, "Alphabetisierung in Brandenburg-Preußen 1600–1850: Zu den Grundlagen von Kommunikation und Rezeption," in *Wissen ist Macht: Herrschaft und Kommunikation in Brandenburg-Preußen* (Berlin, 2001), 49–67.

Winter, Jay, *Remembering War: The Great War and Historical Memory in the Twentieth Century* (New Haven, CT, 2006).

Wishon, Mark, *German Forces and the British Army: Interactions and Perceptions, 1742–1813* (Basingstoke, 2013).

Witte, Bernd, "Ein preußisches Wintermärchen: Theodor Fontanes erster Roman *Vor dem Sturm*," in *Theodor Fontane, am Ende des Jahrhunderts*, ed. Hanna Delf von Wolzogen and Helmuth Nürnberger, 3 vols. (Würzburg, 2000), 1:143–156.

Wittmann, Reinhard, *Buchmarkt und Lektüre im 18. und 19. Jahrhundert: Beiträge zum literarischen Leben, 1750–1880* (Tübingen, 1982).

Geschichte des deutschen Buchhandels: Ein Überblick (Munich, 1991, repr. 2011).

"Was there a Reading Revolution at the End of the Eighteenth Century?," in *A History of Reading in the West*, ed. Guglielmo Cavallo and Roger Chartier (Amherst, 1999), 284–312.

Wohlfeil, Rainer, *Handbuch zur deutschen Militärgeschichte 1648–1939*, vol. 2: *Vom stehenden Heer des Absolutismus zur Allgemeinen Wehrpflicht, 1789–1814*, ed. Hans Meier-Welcker (Frankfurt/M., 1964).

Wolfes, Matthias, *Öffentlichkeit und Bürgergesellschaft: Friedrich Schleiermachers politische Wirksamkeit*, 2 vols. (Berlin, 2004).

Woodford, Charlotte and Benedict Schofield, eds., *The German Bestseller in the Late Nineteenth Century* (Rochester, NY, 2012).

Woolf, Stuart J., *Napoleon's Integration of Europe* (London, 1991).

Wulf, Rüdiger, "'Hurra, heut ist ein froher Tag, des Kaisers Wiegenfest!': Schulfeiern zum Kaisergeburtstag und zum Sedantag des Kaiserreichs," in *"Furchtbar dräute der Erbfeind!": Vaterländische Erziehung in den Schulen des Kaiserreichs 1871–1918*, ed. Jochen Löher and Rüdiger Wulf (Dortmund, 1998).

Wülfing, Wulf, "Die heilige Luise von Preußen: Zur Mythisierung einer Figur der Geschichte in der deutschen Literatur des 19. Jahrhunderts," in *Bewegung und Stillstand in Metaphern und Mythen. Fallstudien zum Verhältnis von elementarem Wissen und Literatur im 19. Jahrhundert*, ed. Jürgen Link and Wulf Wülfing (Stuttgart, 1984), 233–275.

Würffel, Reinhard, *Lexikon Deutscher Verlage von A–Z* (Berlin, 2000).

Youens, Susan, *Schubert's Poets and the Making of Music* (Cambridge, 1999).

Zamoyski, Adam, *Moscow 1812: Napoleon's Fatal March* (New York, 2004).

Ziegler, Edda and Gotthard Erler, *Theodor Fontane: Lebensraum und Phantasiewelt – Eine Biographie* (Berlin, 1996).

Zimmer, Hasko, *Auf dem Altar des Vaterlands: Religion und Patriotismus in der deutschen Kriegslyrik des 19. Jahrhunderts* (Frankfurt/M., 1971).

Ziolkowski, Theodore, *Berlin: Aufstieg einer Kulturmetropole um 1810* (Stuttgart, 2002).

Name Index

Alexander I (1777–1825), Emperor of Russia (1801–25), 34, 414
Alexis, Willibald (pseudonym of Georg Wilhelm Heinrich Häring) (1798–1871). *See* Häring
Altenstein, Karl Siegmund Franz Baron vom Stein zum (1770–1840), Prussian Minister of State (1808–1810), 47
Anderson, Benedict, 10
Andreae, Friedrich (1789–1939), academic historian, 306
Apel, Theodor (1811–1867), Saxon writer and local historian, 408
Archenholz, Johann Wilhelm (1741–1812), Prussian officer and publicist, 51
Arndt, Ernst Moritz (1769–1860), historian and writer, 49–50, 76, 80, 91–92, 94, 99–100, 103–104, 113, 116–117, 123–124, 130, 135, 143–144, 146–148, 165, 173–175, 211–212, 240, 273, 277–278, 325–328, 336, 407, 409
Arnim, Achim von (1777–1837), poet, novelist and journalist, 277–278
Ascher, Saul (pseudonym: Theodisius) (1767–1822), philosopher, publisher and writer, 113–114, 119, 127–128
Asisi, Yadgar, 398
Assmann Aleida, 24, 26, 402, 412
Assmann, Jan, 23
Auerbach, Berthold (1812–1882), writer and novelist, 257

Beauharnais, Hortense de (1783–1837), stepdaughter of Emperor Napoleon I, 343

Beauharnais, Joséphine de (1763–1814), first wife of Emperor Napoleon I, 343, 414
Becker Rudolph Zacharias (1752–1822), publisher, 153
Beethoven, Ludwig (1770–1827), composer and musician, 331
Béguelin, Heinrich von (1765–1818), Prussian official, 43
Beitzke, Heinrich (1817–1895), historian, 291–294, 298
Bell, David A., 11, 301
Bergk, Johann Adam (1769–1834), private scholar, historian and philosopher, 283–284
Bismarck, Otto von (1815–1898), Minister President of Prussia (1862–90), Chancellor of the North German Confederation (1866–71) and the German Empire (1871–90), 259, 295
Bland, Caroline, 379
Blücher, Gebhardt Leberecht von (1742–1819), Prussian general, 93, 135, 322, 376, 414
Bonaparte, Jérôme (1784–1860), King of Westphalia (1807–13), 392
Bonaparte, Napoleon (1769–1821). *See* Napoleon.
Boost, Philipp Friedrich (?), Hessian professor, 52
Börne, Ludwig (1786–1837), journalist and literary critic, 255
Breier, Eduard (1811–1886), Austrian writer, 368–369
Brentano, Clemens (1778–1842), poet, novelist and journalist, 122, 277–278

Subject Index